Aetat LXI

Danl Webster

New York, D. Appleton & Co.

LIFE

OF

DANIEL WEBSTER.

BY

GEORGE TICKNOR CURTIS,

ONE OF HIS LITERARY EXECUTORS.

VOLUME I.

SECOND EDITION.

NEW YORK:
D. APPLETON AND COMPANY,
90, 92 & 94 GRAND STREET.
1870.

PREFACE.

MR. WEBSTER, who died on the 24th of October, 1852, made the following provision in his will, which he executed a few days before his death:

"I appoint Edward Everett, George Ticknor, Cornelius Conway Felton, and George Ticknor Curtis, to be my literary executors; and I direct my son, Fletcher Webster, to seal up all my letters, manuscripts, and papers, and, at a proper time, to select those relating to my personal history and my professional and public life, which, in his judgment, should be placed at their disposal, and to transfer the same to them, to be used by them in such manner as they may think fit. They may receive valuable aid from my friend George J. Abbott, Esq., now of the State Department."

After the probate of the will, Mr. Fletcher Webster transferred to the literary executors all the papers which were supposed to be embraced within the purpose of this provision; and steps were taken to collect from other sources whatever else might be in existence which would be important to the preparation of a Life of Mr. Webster. The result was the accumulation of a large mass of papers and documents of a very important character, among which were a number of exceedingly interesting reminiscences in MS., furnished by the surviving few who had known Mr. Webster from his youth. Great pains were taken in collecting these materials, which were chiefly gathered by Mr. Ticknor, acting for his associates in the literary executorship. The whole of these collections, with the exception of those which belonged to Mr. Ticknor's personal relations with Mr. Webster, were then passed over to Mr. Everett, with the full understanding, however, that every thing else would be at his service whenever he should think it proper to undertake the writing of a Life of Mr. Webster.

As I was the draughtsman of Mr. Webster's will, and as he conversed freely with me respecting all of its provisions, I may mention what occurred in reference to this literary executorship. After naming Mr. Everett and Mr. Ticknor as the friends whom he most desired to place in this relation, he dictated to me the substance of the clause as it now stands. When it had been written down, he added, after a short pause: "Put in also Professor Felton's name and your own; it is the only way I have to mark my affection for him and for you, and four will be as good as two." When I assented to this addition of my own name, there seemed to me scarcely a remote possibility that it would fall to me to perform the office which was evidently in Mr. Webster's contemplation in making this provision; and, when the will had taken effect, and for years afterward, it was always tacitly assumed among us that Mr. Everett would, at some period, be the person on whom that office would devolve. But Mr. Everett did nothing, I believe, after this time, toward the preparation of a full Life of Mr. Webster. Nothing, at least, was found, after his own lamented death, to show that he had begun to write one. His numerous avocations, public and private, and perhaps a continuing doubt whether the period had arrived when a Life of Mr. Webster could be judiciously undertaken, led him to postpone a task for which he was eminently fitted, which his associates in the literary executorship were always unanimously anxious to have him assume, and for which they were eager to afford him all the aid in their power. It should not be forgotten, however, that one part, of what may be considered his duty to his illustrious friend, had been already performed by him, with all the diligence and devotion of his own time to the concerns of others that marked his character. In 1851, when filling the very laborious and responsible office of President of Harvard College, Mr. Everett had edited a full collection of Mr. Webster's Works, to which he prefixed a beautiful and carefully-written biographical memoir. At a later period, he sanctioned the publication, in 1857, by Mr. Fletcher Webster, of two volumes of Mr. Webster's Correspondence, and partly assisted in carrying them through the press. In the preface to that publication, it was suggested that the letters embraced in it would be of value as a collection of materials for a Biography of Mr. Webster, when the time should arrive for the composition of such a work.

Mr. Felton, who in 1860 became President of Harvard College, died on the 26th of February, 1862, mourned by the lovers of learning in our own country, and by not a few in foreign lands. The death of Mr. Everett, in 1865, occurring suddenly in the midst of unofficial and voluntary patriotic labors during our great civil war, revealed to Mr. Ticknor and myself the necessity for an immediate attention to the implied injunctions of Mr. Webster's will. I scarcely need to say—I shall be credited where we are both known—that, if my kinsman had consented to undertake the office which one of us had thus become bound to discharge, my own gratification would have been proportionate to what must now be my regret. But his decision was made with the promptness with which he decides all questions of duty; and thus was devolved upon me the performance of a labor for which three persons had been named before me. As soon as this arrangement was definitely concluded, in the winter of 1865–'66, all the papers were forwarded to me by Mr. Ticknor, and I commenced the following work. It has been prosecuted with such diligence as the cares of an engrossing profession have allowed me to bestow upon it.

My own opinion was, that the time had arrived both for writing and publishing a Life of Mr. Webster. For writing it the time had certainly arrived, if there was any one who, possessing the requisite knowledge of Mr. Webster's history, and having enjoyed his confidence, might be able to undergo the labor. In some of the necessary qualifications I could not regard myself as entirely wanting, however deficient I might be in others. I had known Mr. Webster intimately for many years, during that period of his life when he was the most communicative to those in whom he placed confidence. I had lived from my youth in close association with his nearest friends, in Boston, and I could easily have access to others who were much trusted and loved by him, in this city, and who could give me their aid and counsel. Finally, he had, in his last moments, marked his affection for me in the strongest manner, by many other acts besides that of placing me on the list of those with whom he meant to leave the care of his name and fame. Ten years had passed since his death, and his eldest son, long the survivor of all his children, had fallen on the field of battle, defending, in arms, that Government and Constitution which the father had, with so much renown, defended in the Senate, in the Cabinet, and in the Forum. It did not seem to me that I could properly hesitate to undertake, at whatever sacrifice or risk, the duty that had been thus unexpectedly cast upon me.

Nor does it seem to me, now that this work has been written, that there ought to be delay in its publication. Nearly seventeen years have elapsed since Mr. Webster's death. If all who acted with him in public affairs have not yet passed away, there has occurred in this country, since his decease, one of those catastrophes which make a wide chasm in the history of a nation, and which separate periods not actually remote from each other, as if a century had intervened. Mr. Webster's life ended as the era of patriotic efforts to avert from our country the disasters of internal conflict and civil war was about to close, and when such efforts were about to prove of no avail. To that era he belongs, and in it he stands a grand historical figure, toward whom the eyes of men will be more and more directed as they contemplate what was done to deepen the foundations of our constitutional Republic by those who received it from its immediate founders. We cannot too often revert to the study of their principles, the recollection of their measures, and the appreciation of their services. Above all, we cannot too soon seek to do justice to the memory of a great man, who for nearly forty years was one of the most conspicuous of our statesmen; and whose intellect, by the admission of all, impressed itself upon the age in which he lived with an influence inferior to that of none of his countrymen, and to that of very few of his contemporaries in any portion of the globe.

It is not alone, however, because Mr. Webster was a great

statesman, that a life of him may be important or interesting. He had the singular and rare fortune to be as eminent in the profession of the law as he was in the capacity of a statesman. Through his whole life, these two functions, seldom united to a high degree in the same person, were displayed in constant activity, and each was constantly adding to his reputation, and increasing his influence.

But when this has been said of Mr. Webster, all that made up his public character and renown has not been said. For, as if to complete the compass of his extraordinary endowments, he was an orator in the sense in which Demosthenes, Cicero, Chatham, and Burke, were orators.

If to enlighten, instruct, and elevate popular assemblies or public bodies by spoken discourse, that becomes part of the literature, and is indestructibly associated with the language of a people—if, to create those masterpieces of speech which are preserved by diction, eloquence, reasoning, and thought, that men will not "willingly let die"—if this constitutes oratory, Mr. Webster stands, by the judgment of mankind, among those who have wielded this great power in ancient or in modern times. What he was, however, as an orator, as a lawyer, and as a statesman, would fail to be an adequate portrayal of him, if it were not accompanied by some delineation of what he was as a man. His great intellectual endowments and conspicuous civil functions were united with a character of equally marked peculiarities, and his private life was as full and capacious as that which was known to the public; and it is that which is the most vividly and fondly remembered by those who were intimately associated with him.

If our literature were to remain without a suitable biography of such a man until all those who had known him have ceased to be able to attest and to describe him as he was, it would be marked by a void which some future generation might undertake to fill without the full means of doing justice to him and to his relation to his times. In this department of letters, it is possible that something is gained by the absence of any personal connection between the biographer and his subject; but it is also certain that much is lost when the greater impartiality of the writer is necessarily accompanied by an inferior knowledge of those motives of action, those principles of conduct, and those traits of character which constitute the essential individuality of him who is to be described. The world is generally agreed that lives of distinguished men, which are written by those who fulfil in them an office of friendship, even if they are to be taken with some allowance, possess a balance of advantages. To the criticism, which embraces this general principle, I do not fear to trust myself in all that I have said concerning Mr. Webster. No tie of kindred existed between him and myself; and I am not conscious of the presumption of supposing that I can gain or lose by the judgments that may be formed respecting any portion of his career, any act of his life, or any feature of his character. At the same time, it would be an affectation, if I were not to avow that the writing of this work has been with me a labor of love.

In its prosecution, I have had the benefit of a thorough revision of what I have written by Mr. Ticknor, whose interest both in the subject and in the writer has been with him a double motive for the attention he has bestowed upon my work. All who know the strength of his memory, the soundness of his judgment, and the severity of his taste, will appreciate, as I do, the advantage I have derived from his assistance. No part, however, of this work, it should be understood, has proceeded from his pen, excepting the passages which are expressly quoted from his reminiscences, which were written immediately after Mr. Webster's death, in 1852, but have been hitherto unpublished.

My thanks are also due to the Hon. R. M. Blatchford, the Hon. Hiram Ketchum, and Charles A. Stetson, Esq., of this city; and to the Hon. Peter Harvey and Franklin Haven, Esq., of Boston—all dear and cherished friends of Mr. Webster—for the communication of important materials and information.

The Right Hon. John Evelyn Denison, Speaker of the House of Commons, one of Mr. Webster's English friends, with whom he most frequently corresponded, has kindly placed at my disposal the letters which passed between them.

To George J. Abbott, Esq., formerly of the State Department, and now United States Consul at Sheffield, England—who acted for a long time as Mr. Webster's private secretary, and was with him at Marshfield at the time of his death, who enjoyed Mr. Webster's full confidence, and was much beloved by him—I have to express the cordial thanks of the surviving literary executors for the services anticipated in the reference to him made in Mr. Webster's will.

Although some of the letters which are embraced in this work have been in print since the year 1857, and a few of them had been published previously, their use, in the connection in which they are here found, was essential to the development of Mr. Webster's history, and the illustration of his character. A great many others of Mr. Webster's letters are now published for the first time.

The portrait, which has been engraved for the first volume of this work, was painted by Healy, soon after the negotiation of the Treaty of Washington. Mr. Webster was painted many times, at different periods of his life, by other artists, but by no one better than by Mr. Healy, to whom he sat several times. The picture, of which I have made use, was kindly lent for the purpose by Mr. Blatchford.

The various illustrations, in woodcut, contained in the body of the work, are from photographic views taken expressly for this purpose. They embrace "Elms Farm," and the burial-place of the Webster family, at Franklin, New Hampshire; Mr. Webster's house, in Summer Street, Boston; the "Green Harbor" estate, at Marshfield; and the monuments erected at the tomb in which lie the remains of Mr. Webster, Mrs. Grace Webster, and their children.

Mrs. Caroline Le Roy Webster, after the death of her husband, transferred to the trustees, under Mr. Webster's will, her interest in the estate at Marshfield, and came to reside in the city of New York, where she still survives, surrounded by tho respect and interest of a large circle of friends.

NEW YORK, *Sept.*, 1869.

CONTENTS OF VOLUME I.

CHAPTER VII.

1815–1816.

CHAPTER VIII.

1816–1819.

CHAPTER IX.

1820–1822.

CHAPTER X.

1823–1824.

CHAPTER XI.

1824–1825.

CHAPTER XII.

1825–1826.

CHAPTER XIII.

1826–1827.

CHAPTER XIV.

1827–1828.

CHAPTER XV.

1828–1829.

CHAPTER XVI.

1829–1830.

CHAPTER XVII.

1830–1831.

CHAPTER XVIII.

1831–1832.

CHAPTER XIX.

1832–1833.

LIFE OF DANIEL WEBSTER.

CHAPTER I.

1782–1797.

BIRTH AND PARENTAGE—BOYHOOD—EARLY EDUCATION—ENTERS DARTMOUTH COLLEGE.

NEAR the centre of New Hampshire, where two moderate rivers unite, and form the Merrimac, a company of persons from Kingston, after the peace of 1763, obtained from the royal governor of the province a grant of a township of land, to which the name of Stevenstown was first given, from the name of Colonel Stevens, their leader. Among these persons was Ebenezer Webster, who was born in Kingston in 1739, the son of a farmer and freeholder of the same name. Like many of the young men of New England, he, in early life, enlisted in the provincial troops, raised to take part in the French War; and became a private in one of the companies of "Rangers," which were commanded by Major Robert Rogers, and which served under Sir Jeffrey Amherst in the invasion of Canada.[1] He rose to the rank of captain before the end of the war. At the peace he returned to his native town, was married, and joined the company of settlers who went northward into the wilderness, and founded the town of Stevenstown, the name of which was afterward changed to Salisbury. The township, as originally laid out, was four miles wide, along the west bank of the Merrimac, and extended southwestwardly for nine miles, nearly to the top of the Kearsarge Mountain. The portion of this grant, which Ebenezer Webster obtained for himself, lay farther to the north than any of the others, so that, after his log house was built upon it, there was no civilized neighbor between him and Montreal.

The family of Webster, from which this pioneer of New Hampshire was descended, appear to have been first settled at Hampton, on the coast, about 1636, or sixteen years after the landing of the Pilgrims at Plymouth. Their most remote known ancestor was Thomas Webster, from whom the descent to Ebenezer Webster can be regularly traced in the church and town records of Hampton, Kingston, and Salisbury. They were originally Scotch; but they probably emigrated to this country from England.

Precisely how long Ebenezer Webster continued to live in the log house, which he must have erected about the year 1764, cannot now be determined; but that house was his home from the time when it was built until near the close of the Revolutionary War. From it he buried his first wife, Mehitable Smith, who died in March, 1774; and to it he brought Abigail Eastman, who became his second wife in August of the same year. It was on a hill, three miles westwardly from the river. The region about it was mountainous; the winters were long and dreary; the depth of snow was often prodigious, and there were no regular roads for communication with the country below. The land was poor. Of comfort there was little to be gained there. Of the necessaries of life, what could be had were purchased with severe toil, hardship, and often danger, or

[1] From the journals of Major Rogers, a rare and curious book, printed in London, in 1765, it may be inferred that the enlistment of Ebenezer Webster occurred in 1760, or when he was about two-and-twenty.

at least with the apprehension of danger; for, although the peace of 1763 had put an end to the wild and cruel forays of the Northern Indians into the settlements of New England, the memory of those terrible midnight raids had not yet passed away, and, in the forest that stretched from Ebenezer Webster's farm to the frontier of Canada, there still lurked, if not roving bands, roving individual savages, whose visits, when innocent of blood, too well suggested the horrors of a time not long gone by.[1] In such scenes, and in such a life, he who had "come home from the wars" with strong elements of character to settle down as a farmer on the outposts of civilization, to be one of the founders of a new town, to have children born to him, to know sorrow, to struggle and to toil, was not unlikely to become a devoted parent, a patriotic and respected citizen, and a devout man. All these qualities and characteristics, in fact, belonged to Ebenezer Webster. He is described, too, as a man of great firmness, whose bearing and manner were decisive;[2] tall and erect, with a full chest, black hair and eyes, and rather large and prominent features. Of education, save what he had given to himself, he had none; for it is recorded of him that he never saw the interior of a school-house in the capacity of a pupil. Yet it is known that some of the earliest records of the town of Salisbury are in his handwriting; and by the middle period of his life he was sufficiently well educated to fulfil, from that time to his death,

[1] When speaking once, at length, of his father and mother and their life in the log house, Mr. Webster said: "They endured together in this hut all sorts of privations and hardships; my mother was constantly visited by Indians who had never before gone to a white man's house but to kill its inhabitants, while my father perhaps was gone, as he frequently was, miles away, carrying on his back the corn to be ground, which was to support his family."—(*MSS. in the author's possession.*)

[2] The following anecdote, illustrating his decision of character, is taken from a Memoir of him, published in the *New-Hampshire Statesman*, in 1858, by George W. Nesmith, Esq. In 1791, he was appointed at the head of a committee of the town and the church, to settle a clergyman, the Rev. Thomas Worcester. A council, after the manner of the churches in New England, was assembled to perform the ordination. But a dispute arose between the council and Mr. Worcester on a point of doctrine, and a long time was spent in the discussion, the people waiting impatiently without for the ordination to proceed. At length Judge Webster was appointed to wait upon the council, and inquire into the cause of the delay. He appeared before them, and heard their statement. "Gentlemen," said he, "the ordination must come on *now*, and, if you cannot assist, we must try to get along without you. The point under discussion must be postponed to some other day." The ordination ceremonies proceeded without any further delay.

with entire respectability, the functions of a legislator and a magistrate.[1]

He had been married a second time, as I have said, not long before the shock sent through New England from Bunker Hill was felt in her remotest borders, and her yeomanry sprang to arms. Captain Webster was among the first of them to obey that summons. He raised a company in his own town, the population of which had then become so considerable that it could furnish two hundred men; and, with the other New-Hampshire troops, he and the company which he commanded were out in nearly every campaign of the Revolutionary War. He fought at Bennington under Stark, and at White Plains; and he was at West Point when Arnold's attempt to surrender that post to the British occurred.[2] In the militia of New Hampshire he held the rank of colonel; but, in his own neighborhood, he was for a long time generally called "the captain."

How much he was at home during the war it would of

[1] One of his townsmen thus described him in a letter addressed to the son-in-law of Ezekiel Webster, Professor Sanborn of Dartmouth College, in 1853: "Of his father, Hon. Ebenezer Webster, I have a perfect recollection, as to form and features. His stature was nearly six feet. He was compact, robust, and well-proportioned, and, late in life, inclined to corpulency. His complexion was dark, a broad projecting forehead, eyes large, black, and piercing, overshadowed by heavy brows. With respect to intellect, he was a perfect example of a strong-minded, unlettered man; of sound common sense, correct judgment, and tenacious memory; all of which desirable qualities were for him, to some extent, a substitute for education. He was a resolute, determined character, and never easily turned from his purpose, when once convinced that it was right." — (*Letter by Mr. Thomas H. Pettingill. Correspondence of Daniel Webster*, vol. i., p. 59.)

[2] "A sergeant of his company informed me that he was among the first [at Bennington] to scale the Tory breastwork, as it was called; and that, when he came out of the battle, he was so covered with dust and powder that he could scarcely be recognized." (Mr. Pettingill, *ut supra.*) In 1840, while travelling in the southwestern part of New Hampshire, and anxious to reach his destination, Mr. Webster, while ascending a hill, observed an aged man before him who was driving a fine horse. His name was Boynton. Leaving his own vehicle, Mr. Webster jumped into Mr. Boynton's wagon; so that "the first thing I knew," as the old man said afterward, "he was sitting beside me." But he did not know his passenger at that time, although he engaged to drive him to Wilton. As they went along, conversing about people in New Hampshire, Mr. Boynton observed that he had known "Old Judge Webster, the father of Daniel;" he had been "out in the Continental War with him. I remember," said he, "that he stood guard before General Washington's headquarters the night after Arnold's treason. In the morning General Washington asked him to take a glass of wine with him; and I don't believe he slept a wink the night after that." (MSS.) It was a well-known tradition in New Hampshire, derived from one of his soldiers, that when he was posted for that night as officer of the guard, at headquarters, Washington said to him, "Captain Webster, I believe I can trust *you*."—(*Mr. Nesmith's Memoir in the New-Hampshire Statesman, ut supra.*)

course be impossible to ascertain now. But the domestic events which mark this portion of his life, and render his name and character of interest to the world, were the births of his two sons, Ezekiel and Daniel, who were the only sons of his second marriage. The former was born on the 11th of April, 1780, and the latter on the 18th of January, 1782.[1] From a collation of all the evidence respecting the place in which Daniel was born, it appears that his brother Ezekiel and one of his sisters were born in the log house; that their father built a second house, usually called a "frame" house, near the same spot; and that, in this second house, Daniel was born. In about a year after his birth his father removed to the bank of the Merrimac, to the house in which he died.[2]

"Elms Farm," as it was afterward called, from the numbers of fine elms which are upon it, is the place to which Captain Webster removed in 1783. It is situated in a valley, at a bend of the Merrimac, two and a half miles below the head of that river. It was originally a part of the township of Salisbury; but in 1828 a new town, including this farm, was set off from the eastern end of Salisbury, and called Franklin. The place was bought by Mr. Webster's father, of a family whose name was Call. They were the first settlers upon it; and, many years before they sold it, they had suffered terrible cruelties there at the hands of the Indians.[3] High ranges of hills enclose

[1] The children of Ebenezer Webster, by his first marriage, were five—Olle, a daughter, and Ebenezer, a son, who died young; Susannah, born October, 1766, married to John Colby; David, and Joseph. The children of the second marriage were Mehitable, Abigail, married to Mr. Haddock, Ezekiel, Daniel, and Sarah; Mehitable and Sarah died unmarried.

[2] A sketch of the house in which Mr. Webster was born, drawn by Charles Lanman, Esq., and sanctioned by Mr. Webster, is prefixed to the first volume of his works. The cut at the head of the present chapter is a view of "Elms Farm," as it now appears.

[3] Mr. Webster, in a letter written from this spot to President Fillmore, in July, 1852, says: "Under my eyes, at this moment, is the site of one of the last forts, built on the frontiers to protect the inhabitants of this and the neighboring towns against the Indians. The Indians made constant attacks, often so suddenly, that they could not be resisted. A Mrs. Call was killed by them on this spot, about the year 1775. The cellar of her cabin is close by my house. She was an elderly woman, and her husband and her son were at work in the field, not half a mile off. Her daughter-in-law, with her child in her arms, seeing the Indians coming, jumped in behind the chimney, hushed her baby, and so avoided discovery, and escaped death. This baby, whose name was John Call, I knew very well when I was a boy. My father bought this place of that family. This is one of the very many border stories to which I have listened of winter evenings, in the early part of my life. You will perceive, my dear sir, that I am old enough to begin to become

the river on both sides, but leaving a broad "intervale" of meadow. The two streams which form the Merrimac have retained their Indian names. One, the Pemigewasset, rises in the White Mountains, and flows down their southern slopes, "the beau ideal of a mountain stream," as Mr. Webster has described it—"cold, noisy, winding, and with banks of much picturesque beauty."[1] The other, the Winnepiseogee, is the outlet of the great lake of the same name, which discharges its waters westwardly, until they unite with those of the mountain torrent, making a circuit of about a hundred miles before they reach the sea, through the Merrimac, at Newburyport. Concord, the legislative capital of New Hampshire, is fifteen miles below Franklin, on the same side of the river. From a high sheep-pasture on the Webster farm, through a wide opening in the hills, beyond the Kearsarge Mountain, in a northwesterly direction, Ascutney Mountain, in Vermont, is visible; and from the same spot, looking nearly northeast, Mount Washington, the highest peak of the White Mountains, shows its snowy summit. On this farm the boyhood of Daniel Webster was passed.

No account of his origin can be complete without some attempt to find in his race those remarkable physical traits which distinguished his person through life, and which are so well known to the world, in their unison with his intellectual and moral nature. Fortunately, we have his own account of the physical peculiarities of his family, given with his accustomed clearness in a few sentences of his autobiography. From these many of my readers may be surprised to learn that the Websters of New England have, in general, "light complexions, sandy hair, a good deal of it, and bushy eyebrows;" and that they "are rather slender than broad or corpulent."[2] But he tells us that his father and his father's brothers were very unlike in their personal traits; that his father resembled his grandmother, while his uncles resembled his grandfather.

garrulous; for it is certain that Mrs. Call's murder, by the Indians, a hundred years ago, has little to do with the legislation or diplomacy of the present time."—(*Correspondence*, ii., 535.)

[1] Letter to Mr. Blatchford, from Franklin, May 3, 1846.—(*Correspondence*, ii., 225.

[2] Dr. Noah Webster, the eminent lexicographer, was of a collateral branch of this family.—(*Biographical Memoir*, *Works*, i.)

This grandmother, his father's mother, was Susannah Bachelder, a descendant of the Rev. Stephen Bachelder, in the county of Rockingham. She had black hair and black eyes, and was a woman of uncommon strength of character. Her son, Mr. Webster's father, inherited from her the "Bachelder complexion;" her other sons had the Webster characteristics. The same division of the parental traits took place in Mr. Webster's own generation. He himself has said that, of his four brothers, only one was dark like himself; the other three "ran off into the general characteristics belonging to the name."[1] In fact, however, I have understood that his own brother Ezekiel, who is represented as a model of manly beauty, although his complexion was not so dark as Daniel's, had black hair.

For which of these two brothers there appeared to be the best chance of health and longevity, in their earlier years, their contemporaries would not have doubted. Ezekiel was a robust youth, grew nearly to manhood in the healthy labors of a farmer's son, who was destined for a farmer himself, was afterward educated, and studied and practised the law; but he died instantly, without any apparent illness, at the age of forty-nine. Daniel was a sickly child, and for that reason was not put to work upon the farm so much as his brother; yet he lived to be a man whose physical constitution and frame seemed to be a fitting tabernacle for so great an intellect; and his last illness, in his seventy-first year, was almost the only acute one that he was ever called to endure after he had grown up.

Of the mother of Daniel Webster, there is important testimony from her sons. That she was a woman of clear and vigorous understanding, that she was a tender and self-sacrificing mother, and that to her was referred the final decision of a question that was to affect not only their welfare, but her own and that of every other member of her family, are well authenticated facts.

But it was from his father chiefly, I suppose—from that "Bachelder complexion," physical and moral—that Daniel

[1] Autobiography.

Webster derived the marked qualities of his nature;[1] and to the father I therefore now return, in order to give my readers some idea of the feeling with which his son ever regarded him, before I enter upon the narrative of that son's childhood and youth. To me there is something singularly attractive in the image of that tall, dark man, in form and presence one of the noblest of the earth,[2] standing on his not too fertile New-Hampshire acres, looking abroad into the world, and comparing himself with men for whom Nature had done less than she had for him, but whom education had placed where he could not be their competitor. I seem to see his deep, black eye fall tenderly on the boys who are growing up around him, marking the elder for the stay and staff of his age in the labors of home, and setting apart the younger for a life of books and learning and fame. He has no concealments from his household; and, as time rolls on, all come to know his plan. It suits the circumstances, it is in accordance with the habits of a New-England family. Nevertheless, it is a great undertaking in such a house, to send even one son "to college." But this man is full of resolution. He has a complexion, as General Stark said of him, "which burned gunpowder will not change," and a heart, as his great son said of him, "which he seemed to have borrowed from a lion." Moreover, he is one of that kind of men who live for their children; and he knows that in his laborious life he has nothing else for which to live. His own want of early education, he thinks, shall be compensated by that which he will give to this intelligent, though feeble, youngest boy; and he and the elder lad will extort from their "stubborn glebe" the means of accomplishing this work of love.

He came, it may readily be supposed, not suddenly or hastily to this resolution. To the age of fourteen, Daniel—who

[1] Writing to his son Fletcher, in 1840, respecting the name to be given to his eldest grandson, Mr. Webster said: "I believe we are all indebted to my father's mother for a large portion of the little sense and character which belongs to us. Her name was Susannah Bachelder; she was the daughter of a clergyman, and a woman of uncommon strength of understanding. If I had had many boys, I should have called one of them 'Bachelder.'" The boy in question, Mr. Fletcher Webster's eldest son, was named for his grandfather.

[2] Mr. Webster always said that his father was the handsomest man he had ever seen, excepting his brother Ezekiel.

had been taught to read at home, by his mother or his elder sisters, so early that he never afterward could remember when he could not read the Bible—had no other advantages of education than such as he could obtain at the poor town-schools, which were kept only during a part of the year. But his own words will best describe how this was managed, and to what it amounted:

"I do not remember when or by whom I was taught to read, because I cannot, and never could, recollect a time when I could not read the Bible. I suppose I was taught by my mother, or by my elder sisters. My father seemed to have no higher object in the world than to educate his children to the full extent of his very limited ability. No means were within his reach, generally speaking, but the small town-schools. These were kept by teachers, sufficiently indifferent, in the several neighborhoods of the township, each a small part of the year. To these I was sent with the other children.

"When the school was in our neighborhood, it was easy to attend; when it removed to a more distant district, I followed it, still living at home. While yet quite young, and in winter, I was sent daily two and a half or three miles to the school. When it removed still farther, my father sometimes boarded me out in a neighboring family, so that I could still be in the school. A good deal of this was an extra care, more than had been bestowed on my elder brothers, and originating in a conviction of the slenderness and frailty of my constitution, which was thought not likely ever to allow me to pursue a robust occupation.

"In these schools, nothing was taught but reading and writing; and, as to these, the first I generally could perform better than the teacher, and the last a good master could hardly instruct me in; writing was so laborious, irksome, and repulsive an occupation to me always. My masters used to tell me that they feared, after all, my fingers were destined for the plough-tail."[1]

Such was the life of the boy Daniel Webster at about the period when the foundations of the Constitution of the United States were laid. The strong good sense and intelligent patriotism of the father acted upon that great national event.[2] His townsmen had been accustomed to intrust to him

[1] Autobiography, written by Mr. Webster in 1830.

[2] Mr. Webster once repeated to me, with great pride, a little speech made by his father before giving his vote for the Constitution, and requested me, if I ever had an opportunity, to do something to perpetuate it. It is well known that when the convention of New Hampshire first assembled, in February, 1788, a

such public stations as they had to bestow, and he sat in the convention of New Hampshire, which ratified the Federal Constitution, while his little son at home was playing among the cowslips in the sweet meadows of the Merrimac. When the father gave his vote for "the more perfect Union" which the new frame of government was to establish, the early years of his child, who was to instruct the intellect of the nation in its principles, had so little promise of health, that, as he grew up, play was necessarily allowed to be his chief vocation.

The boy became an adept in it. He played all through the long summer days when he could not work, having for his chief companion, in his field-sports, a certain battered old British soldier and sailor, who had deserted from the king's colors at Bunker Hill, and, having come with a New-Hampshire regiment at the close of the war, had settled himself in a little cottage on the Webster farm. From this man, or with him, he learned the art of angling, which remained a passion with him through life. He apostrophizes this odd character in his autobiography, as Hamlet did Yorick.

> "Thou hast carried me on thy back a thousand times,"

was a phrase that rushed to his memory when, after he had become a pillar of the state, he wrote this account of Robert Wise:

> "Early and deeply religious, my father had still a good deal of natural gayety; he delighted to have some one about him that possessed

majority of the delegates were found to be under instructions from their towns to vote against the Constitution. This was the case with Colonel Webster. But the convention was adjourned to meet again in June; and, in the mean time, Colonel Webster obtained from his constituents permission to vote according to his own judgment. When the vote was about to be taken, he rose, and said: "Mr. President, I have listened to the arguments for and against the Constitution. I am convinced such a government as that constitution will establish, if adopted—a government acting directly on the people of the States—is necessary for the common defence and the general welfare. It is the only government which will enable us to pay off the national debt—the debt which we owe for the Revolution, and which we are bound in honor fully and fairly to discharge. Besides, I have followed the lead of Washington through seven years of war, and I have never been misled. His name is subscribed to this Constitution. He will not mislead us now. I shall vote for its adoption."

I have taken the words of the speech from Mr. Nesmith's Memoir. They are substantially the same with those repeated to me by Mr. Webster. Judge Webster was one of the electors of the President in New Hampshire, when Washington was first chosen to that office.

a humorous vein. A character of this sort, one Robert Wise, with whose adventures, as I learned them from himself, I could fill a small book, was a near neighbor, and a sort of humble companion for a great many years. He was a Yorkshire man; had been a sailor; was with Byng in the Mediterranean; had been a soldier; deserted from the garrison of Gibraltar; travelled through Spain and France and Holland; was taken up afterward, severely punished, and sent back to the army; was in the battle of Minden; had a thousand stories of the yellow-haired Prince Ferdinand; was sent to Ireland, and thence to Boston, with the troops brought out by General Gage; fought at Bunker Hill; deserted to our ranks; served with the New-Hampshire troops in all the succeeding campaigns, and, at the peace, built a little cottage in the corner of our field, and lived there to an advanced old age. He was my *Izaac Walton.* He had a wife, but no child. He loved me, because I would read the newspapers to him, containing the accounts of battles in the European wars. He had twice deserted from the English king, and once at least committed treason as well as desertion; but he had still a British heart. When I have read to him the details of the victories of Howe, and Jervis, etc., I remember he was excited almost to convulsions, and would relieve his excitement by a gush of exulting tears. He finally picked up a fatherless child, took him home, sent him to school, and took care of him, only, as he said, that he might have some one to read the newspaper to him. He could never read himself. Alas, poor Robert! I have never so attained the narrative art as to hold the attention of others as thou, with thy Yorkshire tongue, hast held mine. Thou hast carried me many a mile on thy back, paddled me over and over, and up and down the stream, and given whole days in aid of my boyish sports, and asked no meed but that, at night, I would sit down at thy cottage door, and read to thee some passage of thy country's glory! Thou wast indeed a true Briton."[1]

It was in this happy childhood that he began those habits of minute observation of nature, which all who ever knew him knew to be one of his strongest characteristics, and one of his greatest pleasures. Then, for example, he saw and never forgot how the salmon and the shad, as they came up the Merrimac, "shook hands, and parted" at the confluence of the two streams which make that river, "the shad all going into the lakes, and the salmon all keeping up the mountain torrent, which they continued to ascend, as used to be said, until their back fins were out of the water."[2] Then, too, he first began to notice how the river was deepening its channel; a phenomenon

[1] Autobiography.

[2] Letter to Mr. Blatchford, *ut supra.*

in what he calls "the philosophy of streams," which he continued, at intervals, to note from those banks for fifty years.[1] Then, also, he must have acquired that strong love of agriculture which never left him; for at no period of his life, after boyhood, could he have seen much of practical farming, until he became possessed of his father's property; and I imagine that this is not a propensity which educated men often acquire after they have become cultivated and busy men of the world. In this easy and expanding life, overcoming, each year, something of the ailments of his childhood, he grew to be fourteen years of age, and imbibed most of those tastes which ever afterward drew him, when he could release himself from contact with man, into the closest communion with Nature.

In this period also we are to find the early influences which gave a peculiar tinge and fervor to his patriotic feelings—feelings that always carried his love of country, by emotions whose sources lay deep in an emotional nature, to the history of what had been done and suffered in order to make a country. For we are to remember that at his paternal fireside sat and talked, in the long winter evenings, one who had been an actor, first in the great war by which our fathers helped the crown of England to extinguish the power of France on this continent, and then in that other war for independence, by which the unrequited and misgoverned provinces severed themselves from the parent state. Whoever seeks to know what it was in the formation of the character of Daniel Webster that gave such a glow to the eloquence, and such a breadth to the patriotism of his after-years, whenever and wherever American history connected itself with American nationality, must go back to that fireside, and listen in imagination to the tales which his young heart drank from his father's lips.

Finally, we must go to this period as the time when the religious tendencies, which Nature had implanted in his temperament, received their first impulses and their early development. Whatever may have been his imperfections or his failings, his religious feelings were always deep and fervent; and in all the successes or vicissitudes or sorrows of his life, they

[1] Letter to Mr. Blatchford, *ut supra*.

grew stronger and stronger to the hour of his death. All that need now be said of the special form of Christian faith under which his childhood was passed is, that it was doubtless that which was derived from the Puritans. But its spirit, as it prevailed in his father's house and in his father's life, is all comprehended in two emphatic words, which he applied to his parent, and which described him as "religious, but not sour."[1]

What he had learned of books, at this time, we are partly told by himself in his autobiography. A small circulating library had been established in the neighborhood by his father and other persons, and among the books which he obtained from it was the *Spectator*. Fond of poetry, he went at once to the criticism on Chevy Chase, for the sake of the verses which are cited. "I could not understand," he says, "why it was necessary that the author of the *Spectator* should take such great pains to prove that Chevy Chase was a good story; that was the last thing I doubted." Of other poetry, he knew the psalms and hymns of Dr. Watts; and he informs us that he could repeat them at ten or twelve years of age. There never was, in truth, a time in his subsequent life when he could not repeat them, as many can attest who have heard him do so with

[1] "He had in him," says Mr. Webster, what I collect to have been the character of some of the old Puritans. He was deeply religious, but not sour. On the contrary, good-humored, facetious, showing even in his age, with a contagious laugh, teeth all as white as alabaster, gentle, soft, playful, and yet having a heart in him that he seemed to have borrowed from a lion. He could frown—a frown it was—but cheerfulness, good-humor, and smiles composed his most usual aspect."—(*Letter to R. M. Blatchford, Esq., May* 3, 1846. *Correspondence*, vol. ii., p. 227.)

Mr. Nesmith relates the following specimen of his humor: He had a nephew, Stephen Bohonon by name, who had been a soldier in his company at West Point, and afterward lived at the "South Road" village, in Salisbury. One day, having some business with his nephew, he went to this village, and found him teaching the young people of the neighborhood to dance. He entered the hall where the dancing was going on, and, after waiting a short time, finished his business with his nephew, and returned home. Soon the rumor was circulated that Judge Webster had been seen in a dancing-hall. A member of his church entered a complaint, requiring satisfaction for this reproach. Parson Worcester suggested a written acknowledgment. Judge Webster replied that he would put nothing on file, but that he would make an oral confession before the congregation. Accordingly, on the next Sunday, after the forenoon exercises were closed, he rose in his place, and said: "A few days since, I had some business with my nephew, Stephen Bohonon; went up to his house, found him in the hall of the tavern, instructing the youth in dancing. They were in the midst of a dance when I entered the hall. I took a seat, and waited until the dance was closed; took the earliest opportunity to do my errand with Stephen; found the young people civil and orderly; saw nothing improper. Now, if, in all this, I have offended any of my *weaker* brethren, I am sorry for it."—(*New-Hampshire Statesman.*)

singular felicity, sometimes with a serious and sometimes with a humorous application. No other sacred poetry ever appeared to him so affecting and devout.

He also read, at this time, Pope's "Essay on Man," and learned to repeat the whole of it. This was done systematically; for, he says, "we had so few books, that to read them once or twice was nothing. We thought they were all to be got by heart." But with a fondness of recollection, that will cause all who remember the arrival of a new year's almanac in such a home to understand him when he pronounces it "an acquisition," he relates how he one night rose from his bed, after a dispute with Ezekiel about a couplet of poetry at the head of the April page in the new annual, groped his way to the kitchen, lighted a candle, and went to find the little pamphlet in a distant room. He reached the object of his search, ascertained that he was wrong in his quotation, returned to his chamber, blew out his candle, and went to bed. But, in his literary eagerness, he had come very near burning down the house. A spark from the candle had set fire to some cotton clothes in the room where the almanac had been left, and where his maternal grandmother, of the age of eighty, was sleeping. The flames had caught some of the furniture, and even part of the woodwork of the room. Luckily, he saw the light before he fell asleep. It was at two o'clock in the morning, and in midwinter; and winter in New Hampshire is no genial season. He sprang from his bed, and roused the family by a sharp cry. His father's presence of mind saved the house.

Beyond such acquisitions as were made at home, and the very little that he obtained at the town schools, he is not known to have had any other learning down to the time when his father determined to send him away for other advantages. But I must not leave this period of his first school-days without mentioning his masters, whose names have been rescued from oblivion by their connection with his, and by his affectionate fidelity to all early associations. Two of them were Thomas Chase and James Tappan. Of neither of these pedagogues, however, could it probably be said that the neighbors were much astonished by what they carried in their heads.

The good folk of Salisbury were well aware that there were

institutions and teachers not far off, that could do rather more for their children, when the time came, than Master Chase or Master Tappan. But the district schools of New England have been, from the first, the intellectual nurseries of the land; and it was in these that the two worthies above named dispensed such food for infant minds as they had to give. It is related of Thomas Chase, by Mr. Everett, I presume on Mr. Webster's authority, that he could read tolerably well, and wrote a good hand, but that spelling was not his *forte.*[1] As Mr. Webster was but three or four years old when he attended Master Chase, the orthography of the teacher was not perhaps of the last importance. Tappan came after him, and had somewhat higher qualifications. He lived to a very advanced age, to be always tenderly remembered by his pupil, and to receive from him more substantial tokens of affectionate recognition than the words, however graceful and touching they were, that came to the aged teacher from a pen whose faculty of expressing sympathy and kindness and consolation was scarcely less than its power to address and control the understandings of men.

There was also a third master, whose name Mr. Webster has commemorated in an especial manner, in connection with the first time that he ever saw a copy of the Constitution of the United States. This was William Hoyt, who taught the school in Salisbury for many years, and who also fulfilled the function of keeping a small shop. Mr. Webster has not directly said that he attended Hoyt's school, but, from his account of him, it is no doubt to be inferred that he did:

"William Hoyt was for many years teacher of our country school in Salisbury. I do not call it village school, because there was at that time no village; and boys came to school in the winter, the only season in which schools were usually open, from distances of several miles, wading through the snow or running upon its crust, with their curly heads of hair often whitened with frost from their own breath. I knew William Hoyt well, and 'every truant knew.' He was an austere man, but a good teacher of children. He had been a printer in Newburyport, wrote a very fair and excellent hand, was a good reader, and did teach boys, that which so few masters can or will do, to read well themselves. Beyond this, and perhaps a very slight knowledge of grammar, his attainments did not

[1] Biographical Memoir, Works, vol. i., xxi.

extend. He had brought with him into the town a little property, which he took very good care of. He rather loved money; of all the cases of nouns, preferring the possessive. He also kept a little shop for the sale of various commodities, in the house exactly over the way from this. I do not know how old I was, but I remember having gone into his shop one day, and bought a small cotton pocket-handkerchief with the Constitution of the United States printed on its two sides. From this I learned either that there was a constitution, or that there were thirteen States. I remember to have read it, and have known more or less of it ever since. William Hoyt and his wife lie buried in the graveyard under our eye, on my farm, near the graves of my own family. He left no children. I suppose that this little handkerchief was purchased about the time I was eight years old, as I remember listening to the conversation of my father and Mr. Thompson upon political events which happened in the year 1790."[1]

About the year 1791, his father, who had been a member of both Houses of the State Legislature at various times, was made a Judge of the Court of Common Pleas for the county in which he lived. It was the practice in New Hampshire, at that day, to constitute this court by the appointment of a lawyer as presiding judge, and to associate with him two assistant judges, who were generally called "side justices." The latter were commonly selected from among the substantial farmers. They sat in court at the trial of causes; and, as all the judges had the right, if they chose to exercise it, to sum up the case to the jury, the several members of the court might differ on the law, as well as the jury on the facts. There was, however, much business transacted at those courts which was not strictly judicial, but rather administrative and prudential, relating to the affairs of the county, and requiring strong good sense, integrity of purpose, and activity of mind—qualities which Judge Webster pos-

[1] Memorandum dictated to Mr. Blatchford, at Franklin, October 29, 1850.—(*Correspondence*, ii., 398.)

It was a good deal the practice in the latter part of the last, and the beginning of the present century, to print such documents on the cotton handkerchiefs sold through the country. Many of my readers will remember the Declaration of Independence, Washington's Farewell Address, as well as the Constitution, so printed. It may have been a rude, but it was a happy thought, with whomsoever it originated. Paper was dear; and a cotton handkerchief could be made and printed for a few cents. But I fear that, however durable may have been the impression produced by a few readings on the mind of such a boy as Daniel Webster, the impression of the types on his pocket-handkerchief could not have lasted long after its first immersion in water. My own recollection of these specimens of our infant manufactures is, that they were very attractive to the youthful mind, but that the housewives generally held that they "wouldn't wash."

sessed in a remarkable degree. The position of "side justice," when filled by such a man, was a highly useful and respectable one. There was a salary attached to the office, amounting to three or four hundred dollars a year, which Mr. Webster says was "a sum of the greatest importance to the family." It is not probable that this increase of his income caused Judge Webster to decide immediately to give Daniel a collegiate education, but there can be no doubt that, when the time came for that decision, he felt that this salary would be a very important aid to him in carrying out his plan. If his pecuniary circumstances had been such as to enable him to devote the whole of this sum to his youngest son's expenses at college, it would have been quite sufficient for the purpose. But this was not the case. The sequel did not show that the judicial salary could meet what the excellent parent finally had to do.

Daniel was eleven years old when this improvement in his father's affairs took place. He passed three or four years more in the kind of life which he thus describes: "I read what I could get to read, went to school when I could; and, when not at school, was a farmer's youngest boy, not good for much for want of health and strength, but was expected to do something."[1] At the end of this time, in the summer of 1795, his father disclosed to him his purpose to give him a better education than he had been able to afford to his elder sons. But it does not appear, by what can be gathered from a collation of Mr. Webster's autobiography and portions of his correspondence, that he understood at this time that he was to be sent to college, or that his father mentioned the subject of his education to him in reference to such a step. What occurred in 1795, however, can be related by no one else as he has related it, and I therefore transcribe his own touching account of it:

"Of a hot day in July, it must have been in one of the last years of Washington's administration, I was making hay with my father, just where I now see a remaining elm-tree. About the middle of the forenoon the Honorable Abiel Foster, M. C., who lived in Canterbury, six miles off, called at the house, and came into the field to see my father. He was a worthy man, college-learned, and had been a minister, but was not a

[1] Autobiography.

person of any considerable natural power. My father was his friend and supporter. He talked a while in the field, and went on his way. When he was gone, my father called me to him, and we sat down beneath the elm, on a hay-cock. He said, 'My son, that is a worthy man; he is a member of Congress; he goes to Philadelphia, and gets six dollars a day, while I toil here. It is because he had an education, which I never had. If I had had his early education I should have been in Philadelphia in his place. I came near it as it was. But I missed it, and now I must work here.' 'My dear father,' said I, 'you shall not work. Brother and I will work for you, and will wear our hands out, and you shall rest.' And I remember to have cried, and I cry now at the recollection. 'My child,' said he, 'it is of no importance to me. I now live but for my children. I could not give your elder brothers the advantages of knowledge, but I can do something for you. Exert yourself, improve your opportunities, learn, learn, and, when I am gone, you will not need to go through the hardships which I have undergone, and which have made me an old man before my time." [1]

When the next spring arrived, his father took an important step, but still without informing him that he was to be prepared for college, and apparently without having definitively decided that point in his own mind. In 1781 there had been founded at Exeter, by the Honorable John Phillips, an institution, which has ever since been known as the Phillips Exeter Academy. It has always been conducted like some of the great schools in England; that is to say, the boys are lodged in the houses of respectable families in the town, and they attend a school that is held in the academy building erected for the purpose, and furnished with appropriate rooms for the different classes. Its principal, in Mr. Webster's time, and for forty years afterward, was Dr. Benjamin Abbot, one of the most eminent instructors of youth that this country has produced.

To this institution young Webster was taken by his father in May, 1796.[2] He had never been from home before, and the change, he says, overpowered him. He found himself among ninety boys, who had seen more, and appeared to know more than he did; "and I scarcely remained," he adds, "master of my own senses." But this probably soon wore off, on all occa-

[1] Letter to Mr. Blatchford.—(*Correspondence*, ii., 228.)

[2] Mr. Webster had an elder half-brother, whose name was Joseph, and who was accounted the wit of the family. He was in the habit of saying that Daniel was sent to school in order to make him "equal to the rest of the boys."

sions, at least, but one. He was put into the lowest class, and began English grammar, writing, and arithmetic. The following anecdote is given by Mr. Everett, as a proof of the rapidity of his progress: At the end of a month, the usher[1] said to him one morning, "Webster, you will pass into the other room, and join a higher class;" and added, "Boys, you will take your final leave of Webster—you will never see him again."[2] That he was transferred to a higher class, in rather a marked manner, was told by himself to one of his early friends, who has added the following explanation of the occurrence, as he received it from Mr. Webster:

"The incident related by Mr. Everett, in his Memoir of Mr. Webster, respecting his elevation to a higher class, at the end of the first month at the academy in Exeter, needs, I think, a little correction or explanation, in order to present its most important bearing upon his future life. When his first term at Exeter was near its close, the usher said: 'Webster, you may stop a few minutes after school; I wish to speak to you.' When the other scholars had gone, the usher asked him whether he intended to return to the academy after the vacation. The answer indicated something like reluctance. It had not escaped the observation of the usher, that Webster's rustic manners and unfashionable raiment had drawn upon him the ridicule of some of his associates, who, in every respect, except habiliments and external accomplishments, were greatly his inferiors. The inference was justly drawn that the academy was in danger of losing an estimable and promising pupil, while it retained others who gave no promise of doing honor to that distinguished seminary. The usher, therefore, judiciously and kindly remarked to Mr. Webster that he was a better scholar than any in his class; that he learned more readily and easily than they did; and, if he would return at the commencement of the next term, he should be put into a higher class, and should no longer be hindered in his progress by those boys who cared more for play and dress than for solid improvement. 'These were the first truly encouraging words,' said Mr. Webster, 'that I ever received with regard to my studies. I then resolved to return, and pursue them with diligence and so much ability as I possessed.' Probably the kindness and good judgment of the usher had an important influence upon the whole course of Mr. Webster's after-life."[3]

In October he went home for a short vacation, and then

[1] Nicholas Emery, afterward an eminent lawyer and judge in Portland, Maine.

[2] Biographical Memoir.—(*Works*, i., xxiv.)

[3] Letter by J. W. McGaw, Esq., of Bangor, November 16, 1852.—(*Correspondence*, i., 48–52.)

returned to the academy, and began the Latin grammar. Dr. Abbot was absent on account of indisposition, and a very young usher was fulfilling a part of the doctor's duties. This was Joseph Stevens Buckminster, whose early maturity, personal graces, scholarship, piety, and eloquence, left an impression in New England that is even now but little weakened, although more than half a century has elapsed since his character became sanctified in that community, by an early death, at the age of twenty-eight.[1] In 1796, Buckminster was an advanced pupil of the academy, where he had won great distinction as a scholar, and where his moral excellence, and the fascination of his manners, had made him the idol of all connected with the institution.

To this youthful and brilliant teacher, younger than himself, Webster's first exercises in Latin were recited. It was Buckminster who first endeavored to overcome in the pupil a native diffidence, which will astonish any reader, who now learns, for the first time, that Daniel Webster could not, when a boy, make a school declamation. This fact, which would scarcely be credited on any other testimony than his own, was recorded by him in his autobiography with perfect frankness, and with his usual precision, and is therefore to be accepted just as he states it:

"I believe I made tolerable progress in most branches which I attended to while in this school; but there was one thing I could not do—I could not make a declamation. I could not speak before the school. The kind and excellent Buckminster sought, especially, to persuade me to perform the exercise of declamation like other boys, but I could not do it. Many a piece did I commit to memory, and recite and rehearse in my own room, over and over again, yet, when the day came, when the school collected to hear declamations, when my name was called, and I saw all eyes turned to my seat, I could not raise myself from it. Sometimes the instructors frowned, sometimes they smiled. Mr. Buckminster always pressed and entreated, most winningly, that I would venture, but I could never command sufficient resolution. When the occasion was over, I went home, and wept bitter tears of mortification."[2]

It would have been interesting if he had added a few

[1] Buckminster was born May 26, 1784; entered Harvard College in July, 1797; graduated in 1800; died in 1812.

[2] Autobiography. — (*Correspondence*, vol. i., p. 9.)

words more, and had given us his own recollection of the time when this timidity gave way, and the means which he took, if he ever took any, to overcome it. The image of Demosthenes, breaking up the impediments in his speech, occurs at once to the mind. But there is probably no parallel between the two cases. Mr. Webster's difficulty was doubtless in some degree connected with the state of his physical system; but, I imagine that, as he grew stronger, it disappeared at once, and without his being conscious of the change. The circumstances, too, by which he was surrounded, may have had something to do with his inability to speak before the school. He came there a rustic boy of fourteen, independent, but shy, did not mix a great deal in the sports of the other boys, and was perhaps less well clad than most of them. The tyranny which a great public school can exercise over its better and more sensitive members is proverbial; and it is not less a tyranny, in such cases, because it may be an unintentional one. Mr. Webster has not analyzed the feeling which made it impossible for him to ascend the platform at Exeter; but two of his early friends, one of whom was with him at the school, have stated facts which warrant my suggestions.[1] I judge it to have been a temporary embarrassment, of which he never was specially conscious afterward, because there is no record, so far as I am informed, of his having at a later period subjected himself to any discipline on account of such a feeling, as there is also no tradition of his having experienced it after he entered college. On the contrary, he became at Dartmouth a very easy and impressive speaker and debater. But the remainder of his preparatory education, before he went to college, was passed under a private tutor; and he was not, therefore, in a situation to be exercised in public declamation until he joined that institution.

He remained at Exeter only about nine months. In December, 1796, or January, 1797, his father came for him, and took him home. He had remained at the academy long enough, however, to form some friendships with persons with whom he was afterward associated in public or private

[1] See the letter of James H. Bingham, Esq. (*Correspondence*, i., 54); and the extract quoted above, from J. W. McGaw, Esq.

life.[1] He has nowhere assigned any reason why he was removed from Exeter. His progress there must have been entirely satisfactory to his father, his teachers, and himself. But probably the expense, although moderate, must have had some influence with his father, who found that he could command from a clergyman in his own neighborhood good instruction on easier terms. The state of his health, too, may have rendered it desirable that he should be nearer home; or it may have been thought that, as he was now fifteen years old, he could be carried forward faster by a private tutor than he could be in a great public school.

For some, or all of these reasons, his father determined, in February, 1797, to place him with the Rev. Samuel Wood, the minister of the adjoining town of Boscawen. The distance was about six miles from their home. On the way thither his father first disclosed to him the plan which he had formed of giving him a collegiate education. "I remember," he says, "the very hill which we were ascending, through deep snows, in a New-England sleigh, when my father made known this purpose to me. I could not speak. How could he, I thought, with so large a family, and in such narrow circumstances, think of incurring so great an expense for me? A warm glow ran all over me, and I laid my head on my father's shoulder, and wept."[2]

Of the qualifications of Dr. Wood for the charge which he had undertaken, we can judge only from the very little which Mr. Webster has said with respect to the state of his preparation when he entered college. It was doubtless a period, as Mr. Everett has observed, when the general standard of classical attainments in our country was exceedingly low—far lower than it had been for several generations succeeding the first settlement of the country; and it was long after Mr. Webster had entered upon the active duties of life before there began to be any improvement in this respect. Dr. Wood was as good a scholar, it is fair to presume, as most clergymen in New Eng-

[1] He mentions, in his autobiography, "J. W. Bracket, late of New York, deceased; William Garland, late of Portsmouth, deceased; Governor Cass, of Michigan; Mr. Saltonstall [of Salem]; and James H. Bingham, now of Claremont, N. H."

[2] Biographical Memoir.—(*Works*, i., xxiv.)

land at that day; and it is equally safe to assume that he was not a better one. When Mr. Webster says that he got "a mere breaking in," and that he went to college "miserably prepared, both in Latin and Greek," we are to remember two things: first, that he remained with Dr. Wood only six months, and that at Exeter he had but a short training in the Latin grammar and none in the Greek; secondly, that at college, and afterward, as will hereafter appear, he became a very good Latin scholar at least, and was therefore very likely to depreciate the acquisitions which he carried with him when he left Dr. Wood.[1] In his autobiography he says:

"Mr. Wood put me upon Virgil and Tully, and I conceived a pleasure in the study of them, especially the latter, which rendered application no longer a task. With what vehemence did I denounce Catiline! with what earnestness struggle for Milo! In the spring I began the Greek grammar, and at midsummer Mr. Wood said to me: 'I expected to keep you till next year, but I am tired of you, and I shall put you into college next month.' And so indeed he did, but it was a mere breaking in; I was indeed miserably prepared both in Latin and Greek; but Mr. Wood accomplished his purpose, and I entered Dartmouth College, as a freshman, August, 1797.[2]

While he was at Dr. Wood's an incident occurred which shows the humorous indulgence of his father's treatment of him, and which I should mar if I were to attempt to repeat it in any other than the colloquial way in which he related it to some friends, on a drive from Boston to Salem, in 1825:

"My father sent for me in haying-time, to help him, and put me into a field to turn hay, and left me. It was pretty lonely there, and, after working some time, I found it very dull; and, as I knew my father was gone

[1] In 1825 he spoke of Mr. Wood as "a man of some learning."—(*MSS.*)

[2] Dr. Wood, who was also Ezekiel Webster's tutor, and afterward his pastor, was a man of great excellence of character; "distinguished," says Professor Sanborn, "for his rare Christian virtues. He was one of the excellent of the earth. During his long and successful ministry at Boscawen, he fitted more than one hundred young men for college. Those who could not pay the debt, he trusted; and to some very indigent pupils he forgave the debt. He was not an eminent scholar, though a lover of learning. He could appreciate genius without feeling its fires in his own bosom. By his unwearied diligence and fidelity he succeeded in making good scholars. He labored from principle—from an ever-present conviction that he must do all within his power to benefit the rising generation. It was the boast and glory of his life that he was the tutor of Ezekiel and Daniel Webster. He loved them as children; they honored him as a father."—(*Correspondence*, i., 35.)

away, I walked home, and asked my sister Sally if she did not want to go and pick some whortleberries. She said yes. So I went and got some horses, and put a side-saddle on one, and we set off. We did not get home until it was pretty late, and I soon went to bed. When my father came home he asked my mother where I was, and what I had been about. She told him. The next morning, when I awoke, I saw all the clothes I had brought from Dr. Wood's tied up in a small bundle again. When I saw my father he asked me how I liked haying. I told him I found it 'pretty dull and lonesome yesterday.' 'Well,' said he, 'I believe you may as well go back to Dr. Wood's.' So I took my bundle under my arm, and on my way I met Thomas W. Thompson, a lawyer in Salisbury; he laughed very heartily when he saw me. 'So,' said he, 'your farming is over, is it?'"[1]

After this exploit in haying and picking whortleberries, there remained but six weeks in which to finish his preparation for college; and it appears that Dr. Wood thought it expedient to have some assistance for his Greek. "Well, sir," continued Mr. Webster, conversing in 1825 about his early life, "I went to Dr. Wood's, and, as my father had consented to my going to college, he got a young man of the name of Palmer, a senior in Dartmouth, to come and teach me Greek. I knew nothing at all about it, and I had just six weeks to prepare in. But I went to work, and entered in '97, when I was fifteen."

At Boscawen he had found another circulating library, and he read a great many of the books which it contained. But he mentions one only—"Don Quixote." It was the common translation, and in an edition of three or four duodecimo volumes. "I began to read it," he says in the autobiography, "and it is literally true that I never closed my eyes until I had finished it; nor did I lay it down, so great was the power of that extraordinary book on my imagination."

Such was the youth Daniel Webster when he entered Dartmouth College. In the ancient languages, the Latin grammar, the first six books of the "Æneid," Cicero's four Orations against Catiline, a little Greek grammar, and the four Evangelists of the Greek Testament, were his whole stock. In mathematics he had nothing but the small amount of arithmetic which he might have obtained at the town-schools and at Exeter. Of geography and history he had almost nothing but what he

[1] MSS. account of a drive from Boston to Salem, in 1825, preserved by Mr. Ticknor.

had picked up in his desultory reading. In English literature we have certain knowledge that he had read some of Addison's prose, one of Pope's larger poems, the devotional poetry of Dr. Watts, and a translation of "Don Quixote." I have sought diligently to find the earliest period at which he first knew any thing of Milton and Shakespeare—poets whose imagery, sentiments, language, and lines became afterward so inwrought with his intellectual being that they sprang into his discourse, sometimes in unbidden and unconscious quotation, and sometimes with a purposed use of riches which he had stored in one of the most retentive memories ever possessed by man. But I find no evidence that his knowledge of Milton and Shakespeare began at this early age. It is certain, however, that, before he went to Dartmouth, he must have had some miscellaneous reading of which we have no account. That he read every thing he could get to read, he has told us; and, although the two circulating libraries, which came within his reach, at Salisbury and at Boscawen, must have been rather meagre collections, we may safely infer that he devoured whatever he could find in them that could attract a lad of his years. For he tells us: "In those boyish days there were two things which I did dearly love, viz., reading and playing—passions which did not cease to struggle when boyhood was over (have they yet, altogether?) and, in regard to which, neither *cita mors* nor the *victoria laeta* could be said of either." [1]

[1] ——— "*horae*
Memento cita mors venit, aut victoria laeta."
HORACE, *Sat.* i., 7, 8.

CHAPTER II.

1797–1801.

COLLEGE LIFE—RANK AS A STUDENT—DEVELOPMENT AND ACQUISITIONS.

WE now enter upon a period, in the life of Mr. Webster, through which it is necessary to move with careful steps. The extraordinary elevation to which he rose has tended to invest his college-life with an uncommon interest, and to surround it with impressions which, however pleasing in their apparent conformity with what he afterward became, must be examined with fidelity. For those who knew him, and acted with him only after his mind was in its full maturity, and those who knew him only through the glory of his vast reputation, could not well conceive that there ever was a time, after his intellect began to be manifested at all to the observation of others, when it was not, in a degree corresponding to its subsequent exhibitions, of the same preëminent qualities and powers. Thinking and speaking of him as a prodigy, such as Nature can vouchsafe but once, men easily believed that, at all times, and in every period of his existence, he must have stood in the same relative superiority to his fellows, in which they saw and felt that he stood when they could compare him with others or themselves.

It is well known that there have been those, among the contemporaries of his youth, who have thought that his future greatness was then foreseen and predicted. But such a suggestion, even in regard to such a man, may challenge a dissent that springs from no love of disparagement; and, accordingly, there have been others who lived at the same period, and in the same associations, who have not admitted that, at college, he stood in all respects far above his competitors, and who have thought it unwise to hold him up as an example of mere genius, ascending at once to the highest pinnacles of fame, without the toil and the patient submission to routine, by which distinction is most commonly supposed, and should ordinarily be held, to be best achieved.

The purpose of biography is, or should be, truth. Eulogy and praise are not to be discarded from it, if they can rest on solid foundations. But such foundations must be explored without preconceived theories. He who admits into his descriptions of a great man's life and character the influence of any opinion concerning their example, or who is anxious about methods of education or the best means of self-culture, admits into his office that which will not be unlikely to disturb its performance. As little should there be an effort to maintain any favorite idea of one's own, concerning what must have been the early intellectual and moral development of a man like Daniel Webster. We do not know enough of all the laws that govern the growth of a human mind, to be able to reason backward, from what we have known of it in its maturity, to the times and the processes through which it began to approach the perfect stature in which it has stood before us. We can no more reason in this way, concerning the mind, than we can in regard to the body. Who that ever saw the physical frame of this man in the middle period of his days—filled with life and health, as capacious of labor as of the enjoyment of all that the senses can enjoy, perfect in grace and dignity, speaking in every motion and in every look of power and energy and vitality—could have argued from it back to his earliest years, and have found, without other guide, the feeble and even sickly childhood, with which we know that his earthly existence began? In the history of the mental, as of the physical constitution, we must investigate facts. Evidence is to be carefully sifted and weighed; the opinions and narrations of those who are competent to inform us must be examined and compared, and, above all, if he whose history we desire fully to know has left us his own testimony, given with full justice to others, and with no undue bias toward himself, we are bound to regard it as of great weight, in forming our estimate of what he may have been at a period so remote from the time in which he may have spoken or written concerning his early life.

In the case of Mr. Webster, there is strong reason for relying on his own statements respecting himself. He was an eminently just man; and he never was accused of vanity. He was not unconscious of what he was, or insensible to what he had done in the world, or indifferent about his reputation. But he never sought praise at the expense of others, whether it was the praise that attends the exhibition of mere talent, or that which follows the exhibition of mere industry. He was at once too grand and too simple in his nature to court a cheap applause; and, in speaking of himself at any time, or about any time in his life, if he ever failed in impartiality, he erred against himself, and against no one else. One thing is certainly true of him—and it is, that, in his opinions respecting the means by which he laid the foundation of his extraordinary success, he always gave the utmost importance to the amount of labor which he very early accustomed himself to perform, to the power of labor which he cultivated and increased as he grew in years, and to the command which it gave him over his intellectual faculties. It would have been the last thing which he could ever have desired, to be handed down to posterity as a man of genius who never needed the discipline to which common minds must submit. He never exhibited any of that weakness which has sometimes led men of the highest endowments to conceal their preparation for particular efforts at the bar, or in the senate, or which has craved, at the expense of probability or of truth, a reputation for doing great things out of the inspiration of the moment. Probably few men have ever lived who exceeded Mr. Webster in the power of immediately entering on the discussion of an important subject with very little previous notice of the duty and its demands. But, when he did so, he drew upon stores which he had garnered up in his intellectual resources for years, and it was the discipline of years, long gone by, that enabled him so to use his faculties as to bring those stores instantly to the uses of the hour. He would not have had it understood to be otherwise. I do not mean to say that he was never, or that he was rarely, indebted to that high exaltation of the intellect which comes when in the presence of an audience the mind assumes its greatest intensity of action; which clothes a syllogism in poetic fire, or adorns a train of reasoning with a flow of eloquence, more perfectly than all that study or the closet can do. No great orator, of ancient or of modern times, probably felt more deeply, or displayed more strikingly, in extemporaneous discourse, the effect of what is called inspiration. But I point now merely to that feature of his character which made him entirely free from a vulgar appetite for unmerited fame, and which rendered a false pride, in respect to the present or the past, a stranger to his breast. A man who had this strength and this moral simplicity could surely speak, in his manhood or in his age, of what he was at fifteen or at twenty, in a way that renders his testimony of inestimable value to those who would know him as he was.

There are some other general observations which must be made before the narrative of his college life proceeds, because they are necessary to a correct understanding of the kind and degree of development which he attained at Dartmouth.

An American college is conducted, in some respects, differently from the corresponding institutions in most parts of Europe. No comparison is here intended to be drawn in respect to the advantages of different systems of education, but it is intended merely to describe the kind of institution at which Mr. Webster received his academic education. In most of our colleges there is a *curriculum*, or prescribed course of studies, in the ancient and modern languages, in mathematics and the exact sciences, in mental and moral philosophy, in history, in rhetoric, and in some other branches. In these the student is required to prepare lessons, and to attend daily examinations, which are called "recitations." A daily record is kept of the performance of each student at the particular recitation; and the summary of this record, together with the results of personal deportment and punctuality of attendance on prescribed exercises, determines the relative rank of the students, and their title to the academic honors which the college, in its official capacity, bestows. Lectures are also delivered by the professors in their several departments, some of which the students are required to attend, while on others the attendance is voluntary.

In addition to these means of culture and discipline, there are others furnished by the college, which have a very important influence in the training of our young men. Among these are the public "declamations," which take place before the whole college at stated and frequent times, and in which each student is required to bear his part; the "exhibitions," which occur at certain periods in the college course, and the "commencement" exercises, with which the four years of college life terminate, and at which the degree of Bachelor of Arts is conferred upon each student, who has performed the college course without serious dereliction, and without incurring the necessity of being deprived of such a diploma by misconduct. At the exhibitions and the commencement exercises, the students, on whom the distinction falls, by the award of the College Faculty, deliver their own compositions in the form of orations and addresses in English, or Greek, or Latin; and these appointments constitute the college honors that are the objects of competition among the young men who contend for them. The performances are delivered upon a public stage, and there is always a public audience in addition to the faculty and members of the college.

In many of our colleges, also, there are voluntary societies among the students, which have existed for a long time, and which are conducted with great spirit and emulation, for purposes of general culture in writing and speaking, and for practice in the art of debating. Over these the college exercises no official control. The existence and operation of these voluntary associations—which are often carried on so effectively as to produce an important influence on the development of individuals, aside from all that part of education of which the college takes official cognizance—will account for the fact that a young man may have a high repute among his fellows for talent or scholarship, and may yet fail to achieve the highest honors of his college. But when this occurs, it will almost always be found that he who enjoys such a reputation among his fellow-students has gained it on account of his acquirements beyond the college course, and by his superiority in writing and debate; while he who wins a high college appointment, wins it on account of his exactness in the recitation-room. The two distinctions are rarely united in the same person.

Dartmouth College, when Mr. Webster entered it, was such an institution as I have above described, excepting that it had no provision for teaching the modern languages, and that, in the mathematics and the exact sciences, its course was exceedingly meagre.[1] When young Webster was fairly entered as a Freshman, his class went on with the seventh book of the "Æneid," and with the remainder of the Greek Testament. The studies through the Freshman and Sophomore years continued to be in Latin and Greek, with Pike's Arithmetic and Algebra. But from all the sources of information that are accessible, it seems that he did not rise into immediate and prominent distinction during these first two years of his college course. He was a good scholar, and punctual in his attendance on all exercises; but it appears, on the testimony of one entitled to know, that he was not spoken of at this time as the best scholar in his class, or indeed that any one else was so spoken of; and the estimation in which the College Faculty held him at this period is proved by the fact that, at his Sophomore exhibition, neither of the two principal appointments was assigned to him.[2]

There are extant a few verses which he addressed to one of his college friends, George Herbert, as a farewell, when he was leaving the college for the winter vacation in his Sophomore year, December, 1798. They exhibit no more poetic talent, or power of versification, or vigor of mind, than any lad of sixteen might show who had been similarly educated.

But there is a striking contrast between them and another

[1] Upon this Mr. Ticknor observes: "In *every* department, when Mr. Webster was at Dartmouth, the teaching was 'exceedingly meagre.' Pike's Arithmetic was a miserable book. I doubt whether he [Mr. W.] ever dealt with algebra." But Dr. Merrill, who was Webster's rival for the college honors, expressly mentions algebra.

[2] I state these facts on the authority of the Rev. T. A. Merrill, D. D., of Middlebury, Vermont, who was one of his class-mates, and who, in 1853, soon after Mr. Webster's death, wrote for the literary executors quite a full account of Mr. Webster's college history, which now lies before me in MSS.

short piece written and addressed to the same friend, a little more than a year afterward. The latter displays a great advance in his power of expression and thought, and, if the verses are, as the verses of most youths are, somewhat imitative, they do not lack the elements of real poetry. Some of his companions then thought, and have always believed, that the Muses had been lavish of their gifts to him, and that he did not cultivate them as he should have done. But the truth is, in respect to most of his rhymes that remain, although Nature had made him, in one sense, a poet, and although the prose of his whole life shows how strong were his imaginative tendencies, and how poetical his gravest eloquence often was, there is nothing that can, critically speaking, be dignified by the name of poetry. Whenever he wrote any thing serious in the form of verse, during his college life, or afterward, he was accustomed to laugh at it; and when he wrote any thing comic, his sense of the ludicrous was so strong, and his power of embodying it so exuberant, that he made others laugh with him as heartily as he did himself. But he undoubtedly possessed, at an early age, a faculty of description, in the forms of verse, akin to that which he could always use with wonderful force in prose composition or extemporaneous speaking. There is a tradition of a poem which he read in his junior year, on a battle between an English and a French ship-of-war, in which the latter was sunk, "that held the professor and the class," says one who heard it, "in apparent amazement. I almost shudder," continues his class-mate, "as, fifty-four years after, I seem to see the French ship go down, and to hear her cannon continue to roar till she is absolutely submerged."[1]

But not to anticipate the two later and most important years of his residence at Dartmouth, the reader must now go home with him to the paternal roof, at the spring vacation, in May, 1799, during his Sophomore year; for it was then that a domestic episode occurred in his life, which affected it through many a long year of generous and manly resistance against the ills of poverty.

The affection that had existed between Ezekiel and Daniel Webster, from their childhood, was such as even brothers whc

[1] Dr. Merrill's MSS.

are nearly of an age rarely feel. Whether it was that the younger had, from infancy, stood more than commonly in need of the strong protection of the older and stouter boy, or whether it was the effect of companionship operating upon natures with whom "blood was thicker than water" to a degree not often exceeded in the family tie, they loved each other, until death divided them, as men seldom do or can. They were the sons of an old man, who had become, to repeat his own homely but strong expression, "old before his time;" children of his age, and probably the first of his children who had given much promise of future usefulness, as Daniel was certainly the first of his sons for whom he thought himself called to afford the means of education. The reader already knows the plan which he had formed for his declining years. Ezekiel was to remain at home, and carry on the farm; Daniel was to be educated for one of the learned professions. But as the ample page of knowledge began to unfold itself before the eyes of the young student, and he saw the wide gulf that was to open between himself and his elder brother, his heart was moved. He believed that Ezekiel's talents were as good as his own, and he could not bear to think of him as destined to an inferior lot in life. When he came home for the vacation, he found that his brother felt the unpromising character of his prospects, and that there was a struggle between duty to his parents and the aspirations of a really superior mind. Daniel was unhappy about this state of things. He had a consultation with his brother, after they had gone to bed, which lasted through the whole night, and until after sunrise, neither of them having shut his eyes. Mr. Webster says of his brother, in the autobiography:

"He had thought of going into some new part of the country. That was discussed and disagreed to. All the *pros* and *cons* of the question of remaining at home were weighed and considered, and, when our council broke up, or rather got up, its result was that I should propose to my father that he, late as it was, should be sent to school also, and to college. This, we knew, would be a trying thing to my father and mother and two unmarried sisters. My father was growing old, his health not good, and his circumstances far from easy. The farm was to be carried on, and the family taken care of; and there was nobody to do all this but him, who was regarded as the main stay—that is to say, Ezekiel. However, I ventured on the negotiation, and it was carried, as other things often are, by the earnest and sanguine manner of youth. I told him that I was unhappy at my brother's prospects. For myself, I saw my way to knowledge, respectability, and self-protection; but, as to him, all looked the other way; that I would keep school, and get along as well as I could, be more than four years in getting through college, if necessary, provided he also could be sent to study. He said at once he lived but for his children; that he had but little, and on that little he put no value, except so far as it might be useful to them. That to carry us both through college would take all he was worth; that, for himself, he was willing to run the risk; but that this was a serious matter to our mother and two unmarried sisters; that we must settle the matter with them, and, if their consent was obtained, he would trust to Providence, and get along as well as he could."

All was now referred, therefore, to the decision of the mother; and her decision involved the family means for her whole remaining life, and for the lives of her unmarried daughters. Her husband told her that the farm was already mortgaged to meet the expenses of Daniel's education; and that if Ezekiel, too, were sent to college, it would take all that they had. Her answer was ready: "Well," said she, "I will trust the boys."[1]

Perhaps there is nowhere a tablet in the Temple of Fame, on which any thing more touching than this act of maternal heroism has been or can be inscribed. Thenceforward there was a long period of anxiety and privation for all of them. But its compensations came. The father lived to know that his sons were to take their places among the most honored of their native State. The mother lived longer, to behold the opening of that great career which was before the younger, and to find repose and every comfort in the house of her elder son. The sisters lived to find how safe had been their reliance on fraternal gratitude and honor. On the early grave, therefore, to which one of these brothers went suddenly down, in the prime of a useful and honorable, although a less distinguished life, and on the tomb in which the other, when full of years and honors, and with all the renown that a statesman can reap, was laid by a mourning nation, it should be written that a mother's sagacious faith in the future of her sons supplied to a father's courage all that was needed for one of the largest parental

[1] MS. notes, by Mrs. Ticknor, of Mr. Webster's conversation, in 1825.

sacrifices that the lives of educated men, in any country, have ever had to show.

Perhaps the reader may now think that the question of Daniel Webster's exact rank as a college student has sunk into insignificance. Here was a youth, scarcely more than seventeen years of age, so strong in fraternal affection, so firm in his self-reliance, so capable of looking forward to estimate the future for his brother and himself, that he could tell his aged father that he would assume the burdens that this great sacrifice was to cast upon the family. We are concerned, in this investigation of his life, with the growth of character, as well as with the growth of his mind, or his acquisitions of knowledge; and when we go back with him to his college, we are to remember that, although a boy in years, in moral stature he is already a man. He might have, it is known that he did have, other methods of discipline, other objects of ambition, other desires for knowledge, than those which were limited or satisfied by the academic prizes. He began to fight the great battle of life almost before the down was upon his lip; and if he fought it in his own way, or chose his weapons for himself, or burnished his armor more variously than his comrades, it was because the responsibility of the contest had come upon him so early, and so gravely; and because Nature had given him the strength, and pointed him the way.

Ezekiel Webster, who was at the age of nineteen when the consent of his parents was given to the plan for his education, immediately began to attend a small academy, then recently established, in Salisbury. He remained at this school for two terms, and then went to reside with Dr. Wood, with whom his preparation for college was finished. "His intellectual character," his brother informs us, "as it afterward developed itself, was not early understood, at least not in its full extent. He was thought to have good sense, but not to have, and perhaps had not, great quickness of apprehension."[1] He was at first distrustful of himself, and appears to have been in the habit of writing to Daniel, as if the latter, with superior powers, and earlier advantages, could not appreciate what he had to contend with. Daniel would never admit that his brother was his

[1] Autobiography.

inferior in natural abilities. It is singular to see the order of Nature thus reversed in their relative situations, and to find the younger generously and judiciously performing the duties of mentor to the elder. "You tell me," writes Daniel, "that you have difficulties to encounter which I know nothing of. What do you mean, Ezekiel? Do you mean to flatter? That don't become you; or do you think you are inferior to me in natural abilities? If so, be assured you greatly mistake. Therefore, for the future, say in your letters to me, 'I am superior to you in natural endowments; I will know more in one year than you do now, and more in six than you ever will.' I should not resent this language. I should be very well pleased in hearing it; but be assured, as mighty as you are, your great puissance shall never insure you a victory without a contest."[1]

Ezekiel was certainly not the equal of Daniel at any period of their lives; but he was a man of fine intellect, and, notwithstanding all the difficulties with which he had to contend, he entered Dartmouth College in March, 1801, six months before his brother was graduated, so well prepared, and with such admirable habits of study, that he immediately took, and always retained, so long as he could remain at the college, a high rank in his class.[2] His father's means were from the first inadequate to meet the expenses of both his and Daniel's education. But the compact which had been made at the family altar came at once into operation. Daniel was now able to earn a little more than he needed to spend. He superintended a small weekly newspaper, printed in Hanover, and called *The Dartmouth Gazette*, during the year 1800, which was his junior year. What he received for this literary service paid his own board for the year, and so far relieved the family burdens. In the winter vacation of the same year, he taught a school in Salisbury, and the money thus earned helped to defray Ezekiel's expenses at Dr. Wood's. This was the beginning of that remarkable struggle, which lasted for several years, and through which

[1] Letter to E. Webster, April 25, 1800. —(*Correspondence*, i., 83.)

[2] In Mr. Webster's *Correspondence*, vol. i., p. 31, there is an account of Ezekiel Webster's college reputation written by his son-in-law, Professor Sanborn, in 1857. It will give the reader some idea of that beloved brother, whose name Mr. Webster desired might be associated with his own, so long as his own might endure.

these brothers mutually aided each other by turns, until both had acquired the profession of their choice; for, as Mr. Webster once humorously expressed their frequent interchange of study and of labor for their joint support, as they had but one horse between them, they "rode in tie."[1]

On his return to the college, after the spring vacation of 1799, Daniel appears to have entered upon the discipline of his powers of communication, and to have developed them with great rapidity. For this, the society long known in that institution as "The United Fraternity," afforded him all the needful facilities. He became at once distinguished as a debater, and, before the close of his junior year, he was accounted by far the best writer and speaker in the college. The compass and force of his arguments, in extemporaneous discussion, were acknowledged by all who had the opportunity of hearing him in his society. He manifested, then, in kind, the same completeness and fulness in his views, and the same power of expressing them, which he displayed through life. Although not required to do so, he was in the habit of writing his own declamations for the college stage. "He was accustomed," said one of his class-mates, "to arrange his thoughts in his mind, in his room or his private walks, and to put them upon paper just before the exercise was called for. When he was required to speak at two o'clock, he would frequently begin to write after dinner, and, when the bell rang, he would fold his paper, put it in his pocket, and go in, and speak with great ease. In his movements, he was rather slow and deliberate, except when his feelings were aroused; then his whole soul would kindle into a flame."[2] Indeed, the testimony of all who were living at the time of Mr. Webster's death, and who had been with him at Dartmouth, is uniform on this point: "We used to listen to him," said another of them, "with the deepest interest and respect, and no one ever thought of equalling the vigor and flow of his eloquence."[3]

That he carried on courses of reading and study, adapted to

[1] A New-England phrase, which means that two people, who have but one animal between them, alternately ride and walk.

[2] Letter by Mr. Elihu Smith, to Professor Sanborn.—(*Correspondence*, i., 46.) Written from Pomfret, in Vermont, November 10, 1852.

[3] Hon. Henry Hubbard, ex-Governor of New Hampshire.—(*Correspondence*, i.)

the training which he sought to give himself, is equally well authenticated. He did not neglect the college studies, but he went beyond them. He mastered any subject or book as if by intuition. He gave himself especially to history, in pursuing which he burnt the lamp to very late hours.[1] He studied politics as few young men of the same age have ever studied them.[2] There are passages in his letters, written at this time (1800), which show how closely he observed, and how deeply he was affected, by what was then taking place in Europe. Observations and reflections, that might have flowed from his pen at any age, are to be found scattered through his college correspondence. It was at the period, when Bonaparte, for example, had just returned from Egypt, and the colossal power, which he had grasped as soon as he had reached Paris, began to overshadow even this distant republic, agitated as it had been by sympathies with the French Revolution, that had prepared the way for his ascent to a despotic throne, and his attempt at universal dominion. This young American student saw it, and comprehended it in its relations to his own country. He had been bred up at home, in the school of what was called the Federal party, and had been, therefore, predisposed to the Washingtonian policy of keeping the interests of this country free from entanglements with European politics. But after making every allowance for the effects of early education and home influences, when we read in the letters of a young student of eighteen, a junior undergraduate in Dartmouth College, that he understood the dangers to which his country was exposed, through her necessary commercial relations; that he saw how essential to her safety was internal harmony, and that her liberties could be made the sport of European powers, only when "American blood shall be made to flow in rivers by American swords," we may recognize whose youth it was, that began thus early and fervently to pray that "the bonds of the Federal Union might be strengthened."

[1] Dr. Merrill. MSS.

[2] Among the books which he read at this time, there was one which deeply affected him—Mallet du Pan's "History of the Destruction of the Helvetic Union." What this revealed to him of French ambition, and the fate of republicanism in Europe, may be seen in one of his letters to a college friend, to whom he poured forth the feelings excited by what had befallen Switzerland.—(*Correspondence*, i., 81.)

His reputation in the college and its neighborhood, as a writer and speaker, led the people of the town of Hanover to invite him to deliver an oration on the 4th of July, 1800. This, which was his first public performance, was printed. As might be expected, it shows, in style and expression, marks of the unripe taste of a youth of eighteen; but, in power of thought, and strong grasp of the subject, it gives no uncertain promise of the productions of a later period. The oration begins with a rapid sketch of the history of the country, closing with the glorious success of the Revolution. Several of the soldiers of the Revolution were present, who were addressed in terms of glowing admiration and gratitude. Many of the deceased patriots of the Revolution were commemorated, and the loss which the country had recently sustained, in the death of Washington, was lamented in two or three paragraphs of somewhat high-flown language, such, however, as older speakers in those days were very apt to use. The closing paragraphs were strongly Federal in their tone, full of denunciation of France and of Bonaparte, whom the young orator calls "the gasconading pilgrim of Egypt." The faults of the discourse are such as an audience, in sympathy with its sentiments, would easily overlook; and it was, doubtless, heard with enthusiastic favor.

There is one other of Mr. Webster's college productions, which was printed at the time. This was a eulogy pronounced at the funeral of his class-mate, Simonds, who died at Hanover, in June of their senior year. There is, perhaps, nothing that so profoundly moves a band of college youths as the death of a class-mate, especially if it take place at the institution. In such a closely-united circle of generous and aspiring young men, in the morning of life, Death seems to come with an especial shock; and if his shaft is aimed at one who has given more than ordinary promise, and is more than usually beloved, there will be, inevitably, from the nature of the emotions excited, more than from any desire to ape the customs of the larger and older world, an expression of what is felt, in the formal funeral oration, or other ceremony of that kind. The case of Simonds, excepting in the circumstances of his death, was just such a one as that of which Landor afterward said, all that can be said in such cases, when he wrote the beautiful epitaph, in five words of his masterly Latin, over the poor Oxford scholar, who had wandered out in the fields, and died of exhaustion:

> "Literarum quaesivit gloriam,
> Dei videt."

This is what young Webster was appointed to say over his class-mate Simonds, and what he did in substance say, in the more expanded form of a public eulogy. I know of but one copy now in existence. It is natural, unaffected, full of feeling, and of a strong religious faith. It is not, in my judgment, open to the criticism which he afterward made upon his printed college performances, of being in "bad taste" in respect to its style. Of course, it has not the same simplicity which he afterward reached; there are words which he would have expunged, and sentences which he would not have constructed ten years afterward. But it might, if he had chosen to have it so, have been seen by the world at any period of his life, as a not unworthy forerunner of his more mature productions, for it is marked throughout by the elevation of thought, as well as the tenderness of feeling, that belonged to his character.[1]

The reader is now prepared to understand what was his relative position as a scholar when he approached the termination of his college career. He was not the first scholar in his class, as the faculty, by their rules, were obliged to account scholarship on the college records; but he was the most prominent person in the college in respect to general attainments; and, as an orator, he had no equal. How, then, it will be asked, did it happen that he took no part in the Commencement exercises? And why does he say—in mentioning in his

[1] The copy of this eulogy, which I have seen, belongs to Mr. Ticknor. "In 1820," says Mr. Ticknor, "I happened to dine with Mr. Webster at his own house, while the convention, to revise the Constitution of Massachusetts, of which he was the leading member, was in session; and, sitting next to him after dinner, I told him, in the course of conversation, that I had recently found among some old pamphlets a copy of the oration which he delivered in his senior year on the death of his class-mate Simonds. He looked surprised, and turned suddenly, and rather sternly toward me, and said: 'Have you? I thought, till lately, that, as only a few copies of it were printed, they must all have been destroyed long ago; but, the other day, Bean, who was in college with me, told me he had one. It flashed through my mind that it must have been the last copy in the world, and that if he had it in his pocket it would be worth while to kill him, to destroy it from the face of the earth. So I recommend you not to bring your copy where I am.'"—(*MSS. Recollections of Mr. Webster, by Mr. Ticknor.*)

autobiography that this was "owing to some difficulties"—"*haec non meminisse juvat?*"

The circumstances which he did not think it worth while to recall are now before me, clearly related by one of his classmates, who remained at the college as a tutor for three years after he was graduated, and who therefore had full means of knowing both sides of the affair, the views of the faculty, and the feelings of the class. From his narrative I abridge the following statement:

In the arrangements of the faculty, the four principal appointments had long been ranked as follows—the Salutatory Oration, in Latin, as the first; the Philosophic, in English, as the second; a Greek Oration, as the third; and the Valedictory, in English, as the fourth. It was their practice to assign the first three, and then to call upon the class to choose the Valedictory Orator. It was understood by the class that, in other colleges, the Valedictory was regarded as the first in rank of all the appointments. This circumstance, and the fact that the class expected to make the appointment, would lead a young man of Webster's accomplishments and popularity to prefer it; and the class would have preferred that he should have it. But previous classes had quarrelled so seriously in choosing the Valedictory Orator, that the faculty determined to make this appointment themselves. Webster's rank as a scholar, in the estimate which the faculty felt obliged to make, did not entitle him to the Latin Oration, notwithstanding his relative proficiency in that language; at the same time he stood too high upon the record to make it proper for them to appoint him to the Valedictory, which, for this occasion, they ranked as the fifth of the academic honors. There was, too, an obvious unfitness in making a young man, who was so impressive a speaker in his own tongue, pronounce a public performance in a dead language; while the habits and policy of the college made it necessary to give an honorable precedence to Latin and Greek. Accordingly, the faculty undertook to solve the difficulty, by offering to Webster a choice of a poem in English or an oration in English on the fine arts; and they gave the Valedictory to another member of the class, not suspecting that Webster and his friends would not be gratified. But a poem had never ranked with the first four appointments, and if Webster had selected in place of it the English oration which was offered to his choice, he would, by his own act, have placed himself second on the list of the college honors. This dilemma the faculty did not foresee, or did not appreciate.

As not unfrequently happens on these occasions, a great excitement followed among the members of the class. Several of them applied to be excused from speaking on the day of Commencement, and were excused. Webster was one of them. His friends did not claim that he was entitled to the Latin Oration; but they had marked him for their Valedictory Orator, and considered themselves aggrieved by the refusal of the faculty to intrust them with the appointment, according to an established usage. Webster himself was placed in too embarrassing a position toward his competitors to allow of his exercising the choice which the faculty had given him. Apparently he had no other feeling about the whole affair, for I find no trace in his correspondence of any bitterness toward the faculty or any one else; and his attachment to his Alma Mater, which never flagged, became historical, inspiring one of the grandest of his forensic efforts, when he was called upon, in less than twenty years afterward, to defend her interests and her chartered rights before the highest judicial tribunal in the country.

It is well observed by the gentleman, whose narrative I have followed, that the whole matter turns to Webster's honor, if he did nothing improper himself; and it is therefore incumbent on me to state that there is no foundation for the story of his having destroyed his diploma in disgust and anger after the Commencement exercises were over. If this rumor ever had so much origin as to be a college tradition, it is refuted by evidence that ought to be regarded as decisive; for it is certain that it was not heard of at Dartmouth at the time, or for several years afterward.[1]

The friendships which he formed, when in college, with

[1] Dr. Merrill, his class-mate, from whose account I have taken the facts respecting the appointments, says of this story: "I never believed it, and probably never shall believe it, unless some person reports it directly from Webster himself, as one of the witnesses. I was an intimate friend and correspondent, and continued to reside at the college for three years, but never heard of the story for more than a quarter of a century." (MSS.) The Rev. Elihu Smith, another of his class-mates, said: "I have no doubt the report is false. I stood by

some of the members of his own class, and with two or three young men who were in other classes, were peculiarly strong, and lasted through his life. But perhaps my readers may be curious to know what associations he had with young persons of the other sex, and whether his heart, at this susceptible period, remained wholly his own. There was a small society of young ladies in Hanover, during his junior and senior years, with whom he and his college friends were on terms of intimacy. They appear, however, in his correspondence by their Christian names alone; and probably no diligence on my part, if I were to use it, after the lapse of sixty-five years, to acquire further information concerning them, would be rewarded with much success.[1] But there was gayety in the little town of Hanover in those days, of that modest and moderate sort which consisted with the habits of a seat of learning, and of a religious community. An evening visit, or a social tea-table, a walk, or a drive, were matters of course; and young women could converse with young men without the necessary presence of a superintending eye or ear, because the young of both sexes, from the very purity of the atmosphere in which they were born and educated, and had always dwelt, were fit to be intrusted in a large degree with their own conduct. Hence it has often happened among us that the tenderest and most enduring of all ties have been formed by our educated men at a very early age; and, however strangely it may sound elsewhere, it has been no uncommon occurrence, in all parts of our country, for a young man to leave college with his destiny fixed in at least one very important affair of life, rendering it necessary

his side when he received his degree with a graceful bow; and, such was my connection with him in our society affairs, that if he had destroyed it afterward, I should certainly have known it."—(*Rev. E. Smith to Professor Sanborn, November* 10, 1852. *Correspondence*, i., 46.) Mr. Webster's character and deportment in college, in regard to which the testimony is uniform, were entirely inconsistent with the perpetration of such an act. "No one," says Mr. Smith, "presumed to bring a railing accusation against him." The Honorable Samuel Fessenden, who entered Dartmouth College in 1803, and who personally knew many of Mr. Webster's friends still remaining at Hanover, and who had a strong interest in him, from having been acquainted with him at Fryeburg, observed, in a letter written to one of the literary executors, in December, 1852: "I never heard of his resentment manifesting itself in tearing up his diploma."

[1] To the remark made in the text, there is one exception. One of the ladies of this little circle, a distant connection of my own, is mentioned in his letters by her full name, Mary Woodward. She was a woman of much talent, and high character, but married unfortunately.

for him to hasten with all speed into a settled position in the world.

This did not happen, however, to Daniel Webster; and, after a close scrutiny of his most confidential letters, it is quite clear that, although he may have been a little interested, he escaped, on the whole, unharmed. Perhaps this was owing to the fact that there were two charmers when there should have been but one. That there were two, that he was a little in doubt, that they perplexed him and he them, and that it was chiefly fun and innocent frolic on all sides, is manifest enough. Possibly the dignity of my subject might have excluded this inchoate piece of romance. But as there were rumors which had their day, and he wrote about them half seriously and half playfully, the reader may as well see how he dismissed them. One of the young ladies whom he had most admired was, it would appear, a visitor from Salem; and he thus gives a characteristic close to a letter to his friend Bingham, written in the winter of his senior year:

> "Salem! enchanting name! who would have thought that from the ashes of witches, hung a century ago, should have sprung such an arch coquette as should delight in sporting with the simplicity of
>
> "DANIEL WEBSTER."[1]

With respect to his own opinions about his college acquirements and standing, I find four occasions on which he said or wrote something directly, and the tenor of the whole is uniform. The first occurred in 1802, when he had been graduated only a year. It was observed to him that his scholarship in college had always been regarded as of the highest grade, which was not true of a gentleman then at the bar, whom he had expressed a hope of some day equalling in his professional career. He said:

> "Ay, but the opinion of my scholarship was a mistaken one. It was over-estimated. I will explain what I mean. Many other students read more than I did, and knew more than I did But so much as I read I made my own. When a half hour or an hour, at most, had elapsed, I closed my book, and thought over what I had read. If there was any thing peculiarly interesting or striking in the passage, I endeavored to recall it, and lay it up in my memory, and commonly could effect my object. Then, if, in debate or conversation afterward, any subject came

[1] Correspondence, i., 87.

up on which I had read something, I could talk very easily so far as I had read, and then I was very careful to stop. Thus greater credit was given me for extensive and accurate knowledge than I really possessed."[1]

The next occasion was in 1825, when he said:

"My Greek and mathematics were not great while I was in college, but I was better read in history and English generally than any of my class, and I was good in composition. My Latin was pretty strong too."[2]

In his autobiography he says:

"I was graduated in course, August, 1801. Owing to some difficulties —*haec non meminisse juvat*—I took no part in the Commencement exercises. I spoke an oration to the Society of the United Fraternity, which I suspect was a sufficiently boyish performance.

"My college life was not an idle one. Besides the regular attendance on prescribed duties and studies, I read something of English history and English literature. Perhaps my reading was too miscellaneous. I even paid my board for a year by superintending a little weekly newspaper, and making selections for it from books of literature and from the contemporary publications. I suppose I sometimes wrote a foolish paragraph myself. While in college, I delivered two or three occasional addresses, which were published. I trust they are forgotten; they were in very bad taste. I had not then learned that all true power in writing is in the idea, and not in the style, an error into which the *Ars rhetorica*, as it is usually taught, may easily lead stronger heads than mine."[3]

In 1851, eighteen months before his death, writing to his class-mate, Dr. Merrill, he said:

"I assure you, my dear old friend, that I hear from you with pleasure. You are no shepherd, and certainly I am no king. But we are friends, born in the same country, about the same age, and educated at the same college. We embraced different professions, which we have pursued now for a long time; and Providence has graciously blessed us both with a great share of health and happiness. At our time of life the mind often turns to the past. I find that I think now, much more frequently than twenty or thirty years ago, on college scenes and college friends. I look over the catalogue, call to mind the dead, and inquire after the living. I well remember that I did not keep up with you in the stated course of collegiate exercises. Your lessons were better learned, and you were a great favorite with Professor Smith and the other members of 'the authority,'

[1] Letter from J. W. McGaw, Esq., to Professor Sanborn, November, 16, 1852. —(*Correspondence*, i., 51.) Mr. McGaw was a young lawyer at Fryeburg, Maine, when Mr. Webster resided there as teacher of an academy, and they lived much together.

[2] Ticknor MSS.; notes of the conversation on the drive to Salem.

[3] Correspondence, i., 11.

from the exact punctuality of all your performances. I believe I was less industrious; at any rate, I indulged more in general reading, and my attainments, if I made any, were not such as told for much in the recitation-room. After leaving college, I 'caught up,' as the boys say, pretty well in Latin; but in college, and afterward, I left Greek to Loveland, and mathematics to Shattuck. Would that I had pursued Greek till I could read and understand Demosthenes in his own language!"

From youth to age did he thus always speak when he spoke of himself; with that moderation and modesty, that delicacy toward others, that unwillingness to advance pretensions, which are the characteristics of true greatness, and which, in him, were unmingled with condescension or affectation. If we take the sum of his own testimony, and enlarge it by that of others who knew him at Dartmouth, and who could say what he could not say, adding also what we can learn from such of his writings as have survived from that time, we find that he left the institution with but a small amount of Greek, but very well grounded in Latin; that his acquisitions in English history and English literature were extensive; that his powers as an orator were already developed to a degree rarely witnessed in a young man of nineteen; that his style of writing was flowing and easy, but far from that chaste, compact, and perspicuous manner which he afterward attained; that he had become already a practised debater; that his faculty for labor was something prodigious, his memory disciplined by methods not taught him by others, and that his intellect was expanded far beyond his years. He was abstemious, religious, of the highest sense of honor, and of the most elevated deportment. His manners were genial, his affections warm, his conversation was brilliant and instructive, his temperament cheerful, his gayety overflowing. He was beloved, admired, and courted by all who knew him; and, finally, when he went forth from his college, whatever may have been the discouragements of his narrow fortunes, he was followed by those who had marked his genius and measured his character, as a young man who was soon to be heard of with distinction on the high places of the world.

CHAPTER III.

1801--1807.

BEGINS THE STUDY OF THE LAW IN SALISBURY—TEACHES A SCHOOL IN MAINE—ENTERS THE OFFICE OF MR. GORE IN BOSTON—ADMISSION TO THE BAR—REFUSES A LUCRATIVE OFFICE—PRACTISES IN BOSCAWEN—DEATH OF HIS FATHER—REMOVAL TO PORTSMOUTH.

LEAVING his brother Ezekiel at college in the Sophomore class, Mr. Webster returned to his father's house immediately after he was graduated, in August, 1801, and commenced the study of the law in the office of Thomas W. Thompson, Esq., a lawyer in Salisbury, his father's neighbor and friend. He chose this profession in compliance with the wish of his father, who did not, however, make that wish known to him in any other than the most delicate manner. His other friends urged it strongly; and the nearness of a very good lawyer's office to his father's house probably had some influence on his decision. But his own inclination to the law was not at first very strong. The tenor of his correspondence at this period shows, at least, that he would gladly have spent some further time in exploring the wider fields of literature. Yet he "precipitated" himself "into an office," as he said at the time, and immediately began such a course of elementary law-reading as the books and the methods of that day afforded.

Mr. Thompson, the gentleman with whom he began to study his profession, was a lawyer in good country practice, an assiduous man of business, and a person of cultivated mind.[1] He possessed a tolerably good law library, and a much better one in general letters and history. The first works which Mr. Webster read in the law were in the department of the Law of Nations—being Vattel, Burlamaqui, and Montesquieu. These were followed by a part of Blackstone's Commentaries, and he read, at the same time, the historians Hume and Robertson. Nothing could have been better at that period for a student before entering upon the principles of the municipal and common law. He read Shakespeare, too, a good deal at this time, some of the poetry of Cowper, and Pope's translation of the Iliad. His knowledge of Shakespeare and of Milton commenced while he was at Dartmouth. He now began to quote them familiarly in his letters. He also read, during the autumn of this year, a large amount of what he calls "miscellaneous stuff of no great account." His dog and gun and his fishing-rod filled up his leisure hours.[2]

But reading and shooting or fishing were not the sole vocations of a young law-student in those days. He was expected to look after the minor affairs of the office business, and a part of his professional education consisted in "making writs." There was another and older student in the office, Daniel Abbot, afterward a leading lawyer and most estimable citizen of Nashua, and a life-long friend of Mr. Webster. On one occasion, Mr. Thompson and Mr. Abbot were both absent, and the entire charge of affairs devolved on Webster, who thus indulged his wit upon a case that fell into his hands:

> "I have made some few writs, and am now about to bring an action of trespass for breaking a violin. The owner of the violin was at a husking, where
>
> 'His jarring concord and his discord dulcet'
>
> made the girls skip over the husks as nimbly as Virgil's Camilla over the tops of the corn, till an old surly creature caught his fiddle, and

[1] He was graduated at Harvard College in 1786, and was for three years afterward a tutor in that university.

[2] "With the assistance of my first minister, Mr. Gallatin, formerly called Leo, I have dismissed from the office of this life a few Federal partridges, pigeons, and squirrels, and have drawn from the abundance of Merrimac a few anti-Federal fishes—no loaves—such as sword-back, perch, and flat-headed demi-semi-crotchet quavers, *alias* scaly flat-sides."—(*Letter to James H. Bingham, September* 22, 1801.) The fun of this consists in some allusion to the party politics of the time.

broke it against the wall. For the sake of having *plump witnesses*, the plaintiff will summon all the girls to attend the trial at Concord."[1]

But this pleasant and profitable life for our young student was soon to be interrupted.

As the winter came on, it brought with it Ezekiel's accumulating expenses at college. In December, Daniel thus writes to his friend Bingham, to whom he was accustomed to impart his troubles:

"Having found myself at home after commencement, I found, on consideration, that it would be impossible for my father, under existing circumstances, to continue Ezekiel at college. Drained of all his little income by the expenses of my education thus far, and broken down in his exertions by some ever-lamented family occurrences, I saw he could not afford Ezekiel means to live abroad with ease and independence; and I knew too well the evils of penury to wish him to stay half-beggared at college. I thought it therefore my duty to suffer some delay in my profession for the sake of serving my elder brother, and was making a little interest in some places to the eastward for an employment. My father, however, determined to hire a few hundreds till future days, being very averse to my leaving him. He accordingly rode to Exeter, told his Excellency[2] of the state of affairs, and the good governor helped him to what he wanted on reasonable terms. This was much more favorable than I expected, and I have now hopes of continuing here for the present."[3]

Whether it was that the supply obtained from "the good governor's" friendly aid was insufficient, or whether some unexpected demand broke down the family resources with the weight of the last feather, the result was that Daniel was obliged, before the new year came in, to quit his studies, mount his horse, and go forth in quest, not of adventures, but of the vulgar article money. It was a hard trial for him. He had been four months with Mr. Thompson, and very profitable months they had been to him. He was going on rapidly in his studies of all kinds, and he felt more at ease, after his father's visit to Governor Gilman, than he had felt for a long time. But duty and affection

[1] Letter to Bingham, October 26, 1801.

[2] John Taylor Gilman, Governor of New Hampshire from 1797 until 1807, and from 1813 to 1815. He was a very decided Federalist; but his popularity was so great, and his character so much respected, that he was more than once elected governor when his party was in the minority.

[3] Letter to Bingham, December 8, 1801.

both demanded the sacrifice, and he made it instantly and cheerfully.

He had been written to, and offered the charge of an academy in Fryeburg, Maine, which was at that time a "Province" of Massachusetts. This town is at the head of the Saco River, not far from the border of New Hampshire, near the foot of the White Mountains, and opposite to the town of Conway. He purchased a horse for twenty-five dollars, and, with his wardrobe and such books as he could carry in his saddle-bags, made his way across the country. He found the village of his destination a new one, but it was growing rapidly, and had already an intelligent population, in which the learned professions were all duly represented by "men of information and conversable manners," as he described them in one of his letters. His salary was fixed at the rate of three hundred and fifty dollars a year, but his engagement was for only six months. As he had come there to earn money, he availed himself of an accidental source of further supply, in the humble occupation of copying deeds. It so happened that he went to board in the family of James Osgood, Esq., registrar of deeds for the then newly-created county of Oxford. This gentleman, Mr. Webster tells us in his autobiography, "was not *clerical* in and of himself, and his registration was to be done by deputy."

"The fee for recording at full length a common deed, in a large fair hand, and with the care requisite to avoid errors, was two shillings and three pence. Mr. Osgood proposed to me that I should do this writing, and that of the two shillings and three pence for each deed I should have one shilling and six pence. I greedily seized on so tempting an offer, and set to work. Of a long winter's evening I could copy two deeds, and that was half a dollar. Four evenings in a week earned two dollars; and two dollars a week paid my board. This appeared to me to be a very thriving condition, for my three hundred and fifty dollars' salary as a school-master was thus going on without abatement or deduction for *vivers*. I hope yet to have an opportunity to see once more the first volume of the records of deeds for the county of Oxford. It is now near thirty years since I copied into it the last 'witness my hand and seal,' and I have not seen its outside since. But the ache is not yet out of my fingers, for nothing has ever been so laborious to me as writing, when under the necessity of writing a good hand." [1]

[1] Autobiography.

Certainly this is not the first instance, as it will not be the last, in which a similar labor has been, or will be, submitted to, by young men of education contending against adverse fortunes. But we naturally inquire for the motive that could have made such a drudgery possible to one whose extraordinary gifts of Nature had been enlarged and enriched by the delights of learning. On the other side of the range of hills that lay between his new abode and the college which he had recently left was that brother, for whose education he had made himself responsible to his parents; while at home was an anxious and aged father, now left without the prop on which he had meant to lean. The whole secret of this endurance, therefore, is comprehended in the following occurrence:

"In May of this year (1802), having a week's vacation, I took my quarter's salary, mounted a horse, went straight over all the hills to Hanover, and had the pleasure of putting these, the first earnings of my life, into my brother's hands for his college expenses. Having enjoyed this sincere and high pleasure, I hied me back again to my school and my copying of deeds."[1]

It was on this visit to Hanover that my kinsman, George Ticknor, Esq., who, excepting myself, is now the sole survivor of his four literary executors, first saw him. As I shall have frequent occasion to quote from Mr. Ticknor's recollections of him, extending through a period of fifty years, and now forming, in manuscript, some of the most important and interesting of the materials before me, I avail myself of his mention of the time when the acquaintance and friendship between Mr. Webster and himself began. He observes:

"The first time I ever saw Mr. Webster was in Hanover, in May, 1802. All that I remember of him then is, that the students of the college, whom I was in the habit of seeing, were very proud and very fond of him. It was a knot of young men, among whom was Mr. Henry Hubbard, afterward Governor of New Hampshire; Amos Twitchell, afterward a distinguished surgeon; his own brother Ezekiel, and others, living in the old Kinsman House; at least I saw them there. He was returning from Fryeburg, where he had kept school. He was thin, and had not the appearance of being a strong man. He remained in Hanover only two or three days. The young men seemed rejoiced to have him with them, and

[1] Autobiography.

treated him very caressingly and affectionately. He had been graduated only one year." [1]

Mr. Webster returned to Fryeburg, and remained there in the same occupations until the following September. From three persons who knew him there, and who were ever afterward numbered among his cherished friends, we learn something of interest concerning him. One of them was Jacob W. McGaw, Esq., then a young lawyer in Fryeburg, with whom he lived at Mr. Osgood's. "Here," said Mr. McGaw, "was laid the foundation of that friendship, which, by his generous indulgence, has remained constant and uninterrupted till the time of his death, notwithstanding the very great changes which occurred in our relative positions, by reason of his constant elevation from one grade of honor to another, till he attained a standing from which human greatness knows no progress." Another was Samuel Osgood, son of the registrar, a young man who was near his own age, and who was just then completing his preparation to enter college at an advanced standing. With this gentleman, who became an eminent divine at Springfield, in Massachusetts, he contracted a friendship which was mutually preserved amidst all the changes of their lives. The third was the Honorable Samuel Fessenden, of Portland, son of the Rev. William Fessenden, of Fryeburg, who was Secretary of the Board of Trustees of the Academy. Mr. Samuel Fessenden was nearly of the same age with Mr. Webster, and they were strongly attached to each other. "If I ever loved a man," Mr. Fessenden wrote after Mr. Webster's death, "not a near relative, and out of the pale of kindred, that man was Daniel Webster." [2]

Mr. McGaw tells us that "he had not then attained the full development of manhood. Neither the physical nor intellectual expression of his countenance had become so striking as in subsequent life. His cheeks were thin, and his cheek-bones high. There was nothing specially noticeable about him then except his full, steady, large, and searching eyes. Nobody could see those eyes and ever forget their appearance, or him who pos-

[1] MSS.—Mr. Ticknor was then passing a summer near Hanover (previous to his entering the college), on a visit with his father and mother.

[2] MSS.

sessed them. His gentleness, modesty, and social habits won for him the good-will of his acquaintances and pupils."

"He was always," says Dr. Osgood, "dignified in his deportment. He was usually serious, but often facetious and pleasant. He was an agreeable companion, and eminently social with all who shared his friendship. He was greatly beloved by all who knew him. His habits were strictly abstemious, and he neither took wine nor strong drink. He was punctual in his attendance upon public worship, and ever opened his school with prayer. I never heard him use a profane word, and never saw him lose his temper."

Mr. Fessenden, in a letter addressed to the literary executors, after Mr. Webster's decease, observes:

> "The first I ever knew of Daniel Webster was immediately after he left college, and was employed by my father, the secretary of the Trustees of Fryeburg Academy, to become the principal instructor in that institution. He was not, when he commenced, twenty years old. I heard no one complain that his scholarship was not adequate to the duty he had assumed. On the contrary, I heard the Rev. Dr. Nathaniel Porter, of Conway, and my father, the Rev. William Fessenden, of Fryeburg, both of whom were good scholars, and the former, Dr. Porter, a very great man, say that Daniel Webster was then a very good scholar for one of his years. He did, while at Fryeburg, exhibit traits of talent and genius which drew from those two divines, and from other professional gentlemen, unqualified praise of his powers of mind. I remember very distinctly hearing my father remark that, if Mr. Webster should live, and have health, and pursue a straightforward course of industry and virtue, he would become one of the greatest men this country had produced."

His reading at Fryeburg was chiefly in history and politics, and English literature. He began then to investigate carefully some parts of the political history of the United States. He read Adams's Defence of the American Constitutions, Williams's Vermont, and Mosheim's Ecclesiastical History; and he continued his reading of Blackstone's Commentaries. Here, too, he found Mr. Ames's celebrated speech on the British treaty, and committed it to memory. He read the *Spectator* and the *Tatler*, and the whole of Pope's poetical works, with many other things. Some idea of his industry may be formed from this list, when we remember that he was at the same time teaching a school, and copying deeds four evenings in the week.

All his hours that could be spared from labor, or necessary recreation, were spent in study or in meditation in the fields, and he rarely went abroad in his rambles without a book.[1]

What he was as a teacher, is sufficiently attested by the fact that he was earnestly pressed to remain on an increased salary. "A compensation annually of five or six hundred dollars," he writes to Bingham, "a house to live in, a piece of land to cultivate, and, *inter nos solos*, a clerkship of the Common Pleas, are now probably within the reach and possession of your friend."

I cannot say that he hesitated much, but he did honestly put down upon paper both sides of the question.

Mr. McGaw was always of opinion that he did not at this time feel very strongly the promptings of ambition, or entertain any very sanguine expectations of future eminence; or that, if he had such expectations, he concealed them. In proof of this, he refers to several occasions on which Mr. Webster evinced in conversation a very moderate estimate of himself and his future prospects. But we are to remember that, over all his youth, poverty had cast its discouraging shadow, and that the vigor and elasticity of even his spirit must have been occasionally chilled by it. We are to recollect, too, some points of his character which never changed. He was always a serious man in every serious affair of life. Whatever may have been his consciousness of superior intellectual powers, he never treated any thing contemptuously, which obliged him to put himself on a level with others for the purpose of measuring the exertion which he had to put forth. Whatever he may have thought of this offer, which the good people of Fryeburg doubtless made as tempting as they could, he met it with no disdain, even when writing of it to one of his most intimate friends. But he was drawn away from it, first, by his father's desire to have him embrace the profession of the law; and secondly, as I have no doubt, by that mysterious power, which operates unconsciously upon men of great intellect in their youth, leading them toward the destiny which genius creates for them, and carrying them away from the proffered comfort of obscure and inferior stations to further efforts and continued privation, until the loftier sphere, which has been scarcely revealed to their vision, is entered in triumph at last. So, at

[1] Dr. Osgood.

least, I interpret the sober views which the young Webster thus expressed to his friends, before he finally decided not to make himself for life school-master and denizen of Fryeburg, and Clerk of the Common Pleas for the county of Oxford:

"What shall I do? Shall I say, 'Yes, gentlemen,' and sit down here to spend my days in a kind of comfortable privacy, or shall I relinquish these prospects, and enter into a profession, where my feelings will be constantly harrowed by objects either of dishonesty or misfortune; where my living must be squeezed from penury (for rich folks seldom go to law), and my moral principle continually be at hazard? I agree with you that the law is well calculated to draw forth the powers of the mind, but what are its effects on the heart? Are they equally propitious? Does it inspire benevolence, and awake tenderness; or does it, by a frequent repetition of wretched objects, blunt sensibility, and stifle the still small voice of mercy?

"The talent with which Heaven has intrusted me is small, very small, yet I feel responsible for the use of it, and am not willing to pervert it to purposes reproachful and unjust; nor to hide it, like the slothful servant, in a napkin.

"Now, I will enumerate the inducements that draw me toward the law: First, and principally, it is my father's wish. He does not dictate, it is true, but how much short of dictation is the mere wish of a parent, whose labors of life are wasted on favors to his children? Even the delicacy with which this wish is expressed gives it more effect than it would have in the form of a command. Secondly, my friends generally wish it. They are urgent and pressing. My father even offers me—I will sometime tell you what—and Mr. Thompson offers my tuition gratis, and to relinquish his stand to me.

"On the whole, I imagine I shall make one more trial in the ensuing autumn. If I prosecute the profession, I pray God to fortify me against its temptations. To the winds I dismiss those light hopes of eminence which ambition inspired, and vanity fostered. To be 'honest, to be capable, to be faithful' to my client and my conscience, I earnestly hope will be my first endeavor. I believe you, my worthy boy, when you tell me what are your intentions. I have long known and long loved the honesty of your heart. But let us not rely too much on ourselves; let us look to some less fallible guide to direct us among the temptations that surround us." [1]

In September, Ezekiel came to Fryeburg, and the two brothers made a journey together to the lower part of Maine, and then returned to Salisbury. Ezekiel soon after went back to college, and Daniel resumed his place in Mr. Thompson's

[1] Letter to Bingham, May 18, 1802.

office, where he remained until February or March, 1804. What his studies had thus far been in the law, the reader has seen. Mr. Thompson now made one mistake in directing his reading, to which Mr. Webster thus refers in his autobiography: "He was an admirable man, and a good lawyer himself, but I was put to study in the old way, that is, the hardest books first, and lost much time. I read Coke-Littleton through without understanding a quarter part of it." But he had already mentioned in the same paragraph that he had read two or three volumes of Blackstone's Commentaries; and the criticism therefore, which follows, and is now to be quoted, was intended to point out the inexpediency of making Coke a text-book after Blackstone, with nothing between them to instruct the pupil in the application of the principles of the common law to the transactions of life which form the subjects of ordinary litigation. The best book which Mr. Webster could then find within his reach, for this purpose, was Espinasse's Nisi Prius; and, inferior as this was to the numerous text-books since written, it answered very well. His resort to it shows that he did not mean to have it understood, from his observations about Coke, that Mr. Thompson had neglected to inform him that Blackstone's Commentaries was the proper book with which to begin his legal studies. In fact, his correspondence shows that he began Blackstone when he first entered Mr. Thompson's office, in the autumn of 1801. In the Autobiography he says:

"Happening to take up Espinasse's 'Law of Nisi Prius,' I found I could understand it, and, arguing that the object of reading was to understand what was written, I laid down the venerable Coke, *et alios similes reverendos*, and kept company for a time with Mr. Espinasse and others, the most plain, easy, and intelligible writers. A boy of twenty, with no previous knowledge of such subjects, cannot understand Coke. It is folly to set him on such an author.

"There are propositions in Coke so abstract, and distinctions so nice, and doctrines embracing so many conditions and qualifications, that it requires an effort, not only of a mature mind, but of a mind both strong and mature, to understand him. Why disgust and discourage a boy by telling him that he must break into his profession through such a wall as this? I really often despaired. I thought I never could make myself a lawyer, and was almost going back to the business of school-keeping. A friend has recently returned to me a letter, written by me to him at that time, showing my feelings of despondence and despair. Mr. Espinasse, however, helped me out of this in the way I have mentioned; and I have always felt greatly obliged to him."

He had not gone far, however, in his law studies, before he made another discovery which was quite characteristic of him, because it denoted a principle upon which he had been accustomed in college to discipline and to store his memory on other subjects. "Here give me leave," he writes to Bingham, "to pronounce a wise opinion, viz., that the best way to study law is in relation to particular points. I had read the statute of limitations, I do not know how many times, nor how many more times I might have read it among others, without discovering that it did not affect a sealed instrument, unless I had looked with reference to that particular inquiry. It is very much so, I believe, with history. We read page after page, and, retaining a slender thread of events, every thing else glides from the mind about as fast as the eye traces the lines of the book, yet, when we examine a particular occurrence, or search after a single date, the impression is permanent, and we have added one idea to the stock of real knowledge."[1]

Of his other reading, while he remained in Mr. Thompson's office, we get some sketches, also from his own pen:

"I do not know whether I read much during this year and a half besides law-books, with two exceptions. I read Hume through, not for the first time; but my principal occupation with books, when not law-books, was with the Latin classics. I brought from college a very scanty inheritance of Latin. I now tried to add to it. I made myself familiar with most of Tully's Orations, committed to memory large passages of some of them; read Sallust and Cæsar and Horace. Some of Horace's Odes I translated into poor English rhymes; they were printed. I have never seen them since. My brother was a far better Latin scholar than myself, and, in one of his vacations, we read Juvenal together. But I never mastered his style, so as to read him with ease and pleasure. At this period of my life I passed a great deal of time alone. My amusements were fishing and shooting and riding; and all these were without a companion. I loved this occasional solitude then, and have loved it ever since, and love it still. I like to contemplate Nature, and to hold communion, unbroken by the presence of human beings, with 'this universal frame—thus wondrous fair.' I like solitude also, as favorable to thoughts

[1] Letter to Bingham, December 21, 1802.—(*Correspondence*, i., 127.)

less lofty. I like to let the thoughts go free, and indulge excursions. And when *thinking* is to be done, one must, of course, be alone. No man knows *himself* who does not thus sometimes keep his own company. At a subsequent period of life, I have found that my lonely journeys, when following the court on its circuits, have afforded many an edifying day."

No man, who ever rose to great eminence in the profession of the law, has entered it through an experience more dangerous to an elevated and generous view of the objects which a young lawyer should set before him. If a hard and pinching necessity could ever excuse the growth of a sordid desire for gain, and the pursuit of it by ignoble means, they would have been excused in him.

For nearly two years Mr. Webster studied the law in a country village, where the lowest and speediest of its modes of gaining money must have been the chief aspect in which it appeared to him as a calling.

But his nature was one that could not be satisfied with the acquisition of any profession, merely because it offered the speediest prospects of gain. Poor as he was, and plainly as he must have seen that the sharp weapons of the law, in his hands, might be turned rapidly to account, he did not keep himself from those elegant studies which bring in their immediate riches to the mind alone. He turned from the statute of limitations and the writs of a country office to the Latin classics, to history, to poetry, to whatever would keep him from losing the love of letters, which he had so eagerly and so fully cultivated from his boyhood. Instead of being attracted, he was repelled by the facilities which the lower departments of legal practice appeared to afford for making money; for he saw that they were chiefly concerned with those whom he described as "the very refuse and remnant of mankind." He complains, too, that "law-reading has no tendency to add the embellishments of literature to a student's acquisitions. Our books," he adds, "are written in a hard, didactic style, interspersed on every page with the mangled pieces of murdered Latin, and as perfectly barren of all elegance as a girl's cheek is of beard.[1] The morality of the profession is, too, a matter

[1] There was nothing for the student then but what had come to us from England. He lived to see other writers arise on this side of the Atlantic, of whom he would not have made this criticism. Have we paid back the debt?

of doubt, or rather it is a matter of no doubt at all. Mr. Bennett says that a lawyer, who preserves his integrity unspotted, deserves a place in the calendar of saints. If this calendar were entirely made up of lawyers, I fancy it would be a short, a very short list, not so long, if you take the whole world over, as a catalogue of Freshmen, and yet this is the profession to which I am devoting myself." But, in the midst of these disheartening views, he consoles himself with the reflection that, "if one can keep up an acquaintance with general literature in the mean time, the law may help to invigorate and unfold the powers of the mind."

He found that great help in due time. He mastered Coke without serious difficulty, after he had learned to apply his severe abstractions; and he read him, too, in black-letter.[1] He "laid hands heavily"—to borrow his own expression—on the special pleading of the common law; a science which few of our young lawyers of the present day have an opportunity of studying for practical use, and which, as an aid to mental discipline, and as a system of logical devolution of the issues of a strictly legal controversy, is entirely unequalled by any of the modern devices which have supplanted it. Mr. Webster was always one of the best special pleaders of his time; and he owed his knowledge of the intricacies and the order of that method of pleading to the diligence with which he worked it out in the Latin pages of Saunders, translating and copying as he read. Yet with these graver studies he continued to make rhymes for his own amusement, and for the sake of "keeping alive," as he said, "some taste for the *belles lettres*." But he had no inclination to be drawn before the public as a poet. He was invited, in the winter of 1803, to deliver a poem before

[1] He could not always restrain his fun over some of the doctrines of the English law: "The law question that now puzzles us in this quarter is, whether Bonaparte, when he shall have gone to John Bull's palace, and taken hold of the ring of the door in the name of seisin of the whole island, will be such a king against whom it will be treason in an Englishman to fight. But they may settle this among them; you and I will not give an opinion without a fee."—(*Letter to Bingham, October* 6, 1803. *Correspondence*, vol. i.) I suppose that when he mooted this interesting question, he must have had before him Coke's Observations on the Statute 25, Edward III., *de proditionibus;* where that "prince of the law," as he calls stout old Sir Edward, lays down how treason may be committed against the king in possession, although done in behalf of the king who ought to be in possession; and how a pardon by the king *de jure* is no pardon if he be not also king *de facto*.—(See 3*d Inst.*, 617.)

the Phi Beta Kappa Society of Dartmouth, at their next anniversary. Writing to his class-mate Merrill, he says:

"John Porter, in his official capacity, has notified me of the wishes of the P. B. to write them a poem. If six of the nine Muses were to stand at my elbow, and promise that, according to their best discretion, they would inspire every line, word, and syllable, semicolon and comma, I should not choose to write a poem. I left making *rhymes* when I left college; and, as to *poetry*, I do not know that I ever made any."

As time sped on with him, although he could not quite shake off all the influences of his narrow fortunes, he began to be less discomfited by them, and also to have some perception of what the jurisprudence of his country was to become. "What you have said," he replies to Bingham, "of the obstacles in the way to eminence in this country, has much to support it. But what then? Must we sit down contented in the lonely valley of inferiority? This is a cold, poor, comfortless place. If the hill of difficulties be so high that we cannot climb over it, yet perhaps we can make a shift to creep round it. At all events, it is worth the trial. I do not soon expect to see in America a Locke, a Newton, a Pope, or a Sir Joshua. But Mansfields and Kenyons, I believe, we shall rear in the next age. And the reason of the difference is, that eminence will be sought with more ardor in the lucrative professions, than in the abstract sciences and the fine arts." Still, for himself, his expectations, so far as they were expressed to his friends, continued to be moderate and subdued. "Yet, Merrill," he writes a year later, "you and I have some ambition; so has, or ought to have, every one. So much ambition as shall prompt to laudable exertion and industry; so much as is well consistent with the duties and the honest pleasures of life, as induces a wish to make ourselves respected by our friends and not entirely despised by our enemies; and, on the score of property, so much ambition as instigates to the acquirement of a decent, competent estate, enabling us to treat our friends as they deserve, and to live free from embarrassment; this degree of ambition is rational and necessary."

Was this all that at the age of two-and-twenty he had proposed to himself? Did his description of a "rational and necessary ambition" comprehend all that burned within him, or was there still something that he held in reserve, even with his youthful companions, and that urged him on to a more brilliant future than that which he depicted as their common lot? His correspondence with his college friends was entirely free and intimate, and he probably expressed in it, as openly as any man ever expresses in such letters, the feelings of his heart. Apparently he was not at this time looking, in his own thoughts, for the great prizes in the lottery of life. He was a diligent and laborious student, devoted to the acquisition of knowledge both in and out of his profession. He did not mean to take an inferior position in it, and he did not confidently expect to ascend to its highest honors. He was not, at this time, looking to any of the chief cities or the large towns as his future theatre. He knew that while his father lived, and perhaps for a much longer period, he must be where he could minister to the comfort of those who had now such strong claims upon his presence and his care. The life of a country lawyer, therefore, was the sphere that appeared to him to be before him. Still the great powers which he had so sedulously cultivated, and which stirred within him half-conscious of their destiny, craved a larger development, wider fields of observation, and more ample means of culture, than his native village could afford. He had a strong desire to finish his studies in Boston; and thither his hopes and his plans tended for some time in the autumn and early winter of 1803. But he had to wait, as he said, until "something like a miracle" should put the means into his hands.

The "miracle" came in the shape of an accidental turn of his brother's affairs. Ezekiel had worked hard to maintain himself at college, and had been helped by all at home, until help was no longer possible. Something had to be done by one or the other of the brothers to recruit their exhausted finances. Ezekiel passed the winter vacation of 1803–'4 in teaching a school in Sanbornton; and in February, Daniel went to Boston, to seek some employment for himself or his brother. It chanced that a young college friend of theirs, Dr. Cyrus Perkins, afterward a distinguished physician in Boston and New York, had been for some time teaching a small private school in Boston, in what was then called "Short" Street.[1] He had obtained the mastership of

[1] Since a part of "Kingston" Street.

one of the public schools, and offered to relinquish his private school to Ezekiel Webster.

This arrangement was at once concluded, as soon as Daniel could return to Salisbury; and Ezekiel went immediately to Boston, although at the risk of not obtaining his degree at the ensuing college commencement.

Ezekiel being thus settled for a time in Boston, Daniel appears to have turned his thoughts toward the city of New York. But his brother earnestly opposed this plan, and thus advised his coming to Boston:

"Agreeably to your injunction, I have thought and meditated upon your letter for three days, and for no inconsiderable portion of three nights, and I now give you the result as freely as I wish your welfare. I am directly opposed to your going to New York, and for several reasons. First, the expensiveness of a journey to that city, and of a residence in it, is, with me, a material objection; secondly, the embarrassments to which you will be liable, without friends to assist, or patronage to support you; thirdly, I fear the climate would be injurious to your constitution. I have now told you what I would not have you do; and I also tell you what I wish you to do. I would have you decamp immediately with all your baggage from Salisbury, and march directly to this place. This is the opinion which I have maturely formed, for which a thousand reasons might be urged. They are too numerous to be mentioned, nor is it perhaps necessary, for I say to you imperatively, 'Come.' It is the easiest thing in the world for a fellow of any enterprise or ability to support himself here very handsomely, without descending to any business incompatible with the situation of a gentleman. Here, too, is the focus of information. . . . I will state to you a single circumstance which, I think, will remove all doubt about paying your way. I have now eight scholars in Latin and Greek, whom I shall be obliged to dismiss if I cannot have an assistant, and I dare not at present hire one. The tuition of these eight scholars will pay for your board. They recite twice in a day, and it will take you about three-fourths of an hour to hear them each time. Here, then, you can support yourself by the labor of one hour and a half each day. If you will spend that time in my school daily, I will board you at as genteel a boarding-house as you can wish, or the place affords. Consult father, the family, and your friends, and start for Boston the next day after the receipt of this letter. Another such an opportunity may never occur. Come, and, if you don't find every thing to your liking, I will carry you back to Salisbury with a chaise and six, and pay you for your time. I must say again, consult father. If he approves, take the patriarchal blessing, and come." [1]

[1] Ezekiel to Daniel, April 4, 1804.

Mr. Webster says in his Autobiography:

"Accordingly, I went to Boston in July, to pass a few months in some office. I had not a single letter, and knew nobody in the place to which I was going, except Dr. Perkins, then a very young man, and, like myself, struggling to get on. But I was sanguine, and light-hearted. He easily persuades himself that he shall gain who has nothing to lose, and is not afraid of attempting to climb, when, if he fail in his first step, he is in no danger of a fall. Arrived in Boston, I looked out for an office wherein to study. But, then, as I knew none of the legal gentlemen, and had no letter, this was an affair of some difficulty. Some attempts to be received into a lawyer's office failed, properly enough, for these reasons; although the reminiscence has since sometimes caused me to smile."

Mr. Ticknor observes, that Mr. Webster made but one such unsuccessful application, and that he was in the presence of the gentleman but for a moment, who never remembered the occurrence afterward. There was one member of that bar, however, who had a quicker penetration, although his associations and habits might perhaps have made access to him under such circumstances even more difficult than to others.

Christopher Gore, whose pupil Mr. Webster became in Boston, was the first district attorney of the United States for Massachusetts, having been appointed to that office by Washington in 1789. In 1796 he was sent to England as a commissioner under Jay's treaty, for the settlement of claims of citizens of the United States for spoliations by British cruisers during the wars of the French Revolution. He remained in London in the discharge of that duty for nearly eight years; and, during an absence of the American minister in 1803, he acted as *chargé d'affaires.* He was a man of good fortune, a scholar and a courtly and polished gentleman, whose information and manners exhibited the fruits of much intercourse with the world. He was, too, an excellent commercial lawyer, fond of the practice of his profession, in which his standing was eminently respectable. On his return to Boston, shortly before Mr. Webster applied to be received as his pupil, he had resumed his practice. Five years afterward, in 1809, he was elected Governor of Massachusetts by the Federal party, but in the next year he was defeated by Mr. Gerry, the candidate of the Democratic party.[1] From 1813 to 1815 he was a member of the Senate of the United States. It was a most fortunate thing for Mr. Webster that he came in contact with such a man. Mr. Gore was, doubtless, the first person he had then met, who, to great refinement of manners and complete knowledge of the world, united a general scholarship. Mr. Webster said of him:

"Since I left John Wheelock,[2] I have found no man so indefatigable in research. He has great amenity of manners, is easy, accessible, and communicative, and, take him all in all, I could not wish a better preceptor."[3] This was said, when Mr. Webster had been four months in Mr. Gore's office; and his estimate of Mr. Gore never changed. That they appreciated each other from the first, is quite apparent from the narrative which Mr. Webster has left us of the mode in which their acquaintance began.

"Mr. Gore had just then returned from England, and renewed the practice of the law. He had rooms in Scollay's Building, and, as yet, had no clerk. A young man, as little known to Mr. Gore as myself, undertook to introduce me to him. In logic, this would have been bad. *Ignotum per ignotum.* Nevertheless, it succeeded here. We ventured into Mr. Gore's rooms, and my name was pronounced. I was shockingly embarrassed, but Mr. Gore's habitual courtesy of manner gave me courage to speak. I had the grace to begin with an unaffected apology; told him my position was very awkward, my appearance there very like an intrusion; and that, if I expected any thing but a civil dismission, it was only founded in his

[1] It used to be said that Mr. Gore lost his election as governor, when he was a candidate a second time, by reason of his having made a canvassing tour through the State in a coach-and-four, attended by servants in livery, and escorted by a troop of horse. When he left the office of governor, he retired to an elegant country-seat in Waltham, about nine miles from Boston, where he lived for the residue of his life. He died in 1827. His chariot, with its crimson hammer-cloth, his four long-tailed bays, liveried coachman, and mounted footmen are among my earliest recollections. But these manners were not adopted by Mr. Gore in a spirit of ostentation, nor were they altogether singular in those days. In him, as in others, they were the dignified accompaniments of a life of refinement and social distinction. But they certainly were not calculated to win votes at a popular election, at a time when party spirit ran very high. Mr. Gore, however, never laid them aside in consequence of his defeat, and he always retained the sincere respect of the people of Massachusetts. Dying without children, he left the bulk of his fortune to Harvard College. The modern library of the university, built from his munificent donation, was called in his honor Gore Hall.

[2] The President of Dartmouth College.

[3] Letter to Merrill, November 30, 1804.

known kindness, and generosity of character. I was from the country, I said; had studied law for two years; had come to Boston to study a year more; had some respectable acquaintances in New Hampshire, not unknown to him, but had no introduction; that I had heard he had no clerk; thought it possible he would receive one; that I came to Boston to work, not to play; was most desirous, on all accounts, to be his pupil; and all I ventured to ask at present was, that he would keep a place for me in his office till I could write to New Hampshire for proper letters, showing me worthy of it. I delivered this speech *trippingly* on the tongue, though I suspect it was better composed than spoken. Mr. Gore heard me with much encouraging good-nature. He evidently saw my embarrassment; spoke kind words, and asked me to sit down. My friend had already disappeared. Mr. Gore said, what I had suggested was very reasonable, and required little apology. He did not mean to fill his office with clerks, but was willing to receive one or two, and would consider what I had said. He inquired, and I told him, what gentlemen of his acquaintance knew me and my father in New Hampshire. Among others, I remember I mentioned Mr. Peabody, who was Mr. Gore's class-mate. He talked to me pleasantly for a quarter of an hour; and, when I rose to depart, he said: 'My young friend, you look as though you might be trusted. You say you came to study, and not to waste time. I will take you at your word. You may as well hang up your hat at once; go into the other room; take your book, and sit down to reading it, and write at your convenience to New Hampshire for your letters.'"

This immediate confidence could not have been wholly the effect of a morning of good-nature, with an easy gentleman who happened to be quite at leisure and was willing to trust to accident for a clerk. The young man who presented himself thus unheralded, before a person of Mr. Gore's fastidious perceptions, could have been no rustic bumpkin, notwithstanding the air of embarrassment which his own modesty of narration has thrown around the scene. Learning and mental discipline, such as he had enjoyed, do not pour their riches into such a nature as his, without affecting the outer man; and genius and gentlemanly culture may be detected as quickly as their opposites, by one who is accustomed to note their manifestations. We know, too, that later there was a magnetism, in the presence of Mr. Webster, which all men felt, and which has been felt where his name was for the moment unknown. The same influence may have existed in his younger days; or a keen and practised observer, like Mr. Gore, might have seen in his eye, which it was said no man, even then, ever saw and forgot, some revelation of the intellect and character within.[1]

But whether this speculation is fanciful or well founded, the pleasing character of the anecdote remains. It connects, by an incident honorable to both, the name of the great statesman with the name of a man whose pure and elevated character made him one of the ornaments, as his love of letters made him one of the benefactors, of the society in which he lived and died. Mr. Gore was well fitted to direct the studies of such a pupil, and to supply and point out to him those sources of knowledge which could not have come within his reach in New Hampshire.

"I was conscious," continues the autobiography," of having made a good stride onward, when I had obtained admission into Mr. Gore's office. It was a situation which offered to me the means of studying books and men and things. It was on the 20th of July, 1804, that I first made myself known to Mr. Gore; and, although I remained in his office only till March following, and that with considerable intervening absences, I made, as I think, some respectable progress.

"In August the Supreme Court sat. I attended it constantly, and reported every one of its decisions. I did the same in the Circuit Court of the United States. I kept a little journal at that time, which still survives. It contains little besides a list of books read.

"In addition to books on the common and municipal law, I find I read Vattel for the third time in my life, as is stated in the journal, Ward's 'Law of Nations,' Lord Bacon's 'Elements,' Puffendorff's 'Latin History of England,' Gifford's Juvenal, Boswell's 'Tour to the Hebrides,' Moore's 'Travels,' and many other miscellaneous things.[2]

"But my main study was the common law, and especially the parts of it which relate to special pleading. Whatever was in Viner, Bacon, and other books then usually studied on that part of the science, I paid my respects to. Among other things I went through Saunders's Reports, the old folio edition, and abstracted, and put into English, out of Latin and Norman-French, the pleadings in all his reports. It was an edifying work. From that day to this the forms and language of special pleas have been quite familiar to me. I believe I have my little abstract yet.

[1] Mr. Webster mentioned, with some glee, in one of his letters written at the time, that, in consequence of his name not being distinctly pronounced by his companion who introduced him, he had been in the office a week before Mr. Gore knew his name. "This," he added, "I call setting out in the world. . . . But I most devoutly hope that I shall never have to set out again."—(*Letter to Bingham, August* 4, 1804.)

[2] He might have added to this list "Gibbon's Life and Posthumous Works," by Lord Sheffield, and Paley's "Natural Theology." He called the "'Natural Theology' an ingenious little thing."—(*Letter to Merrill, May* 14, 1805. *Correspondence*, vol. i.)

"I remember, one day, as I was alone in the office, a man came in, and asked for Mr. Gore. Mr. Gore was out, and he sat down to wait for him. He was dressed in plain gray clothes. I went on with my book till he asked me what I was reading, and, coming along up to the table, I held out my book, and he took it and looked at it. '*Roccus*,' said he, '*de navibus et naulo*. Well, I read that book, too, when I was a boy;' and proceeded to talk not only about 'ships and freights,' but insurance, prize, and other matters of maritime law in a manner 'to put me up to all I knew,'[1] and a good deal more. The gray-coated stranger turned out to be Mr. Rufus King."[2]

Men, indeed, as he has said, were the objects of his study, as well as books. The leaders of the Boston bar, at that time, were Theophilus Parsons, afterward the celebrated Chief Justice of Massachusetts; Samuel Dexter, the great advocate who, at a later period, argued against the Embargo for his townsmen, and "put his whole heart" into the cause;[3] Harrison Gray Otis, fluent, rapid, classical, a graceful orator, and one of the most ingenious of lawyers; James Sullivan, a strong, laborious, and earnest man; and Daniel Davis, a skilful criminal lawyer, of much experience and ability as a public prosecutor, and for a long time Solicitor-General of the State. How closely Mr. Webster observed these men, and how accurately he measured them, his diary, kept while he was in the office of Mr. Gore, abundantly proves. Although he might afterward, if he had undertaken it, have drawn more elaborate portraits, I doubt if he would at any subsequent period have changed any thing that he then set down. In two or three instances he sketched these eminent lawyers by a few strokes of his pen, which at once discriminate them.[4] But a kindred intellect led him to a closer comparison of Dexter and Parsons.

Besides attending the courts and studying the law, Mr. Webster had, for a time at least, one other occupation in Boston while he was in the office of Mr. Gore. In August, 1804, it became necessary for his brother Ezekiel to go to Hanover, in order to take his degree; and, during his absence, Daniel took

[1] For the origin of the phrase, *to put a man up to all he knows*, see post.

[2] Autobiography.

[3] Second speech on Foot's resolution. —(*Works*, iii., 329.)

[4] One of his short descriptions—refering to a gentleman then at the Boston bar—embodies a manner that is not rare in any age with men of a certain vehemence of temperament: "He rolls on his cause with an immense labor, deals in much sour invective, and acts in that way, as if he supposed the court and jury against him."

charge of the little school in Short Street. Edward Everett was one of the pupils of the school at that time; and in this relation the friendship between Mr. Webster and that distinguished scholar and statesman began, nearly fifty years before Mr. Webster's death. George Ticknor was not a pupil of the school, but in 1804–'5 he received private instruction in Greek from Ezekiel Webster, and at his father's house both the Websters and their friend Perkins were frequent visitors. That the younger Webster mingled to some extent in the other society of the town, is apparent from his correspondence; but his circle of acquaintance was not large, and he was too busy to increase it. He appears to have been absent from Boston in November, 1804, on an excursion to Albany, in company with a gentleman who had some occasion for his services. They travelled in a private carriage through Springfield to Albany, and thence came down to Hudson, from which place they returned by way of Hartford and Providence to Boston.

The following letter was written to his brother from Albany:

[TO EZEKIEL WEBSTER.]

"Albany, *November* 15, 1804.

"Dear Zeke: Like other invalids, we have made it an important point to visit the Springs. Yesterday we were at New Lebanon. The health of both of us is much benefited by a visit to the medicinal waters of that place. We drank, I believe, nearly a teaspoonful apiece, and, after washing it down with a draught of wine, we really thought we felt better. This place, New Lebanon, and Saratoga, will be the Bath and Spa of America. They are now the resort of the well as well as the sick—of the gay, the rich, and the fashionable. Where you look to see every nook and corner crowded by cripples and consumptive skeletons, you find taverns, assembly-rooms, and billiard-tables.

"Albany is no despicable place. To be sure, it is irregular, and without form. Its houses are generally old and poor-looking—its streets are rather dirty—but there are many exceptions. A part of the town is very high, overlooking the river in a very pleasant manner, and affording many fine seats. Some handsome buildings ornament the town. The Dutch Reformed Church and the new State Bank would not disgrace State Street. Here are all sorts of people—both Greek and Jew, Englishman and Dutchman, Negro and Indian. Almost everybody speaks English; occasionally, though, I have heard them talk among themselves in a *lingo* which I never learned even at the Indian charity school. The river here is half a mile wide—that is, I should think so; and, if I think wrong, you must look at Dr. Morse, and correct me.

"To-morrow, weather being fair, we set out on our return. We shall probably go by way of Hudson, Hartford, etc.

"Before I get back to Boston, the time will expire in which I was to pay Mr. Howard, Codman's Wharf, for the sugar,[1] etc. He was promised his cash by the 20th instant. If you will borrow it somewhere, and pay him, perhaps I can replace it when I arrive. I am peculiarly desirous of being punctual in this case, because Mr. C. was surety to Mr. Howard that I should be so. Pray get it paid somehow before the sun goeth down the 20th. It is about eighteen dollars.

"Call in at Mr. Chamberlain's, and give him and his family my love. I shall be glad to get back again, tell them.

"Adieu, honest fellow. "D. WEBSTER.

"And there went abroad over all the land an evil spirit, and it deluded many. Oh, good old mother Massachusetts!"[2]

This excursion gave Mr. Webster an opportunity to see a part of the country which he had never visited before, and, of course, it was the first time he had ever been out of New England. His companion defrayed the expenses of the journey, and at the end of it Mr. Webster wrote to Bingham: "I put my hand in my pocket and found one hundred and twenty dear delightfuls, all my own, yes, every dog of 'em. I am so proud to have a dollar of my own, I was determined to tell you of it."[3]

As he was thus going on toward the period of his admission to the bar, the worthy father at home, anxious and embarrassed in his affairs, was suddenly cheered by a plan for his son's settlement in life, which would place them all in a position of easy independence. The other judges of the court of which he was a member had great regard for him, and, the clerk of their court having died, they offered the place to Judge Webster for his son

[1] Supplies for his father's family.

[2] Great political changes took place in Massachusetts at this time.

[3] Letter to Bingham, January 2, 1805. From an unexpected quarter we may learn the exact *per diem* which made up this "dear delightful" sum. In a simple-hearted, affectionate letter from home, written by his sister Sarah (she of the whortleberry incident), there is a passage which reads as follows:

"Before we received your letters by the mail, we heard that you were gone to New York with a gentleman, at the moderate price of seven dollars a day for your company. It seems, Daniel, that your company is very agreeable in Boston as well as in Salisbury. We should all be willing to give as much to see you in this town, if we had the change as handy as you have in Boston." And then the good girl tells him the very little of country news in her small sphere—how the people move on in the same old way as when he was at home; and how they sometimes have "junkets," and sometimes "freewillers' meetings," which last, being interpreted, were a kind of "love-feast" among a portion of the Baptists, not participated in, probably, by the orthodox Webster family. There is a postscript to the lady's letter, but it was dictated and signed by the father; and it reveals a cause for the satisfaction with which Daniel regarded his earnings.

Daniel. The joyful news was quickly communicated to the latter in Boston. Here was another temptation, and a stronger one than the Fryeburg preferment held out; for it was a better situation, and it was one, moreover, that would put him at once where his parents and his sisters could have the benefit of his society as well as his pecuniary aid. But I cannot relate his perplexities and contradictory feelings as he has related them himself, and I therefore compile a narrative of the manner in which he met this singular event in his life, from the two ample sources that are before me. One of these accounts, which is contained in his Autobiography, has been published several years. The other, which is in some respects still more graphic and detailed, was given in the conversation of 1825, to which I have more than once referred, and which has not hitherto been made public. The colloquial narrative begins in this way:

"In 1804, the Clerk of the Court of Common Pleas of Hillsborough County died, and Chief-Justice Farrar immediately offered the place to me. The receipts of this office were full fifteen hundred dollars a year, and you may imagine that I felt as if my fortune was made. My brother and I were both in debt, our father was old, and his estate mortgaged. I had been looking to this office, but hardly with hope, and here it was—here was the appointment to what, as I may say, had been the ambition of the family ever since the Revolution. It was fifteen hundred a year. Why, I could pay all the debts of the family, could help on Ezekiel—in short, I was independent. I had no sleep that night; and, the next morning, when I went to the office, I stepped up the stairs with a lighter heart than I ever had before. I told Mr. Gore of my good fortune. 'Well, my young friend,' said he, 'the gentlemen have been very kind to you; I am glad of it. You must thank them for it. Certainly they are very good; you must write them a civil letter. You will write immediately, of course.' I told him that I felt their kindness and liberality very deeply; that I should certainly thank them in the best manner I was able; but that I should go up to Salisbury so soon, I hardly thought it was necessary to write. He looked at me as if he was greatly surprised. 'Why,' said he, 'you don't mean to accept it, surely!' The bare idea of not accepting it so astounded me that I should have been glad to have found any hole to have hid myself in; the very centre of Symmes's would have been welcome to me. I told him, as soon as I could speak, that I had no thought of any thing else. 'Well,' said he, 'you must decide for yourself; but come, sit down, and let us talk it over. The office is worth fifteen hundred a year, you say. Well, it never will be any more. Ten to one, if they find out it is so much, the fees will be reduced.[1] You are appointed now by friends; others may fill their places who are of different opinions, and who have friends of their own to provide for. You will lose your place; or, supposing you to retain it, what are you but a clerk for life? And your prospects as a lawyer are good enough to encourage you to go on. Go on, and finish your studies; you are poor enough, but there are greater evils than poverty; live on no man's favor; what bread you do eat, let it be the bread of independence; pursue your profession, make yourself useful to your friends, and a little formidable to your enemies, and you have nothing to fear.'

"I could say nothing to all this, and Mr. Gore's opinion that I could do something as a lawyer encouraged and flattered me. He told me to come the next morning, and talk a little more with him; I went home, and passed another sleepless night.

"The obtaining this office had been a darling object with my father. Its possession would make the family easy; and he had hastened to send me word that the prize was won. I certainly considered it a great prize myself, not that I did not love my profession, not that I did not hate the clerkship, and all clerkships, but simply from a desire to reach that high point of terrestrial bliss, at which I could feel that there was a *competency* for our family, myself included. I had felt the *res angustæ* till my very bones ached. Mr. Gore peremptorily shut me out from this opening paradise.[2] I need hardly say that I acquiesced in his good advice, though it certainly cost me a pang. Here was present comfort, competency, and, I may even say, riches, as I then viewed things, all ready to be enjoyed, and I was called upon to reject them for the uncertain and distant prospect of professional success. But I did resist the temptation; I did hold on to the hope which the law set before me. One very difficult task remained, however, to be performed, and that was to reconcile my father to my decision. I knew it would strike him like a thunder-bolt. He had long had this office in view for me. Its income would make him, and make us all, easy and comfortable; his health was bad, and growing worse. His sons were all gone from him. This office would bring me home, and it would bring also comfort and competency 'to all the house.' It was now midwinter.

"Well, sir," continued Mr. Webster, in 1825, "after talking further with Mr. Gore, I made up my mind to refuse the clerkship at all risks. I went to Mr. Taylor,[3] and told him I wanted some money, and that I should pay him some time or other. He said I should have as much as I wanted.

[1] The MS. adds, "Within two years of this time the fees were reduced."

[2] Mr. Webster, at this time, had no thought of marrying. He had not even met the lady who afterward became his wife. He had been somewhat interested in another lady, who is occasionally referred to in his letters written after he left college, but who was not either of those whom he had known at Hanover. But this affair never proceeded very far, and he had entirely dismissed it from his mind before he went to Boston.

[3] Mr. Joseph Taylor, a connection of the Amory family.

I told him I must have a good deal—three or four hundred dollars. He gave it to me, and, with this in my pocket, I hired a sleigh,[1] and set off for home. I got home one afternoon, just at sunset, and saw my father in his little room, sitting in his arm-chair. He was pretty old then, and tall, and very thin. His face was pale, and his cheek sunken, and his eyes—which were always large, and very black—seemed larger and blacker than I ever saw them. He seemed glad to see me, and, almost as soon as I sat down, he said: 'Well, Daniel, we have got that office for you.' 'Yes, father,' said I, 'the gentlemen were very kind, I must go and thank them.' 'They gave it to you without my saying a word about it.' 'I must go and see Judge Farrar, and tell him I am much obliged to him.' And so I talked about it very carelessly, and tried to make my father understand me. At last he began to have some suspicion of what I meant; and he straightened himself up in his chair, and looked at me as if he would look me through. 'Daniel, Daniel,' said he, 'don't you mean to take that office?' 'No, indeed, father,' said I; 'I hope I can do much better than that. I mean to use my tongue in the courts, not my pen; to be an actor, not a register of other men's acts. I hope yet, sir, to astonish your honor in your own court by my professional attainments.'

"For a moment I thought he was angry. He rocked his chair, slightly; a flash went over an eye, softened by age, but still as black as jet; but it was gone, and I thought I saw that parental partiality was, after all, a little gratified at this apparent devotion to an honorable profession, and this seeming confidence of success in it. He looked at me for as much as a minute, and then said very slowly, 'Well, my son, your mother has always said you would come to something or nothing. She was not sure which; I think you are now about settling that doubt for her.' This he said, and never a word spoke more to me on the subject. I stayed at home a week, paid any little bills that came in, bought what was necessary for the family, promised to come to him again as soon as I was admitted to the bar, and returned to Boston."

The time was now approaching for his admission to the bar, and the choice of a place of settlement. "In some country town in New Hampshire," he writes to one of his friends just before his admission, "I shall probably put off my character of a rover, and fix my feet for a season. Having been for the winter a wandering comet, in the spring I become a falling star, and shall drop from the firmament of Boston gayety and pleasure to the level of a rustic village—of silence and obscurity."[2]

[1] He means that he hired a seat in a country sleigh that had come down to the market. At that time, he says in the Autobiography, "Stage-coaches no more ran into the centre of New Hampshire than they ran to Baffin's Bay."

[2] Letter to Mr. Fuller, March 10 1805.

He was admitted to practice in March, 1805, in the Court of Common Pleas in Boston, on the motion of Mr. Gore. It was the custom then for the patron to make a short speech introducing the pupil to the court. It is a well-known tradition that on this occasion Mr. Gore predicted the future eminence of his young friend. What he said has not been preserved; but that he said what Mr. Webster never forgot, that it was distinctly a prediction, and that it excited in him a resolve that it should not go unfulfilled, we have upon his own authority, although he appears to have been unwilling to repeat the words of Mr. Gore's address.[1] This ceremony being over, he went immediately to Amherst, in New Hampshire, where his father then was, attending a session of the court. It was his wish at this time to settle in Portsmouth; but he resolved not to leave the immediate neighborhood of Salisbury during his father's life. Accordingly, he established himself in the adjoining village of Boscawen; and there, in the spring of 1805, he began the life of a country lawyer.

Before he left Boston, he had made a considerable purchase of books, for which he was to remit the money from New Hampshire. The money was forwarded, but the letter containing it was stolen from the messenger before it reached the hands of Ezekiel. Many letters passed between the brothers, and many plans were devised for raising another sum sufficient to obtain the books. At first, Ezekiel was desired to wait upon the bookseller, explain the loss, and request that the books might be put again upon his shelves. At length it was arranged that Ezekiel should ask Mr. Thacher, a member of the Boston bar, to become surety for the payment; to which that gentleman at once assented.

Furnished with this security, Ezekiel repaired to the bookseller's shop, tendered the indorsement of Mr. Thacher upon his own note, and asked for the books. But the worthy bibliopole refused all security, kindly forwarded the books, and gave all the credit that was asked. He lived to witness Mr. Webster's whole career.[2]

Books, indeed, were quite essential to his existence where he

[1] See the Autobiography. — (*Correspondence*, i., 20.

[2] The bookseller was Mr. Samuel H. Parker.

now was. The life which he led at Boscawen, for two years and a half, would have been insupportable without them. He described it in his letters as "a life of writs and summonses." "Other mechanics do pretty well here," he said, "and I am determined to try my luck among others."[1]

There was no congenial society for him, and he yet wanted that support which other young men, similarly situated, have found, from having formed that tender connection which may be the solace of present silence and obscurity, even when the beloved object is far away. He was not in love, and apparently he was not likely to be. He endured "the burden of perpetual solitude and seclusion," by devoting himself to business and study. His practice extended over three counties, Hillsborough, Rockingham, and Grafton.[2] It amounted to not more than six or seven hundred dollars a year; but this was sufficient for his support, besides leaving a small sum for the increase of his library. His studies during this period were various, and more extensive, I imagine, than they were during the same length of time at any former portion of his life, especially in the law and in history. With what energy he continued to resist the influences of that kind of practice in which most young men must begin their professional life, how he labored at this time to make himself a real lawyer, and how well he estimated the means that were to make him one, his correspondence shows. After reading what is now to be quoted, no one need be surprised that, as soon as he stepped forth from that little village in the interior of New Hampshire, he stood at once the equal and the competitor of men who were many years his seniors, and who had long occupied the foremost places at the bar of New England.[3]

"Study is the grand requisite for a lawyer. Men may be born poets, and leap from their cradle painters; Nature may have made them musi-

[1] He revenged himself upon the writs and summonses by turning them into verse:

"All good sheriffs in the land,
We command,
That forthwith you arrest John Dyer,
Esquire,
If in your precinct you can find him,
And bind him," etc., etc.

He then adds: "If the Legislature will but put our writs into a poetical and musical form, it will certainly be the most harmonious thing they ever did."—(*Letter to Bingham*, January 19, 1806.)

[2] "Scattering business over so much surface," he said, "is like spilling water upon the ground."

[3] Mr. Webster has said in his Autobiography (written in 1829), that, with the exception of instances in which he had been associated with the Attorney-

cians, and called on them only to exercise, and not to acquire, ability; but law is artificial. It is a human science, to be learned, not inspired. Let there be a genius for whom Nature has done so much as apparently to have left nothing for application, yet, to make a lawyer, application must do as much as if Nature had done nothing. The evil is, that an accursed thirst for money violates every thing. We cannot study, because we must pettifog. We learn the low recourses of attorneyism, when we should learn the conceptions, the reasonings, and the opinions of Cicero and Murray. The love of fame is extinguished, every ardent wish for knowledge repressed; conscience put in jeopardy, and the best feelings of the heart indurated by the mean, money-catching, abominable practices which cover with disgrace a part of the modern practitioners of the law. . . . Our profession is good, if practised in the spirit of it; it is damnable fraud and iniquity when its true spirit is supplied by a spirit of mischief-making and money-catching."[1]

BURIAL-PLACE AT FRANKLIN.

His first speech at the bar was made during the first year of his residence at Boscawen, and after the lapse of forty years he remembered with the deepest tenderness that his father heard it.[2] But his father never heard him a second time. He appears to have been unable to go abroad during the succeeding winter, and he died in April, 1806. In a burial-place set apart in his

General of the United States, he had hardly ten times in his life acted as junior counsel.

[1] Letter to Bingham, January 19, 1806.

[2] Letter to Mr. Blatchford, written from Franklin, May 3, 1846.—(*Correspondence*, ii., 225.) He states the same fact in the Autobiography.

own field, "beneath the shadows of a tall pine," he was laid by filial hands. Writing from that spot, when he was nearly of the same age at which his father died, Mr. Webster said: "I neither left him nor forsook him. My opening an office in Boscawen was, that I might be near him. I closed his eyes in this very house. He died at sixty-seven years of age, after a life of exertion, toil, and exposure: a private soldier, an officer, a legislator, a judge, every thing that a man could be to whom learning never had disclosed her 'ample page.'"[1]

It is not easy to determine whether Mr. Webster's first speech, which he says was made when his father "was on the bench," was made in the Court of Common Pleas, of which his father was a judge, or in the Superior Court of Judicature of which the Honorable Jeremiah Smith was the chief justice. The local tradition in the county of Grafton, at the period of Mr. Webster's death, was that his first cause was a case of some notoriety, that was tried in 1805, at Plymouth in that county, in the Superior Court, and that Judge Smith was on the bench.[2] If this was the case in which his father heard him, Judge Webster must have been invited to take a seat on the bench according to the usual courtesy, but he could not have been present in his official capacity, as he was a member of an inferior court. Nor could his son, in the year 1805, have been entitled to argue a cause to the jury in the Superior Court, since he was not admitted as a counsellor of that court until 1807. On the other hand, there is something more authentic than a tradition, respecting a cause which was tried before Chief-Justice Smith, in what was then the county of Hillsborough, in 1806, and in which Mr. Webster was allowed to take the part of junior counsel; and it was after hearing him in this case that Judge Smith is said to have remarked, on leaving the court-house, that "he had never before met such a young man as that."[3] Both of these were civil cases. There is also an account of a very powerful speech which he made in defence of a person

[1] Letter to Mr. Blatchford, written from Franklin, May 3, 1846.—(*Correspondence*, ii., 225.)

[2] My authority for this statement is a letter addressed to one of the literary executors, in 1853, by Mr. Alfred Russell, a gentleman who visited Plymouth at that time, and carefully gathered the tradition of what was there supposed to have been Mr. Webster's first cause.

[3] See Morrison's "Life of Chief-Justice Smith," pp. 179, 180. Boston, 1845

indicted for murder and tried in the Superior Court in Grafton County. It is said that the senior counsel abandoned the cause after hearing the evidence, leaving to Mr. Webster the whole burden of summing up to the jury. But it is scarcely needful to trace the precise degree of accuracy with which these several accounts have come down to us, or to determine which of them is to be regarded as his first cause. It is enough to know that, before he left the interior of the State, he had produced an impression which is even now not effaced, and that different counties have contended for the honor of having been the scene of his first effort at the bar.[1]

In the Autobiography, all that he says further, respecting the period of his residence in Boscawen, is embraced in the following short paragraph:

"The two years and a half which I spent in Boscawen were devoted to business and study. I had enough of the first to live on, and to afford opportunity for practice and discipline. I read law and history; not without some mixture of other things. These were the days of the *Boston Anthology;* and I had the honor of being a contributor to that publication. There are sundry reviews written by me, not worth looking up or remembering."

But, slight as was the interest which, in 1829, he thought might be attached to these things, they are not to be passed over without mention. His contributions to the *Monthly An-*

[1] Although I am unable definitely to assign this honor, I can add to the anecdotes of this period the following account of Mr. Webster's first encounter with Mr. Jeremiah Mason, of Portsmouth, which was given to me by Mr. Mason himself. A man, who had previously held a respectable position in one of the counties where Mr. Webster then practised, was indicted for forgery. Mr. Mason, as the leading counsel in New Hampshire, was sent for, on a special retainer, to defend him. "I had heard," said Mr. Mason, "that there was a young lawyer up there, who was reputed to be a wonderfully able fellow; and was said by the country people to be as black as the ace of spades, but I had never seen him. When they told me that he had prepared the evidence for this prosecution, I thought it well to be careful, especially as the trial was to be conducted by the attorney-general. But when the trial came on, the attorney-general was ill, and the prosecutors asked that Webster should be allowed to conduct the case. I assented to this readily, thinking I ought to have an easy time of it; and we were introduced to each other. We went at it, and I soon found that I had no light work on my hands. He examined his witnesses, and shaped his case with so much skill, that I had to exert every faculty I possessed. I got the man off, but it was as hard a day's work as I ever did in my life. There were other transactions behind this one which looked quite as awkward. When the verdict was announced, I went up to the dock, and whispered to the prisoner, as the sheriff let him out, to be off for Canada, and never to put himself within the reach of that young Webster again. From that time forth I never lost sight of Mr. Webster, and never had but one opinion of his powers."

thology were four; in 1806, a review of a Treatise on Political Economy, by Tunis Mortman; in 1807, a review of the first volume of Johnson's (New York) Reports, and an article on the French language; in 1808, a review of Lawe's Treatise on Pleading.[1]

After his father's death, Mr. Webster waited only for his brother's admission to the bar, so that he could relinquish to him the office in Boscawen, and that his mother and sisters might have a protector at hand. He had assumed the burden of his father's debts; and in the autumn of 1807, Ezekiel took charge of the farm on which the family had been left, and succeeded to the law business at Boscawen. From that time the care of their mother and sisters was shared between them. In September of that year, Daniel removed to Portsmouth. He had been admitted as a counsellor of the Superior Court in the preceding May.[2]

Of Mr. Webster's political principles or his connection with political affairs, down to the time of his removal to Portsmouth, it is necessary to say but little, partly because his political principles were very simple, and partly because his connection with political affairs, before the year 1812, was less than is commonly maintained by young American lawyers. I have already intimated that his father, from having served under Washington in the Revolution, was of that class of men who deemed that they could best discharge their duty to their country by following in the footsteps of Washington in civil affairs. These old officers of the Revolution, after their great chief had retired from public life, endeavored to shape their political conduct by the maxims which they believed had been inculcated in his "Farewell Address." That many of these men, scattered through the country, after the formation of the political parties, gravitated into the Federal party; that they tempered its counsels by their moderation and their sober patriotism; that they gave to its opposition to the measures of

[1] The *Monthly Anthology* was published in Boston, from 1804 to 1811. In the Boston Public Library there is a copy of the work, in which the names of the writers are noted. The *Anthology* was the forerunner of the *North American Review*.

[2] His assumption of his father's debts continued to weigh upon him as a heavy burden for many years. In fact, he did not entirely free himself from it until after he removed to Boston, in 1817.—(*Ticknor MSS.*)

Government, when the Government passed into the hands of their opponents, a consistent adherence to the spirit and purposes of the Constitution, and that they prevented some of the excesses to which an opposition is prone, are facts which require now no formal proof. That this was eminently the tone of the New-Hampshire Federalists, no one will doubt who is acquainted with the political history of that State. It was in that New-Hampshire school of Federal politics that Mr. Webster was educated. To this circumstance, as well as to the breadth and comprehensiveness of his intellect, we are to ascribe the fact, that although he entered public life at a period when party spirit was exceedingly virulent, he was never at any time in his whole career a very warm partisan, and never had any great faith in the utility of parties, while he submitted to them as a necessity, and like a wise and practical statesman regulated his coöperation with them as a choice between evils which he could not prevent. In regard to his connection with political affairs before the year 1812, after having indicated the political school in which it may be said he was born and educated, there is little more to be said. For, although before his removal to Portsmouth, he kept up an intelligent interest in public affairs, and although his range of knowledge on such subjects was far greater than that of most educated men at the same period who were much older in years, yet his active participation in politics was very slight, and his concern in the management of party machinery amounted to almost nothing. He did, in 1804, at the request of his friends, when visiting his father from Boston, write a political pamphlet to promote the election of Governor Gilman, the candidate of the Federalists. It was called "An Appeal to Old Whigs;" being, of course, an exhortation to those who had been Whigs in the Revolution. But even then he felt no very strong party interest in his production.[1] He also, as he has mentioned, delivered an oration on the fourth of July, at three several times between the period of his leaving college and his removal to Portsmouth. But he

[1] He said of it, whimsically enough, a year later, "Last year I wrote a political pamphlet in two days, which I have had the pleasure of seeing kicked about under many tables. But you are one of the very few who know the author of the 'Appeal to the Old Whigs.' Keep the precious secret."—(*Letter to his classmate Bingham, January* 19, 1806. *Correspondence*, vol. i.)

was pressed into this service more on account of his literary and oratorical accomplishments, than on account of his activity or zeal as a politician. None of these discourses are of any importance, excepting in a literary point of view; and, in this respect, all of them that have survived exhibit the growth of his power of expression and an approach to that pure and vigorous English of which he afterward became so great a master. But his political character should not begin to be studied before he wrote the "Rockingham Memorial" in 1812, or at least until the year 1808, when he published a small pamphlet on the Embargo. This chapter, therefore, may be concluded with what he has himself said on the subject of his connection with political affairs prior to 1808:

"I have never held office, popular or other, in the government of New Hampshire. My time was always exclusively given to my profession till 1812, when the war commenced. I had occasionally taken part in political questions, always felt an interest in elections, and contributed my part, I believe, to the political ephemera of the day. Indeed, I always felt an interest in political concerns. My lucubrations for the press go back, I believe, to my sixteenth year. They are, or ought to be, all forgotten, at least, most of them; and all of this early period.

"When I visited my father from Boston, in January or February, 1804, a severe political contest was going on between Governor Gilman and Governor Langdon. The friends of the former, and they were my friends, wanted a pamphlet, and I was pressed to write one. I did the deed, I believe, at a single sitting of a winter's day and night. Among other things of a similar kind, it is certainly not despicable. It is called an "Appeal to Old Whigs." Like other young men, I made fourth of July orations—at Fryeburg, 1802; at Salisbury, 1805; at Concord, 1806, which was published; and at Portsmouth, 1812, published also.

"August, 1812, I wrote the 'Rockingham Memorial.' It was an anti-war paper of some note in its time. I confess I am pleased to find, on looking at it now, for I do not think I have read it in all the twenty years that have rolled by since I wrote it, that it is of a tone and strain less vulgar than such things are prone to be.

"Before this period, I think in 1808, I had written the little pamphlet, lately rescued from oblivion, called 'Considerations on the Embargo Laws.'"[1]

[1] Autobiography.

CHAPTER IV.

1807–1813.

REMOVAL TO PORTSMOUTH—MARRIAGE—THE BUCKMINSTERS—MR. JEREMIAH MASON—BIRTH OF A DAUGHTER—THE EMBARGO—P. B. K. ORATION—WAR OF 1812—THE ENGLISH AND FRENCH DECREES—ROCKINGHAM MEMORIAL—ELECTION TO CONGRESS—RESOLUTIONS ON THE ALLEGED REPEAL OF THE FRENCH DECREES.

ON a Sunday morning in September, 1807, the sexton of the Rev. Dr. Buckminster's church, in Portsmouth, introduced a stranger into the minister's pew, according to the custom of the time. The eldest daughter of the family, on her return from church, observed that "there had been a remarkable person in the pew with her, that he riveted her attention, and that she was sure he had a most marked character for good or for evil." The stranger was Daniel Webster, at the age of twenty-five. His appearance at that time has been thus described, by another lady of the same family, from whom this anecdote is derived: "Slender, and apparently of delicate organization, his large eyes and massive brow seemed very predominant above the other features, which were sharply cut, refined, and delicate. The paleness of his complexion was heightened by hair as black as the raven's wing." He took lodgings very near Dr. Buckminster's house, and in a short time, says the same lady, "there was no longer a problem connected with him."[1]

[1] Mrs. E. Buckminster Lee.—(*Correspondence*, i., p. 438.)

He soon became very intimate in the family of Dr. Buckminster, who was the father of the young usher at Exeter already mentioned. The younger Buckminster was now a distinguished clergyman in Boston, settled over the society worshipping at the church in Brattle Street, and he was one of the founders of the *Boston Anthology*, to which Mr. Webster had been a contributor during his residence at Boscawen. To this association is probably to be traced the interest that was immediately taken in Mr. Webster by the Buckminster family. Mrs. Lee says:

"We soon saw enough of him to appreciate in some degree, young as we were, his extraordinary genius, and the noble qualities of his character. The genial and exceedingly rich humor that he so often exhibited was, perhaps, at this time more prized by us than any other of the diversified talents we admired in him. He soon formed a circle around him, of which he was the life and soul. We young people saw him only rarely, in friendly visits. I well remember one afternoon that he came in, when the elders of the family were absent. He sat down by the window, and, as now and then an inhabitant of the small town passed through the street, his fancy was caught by their appearance and his imagination excited, and he improvised the most humorous imaginary histories about them, which would have furnished a rich treasure for Dickens, could he have been the delighted listener, instead of the young girl for whose amusement this wealth of invention was expended. Hon. Mr. Mason, of Portsmouth, who delighted in the humor so often displayed by Mr. Webster, used to say, that 'there was never such an actor lost to the stage as he would have made had he chosen to turn his talents in that direction.'

"My father, Dr. Buckminster, took the liveliest interest in Mr. Webster, and, as he remarked at this time the apparent frailty of his constitution, he urged upon his young friend his sure remedy for slight indisposition. This was half an hour of wood-sawing before breakfast, with a long two-handed saw, himself holding the end opposite to that of his young friend. We young people were always delighted when this strong medicine was taken before breakfast, for, however disagreeable in itself, Mr. Webster appeared at our breakfast, afterward, with his genial humor unimpaired."

In the following June (1808), Mr. Webster left Portsmouth, on a visit, as his friends supposed, to his native town; and without communicating to them any other intention. He returned, bringing with him a wife.

When his matrimonial engagement was first formed does not distinctly appear, although there is a hint of it in one of his letters written in the previous December: "I have been a young dog long enough, and now think of joining myself, as soon as convenient, to that happy and honorable society of which you are one, the society of married men. Can I do better?"[1] The lady was Grace Fletcher, daughter of the Rev. Elijah Fletcher, of Hopkinton.[2] She had an elder sister, who was the wife of Israel W. Kelly, Esq., of Salisbury, at that time sheriff of the county of Merrimack, and afterward United States marshal for the district of New Hampshire. It was while Miss Fletcher was on a visit to her sister that Mr. Webster first met her, at some time in the year 1807. She was at the period of her marriage at the age of twenty-seven. They were married at Salisbury, June 24, 1808.

Writing as if in the presence of the remaining few who knew this lovely woman, the wife of Mr. Webster's early days and the mother of his children, I borrow, of course, the descriptions of others. To me, the gentle being who shared his early fortunes, and after a union of twenty years was called away from him, is not even a memory; and it is only as her qualities were said to have been reproduced in her daughter, whom I knew, that I can have her in imagination. But there is no need for repetitions of what I have heard. Mrs. Webster's character can be given in the words of those who knew her during her whole married life. Of these, it is needful to quote no one but her own and her husband's early friend, Mrs. Lee, who, in 1856, addressed to Mr. Fletcher Webster a sketch of his mother, which is printed in his father's correspondence:

"Mrs. Webster's mind was naturally of a high order, and whatever was the degree of culture she received, it fitted her to be the chosen companion and the trusted friend of her gifted husband.

[1] Letter to Mr. Fuller, Dec. 2, 1807.

[2] Mrs. Webster's mother, Rebecca Chamberlin, married, first, the Rev. Elijah Fletcher, of Hopkinton. Of this marriage there were four children—three daughters and a son; Grace being the youngest. Mrs. Fletcher again married the Rev. Christopher Paige, of Hopkinton, and bore to him three sons and a daughter. James W. Paige, Esq., who became an eminent merchant in Boston, where he lately died, was the third son of this marriage, and was, consequently, half-brother of Mrs. Grace Webster. He was one of the trustees under Mr. Webster's will, to whom the estate at Marshfield was devised by Mr. Webster for the use of his son and grandson. He first met Mr. Webster in the year 1807, at his mother's house. At that period Mr. Paige's long connection with Mr. Webster began, and it continued of the most intimate and affectionate character to the time of Mr. Webster's death. Mr. Paige died at his house in Summer Street, in Boston, May 19, 1868.

"She was sincerely and deeply religious, and to this divinely operating principle was it to be attributed that she was never elated, never thrown off the balance of her habitual composure by the singular early success of her husband, and the applause constantly following him. I remember a remark of the Rev. Dr. Parker, of Portsmouth: 'that it was a striking peculiarity of Mrs. Webster that she was always equal to all occasions; that she appeared with the same quiet dignity and composed self-possession in the drawing-room in Washington as in her own quiet parlor;' it was only when an unexpected burst of applause followed some noble effort of her husband, that the quickened pulse sent the blood to her heart, and the tear started to her eye. Uniting with great sweetness of disposition unaffected, frank, and winning manners, you will readily believe that no one could approach your mother without wishing to know her; and no one could know her well without loving her.

"When Mr. Webster had brought this interesting companion to Portsmouth, the circle that gathered around them became more intimate, and was held by more powerful attractions. There certainly was never a more charming room than the low-roofed, simple parlor, where, relieved from the cares of business, in the full gayety of his disposition, he gave himself up to relaxation."

It is perhaps not given to us to know with certainty, or to estimate accurately, the happiest period of any man's life, even when we have been personally familiar with the whole of it. But before the reader enters upon the days when Mr. Webster was first drawn into the political arena, he may wish to linger amid the tranquil scenes of domestic and social life which followed his marriage, and filled his residence at Portsmouth with a more than ordinary share of human felicity. All accounts concur in representing this as a period of great happiness for him and his. He himself speaks of those Portsmouth years, long after they had flown and he had tasted the sweets of fame and public honors, as "very happy years;" and the testimony of two of his most intimate friends, who saw him in the enjoyments of this portion of his life—I refer to Mr. Ticknor and Mrs. Lee—is like his own. The elements which made up that happiness were very large. His health was now firmly established. His professional position soon became every thing that the condition of society in his native State could hold out to any man. He had gathered about him ample means of further intellectual culture; he was surrounded by a circle of intelligent and admiring friends; his great powers were expanding with the discipline of his daily avocations; the approbation and affection of his fellow-citizens followed him without check; he had known no affliction greater than the loss of his father,[1] and his domestic life had become complete. Within two years after his marriage, a daughter was born, who received her mother's name. She was a child of uncommon intelligence and beauty, constantly in request among the friends of her parents, and long remembered among them as are the early developed and the early lost. As yet, that sorrow had not darkened his house, and this little girl was among its attractions.

In Mr. Ticknor's Reminiscences of Mr. Webster, I find the following passage relating to this period:

"Between 1809 and 1814, I was frequently in Portsmouth, visiting my friend, Mr. N. A. Haven, Jr. I always saw Mr. Webster on these occasions, dining with him at his own house and elsewhere, and meeting him often in the evening. Sometimes I saw him at his office. He seemed busy, but was always ready for cheerful conversation; and loved to tell humorous stories of his college-life. His office was a common, ordinary-looking room, with less furniture and more books than common. He had a small inner room, opening from the larger, rather an unusual thing. When I first saw him there, he lived in a small, modest, wooden house, which was burned in the great fire in 1813. His parlor was a bright and cheerful room. I remember how proud and fond he seemed of little Grace, his first child, as she sat by the fire with her book; a child of uncommon intelligence, with a brilliant red and white complexion, and deep-set eyes, and hair as black as her father's. He seemed very happy. He had grown a little stouter than he was when I first saw him, and had a more commanding air; but he was always animated, and sometimes full of fun. After the fire he had a somewhat better house; that, I think, was behind Dr. Buckminster's Church. Mrs. Webster was pleasing and animated, and her manner to the friends of her husband, and to us young men, was very kind and cordial."[2]

To those who have known Mr. Webster only in public, or who remember only the stately manner of his ordinary intercourse with men, it is difficult to give an idea of the genial affections which at every period of his life flowed out from him in the domestic circle, and still more difficult to paint the

[1] His sister Sarah, who was nearer his own age than any other member of his family, and to whom he was tenderly attached, died in a little more than four years after he removed to Portsmouth. This loss, therefore, I do not consider as falling within the period particularly adverted to in the text.

[2] MSS.

abounding gayety and humor and fascination of his early days, the eloquence of his unrestrained conversation, and the influence of his personal presence. Yet it is upon these characteristics, more than upon the manifestations of his great public or professional talents, that the reminiscences of his early friends have always dwelt. I can scarcely open one of the numerous communications that are before me from those who knew him as a young man, that does not speak with peculiar zeal of his social powers. It seems as if they felt that the world has set its seal upon all that was great in his genius and majestic in his deportment and character, or imposing in his intellectual achievements and public services, yet that there was a charm, a grace, a perfume in his social existence, which they fear the world has not known, and of which they bear their testimony more fondly than of all things else that cluster about his name.

In Portsmouth, Mr. Webster entered at once into a professional practice that brought him in contact with the first lawyers of that bar. He was soon engaged as leading counsel on one or the other side of nearly every important cause in several of the counties of New Hampshire; he and a few others of the principal members of the Portsmouth bar following the Superior Court on its circuit through the State. Among these was that extraordinary man, of whom little is now known, beyond the borders of New England, by the active generations of American lawyers; but to whose acute and powerful mind, through the discipline of opposing conflicts at the bar and the associations of an intimate friendship, Mr. Webster has impressively recorded his own obligations, as he always acknowledged them in private conversation. This was Mr. Jeremiah Mason, who was by fourteen years Mr. Webster's senior, and who was the admitted head of the legal profession in New Hampshire, when Mr. Webster went to Portsmouth, as he was also one of the greatest lawyers that New England has ever produced. Since it was my fortune to have known both of these very eminent persons, to have heard them repeatedly at the bar, and to have conversed with each of them respecting the other, I may, before quoting what Mr. Webster has written concerning Mr Mason, express my sense of its entire justness.

In stature, Mr. Mason, in the prime of life, stood six feet and seven inches. His frame was proportionately massive; his movements were slow and deliberate; and, as if from the inconvenience of always towering above the majority of mankind, he had a habit of stooping a good deal. This peculiarity, and an absence of most of the external signs of great mental exertion, made him often appear like a man who did not choose to put forth more than half of his natural strength of body or of mind. His countenance was almost as heavy as that of Dr. Johnson; while in the grasp of his intellect, in his sententious wisdom, and in a certain contempt for every thing that was not absolutely true when measured by the severest standards, he was not unlike that celebrated person. His head did not appear to be large, in comparison with the majestic proportions of his body; and the forehead, contrary to the usual rule in men of great intellect, was somewhat retreating. A stranger, seeing him in public, seated in a posture which denoted an apparent sluggishness of temperament, might have taken him for a dull man, if the constant watchfulness of his eyes had not revealed the unceasing alertness and activity of his mind. As his imposing form rose slowly, and he straightened himself by degrees to as great a height as he ever permitted himself to attain, all doubt as to what he was, or what he was about to do, vanished from the spectator's thoughts, when the first words reached his ears. He had no rhetoric whatever. He used no gestures. His pronunciation was quaint, sometimes provincial; but his choice of language was unerring. He disdained every ornament but the ornament of perfect clearness. His discourse was the embodiment of pure reason, the expression of an irresistible logic. When he dealt with evidence, he made it crush the intellect of his hearer into conviction. When he dealt with principles of law, he handled them with such a simplicity, and made them so lucid, and fitted them so exactly to his case, that one could scarcely avoid believing that, if on the particular occasion he was wrong, the law itself had always been wrong.

He was, indeed, a consummate master of the common law. In the other parts of jurisprudence, he was not what would be accounted very learned; at least, there were many men of his time who knew more of what the books contained, in several of the departments of legal lore. But he was always sufficiently furnished to do justice to any cause that he undertook, and he brought to every cause in which he saw fit to engage a power of reasoning and of discrimination, and a depth of insight, that made him a most formidable adversary. He once accepted a seat in the Senate of the United States, where he served from 1813 to 1817, and where his great abilities, his wise counsels, and elevated character gave him a large influence. Being a Federalist, and a change of parties having taken place in the State, he was not reëlected. He returned to the practice of his profession in New Hampshire, and to the enjoyments of a private station, in which he was widely known as the most eminent citizen of the State. In 1832, at the age of sixty-four, he removed to Boston, where he commanded a large practice in the courts for a period of about six years. At the end of that time, having accumulated such fortune as he deemed needful, he retired from the more active duties of his profession, and lived to the age of eighty, with dignity and ease, with all his faculties unimpaired, and imparting to those who had the advantages of his society the fruits of his singular wisdom and sagacity, which touched with equal power every public question and every private interest. He died on the 14th of October, 1848.

Of this great antagonist of his early professional career and of this friend with whom he never had a moment's personal difference, Mr. Webster made a record in his Autobiography, which he was well aware would remain private while either of them lived, but which he intended should stand as his deliberate judgment. It was written nearly twenty years before Mr. Mason's death; but it is well known that Mr. Webster never changed the estimate which he then so carefully placed on record, as I am confident that he never could have had subsequent reason for changing it:[1]

[1] In a playful letter, written by Mr. Webster to Mr. Mason, in 1830, from Washington, he says: "I have been written to, to go to New Hampshire, to try a cause against you next August. . . . If it were an easy and plain case on our side, I might be willing to go; but I have some of your pounding in my bones yet, and don't care about any more till that wears out."—The profound respect of these great men for each other was founded in their intellectual equality. Mr. Mason never suppressed his contempt when he felt it. One of his Portsmouth neighbors was accustomed to say, that he had often

"I lived in Portsmouth nine years, wanting one month. They were very happy years. Circumstances favored me at my first beginning there. Owing to several occurrences, there happened to be an unfilled place among leading counsel at that bar. I did not fill it; but I succeeded to it. It so happened, and so has happened, that, with the exception of instances in which I have been associated with the Attorney-General of the United States, for the time being, I have hardly ten times in my life acted as junior counsel. Once or twice with Mr. Mason, and once or twice with Mr. Prescott,[1] once with Mr. Hopkinson,[2] are all the cases which occur to me.

"Indeed, for the nine years I lived in Portsmouth, Mr. Mason and myself, in the counties where we both practised, were on opposite sides, pretty much as a matter of course. He has been of infinite advantage to me, not only by his unvarying friendship, but by the many good lessons he has taught, and the example he set me in the commencement of my career. If there be in the country a stronger intellect, if there be a mind of more native resources, if there be a vision that sees quicker, or sees deeper into whatever is intricate, or whatsoever is profound, I must confess I have not known it. I have not written this paragraph without considering what it implies. I look to that individual, who, if it belong to anybody, is entitled to be an exception. But I deliberately let the judgment stand. That that individual has much more habit of regular composition, that he has been disciplined and exercised in a vastly superior school, that he possesses even a faculty of illustration more various and more easy, I think may be admitted. That the original reach of his mind is greater, that its grasp is stronger, that its logic is closer, I do not allow."

The person with whom Mr. Webster here intended to compare Mr. Mason was Chief-Justice Marshall. When this is known, and it is recollected that, from the age of twenty-five, for a period of nine years, Mr. Webster was in almost daily conflict with the professional adversary whom he thus described, it is not difficult for us to appreciate the nature of the training. Mr. Mason compelled, in those who had to meet him, the utmost diligence of preparation, and the utmost vigilance in the trial of their causes. To be lacking in any thing that study of the case could have insured, or to relax the attention, where he was the opponent, was certain defeat. Mr. Mason, too, was in

heard him speak of persons of very high consideration in the country as "little ——," and "little ——;" but that he never heard him say "little Webster."

[1] The Hon. William Prescott, father of the historian.

[2] Joseph Hopkinson, of Philadelphia. This refers to the Dartmouth College case, in which Mr. Webster, in one sense, acted as "junior," that is, he opened the cause, and Mr. Hopkinson closed it. But the opening argument, as not infrequently happens, was the decisive one. This occurred in 1818.

himself a study for a young man educated as Mr. Webster had been; for, although there was much in his manner that might be observed and avoided, there was also that which could be noted to advantage. I well recollect a description Mr. Webster once gave me, of a change which he said he deliberately made in his own style of speaking and writing. He observed that, before he went to Portsmouth, his style was florid—he even used the word "vicious"—and that he was apt to make longer sentences and to use larger words than were needful. He soon began, however, to notice that Mr. Mason was, as he expressed it, "a cause-getting man." "He had a habit," said Mr. Webster, "of standing quite near to the jury, so near that he might have laid his finger on the foreman's nose; and then he talked to them in a plain conversational way, in short sentences, and using no word that was not level to the comprehension of the least educated man on the panel. This led me to examine my own style, and I set about reforming it altogether."

As we are now arrived at the period when Mr. Webster began to take a more active interest in political questions than he had previously exhibited, it will be necessary to describe briefly the condition of public affairs, the situation of the people who subsequently proffered him a seat in Congress, and their and his relation to the public questions of the time.

During the European wars which followed the French Revolution, Washington had with difficulty preserved this country in an attitude of neutrality, and in that attitude had handed it over to his successor in the presidency, the elder Adams. Through the administration of the latter, commencing in 1797 and ending in 1801, the two political parties, known in our subsequent history as the Federalists and the Democrats, had become perfectly well defined;[1] and the triumph of the latter, in the election of Mr. Jefferson, established them as the

[1] In the political nomenclature of that period, the party which elected Mr. Jefferson President of the United States were at first called "Republicans," and Mr. Jefferson himself always adhered to this designation. It was originally adopted for the purpose of expressing opposition to the supposed *monarchical* tendencies of some of the leading Federalists. But the term "Democrats" was that by which this party were usually distinguished at the time of Mr. Webster's entrance into public life, and this term will accordingly be used in the present work.

governing party of the country for the long period of sixteen years. Mr. Jefferson's administration, beginning in 1801 and ending in 1809, commenced about two years before the gigantic war which England waged against Bonaparte from 1803 to 1815, and which extended to the middle of Mr. Madison's second presidency; Mr. Madison having succeeded Mr. Jefferson in 1809, and going out of office in 1817. Mr. Jefferson, therefore, was President of the United States when Mr. Webster, in 1807, became a citizen of a town on the coast of New England, the people of which were largely engaged in maritime commerce, and warmly sympathized in the political opinions then in vogue in most of the commercial towns of that region. These opinions were chiefly those of the Federalists. The bearing, upon the interests of these communities, of the events which were then taking place in Europe and which strongly affected the relations of this country with the two great antagonist powers then struggling for an exclusive control of the ocean, makes it needful to recall the precise attitude in which their measures had placed our commerce, at the moment when, in 1807, it was arrested by the Embargo.

On the 16th of May, 1806, the British Government—in retaliation for the previous occupation of Hanover by the troops of Prussia, a country then under the control of Bonaparte, and in consequence of the exclusion of British ships from Prussian ports—by an Order in Council, declared the coasts of Prussia in a state of blockade, and also declared another blockade of the coasts of the Channel from Ostend to the mouth of the Seine. Napoleon's counter-Decree, issued from Berlin, November 21, 1806, placed the British Islands in a state of blockade, prohibited all commerce and communication with them, and declared that no vessel coming directly from England or any of her colonies, or touching there after the publication of the decree, should be received into any French harbor. This was followed, on the part of England, by another Order in Council, issued January 7, 1807, excluding all neutral vessels from trade with any port belonging to France or her allies, from which British vessels were excluded.

Then came another Order in Council, dated November 11, 1807, which declared all ports and places of France and her allies, from which the British flag was excluded, as subject to the same restrictions, in respect of trade and navigation, as if actually blockaded in the most strict and vigorous manner, and prohibited all trade in articles the produce or manufacture of such countries or colonies. Finally, this series of violent manifestoes was made complete, by the famous Milan Decree, issued by Bonaparte, December 17, 1807, by which every vessel, of whatever nation, that should have submitted to be searched by British cruisers, was declared to have lost the neutral character; every neutral vessel sailing between British ports, with any species of cargo, was declared to be good prize; and these rigorous measures were to be continued toward every neutral nation, until it had caused England to respect the rights of its flag.

These stupendous assumptions of a power which the public law gave to neither of the belligerents, operated more injuriously upon the commerce of the United States than upon that of any other country in the world. In fact, we were then almost the only carrying nation that was not directly or indirectly a party to the war; and we had, in consequence, ever since it began, possessed a large part of the carrying trade of the globe. We were thus reduced to the dilemma of being driven from the seas, or of compelling one or both of the belligerents to recede from their unwarrantable positions. Which of them was originally or was most in the wrong; against which it was our policy to fight, or to which it was expedient to lean; and what were the measures, short of actual war, that ought to be adopted by us, were the questions on which our political parties differed from the moment when our commerce began to feel the effects of a contest that involved every part of the European world and nearly every colonial dependency of a European power. Many of the commercial classes in this country naturally felt that the aggressions of France and the ambition of Bonaparte had originally created this enormous disturbance in the relations of nations; and they as naturally believed that affairs were not to be improved by our siding with France against England. In the Eastern States, the commercial towns were generally the political strongholds of the Federalists; and the Federalists had been, from the first, distrustful of a French alliance, opposed to the schemes of Bonaparte, and desirous to have our difficulties with England accommodated, upon principles that would at once save our national rights and prevent us from becoming absorbed into the vortex of European politics and wars.

But the Federalists were in a political minority in the country. The nation at large, whether from the effect of its old contest with England, or from the sympathies awakened by the early experiment of the French to possess and live under republican institutions, did not decidedly recoil from the absolute and despotic power which the empire subsequently established both over France and over a large part of Europe; and perhaps nothing was ever more skilfully done, than when the founder of that empire, in launching his final bolt against England, warned the people of this country that, if they desired to see the day when their rights as neutrals would be again respected, they must extort their admission from England, but that from him, until they had done this, they had nothing to expect.

Some occurrences between this country and England, which had happened or were happening when the full consequences of these measures began to be felt on this side of the Atlantic, largely contributed to the effect which Bonaparte expected to produce. In June, 1807, the causeless attack on the Chesapeake by the Leopard, off the capes of Virginia, had filled the whole country with indignation against the English, at a moment when our people were most excited by the pretension of a right to search our vessels for British seamen and deserters. Mr. Jefferson at once sent orders to the American ministers in England to demand reparation for the outrage on the Chesapeake; and on the 2d of July he issued his proclamation excluding British vessels-of-war from the waters of the United States. He summoned Congress, in an extraordinary session, to meet on the 26th of October. In the mean time, both Napoleon's Berlin Decree of November 21, 1806, and the English Order in Council of January 7, 1807, were in operation; but when Mr. Jefferson sent his message to Congress, at the opening of the special session, in consequence of the more direct and immediate aggressions of the English upon our commercial rights and the recent affair of the Chesapeake, he directed the attention of that body almost exclusively to the complaints which we had to make against Great Britain; and, taking severe notice of her late interdiction of all trade by neutrals between ports not in amity with her, he mentioned the French Decree of November 21, 1806, incidentally only, as a document that had already been laid before Congress. The consequence was, that our grievances against England, and the measures proper to be adopted in relation to them, formed the chief topic of popular excitement, at the time when intelligence of the still more stringent Order in Council of November 11, 1807, was received at Washington, and when the President, by his message of December 18, 1807, recommended the Embargo. This recommendation, which was made one day before the date of Napoleon's Milan Decree, together with the pending controversies with England, gave to the Embargo the appearance of a measure directed against the latter power; when, in truth, it was claimed by the Administration to be necessary to prevent the departure of our vessels from our own ports, in order to save our commerce from exposure to the depredations of both the belligerents. The bill, laying an indefinite embargo on all vessels in the ports of the United States, was promptly carried through Congress, and became a law on the 22d of December, 1807.

No measure of the Federal Government, since the adoption of the Constitution, had ever appeared, to most of those on whose interests it directly operated, so sudden, so unnecessary, and so oppressive, as the Embargo. It fell upon the Eastern States with a terrific weight. Six towns in New England possessed more than a third of the tonnage of the whole Union. At one blow, this great mass of shipping was rendered almost valueless. The numerous classes, who were dependent on its active employment for their livelihood, were suddenly deprived of their long-accustomed means of earning their daily bread. When we consider the conflicting opinions that had prevailed for years concerning the policy that ought to be pursued by our Government toward the respective belligerents; when we remember that, on the laying of the Embargo, one portion of the people felt called upon to justify a measure that inflicted unparalleled suffering upon another portion; when we recall the new, and then singular question, whether a constitutional power to regulate commerce embraces a power to indefinitely inhibit it—in short, when we endeavor to estimate all the elements of agitation and excitement that then pervaded our politics, we shall have no cause for being surprised at the angry crimination of parties, as we can have, in truth, no reason for assuming that all the right, or all the wrong, was on either side. It is easy to arraign the Federalist or the Democrat of that period, if we choose to identify ourselves with his opponent. But we shall find, if we survey such periods with impartiality, that, even in times of difficulty and danger, the call of patriotism will not always make men endure patiently the destruction of all their pecuniary interests, when they firmly believe that other measures might have been adopted to avert the injury; and that, when other men have fixed opinions that the measures of Government are necessary and right, they will inevitably erect a very high and exacting standard of patriotism, by which they will require the sufferers to restrain their opposition to measures which they themselves uphold. In such a state of things, there will be excesses on both sides. It is the part of a wise posterity, in looking back to the political contests of a former generation, not to disregard the possibility of error that belongs to human nature, whatever may have been the badges that it wore, or the political classification under which it was known.

It has already been said that Mr. Webster's public character should not be considered as beginning at least before the year 1808, when he published a small pamphlet on the Embargo. This production appeared at a period when the restrictions imposed by Congress upon the commerce of the country were without limitation in point of time, and when it was suffering from a paralysis, for which no prospect of relief could be discerned in the apparent policy of the Administration. The topics discussed by Mr. Webster related to the distinction, in point of constitutional power, between an unlimited and a limited Embargo; the real and the ostensible causes of the present one, and the ruinous effects which it had produced.[1]

[1] I do not discover why Mr. Webster did not put his name to this pamphlet. But it may be conjectured that, as many of the Republican or Democratic party,

For some time after the publication of this pamphlet, Mr. Webster does not seem to have taken any active part in political discussions, nor did he appear before the public in any capacity until 1812, excepting as an orator of the P. B. K. Society of Dartmouth, in the summer of 1809—a purely literary occasion. I take from Mr. Ticknor's Reminiscences the following brief notice of this performance:

> "In 1809 I was at Hanover, when Mr. Webster went there to deliver his Phi Beta Kappa oration. Mrs. Webster, Mr. and Mrs. Jeremiah Mason, and several other friends, were with him. They made a very merry party. Some of them stayed at the Olcotts', and others at Dr. Smith's. They were objects of great interest in the village through the whole time they remained there. Mr. Webster's manner in speaking was very fine—fresh, earnest, and impressive (I was then eighteen years old); his oration was very much admired and praised; but it seemed to me, at the time, that the excitement he created and the homage he received were due rather to their affection for the man, and their great admiration of him, than to the merit of that particular performance."

The original manuscript of this discourse now lies before me, just as it was written on the journey from Portsmouth to Hanover; for, in truth, Mr. Webster had accepted the engagement in the midst of a very busy professional practice, and, when he left Portsmouth, he had scarcely put pen to paper. The oration was written at the inns on the journey, although composed, doubtless, as was his frequent custom, during the drive of each day. It bears the marks of this haste, and, apart from the manner in which it was delivered, it was certainly, on the whole, as Mr. Ticknor intimates, not a very remarkable performance. But it contained touches of the power which afterward became so characteristic, and which has preserved so many of his written discourses after all the adventitious accompaniments of the occasion and the delivery have

in New England as well as elsewhere, had already begun to waver in their political faith in the propriety of this measure, it may have been thought expedient to furnish them with arguments without indicating that they came from a Federal source. In his Autobiography, he speaks of it as "the little pamphlet lately rescued from oblivion." Whether it was then (1830) brought forward with friendly or unfriendly motives I do not know, or in what way it had been "rescued." The only copy of it that I have seen is in the Library of the Massachusetts Historical Society, which is one of the original impression. The opinions expressed in it, concerning the unconstitutional character of an embargo, not limited in duration, Mr. Webster never changed.

been long separated from their text. The subject which he selected was the "State of our Literature." After adverting to the fact that neither our own country nor the age was distinguished by uncommon literary zeal, he entered upon a discussion of the causes which then impeded the cultivation of letters and science in America. The following passage, in which he answered what was then a domestic apology for the prevailing "apathy in the pursuit of literary and scientific objects," may be quoted; for it reminds us of the great thoughts that were afterward so imposingly developed in his Plymouth discourse:

"It has indeed been said that America is yet too young to imbibe an ardor for letters; that she can hardly expect even works of mediocrity, for years yet to come; that seven centuries from the foundation of Rome were scarcely sufficient to produce Horace and Virgil, Hortensius and Cicero; that when as many years have rolled by, from the landing of our fathers, as from Romulus to Augustus, we may then expect great poets, orators, and historians. No reasons from analogy can apply among nations so entirely dissimilar. Rome set out in the career of national existence completely barbarous. She got up out of her cradle an infant savage, with all the wolf in her blood. She was profoundly ignorant of first elements. She began at her alphabet. America, on the contrary, commenced her existence at a time when the sources of knowledge were unfolded, and the human mind was bounding forward in the path of improvement. Her first colonists were scholars. Raleigh, Smith, Penn, Robinson, are not names found in the first page of Roman history. No nation can trace so certain and so honorable an ancestry as America. It runs not back to clans of ravishers and robbers, nor to the lair of the foster-mother of Romulus. Nor is it enveloped in feudal ignorance or Druidical mystery. It is the plantation of enlightened men, from the best-informed nations of Europe, in a new country, who were anxious to strew the seeds of knowledge at the birth and beginning of their republic."

This extract is sufficient to enable the reader to mark the period when Mr. Webster had acquired the style for which he was distinguished through life. The short, pregnant sentences, the choice and expressive words, the rejection of superfluous phrases, are here as conspicuous as they are in any thing that he ever wrote.[1]

[1] In some rough notes written by Mr. Webster in 1831, for the use of a friend, I find the following, relating to this oration: "As far as I remember, I had hardly put pen to paper when I left Boscawen [Portsmouth] to deliver it. Much was written on the road, and many things were conned over and delivered

The period which intervened between 1809 and 1812 was, as I have already said, exclusively devoted by Mr. Webster to the practice of his profession. But the year 1812 brought with it a great change in the situation of the country, and a community like that of Portsmouth could not leave such a man as Mr. Webster in the occupations and enjoyments of private life. In June of that year, on the recommendation of Mr. Madison, then President of the United States, Congress had declared war against England—a war which the supporters of the Administration had long regarded as inevitable and necessary, but which their opponents had as steadily sought to avert. The Embargo, which commenced in 1807 under Mr. Jefferson, had produced no effect on the course of England and France toward the neutral commerce of the United States. It was relaxed in 1809, in respect to our trade with other countries; but against England and France a system of the strictest non-intercourse was substituted for it, by an act passed on the 1st of March, 1809, which was to continue until the end of the next session of Congress. It was announced, in this law, that in case either England or France should so revoke or modify her edicts as that they should cease to violate the neutral commerce of the United States, the President was authorized to reopen the trade with the nation so doing, by proclamation.

The position thus taken involved us in such a way in the dealings of the two belligerents with each other, in respect to their injurious edicts, that France was enabled to exercise over our course, by her menaces, her flattery, and her duplicity, a far greater influence than should ever have been permitted to her. As soon as Napoleon heard of our Non-intercourse Act of March 1, 1809, he immediately seized and sequestered all the American vessels then in France, with their cargoes, by way, as he said, of reprisal. Congress then modified the authority given to the President, by a new act passed on the 1st of May, 1810, which provided that, in case either Great Britain or France should, before the 3d of March, 1811, so

which were never written at all. I have turned down two leaves and marked short passages. I find, on one of them, a good round abuse of the *press*, which it may be prudent to omit." I do not find any distinct allusion to the press, but I presume Mr. Webster referred to a passage in which he introduced a vigorous denunciation of the corrupting effect of party politics.

revoke or modify her edicts as that they would cease to violate the neutral commerce of the United States, the President might declare the fact by proclamation; and that, if the other nation did not do the same thing within three months thereafter, the President might put the Non-intercourse Act in force against her. A copy of this law was immediately forwarded to the American minister in Paris, and he was instructed to say to the French Government that they now had an opportunity, by repealing their edicts as to the United States, to see the latter put their Non-intercourse Act in force against England, in order to compel her to abandon her Orders in Council. At the same time, our minister was directed to combine, with his application for a repeal of the French Decrees, a demand for restitution of the American property that had been sequestered in France.

Napoleon adroitly seized upon this overture. On the 5th of August, 1810, his foreign secretary wrote to our minister, that as Congress had now retraced their steps, and had opened the trade of France to American ports, and engaged to oppose whichever of the belligerent powers that should refuse to acknowledge the rights of neutrals, he was authorized to declare the Decrees of Berlin and Milan revoked, and that after the 1st of the ensuing November they would cease to have effect; it being understood, he added, that, in consequence of this declaration, the English should revoke their Orders in Council and renounce the new principles of blockade which they had wished to establish, or that the United States, conformably to their Non-intercourse Act, should cause their rights to be respected by the English. He further expressed the satisfaction of the Emperor in making known this determination, and added that His Majesty loved the Americans, and that their prosperity and their commerce were within the scope of his policy. But no copy of any repealing decree was furnished to the American minister, and he consequently could not enable his colleague in London to exhibit to the British Government any thing but the conditional and equivocal French note of August 5, 1810. As late as the 7th of September, all that could be further drawn from the French secretary was, that the Berlin and Milan Decrees would not be applied to American vessels, if they could be considered as American, but that they would be treated as hostile if they had submitted to be visited by British cruisers under the Orders in Council.

But the British Government did not consider that this proceeding could be made the ground for exacting from them a repeal of their Orders in Council, in compliance with a promise which they had previously given to repeal them, when satisfied of the revocation of the French Decrees. They construed the French declaration in one of the ways of which it was certainly susceptible, namely, as a conditional revocation; the condition being, as they viewed it, that, before the French Decrees should cease to operate, Great Britain must have repealed her Orders in Council, and also must have renounced those principles of blockade which the French alleged to be new. They said that the United States could not be warranted in putting their Non-intercourse Act in force against England, and not against France, under such a condition as France had now added to the American claim.

At home, the President, relying on the French declaration, on the 2d of November, 1810, issued his proclamation, announcing that the French Decrees had been so revoked as to cease to violate the neutral commerce of the United States, and declaring our trade open with France and her dependencies. On the same day the collectors of the customs throughout the Union were instructed to put the Non-intercourse Act in force, after the 2d of the ensuing February, against British vessels, and all the productions of Great Britain and her dependencies, if the revocation of the English Orders in Council had not in the mean time been announced. When informed of this step, Napoleon did nothing more than to direct his prize courts to suspend the further execution of the Berlin and Milan Decrees, in the cases of American vessels, until the 2d of February, but to hold the American prizes in a state of sequestration until that day. His cruisers were not directed to cease making captures of American property sailing in contravention of his decrees. The Emperor reserved to himself to determine, on the 2d of February, "with regard to the definitive measures to be taken for distinguishing and favoring the American navigation."

While these things were taking place in France and in

America, our minister in London, Mr. Pinckney, was engaged in claiming from the English ministry a repeal of their Orders in Council, upon the ground of the French declaration of August 5, 1810, and was receiving in substance the answer which has already been recapitulated. This discussion lasted from the middle of August, 1810, until the last of February, 1811, when Mr. Pinckney, convinced that nothing could be done, asked for an audience of leave from the Prince Regent, which was granted on the 1st of March, and he prepared to return home. But, before his departure, the appointment of Mr. Foster as minister plenipotentiary to the United States was announced to him, with the intimation, however, that Mr. Foster, while instructed to adjust, if possible, all matters of difference with the United States, would not be authorized to relinquish any of the principles on which the British Government held it to be impossible for them to repeal their Orders in Council under the conditions which they understood to have been dictated by France. They desired, they said, to relinquish those orders whenever it could be done without involving the sacrifice of their essential maritime rights and interests.

Meanwhile, in the absence of satisfactory proof that the French Decrees had been repealed, more than twenty-five American vessels, with their cargoes, were condemned by the English Admiralty Court, in May and June of that year (1811), for violation of the Orders in Council. Other occurrences tended to increase the popular irritation against England on this side of the Atlantic. In May, a conflict took place between our frigate the President and the British cruiser the Little Belt. This affair was the counterpart of that of the Chesapeake and the Leopard; but, in this instance, the superiority of force was on our side, and the combat grew out of an attempt by our frigate to ascertain the nationality of the Little Belt. When, therefore, Mr. Foster arrived in Washington, in July, 1811, he had to deal with the cases of the Chesapeake and the Little Belt, the grievances arising from the impressment of seamen out of our vessels, the demand of our Government for a repeal of the Orders in Council, and other topics of serious difference. The great obstacles to any adjustment, however, were found in the right of search insisted on by Great

Britain, and the position in which the repeal of the Orders in Council had been placed by what had already occurred. A long negotiation, extending from July, 1811, to June, 1812, in which the divergence still turned on the point whether the French Decrees had, in truth, been repealed—each side presenting what it regarded as proof of its own view of that question—resulted in nothing.[1] The act of Congress which declared war against England, passed on the 18th of June, 1812, proceeded upon the idea that a state of actual hostilities had for some time existed, and recognized a war as well as established one.

These explanations will be sufficient to show the attitude of the question relating to the policy or the propriety of the war, as it was viewed among us by those who supported and those who opposed it: the one side alleging that France, however oppressively she had conducted toward us in the past, had at length removed her obnoxious decrees as against us, and that England was now wholly in the wrong; the other side affirming that France had, in sheer duplicity, caused us to make war on England, the result of which, besides its injurious effects on all our other interests, would be an unnatural alliance between our Government and the Emperor Napoleon. It was in this state of the public feeling that Mr. Webster entered political life. His first appearance as a public speaker, after the commencement of the war, was on the 4th of July, 1812, when he was invited to deliver an oration before the "Washington Benevolent Society" of Portsmouth.

This address contained a firm but temperate statement of the grounds of opposition to the war. But it also contained more; for, young as Mr. Webster was—he was but just turned of thirty—he had already mastered the great purposes for which the Federal Government had been established under the Constitution, and he knew how to deduce from those purposes the duties which, by plain implication, they impose upon any administration that undertakes the conduct of a war against

[1] Of this prolonged and dreary correspondence, the *Annual Register* observed, with great truth and impartiality, that "both parties boasted of their moderation and forbearance; both alleged the reason and justice of their cause; yet both were, in fact, determined by motives of state-policy operating exclusively upon themselves."—(*Annual Register for* 1812, vol. liv., p. 194.)

a maritime power. "Maritime defence, commercial regulation, and national revenue, were laid," he said, "at the foundation of the national compact. They are its leading principles, and the causes of its existence. They were primary considerations, not only with the convention which framed the Constitution, but also with the people when they adopted it. They were the objects, and the only important objects, to which the States were confessedly incompetent. To effect these by the means of a national government was the constant, the prevalent, the exhaustless topic of those who favored the adoption of the Constitution."

After showing that the interests of commerce had been intrusted to the safe keeping of the General Government, not for confinement and restriction, but for encouragement, protection, and manly defence, he proceeded to notice the departure from Washington's political system, that had been evinced by the neglect into which the navy had been suffered to fall during the administration of Mr. Jefferson.

"In the system of Washington was also embraced a competent provision for maritime and naval defence. He saw that we had no other grounds to look for safety or security than in our own power to protect ourselves, and to punish wrong wherever it was offered. A navy, sufficient for the defence of our coasts and harbors, for the convoy of important branches of our trade, and sufficient also to give our enemies to understand, when they injure us, that they also are vulnerable, and that we have the power of retaliation as well as that of defence, seems to be the plain, necessary, indispensable policy of the nation. It is the dictate of nature and common sense, that means of defence shall have relation to the nature of the danger. In the administration of Washington, whose habit it was rather to follow the course of Nature than to seek to control it, beginnings were made, bearing proportion to what our trade then was, and looking forward to what it would be. Even at that time, the quantity of our navigation justified respectable naval preparations. The quantity of shipping, owned by the single neighboring county of Essex, as early as that period, would bear comparison with the whole navigation of England in the reign of Elizabeth, when the Armada of Spain was defeated by the English navy.

"If the plan of Washington had been pursued, and our navy had been suffered to grow, as it naturally would have done, with the growth of our commerce and navigation, what a blow might at this moment be struck, and what protection yielded, surrounded as our commerce now is with all the dangers of sudden war! Even as it is, all our immediate hopes of glory or conquest, all expectation of events that shall gratify the pride or spirit of the nation, rest on the gallantry of that little remnant of a navy that has now gone forth, like lightning, at the beck of Government, to scour the seas.

"It will not be a bright page in our history, which relates the total abandonment of all provision for naval defence, by the successors of Washington. Not to speak of policy and expediency, it will do no credit to the national faith, stipulated and plighted as it was to that object, in every way that could make the engagement solemn and obligatory. So long as our commerce remains unprotected, and our coasts and harbors undefended by naval and maritime means, essential objects of the Union remain unanswered, and the just expectation of those who assented to it, disappointed.

"A part of our navy has been suffered to go to entire decay. Another part has been passed, like an article of useless lumber, under the hammer of the auctioneer. As if the millennium had already commenced, our politicians have beaten their swords into ploughshares. They have actually bargained away in the market essential means of national defence, and carried the product to the Treasury. Without loss by accident or by enemies, the second commercial nation in the world is reduced to the humiliation of being unable to assert the sovereignty of its own seas, or to protect its navigation in sight of its own shores. What war and the waves have sometimes done for others, we have done for ourselves. We have taken the destruction of our marine out of the power of fortune, and nobly achieved it by our own counsels!"

Why he began thus early to insist on measures of naval defence, will be understood by those who remember that the tendency was at first to make this a war on the land, and that the project of invading Canada was already foreshadowed at the time he delivered this address. Yet at this moment our merchant-vessels were scattered over every sea, and it has been remarked by one of our own writers, who was entirely conversant with the subject, that "no other instance can be found of so great a stake in shipping with a protection so utterly inadequate."[1]

This discourse is also important in another respect, for Mr. Webster took occasion in it to state the true principles which govern that question in political ethics which relates to the just boundaries of political opposition in a time of war. These principles he enunciated so clearly, that all can see in them the

[1] Cooper's "History of the American Navy." He states that at the commencement of the war we had only seventeen cruising vessels on the ocean, nine of them being of a class less than frigates.

rules by which his own conduct as a public man was regulated, from the beginning of his career until its close:

"With respect to the war in which we are now involved, the course which our principles require us to pursue cannot be doubtful. It is now the law of the land, and as such we are bound to regard it. Resistance and insurrection form no part of our creed. The disciples of Washington are neither tyrants in power nor rebels out. If we are taxed, to carry on this war, we shall disregard certain distinguished examples, and shall pay. If our personal services are required, we shall yield them to the precise extent of our constitutional liability. At the same time, the world may be assured that we know our rights, and shall exercise them. We shall express our opinions on this, as on every measure of Government—I trust, without passion; I am certain, without fear. We have yet to learn that the extravagant progress of pernicious measures abrogates the duty of opposition, or that the interest of our native land is to be abandoned by us in the hour of her thickest dangers, and sorest necessity. By the exercise of our constitutional right of suffrage, by the peaceable remedy of election, we shall seek to restore wisdom to our councils, and peace to our country.

"Standing thus pledged by our principles to obey the laws, and to perform the whole duty of faithful citizens, we are yet at liberty to declare fully and freely the grounds on which we lament the commencement and shall deplore the continuance of the present contest. We believe, then, that this war is not the result of impartial policy. If there be cause of war against England, there is still more abundant cause of war against France. The war is professedly undertaken, principally, on account of the continuance of the British Orders in Council. It is well known that those orders, odious as they are, did not begin the unjust and vexatious system practised upon neutrals, nor would that system end with those orders, if we should obtain the object of the war, by procuring their repeal. The decrees of France are earlier in point of time, more extravagant in their pretensions, and tenfold more injurious in their consequences. They are aggravated by a pretended abrogation, and, holding our understandings in no higher estimation than our rights, that nation requires us to believe in the repeal of edicts, the daily operation of which is manifest and visible before our eyes."

The discourse was closed with a vigorous denunciation and protest against a French alliance, or the establishment of a common interest between our free republican institutions and the absorbing despotism and ambition of the French empire.

Regarded as the point from which Mr. Webster's political career began, this address stands in a very important relation to his history. Whatever differences of opinion may have prevailed heretofore, or may exist now, in respect to the origin, necessity, or expediency of the War of 1812, no liberal and just man can well deny that there were grounds of opposition to it on which a patriotic statesman could enter the public service of a community whose opinions had been from the first adverse to the policy which had led to it, and whose interests were believed to have been sacrificed to that policy. No such man can deny that Mr. Webster's statement of those grounds was temperate and thoughtful, marked alike by a true fidelity to the duties which a citizen owes to the government of his country, and a manly assertion of the duties which that government owes to the interests which it is appointed to protect. It is not correct to regard the maritime interests of this country at that period as bearing so small and insignificant a proportion to what may be considered as the sum of all the industry of the country, as to draw down upon men who held those interests, on account of their opposition to the war, the censure that is justly applied to a factiously sectional resistance against great national measures. The object for which the war was avowedly begun was the vindication of our rights and the protection of our interests as a commercial people. Those interests were so large that a single State then possessed four times as much shipping as was owned by England in the reign of Elizabeth. Nor was the relation of our shipping to the producing industry of the country one that should have caused its anxiety to be treated as a narrow and selfish local jealousy. In the year preceding the declaration of war (1811), the value of five principal articles of our exports, of domestic production, exceeded forty-five millions of dollars;[1] a larger amount, with two exceptions, than had ever been sent out of the country in a single year since the adoption of the Constitution. Surely it cannot be said that it was unreasonable in our own merchants to expect to be the carriers of this mass of our own exports, and of the imports for which it was exchanged; or that their criticism of a public policy, which was believed to deal unwisely with these great maritime concerns, had no relation to the producing interests of the whole Union. That the war finally resulted in what could be regarded as a success, is due, in a large measure, to the

[1] They consisted of cotton, tobacco, flour, rice, and manufactures.

employment and the achievements of the navy; that arm of national defence which is at once fostered by a great national commerce, and can alone effectually vindicate the rights of a commercial people.

Mr. Webster's address before the Washington Society immediately passed through two editions. It led to his appointment as a delegate from the town of Portsmouth to attend an assembly of the people of the county of Rockingham, which was convened in the following August, for the purpose of expressing to the Government, in a direct manner, their opposition to the war, and their opinions respecting the means by which it should be brought to a speedy and honorable termination. This was done in the form of a memorial, addressed to the President of the United States, and signed by a committee representing more than fifteen hundred delegates. The paper adopted for this purpose was written by Mr. Webster, and is the document referred to in his Autobiography, and then and since known as "The Rockingham Memorial." Its length and character, and the character of the assembly—which was what would now be called a mass convention—show that he had been selected to prepare it before the day of the meeting. Many persons of distinction in that part of the State, much older than himself, were named on the committee, but he was placed at its head, and reported the memorial. It was a carefully-written document, reviewing thoroughly the course of policy which had brought about the war; explaining the grounds of opposition to it which the people in whose name it spoke felt themselves justified in assuming; pointing out and remonstrating against its tendency to produce an alliance with France; urging immediate naval preparations, and a reliance on that means of defence; and recommending the adoption of a system that would speedily restore the blessings of peace and commerce. On the subject of fidelity to the Union, it thus stated the principles of those who, in this manner, as citizens of a free republic, addressed themselves to its chief magistrate:

"We are, sir, from principle and habit, attached to the Union of the States. But our attachment is to the substance, and not to the form. It is to the good which this Union is capable of producing, and not to the evil which is suffered unnaturally to grow out of it. If the time should ever arrive when this Union shall be holden together by nothing but the authority of law; when its incorporating, vital principle shall become extinct; when its principal exercises shall consist in acts of power and authority, not of protection and beneficence; when it shall lose the strong bond which it hath hitherto had in the public affections; and when, consequently, we shall be one, not in interest and mutual regard, but in name and form only—we, sir, shall look on that hour as the closing scene of our country's prosperity.

"We shrink from the separation of the States, as an event fraught with incalculable evils, and it is among our strongest objections to the present course of measures, that they have, in our opinion, a very dangerous and alarming bearing on such an event. If a separation of the States ever should take place, it will be on some occasion when one portion of the country undertakes to control, to regulate, and to sacrifice the interest of another; when a small and heated majority in the Government, taking counsel of their passions, and not of their reason, contemptuously disregarding the interests and perhaps stopping the mouths of a large and respectable minority, shall, by hasty, rash, and ruinous measures, threaten to destroy essential rights, and lay waste the most important interests.

"It shall be our most fervent supplication to Heaven to avert both the event and the occasion; and the Government may be assured that the tie that binds us to the Union will never be broken by us."

Toward the President himself this memorial was courteous and dignified in its tone. It pressed indeed the *argumentum ad hominem*, by reminding the President of the opinions which he had frequently expressed, when advocating the adoption of the Constitution, of the necessity for an acquisition of maritime strength, in providing and maintaining a national navy. The neglect into which the navy had been suffered to fall, by those with whom Mr. Madison had politically acted since the Administration of the elder Adams went out of power, fully justified this personal appeal. But it was couched in terms of the utmost respect; and as Mr. Webster soon after entered Congress, and stood at once and always remained in friendly personal relations with Mr. Madison, it is certain that the latter would have concurred in Mr. Webster's own observation—made nearly twenty years afterward—that there was nothing in this paper which the writer ever needed to regret. It marks the character of the opposition which he continued to maintain to the Administration of Mr. Madison, so long and so far as he maintained any.

Among the purposes for which the Rockingham convention

was assembled, was the nomination of candidates for the approaching general election. Mr. Webster was nominated as a Representative to the Thirteenth Congress, to which he was subsequently elected, and in which he took his seat on the 24th of May, 1813.[1]

There were several young men in this Congress of high talent, some of whom were afterward known to fame. The two persons were there, with whose names Mr. Webster's has been more associated than with those of any others of his contemporaries, as standing upon the same plane of intellect. Henry Clay was the Speaker of this House, and John C. Calhoun was the leading member upon the floor, both being on the side of the Administration. Among those of lesser mark, but still prominent then and always while they lived, were William Gaston, of North Carolina; John McLean, of Ohio; John Forsyth, and George M. Troup, of Georgia; Charles J. Ingersoll, of Pennsylvania; and Felix Grundy, of Tennessee.

One of the first acts of Mr. Webster, on entering Congress, was, to introduce certain resolutions, calling upon the Executive for information respecting the time and mode in which the repeal of the French Decrees had been communicated to our Government. As this whole matter stood before the public at the time of the declaration of war, it appeared either that our Government had been deceived by the French ministry, or that they were in possession of a repealing decree when the war was declared, and had withheld it; for no such decree had made its appearance until after the declaration of war had passed through Congress. Mr. Webster considered that the reputation of the country was involved in this affair, because the French foreign secretary had declared to the American minister in Paris, on the 1st of May, 1812, that a copy of the repealing decree had been furnished to his predecessor, and that another had been transmitted to the French minister at Washington at the time of its date, which was April 28, 1811. Mr. Webster, therefore, for the purpose of eliciting all the facts, and in order to have them

[1] A law of the previous Congress had appointed the next meeting of that body to be held May 24, 1813. The first session of the Thirteenth Congress commenced on that day, and was terminated on the 2d of August. The second session commenced December 6, 1813.

placed in their true light before the country, so framed his resolutions that, if they were answered at all, the whole matter must be disclosed. The resolutions were introduced by him on the 10th of June, 1813, accompanied by some temperate remarks concerning the doubt in which this matter was then enveloped.[1]

A long and somewhat angry debate ensued, in which Mr. Calhoun led the defence of the Administration with great spirit and warmth. He was at first somewhat disposed to stifle the inquiry. But the House was not in a mood to do this. The war was not at that time so popular that the members could refuse an inquiry into the measures that had led to it. Indeed, the declaration of war had originally passed a House of one hundred and twenty-eight members by a majority of thirty votes only, and a Senate of thirty-two members by a majority of six; while an amendment to include France in the war was negatived in the Senate by the meagre majority of four. The friends of the Administration were now, therefore, in a new Congress, obliged to meet this inquiry, without having at their command such a popular enthusiasm for the war as might have justified their refusal, if such enthusiasm had existed. The debate on the resolutions continued at intervals until the 21st of June, but they were all finally passed as they were introduced, by very large

[1] What Mr. Webster said on this occasion strongly attracted the attention of Chief-Justice Marshall. Nearly twenty years afterward, when Mr. Webster's collected speeches were first published, it appears from the following letters that the Chief Justice was disappointed at finding this one omitted from the volume:

[FROM CHIEF-JUSTICE MARSHALL.]

"*January* 23. 1831.

"DEAR SIR: I have just received the copy of your 'Speeches and Forensic Arguments,' and am much flattered by this mark of your attention. I beg you to present my compliments to Mrs. Webster; and to say that I think myself, in part, indebted to her for it. At all events, she has, I perceive, had some agency in conferring the favor.

"I shall read the volume with pleasure, and preserve it with care.

"Will you allow me to say that, on looking over the contents, I felt at the first moment some disappointment at not seeing two speeches delivered by you in the first Congress, I believe, of which you were a member.

"With great and respectful esteem,

"I am, your obedient,

"J. MARSHALL."

[FROM JUDGE STORY.]

"WASHINGTON, *January* 23, 1831.

"MY DEAR SIR: After the Chief Justice (Marshall) had received the volume of your speeches this morning, he came into my chamber, and told me he had been looking over the index, and noticed two omissions of speeches which he remembered you had made in Congress at an early period of your public life, and which he had then read. One was on some resolutions, calling upon President Madison for the proof of the repeal of the Berlin and Milan Decrees; the other, on the subject of the Previous Question. He observed: 'I read these speeches with very great pleasure and satisfaction at the time. At the time when the first was delivered, I did not know Mr. Webster; but I was so much struck with it, that I did not hesitate then to state that Mr. Webster was a very able man, and would become one of the very first statesmen in America, and perhaps the very first.'

"Such praise from such a source ought to be very gratifying. Consider that he is now seventy-five years old, and that he speaks of his recollections of you some eighteen years ago with a freshness which shows you how deeply your reasoning impressed itself on his mind. Keep this *in memoriam rei*.

"Yours very truly,

"JOSEPH STORY.

"The Hon. Daniel Webster."

majorities. Mr. Webster had intended to close the discussion upon them, but he found it unnecessary.[1]

Mr. Jeremiah Mason had been recently chosen a Senator from New Hampshire, and he arrived and took his seat in the Senate while these resolutions were under discussion in the House. The answer to them was made by the Secretary of State, Mr. Monroe, on the 12th of July. It disclosed the fact that our Government had received no intelligence of the repealing decree of April 28, 1811, until the 13th of July, 1812, nearly a month after the declaration of war against England. It followed, therefore, that our reliance on the action of France was based wholly upon the declaration of August 5, 1810, which, it was argued by Mr. Monroe, had fully satisfied every claim of the British Government according to their own principles, and ought to have been received by them as sufficient cause for a repeal of their Orders in Council. On this point there was of course a great difference of opinion between those who favored the war against England and those who believed that France ought to have been selected as our enemy, or at least that she should have been dealt with in a very different way from that which had been adopted. It is in the highest degree probable that, if there had been no such existing cause of irritation against England as her oppressive pretension of a right to search our vessels for seamen whose allegiance she claimed, there would not have been the same inclination to push matters to an extremity with her, by adopting so untenable a ground in reference to the French Decrees. The French declaration of August 5, 1810, was deceptive, and was intended to be so;[2]

[1] "You have learned the fate of my resolutions. We had a warm time of it for four days, and then the other side declined further discussion. I had prepared myself for a little speech, but the necessity of speaking was prevented. I went with Rhea, of Tennessee, to deliver the resolutions to the President. I found him in his bed, sick of a fever. I gave them to him, and he merely answered that they would be attended to."—(*Letter to Ezekiel Webster, June* 28, 1813.)

[2] Mr. Madison had become convinced of this before our declaration of war against England. In a private letter to Mr. Jefferson, written May 25, 1812, he said; "France has done nothing toward adjusting our differences with her. It is understood that the Berlin and Milan Decrees are not in force against the United States, and no contravention of them can be established against her. On the contrary, positive cases rebut the allegation. *Still, the manner of the French Government betrays the design of leaving Great Britain a pretext for enforcing her Orders in Council.* And in all other respects the grounds of our complaints remain the same. The utmost address has been played off on Mr. Barlow's hopes and wishes," etc.—(*Writings of Mr. Madison*, vol. ii., p. 535.) This letter

and, as each of the belligerents rested the apology for its injurious edicts upon the law of retaliation and self-defence, a neutral, that could present to one of them no better proof of the sincerity and good faith of its adversary than that French declaration, had but a weak practical ground on which to depend, however strong might be the argument against the inherent illegality and wrong of the whole system on which the edicts were justified by either of the two powers.[1]

discloses two remarkable facts: one, that the President still clung to the idea that the French Decrees were not enforced against us after August 5, 1810, notwithstanding our vessels were still remaining under sequestration, and no redress could be obtained; the other, that the President had at length penetrated the design of the French Government, namely, not to have the English Orders in Council repealed. But we had gone too far in the direction in which France wished us to go to retrace our steps, although the President's private opinion of her conduct and designs did not now differ much from that entertained by the Federalists. What his opinion was will appear further by an extract from a private letter which he wrote to Mr. Barlow under date of August 11, 1812: "The conduct of the French Government, explained in yours of the ———, on the subject of the decree of April, 1811, will be an everlasting reproach to it. It is the more shameful as, departing from the declaration to General Armstrong [August, 1810], of which the enforcement of the non-importation was the effect, the revoking decree assumes this as the cause, and itself as the effect; and thus transfers to this Government the inconsistency of its author-" —(*Ibid.*, p. 540.) Yet, when this subject was brought before Congress at the next session, not only did the Secretary of State argue that the conduct of France had deprived Great Britain of all reasonable pretext for continuing her Orders, but the whole force of the Administration was exerted on the floor of the House in support of that view, as the splendid abilities of Mr. Pinkney had been exerted previously in London in the same line of argument. As we now know the private feelings and convictions of Mr. Madison, the opponents of his Administration ought to be relieved of the charge of factiousness, even if they did maintain that the conduct of France had been animated by a purpose to lead us into a war with England.

[1] There is a judgment of Sir William Scott, pronouncing condemnation in 1811 of certain American vessels under the Orders in Council, in which that most able judge employed his acute and powerful intellect in framing a justification for those orders upon the doctrine of retaliation. The question had been presented to him in the argument, what would be his duty as an admiralty judge, under Orders in Council that were repugnant to the law of nations. After admitting that his court was bound to administer the law of nations to the subjects of other countries in their relations with Great Britain, he parried the question that had been pressed upon him by saying that the king in council had legislative authority over the court; that the law of nations constituted the unwritten law, and the king's Orders in Council the written law of the court; and that there was in this instance no repugnance between these two laws, because the king's orders and instructions were to be presumed, under the given circumstances, to conform themselves to the principles of the unwritten law. But as it could not escape a mind of such penetration that this led directly to the consequence that the legislative will of a single belligerent may dictate what the law of nations is, so as to bind the judicial action of a tribunal that sits to administer that law between its own sovereign and the subjects of other countries, he proceeded to say, further, that the Orders in Council which he had then to enforce were not repugnant to the law of nations, because they were *retaliatory*. This was at least an admission that the doctrine of *presumption* was not quite sufficient, and that it was necessary to find in the law of nations itself some principle that would make the orders conformable to what a belligerent may lawfully do. He

The British Orders in Council were repealed on the 23d of June, 1812, professedly upon the ground that the French Decrees had been repealed on the 28th of April, 1811. When the answer of our Secretary of State to Mr. Webster's resolutions was received in the House of Representatives, on the 12th of July, 1813, it was referred to the Committee on Foreign Relations, of which Mr. Calhoun was chairman, with an order to print five thousand copies of it. Mr. Webster, who had remained for some time longer than he had intended, waiting for the answer of the secretary, had then left Washington on his return home, supposing that the subject would not be again brought before the House during that session. On the day fol-

found this principle in the doctrine of *retaliation*. He frankly admitted that the orders would be unjust if they ceased to be retaliatory; and that they would cease to be retaliatory from the moment the enemy should retract in a sincere manner those measures of his against which they were intended to retaliate. This doctrine, applied to the real circumstances of the case, amounts to this, that whenever a belligerent chooses to say that the hostile measures of his adversary require him, in self-defence, to resort to measures of retaliation, his right of retaliation is superior to all the rights of all the neutral nations; and that until the neutral nations can, by forcing his adversary to change his course, relieve him of the necessity of retaliating, they must submit to the entire displacement and overthrow of the rights which, but for this effect of his right of retaliation, would belong to them. But it is obvious that if the unwritten law of nations embraces this principle, there are no such things as the rights of neutrals, or rights which belong to nations which are not at war, when some nations are at war. It is, however, quite certain that the law of nations does affix limits to the operation of retaliatory measures upon the rights of nations that are not engaged in the war; and the real question in relation to the English Orders and the French Decrees was, whether, admitting that they were retaliatory, or claimed to be such, they were within or without the limitations which the law of nations has established as the sphere in which the proceedings of nations at war can affect the rights of nations that are not at war. At the present day there would be very little hesitation on the part of this country in saying to any two belligerents, that this doctrine of retaliation has limits which must be respected. That we did not at that time so act toward both England and France, without complicating ourselves in efforts to make one of them recede in order to remove the other's claim of retaliation, must be imputed to our comparative weakness. Those who opposed the war with England would have preferred to have our Government deal at once with the original and inherent wrong in the conduct of both the belligerents, especially as they felt that the insults heaped upon us by France were even more aggravated than the injuries done to us by England; and, if we had been then what we are now, it is probable that the nation would have tolerated no selection of either adversary, but would have left each to choose for itself our friendship or our hostility. As it was, we were led, by a variety of causes, some of which our Administration could not control, to choose for ourselves the hollow and contemptuous friendship of France and the open enmity of England. (I have not been able to find this judgment of Sir William Scott in the regular reports of his court. But a copy of it was transmitted by our *chargé* at London to our Secretary of State, in June, 1811, and it is given in the annals of Congress, Twelfth Congress, 1811–'12, Appendix, p. 1742. It was pronounced on the 30th of May, 1811, preparatory to a decree condemning the brig Fox and a large number of other American vessels which had been seized under the Orders in Council.)

lowing the reference, Mr. Calhoun made a report, which took the ground that the pressure of our measures and the determination of Congress to redress our wrongs by arms, and not the repeal of the French Decrees, had broken down the Orders in Council. The report closed with recommending the passage of a resolution approving the conduct of the Executive in relation to the various subjects embraced in Mr. Webster's resolutions. Several efforts were subsequently made to have this report considered, but the House refused to act upon it at this session. On the 2d of August, Congress adjourned until the first Monday in the ensuing December.[1]

Although Mr. Webster had been present in this Congress but for a few weeks, he had already become a marked man. He had taken his stand as one of the leading opponents of the war, and had at the same time shown to the House and to the country what the character of his opposition was to be. His firmness in carrying this inquiry through the House had satisfied every one that he was not a person to be turned from his purpose in any matter in which he believed the honor of the country to be involved; while it was equally apparent that he intended to hold the Administration to nothing but its just degree of responsibility to public opinion in respect to the course of its action previous to the war. In future sessions, it was to become his duty to oppose measures connected with the conduct of the war, which he believed to be in conflict with the fundamental rights of the citizen, or in contravention of a sound public policy.

[1] The temper of the public mind in this country at the time of the adjournment may be learned from Mr. Madison's private letter to Mr. Barlow, already referred to, which was written in the same month: "In the event of a pacification with Great Britain, the full tide of indignation with which the public mind here is boiling will be directed against France, if not obviated by a due reparation of her wrongs. War will be called for by the nation almost *una voce*. Even without a peace with England, the further refusal or *prevarications* of France on the subject of redress may be expected to produce measures of hostility against her at the ensuing session of Congress. This result is the more probable, as the general exasperation will coincide with the calculations of not a few, *that a double war is the shortest road to peace*."—(*Writings of Madison*, vol. ii., p. 541.)

CHAPTER V.

1813–1814.

MR. WEBSTER'S LIFE AT PORTSMOUTH—BIRTH OF DANIEL FLETCHER—GREAT FIRE IN THE TOWN—CONGRESS OF 1813–'14—RESOLUTIONS ON FRENCH DECREES—MILITARY TRIALS FOR TREASON—ENCOURAGEMENT OF ENLISTMENTS—MODIFICATION OF THE EMBARGO—REPEAL OF THE RESTRICTIVE SYSTEM—DOMESTIC MANUFACTURES—PRACTICE IN SUPREME COURT—RETURNS HOME.

MR. WEBSTER reached his home in Portsmouth, from the special session of 1813, at about midsummer, and immediately resumed his usual avocations. His children were now two—Grace, who has been mentioned in the last chapter, and Daniel Fletcher, who was born July 23, 1813. Of his life at this time, we have already had some reminiscences from the pen of Mr. Ticknor.

The summer and autumn passed on as usual, but in December he was again on his way to attend the regular session of Congress, leaving Mrs. Webster and the children at home. While he was on this journey, a great conflagration swept over a considerable part of the town of Portsmouth, and his house was burnt, with others. The house had been purchased by Mr. Webster a short time before, for the sum of six thousand dollars. In addition to its furniture, his library was also lost; and, as there was no insurance on any part of the property, all that he had of worldly goods was completely gone. Mrs. Webster and the children found a temporary home in the family of

Mr. Mason. In the mean time, the news of the fire, which had been attended with some appalling circumstances, had reached Washington, where Mr. Webster, on his arrival, first met the account. Before he could open his letters, his firmness was put to a great trial, by the somewhat exaggerated statements of those who hastened to give him information. But a cheerful letter from his wife, advising him not to return, reassured him; and "finding nothing lost," he says, "but house and property," and considering how critical were the public affairs, he commended his little family to their friends, and remained at Washington through the winter.

There was, indeed, no little need for such men, even if they were not political friends of the Administration. The war, although there had been some brilliant successes on the Lakes and one important victory on the ocean, had not been prosperous on the land. In Europe, the star of Bonaparte was no longer in the ascendant—disaster had overtaken him; and England, at the head of the great combination that was now closing around him, was not unlikely to be in a situation to carry on her contest with us more vigorously than before. Our Administration, not a strong one, was in want of both men and money. Perplexed, and not sure of an undivided support from its own party, it was in danger of following counsels insufficiently weighed. It was conducting the first important war that had been undertaken since the establishment of the Constitution; and on that war the sentiments of the people were by no means unanimous. New measures were to be brought forward, new powers were to be exercised, which might subject the Constitution to a severe test. These measures were to undergo the ordeal of discussion by the representatives of a people who had been accustomed to the utmost freedom of debate and criticism; who had not learned to surrender that freedom to the demands of official judgment; and who would be certain to insist that the hitherto untried powers of war, embraced in the Constitution, should not be pressed to its injury and its possible overthrow. If the war was to go on, its policy was to be settled; and perhaps there never has been a war conducted by a constitutional government and in behalf of a free people, in which the restraining influence of a vigilant and upright opposition was more needed than it was in giving direction to the forces and consistency to the aims of this one. It was a period from which the people of this country can learn many lessons. Rash men, in and out of Congress, there doubtless were, in the opposition, who said and did rash things. Pure and patriotic men there were, connected with the opposition, who committed the mistake of leading movements that were not fully explained; who trusted too implicitly to the excellence of their own motives and the weight of their own virtues, and left that which could be misapprehended or distorted to work injury in the minds of the unsatisfied. But through the whole of that conflict there were men in the Federal party, in both Houses of Congress, who fulfilled the true function of an opposition; who made the limits of opposition so clear, that they incurred no merited obloquy; who were never connected with any occurrence that should cause their judgments as statesmen to be impugned; who spoke firmly, but always temperately; and who never spoke but to save a constitutional principle, or to insure a wiser policy. Of these, Mr. Webster was one of the foremost; on the floor of the lower House he was the first.

He had not lost sight of his resolutions of the last session, which called for information respecting the repeal of the French Decrees. The Secretary of State, Mr. Monroe, had not confined himself to furnishing the facts inquired for, but had entered into an elaborate defence of the war. Without some action upon his answer, the inference would be that it was regarded as conclusive upon the judgment of the House and of the nation. The House had now, with a near approach to unanimity, ordered an inquiry into the causes of the failure of our arms. Mr. Webster deemed it equally important that there should be a discussion of the grounds of the war. "If," he said, "its advocates can show satisfactorily that this war was undertaken on grounds plainly and manifestly just; if they can show that it was necessary and unavoidable; that it is strictly an American war; that it rests solely on American grounds; and that it grew out of a policy just and impartial as it related to the belligerents of Europe—if they ever make all this manifest, the war will change its character. It will then grow as energetic as it now is feeble. It will then become the cause of the people, and not the cause of a party." He therefore sought and obtained a reference of the secretary's answer to a committee of the whole. This occurred on the 3d of January, 1814. But the discussion was never allowed to take place.

Before many days had elapsed, Mr. Webster felt called upon to speak in terms of indignant rebuke of a project which he and such men as Gaston, Stockton, Hanson, and Cheves regarded as a proposition deliberately to violate the Constitution. The country was filled with rumors of treasonable practices by persons who were said to have given information to the enemy, that had assisted his military movements. The party spirit, that ruled a majority of the House of Representatives, permitted a resolution to be introduced, contemplating the extension of the rules and articles of war, relating to spies, to citizens of the United States. This was tantamount to the establishment of a military jurisdiction for the trial of citizens charged with the offence of treason. Robert Wright, of Maryland, was the member who introduced the resolution, instructing a committee of the whole to inquire into the expediency of so extending the military jurisdiction. Mr. Stockton instantly denounced it as a proposition unfit to be even referred to a committee. Other gentlemen followed him in the same strain, when Mr. Webster arose and delivered a short speech, which is probably very imperfectly preserved, but of which enough remains to vindicate his opposition to the measure. After declaring his readiness to provide additional legal punishments for any description of offences, he proceeded to show that the offences which were alleged to have given occasion for this inquiry constituted the crime of treason, as it stands defined in the Constitution, and that this resolution was one to change the forum for the trial of that offence:

"If illegal intercourse with the enemy existed, he should go as far as any one in applying constitutional remedies to that evil. But this resolution proposes, in effect, to consider whether it is not expedient to try accusations for treason before military instead of civil tribunals. However glaring may be the idea, yet such is in truth the real nature of the proposition. It is to change the forum for the trial of treason. The mover of the resolution and the gentleman from the State of Georgia (Mr. Troup) have not left any doubt on this subject. They have alluded to cases which they suppose the resolution to embrace, and for which they deem it necessary to provide military punishment. But what is the nature of those cases? Are they not cases of treason? It is said information has been communicated to the enemy, very material to him, respecting the operation of our own forces, by citizens of the United States. Signals are said to have been made for this purpose on the St. Lawrence and elsewhere. Do gentlemen suppose that the act of communicating to the enemy important intelligence, whether by signals or otherwise, whereby he is the better able to defend himself or attack his adversary, is not treason? Certainly, sir, all such offences as gentlemen have mentioned are provided for by law, and adequate penalties annexed to their commission. The simple question before us is, whether we will consider the propriety of taking the power of trying for these offences from the courts of law, where the Constitution has placed it, and confer it on the military. Sir, the proposition strikes me as monstrous. I cannot consent to entertain the consideration of it even for a moment. It goes to destroy the plainest constitutional provisions. If it should prevail, I should not hesitate to pronounce it a most enormous stride of usurpation. Nothing in any government called a free one, even in the worst of times, has exceeded it. I am utterly shocked at the arguments offered in favor of it. When the mover was asked why, in the cases he mentioned, the offenders could not be punished for treasonable practices, I understood him to answer that, on trials for treason in the courts of law, the testimony of two witnesses is required; but, if the trial could be transferred to a military tribunal, the two witnesses could be dispensed with. Are we now gravely to consider a proposition of which this is among the professed objects? The gentleman from Georgia (Mr. Troup) observed that, when persons had been apprehended for offences, they had been rescued by *habeas corpus* issued by the civil magistrate. And are we to deliberate whether it be not proper for us to prevent the delivery of the citizens of this country from illegal arrests and imprisonment by the interposition of their great constitutional remedy, their writ of *habeas corpus?* The Constitution contains no provision more valuable; it makes no injunction more direct and imperative than those respecting trials for treason, and the benefit of the *habeas corpus.* Treason is not left to be defined, even by the highest courts of law. It was foreseen that, in times of commotion, victims might be sacrificed to constructive treason; that doctrine which, in other places and in other times, has shed so much innocent blood, and which brought Algernon Sydney to the scaffold. The Constitution, therefore, defines treason, and prescribes the mode of proof. But what is there in the worst cases of construction of treason that can be compared, in point of enormity, to the proposition now before us? This is not to give a latitude of construction to the judge; it is to take the cause away from the judge, and carry it to the camp. Instead of indictment, arraignment, and trial, it proposes the summary process of martial law. If the proposition should pass into a law, it takes away the constitutional definition of the offence; it takes away the prescribed mode of proof; it takes away the trial by jury; it takes away the civil tribunal and establishes the military. On a resolution of this sort, I cannot believe the House will consent to deliberate."

Mr. Wright's resolution was referred, by the small majority of eleven votes, and was made the order of the day for the ensuing Friday. But, after what had occurred, no one ventured to bring it up in Committee of the Whole, and it was never acted upon further.[1]

A little later, when a bill to encourage enlistments into the army, by giving very high bounties, was before the House, Mr. Webster delivered a speech on the whole subject of the war, which was of an exceedingly elevated and commanding tone.[2]

The first attempt at the conquest of Canada had failed. Still, the invasion of Canada appeared to be an essential object with the Administration and a majority of its supporters in Congress; for an amendment offered to the bill, to restrict the employment of the troops to be enlisted to the defence of our own territory and frontiers, was rejected by a decisive vote. Mr. Webster had, therefore, to address himself to what he deemed an erroneous policy in the conduct of the war, as well as to speak incidentally on its general merits. These two topics were inseparably connected, because the known differences of opinion respecting the original expediency of the war, and its avowed objects, pointed to the necessity for a change in the

[1] I observe with pain the name of Mr. Calhoun among those who voted for a reference of this resolution. In any other than a time of high party excitement, he could not have been persuaded to give that vote, for he was devotedly attached to the principles of constitutional liberty. Mr. Clay was in the chair. As there was a clear majority for the resolution, he was not called upon to vote, and did not. Among the stories told at that time and repeated in this debate, it was said that Judge Ford, living somewhere near the St. Lawrence, had, when General Wilkinson's army was descending that river, hoisted a light in his upper story, which gave the British information, and that Wilkinson's army was soon fired upon from the Canada shore. Such tales found a ready credence with some of the Administration members, while others probably voted for the resolution in order to terrify the opponents of the war. The character of Judge Ford was vouched for by several of the most prominent members of the House. He was formerly of New Jersey, and was now a person of eminence in the region where he lived, and had written and spoken a great deal against the war. Perhaps the light which he "hoisted in his upper story" was metaphorical.

[2] Speech on the Encouragement of Enlistments, January 14, 1814. The speech is very well reported in the Annals of Congress. (Thirteenth Congress, vol. i., pp. 940 *et seq.*) It was not a prepared speech, but this report was corrected by Mr. Webster. He had no intention of speaking until nine o'clock that morning, and he addressed the House at two. (*Correspondence*, i., p. 239; letter to his brother Ezekiel Webster.)

policy which had hitherto governed its prosecution. Of the large circumspection with which a question of war should be approached by the Government of this Union, Mr. Webster spoke in terms that can never lose their importance while that Government remains what it is:

"We are told that our opposition has divided the Government and divided the country. Remember, sir, the state of the Government and of the country when war was declared. Did not difference of opinion then exist? Do we not know that this House was divided? Do we not know that the other House was still more divided? Does not every man, to whom the public documents were accessible, know, that in that House one single vote, if given otherwise than it was, would have rejected the act declaring war, and adopted a different course of measures? A parental, guardian government would have regarded that state of things. It would have weighed such considerations; it would have inquired coolly and dispassionately into the state of public opinion in the States of this confederacy; it would have looked especially to those States most concerned in the professed objects of the war, and whose interests were to be most deeply affected by it. Such a government, knowing that its strength consisted in the union of opinion among the people, would have taken no step of such importance without that union; nor would it have mistaken mere party feeling for national sentiment.

"That occasion, sir, called for a liberal view of things. Not only the degree of union in the sentiments of the people, but the nature and structure of the Government; the general habits and pursuits of the community; the probable consequences of the war, immediate and remote, on our civil institutions; the effect of a vast military patronage; the variety of important local interests and objects—these were considerations essentially belonging to the subject. It was not enough that Government could make out its cause of war on paper, and get the better of England in the argument. This was requisite, but not all that was requisite. The question of war or peace, in a country like this, is not to be compressed into the compass that would fit a small litigation. Incapable, in its nature, of being decided upon technical rules, it is unfit to be discussed in the manner which usually appertains to the forensic habit. It should be regarded as a great question, not only of right, but also of prudence and expediency. Reasons of a general nature, considerations which go back to the origin of our institutions, and other considerations which look forward to our hopeful progress in future times, all belong, in their just proportions and gradations, to a question, in the determination of which the happiness of the present and of future generations may be so much concerned. I have heard no satisfactory vindication of the war on grounds like these. They appear not to have suited the temper of that time. Utterly astonished at the declaration of war, I have been surprised at nothing since. Unless all history deceived me, I saw how it would be prosecuted when I saw how it was begun. There is in the nature of things an unchangeable relation between rash counsels and feeble execution.

"It was not, sir, the minority that brought on the war. Look to your records from the date of the Embargo in 1807 until June, 1812. Every thing that men could do they did to stay your course. When at last they could effect no more, they urged you to delay your measures. They entreated you to give yet a little time for deliberation, and to wait for favorable events. As if inspired for the purpose of arresting your progress, they laid before you the consequences of your measures, just as we have seen them since take place. They predicted to you their effects on public opinion. They told you that, instead of healing, they would inflame political dissensions. They pointed out to you also what would and what must happen on the frontier. That which since has happened is but their prediction turned into history. Vain is the hope, then, of escaping just retribution, by imputing to the minority of the Government, or to the opposition among the people, the disasters of these times. Vain is the attempt to impose thus on the common sense of mankind. The world has had too much experience of ministerial shifts and evasions. It has learned to judge of men by their actions, and of measures by their consequences."

Recurring to the imputations cast upon the opposition—imputations to which an opposition is commonly subjected—he asserted the duty and the right of free discussion in a manner equally worthy of being remembered at all times and under all circumstances:

"If the purpose be, by casting these imputations upon those who are opposed to the policy of the Government, to check the freedom of inquiry, discussion, and debate, such purpose is also incapable of being executed. That opposition is constitutional and legal. It is also conscientious. It rests in settled and sober conviction that such policy is destructive to the interests of the people, and dangerous to the being of the Government. The experience of every day confirms these sentiments. Men who act from such motives are not to be discouraged by trifling obstacles, nor awed by any dangers. They know the limit of constitutional opposition—up to that limit, at their own discretion, will they walk, and walk fearlessly. If they should find, in the history of their country, a precedent for going over, I trust they will not follow it. They are not of a school in which insurrection is taught as a virtue. They will not seek promotion through the paths of sedition, nor qualify themselves to serve their country in any of the higher departments of its Government by making rebellion the first element in their political science.

"Important as I deem it to discuss, on all proper occasions, the policy of the measures at present pursued, it is still more important to maintain the right of such discussion in its full and just extent. Sentiments lately sprung up, and now growing fashionable, make it necessary to be explicit on this point. The more I perceive a disposition to check the freedom of inquiry by extravagant and unconstitutional pretences, the firmer shall be the tone in which I shall assert and the freer the manner in which I shall exercise it. It is the ancient and undoubted prerogative of this people to canvass public measures and the merits of public men. It is a 'home-bred right,' a fireside privilege. It has ever been enjoyed in every house, cottage, and cabin in the nation. It is not to be drawn into controversy. It is as undoubted as the right of breathing the air, or walking on the earth. Belonging to private life as a right, it belongs to public life as a duty; and it is the last duty which those whose representative I am shall find me to abandon. Aiming at all times to be courteous and temperate in its use, except when the right itself shall be questioned, I shall then carry it to its extent. I shall then place myself on the extreme boundary of my right, and bid defiance to any arm that would move me from my ground. This high constitutional privilege I shall defend and exercise within this House and without this House, and in all places, in time of war, in time of peace, and at all times."

Passing, then, to the futility of all projects for the conquest of the neighboring British provinces, he proceeded to the connection between the avowed object of the war—the defence of our maritime rights—and the great purpose for which the Government had been created, the protection and encouragement of commerce. This purpose, he argued, is defeated by every measure of embargo and restriction, and can be answered in a time of war only by coping with the enemy on the ocean. The speech was closed with an impressive appeal to the House for a change in the mode of carrying on the war, and with an explicit declaration of his own purpose to support measures which he could approve, and such measures only:

"The faith of this nation is pledged to its commerce, formally and solemnly. I call upon you to redeem that pledge, not by sacrificing while you profess to regard it, but by unshackling it, and protecting it, and fostering it, according to your ability, and the reasonable expectations of those who have committed it to the care of the Government. In the commerce of the country the Constitution had its growth; in the extinction of that commerce it will find its grave. I use not the tone of intimidation or menace, but I forewarn you of consequences. Let it be remembered that, in my place, this day, and in the discharge of my public duty, I conjure you to alter your course. I urge to you the language of entreaty. I beseech you by the best hopes of your country's prosperity, by your regard for the preservation of her Government and her Union, by your own ambition, as honorable men, of leading hereafter in the councils of a great and growing empire; I conjure you, by every motive which can be addressed to the mind, that you abandon your system of restrictions—that you abandon it at once, and forever.

"The humble aid which it would be in my power to render to measures of Government shall be given cheerfully, if Government will pursue measures which I can conscientiously support. Badly as I think of the original grounds of the war, as well as of the manner in which it has been hitherto conducted, if, even now, failing in an honest and sincere attempt to procure just and honorable peace, it will return to measures of defence and protection, such as reason and common sense and the public opinion all call for, my vote shall not be withholden from the means. Give up your futile projects of invasion. Extinguish the fires that blaze on your inland frontier. Establish perfect safety and defence there by adequate force. Let every man that sleeps on your soil sleep in security. Stop the blood that flows from the veins of unarmed yeomanry and women and children. Give to the living time to bury and lament their dead in the quietness of private sorrow. Having performed this work of beneficence and mercy on your inland border, turn, and look with the eye of justice and compassion on your vast population along the coast. Unclinch the iron grasp of your Embargo. Take measures for that end before another sun sets upon you. With all the war of the enemy on your commerce, if you would cease to war on it yourselves, you would still have some commerce. That commerce would give you some revenue. Apply that revenue to the augmentation of your navy. That navy will, in turn, protect your commerce. Let it no longer be said that not one ship of force, built by your hands, yet floats upon the ocean. Turn the current of your efforts into the channel which national sentiment has already worn broad and deep to receive it. A naval force, competent to defend your coast against considerable armaments, to convoy your trade, and perhaps raise the blockade of your rivers, is not a chimera. It may be realized. If, then, the war must be continued, go to the ocean. If you are seriously contending for maritime rights, go to the theatre where alone those rights can be defended. Thither every indication of your fortune points you. There the united wishes and exertions of the nation will go with you. Even our party divisions, acrimonious as they are, cease at the water's edge. They are lost in attachment to national character on the element where that character is made respectable. In protecting naval interests by naval means, you will arm yourselves with the whole power of national sentiment, and may command the whole abundance of the national resources. In time you may enable yourselves to redress injuries in the place where they may be offered; and, if need be, to accompany your own flag throughout the world with the protection of your own cannon."

In thus calling upon the Administration to abandon the

system of commercial restrictions, and to go to the ocean as the proper theatre of the war, Mr. Webster made it manifest that no half-way measures could receive his support. In a very short time the Administration found it necessary to introduce a proposition to modify the Embargo; and the vote given upon it by Mr. Webster affords a remarkable illustration of the fidelity and consistency with which he always adhered to his convictions respecting the limits of constitutional powers. He never at any time in his life believed that an embargo, unlimited in duration, and capable of being removed only by an act of Congress assented to by the whole legislative power, is authorized by the Constitution. The existing Embargo, enacted on the 17th of December, 1813, was not exactly of this character, like that of 1807; but it embraced the whole coasting as well as the whole foreign trade of the United States. The consequence was, that there could be no commerce by water between different States, or between different ports of the same State. In the course of the winter, a population of seven thousand persons, on the island of Nantucket, were in great extremities for want of the necessaries of life. This island, belonging to Massachusetts, fifteen miles long, and three miles wide, and thirty miles from the main-land, afforded no fuel, and produced scarcely any provisions. The inhabitants had been engaged in the whale-fishery ever since its first settlement, and had always depended for their supplies upon the nearest towns on the coast. Thirty of its principal citizens were now in the town of New Bedford, unable, in consequence of the Embargo, to reach their families. This perilous state of things, of which it can only be said that it was not (although it should have been) foreseen, required special relief. A bill was introduced to authorize the President to grant to the people of Nantucket certain privileges of commerce with the main-land during the existence of the Embargo. Mr. Webster voted against it, because he considered that part of the Embargo which interdicted the coasting trade as unconstitutional and void. He never would consent, he said, to pass any law, giving to our citizens a privilege which they enjoyed under the Constitution, and of which they could not be rightfully divested. Seven other members voted with him upon the same ground; all the other members voting for the bill.

But, before the end of the session, and in less than three months from this modification of the Embargo, Mr. Webster had the satisfaction of seeing the Administration change its whole course on this subject, and of taking part in what he styled "the funeral ceremonies of the restrictive system." The Embargo of December, 1813, had been passed on the recommendation of President Madison, upon the ground that supplies found their way to the enemy from our own ports, and that British productions were brought into the United States from neutral countries, and even in British vessels disguised as neutrals. But the experience of only four months demonstrated the entire uselessness, as a war measure, of placing our whole commerce in a condition of paralysis, and also demonstrated its direct effect of depriving the Government of revenue. The President now recommended a repeal of the Embargo. Mr. Calhoun, who led for the Administration on the floor of the House, as chairman of the Committee on Foreign Relations, undertook the duty of explaining the reasons for this change of policy. His part was a difficult one to perform; for the opponents of the Embargo had from the first, and as often as it was renewed, pointed out the consequences which had always attended it. But Mr. Calhoun proceeded in his task with great skill and address. He frankly admitted that, in his own opinion, the Embargo was originally fitted to produce an effect on the conduct of the belligerent nations of Europe toward ourselves, so long only as we remained actually at peace with them; and that it ought to have been abandoned when we went to war with England. This admission of its futility, as a measure of war, made it necessary for him to find, in the condition of things in Europe, when the Embargo was laid, and in the changes which had since taken place in Europe, both a justification for laying it, and a reason for now abandoning it. In order to find the former, he went back to the state of Europe in 1807, when we first began the restrictive system under Mr. Jefferson, and when, all the European powers being arrayed against England, there was no nation but ourselves interested in the support or defence of neutral rights. As there was then no prospect of producing any impression by it on neutral powers—there being no neutrals—and as Great Britain might be made to feel its effects, it was, he argued, as a means of preventing a war with her, a wise and proper measure. Then, inserting gracefully the admission that, as a war measure, the restrictive system, in his own opinion, might have been abandoned earlier, he proceeded at once to the state of things now existing in Europe, in which there were many nations of great power in a neutral condition, or acting with England against France, interested, like ourselves, in the restoration of neutral rights, with whom it was now our best policy to open commercial intercourse. He dwelt particularly on the importance of cultivating the good-will of the Emperor of Russia, who, being now the ally of England, would have an important influence in inducing her to bring her war with us to a termination, in which our objects, of reëstablishing neutral rights and the freedom of the seas, would be accomplished.

There are few specimens of parliamentary tact, on the records of any deliberative assembly, more ingenious than this speech of Mr. Calhoun in favor of repealing the Embargo of December, 1813. But he forgot, perhaps he wished to forget, that it *was* the Embargo of December, 1813, which he was about to repeal. He forgot that the very assertion of the President, when he recommended this as a war measure, was, that there were neutral nations, under whose flag and through whose ports an indirect commerce between Great Britain and ourselves was then alleged to be going on, which weakened us and strengthened her as belligerents, and which must therefore be suppressed, at whatever expense to those neutral nations. All that Mr. Calhoun said, respecting the importance of conciliating and helping the nations that were neutrals, in April, 1814, when he proposed the repeal, was true and sound; but it was just as true and sound in December, 1813, when this Embargo was laid. Moreover, Bonaparte had been driven out of Russia in the winter of 1812–'13; and when we laid this particular Embargo of December, 1813, putting an end to all lawful commerce with all nations, a large part of Northern Europe was preparing to combine against him, and their territories could no longer be used by him as the sphere of his own restrictive policy.

When, therefore, Mr. Webster rose to answer Mr. Calhoun, it was quite natural that he should congratulate his friends on the approaching triumph of their principles, and that he should claim the vote about to be given as a high tribute to the correctness of their opinions and the consistency of their conduct Accepting the issue tendered by Mr. Calhoun in going back to the origin of the restrictive system of embargoes and non-intercourse, Mr. Webster proceeded to say that it was originally offered to the people of this country as a kind of political faith; to be believed in, but not examined; to be acted upon, and not reasoned about. To deliberate on it was to doubt; and to doubt was heretical. It stood upon the trust reposed in its authors, not upon any merit which could be discovered in itself. It had been from the beginning a kind of party superstition, and, as such, it had been adhered to, as a measure of war, although it was now admitted that it was unfitted for such a purpose.

He then stated with much force the fundamental objection to this system that had always been urged against it by its opponents, that its measures were ruinous to ourselves, that they were inoperative on others, and that they did not spring from a purely American policy. It was an imitation of the Continental system of France, and was, in fact, a means of coöperation with her in her conflict with England. The commencement of the Continental system of restriction followed immediately on the subjugation of Prussia, and the humiliation of Russia;[1] and our Embargo of 1807 came in, and contributed all that we could contribute to make that system effectual. It was now clear that our restrictive policy depended for its success on another and a mightier system. Incapable itself of directly producing any great effect on the interest of England, it might yet contribute to that end by its coöperation with her European enemy. It was now admitted that it must fall, because great changes had taken place. Those changes, Mr. Webster said, were neither more nor less than the overthrow of French power, and the deliverance of nations long oppressed by its despotic spirit. How unnatural, he continued,

[1] At the decisive battle of Austerlitz, December 2, 1805, in which a great victory enabled Napoleon to extort the treaty of Presburg.

how perverse, how radically false must be a system of measures which has opposed our interests to the general interests of mankind, and reduced us to that miserable condition that, unless we would wish to see our own Government disconcerted, and its hopes disappointed, we must rejoice, not in the general liberty and prosperity of nations, but in the progress of successful usurpation ![1] Even without regard to the character of the Government with which this system was uniting us, it was, in its own nature, radically wrong and reprehensible; for it had a direct tendency to diminish our own independence and self-respect, and to make us rely on the efforts and success of others for the maintenance of our own rights. If it had been seen, at its first introduction, as was now impliedly admitted, that it depended for its success on the condition of European politics, that it owed its support to the continuance of French power over the Continent, and that, with any considerable diminution of that power, it would become futile and contemptible—the people of this country, he declared, from a sentiment of national independence, would have rejected it with scorn.

Whatever may be thought of the motives with which our restrictive system was originally adopted, it must be allowed, I think, that Mr. Calhoun had laid open the ground for this retort, and that Mr. Webster assigned the true character to its tendencies and the true objections to it that had always existed. Down to the latest moment, it had constantly been maintained by the supporters of the present and the preceding Administration, that the continuance of this system did not depend on events in Europe; that to refer to them was uncharitable and unjust; and that the system must be adhered to, now that we were at war. "But now," said Mr. Webster, "in a moment, in the twinkling of an eye, the whole system is dissolved; and all its crowds of laws and supplements, and its garniture of

[1] In that heroic address, issued by the Emperor Alexander to his people, announcing the capture of Moscow by the French, there was a prophetic sentiment which foretold the deliverance of Europe through the sufferings of Russia: "In the present miserable state of the human race," said the Czar, "what glory awaits the nation which, after having patiently endured all the evils of war, shall succeed, by the force of courage and virtue, not only in reconquering its own rights, but in extending the blessings of freedom to other states; and even to those who have been made the unwilling instruments of attempting its subjection!"

messages, reports, and resolutions of public bodies, are tumbling undistinguished into a common grave."

This animated but perfectly courteous discussion was continued by a reply from Mr. Calhoun and a rejoinder from Mr. Webster, the former contending that the war and the restrictive system were both means to the same end—the coercion of England into a disposition to respect the rights of neutrals; that whether one or the other was to be pursued was a matter of election, to be decided by a sound discretion. He repelled the idea that the House or the Government had coöperated in the views of France, and trusted that Mr. Webster would believe that, as honorable men, his opponents meant to stand on American ground. Mr. Webster said that he had made no observations respecting motives; that he had pointed out the necessary tendencies of the system; that we should have asserted our rights by our own strength, and not, even for the purpose of effecting a great object, have resorted to a course of measures dependent for their success on foreign events, which had made our policy so vacillating that our statutes "frowned at each other on the record in the most positive spirit of contradiction."

The bill for repealing the Embargo and the Non-Intercourse Acts was then passed by a very large majority.[1]

This debate was also marked by an interesting feature that exhibits the then relative positions of Mr. Calhoun and Mr. Webster on the subject of protection to domestic manufactures. The tariff that was at that time in operation as a war tariff was a system of double duties; the duties having been raised to twice their former standard for the sake of more revenue. But, as they were arranged, they had no special reference to the protection of our own manufactures. The Embargo and Non-Intercourse laws, however, had of course operated as a system of very efficient protection; and, now that they were to be repealed, great anxiety was felt as to the effect of that repeal on our manufactures. On the day previous to this debate on the restrictive system, the House had adopted a resolution directing the Secretary of the Treasury to report to Congress, at its next session, a general tariff of duties, conformably to what might then be the situation of the general and local interests of the

[1] April 7, 1814.

United States. In his speech introducing the bill to repeal the Embargo, Mr. Calhoun had said, in reference to the fears of the manufacturing interests, that this resolution was a strong pledge that the House would not suffer the manufacturers to be unprotected in case of a repeal of the restrictive system; and that he himself hoped that at all times and under every policy they would be protected with due care. Mr. Webster, in reply to this, said that with respect to manufactures it was necessary to speak with some precision. He was not their enemy; he was their friend, but he was not for rearing them, or any other interest, in hot-beds. He would not legislate precipitately, even in favor of them; above all, he would not profess intentions in relation to them which he did not purpose to execute. He felt no desire to push capital into extensive manufactures faster than the general progress of our wealth and population propels it. After adding some general remarks on the character and effects of great manufacturing towns, as contrasted with the influences of agricultural pursuits, he closed this part of the discussion as follows:

> "I have made these remarks, sir, not because I perceive any immediate danger of carrying our manufactures to an extensive height, but for the purpose of guarding and limiting my opinions, and of checking, perhaps, a little the high-wrought hopes of some who seem to look to our present infant establishments for 'more than their nature or their state can bear.' It is the true policy of government to suffer the different pursuits of society to take their own course, and not to give excessive bounties or encouragements to one over another. This, also, is the true spirit of the Constitution. It has not, in my opinion, conferred on the Government the power of changing the occupations of the people of different States and sections, and of *forcing* them into other employments. It cannot prohibit commerce any more than agriculture, nor manufactures any more than commerce. It owes protection to all. I rejoice that commerce is once more permitted to exist; that its remnant, as far as this unblessed war will allow, may yet again visit the seas, before it is quite forgotten that we have been a commercial people. I shall rejoice still further when I see the Government pursue an independent, permanent, and steady system of national politics; when it shall rely for the maintenance of rights and the redress of wrongs on the strength and resources of our own country, and break off all measures which tend, in any degree, to connect us with the fortunes of a foreign power."

It is important to remember that this was said in 1814,

when no "hot-bed" system had been, if such was afterward, resorted to.

This session of Congress ended on the 18th of April, 1814. It was during this winter that Mr. Webster began that long course of practice in the Supreme Court of the United States which was seldom entirely interrupted from that time forward, although there came to be periods when his public and official duties obliged him to make great sacrifices in respect to his professional emoluments. At this period the court commenced its sessions in the month of February. Its term in the present year was closed about the middle of March. Mr. Webster was employed in several prize cases, none of which, however, involved very important questions.[1] We get the following item of interest from his correspondence with his brother: "There is no man in the court that strikes me like Marshall. I have never seen a man of whose intellect I had a higher opinion."[2] After the adjournment of the court, Mr. Webster went with a few other gentlemen to dine with Judge Washington, at Mount Vernon.[3]

[1] *Correspondence*, i., 244.

[2] For some very interesting descriptions of the other judges of that time, as well as of the Chief Justice, see the letters of Judge Story, given in his life by his son, Mr. W. W. Story, vol. i., pp. 166, *et seq.* These letters were written before Judge Story was on the bench, and while he was a member of Congress. He became a member of the court in 1811.

[3] Letter to E. Webster.—(*Correspondence*, i., 244.) There is an error in the date of this letter in the printed copy. It should be *March* 29, 1814, instead of *May*. Mr. Webster was not in Washington after the end of the session of Congress.

CHAPTER VI.

1814–1815.

EXTRAORDINARY SESSION OF CONGRESS—BURNING OF THE CAPITOL BY THE ENGLISH—PEACE NEGOTIATIONS—THE HARTFORD CONVENTION—A LAND TAX—CONSCRIPTION—ATTEMPT TO CREATE A NATIONAL BANK.

THE Thirteenth Congress was assembled by proclamation of the President in an extraordinary session, on the 19th of September, 1814. Grave events had occurred. In the preceding August, the enemy had landed a force fifty miles below Washington, which marched to the city, burned the capitol, the President's house, and some of the other public buildings, and then retired. The President's message, at the opening of the session, took notice of this "destruction of public edifices, protected, as monuments of the arts, by the laws of civilized warfare;" and, repelling the idea that any disgrace could attach to ourselves from this occurrence, it proceeded to recapitulate the successes which we had met with elsewhere. Adverting to the great numbers of the militia that had necessarily been called into the field, the message recommended an increase of the regular army and a classification of the militia for active service. Adverting to the state of the finances, it called for pecuniary supplies on a scale commensurate with the extent and character which the war had assumed.

The diplomatic relations of the war had been somewhat changed since the last adjournment of Congress. An offer of mediation by the Emperor of Russia, made in March, 1813, had been accepted by our Government, and commissioners had been sent to Europe to await the result of this proposal. The British Government declined the mediation, and proposed to treat directly with the United States. Accordingly, in January, (1814), a new commission was sent to our plenipotentiaries, who were then at Gottenburg. It was not, however, until August, that the British and American commissioners met, at Ghent; and when the session of Congress began in September, the negotiation was in progress, but with little prospect of a successful result. The measures of the session, therefore, related to the further prosecution of the war—or, as must be the case with nearly all measures in a time of war, they related directly or indirectly to the procurement of men and money.

Mr. Webster's policy was a policy of watchfulness. He was a member of the opposition, but an independent one. Although classed with the Federal party and generally acting with it, he was bound by no party trammels. He was totally unconnected with any measures of the New-England Federalists, which, whether justly or unjustly, were then and have since been regarded as objectionable. He left his home for this session of Congress before the famous "Hartford Convention" was talked of or contemplated.[1] When he heard afterward that such a

[1] For the benefit of readers not familiar with our political history, to whom the name of the "Hartford Convention" will, of itself, carry no meaning, it may be well to explain that this was an assembly of delegates from some of the New-England States, which met at Hartford, in Connecticut, in the winter of 1814–'15, and sat with closed doors. It was composed of men of very high personal characters, belonging to the Federal party. It was then believed by their political opponents that their meeting had a treasonable object, namely, to withdraw the New-England States from the Union, on account of the war with Great Britain. This purpose has been denied, and explanations have been made; but the supposed treasonable character of the meeting has passed into a kind of popular maxim. Although Mr. Webster had no connection with it, and, in fact, disapproved of it, he never at any time regarded it as seditious or treasonable. He knew the chief persons who composed it too well to believe that they were a knot of traitors. They were, in truth, some of the most eminent and virtuous citizens of New England, whose error consisted in holding a meeting of prominent and important men, in a time of war, to deliberate secretly on public affairs, when the administration of the Government was in the hands of the opposite party. Under such circumstances, they could not "escape calumny."

At different times in Mr. Webster's life efforts were made, by persons unfriendly to him, to connect him in some way with this assembly. Among these efforts, it appears that, about the year 1835, it was rumored that a Mr. Chamberlin, of New Hampshire, had received a letter from Mr. Webster, approving of the Hartford Convention. Mr. Chamberlin had died; but his papers were searched, and the letter, or *a* letter, was found, and brought to the city of New York, where a caucus was held over it. But, as it did not contain any mention of the Hartford Convention, it was not published.

meeting was proposed, he advised the Governor of New Hampshire not to appoint delegates to it. The State was, in fact, not represented, as a State, in that convention; although two of the counties on the Connecticut River, a hundred miles from Mr. Webster's residence, sent members to it. Mr. Webster had no connection with it whatever. This will account for a fact mentioned in the following extract from Mr. Ticknor's MS. "Recollections" of Mr. Webster, which gives some interesting sketches of his position and occupations during this session of Congress:

"In January and February, 1815, I passed some time at Washington. I lived at Crawford's Hotel, in Georgetown, which was then a sort of headquarters of the Federal members of Congress. Mr. King and Mr. Gore, members of the Senate, lived there with their wives, in a kind of state now unknown; each of them keeping a coach-and-four, and driving every morning to the humble chamber in which the Senate then met in consequence of the destruction of the capitol by the British. At the same hotel lived Mr. Mason, Mr. Webster, and several other distinguished Federal members of Congress. Mr. Webster, who had then been in Congress only a little more than two years, was already among its foremost men, and stood with Gaston and Hanson to lead the opposition in debate, on the floor of the lower House. Most of the Federal members at that time had ceased to visit at the President's house. Mr. Webster, however, thought it proper to continue to do so, and then and always maintained friendly relations with Mr. Madison, and spoke of him with respect. His society was much sought. His relations with Mr. Gore, dating from the period of his studying the law, and his intimate friendship with Mr. Mason, never at any moment interrupted or disturbed, made him a most welcome member of that brilliant circle, which generally met in the evening in the private parlor belonging to Mrs. King and Mrs. Gore, which was rather an elegant drawing-room, for the time.

"As I had passed two days at Hartford, in the same private quarters with Mr. Cabot, Mr. Otis, and several of the principal members of the Hartford Convention, then in session, the gentlemen, Mr. Gore and Mr. Mason especially, were very curious to learn from me any thing that I might know respecting that remarkable body. But I had no information to give them. I was travelling with Mr. S. G. Perkins, and for that reason alone lived

These facts were afterward communicated to Mr. Webster by a political opponent. Such was always the fate of attempts to identify him with that meeting. The impossibility of his having been connected with it, and his disapprobation of it, are stated in his Correspondence, vol. i., pp. 11, 184. The fact stated by Mr. Ticknor, of Mr. Webster's and Mr. Mason's entire ignorance of what was going on at Hartford, is new and striking. As I shall not again allude to this topic, I may here refer the reader to Mr. Webster's speech in reply to Mr. Hayne (*Works*, iii., 314, 315), for his views respecting the Hartford Convention.

with Mr. Cabot and his friends, who communicated none of their secrets to either of us. Mr. Gore, and more especially Mr. Mason and Mr. Webster, expressed their dissatisfaction with the meeting of the convention and more particularly that they received no information by correspondence from its members. They gave this as a reason for asking information concerning it, from me.

"Mr. Webster's room was next to Mr. Mason's. They dined at a congressional mess in the same house. Mr. Gore and Mr. King and their ladies had a private table together, to which they often invited friends. I heard Mr. Webster several times in the House, not in formal speeches, but in that very deliberate conversational manner, and with the peculiar exactness of phraseology, which marked him as a public debater to the end of his life. He did not fail then, any more than afterward, to command the attention of the House. The subjects on which he spoke related to the common course of business, and were not exciting or particularly interesting. I dined repeatedly at the congressional mess, of which he was one. I met him at Mr. Gore's table and elsewhere. In the mess he was very amusing, talking gayly, and as if no care rested upon him. Everywhere he was liked as a social companion.

"He was at this time much occupied with the study of English politics. Volumes of the 'Annual Register,' and the 'Parliamentary Debates,' covered his table; and while I was in Washington he read through Brougham's 'Colonial Policy of the European Powers,' parts of which he praised to me, while with other portions he was much dissatisfied. When conversing with the other members with whom I constantly saw him, he seemed to me to know more about the details of business before the House than any of them. I mean that he appeared to know more what was to come up next, or soon, facts which I was anxious to learn."

In the first debate of a general character in which Mr. Webster took any part at this session, his position as an opponent of the Administration and its policy was defined with so much precision, that no vote or action of his was likely to be, as in fact none was, at the time, misapprehended or misrepresented. A proposition came before the House at an early period in the session to grant a new land tax of twice the amount of the last one. In assigning his reasons for voting against it, Mr. Webster said that although majorities in legislative bodies sometimes believed it to be in their power to place dissenting members in a situation in which their conduct would be liable to unfavorable construction, there was rarely any serious difficulty attending such occasions, and on the present one there was no difficulty at all. He did not feel himself under any necessity either of obstructing the passage of the taxes through the House, or of taking upon himself any portion of the responsibility of laying them. A case might arise in which it would be for those who had been the minority to say whether the supplies should be granted or withheld. This was not such a case; it was certain that the taxes would be granted; and, therefore, as he had not the power of withholding supplies until a change of measures in carrying on the war could be compelled, he did not think it fit, by adding his vote to the vote of the majority, to be deemed to sanction the measures of the Administration, through a voluntary support of its plans of finance. He would have the power and strength of the nation called forth and guided by different hands, to compel England to make a peace that would be honorable and fair. But, as he could not have this, and as the supplies did not depend upon his vote, he held himself at liberty not to approve, without reason, the course that was pursued.

At the time when he so voted against the taxes, the President had recently transmitted to Congress information of the state of the negotiation at Ghent. This intelligence did not satisfy Mr. Webster that such a peace was demanded on our part as we ought to demand, or that England meant to accede to such a peace.[1] He did not consider the Administration able to carry on the war successfully, and did not choose by his vote to express his confidence in them. He thought the President ought to be assisted by a much stronger Cabinet; and, looking at the actual condition of the negotiations at Ghent, he believed that different measures at home were essential to the procurement of a peace that should close forever all existing controversies. He marked out his course respecting the taxes accordingly, and assigned his reasons for voting against them. In doing so, he acted in no spirit of party; in fact, he acted quite as independently of his own party as of the party of the Administration, for most of the Federal members voted for the taxes.

As a question of political ethics, there can be no doubt that a statesman, in such governments as ours, is perfectly entitled to give effect to his opinions respecting the measures of an ad-

[1] Correspondence, i., 245.

ministration by voting against taxes, even if they are war taxes. The question whether such a vote, under such circumstances, is right, is totally different from the question whether it will be popular. A mere politician will be very unlikely to vote against war taxes. If he does not, the reason is patent. Applying the standard of popularity, his action in voting supplies is right. Applying a different standard, and supposing the opinions avowed to be honestly held, a vote against war taxes needs no defence. The distinction between the governing motives involves the whole difference between a politician and a statesman; although all the members of an opposition who vote for supplies to carry on a war may not be mere politicians, and all who vote against them may not be statesmen. With respect to the judgment to be formed concerning the individual, if he was a person of sufficient elevation and independence of character to assume the risk of unpopularity, we must look beyond that to higher and larger considerations.

Among the measures that were proposed at this session for obtaining men, a plan for a conscription or compulsory draft, that was much debated in both Houses, at once arrested Mr. Webster's attention, and he determined to resist it as a usurpation. The Secretary of War, Mr. Monroe, in his report at the beginning of the session, had recommended a plan for a forcible draught of the whole free male population of the United States, between the ages of eighteen and forty-five, for the purpose of recruiting the regular army. The bill which was introduced in the Senate, and which passed that body, was not exactly of this character, but it was a plan for a classification of the militia, and for a system of drafting individuals, including minors, from the different classes, to be formed into regiments and brigades. Both plans involved the principles of conscription, and in both Houses the discussion involved the question of the constitutional authority of Congress either to fill the regular army in that mode, or to make a compulsory draft of individuals from the militia of the States. The supporters of the Administration generally asserted these powers in their fullest extent; the members of the opposition denied them. Mr. Webster's speech on this subject has not been preserved. It was made on the 9th of December (1814), on a motion to indefinitely postpone the bill, and it was written out by him afterward. But it was never published, and the manuscript is not now to be found. That Mr. Webster regarded both of these forms of conscription as entirely unauthorized by the Constitution, is apparent from his correspondence, from the arguments of his friends in each of the two Houses, and from the allusions to his opinions made by the friends and the opponents of the measure in the course of the discussion. Neither of the two plans ever took effect, as the public sentiment entirely accorded with the arguments of the opposition. In 1831, Mr. Webster referred with some apparent satisfaction to his agency in defeating this measure, in these words: "I had a hand, with Mr. Eppes and others, in overthrowing Mr. Monroe's *conscription* in 1814."[1]

A subject to which great political interest was once attached, and one on which Mr. Webster at various times acted a very important part—a national bank and the currency of the country—now claims the reader's attention. It may be well, therefore, to preface the narrative of what took place at this session,

[1] MS. letter (see also the printed Correspondence, vol. i., pp. 245–248). This question of the constitutional authority of the Federal Government to demand compulsory military service of the citizens of the States was discussed with great ability by the opposition, in 1814, and their arguments were unanswered. In recent times, it has not been sufficiently considered that the exercise of such a power displaces the authority of the States over their militia, and, when exercised over minors, that it annihilates the rights of the parent or guardian, which are exclusively under the control of the State. In 1814, the most eminent constitutional lawyers in Congress, on the opposition side, maintained that the Federal power "to raise armies" is, by the necessary effect of the whole constitutional scheme relating to the militia, to be regarded as extending only to the raising of regular armies by contracts of enlistment; that the citizen owes compulsory military service to his State, in its militia; and that the Federal Government has a defined power of reaching that compulsory service through the organized militia of the States, by calling it forth on the occasions provided for by the Constitution, and can reach it in no other way. On this subject, the speeches of Mr. Mason, Mr. Gore, and Mr. Daggett, in the Senate; and of Messrs. Stockton, Grosvenor, Sheffey, and Cyrus King, in the House, are especially valuable. Mr. Mason's argument was the most important one that he ever made on a constitutional question. The bill was indefinitely postponed in the Senate, on the motion of Mr. Rufus King, December 28, 1814. Of this occurrence, Mr. Webster wrote, on the 9th of January: "Mr. King is getting a good deal of popularity for having moved the postponement of Giles's bill; it was accidental and unpremeditated, and there was no debate. After we passed the bill, with amendments, it was bandied about several days from House to House, on account of the disagreeing votes relative to the amendments. Being one day before the Senate, and it being known that public sentiment had terrified the vehement Senators, Mr. King made the motion. Some members happened to be out, it was immediately put and carried."—(*Correspondence*, i., 249. See further, in the Index, *verb.* "conscription.")

by quoting a part of a memorandum written by him in 1831, which is now in my possession. It explains the leading principle on which he began and ever afterward continued to act upon this subject:

"One of the first things which engaged my attention, after I had become a member of Congress, was the currency of the country. It had become greatly deranged. The old Bank of the United States had expired in 1811, and on that occurrence a great mass of additional banking capital had been put in operation in the several States. Upon the breaking out of the war, most of the State banks had suspended specie payments. This was followed by the greatest irregularity and disorder in the currency of the country. Bank paper was depreciated on a scale rapidly descending from North to South. The banks of Boston paid specie on demand, and of course their paper was equivalent to specie. But the notes of the New-York banks were ten *per centum* below specie value, those of Philadelphia fifteen, Baltimore twenty, and Washington twenty-five. Taxes, duties, and debts to the Government were everywhere paid in the bills of the local banks. This was undoubtedly all against law, because bank notes were not money, and because, so far as respected custom-house duties, there was an express statute, of long standing, requiring them to be paid in gold and silver coin. One effect of this monstrous derangement of the currency was that, in some quarters, the public burdens were discharged at ten, twenty, or twenty-five per cent. less payment than in other quarters. Throughout all the debates on the bank question, I kept steadily in view the object of restoring the currency, as a matter of the very first importance, without which it would be impossible to establish any efficient system of revenue and finance. The very first step toward such a system is to provide a safe medium of payment. I opposed, therefore, to the full extent of my power, every project for a bank so constituted that it might issue irredeemable paper, and thus drown and overwhelm us still more completely in the miseries and calamities of paper money. I would agree to nothing but a specie-paying bank."

The first Bank of the United States, chartered in 1791 for twenty years, had given rise to a fundamental difference of opinion in the Cabinet of President Washington on the question of the constitutional power of Congress to create such an institution. Hamilton was its principal advocate, and Jefferson its principal opposer. In 1811, the party which had originally opposed the bank defeated the renewal of its charter. In 1814–'15, the exigencies of the Administration strongly demanded such an institution, and a bill to create one was introduced. Congress was at that time divided into three parties on this subject. The first consisted of those who were against a bank under any form. The number of these persons was considerable. They belonged generally to the friends of the Administration. They voted, therefore, for the bank, or rather with its friends, on all preliminary and incidental questions, but on the final passage they voted against the bill. Accordingly, there was always a body of members who, from their original opposition to any national bank, were at last to be found voting against any project of the kind.

Second, there was a party among the supporters of the Administration who were in favor of a bank, provided it should be such a one as they thought would not only regulate the currency and facilitate the operations of Government, but would also afford present and important aids by heavy loans, for which purpose it was to be relieved from the necessity of paying its notes in specie. This party, therefore, was in favor of an irredeemable paper currency.

The third party consisted of those who were willing to create a bank with a reasonable amount of capital, compelled always to redeem its notes in specie, and at liberty to judge for itself when it would and when it would not make loans to the Government. With these Mr. Webster acted.[1]

The bill to incorporate a national bank was first introduced in the Senate, where it was passed by a majority of two votes. As it came into the House, it was a bill which proposed to constitute a bank with a capital of fifty millions of dollars, of which four millions only were to be specie, and the residue to consist of Government stocks, then much depreciated. Government was to have the power to borrow from the bank thirty millions. The notes of all banks south of New England being from ten to twenty-five per cent. below the specie standard, specie had disappeared from circulation. On the notes of the proposed national bank specie was not required to be paid until the last payment on its stock had been completed; and the Government was to have the power at all times to make any regulations which it might think proper in regard to specie payments. As such a bank, in the existing circumstances of

[1] This statement of the condition of parties in that Congress is taken almost *verbatim* from Mr. Webster's own memorandum.

the country, could not go into operation, if it paid specie on its bills, because its specie would be drained at once; and as the Government, when it had borrowed thirty millions of its paper, must protect it by continuing the exemption from paying specie, the scheme was one to create an irredeemable paper circulation, founded on depreciated Government stocks.[1]

The discussion on this bill began in the House on the 9th of December (1814), and was continued with various interruptions until the 24th, when it was reported by the Committee of the Whole, amended. Mr. Webster had gone to Baltimore to pass Christmas. He was sent for by his friends, rode to Washington on horseback in the night of Monday, the 26th, and was in the House on the morning of Tuesday, the 27th.[2] On the 29th, the bill was put on its final passage, and Mr. Webster had just moved its recommitment with certain instructions, when the House adjourned. On the same night, Mr. Brent, a Senator from Virginia, died. Yet so great was the anxiety to pass this bill, that the House when it assembled on the following day, although the death of Mr. Brent was announced, refused to adjourn until a message came from the Senate respecting arrangements for the funeral, when, on motion of Mr. Pleasants, of Virginia, the bill was laid upon the table. No business was transacted until Monday, the 2d of January. On that day, Mr. Webster made a speech against the bill, on his motion to recommit it with instructions.

This speech, a vigorous exposition of the bad features of such a bank, is contained in the third volume of Mr. Webster's works, and it is therefore not needful to make extracts from it. It prevented the passage of the bill; for, although the House refused to recommit it, and came to a direct vote on the question of its final passage, the vote stood eighty-one yeas, to eighty nays. Amidst profound silence, the Speaker, Langdon Cheves, of South Carolina, rose, and, after stating briefly but impressively his reasons for voting against the bill, announced that it was lost, by a tie. Mr. Calhoun, although not an advocate

[1] A bill of the same character had been rejected by the House on the 28th of November. It was then introduced into the Senate, and, having passed that body, without any material alteration, it came before the House on the 9th of December.

[2] The distance is forty miles. He went on horseback because the roads were then very bad.

for this particular bill, was deeply concerned about the situation of the Government, and its humiliating condition from the want of resources to carry on the war. He felt, however, that he could rely on Mr. Webster's willingness to give the Administration a proper bank, which Mr. Webster had repeatedly avowed in the course of this discussion. As soon as the vote was announced, he walked across the floor of the House to the spot where Mr. Webster stood, and holding out both his hands to Mr. Webster, and telling him that he should rely on his assistance in preparing a new bill, burst into tears, as Mr. Webster assured him the assistance should not be withheld.[1] The pledge was personally redeemed; but the close of the war, which was nearer at hand than was then known to either of them, put an end for a time to discussions about a bank, after some further efforts had been made to create one.

These efforts followed a motion, made on the day after this bill was rejected, to reconsider the vote. Mr. Webster voted against the reconsideration, but it was carried, and he then voted for the recommitment of the bill to a select committee, in order to have it altered. The new bill, reported by the select committee on the 6th of January (1815), reduced the capital to thirty millions, made many important changes in respect to the payments of the capital, and struck out the provision which enabled the Government to borrow thirty millions from the bank, with its accompanying power of authorizing a suspension of specie payments. This being a real specie-paying bank, Mr. Webster and his friends voted for it, and it was passed on the 7th of January by a very large majority. After some disagreement between the two Houses, which was finally reconciled, the bill was passed by the Senate and sent to the President, who returned it on the 30th, without his signature, assigning his reasons. The grounds of the "veto" were chiefly two: first, that the capital of the bank, in respect to the media in which it was to be paid, was not well compounded; second, that, being obliged to pay specie on its bills, it could not furnish a circulating medium that could be relied on during the war, nor furnish loans, or means of anticipating the rev-

[1] My authority for this anecdote is Mr. Ticknor, who received it from Mr. Webster himself, and made a record of it.

enue. The Senate then refused to pass this bill over the "veto," and immediately proposed another, which was in substance like the bill that had been first rejected in the House; or in other words, it was a bill for a paper bank. On this bill, a new struggle began in the House on the 12th of February, and it was much pressed and hurried. But, on the 17th, news of the treaty of peace having been received, the bill was indefinitely postponed. Thus ended for the present the efforts of the Administration to obtain a national bank. On the 3d of March (1815), the Thirteenth Congress expired.

From this narrative it will be seen that Mr. Webster was not unwilling, during the war, to afford to the Administration a national bank, if they were willing to take one which he thought fit to be created. On the point of constitutional authority to create such an institution, Mr. Webster did not differ from President Madison, who, in his "veto" message, held this question to be precluded by repeated acts of all branches of the Government and a concurrence of the general will of the nation. The issue between Mr. Webster and the Administration, therefore, was wholly on the details of the measure, and chiefly on the question of creating a paper currency not redeemable in specie. Writing to his brother, after the loss of the bill which he was so instrumental in defeating, he said: "A hundred of the narrowest chances alone saved us from a complete paper-money system, in such a form as was calculated and intended to transfer the odium of depreciation from the Government to the bank."[1] Writing after the President had refused to sign the subsequent bill for which he voted, he said: "the President has negatived the Bank Bill. So all our labor is lost. I hope this will satisfy our friends, that it was not a bank likely to favor the Administration."[2]

This, then, must be considered the starting-point of all Mr. Webster's public conduct on this subject. He had entered Congress with a firm opinion that a paper currency, not redeemable in specie on demand, is a source of incalculable evil to the community and the Government. He did not believe that the

[1] Letter to E. Webster, January 22, 1814.

[2] Letter to the same, January 30, 1814.—(*Correspondence*, i., 250, 251.) The meaning of Mr. Webster, in the letter last quoted, was, that this was not a bank likely to be in favor with the Administration, or to suit it.

exigencies of war, or any other exigencies, could justify such a departure from all the sound principles of finance; and he was especially unwilling to create a national institution whose notes, certain to be depreciated, were to be received by the Government in payment of its dues. What he did, and with what success, to bring about a better state of things in this respect, will be seen hereafter.

CHAPTER VII.

1815-1816.

FOURTEENTH CONGRESS—NATIONAL BANK—SPECIE RESOLUTIONS—TARIFF OF 1816—DEATH OF MR. WEBSTER'S MOTHER—CHALLENGED BY MR. RANDOLPH—RETIRES FROM CONGRESS—REMOVAL TO BOSTON.

IN 1831, Mr. Webster said that he had seen no such Congress for talents as the Fourteenth.[1] It commenced its first session in December, 1815. Mr. Clay, after taking part in the negotiation of the treaty of Ghent, had returned to Congress, and was again Speaker. Mr. Calhoun had also been reëlected. The celebrated John Randolph, of Roanoke, a man of genius and with more than the usual eccentricities of genius, was again in Congress. Mr. Pinkney, then the first lawyer in the United States, and enjoying by far the largest practice at the bar of the Supreme Court, was a member of this Congress until April, when he resigned his seat to accept the mission to Russia. Joseph Hopkinson and John Sergeant, of Pennsylvania; Alexander C. Hanson, of Maryland; Daniel Sheffey, of Virginia; Henry Southard, of New Jersey; William Lowndes, of South Carolina; William Gaston, of North Carolina; John McLean, of Ohio; Samuel R. Betts, of New York; John Forsyth, of Georgia; and many other able men were on the roll of a House which, even without the names of Clay, Calhoun, Randolph, Pinkney, and Webster, would have been accounted no ordinary assembly. Mr. Calhoun and Mr. Webster, on opposite sides,

[1] MS. letter.

exercised the largest influence on the course of business, although Mr. Randolph was a much more frequent speaker than either of them. Mr. Clay participated a good deal in the discussions, especially in Committees of the Whole. Mr. Pinkney made but one speech while he was a member of this House—a very profound one, on the treaty power, in reference to a bill to regulate commerce with Great Britain, which was supposed to be necessary in order to carry out the convention of July 3, 1815.[1]

Mr. Webster, who had been reëlected for New Hampshire, did not take his seat until the 7th of February (1816), although he was in Washington in the early part of January with Mrs. Webster. They were recalled by the illness of their little daughter Grace, who had been left with some friends near Boston. On the child's recovery, Mr. Webster returned to Washington, and found the subject of a national bank again before Congress. This was the bill which incorporated the last bank of the United States that was ever created. As Mr. Webster found it before the House, it was a bill possessing the same objectionable features which he had opposed in the preceding Congress. Having already quoted from a memorandum written by him in 1831, in explanation of his course on the former bill, I resort to the same paper for the purpose of using his own words in reference to the present one:

"On the introduction of the bill to incorporate the present bank, I opposed its proposed amount of capital—fifty millions—as being unnecessarily large, and still more vehemently the power proposed to be given to the

[1] The strange insolence of Mr. Randolph—it can be called by no other name—was exercised toward Mr. Pinkney on this occasion, by commencing his reply to that most distinguished person in this way: "I give up to the gentleman from Maryland—I am told he is from Maryland—those fanciful and fine-spun theories," etc. At the moment of this supercilious affectation of ignorance respecting Mr. Pinkney's representative character, he stood at the zenith of his great fame as a lawyer, had been Attorney-General of the United States, and minister to Great Britain, and his name was as much identified with the State of Maryland and the city of Baltimore as it was possible for the name of any man to have a local habitation. But Randolph often descended to very puerile insults for the mere sake of giving annoyance. Notwithstanding he boasted himself to be "one of the best shots in Virginia," it is probably due to the conviction of his partial insanity, among those of his contemporaries who admitted the practice of duelling, that he died in his bed. But he was visited sometimes with deep and extreme compunctions, after having outraged all propriety, which made him break out in further eccentricities, that were often as touching as his previous conduct had been provoking.—(See the account of his singular magnanimity and tenderness during and after his duel with Mr. Clay, as given in his Life by Mr. Garland; and also the correspondence attending his challenge of Mr. Webster, given in the present chapter, *post.*)

President of the United States, to authorize a suspension of specie payments. In both these respects, my opposition, with that of others, was successful: the proposed amount of capital was reduced, and the power to authorize a suspension of specie payments was stricken out. It was also my opinion that the Government should have nothing to do with the appointment of directors, as it had not in the first bank. As the Government itself was to be a large subscriber to the present institution, it was by some deemed reasonable that it should have its proper voice in the annual constitution of the board of directors. But I was opposed to the subscription to the stock on the part of the Government, and this, together with the appointment of Government directors, and a hope of other useful changes in the charter, influenced my final vote, which is known to have been against the bill. I was at special pains to convince Congress and the country that a paper bank would be ruinous; a bank with an inordinate amount of capital, such as fifty millions, dangerous; and that all hope of restoring the currency of the country, even by means of the best-conducted bank, futile, until the Government itself should execute existing laws, and require payment of debts and taxes in legal coin, or in the paper of specie-paying banks."

In the speech which Mr. Webster made upon this bill on the 28th of February (1816), he said:

"It was a mistaken idea which he had heard uttered on this subject, that we were about to reform the national currency. No nation had a better currency than the United States; there was no nation which had guarded its currency with more care, for the framers of the Constitution, and those who enacted the early statutes on this subject, were hard-money men; they had felt, and therefore duly appreciated, the evils of a paper medium; they therefore sedulously guarded the currency of the United States from debasement. The legal currency of the United States was gold and silver coin. This was a subject in regard to which Congress had run into no folly. What, then, was the present evil? Having a perfectly sound national currency—and the Government have no power, in fact, to make any thing else current but gold and silver—there had grown up in different States a currency of paper issued by banks, setting out with the promise to pay gold and silver, which they had been wholly unable to redeem. The consequence was, that there was a mass of paper afloat, of perhaps fifty millions, which sustained no immediate relation to the legal currency of the country—a paper which will not enable any man to pay money he owes to his neighbor, or his debts to the Government. The banks had issued more paper than they could redeem, and the evil was severely felt. He declined occupying the time of the House to prove that there was a depreciation of the paper in circulation; the legal standard of value was gold and silver; the relation of paper to it proved its state, and the rate of its depreciation. Gold and silver currency is the law of the land at home and the law of the world abroad; there could in the present state of the world be no other currency. In consequence of the immense paper issues having banished specie from circulation, the Government has been obliged, in direct violation of existing statutes, to receive the amount of their taxes in something which is not recognized by law as the money of the country, and which is, in fact, greatly depreciated. This was the evil.

. . . .

"In his opinion," Mr. Webster said, "any remedy now to be applied to this evil must be applied to the depreciated mass of paper itself; it must be some measure that would give heat and life to this mortified mass of the body politic. The evil was not to be remedied by introducing a new paper circulation; there could be no such thing as two media in circulation, the one credited and the other discredited. All bank paper derives its credit solely from its relation to gold and silver; and there was no remedy for the state of depreciation of the paper currency but the resumption of specie payments. If all the property of the United States was pledged for the redemption of these fifty millions of paper, it would not thereby be brought up to par; or if it were, that would happen which had never yet happened in any other country. An issue of Treasury notes would have no better effect than the establishment of a new bank paper. At a period anterior to the reformation of the coin in England, when existing coin had been much debased by clipping, an attempt had been made to correct the vitiated currency by throwing a quantity of sound coin into circulation with the debased; the result was, that the sound coin disappeared, was hoarded up, because more valuable than that of the same nominal value which was in general circulation.

. . . .

"The State banks not emanating from Congress, what engine could Congress use for remedying the existing evil? Their only legitimate power was, to interdict the paper of such banks as do not pay specie from being received at the custom-house. With a receipt of forty millions a year, if the Government was faithful to itself and to the interests of the people, they could control the evil; it was their duty to make the effort; they should have made it long ago, and they ought now to make it.

. . . .

"The whole strength of the Government ought to be put forth to compel the payment of the duties and taxes in the legal currency of the country. In regard to the plan of the proposed bank, he would consent to no bank which to all intents and purposes was not a specie bank; and in that view he was in favor of the proposed amendment. He expressed some alarm at the stock feature of the bank, which would enable and might induce the existing bank corporations to come forward and take up the whole stock of this national bank.[1] He should be glad to see a bank established

[1] At the foot of the memorandum of 1831, I find the following, in Mr. Webster's handwriting, in reference to the prediction of excessive speculation in the

which would command the solid capital of the country. There were men of wealth and standing who would embark their funds in a bank constituted on commercial specie principles, but who would not associate in such an institution with the stockholders in the country [banks] any more than a good currency would associate with a bad one."

On the 5th of April, after the bill, which had passed the House, had been returned from the Senate with some modifications, Mr. Webster stated his objections to it on account of the participation of the Government in its direction and management. It was passed, however, on that day, Mr. Webster voting against it, and it soon afterward received the signature of the President. Mr. Calhoun immediately introduced a bill to require the collection of the revenue in the lawful money of the United States. This bill was rejected. Mr. Webster then presented his resolutions of April 26, 1816, which required all dues to the Government to be paid in coin, or in Treasury notes, or in the notes of the Bank of the United States. They were adopted by a large majority. His great object in this measure is thus stated in the memorandum of 1831:

"The peace did not put an end to the disorders of the currency. The State banks did not resume specie payments. The present Bank of the United States was incorporated; and it was under these circumstances that I brought forward the resolutions of April, 1816. When introduced, they bore a preamble which, I dare say, appears on the Journal, and which may perhaps be worth looking up. This was dropped in the progress of the measure, as it was thought to be unimportant, and as it implied some sort of censure on the past administration of the Treasury. The resolutions had all the desired effect. They brought about an entire change in the currency of the country. Duties and taxes, debts for lands, etc., were then equally borne and equally paid. After some years of unfortunate management, the national bank took a good direction; and from that time to this the United States have had a currency perfectly sound and safe, and more convenient, and producing local exchanges at less expense, than any other nation is or ever was blessed with."

It required no little strength of argument, power of illustration, and force of character, to lead a House, which had just rejected a similar measure in the form of a bill, to assert the

stock of the proposed bank: "The early history of the bank shows that if it was not foresight, it was at least singularly fortunate guessing, which predicted enormous subscriptions to the proposed institution for purposes of speculation, and out of all proportion to the real ability of the subscribers."

same principle in the form of a resolution. But Mr. Webster had mastered this subject, and he was exceedingly in earnest about it. While he was able to show that the superior soundness of the banks in his own section of the country, which paid their bills in specie, was the very cause that made the payment of taxes and duties in that section twenty-five per cent. higher than in other parts of the Union, so long as the Government continued to receive depreciated paper, he was also able to convince the House that this state of things must be changed, or it would affect the stability of the Government. He said:

"It is our business to foresee this danger, and to avoid it. There are some political evils which are seen as soon as they are dangerous, and which alarm at once as well the people as the Government. Wars and invasions, therefore, are not always the most certain destroyers of national prosperity. They come in no questionable shape. They announce their own approach, and the general security is preserved by the general alarm. Not so with the evils of a debased coin, a depreciated paper currency, or a depressed and falling public credit. Not so with the plausible and insidious mischiefs of a paper-money system. These insinuate themselves in the shape of facilities, accommodation, relief. They hold out the most fallacious hope of an easy payment of debts, and a lighter burden of taxation. It is easy for a portion of the people to imagine that Government may properly continue to receive depreciated paper, because they have received it, and because it is more easy to obtain it than to obtain other paper, or specie. But on these subjects it is that Government ought to exercise its own peculiar wisdom and caution. It is supposed to possess, on subjects of this nature, somewhat more of foresight than has fallen to the lot of individuals. It is bound to foresee the evil before every man feels it, and to take all necessary measures to guard against it, although they may be measures attended with some difficulty, and not without temporary inconvenience. In my humble judgment, the evil demands the immediate attention of Congress. It is not certain, and in my opinion not probable, that it will ever cure itself. It is more likely to grow by indulgence, while the remedy which must in the end be applied will become less efficacious by delay.

"The only power which the General Government possesses of restraining the issues of the State banks is, to refuse their notes in the receipts of the Treasury. This power it can exercise now, or at least it can provide now for exercising it in reasonable time, because the currency of some part of the country is yet sound, and the evil is not yet universal. If it should become universal, who that hesitates now will then propose any adequate means of relief? If a measure, like the bill of yesterday, or the resolution of to-day, can hardly pass here now, what hope is there that any efficient measures will be adopted hereafter?"

At this session of Congress an important change took place in the tariff by the passage of an act which was the first in the series that came afterward to be regarded in South Carolina as oppressive and unconstitutional. Mr. Webster's relation to the tariff of 1816 is to be understood by examining the efforts which he made and the votes which he gave upon the details of the bill. It was an Administration measure, founded chiefly on a scheme prepared and submitted to Congress by the Secretary of the Treasury, Mr. Dallas, in which the protection and encouragement of manufactures was avowedly the leading object. It was warmly advocated by the principal members from South Carolina, including Mr. Calhoun and Mr. Lowndes. The bill, as reported by the Committee of Ways and Means, proposed to lay a duty of twenty-five per cent. *ad valorem* on all cotton and woollen manufactured goods; which, on motion of Mr. Clay, was increased, as to manufactures of cotton, to thirty per cent. It was apparent to Mr. Webster that such a duty would put an end to the importation of India cottons, a business in which a large amount of shipping was then employed. He was satisfied, too, that a duty so high as that proposed would expose the manufacture of cotton goods in this country to the danger of a fluctuating policy, as he did not believe that such a duty could be permanent. The latter effect he thought he could avert; the former he could not prevent, for it had become manifest that those who advocated this measure intended to exclude as many of the foreign fabrics as they could. A duty of even twenty per cent. was sufficient to exclude the India cottons, and therefore it was not probable that Mr. Webster could obtain a graduation of the duties to any lower point. He proposed, consequently, to fix the duties on cotton goods at thirty per cent. *ad valorem* for two years from the 30th of June, 1816, at twenty-five per cent. for the two years next succeeding, and at twenty per cent. after the expiration of the last period. If protection was to be given, he wished it to be permanent. Mr. Calhoun and Mr. Lowndes were of opinion that an ultimate and permanent duty of twenty per cent. would be sufficient for the protection which they sought, and Mr. Webster's proposition was agreed to by a large majority.[1] Subsequently, in justice to those who had embarked in the India trade before this great change of policy could have been anticipated, Mr. Webster advocated and voted for a provision admitting India cottons that might arrive in this country before the 1st of March, 1817, in vessels that sailed from the United States before the 1st of February, 1816, on the payment of a duty of thirty-three and one-third per cent. on their cost, and on twenty per cent. added to their cost. In this shape, the tariff of 1816 went into operation, and under it the importation of India cottons was extinguished.

With the same general view of securing such a system as would be likely to be permanent, and would inflict the least injury on the navigating interests, Mr. Webster voted for reductions of the duties proposed by this bill on woollen goods, iron, and hemp. He does not appear to have entered into the discussion on the general principle of protection. Mr. Calhoun asserted its policy, and did not question the constitutional power. Mr. Webster did not question the constitutional power any more than Mr. Calhoun; and with respect to the policy, finding that it was to prevail, he sought to mitigate the effects of so great a change, and to prevent a future reaction.

Mr. Webster appears to have taken an active part in but one other measure of this session. This related to a matter which must now be looked upon with singular interest, as it marks the early beginnings of a steam navy, and the conceptions in regard to it which then prevailed. A proposition was introduced to authorize the building of three steam "batteries." The idea seems to have been entertained by the naval committee, and by many other members, that these structures would necessarily be stationary, or nearly so; and the question was, whether they should by law be required to be built and kept at the mouth of the Chesapeake, or at the mouth of the Mississippi. Members objected to its being left in the discretion of the President to direct the place of building and using them. One gentleman said that steam-frigates might possibly move

[1] A change was afterward made, before the bill finally passed, so as to levy a duty of twenty-five per cent. *ad valorem* for three years from June 30, 1816, and a duty of twenty per cent. thereafter.

from New York to Philadelphia, but it would be impracticable to navigate the coast with them to New Orleans, a voyage to which, from any of the other cities, was as difficult and dangerous as one across the Atlantic. Mr. Webster appears to have better understood what could be done. He had satisfied himself, on the statements of experienced persons, that steam-frigates could be built to move anywhere. He thought, therefore, that these vessels should be treated as strictly a part of the navy, and be placed entirely under the control of the President. He moved to modify the bill accordingly, and his motion was adopted by a large majority.[1]

Before Mr. Webster left Washington, at the close of this session, he heard of an alarming illness of his mother, who had resided with his brother Ezekiel, at Boscawen, since the death of their father. "If," he wrote to his brother, "she should be living on the receipt of this, tell her, I pray for her everlasting peace and happiness, and would give her a son's blessing for all her parental goodness. May God bless her living or dying. If she does not survive, let her rest beside her husband and our father." The good lady did not survive; and on the 28th of April she was laid at the appointed place, in the burial-ground at Franklin, where a plain inscription still marks her grave and that of her husband.

It was during this session that Mr. Webster received a challenge from Mr. Randolph; the sole instance in which a message of that character was ever sent to him. He was not, at any period of his life, likely to be much embarrassed or disconcerted by a demand of this nature, for he never gave any real occasion for one. He, moreover, held the practice of duelling in great contempt. On this occasion, it was apparent to all who witnessed what occurred in the House between Mr. Webster and Mr. Randolph, that the latter had no just ground for requiring an explanation; for, as soon as it was known that he had sent Mr. Webster a challenge, several gentlemen, friends of both parties, came forward and effected an amicable adjustment of the difficulty. The sedate and firm answer of Mr. Webster to Mr. Randolph's message made it apparent that there was no real cause for Mr. Randolph's sensitiveness, and it also disclosed

[1] April 14, 1816.

Mr. Webster's sentiments respecting this form of obtaining "satisfaction."[1]

[MR. WEBSTER TO MR. RANDOLPH.]

"SIR: For having declined to comply with your demand yesterday in the House, for an explanation of words of a general nature, used in debate, you now 'demand of me that satisfaction which your insulted feelings require,' and refer me to your friend, Mr. ——, I presume, as he is the bearer of your note, for such arrangements as are usual.

"This demand for explanation, you, in my judgment, as a matter of right, were not entitled to make on me; nor were the temper and style of your own reply to my objection to the sugar tax of a character to induce me to accord it as a matter of courtesy.

"Neither can I, under the circumstances of the case, recognize in you a right to call me to the field to answer what you may please to consider an insult to your feelings.

"It is unnecessary for me to state other and obvious considerations growing out of this case. It is enough that I do not feel myself bound, at all times and under any circumstances, to accept from any man, who shall choose to risk his own life, an invitation of this sort; although I shall be always prepared to repel in a suitable manner the aggression of any man who may presume upon such a refusal.

"Your obedient servant,

"DANIEL WEBSTER."

After this note had been delivered to Mr. Randolph, and the whole affair had been adjusted, Mr. Webster, who had kept no copy of his part of the correspondence, wrote to Mr. Randolph, at the close of the session, to request one. The following reply, marked by the generous feelings and morbid characteristics of the writer, reached Mr. Webster on his return to Boston:

[MR. RANDOLPH TO MR. WEBSTER.]

"DAVIS, NINE MILES FROM WASHINGTON, ON THE BALTIMORE ROAD, *August* 30, 1816.

"SIR: Your polite and friendly note was put into my hands this morning, under circumstances that did not permit me to write. I now regret very

[1] I have said in the text that Mr. Webster held the practice of duelling in great contempt. I did not deem it necessary to say that he had also a high moral and religious disapprobation of it. As a specimen of the mode in which he was accustomed to ridicule it, among his friends, the following piece of drollery may be found in a letter to his son Fletcher, on one of those occasions which were formerly so frequent in Washington: "I understand there is a man here from Missouri, a Colonel S., who means to have a fight with Mr. Benton, and, if Mr. Benton will not have a regular duel, intends to fight him *ex parte*."—(Jan. 15, 1836. *Correspondence*, ii., 17.)

much that I did not leave Georgetown with you this morning. I have just dined where you breakfasted this morning, with a most pleasant party. That reflection seems to add to the uncomfortable feeling of solitariness that now assails me. Below you have the 'copy' of the paper which you desired me to forward to you. Accept my acknowledgments for the terms in which that request is made, and believe me, with very high respect and regard,

"Your obedient servant,

"JOHN RANDOLPH, of Roanoke."

The session of Congress terminated on the 30th of April, 1816. Before it ended, Mr. Webster had decided upon a very important change in his own life and position; upon no less a change than to remove from his native State and to retire from public life. He was now thirty-four. He had lived in Portsmouth nine years, in happiness and success. He had risen to a position of great distinction and usefulness, for so young a man, and all that New Hampshire could bestow upon him was doubtless within his reach. But in his profession the State of his birth had not given him, and could not give him, the field which his talents and the wants of his increasing family required. His local practice in New Hampshire had never been worth more than two thousand dollars a year, and it was scarcely capable of being made to yield a larger income. The loss of all his property by the fire of 1813 had made it necessary for him to seek larger resources. Whether he looked for still higher distinction in the political world, at some future time, or meant never to return to it, I do not know; but I am satisfied that at this period he had not an absorbing taste for public life, or a fixed political ambition. At all events, he appears to have determined to pass some years in exclusive devotion to his profession, and he therefore looked about for the best position for this important object. He hesitated between the cities of New York, Albany, and Boston; but he finally chose the latter; and, having made his decision, he proceeded immediately to carry it out. In June (1816), he went there with Mrs. Webster, to select a house, and in August he removed with his family.[1]

[1] The house in which he first resided in Boston was on Mt. Vernon Street, at the summit of Beacon Hill, and a few rods northwest of the State-House. It is still standing, just as it was when he entered it more than fifty years ago.

CHAPTER VIII.

1816–1819.

CONGRESS IN 1816–'17—DEATH OF LITTLE GRACE—RETIRES FROM PUBLIC LIFE—BIRTH OF HIS DAUGHTER JULIA—POSITION AT THE BOSTON BAR—SOCIAL LIFE—DARTMOUTH COLLEGE CASE—ROBBERY OF MAJOR GOODRIDGE.

AT the time when Mr. Webster took up his residence in Boston, he had numerous engagements in the Supreme Court of the United States, and, as the full term for which he had been reëlected as a member of Congress from New Hampshire had not expired, he went again to Washington, in December, 1816, accompanied by Mrs. Webster. He took some part in the proceedings of the session until the first week in January, when the illness of their daughter again brought the parents home. This child, always precocious and always delicate, was now to be taken from them. She had been declining for some time, and was at length pronounced by the physicians to be in a consumption. I borrow the words of Mrs. Lee, who was rarely absent when sorrow came near to those whom she so loved and honored:[1]

"I can hardly trust myself to speak of this child, so little to be relied on are the reports of precocious children. But as I recall some of the peculiarities of this little girl, she certainly appears, at three and four

[1] The death of this child occurred in January, 1817. A singular fatality seemed to attend the name of Grace Webster. A daughter of Mr. Everett, to whom this name was given, a precocious child, like Mr. Webster's, died in 1836. Mr. Webster's eldest grand-daughter, the second child of his son Fletcher, also bore the name of Grace, and died in 1844, at nearly the same age with the first one of the name

years old, wonderfully intelligent, and a most agreeable companion. There was no one so much in demand as the little Grace—her mother's friends constantly sending for her, and delighting themselves with her sweet simplicity; and, if such an expression can be allowed, her infantile sagacity. Her young soul seemed to dwell very near the Author of her being. Her mother once said to a friend, 'I wish I could feel the presence of God as little Grace seems to feel it.' Not only did 'heaven lie about her in her infancy,' but she knew that God was always near her. Another peculiarity was the tenderness she felt for the poor and unhappy. Beggars were frequent at this time. There were few relief societies, and begging from door to door was not forbidden. Grace would never consent that an asker of charity should be sent away empty. She would bring them herself into the house, see that their wants were supplied, comfort them with the ministration of her own little hands, and the tender compassion of her large eyes. If her mother ever refused, those eyes would fill with tears, and she would urge their requests so perseveringly, that there was no resisting her.

"But God's hand soon beckoned her away. Her parents had left Portsmouth for their residence in Boston, and Mr. Webster had gone the second time from New Hampshire to serve a session in Congress, when that insidious disease, to which delicate organizations so often become a prey, began to impair the health of the little Grace. The progress of the disease was so rapid, that her parents had only time to hasten from Washington to their house in Boston, where their child, whose short life had been lived, as it were, on the threshold of heaven, passed with gentle and painless steps within the veil which hides from us the great mysteries of the future. Grace woke from a sweet sleep, and asked for her father. He was instantly called, and, placing his arm beneath her, he drew her toward him, when a singular smile of love and sweetness passed over her countenance, and her life was gone. Mr. Webster turned away from the bed, and great tears coursed down his cheeks. I have three times seen this great man weep convulsively. Another time was when death deprived him of that brother, so tenderly loved, with whom, as we learn from the Autobiography, and from his own lips, there was so close a union, that, till both of them had families, which drew them from each other, there had been between them but one aim, one purse, one welfare, and one hope."

Mr. Webster went again to Washington, immediately after the burial of his child, and confined himself almost exclusively to his duties in the Supreme Court.

At this session, Mr. Calhoun brought forward his plan, which was intended to lay the foundation for a general system of "internal improvements," by setting apart the bonus and dividends to be derived from the United States Bank, as a permanent fund for that purpose; and, at the same time, he argued elaborately in support of the constitutional power of Congress to make appropriations for such objects. Mr. Webster voted for the bill on its passage. It was returned by President Madison without his approval; the ground of the "veto" being that the power is not expressly given in the Constitution, and cannot be deduced from any part of it without an inadmissible latitude of construction, and a reliance on insufficient precedents. Mr. Webster examined the whole subject with care, for the purpose of forming his own opinions upon it, although he does not appear to have taken any part in its public discussion at this time. He reached the conclusion that Congress has power to accomplish or to aid in accomplishing the objects which have been commonly designated in our legislative history as "internal improvements;" a conclusion which was sufficiently manifested by his final vote sustaining Mr. Calhoun's bill against the "veto" of the President. The measure failed to receive the requisite constitutional vote.[1]

The session of Congress was terminated on the 3d of March, 1817; and with it ended Mr. Webster's connection, for the present, with public affairs. As soon as the Supreme Court had risen, he returned to Boston.

Released from all public cares, he now began a career of great professional distinction. Business of the most important character flowed in upon him, from the natural influence of his high reputation, of his diligence and learning, of his great powers as an advocate, and his many personal accomplishments. The position which he at once occupied at the Boston bar was that of an equal and a competitor with the oldest and most eminent of its members. In a short time he was in the receipt of a very large professional income.[2] Of his domestic and so-

[1] See the account given by Mr. Webster, in his second speech on Foot's resolution, of the formation of his opinions and the shaping of his political course, on this and other constitutional questions, in 1816, "*Teucro duce.*"—(*Works*, iii., 297.)

[2] Mr. Webster's fee-book from August, 1818, to August, 1819, foots up $15,181. But as he is known not to have been very careful in keeping accounts, and as nearly all lawyers, who practise much as advocates and counsellors, receive more than finds its way into their account-books, unless they are kept with great accuracy, I am satisfied that his income, from 1818 until he again entered Congress in 1823, could not have been, on an average, much less than $20,000 a year. The customary fees of such counsel at that time were about one-half of what they are now.

cial life, during this period of his retirement from Congress, there are some interesting sketches by Mrs. Lee and Mr. Ticknor, which will find their appropriate place here, before I commence the description of the intellectual labors with which this period was filled. Mrs. Lee writes:

"Mr. Webster says in his Autobiography, that after he had finished his session in Congress from New Hampshire, he came to Boston and gave himself with diligence to the business of his profession.

"He was now thirty-five years old, and certainly in the perfection of all the powers of body and mind. The majestic beauty of his countenance was never more striking than at this period. There is a miniature taken at this time, which gives a most agreeable impression of his features, but which those who knew him in the later years of his life would hardly accept as a perfect likeness. The noble expansive brow and deep-set, melancholy eyes do justice to those features; but the tender, flexible lips, although expressing the sweetness of his character at that period of his life, have not the expression of intense firmness which afterward gave such character to his countenance.

"As I had the privilege of being often a visitor in his family, a recapitulation of the course of his every-day life may be more interesting to you than any thing else.

"Mr. Webster was always an early riser. There is an eloquent letter which expresses his true feeling upon the influence of the morning hours. Like most of the great and good people we read of, the hours of the early morning were [to him] the most cheerful of the day. The drowsy in his own house were awoke by his joyous voice singing some cheerful carol, such as,

'The east is bright with morning light,
Uprose the king of men with speed,' etc.

"At breakfast, before the cares of business began, he was cheerful but thoughtful, courteous and genial toward every one; listening to the prattle of the children, and kindly attentive to all their little requests. When he returned, at two or three o'clock, weary from the courts, or from his office, the promptly ready service of Hannah, a woman who had been in his family many years, was always welcome. She knew the sound of the door when opened by Mr. Webster, and it was scarcely closed before she was at his side. He was dependent upon services prompted by affection, and loved those spontaneous offerings which came from the heart.

"After dinner, Mr. Webster would throw himself upon the sofa, and then was seen the truly electrical attraction of his character. Every person in the room was drawn immediately into his sphere. The children squeezing themselves into all possible places and postures upon the sofa, in order to be close to him; Mrs. Webster sitting by his side, and the friend in the house or social visitor, only too happy to join in the circle. All this was not from invitation to the children, he did nothing to amuse them, he told them no stories; it was the irresistible attraction of his character, the charm of his illumined countenance, from which beamed indulgence and kindness to every one of his family. In the evening, if visitors came in, Mr. Webster was too much exhausted to take a very active part in conversation. He had done a large amount of work before others were awake in the morning, and in the evening he was ready for that sweet sleep which 'God gives to His beloved.'"

In January, 1818, Julia, the only daughter of Mr. Webster who lived to the age of womanhood, was born in Boston, in the house on Mt. Vernon Street which he first occupied in that town. Of his life at this time, Mr. Ticknor observes:

"Soon after I returned from Washington, in 1815, I went to Europe, and did not come back till 1819. Mr. Webster was then living in Boston in Mt. Vernon Street. Two days after I arrived, I met him at dinner at Mr. Isaac P. Davis's, who then lived in the Wheeler House in Boylston Street. Judge Story, Mr. George Blake, Mr. Willian Sullivan, and a few others, made the party. Such a party could not have sat down together at a private table when I left home. It was what was called 'the era of good feelings.' Mr. Webster had been very instrumental in producing this state of things in the country. Mr. John Lowell, in the summer of 1817, told me, in Paris, that Mr. Webster, in a private visit to Mr. Monroe, just before leaving Washington, when he ceased to be a member of Congress, asked the President to make a visit to the North. The President objected, on the ground that a person of his political opinions would be very unwelcome there. Mr. Webster replied that he thought it would be better if party feeling were diminished in the United States, and that this was a favorable opportunity to diminish it—he believed that the President would be kindly received without distinction of party, and that such a circumstance would tend much to allay all political bitterness. 'The country,' he said, 'was much too busy and too eager in its prosperity, to give much time to quarrelling about things chiefly bygone.' They had much conversation on the subject. Mr. Webster told the President that he thought he could venture to speak freely, as he had already left Congress, and should in future give his attention to his profession and private affairs. Mr. Monroe thanked him, and said he would consider the matter. The result was, President Monroe's well-known journey to the North.

"On relating the conversation with Mr. Lowell to Mr. Mason some years afterward, he told me that he was aware at the time of Mr. Webster's course and influence in the matter, and that at his (Mr. Webster's) instance he had personally invited Mr. Monroe to visit him at Portsmouth, and did what he could to make his tour agreeable and useful.

"At the dinner at Mr. Davis's, Mr. Webster talked a good deal about Europe—all I remember of his conversation is, that he had a very accurate idea of the difference between a European and an American village – of the results of building with destructible materials, like pine wood, or of more lasting materials like brick and stone, and of the effect upon the character of a people, which followed from having the same family for successive generations live in the same place, in narrowing their minds."

The period which is now to be described extends from the summer of 1817 to Mr. Webster's return to Congress, in 1823, as a Representative from Massachusetts. It was filled with an extraordinary amount of intellectual activity. It comprehends the celebrated argument in the Dartmouth College case, in the Supreme Court of the United States, which raised him immediately to the very highest rank as a constitutional lawyer; his service in the constitutional convention of Massachusetts, in which his powers as a statesman, a legislator, and a debater, were displayed with singular brilliancy, and employed with singular usefulness; his discourse at Plymouth, which placed him on the list of the world's great orators; and a vast variety of professional performances, in every department of jurisprudence, and embracing nearly every phase of human affairs that can come within the cognizance of courts of justice. In order to give the reader an adequate idea of the amount and character of the intellectual labor that was crowded into these six or seven years of the prime of Mr. Webster's life, perhaps the best mode will be to describe separately what belongs to his professional and what relates to his other employments.

The professional reader, who is curious to measure the extent of Mr. Webster's practice during the period to which I now refer, will find the number of causes which he argued, *in banc*, in the Supreme Court of Massachusetts, in the Circuit Court of the United States for the First Circuit, and in the Supreme Court of the United States, from 1817 to 1823, by consulting the official reports of those courts for that period.[1] These show a very large employment as leading counsel in those three tribunals; but, of course, they contain no record of the *nisi prius* business in which he must have been engaged, in some degree commensurate with his employment as an

[1] The volumes of the "Massachusetts Reports," from the 13th to the 17th, inclusive, together with the first volume of "Pickering's Reports," the second of "Gallison's Reports," and the first and second of "Mason's Reports," and of "Wheaton's Reports," cover the period referred to.

advocate before the courts *in banc.* All this mass of litigation, although leaving its impress on the jurisprudence of the country—as every well-debated question does, under a system of law that is founded and depends upon recorded precedents—was, with one great exception, unconnected with the relations of the States of this Union to the restraining authority and supremacy of the Constitution of the United States. Such a question was wanting to the complete development of Mr. Webster's power and reputation as a lawyer, and it came from an occasion and a source eminently adapted to call forth his abilities, and to enlist his strongest interest.

Dartmouth College, at which, as we have seen, he received his academic education, was originally a charity school for the instruction of Indians in the Christian religion, founded by the Rev. Eleazer Wheelock, D. D., about the year 1754, at Lebanon, in Connecticut. Its success led Dr. Wheelock to solicit private subscriptions in England, for the purpose of enlarging it, and of extending its benefits to English colonists. Funds having been obtained for this purpose from various contributors, among whom the Earl of Dartmouth, Secretary for the Colonies, was a large donor, Dr. Wheelock constituted that nobleman and other persons trustees, with authority to fix the site of the college. The place selected was on the Connecticut River, at what is now the town of Hanover, in New Hampshire, where large donations of land were made by the neighboring proprietors. A charter for the college was obtained from the crown, in 1769, creating it a perpetual corporation. The charter recognized Dr. Wheelock as founder, appointed him to be the president, and empowered him to name his successor, subject to the approval of the trustees; to whom was also imparted the power of filling vacancies in their own body, and of making laws and ordinances for the government of the college, not repugnant to the laws of Great Britain or of the province, and not excluding any person on account of his religious belief.

Under this charter, Dartmouth College had always existed, unquestioned and undisturbed in its rights as a corporation, down to the Revolution, and subsequently until the year 1815. Whether from political or personal motives springing up outside of the board of trustees of that period, or from some collisions arising within the body itself, it appears that, before Mr. Webster left the State of New Hampshire, legislative interference with the chartered rights of this college was threatened; and its president, Dr. Brown, was anxious to secure his influence and services. Mr. Webster, however, declined to take any part in these disputes as they then stood. But, in the following year (1816), the difficulties, which had become mixed with political interests, culminated in a direct interference by the Legislature. In that year an act was passed, changing the corporate name from "The Trustees of Dartmouth College" to "The Trustees of Dartmouth University;" enlarging the number of trustees, vesting the appointment of some of them in the political bodies of the State, and otherwise modifying the ancient rights of the corporation as they existed under its charter derived from the crown of England.

A majority of the existing trustees refused to accept or to be bound by this act, and brought an action of trover in the Supreme Court of the State, in the name of the old corporation, against a gentleman, Mr. W. H. Woodward, who was in possession of the college seal and other effects, and who claimed to hold them as one of the officers of the newly-created "university." The argument in this case was made in the State court, for the college, by Mr. Mason and Mr. Jeremiah Smith, assisted by Mr. Webster. The decision was against the claim of the college. It was then determined to remove the cause, by writ of error, to the Supreme Court of the United States, under the provisions of the Federal Constitution and laws creating in that tribunal an appellate jurisdiction in cases which, although originating in a State court, involve the construction and operation of the Federal Constitution. This was supposed to be such a case, because it was claimed by the college that the act of the Legislature, modifying its charter, impaired the obligation of a contract; an exercise of power which the Constitution of the United States prohibits to the Legislature of a State.

As soon as it was known in New Hampshire that this very interesting cause was to come before the Supreme Court of the United States, the friends of the college, including their other counsel in the State court, unanimously desired to have it committed to the hands of Mr. Webster. He consented to take charge of it in the autumn of 1817; but the cause was not argued at Washington until February, 1818. In the interval, Mr. Webster gave directions relating to the form and contents of the special verdict, which was to be carried up by the writ of error, and had several conferences with the gentlemen who had argued for the college with very great learning and ability in the State court. He was left entirely at liberty to appoint his associate counsel, and he selected Joseph Hopkinson, of Philadelphia.

To those who might then have been, or to those who may now be uninitiated in the relations of our complex system of Government, this dispute whether the trustees of the college should be one or another set of persons at the command of the State; whether it should be called by its ancient name, or by a new name affixed to it by the legislative power, might seem a rather trivial subject of litigation, not likely to involve principles extending into the indefinite future, and reaching to the very foundations of the rights of property. Such, however, was the character of this celebrated cause; and, in order to exhibit what our constitutional jurisprudence owes to the advocate who carried this case triumphantly through its final arbitrament, it is necessary to refer to the provision of the Constitution which it became his duty to expound, and to the development and application which it had previously received.

The framers of the Constitution of the United States, moved chiefly by the mischiefs created by the preceding legislation of the States, which had made serious encroachments on the rights of property, inserted a clause in that instrument which declared that "no State shall pass any *ex post-facto* law, or law impairing the obligation of contracts." The first branch of this clause had always been understood to relate to criminal legislation, the second to legislation affecting civil rights. But, before the case of *Dartmouth College* vs. *Woodward* occurred, there had been no judicial decisions respecting the meaning and scope of the restraint in regard to contracts, excepting that it had more than once been determined by the Supreme Court of the United States that a grant of lands made by a State is a contract within the protection of this provision, and is, therefore, irrevocable.

These decisions, however, could go but little way toward the solution of the questions involved in the case of the college. They did, indeed, establish the principle that contracts of the State itself are beyond the reach of subsequent legislation, equally with contracts between individuals; and that there are grants of a State which are contracts. But this college stood upon a charter granted by the crown of England before the American Revolution. Was the State of New Hampshire—a sovereign in all respects after the Revolution, and remaining one after the Federal Constitution, excepting in those respects in which it had subjected its sovereignty to the restraints of that instrument—bound by the contracts of the English crown? Is the grant of a charter of incorporation a contract between the sovereign power and those on whom the charter is bestowed? If an act of incorporation is a contract, is it so in any case but that of a private corporation? Was this college, which was an institution of learning, established for the promotion of education, a private corporation, or was it one of those instruments of government which are at all times under the control and subject to the direction of the legislative power? All these questions were involved in the inquiry whether the legislative power of the State had been so restrained by the Constitution of the United States that it could not alter the charter of this institution, against the will of the trustees, without impairing the obligation of a contract. If this inquiry were to receive an affirmative answer, the constitutional jurisprudence of the United States would embrace a principle of the utmost importance to every similar institution of learning, and to every incorporation then existing, or thereafter to exist, not belonging to the machinery of government as a political instrument.

The State court of New Hampshire, in deciding this case, had assumed that the college was a public corporation, and on that basis had rested their judgment; which was, that between the State and its public corporations there is no contract which the State cannot regulate, alter, or annul at pleasure. Mr. Webster had to overthrow this fundamental position. If he could show that this college was a private eleemosynary corporation, and that the grant of the right to be a corporation of this nature is a contract between the sovereign power and those who devote their funds to the charity, and take the incorporation for its better management, he could bring the legislative interference within the prohibition of the Federal Constitution.

It is probable that there was no lawyer in the United States at that moment better qualified to discuss this question than Mr. Webster. He had been from a very early period in his life a great student of English history, and he was thoroughly familiar with the principles of the common law. The question to which class of corporations—public or private—did this college belong—the critical question in the cause—was one to be decided on the principles of the common law, as the governing body of jurisprudence by which the Constitution of the United States is to be interpreted, in its application to public or private rights. It affected, too, every institution of learning in the country that had been similarly endowed and founded; while the particular institution, the fate of which was at stake in the cause, was one which the strongest sympathies of his youth and the fullest convictions of his manhood stimulated him to preserve from the control of party politics and the mischiefs of political legislation. Inspired by these motives, he opened the cause, in the argument of which all that is preserved is contained in the *fifth* volume of his works; a report which gives us only the legal reasoning of a speech that was undoubtedly as remarkable for its beauty, pathos, and eloquence, as it was for its logical power and its wealth of historical and juridical illustration.

Its important positions, stated in their logical order, were these: 1. That Dr. Wheelock was the founder of this college, and as such entitled by law to be visitor, and that he had assigned all the visitatorial powers to the trustees. 2. That the charter created a private and not a public corporation, to administer a charity, in the administration of which the trustees had a property, which the law recognizes as such. 3. That the grant of such a charter is a contract between the sovereign power and its successors and those to whom it is granted and their successors. 4. That the legislation which took away from the trustees the right to exercise the powers of superintendence, visitation, and government, and transferred them to another set of trustees, impaired the obligation of that contract. The arguments of Mr. Wirt, then Attorney-General of the United States, and of Mr. Holmes, for the defendants in error, related chiefly to the points that the charter was not a contract, but a mere appointment to office, the trustees being agents of government, and the property, in fact, given to the public; that if the charter was a contract, it was not impaired by the legislation, which merely gave the trustees new assistants; and that Dr. Wheelock was not the founder, as he never gave any thing. Mr. Hopkinson replied, on all these topics, in a speech of much ability. On the conclusion of the argument, the Chief Justice intimated that a decision was not to be expected until the next term. It was made in February, 1819, fully confirming the grounds on which Mr. Webster had placed the cause. From this decision, the principle in our constitutional jurisprudence, which regards a charter of a private corporation as a contract, and places it under the protection of the Constitution of the United States, takes its date. To Mr. Webster belongs the honor of having produced its judicial establishment.

We look back upon a forensic performance like this, which was followed by a judgment affirming its positions, and fixing them among the foundations of our law, so that its principles have become familiar to us, as if the conception and development of the subject involved less reach of originality and less depth of research and force of reasoning than they really did. But we should judge of the advocate on these critical occasions, in some measure, through the impressions and opinions of those who heard him, and who stood at the same point in our juridical history at which he was himself placed. What they regarded as a very high intellectual achievement, advancing the law by a great stride toward the perfection of which a human and an artificial system of social rights is capable, we may well accept as such upon their testimony. For, while we observe the excitation of feeling produced by the immediate influence of the speech on those who heard it, we must concede to contemporaries a superior appreciation of the difficulties that were to be encountered. Tradition, if it has not always placed this performance at the very head of all Mr. Webster's forensic efforts, has certainly, by the universal testimony of those who heard it, regarded it as one that immediately impressed the highest intellect of the nation with an adequate sense of his power. But, among all the admiration that it called forth from those who were present, there is nothing more happy or more striking than what was said by Mr. Webster's associate in the cause. Writing to the president of the college, after the judgment of the court had fully sanctioned the arguments of its advocates, and placed it in safety for all future time, Mr. Hopkinson modestly disclaimed for himself any other merit, in his reply to their opponents, than that of having followed and enforced the positions taken by Mr. Webster in his opening of the cause. He then added, "I would have an inscription over the door of your building: 'FOUNDED BY ELEAZER WHEELOCK, REFOUNDED BY DANIEL WEBSTER.'"

The most vivid description that is extant of Mr. Webster's manner on this occasion, was given by a gentleman, who was present, to Mr. Choate, in 1853.[1] I quote it entire:

"Before going to Washington, which I did chiefly for the sake of hearing Mr. Webster, I was told that, in arguing the case at Exeter, New Hampshire, he had left the whole court-room in tears at the conclusion of his speech. This, I confess, struck me unpleasantly—any attempt at pathos on a purely legal question like this seemed hardly in good taste. On my way to Washington, I made the acquaintance of Mr. Webster. We were together for several days in Philadelphia, at the house of a common friend; and, as the college question was one of deep interest to literary men, we conversed often and largely on the subject. As he dwelt upon the leading points of the case, in terms so calm, simple, and precise, I said to myself more than once, in reference to the story I had heard, 'Whatever may have seemed appropriate in defending the college *at home*, and on her own ground, there will be no appeal to the feelings of Judge Marshall and his associates at Washington.' The Supreme Court of the United States held its session, that winter, in a mean apartment of moderate size—the capitol not having been rebuilt after its destruction in 1814. The audience, when the case came on, was, therefore, small, consisting chiefly of legal men, the *élite* of the profession throughout the country. Mr. Webster entered upon his argument in the calm tone of easy and dignified conversation. His matter was so completely at his command that he scarcely looked at his brief, but went on for more than four hours with a statement so luminous, and a chain of reasoning so easy to be understood, and yet approaching so nearly to absolute demonstration, that he seemed to carry with him every

[1] Dr. Chauncey A. Goodrich, a professor in Yale College. See the eulogy on Mr. Webster, pronounced by Mr. Choate at Dartmouth College, July 27, 1853, at the request of the authorities and the students.

man of his audience without the slightest effort or uneasiness on either side. It was hardly *eloquence*, in the strict sense of the term; it was pure reason. Now and then, for a sentence or two, his eye flashed and his voice swelled into a bolder note, as he uttered some emphatic thought; but he instantly fell back into the tone of earnest conversation which ran throughout the great body of the speech. A single circumstance will show you the clearness and absorbing power of his argument.

"I observed that Judge Story, at the opening of the case, had prepared himself, pen in hand, as if to take copious minutes. Hour after hour I saw him fixed in the same attitude, but, so far as I could perceive, with not a note on his paper. The argument closed, and I could not discover that he had taken a single note. Others around me remarked the same thing, and it was among the *on dits* of Washington that a friend spoke to him of the fact with surprise, when the judge remarked, 'Every thing was so clear, and so easy to remember, that not a note seemed necessary, and, in fact, I thought little or nothing about my notes.' The argument ended, Mr. Webster stood for some moments silent before the court, while every eye was fixed intently upon him. At length, addressing the Chief Justice, he proceeded thus:

"'This, sir, is my case. It is the case, not merely of that humble institution, it is the case of every college in our land. It is more. It is the case of every eleemosynary institution throughout our country—of all those great charities founded by the piety of our ancestors, to alleviate human misery, and scatter blessings along the pathway of life. It is more! It is, in some sense, the case of every man among us who has property of which he may be stripped, for the question is simply this: Shall our State Legislatures be allowed to take that which is not their own, to turn it from its original use, and apply it to such ends or purposes as they in their discretion shall see fit?

"'Sir, you may destroy this little institution; it is weak; it is in your hands! I know it is one of the lesser lights in the literary horizon of our country. You may put it out. But, if you do so, you must carry through your work! You must extinguish, one after another, all those greater lights of science which, for more than a century, have thrown their radiance over our land!

"'It is, sir, as I have said, a small college. And yet there are those who love it—'

"Here, the feelings which he had thus far succeeded in keeping down, broke forth. His lips quivered; his firm cheeks trembled with emotion; his eyes were filled with tears, his voice choked, and he seemed struggling to the utmost simply to gain that mastery over himself which might save him from an unmanly burst of feeling. I will not attempt to give you the few broken words of tenderness in which he went on to speak of his attachment to the college. The whole seemed to be mingled throughout with the recollections of father, mother, brother, and all the privations and trials through which he had made his way into life. Every one saw that it was wholly unpremeditated, a pressure on his heart, which sought relief in words and tears.

"The court-room during these two or three minutes presented an extraordinary spectacle. Chief-Justice Marshall, with his tall and gaunt figure bent over, as if to catch the slightest whisper, the deep furrows of his cheek expanded with emotion, and his eyes suffused with tears; Mr. Justice Washington at his side, with his small and emaciated frame and countenance more like marble than I ever saw on any other human being —leaning forward with an eager, troubled look; and the remainder of the court, at the two extremities, pressing, as it were, toward a single point, while the audience below were wrapping themselves round in closer folds beneath the bench, to catch each look and every movement of the speaker's face. If a painter could give us the scene on canvas—those forms and countenances, and Daniel Webster as he there stood in the midst—it would be one of the most touching pictures in the history of eloquence. One thing it taught me, that the *pathetic* depends not merely on the words uttered, but still more on the estimate we put upon him who utters them. There was not one among the strong-minded men of that assembly, who could think it unmanly to weep, when he saw standing before him the man who had made such an argument, melted into the tenderness of a child.

"Mr. Webster had now recovered his composure, and, fixing his keen eye on the Chief Justice, said, in that deep tone with which he sometimes thrilled the heart of an audience:

"'Sir, I know not how others may feel' (glancing at the opponents of the college before him), 'but, for myself, when I see my Alma Mater surrounded, like Cæsar in the senate-house, by those who are reiterating stab after stab, I would not, for this right hand, have her to turn to me, and say, *Et tu quoque mi fili! And thou too, my son!*'

"He sat down. There was a deathlike stillness throughout the room for some moments; every one seemed to be slowly recovering himself, and coming gradually back to his ordinary range of thought and feeling."

About a year previous to this argument of a legal and constitutional question of the highest reach, before a court of law, Mr. Webster was employed in a totally different sphere of the functions of an advocate, in the defence of two persons before a jury, indicted under circumstances of a remarkable character, whose guilt was almost unanimously assumed by the public, who were unquestionably innocent, and whose safety depended upon a skilful cross-examination of the prosecutor, and a discussion of probabilities upon evidence. I allude to the dramatic story of the robbery of Major Goodridge.

Goodridge was a person of previous good character and respectable standing, who professed to have been robbed of a large sum of money, at about nine o'clock in the night of December 19, 1816, on the road between Exeter and Newburyport, soon after passing the Essex Merrimac Bridge, on his way from New Hampshire into Massachusetts. Among the proofs of the robbery was a pistol-shot through his left hand, received, as he said, before the robbers pulled him from his horse; he and one of his assailants discharging their pistols at each other on the same instant. He was then, according to his account, dragged from his horse, and across a fence into a field, robbed, and beaten until he was senseless. On his recovery he went back to the toll-house on the bridge, where he appeared to be for a time in a state of delirium. But he had sufficient self-possession to return to the place of the robbery with some persons who accompanied him with a lantern, where his watch, papers, and other articles were found scattered on the ground. On the following day, he went to Newburyport, and remained there ill, at intervals in a state of real or simulated frenzy, for several weeks. Having regained his health, he set about the discovery of the robbers; and so general was the sympathy for him in a very orderly community, that his plans were aided by the innocent zeal of nearly the whole country-side. His first charge was against the Kennistons, two poor men who dwelt in the town of New Market, New Hampshire, on the other side of the river. In their cellar he found a piece of gold, which he identified by a mark which he said he had placed on all his money, and a ten-dollar note which he also identified as his own. The Kennistons were arrested, examined, and held for trial. He next charged the toll-gatherer, one Pearson, as an accomplice; and on his premises, with the aid of a witch-hazel conjuror, he also found some of his gold and papers in which it had been wrapped. Pearson was arrested, examined before two magistrates, and discharged. He then complained against one Taber, a person who lived in Boston. Finally, he followed a man named Jackman to the city of New York, in whose house he swore that he also discovered some of his marked wrappers. The machinery of an Executive requisition was put in motion, and Jackman was brought into Massachusetts and lodged in jail. He and

Taber, and the Kennistons, were then indicted for the robbery, in the county of Essex.

So cunningly had this man contrived his story and arranged his proofs, that the popular belief was entirely with him. The witch-hazel part of his evidence probably did not disincline the populace to believe him. But it is even said that there were few members of the county bar who did not regard the case of the Kennistons as desperate. There were some, however, who believed Goodridge's story to be false; and these persons sent for Mr. Webster to undertake the defence of the accused. The indictment against Taber was *nol. pross'd.* That against the Kennistons came on for trial at Ipswich, in April, 1817. They had nothing on which to rely but their previous good character, the negative fact that since the supposed robbery they had not passed any money or been seen to have any, and the improbabilities which their advocate could develop in the story of Goodridge. The theory of the defence was, that Goodridge was his own robber, and had fired the pistol-shot through his own hand.

In the power of cross-examining witnesses Mr. Webster had no superior in his day; and his reputation in this respect doubtless aided the impression which he produced upon this jury. There were traditions which had come over the border from New Hampshire, of his terrible skill in baffling the deepest plans of perjury and fraud, which excited the jury to the closest attention to his method of dealing with Goodridge. They saw his well-concocted story laid bare, in all its improbable features, while every aid was given to him by Mr. Webster to develop suggestions which could be set off against the theory that the latter meant to maintain. But when all the evidence for and against Goodridge's narrative had been drawn out, and it came to the summing up, there remained two obvious difficulties in the way of that hypothesis. One of them was, that no motive had been shown for so strange an act as a man's falsely pretending to have been robbed, and charging the robbery upon innocent people; the other, that the theory of Goodridge being himself the robber, apparently made it necessary to believe that he had proceeded, in his fraudulent manufacture of proofs, to the extremity of shooting a pistol-bullet through his own hand. These were very formidable difficulties; for the law of evidence, as administered in our criminal jurisprudence, very properly regards the absence of motive for an act, the commission of which depends on circumstantial proof as one of the important things to be weighed in favor of innocence; and as to the shooting, it was certainly in a high degree improbable that a man would maim himself, in order to maintain a false statement that he had been robbed and maimed by some one else. But in grappling with these difficulties, Mr. Webster told the jury that the range of human motives is almost infinite; that a desire to avoid payment of his debts, if he owed debts, or a whimsical ambition for distinction, might have been at the bottom of Goodridge's conduct; and that having once announced himself to the community as a man who had been robbed of a large sum and beaten nearly to death, he had to go on and charge somebody with the act. This was correct reasoning, but still no motive had been shown for the original pretence; and, if there had not been some decisive circumstances developed on the evidence, it is not easy to say how this case ought to have been decided. These circumstances made it unnecessary to believe that, although Goodridge himself discharged the pistol which wounded him, he intended that result. His story was, that the pistol of the robber went off at the moment when he had grasped it with his left hand. Yet, according to the testimony of the physicians who attended him, there were no marks of powder on his hand; and the appearance of the wound led to the conclusion that the muzzle of the piece must have been three or four feet from his hand, while there were marks of powder on the sleeve of his coat, and the ball passed through the coat as well as the hand. This state of the evidence justified Mr. Webster's remark that "all exhibitions are subject to accidents. Whether serious or farcical, they do not always proceed exactly as they are designed to do." Goodridge, he argued, intended to shoot the ball through his coat-sleeve, and it accidentally perforated his hand also. This discredited his story more than any thing else, and convinced the jury that, if he found any of his money on the premises of the Kennistons, he placed it there himself. The Kennistons were acquitted. Goodridge returned to the charge;

Jackman was put on trial at the next term of the court, and the jury disagreed. At his second trial, Mr. Webster defended him, and he was acquitted. These criminal proceedings were followed by an action for a malicious prosecution, instituted by Pearson against Goodridge. Mr. Webster was of counsel for the plaintiff in this case. The evidence was now still more clear against Goodridge; a verdict for a large amount was recovered against him, and the public at last saw the fact judicially established that he had robbed himself. He left New England a disgraced man. No clew to his motive was ever discovered.

Twenty years afterward, Mr. Webster was travelling in the western part of the State of New York; he stopped at a tavern, and went in to ask for a glass of water. The man behind the bar exhibited great agitation as the traveller approached him, and when he placed the glass of water before Mr. Webster his hand trembled violently, but he did not speak. Mr. Webster drank the water, turned without saying another word, and reëntered his carriage. The man was Goodridge.

CHAPTER IX.

1820-1822.

MR. CALHOUN'S VISIT TO BOSTON—PROFESSIONAL POSITION—CONVENTION TO REVISE THE CONSTITUTION OF MASSACHUSETTS—THE PLYMOUTH ORATION—CASE OF LA JEUNE EUGENIE—DEFENCE OF JUDGE JAMES PRESCOTT—ELECTED TO CONGRESS FROM BOSTON.

IN the summer of 1820, while Mr. Webster was diligently occupied in the practice of his profession, Mr. Calhoun, who was then Secretary of War, made an official tour to the North, for the purpose of examining the forts and arsenals of the Federal Government. His reception by Mr. Webster in Boston is thus described by Mr. Ticknor:

"When Mr. Calhoun came to Boston in the summer of 1820, as Secretary of War, to examine the arsenals and forts, Mr. Webster, who then lived in Somerset Street, was particularly hospitable and attentive to him. They had always been on good and kindly terms, even during the war, when they were leading in opposite parties. Whatever collisions they might have had on the floor of the House, were all forgotten at the time of Mr. Calhoun's visit to Boston. Mr. Webster was then earnestly devoted to the practice of his profession, but he was unquestionably not without political aspirations. He was much with Mr. Calhoun; went with him to the arsenal at Watertown, and passed the rest of the only day he could be with him in driving about the neighborhood. A large party of the principal persons in this portion of the country, I recollect, waited long for them at Mr. Webster's to dinner. Mr. Calhoun talked much and most agreeably at table, and it was evident to all of us that Mr. Webster desired to draw him out and show him under the most favorable aspects to his friends. After dinner, a considerable number of young men, particularly of the young lawyers of the town, came in and were presented to Mr. Calhoun. We all said, 'Mr. Webster wishes Mr. Calhoun to be the next President of the United States;' some added, 'He has been driving with him all day, *tête-à-tête* in a phaeton, and they understand one another.' But the positions of such men are stronger than themselves, and they understand one another without words."

In the midst of the professional practice which has been partly described in the last chapter, Mr. Webster was called upon to act a very important part in an entirely new sphere of public duty. He had been hitherto known as a leading member of Congress, and as a very eminent lawyer. In these capacities he had, at the age of thirty-eight, achieved a reputation which can scarcely be regarded as second to that of any man in America, when we take into account both his position at the bar and his position as a statesman. Of all those who were practising in the Supreme Court of the United States in 1820, Mr. Pinkney is the person with whom we naturally compare Mr. Webster. He was much older than Mr. Webster, and as an advocate and a lawyer he was undoubtedly a very great man—inferior to no one who has ever yet addressed that tribunal. That Mr. Webster, before he was forty, became the equal and competitor of Mr. Pinkney, is certainly a fact admitted by their contemporaries, and it marks the position to which Mr. Webster attained by very rapid strides, as if it belonged to him of right. But Mr. Pinkney added another to the list of distinguished lawyers who have not been equally distinguished in parliamentary life. His place, as he himself well knew, and as he once said in Congress, was in courts of justice; and there, in spite of the affectations which covered him with a mantle of small weaknesses, he was regarded, by all who were accustomed to hear him, as a person of prodigious strength. No amount of foppery could obscure the splendor of his intellect or intercept the blaze of light which he poured upon his subject, when he forgot, in the earnestness of his reasoning and the vehemence of his elocution, his strange desire to be considered rather an idle and elegant man of fashion than the indefatigable student and laborious lawyer he really was.[1]

[1] Mr. Justice Story was in the habit of relating the following anecdote: On one occasion, when Mr. Webster and Mr. Pinkney were opposed to each other in

Neither Mr. Clay nor Mr. Calhoun, who were nearer Mr. Webster's age, was greatly distinguished as a lawyer. Mr. Calhoun, in fact, never practised the law; and, down to the year 1820, Mr. Clay, who had become very eminent in political life, was known chiefly as a statesman, and had gathered no special laurels at the bar of the Supreme Court of the United States. Of Mr. Webster, therefore, it may be said, at the period to which I now refer, that, when we regard the double reputation which he had acquired on the floor of Congress and in the courts of law, and consider his age, he was the most conspicuous person in the country. All this reputation was now to encounter new hazards, in new and untried fields of intellectual exertion.

The State of Massachusetts had existed under a free constitution of its own creation, since the year 1780. This constitution, the work of John Adams, Samuel Adams, and other patriots of the Revolution, had been made in the midst of the Revolutionary War, and, of course, before the Constitution of the United States. It was in many respects a model of a free representative government, carefully reconciling popular rights with public order; but the circumstances of the Commonwealth for which it was designed had in forty years undergone some changes. Maine, which had hitherto belonged to Massachusetts as a part of her jurisdiction, had asked and obtained the consent of the latter to a separation. The necessity which this induced for modifying the representative system, and other exigencies growing out of the progress of society and the relations of the State to the Federal Government, caused the assembling of a convention of the people of Massachusetts to revise its constitution. This body met in Boston in November, 1820, and terminated its sessions in January, 1821. Mr. Webster was one of the delegates to it.

the same cause, the latter had an associate who was not remarkable for the brilliancy or importance of his discourse. This gentleman had been speaking for some time, opening his cause in a very prosing manner, and more than one of the judges had even relapsed into something very like a nod, when Mr. Pinkney was called out. As he left the court, he handed his notes to his colleague. Mr. —— went on for some time from his own brief, and the atmosphere of the court became more and more drowsy; the counsel on the opposite side, the judges, and the spectators paying a very languid attention, if any at all. Presently, ceasing to speak from his own notes, Mr. —— stated a new point, and followed it by some observations that caused everybody to take up their pens and open their ears. At that moment a whisper from Mr. Webster became audible through the room—'He has got on the armor of Achilles!'"

A constitutional convention of an American State is a representative body of one chamber, acting for the whole community, in whom resides the power, according to the theory of our institutions, of amending, altering, or abolishing the existing form of the State government and of substituting a new one, subject only to the condition expressly imposed by the Federal Constitution, that the form shall be republican, and to the further implied condition that it shall consist with the rights and authority of the United States. Exercising this ample and original power of moulding the political institutions of society for the purpose, at least, of determining what shall be submitted to the people for their final ratification, such a body eminently demands the highest range of talent and character that the society can furnish. The people of Massachusetts were not unmindful of what they owed to their own interests, or to the science and the cause of good government, in constituting this convention. They wisely excluded no one on account of his present public station. Several of the prominent judges, including Parker, the Chief Justice of the Commonwealth, and both of the Federal judges, Story and Davis, were members. All the learned professions, the merchants, the agricultural classes, the town and the rural populations, were duly represented by a body of delegates whose aggregate weight of character and ability has not been exceeded by that of any assembly that was ever convened in New England. The venerable John Adams, then in his eighty-fifth year, added grace and dignity to the convention as one of its members, and the compliment was paid to him of electing him its president; but he declined the duty of the chair, and the Chief Justice was then substituted as the presiding officer. The convention was necessarily a large body, because the municipalities of the State, consisting of about three hundred towns, had always claimed and exercised the right of separate representation in all political action, and because their corporate existence, in fact, lay at the foundation of the State itself. The number of delegates for each town was fixed at the number by which it was entitled to be represented in the lower House of the Legislature. This gave a convention of nearly five hundred members. So numerous a body of course embraced elements of decidedly radical as well as of strong conservative tendencies. The latter class in general regarded the old constitution as one demanding few alterations or additions; the former naturally favored innovations; so that the chief occasions likely to call forth the abilities of the members would be those which involved the attack or the defence of institutions and principles that lie at the basis of republican government.

But, although these two tendencies of individual minds, the radical and the conservative, were present in this convention—as they must be in every thing that relates to the affairs of society—there were peculiar circumstances attending it, which made it a very different sphere for such a man as Mr. Webster, from a parliamentary and legislative body. A public man who leads in the English House of Commons, or in one of our Houses of legislation, national or State, is generally obliged to do so as the head of a party. To a certain extent his opinions and action are restricted by the principles professed by his party, and the objects at which it aims, whether it conducts or opposes the administration of the time. He may, it is true, have occasion to deal with questions that go deeper than party opinion, and to appeal to that which is common to all parties; he often has to win votes from his opponents as well as from those with whom he is politically associated. Still, the existence of parties is not seldom unfavorable to the exhibition and influence of the higher statesmanship, which finds its best field when native genius for political discussion and practical talent for the application of principles to the condition of the whole society can do their appropriate work without the bias and the trammels arising from that minor organization in the republic that is constituted by a party. In the Massachusetts Convention of 1820 there were fortunately no parties. There was a small minority of highly cultivated and experienced men, who generally acted together, from the natural concurrence of the sentiments of men of that class; and they commonly governed the decisions of the whole body. But the convention was chosen and held at a time when there were no political parties in this country acting as strictly defined organizations. It was in what was called "the era of good feeling;" a current designation of the state of political affairs that existed during the administration of President Monroe, after the old contests and feelings between the Federal and Democratic parties had mostly subsided, and before their successors, the National Republican or Whig, and the modern Democratic parties, had been formed.

This absence of party divisions in the convention was highly favorable to the best interests of the State, and it was especially so to the influence of Mr. Webster and of those who acted with him, upon the institutions of the Commonwealth. It rendered the convention, although an extremely popular body, remarkable for its deliberative character. It was an assembly that listened to and was controlled by argument; that sacrificed prejudice to reason; and, when it saw the right, decided for it, without the influences arising from the intermixture of party objects. To these fortunate circumstances, and to the power which they gave to such a statesman as Mr. Webster, it is in a large degree to be ascribed that the political institutions of Massachusetts remain to this day, in many respects, decidedly more conservative than those of many of her sister States, notwithstanding the spirit of her people in political action is often quite the reverse of what might be argued from the spirit and letter of their constitution. Mr. Webster's activity and success in this convention were thus described by Judge Story, in a letter to a common friend, soon after its session was terminated:

> "Our friend Webster has gained a noble reputation. . . . It was a glorious field for him, and he has had an ample harvest. The whole force of his great mind was brought out, and in several speeches he commanded universal admiration. He always led the van, and was most skilful and instantaneous in attack and retreat. He fought, as I have told him, in the 'imminent deadly breach;' and all I could do was to skirmish in aid of him upon some of the enemy's outposts. On the whole, I never was more proud of any display than his in my life."[1]

Mere ambition, although Mr. Webster certainly was not then or at any other time without ambition, is not to be regarded as the sole spring that moved this great intellectual energy. He was in the vigor of manhood; full of talent of the most various kinds; full of knowledge, as knowledge is derived from books or from the business of life; with forces within him that were irrepressible, and that carried him forward in every

[1] Letter to Mr. Mason, January 21, 1821.—(*Life of Judge Story*, i., p. 395.)

conflict, by their spontaneous action, to the accomplishment of all the good toward which such extraordinary gifts are naturally impelled. At this time of his life there was scarcely ever seen in him any of that solemn repose, amounting to an apparent lethargy, from which in his later years he seemed capable of being aroused only by a strong external pressure. I have heard him described, by those who knew him at this period, as being in manner extremely alert and vivacious, although always dignified and refined. My own recollection of him goes back sufficiently far to enable me to remember the manifestations of power which his countenance, his bearing, and his conversation perpetually gave forth, when he was not absorbed in the abstractions of thought or study; and I can well understand the impressions of those whose recollections were earlier, and which led them to describe him afterward as the most "living" man they had ever known. Yet Mr. Webster was never carried, either by the impulse of great animal spirits or by the force of genius, into the regions of impracticable speculation, or of over refinement in politics, or of mere theories in human affairs. He could be as acute a dialectician as any man whom he ever encountered; but his dialectics were never divorced from those actual conditions of society which limit the office of metaphysics in the science of government.

Among the instances of his application of theoretical reasoning to the circumstances of the community on whose constitution he was acting, a brief reference only can be made here to some of the more important topics on which he exercised a decisive influence over the deliberations and decisions of the convention. One of these related to the question whether the oath of office ought to be made to embrace any other religious test than is implied in the sanction of the oath itself.

The constitution of Massachusetts had hitherto required a declaration of belief in the Christian religion as a part of the oath of office. It is not strange that this should have been established by a people whose earliest polity, from the first planting of their colonies of Plymouth and Massachusetts Bay, approached very nearly to a theocracy. When the constitution of 1780 was formed, the principle of the original equality of all men in respect to civil rights, asserted in the Declaration of

Independence, led to the recognition of certain personal rights, which the Government, representing the whole people, is bound to secure to each individual of the society in return for his civil obedience and service, and his contribution to the public burdens. This principle was embodied in the Bill of Rights which made a part of the Constitution, by asserting the right of all individuals to be protected in the enjoyment of life, liberty, and property, according to standing laws. In progress of time there came to be a vague feeling that the acknowledged rights of persons ought to be deemed to embrace the holding of office; which, in the actual state of society, they could not embrace, if the qualification of belief in the Christian religion were required, since it was known that this belief was not universal. Against this feeling there was arrayed another, which had its origin partly in the old connection between church-membership and civil station, and partly in the opinion of certain classes that the constitution of a people who professed Christianity ought to require of their public officers a declaration of that faith. This feeling was opposed to any relaxation for the sake of making it possible for a few disbelievers to hold public office.

But, between these two opinions, there was on each side a question that needed a clear examination before it could be determined which of them or whether either of them was correct. On the one hand, is it true that the holding of office is or should be made one of the acknowledged rights of individuals on the same ground with the rights of life, liberty, and property? On the other hand, is it necessary to the safety of Christianity, or of civil government, to exclude from office those who are not qualified to profess a belief in that religion? Mr. Webster saw with his usual accuracy that the true answer to the first of these questions reduced the whole matter to an issue of expediency. In making that answer, he vindicated the right of the State to prescribe any qualifications for office that it might see fit to make, by showing that office cannot be claimed by individuals as a personal right, consistently with a freedom of choice in the electors. Practically, he argued, whether a belief in Christianity is or is not required as a constitutional qualification, the people will be governed in their choice by the sentiments which the candidates are understood to hold on this as well as on other subjects, and no one can complain. What the people can practically do, without giving just cause for complaint, they have a right previously to say in their fundamental law that they will do. It is otherwise with the rights of life, liberty, and property, for the protection of which civil society is instituted; while it is not instituted for the purpose of securing to all individuals a right to hold office.

Having thus disposed of the claim to office on the ground of right, he placed the question on grounds of expediency, by maintaining, *first*, that the exclusion of unbelievers is an exclusion for that which may involve the conscience; *second*, that, as a vast majority of the inhabitants of the State were believers in the Christian religion, it was sufficiently certain, without any constitutional requirement, that such persons would ordinarily be chosen to places of public trust; *third*, that a qualification which is practically needless, and is founded in an objection that may involve the consciences of men, is an unnecessary rigor that marks men with opprobrium, and has a tendency to proscription. As he did not propose to strike from the constitution the recognition of the benefits which civil society derives from the institutions of Christianity, he thought that the removal of the religious qualification for office could not be misconstrued. These views prevailed with the convention, and this qualification has ever since been abolished in Massachusetts.

The two most important, however, of the elaborate speeches made by Mr. Webster in this convention related to the basis of the Senate and the independence of the judiciary. With respect to the first of them, taking the whole speech as it was delivered, and as it stands in the report of the proceedings, probably there is not on record, anywhere, a more profound discussion of the principles on which a republican government can be so formed as to embrace means of affording a distinct protection to property. The problem of founding such a government, in part, upon property, without introducing a tendency to oligarchy, was the topic which Mr. Webster undertook to explain on this occasion; and whoever will examine the whole scope of his argument, and will compare it with what has been written and said elsewhere on the relations of property to government—observing the illustrations which he drew from what was then taking place in other countries, and the predictions which he made—will be satisfied of the importance of this speech. The subject came before the convention in consequence of a provision in the constitution of 1780, by which members of the Senate had been chosen in districts in proportion to the amount of taxable property in each district, while members of the House were chosen in proportion to the population of the towns represented. The framers of that constitution had, in this way, met the difficult problem in representative government, which arises when there are, or can be, no personal distinctions on which to found one of the branches of the legislative power. They selected representation by districts, in proportion to taxable property, because this is the only mode in which a difference of origin between two Chambers can be introduced, if the electors of both are to be the same, and the persons to be chosen are to have the same qualifications. In the course of forty years, there had been a considerable increase of the democratic spirit, and it had become necessary to answer those who insisted that this arrangement gave an undue advantage to the richer districts, and that it was, in principle, inconsistent with the character of American institutions. The question was, whether this provision of the old constitution should remain, or whether the representation in both branches of the Legislature should be based on population alone.

Mr. Webster divided this question into two. They were to inquire, he said, first, whether the legislative department was to be constructed with any other check than such as arises simply from dividing it into two Houses; secondly, if there was to be another and further check, in what manner should it be created? He then enforced the necessity, and explained the office, of checks and balances in the legislative department. Their utility, he said, arises from the truth that, in representative governments, that department is the leading and predominating power, whose tendency is to encroach on all the other departments. If all legislative power rests in a single House, it is very doubtful whether any proper independence can be given either to the executive or the judiciary, because there is no sufficient safeguard to insure deliberation and caution in its measures. If two Chambers are chosen upon the same basis, by the same electors, and for the same term of office, they will be actuated by the same feelings and interests; they will be substantially one body, though two in form. And if all legislative power be in one popular body, all other power, sooner or later, will be there also. There can be no sufficient check between two Chambers without some difference of origin, or interest, or feeling; and the great question had been, in this country, where to find, or how to create, this difference in governments entirely elective and popular.

In the actual circumstances of the State, Mr. Webster said, the question was not whether a representation in one branch, by districts, in proportion to their public taxes, was the best mode of constituting the necessary difference between the two branches, but whether it was better than no mode; for the whole practice and spirit of the people were opposed to the introduction of differences in the qualifications of electors, or of the persons to be chosen, or in the manner of making the appointments. They had therefore to consider the question, whether property, not as an element of personal power in proportion to the amount of personal possessions, but in a general sense, and in a general form, should have its weight and influence in political arrangements.

In the discussion of this part of the subject, he exhibited his thorough understanding of the fact that republican government, as it has grown up in this country, rests not more on political constitutions than on the laws which regulate the descent and distribution of property. He maintained then, as he always maintained, that our constitutions are the fruit of the general equality of property which our laws and customs have produced; an equality which began before we had constitutions, and which fixed the future frame and forms of our governments. In the great central fact of the division of the soil among a multitude of small proprietors, tending constantly to produce a general distribution of all property, lay the truth that, in the distribution of political power, the interests of property may be consulted and provided for, without divorcing them from the interests of the people. In all countries, it is true that, in the absence of military force, political power naturally and necessarily goes into the hands which hold the property; in this country, it goes into the hands of the people, because the people, individually, possess property more generally than has been known elsewhere.

In illustration of the effect produced upon republican institutions by the equal or the unequal distribution of property, Mr. Webster resorted to the instances of England and France. In respect to the former, he pointed out tendencies that we have since seen progressing to very decided results; and, in regard to the latter, he made a prediction which came afterward to a literal fulfilment. In England, he said, the process of subdivision of property, which had begun after the abolition of the feudal system and the introduction of commerce, had been retarded within the last half century. Large estates were growing larger, and the number of those who held no property was rapidly increasing. This state of things was destined to have a powerful effect on the British Constitution; because the great inequality of property tended to produce and to increase the danger that those who possessed it would be dispossessed by force; or, in other words, that the government might be overturned. Another half century has nearly elapsed since Mr. Webster expressed these opinions; and we have seen this tendency become the great cause of anxiety to British statesmen, and the controlling reason for changes which have amounted almost to a revolution, thus far fortunately peaceful, but of which we have not yet seen the issues or the end.

In the case of France, the effect of the distribution of property upon the stability and forms of the government was, in Mr. Webster's opinion, destined to be not less striking and still more direct, although the process that was going on was the reverse of that which was to be witnessed in England. The law of descents then prevailing in France tended to the minute subdivision of property, and to the creation of a great number of small proprietors. The opinion then generally held in Europe was, that the masses of the people would become too poor to resist the encroachments of executive power. Mr. Webster entertained an exactly opposite opinion. He predicted that if the government did not change the law, the law in half a century would change the government; and that this change would be not in favor of the power of the crown, as European writers had supposed, but against it. He founded this opinion upon the experience which we have had in this country, that a multitude of small proprietors, acting with intelligence, and the enthusiasm that springs from a common cause, constitute an invincible power, which sooner or later, in the absence of military force, acts upon and controls the political institutions. In six years after this prediction was made, the King of France, at the opening of the Legislative Chambers, declared that the progressive partitioning of lands was essentially contrary to the spirit of a monarchical government, and would enfeeble the guaranties which the charter had given to his throne and his subjects.

The Revolution of 1830 followed, and displaced the elder branch of the Bourbons—a revolution that was made through the influence of the classes described by Mr. Webster as the small proprietors, who were not content with the guaranties of the charter which the King sought to uphold by legislation that would prevent the minute subdivision of property.

The contrast which these two examples presented, when placed in opposition to the state of things in this country, appeared to Mr. Webster to furnish another reason for preserving to property that distinct means of protection which had been introduced by making it the origin of the check which the construction of the Legislature required. All property being subject to taxation, for the purpose of maintaining a system of public education, in which the children of the poor can participate equally with the children of the rich, it was entitled to the respect and care of government, because, in a very important way, it aids in sustaining government by paying for the education of the people.

The effect of this speech and of a very powerful one made by Judge Story, who had preceded Mr. Webster in the discussion, was, that the existing basis of the Senate was retained. It has since been changed: and, whatever may have been the reasons for that change, it has become apparent in Massachusetts, as it has elsewhere, that, where there is no difference of origin between the two branches of a legislative body, there will be no difference of sentiment and feeling: all will be actuated by the same motives and be under the same influences: and thus the practical value of a division into two Chambers will be greatly diminished by the absence of every efficient check.

The constitution of 1780, adopting the practice which had been introduced in England, of making judges removable from office by the crown only on an address of Parliament, had made them removable in like manner by the State Executive on an address of the two Houses of the Legislature. At the same time the term of the judicial office in Massachusetts was during good behavior: and there can be no doubt that it was the original purpose of the people to render the judiciary completely independent of the other departments. An error, however, had crept in, which appeared to mar the theory of independence which the people had intended to establish, and which made that theory practically less operative than it ought to be. It had not been sufficiently considered that the purpose of the change in England, from a naked power of removal by the crown to a power of removal on an address of Parliament, was to shield the judges against the arbitrary influence of the crown; and that this change, while it had avoided one evil, had introduced what was a less but what was still another evil. It had been assumed, in Massachusetts, to be necessary to retain the removal by address, in order to meet cases of incompetency or personal misconduct; impeachment being regarded as the appropriate remedy for official misconduct. If this necessity exists, still, a naked power in a bare majority of the Legislature, to pass an address for the removal of a judge from office, must be allowed to be an imperfection; and this imperfection was increased in the Massachusetts constitution of 1780, by the absence of any provision requiring the reasons to be assigned, or admitting the judge to be heard.

To correct this, Mr. Webster and others of the most prominent members of the convention desired to introduce a provision that would require an address of removal to be passed by the votes of two-thirds of each House. On this proposition Mr. Webster made the speech on the independence of the judiciary, which now stands in the third volume of his works. The proposition was not adopted. On its rejection, Mr. Webster immediately introduced a resolution, declaring that no address for the removal of any judicial officer should pass either House of the Legislature, until the causes for such removal are first stated and entered on the journal, and that a copy thereof shall be served on the person in office, so that he may be admitted to a hearing in his defence before each House. This was adopted, and afterward became a part of the constitution.

On a great many other subjects Mr. Webster took a leading part in this convention. So important, indeed, was his whole action in this body, that it gave him, to use the words of another, "a degree of confidence, respect, and authority, to which few in that ancient Commonwealth could lay claim."[1] The mere amount of labor which he performed, in this revision of the constitution of the State, impressed the members and the public not less than the ease and readiness or the commanding ability which he brought to the work.

But, while his duties in that convention would seem to have been enough to fill the measure of any man's powers, he was at the same time engaged in writing the celebrated discourse which he delivered at Plymouth, on the two hundredth anniversary of its settlement, December 22, 1820. It has been already intimated that this was a new and untried field for Mr. Webster to enter. The orations which he had delivered on the 4th of July, nearly all of them before he was five-and-twenty, may be regarded, as he himself once said of them, as boyish performances. The subject of his P. B. K. oration in 1809, which was a merely literary discourse, and that of his address before the Washington Benevolent Society of Portsmouth in 1812, which was purely political, had neither of them approached in grandeur the theme on which he was now to appear in the character of an orator. Nor had he been, since those comparatively unimportant occasions, in the habit of appearing before the public in that character, or of discussing subjects with a view to any other than business purposes. He was known to be the possessor of great eloquence, to be a profound and original writer, and master of a singularly correct and perspicuous English style. Still, the construction of one of those capital discourses, which, adapted to the demands of

[1] Philadelphia Quarterly Review, 1831.

a great subject, and an important historical event, shall satisfy the thoughts and feelings at once of the most and the least cultivated of a popular audience, and then shall remain, when it comes to be addressed through the press to the wider audience of a nation, a monument of fame to the occasion and the speaker, was what he had not hitherto undertaken.

No occasion or subject, however, could have been presented to Mr. Webster better fitted to call forth his powers as an orator, than the celebration, at the end of two centuries, of the first settlement of New England. A child of New England and her institutions, his nature was yet too large and comprehensive to permit him to present those institutions to the world in any other light than that in which every observer of human progress, and every admirer of human greatness, can recognize what they have done for America and for mankind. At no part of his life had he any tendency to exalt one portion of his country over another; nor did this occasion demand of him any narrow and local spirit of boasting. It found in him an intellect that could grasp the largest of the relations between the foundation of the civil and religious polity of New England, and the growth and expansion of the United States; which could describe without exaggeration, and yet with an epic dignity, the peculiar effects of the colonization, planted from England in America, on the knowledge, the sentiments, and the prospects of civilization.[1]

[1] I deem this the appropriate place to quote Mr. Webster's sentiments respecting the personal characteristics of the early settlers of New England, as I find them expressed in a letter to his nephew, Mr. Haddock, written in 1826:

"In regard to the moral character generally of our ancestors, the settlers of New England, my opinion is, that they possessed all the Christian virtues, but charity; and they seem never to have doubted that they possessed that also. And nobody could accuse their system or their practice but of one vice, and that was religious hypocrisy, of which they had an infusion, without ever being sensible of it.

"It necessarily resulted from that disposition which they cherished, of subjecting men's external conduct, in all particulars, to the influence and government of express rule and precept, either of church or state. That always makes hypocrites and formalists; it leads men to rely on mint and cummin. A man thought it an act of merit, if we may take the blue laws of Connecticut for authority, not to walk within ten feet of his wife in their way to church; as some people, nowadays, think it a merit to restrain their daughters from a village dance; one is quite as sensible and as much to do with religion as the other. Indeed, it is the universal tendency of strong religious excitement, a tendency of our infirm nature, growing out of our weaknesses and our vices, to run into observances and make a strong merit of external acts. Our excellent ancestors did not escape the influence of this propensity; but they had so many other high and pure virtues, that this spot

Nearly fifty years have elapsed since the delivery of this memorable oration; and of those who heard it, and heard it with minds and tastes sufficiently matured to comprehend and enjoy its power and beauty, there can be but few survivors. I am able, however, to quote from Mr. Ticknor a description which brings the scene and the orator vividly before us:

"I went to Plymouth on the 21st of December, 1820, with Mr. and Mrs. Webster, Mr. and Mrs. I. P. Davis, Miss Stockton, Mr. F. C. Gray, and Miss Mary Mason. Where we stopped to dine we overtook fifty or sixty persons, among whom were Colonel Perkins, Mrs. S. G. Perkins, Mr. E. Everett, and many others of our acquaintance. Mr. Webster had been a little uninterested during the morning drive, wearied perhaps by his labors in the convention, and partly occupied with thoughts of the following day. But at the little half-way house, where we all crowded into two or three small rooms, we had a very merry time, and Mr. Webster was as gay as any one. In the evening at Plymouth every thing had the air of a *fête;* the houses of the principal street—in one of which we lodged—were all lighted up, so that the street itself was illuminated by them, and a band of music went up and down, followed by a crowd, while it serenaded the many strangers already collected from a distance for the great centennary anniversary. Old Mr. Samuel Davis, a sort of embodiment of the Pilgrim traditions of the seventeenth century, and others of the principal inhabitants of Plymouth, paid their respects to Mr. Webster in the course of the evening, and made it very agreeable, from the recollections that they brought with them and the conversation that naturally followed.

"In the morning I went with Mr. Webster to the church where he was to deliver the oration. It was the old First Church—Dr. Kendall's. He did not find the pulpit convenient for his purpose, and after making

should not give offence. They were a wonderful people. This very failing, of which I have spoken, leaned so much on the virtues of decision, sense of duty, and the feeling that will bear no compromise with what it thinks wrong, that I forgive it to them. The determined spirit with which they resisted every approach of what they thought evil, was itself a great virtue. 'Of itself it is harmless, but it leads, or may lead, to evil.' This was their answer, and perhaps there is something in it; but then it may be said of almost every thing. The vice of the argument, as an argument, is, that it proves too much. Eating, drinking, sleeping, conversation, are all equally under its condemnation. But though indefensible as a rule of conduct, some general consequences followed from the spirit which accompanied it, which consequences are extremely useful. It sharpened the sight for the discovery of political evils. The tea-tax, for example, was not oppressive, as a tax; it was too small for that. It was opposed on principle. 'It led or might lead to other taxes.' Our fathers acted on system; and the inquiry with them was, not whether the thing was bearable, but whether it was right. I verily believe, although I do not like creeds in religious matters, that creeds had something to do with the Revolution. In their religious controversies, the people of New England had always been accustomed to stand on points; and when Lord North undertook to tax them, they stood on points also. It so happened, fortunately, that their opposition to Lord North was a point on which they all united.

two or three experiments, determined to speak from the deacon's seat under it. An extemporaneous table, covered with a green baize cloth, was arranged for the occasion, and, when the procession entered the church, every thing looked very appropriate, though, when the arrangement was first suggested, it sounded rather odd. The building was crowded: indeed, the streets had seemed so all the morning, for the weather was fine, and the whole population was astir as for a holiday. The oration was an hour and fifty minutes long, but the whole of what was printed a year afterward (for it was a year before it made its appearance) was not delivered. His manner was very fine—quite various in the different parts. The passage about the slave-trade was delivered with a power of indignation such as I never witnessed on any other occasion. That at the end, when, spreading his arms as if to embrace them, he welcomed future generations to the great inheritance which we have enjoyed, was spoken with the most attractive sweetness, and that peculiar smile which in him was always so charming. The effect of the whole was very great. As soon as he got home to our lodgings, all the principal people then in Plymouth crowded about him. He was full of animation and radiant with happiness. But there was something about him very grand and imposing at the same time. In a letter which I wrote the same day, I said that 'he seemed as if he were like the mount that might not be touched, and that burned with fire.' I have the same recollection of him still. I never saw him at any time when he seemed to me to be more conscious of his own powers, or to have a more true and natural enjoyment from their possession.

"At the public dinner the same day, he was not much moved by the great enthusiasm around him, which had chiefly been excited by himself. At the ball that followed, he was agreeable to everybody and nothing more; but when we came home he was as frolicsome as a school-boy, laughing and talking, and making merry with Mrs. Webster, Mrs. Davis, and Mrs. Rotch, the daughter of his old friend Stockton,[1] till two o'clock in the morning. The next day we came back to Boston, but I remember nothing of the return."

The Plymouth discourse was not published until about a year after its delivery. Public expectation had been greatly excited by the accounts of those who heard it, and the commendations of the local press. The following letters, addressed to Mr. Webster by two persons widely differing in their mental characteristics, are but specimens of the manner in which it was received.

[PRESIDENT JOHN ADAMS TO MR. WEBSTER.]

"MONTEZILLO, *December* 23, 1821.

"DEAR SIR: I thank you for your discourse, delivered at Plymouth, on

[1] The first Senator of that family, and signer of the Declaration of Independence, father of the late Commodore Stockton.

the termination of the second century of the landing of our fathers. Unable to read it from defect of sight, it was last night read to me by our friend Shaw.[1] The fullest justice that I could do it would be to transcribe it at full length. It is the effort of a great mind, richly stored with every species of information. If there be an American who can read it without tears, I am not that American. It enters more perfectly into the genuine spirit of New England than any production I ever read. The observations on the Greeks and Romans; on colonization in general; on the West India Islands; on the past, present, and future of America, and on the slave-trade, are sagacious, profound, and affecting in a high degree.

"Mr. Burke is no longer entitled to the praise—the most consummate orator of modern times.

"What can I say of what regards myself? To my humble name, *Exegisti monumentum aere perennius.*'

"This oration will be read five hundred years hence with as much rapture as it was heard. It ought to be read at the end of every century, and indeed at the end of every year, forever and ever.

"I am, sir, with the profoundest esteem, your obliged friend and very humble servant,

"JOHN ADAMS.

"The Honorable Daniel Webster."

[CHANCELLOR KENT TO MR. WEBSTER.]

"ALBANY, *December* 29, 1821.

"MY DEAR SIR: Be pleased to accept my thanks for the receipt and perusal of your Plymouth Discourse, which came by yesterday's mail. The reflections, the sentiments, the morals, the patriotism, the eloquence, the imagination, of this admirable production are exactly what I anticipated; elevated, just, and true. I think it is also embellished by a style distinguished for purity, taste, and simplicity. Excuse me for this once, and I will not trespass in this manner again. I am proud to be able to trace my own lineage back to the Pilgrims of New England, and prouder still that I have been thought deserving of the esteem and friendship of some of the brightest of their descendants.

"Permit Mrs. Kent and me to unite in presenting our best respects, and the compliments of the season, to Mrs. Webster, and be assured of the constant esteem and regard of your friend and most obedient servant,

"JAMES KENT.

"Honorable D. Webster."

Respecting subsequent appreciation, it can only be necessary to say that this discourse has become classical in our literature, and that it is generally regarded as the corner-stone of Mr.

[1] William Smith Shaw, founder of the Boston Athenæum, and for many years its librarian, was a near relative of the two Presidents Adams, and during the administration of the elder he filled the office of private secretary to the President.—(Ticknor's Life of Prescott the historian, p. 9.)

Webster's fame as an orator. In this department he was the founder of his own school, in which no one has become his equal. From that day it became universally known that he who had achieved so much reputation in legislative assemblies, in the forum, and in the councils of the wise in civil affairs, was also to rank among the most eminent of ancient or modern orators; and that whenever men's thoughts and feelings demanded, for some peculiarly high national festival of the reason and the heart, the interpretation and expression of the loftiest eloquence, they were to turn instinctively to him to fill the noblest cravings of their intellectual natures, and to move the deepest sources of their patriotism.

We can only conjecture what the literature of England might have contained if Chatham had been called upon to treat, in a formal, public discourse, such an event as the revolution which finally expelled the Stuarts; or if Burke had been invited to commemorate the defeat of the Armada and all the consequences which flowed from the safety it insured to Elizabeth's Protestant throne. But it has not been the habit of Englishmen to celebrate the deeds of their ancestors through the eloquence of their greatest living orators, as it has been ours. In this department of demonstrative oratory we have been more prolific than any other nation of modern times. Vast numbers of these productions perish, of course, at their birth. But who would have preferred that this national habit had never been formed, and have been content never to have had the Plymouth Discourse, the first Bunker Hill oration, and the eulogy on Adams and Jefferson, of Daniel Webster? The question implies a loss for which we can imagine no compensation. Among the remains of ancient oratory there have come down to us a few master-pieces of public speech, in which we admire the consummate specimens of a national eloquence and the undying fruits of genius. We cannot know whether our own language, after being lost as a vernacular tongue, will be studied as we now study the languages of Greece and Rome. But, if, like them, it has capacities for such preservation, it will be preserved in the productions of its great orators as long as in any other of its forms of prose composition.

After the delivery of the Plymouth Oration in December, 1820, the whole of the year 1821 was filled with private and professional pursuits. Mr. Webster's engagements at this time in the Supreme Court of Massachusetts and the Circuit Court of the United States for the first circuit were incessant. In the latter they embraced, among many other causes of no great public importance, the case of *La Jeune Eugénie*, a vessel captured by an American cruiser on the coast of Africa, for being engaged in the slave-trade, and sailing at the time of capture under the French flag and French papers. She was claimed, in the proceedings instituted in Boston, by French owners; and if such was her national character, she could be condemned only upon the ground that the slave-trade was contrary to the law of nations. Mr. Webster argued that the slave-trade was a violation of the law of nations, first, because it is contrary to the law of nature which is a component part of the law of nations; and secondly, that, having been prohibited to their own subjects by nearly all civilized nations, it might now be deemed contrary to the conventional law of nations. He succeeded in satisfying Mr. Justice Story, before whom the cause was heard, that these were the true principles to be applied to the case; and accordingly, in May, 1822, that very eminent judge pronounced the elaborate opinion which is reported in the second volume of Mason's Reports, and in which he held that the African slave-trade, abstractly considered, is inconsistent with the law of nations, and that a claim founded upon it may be repelled in any court where it is asserted, unless the trade be legalized by the nation to which the claimant belongs.[1]

Another of Mr. Webster's professional engagements during this year consisted in the defence of Judge James Prescott, before the Senate of Massachusetts sitting as a court for the trial

[1] At the time when this case was argued, the case of *Le Louis*, decided in 1817 by Sir William Scott, in which he held that trading in slaves was not a crime by the universal law of nations, had not been published in the regular reports of the High Court of Admiralty, but the decision was cited and commented on in the argument of the case of *La Jeune Eugénie*, and was directly dissented from by Judge Story in his opinion. The second volume of Dodson's Reports, containing this judgment of Sir William Scott, appears to have reached this country soon after the argument of the case of *La Jeune Eugénie*. Writing to Judge Story for a loan of the volume, Mr. Webster said, "I very much fear my Lord Stowell has missed a figure. However, I suppose, as usual, he has given plausible reasons." (Compare 2 Dodson, 210, and 2 Mason, 409.)

of an impeachment. Prescott was for twenty years judge of probate for the county of Middlesex; and, after a course of generally useful and respectable administration of the duties of that office, he was impeached on charges of having taken illegal fees from persons having business in his court. The charge did not extend to bribery, but only to the taking of fees for official services to which no fee was attached by law, and to the holding of special courts not authorized by statute. The whole prosecution involved only some very paltry sums, received or demanded by the judge doubtless imprudently and indelicately; and the impeachment itself developed a very strong illustration of the public inexpediency of compensating judges by fees instead of by fixed salaries—a practice which was then discontinued in Massachusetts in relation to all judges except the judges of probate, but which has since been totally changed in that Commonwealth, as it has been elsewhere. The case was attended with a good deal of excitement and prejudice, but the unfortunate judge could scarcely be said to have acted corruptly. Mr. Webster felt much compassion for him, especially as the articles exhibited against him were somewhat vague. In a very powerful argument, which is preserved among Mr. Webster's works, he reasoned—with that close and penetrating logic which was so characteristic of him, and which was all that he could bring to bear upon a case whose aspect was bad—that the charges had not been set forth and proved with the reasonable accuracy and certainty which the law and the constitution required. In this respect, the argument will always remain an important source of information concerning the principles of accusation and proof that ought to be followed on the trial of impeachments. Its well-known exordium stands as one of the most impressive specimens of Mr. Webster's forensic eloquence.[1]

While Mr. Webster was engaged in the diligent practice of his profession, from which his emoluments at this time were very large, he was unexpectedly and strongly solicited in the autumn of 1822, by many leading gentlemen in Boston, to become their Representative in the next Congress. A meeting of delegates from all the wards of the city appointed a committee to wait upon him and urge his acceptance of a nomina-

[1] Works, v., 502–545.

tion. One of these gentlemen, on the day after this committee was appointed, entered Mr. Webster's office, and found him reading. "Mr. Webster," said his visitor, "I come to ask you to throw down your law-books and enter the service of the public; for to the public you belong. I know what sacrifices we demand of you, but we must rely on your patriotism. We cannot take a refusal."[1] A few days afterward, a formal requisition, signed by all the committee, was presented to him, and he had to make a decision on this, as I believe it to have been to him, not very welcome application. It is not improbable that he may have looked forward to a return to public life in some other position than one which he had formerly filled. He had not ceased to take a strong interest in whatever concerned the country or in what was passing abroad; he was conscious of his own great aptitude for political discussions, and he undoubtedly had that within him for which the exercise of his powers in the walks of his profession, however high they lay along the roads to fame, was not a complete satisfaction. But he had two very good reasons for not being entirely pleased with the invitation of his Boston friends. His circumstances were not so independent as he hoped in a few years more of professional labor to make them;[2] and having once served with distinction in the House of Representatives, and voluntarily retired from it, he did not particularly wish, at the age of forty, to return to that body. But he had become an adopted citizen of Massachusetts, where he had been welcomed with the highest respect and consideration, and he did not think that it became him to reject the proposed honor of representing such a city as Boston in the halls of Congress. He accepted the nomination, and was elected that autumn by a very large majority of the votes.

[1] The late William Sturgis, Esq., the gentleman referred to, was himself my authority for this anecdote.

[2] It has been stated in a previous chapter that Mr. Webster assumed the payment of his father's debts. He would not suffer his father's estate to be declared insolvent, according to the provisions of the New-Hampshire law; and the consequence was, that his father's debts remained a heavy burden upon him, from which he did not free himself until some time after his removal to Boston.

CHAPTER X.

1823–1824.

REËNTERS CONGRESS—SPEECH ON THE GREEK REVOLUTION—TARIFF OF 1824—PROPOSED CHANGES IN THE JUDICIAL SYSTEM—THE CASE OF GIBBONS *vs.* OGDEN—CANDIDACY OF MR. JOHN QUINCY ADAMS—FIRST VISIT TO MARSHFIELD—REËLECTED TO CONGRESS.

ON the return of Mr. Webster to Congress in December, 1823, after a retirement of six years, he brought a great access of reputation; for, although he had been so long out of public station, he had not been withdrawn from the public eye; and the opportunities of distinction, which he had foregone by abstinence from political affairs, had been more than compensated by the fame which he had acquired as a lawyer and an orator, and which now filled the country. His course was likely to be watched with great interest by all, with some degree of jealousy by a few. The "Federal" party, with which he had acted during his former service in Congress, was no longer an existing organization; and such had been the effect of Mr. Monroe's administration on former political distinctions, that there could scarcely be said to be any well-defined "Republican" party remaining. But the old party feelings, although much abated, had not entirely worn themselves out, nor had the old names wholly ceased to be used. A person of so much distinction, therefore, as Mr. Webster, who had been regarded as a Federalist, in coming again into Congress, came among some who were not likely to forget that he had been their political opponent.

Mr. Clay was chosen Speaker. Friendly, although not intimate, personal relations had all along existed between him and Mr. Webster; but Mr. Clay had been an ardent leader during the war on the side of an Administration, some of whose measures Mr. Webster had felt it to be his duty to oppose. Mr. Clay was now one of five or six candidates for the presidency from among whom a choice was to be made, but he probably did not count upon the support of Mr. Webster. The latter entertained a sincere respect for Mr. Clay's public character, and regarded him as a liberal and honorable man, not unfriendly in his general feeling; yet he did not anticipate that, in the organization and arrangement of the affairs of the House, Mr. Clay would venture entirely to disregard old lines of distinction, although he supposed that in his own case the Speaker would not be afraid to shake off any party trammels that might have formerly existed. The result was, that, without any communication between them or their respective friends, Mr. Clay placed Mr. Webster at the head of the Judiciary Committee; an appointment which, under all the circumstances, was the most fit which he could have made, and one that was doubtless made from a sense of its fitness.

In the presidential election that was then approaching, Mr. Webster felt less interest than he did in another subject. He had long been an anxious observer of the heroic struggle which the Greeks had maintained against their Turkish oppressors; he had studied the civil and military aspects of the Greek Revolution with the closest attention: he had become satisfied that the Greeks had character enough to carry them through the contest with success; and he not only felt, in common with the whole people of this country, a warm sympathy in their cause, but he saw, as not many others did, in the principles and policy proclaimed by the allied governments of Europe, and in the general indifference of the statesmen of Europe to the result of this contest, great cause of danger to liberty throughout the world. He determined therefore to do or say something in behalf of the Greeks at an early period of the session.

Before deciding on the step to be taken, he conferred with

Mr. Rufus King, Mr. Clay, and other gentlemen, all of whom approved of what he proposed to do. He also consulted the President; but, as the message, which Mr. Monroe was about to send in to Congress, had taken high ground as to interference by European powers in the affairs of this continent, he was reluctant to have the appearance of interfering in the concerns of the other. This did not weigh much with Mr. Webster, who thought that "we have as much community with the Greeks as with the inhabitants of the Andes and the dwellers on the borders of the Vermilion Sea."[1] The message, however, when it appeared, was found to contain an expression of sympathy for the Greeks, which was closed with something very like an official statement that they were to be regarded as having in fact achieved their independence. "From the facts," said the President, "which have come to our knowledge, there is good cause to believe that their enemy has lost forever all dominion over them; that Greece will become an independent power. That she may attain that rank is the object of our most ardent wishes."[2]

After the House had been in session a few days, Mr. Webster introduced the following resolution:

> "That provision ought to be made by law for defraying the expense incident to the appointment of an agent or commissioner to Greece, whenever the President shall deem it expedient to make such appointment."

After a few explanatory remarks, he desired that the resolution might lie upon the table. It was taken up in Committee of the Whole on the 19th of January. A large and fashionable audience had assembled in the galleries to hear Mr. Webster. It was supposed that he meant to take advantage of the almost universal popular sympathy for the Greeks, and the classical associations of the subject, in order to make a brilliant oration, which would bring him again before the public with renewed *éclat*.[3] Nothing could have been further from his purpose. The crowds which had come to listen to an anticipated display of rhetoric, or the members who supposed that he contemplated a "move" on the political chess-board, were astonished at the

[1] Correspondence, i., 332, 333.

[2] Mr. Monroe's message of December 2, 1823. This was the message which promulgated the famous (so-called) "Monroe Doctrine."

[3] Philadelphia Quarterly for 1831.

development which he made of the subject, and the direction which he gave to it. Instead of addressing himself to the vague sympathies of the popular heart, he proceeded to enlighten and instruct the public mind, not only of America but of Europe, respecting the principles which had been announced by the "Holy Alliance," as the basis on which they intended to resist the efforts of any people to change their government or their political relations. He analyzed all the European Congresses, from that of Paris in 1814, to that of Laybach in 1821, and brought into prominent relief the doctrines which resulted from them—that all sovereigns have an interest and a right to control all nations in any attempt which they may make against the government that is over them. He denounced this principle as an infraction of the public law, and maintained that the liberty of every civilized people on the globe was concerned in putting it down.

This state of things, he contended, called emphatically upon us, not for direct interference, but for an expression of our opinion in terms that could not be mistaken. The present age was characterized by a tendency to limited governments; the enlightened part of mankind had very distinctly evinced a desire to take a share, at least, in the government of themselves. But there was an antagonistic principle at work, which, if not resisted, would prostrate the liberties of the whole civilized world. "They are doctrines," said Mr. Webster, "which have been conceived with great sagacity, they are pursued with unbroken perseverance, and they bring to their support a million and a half of bayonets."

"It was not by war," he continued, "that we were to propagate our sentiments in favor of the liberties of mankind. Formerly, indeed, there was no means of making an impression on nations but by fleets and armies; but the age had undergone a change; there is now a force in public opinion, which, in the end, will outweigh all the physical force that can be brought against it."

He then passed to the modern history of Greece, her sufferings, and the apathy with which the neighboring nations, professedly Christian, had looked on; an apathy, he said, which was a disgrace to Europe. A rapid survey of the progress and present condition of the Greek Revolution followed, which brought him to the position taken in the President's message, with which, he contended, his resolution was in entire harmony, for it proposed nothing but to enable the President to send a commissioner to Greece whenever he should think proper. Its passage would violate no neutrality, break no engagements with the Porte, for we had none; but it would assure the Greeks of our sympathy, and inspire them with fresh constancy in their struggle. "I cannot say, sir," he concluded, "that they will succeed; that rests with Heaven. But, for myself, if I should hear to-morrow that they have failed, that their last phalanx had sunk beneath the Turkish scimetar, that the flames of their last city had gone down into its ashes, and that naught remained but the wide, melancholy waste where Greece once was, I should still reflect, with the most heartfelt satisfaction, that I have asked you, in the name of seven millions of freemen, that you would give them, at least, the cheering of one friendly voice."

When Mr. Webster had concluded his speech, Mr. Clay laid upon the table a resolution which declared that the people of the United States would not see, without serious inquietude, any forcible interposition by the allied powers in behalf of Spain, to reduce the South-American republics to their former subjection. The discussion then went on upon Mr. Webster's resolution concerning Greece. The cry of "Quixotism" was immediately raised, especially by Mr. Randolph, who attacked both Mr. Webster and Mr. Clay with his usual sarcasm. The resolutions of both, he said, led to war. An effort was made to have the committee rise. This called up Mr. Clay, who defended Mr. Webster's resolution as well as his own; the latter he did not mean to press at that time, but he advocated the passage of the former at once. A long discussion ensued, in the course of which Mr. Clay came out in great force in further defence of Mr. Webster's proposition. He saw that much of the opposition to it was personal, and he at once administered a rebuke to the party feeling which dictated that opposition in his most spirited manner. He said:

"I know that, at least, some of the objections to the original proposal are occasioned by the source from which it proceeded. There are individuals in this House who look at the mover of this resolution as if its value or importance were to be measured by inquiring who brought it forward. Sir, I have long had the pleasure of knowing the honorable gentleman who originated this resolution; I have sometimes had the pleasure of acting with him; and I would suggest to those to whom I have alluded, that, if they seek to be regarded as the sentinels of freedom, they must disregard the source from which any measure favorable to its interest may happen to have proceeded, and must take it upon its own intrinsic merits. If a gentleman, who happens to belong to a different party, in political sentiment, shall bring forward a proposition fraught with liberal principles and noble sentiments, is it to be rejected for his sake? If this is the case, we cease to be Republicans; and those who act on principles the reverse of ours will be the men who truly deserve that name; and, sir, if all Republicans must oppose this doctrine, and all Federalists advocate it, I, for one, shall cease to be a Republican, and shall become a Federalist."

Mr. Clay could always be stung by the taunts of Mr. Randolph, and, on this occasion, his indignation kindled all the fires of his eloquence, and pointed it with his utmost scorn, which he doubtless unbridled the more readily, as he was conscious that a great public sentiment existed behind him, that would justify the adoption of Mr. Webster's resolution. His speech was bold, decisive, and uncompromising. "Go home," he said, in conclusion, "go home, if you dare; go home, if you can, to your constituents, and tell them that you voted it down. Meet, if you dare, the appalling countenances of those who sent you here (he meant no defiance), and tell them that you shrank from the declaration of your own sentiments; that you cannot tell how, but that some unknown dread, some indescribable apprehension, some indefinable danger, affrighted you; that the spectres of scimetars and crowns and crescents gleamed before you, and alarmed you; and that you suppressed all the noble feelings prompted by religion, by liberty, by national independence, and by humanity." He could not bring himself to believe, Mr. Clay said, that such would be the feeling of a majority of this House. But, for himself, though every friend of the measure should desert it, and he be left to stand alone with the gentleman from Massachusetts, he would give to the resolution the poor sanction of his unqualified approbation.[1]

[1] Annals of Congress: Eighteenth Congress, 1171–1177.

The discussion was further continued until the 26th of January, when, in consequence of the unwillingness manifested either to adopt Mr. Webster's resolution, or any modification of it, he consented that the Committee of the Whole should rise without taking a vote. But his purpose was answered. He had drawn the attention of the world to the principles on which the Holy Alliance was arrayed against the liberties of nations. His speech, we are told by one who watched its circulation and influence, "besides being printed wherever the English tongue is spoken, has been circulated through South America, and published in nearly every one of the civilized languages of Europe, including the Spanish and Greek."[1] At the time this statement was publicly made (1831), Mr. Webster could coolly review the object which he had in view in making the Greek speech of 1824. The following note, now before me, in MS., from him to the writer of the article in the *Philadelphia Quarterly*, will be read with interest:

"One word about the Greek speech. I think I am more fond of this child than of any of the family. My object, when the resolution was introduced, was not understood. It was imagined that, seeing the existence of a warm public sympathy for the suffering Greeks, the purpose was only to make a speech responsive and gratifying to that sympathy. The real object was larger. It was to take occasion of the Greek Revolution, and the conduct held in regard to it by the great Continental powers, to exhibit the principles laid down by those powers, as the basis on which they meant to maintain the peace of Europe. This purpose made it necessary to examine accurately the proceedings of all the Congresses, from that of Paris, in 1814, to that of Laybach, in 1821. I read those proceedings with a good deal of attention, and endeavored to extract the principle on which they were founded. There is nothing in the book[2] which I think so well of as parts of this speech. Events have shown that some opinions here expressed were well founded. A revolution has taken place, and the people reform their constitution, and then invite an individual to the throne, *on condition* of governing according to the constitution.[3] Belgium is doing the same; Poland is attempting to do the same. This is in the spirit of the English Revolution of 1688; but it is 'flat burglary' according to the law of Laybach.

"I was something of a prophet, too, in regard to the duration of the late French monarchy. See Plymouth Discourse. But enough; I am

[1] Philadelphia Quarterly for 1831.

[2] The edition of his speeches, then recently published, and reviewed by the gentleman to whom the note was addressed.

[3] The case of Louis Philippe.

tired of saying 'I,' 'me,' and 'mine.' My dear sir, if the world cannot see the merits of my illustrious works, why should I (or why should you) trouble ourselves to point them out?"

Before leaving the Greek speech, it may be well to say that it was a common complaint among Mr. Webster's friends, at that time, that he took but little pains in the publication of his speeches. On this occasion Mr. Hopkinson wrote to him:

"You are generally too careless of yourself and your reputation; and, content with doing a thing well, you have too little solicitude about the proof of it to the world. Your views of the character, object, and extent of the Holy Alliance, have particularly attracted public attention for their strength and novelty in many particulars. Develop yourself fully on this subject; it is of vast interest, and may be illustrated with great force by their declarations and conduct for the last two years. It is, in one respect, a misfortune for a man to obtain a high eminence of character; he is required always to maintain it, and this calls for a constant vigilance and effort, which are not always convenient. Besides, few have judgment to know of what a subject is capable, and expect to see the same power displayed, whether an oak is to be uprooted, or a rose plucked from its bush. I agree with Mr. Randolph, in his surprise that you should find so much to be well said on your resolution. It is only a mind of great resources, with a genius creative and prolific, that could have connected it with so much important and interesting matter. Not one of your opponents has met you fairly on your own ground. Some have treated the resolution as an abstract declaration of war, and others have assumed that it would certainly lead to war; and thus, mounted on a monster of their own creation, they have gone off at full speed, spreading devastation and terror in their path. It is thus with men who must speak, and can't argue. Of this *genus* I have seen so many, especially in the great hall of Congress, that I know them from the first jump they take."

Prompted by this friendly advice, Mr. Webster did prepare a suitable report of this speech, which is substantially the same with that now contained in the third volume of his works. But he pruned the actual speech a good deal when this edition was published, in 1851, and perhaps did it some injustice, as he was apt to do, from the severity with which he occasionally handled his own productions. A contemporaneous report, that appeared in the *National Intelligencer*, is somewhat more full, although it wants the animation of the first pronoun.[1]

[1] This report is repeated in the Annals of Congress, Eighteenth Congress, first session.

The President's message, at the opening of this session, had recommended a revision of the tariff; and accordingly an elaborate bill was prepared and first reported to the House, which gave rise to a memorable discussion, in which a high protective tariff first received from Mr. Clay (its principal advocate) the name of the "American system." As Mr. Webster's early relation to this subject has sometimes been misunderstood, it will be necessary to recur to the opinions which he had hitherto held. The reader has already seen that, in 1814, he declared himself not to be in favor of a policy which would force capital into manufactures faster than it would naturally find its way into them without the direct influence of legislation.[1] In 1816, when the principle of protection to domestic manufactures, advocated by Mr. Calhoun, was first introduced into our revenue system as an incidental object of the regulation and imposition of duties on foreign goods, Mr. Webster, as I have already said, confined himself to the procurement of such duties on particular commodities, as would be likely to afford a settled and steady policy in relation to the principal branches of manufacture. From 1816 to 1823 he was, as we have seen, out of Congress. In the mean time, the effect of the tariff of 1816 had been to stimulate the investment of capital still more in manufacturing establishments, especially of cotton and wool, and there were indications that a policy of direct protection and encouragement by the means of still higher duties, laid for this express purpose, would be substituted for the tariff then in operation. Under these circumstances a meeting was held in Faneuil Hall in Boston, in 1820, for the purpose of opposing a still further extension of this principle. Mr. Webster, although not in public position at that time, was invited to attend and address this meeting, because his general sentiments on the subject were known to be opposed to any other measure of protection than that which is incidental to the collection of sufficient revenue for the wants of Government, and which can be adjusted from time to time to the particular situation of all the industries of the country. Previous to this time, the right to afford protection to domestic manufactures against foreign competition was placed by its advo-

[1] *Ante*, chap. v.

cates upon the ground that it is a power incidental to the power of laying and collecting revenue; and Mr. Webster argued, in his speech at Faneuil Hall, that, if protection is an incident to revenue, the incident cannot fairly be carried beyond the principal, and that duties laid for the mere object of protection are beyond the scope of the power under which it was claimed that they might be imposed. This opinion, so far as the revenue power is concerned as the source of protective duties, Mr. Webster substantially held to the end of his life; that is to say, if the power of protection is to be inferred solely from the revenue power, the protection can only be incidental. But, when he first expressed this opinion in 1820, Mr. Madison's papers and other publications, which throw a great deal of light upon the commercial clause in the Constitution, as intended by its framers to embrace the power of protecting domestic industries, had not appeared. This fact is important to be observed, in speaking of Mr. Webster's views of 1820. In what he said in 1820 on the subject of power, he had nothing in view but the revenue power. On the question of policy, he did undoubtedly at that time oppose earnestly the further extension of a principle of legislation which would, as he believed, give an artificial stimulus to some branches of industry, operate to the injury of maritime commerce, and introduce among us the system of prohibitions and monopolies which had long been followed, but which were beginning to be questioned, in England.

From 1820 to 1824, partly in consequence of the changes of capital brought about by the influence of the tariff of 1816; partly by the fall of prices everywhere, consequent upon the general peace in Europe, and the efforts to return to a basis of specie payments both abroad and at home, and from other less palpable causes, there was a general commercial depression throughout this country. The opinion was then embraced by some leading minds, especially by Mr. Clay, that the true remedy for this state of things was to encourage still more the development of manufactures among us, and, by a system of high protection, to raise up a larger home market for agricultural products generally, and also to bring about the employment of our own iron, hemp, and other articles which are consumed in ship-building, to the exclusion of foreign materials. In seeking for a means of naturalizing the arts in this country, Mr. Clay became satisfied that we "must resort to the same method which the wisdom of other nations had found to be alone effectual, namely, adequate protection against the otherwise overwhelming influence of foreign competition." How far Mr. Clay was personally concerned in arranging the details of the tariff bill of 1824 does not appear; but it is certain that when he came forward and made that measure his own, and laid at its foundation the principle of a high protective tariff, as the means of remedying the existing commercial depression, and of launching the country upon a new career of prosperity, he carried the principle in argument to the full extent to which it had been carried in England, and relied mainly upon the example of England as his justification. It is also certain that the tariff bill of 1824 as it stood before the House, was so constructed that many persons, like Mr. Webster, who would have been in favor of some of its provisions had they stood alone, could not vote for others on account of their injurious operation upon interests which they were bound to regard. But the measure was pressed as a whole, and as the establishment of a system, of which the encouragement of manufactures, through the direct operation of high protective duties, was the avowed object and the corner-stone.

Of course, a measure of this kind, so constructed, and brought forward as a system which was confessedly an imitation of that which was supposed, rightfully or wrongfully, to have created the prosperity of England, encountered opposition. As a matter of course, too, introduced as it was at a time when the navigating interests were laboring under the unfavorable effects produced by the tariff of 1816, when the ship-builder needed to purchase his materials at the lowest possible rates, and when the ship-owner needed all the freights that he could command—it must lead those who represented such interests to look carefully at the application of a principle that was now to be carried further than it had ever been carried before. It was equally certain that there must be great differences of opinion upon the question whether the true mode of benefiting the agricultural classes of such a country as this, is, to shut up the consumption of their products within a home market, or even to create a state of things which has a decided tendency in that direction; and that there also must be great doubts whether they are benefited by making it necessary for them to abstain from the use of a foreign manufactured article, in order to avoid the payment of a tax which is imposed for the benefit of a domestic manufacturer. But it is no part of my purpose to enter into the discussion of these great questions of political economy, which have not even yet reached a wholly satisfactory solution; but the general aspects of the subject are here alluded to, as it presented itself in 1824, for the purpose of guarding the reader against any erroneous views of the opinions and course of Mr. Webster on that occasion.

The bill of 1824 had been pending for some time in Committee of the Whole, in a desultory debate on its multifarious provisions and its general principle, when, on the 31st of March, Mr. Clay availed himself of a convenient opportunity to develop the general policy of the measure, and to place himself in the responsible situation of its principal advocate. He began by describing what he considered as a condition of "distress" throughout the country. Characterizing the policy which he meant to recommend, as a "genuine American system," he described those, who thought a foreign market an adequate vent for the surplus products of our labor, as "partisans of the foreign policy." He then proceeded to enforce the principle of protection by the example of England, the country in which it had been most steadily and extensively maintained, and combated the objections which had been made to its introduction here, in a speech of astonishing ability, which is perhaps the most perfect summary of the arguments in its favor that has ever been placed on the records of our legislation.

Mr. Webster began his reply to Mr. Clay, by stating that he represented a district that was highly commercial, and deeply interested in manufactures also; and that such were the complex and conflicting details of this bill, that a vote in its favor would support measures which ought not to be adopted, and a vote against it would oppose measures, some of which might be correct. He did not approve of legislation which, for the sake of inaugurating a new system that was to give a great stimulus to manufactures, dealt in this manner with the existing pursuits of the country. But, passing to the general policy of this measure, he took occasion very distinctly to repel the inference that might be drawn from the application made by Mr. Clay of the terms "American policy" and "foreign policy," as marking an invidious distinction between those who favored and those who opposed this bill. A policy, he said, which America never had tried, which was admitted to be drawn from the example of other countries, could not correctly, if names were things, be described as an American policy; while that which we had hitherto pursued, and which foreign nations had not, was scarcely to be designated as a foreign system. He then took issue with Mr. Clay in respect to the state of the country, which he regarded as one of depression and not distress, denying that there was cause for so gloomy a representation as had been made. He traced the causes of the existing depression, and argued that this bill was not calculated to reach them. It was necessary, he said, to know, when new applications were to be made of the principles of protection, how the measure was to operate on all the interests of the country; what provisions were expected to have the effect of increasing the home market, and what might tend the other way. On these points he had derived little information from the advocates of the measure. But he could not, he said, on this great subject, espouse a side and fight under a flag.

Adverting to the case of England, he contended that the policy of restraints and prohibitions was getting out of repute as the true nature of commerce became better understood, and he established this position by numerous citations from English statesmen of eminence, who were even then beginning to question that policy. The reason why exclusion, prohibition, and monopoly were now suffered to remain in the English system, was, he observed, because a thing wrongly done cannot always be undone; and for the same reason it would be wise in us to take all our measures of this kind with great caution. On this subject he held that there were substantial distinctions which ought to be observed. One is the distinction between entire prohibition and reasonable encouragement. It is one thing, by duties on foreign articles, to awaken a home competition in the production of the same articles; it is quite another thing to remove all competition by the total exclusion of the foreign article. There was again a broad distinction between affording reasonable encouragement to manufactures already existing in the country, and by total prohibition raising up manufactures not suited to the climate, the nature of the country, or the state of the population. Although it might not always be easy to apply these distinctions, yet they were sufficiently clear to indicate the true course of policy.

There were, continued Mr. Webster, some general objections to Mr. Clay's course of reasoning: 1. He seemed to treat all domestic industry as if it were confined to the production of manufactured articles. It was an error to attribute to certain employments the peculiar appellation of American industry. If one man makes a yard of cloth at home and another raises agricultural products and buys a yard of imported cloth, both are the earnings of domestic industry; and it is questionable how far it is proper for Government to decide which is the best mode of obtaining the article, or how far it ought to be left to individual discretion. The various interests and pursuits of society should be allowed to flourish and grow together. They might promote manufactures by causing sudden transfers of capital and violent changes in men's occupations, if they chose to disregard the effect on other interests. Without exceeding the bounds of moderation, they might incidentally, through the revenue power, benefit such manufactures as could be most usefully promoted at home, but his objection was to the immoderate use of the power. 2. Mr. Clay had left out of consideration what had already been done for manufactures. The real aspect of the question was, in regard to each branch of manufactures affected by the bill, whether enough had not already been done, and whether more could now be done without great injury to other interests. In illustration of this view of the subject, he closed with an elaborate examination of the existing condition and prospects of the great branches of manufacture, and the effect of the bill upon the navigating and agricultural interests.

His vote was given against the bill, which had a majority of five only in its favor. In the Senate, the bill was materially modified in respect to many of its details, and, when the House finally concurred in these changes, many of Mr. Webster's objections were obviated.

From this analysis it will be seen in what sense, at this time, Mr. Webster was a "free-trader" on the one hand, or, on the other hand, what description of a tariff he favored. It is to be remembered that this speech of 1824 was made in answer to an argument by Mr. Clay, in which that gentleman had pressed the theory of protection and its benefits to the utmost verge of the practice of England, and this, too, upon a bill that operated so injuriously upon many great branches of industry, that it could not afterward pass the Senate unchanged. Mr. Webster was obliged, therefore, to present the argument that is opposed to an extreme application of the principle of protection. In theory he doubtless concurred with the general sense in which the current of the age was then beginning to flow, in favor of freedom of commercial intercourse and unrestrained individual action, as the best condition for all nations. But he accepted the fact that we had adopted to a certain extent the principle of protection, and were acting upon it; and, therefore, in his view, the true policy of all our legislation on this subject was to adjust the revenue in reference to its bearing on domestic industry, so as neither to introduce an artificial stimulus of some favored pursuits nor to cripple others which were left to their own unaided vigor. As a statesman, therefore, in a general sense, Mr. Webster inclined to the doctrines of what is called "free trade;" as an American legislator, he was not a "free-trader" in 1824 or at any other period. He resisted such an application and extent of the principles of protection as he thought would be injurious; but he did not deny the necessity for some continued exercise of that principle, nor did he combat the constitutional power.[1] Whatever may have been the effect

[1] In a letter from Mr. Gore, addressed to Mr. Webster at this time, we may see how his views on the subject of the tariff were regarded by those who had no extreme opinions on either side: "I thank you for an excellent speech, lately received, on the tariff, replete, in my estimation, with true principles and sound doctrines, which, if acted upon, would promote the individual objects exclusively intended to be fostered, at the same time that the other great interests of the community would be preserved. No one rejoices more sincerely than myself at

of the tariff of 1824 on the pursuits of the country, or on the opinions and conduct of public men, Mr. Webster is not responsible for it.[1]

Mr. Webster's position in the House, as chairman of the Judiciary Committee, brought a great variety of subjects under his immediate cognizance, the most important of which related to certain changes then agitated in respect to the construction and action of the Supreme Court of the United States. There were causes of very considerable anxiety to the friends of the Government, springing from certain dissatisfactions with the relations of that tribunal to the working of the Constitution. The number of the judges had hitherto been seven; and as their discharge of the circuit duties, as well as of the duty of sitting *in banc*, had long been a part of the judicial system, and as the growth of the country had rendered some further provision desirable, the question had arisen, what that provision ought to be. At all times this question involves an enlargement of the number of the judges of the Supreme Court, if they are to retain their connection with the circuits, as one alternative, *or*, as the other, the preservation of a smaller number of the members of that court, and the creation of an independent court, or the appointment of special judges to perform the circuit duties. The disadvantage of a numerous bench for the purpose of sitting as a court of errors *in banc*, and the disadvantage of separating the judges of the Supreme Court from the circuits, in order to limit their number, rendered this a matter of great perplexity. These difficulties were inherent in the subject; there were others, which were perhaps more formidable, arising from the state of men's feelings and opinions.

The function of declaring void and inoperative any law of a State that conflicts with the Constitution of the United States, which was designed by that Constitution to be vested in the

witnessing your advance in the public mind. There is hardly cavil and carping enough to relieve you from the denunciation pronounced against him of whom all speak well."—(May 11, 1824. *Correspondence*, i., 351.)

[1] There was a phrase current at that time which described the kind of legislation to which Mr. Webster and others were willing to assent as a "judicious" tariff. It was bitterly ridiculed by Mr. Clay, who declared that, if the bill then before the House did not pass, no other could at that session, or probably during that Congress. (See Annals of Congress; Eighteenth Congress, 1st Session.)

Supreme Federal Tribunal, and for which the Judiciary Act of 1789 had provided the necessary practical means, had, previous to the year 1824, been exercised several times since the origin of the Government, in cases where the law of a State had been sustained by its own supreme tribunal, and where the appellate jurisdiction of the Supreme Court of the United States had been assumed to have been rightfully given by the twenty-fifth section of the Federal Judiciary Act.[1] This exercise of appellate jurisdiction over the decisions of the State courts, in this class of cases, had given no special dissatisfaction in New Jersey, or Maryland, or New Hampshire, the States in which the most prominent cases of its application had arisen;[2] but when, in the cases of *Cohens* vs. *Virginia* and *Green* vs. *Biddle*, coming from Virginia and Kentucky, the same power had been successfully invoked, State jealousy and pride were touched to the quick in two of their principal strongholds. The dissatisfaction culminated at this session of Congress in efforts to curtail the authority and limit the action of the Supreme Court of the United States; and at the very time when these efforts were made, the validity of the steamboat monopoly of the State of New York was pending before that tribunal in the case of *Gibbons* vs. *Ogden*.

Mr. Webster's position, therefore, as chairman of the Judiciary Committee, was extremely delicate and responsible. He had to meet propositions looking to important changes in the construction of the Supreme Court and the functions of the judges, and other propositions, which contemplated the extinction or the restriction of its appellate jurisdiction over the State courts. With respect to the former, he entertained then and always a strong opinion that the separation of the judges of that court from circuit duties is entirely inexpedient. He considered that the best mode of affording the relief made necessary by the pressure of business upon the circuits, was to appoint circuit judges where that pressure was greatest, and at the same time to have the judges of the Supreme Court per-

[1] The section which declares the cases which may be removed from State courts to the Supreme Court of the United States, and provides for the mode of effecting it.

[2] *New Jersey* vs. *Wilson*, 7 Cranch (from New Jersey); *McCulloch* vs. *Maryland*, 4 Wheaton (from Maryland); *Dartmouth College* vs. *Woodward*, 4 Wheaton (from New Hampshire).

form some *nisi prius* duties. But there was no general concurrence of opinion on these points at this session, and he could only prevent the adoption of measures which he thought objectionable. On the other branch of the subject, he had to oppose, first, a proposed repeal of the twenty-fifth section of the Judiciary Act; and next, a plan requiring the concurrence of a certain fixed number of the judges of the Supreme Court in any decision that should reverse the judgment of a State court on the ground of the constitutional invalidity of a State law. In this opposition he was successful, and this class of cases was left under the provisions of the Judiciary Act of 1789.

During the most exciting period of the debate of 1824, on the tariff, and while Mr. Webster was himself speaking in the House on that subject, he was suddenly called upon to prepare for the argument of the case of *Gibbons* vs. *Ogden* in the Supreme Court, involving the constitutional validity of the laws of New York, which had granted to Fulton and Livingston the exclusive navigation of all the waters within the jurisdiction of that State, by vessels impelled by steam, for a term of years not then expired. Every tribunal in that State to which the question had been submitted, including its "Court of Errors and Appeals," had affirmed that these laws were not an infraction of the constitutional jurisdiction of Congress to regulate commerce between the States. The particular injunction issued in the case, at the instance of those holding the monopoly, restrained a vessel that ran between the city of New York and Elizabethtown, in New Jersey. Mr. Webster had not been employed in the cause in the State courts; but, on its removal to the Supreme Court of the United States, he was retained in it to argue against the validity of the New York laws. The circumstances attending his summons into court in this cause, which was at the time quite unexpected, are thus detailed by Mr. Ticknor in his reminiscences of Mr. Webster:

"In the spring of 1824, Mr. Webster was much concerned in the discussion then going on in the House of Representatives at Washington, upon the tariff. One morning he rose very early—earlier even than was his custom—to prepare himself to speak upon it. From long before daylight till the hour when the House met, he was busy with his brief. When he was far advanced in speaking, a note was brought to him from the Supreme Court, informing him that the great case of Gibbons *vs.* Ogden would be called on for argument the next morning. He was astounded at the intelligence, for he had supposed that after the tariff question should have been disposed of, he would still have ten days to prepare himself for this formidable conflict, in which the constitutionality of the laws of New York, granting a steamboat monoply of its tide-waters, would be decided. He brought his speech on the tariff to a conclusion as speedily as he could, and hurried home to make such preparation for the great law argument as the shortness of the notice would permit. He had then taken no food since his morning's breakfast—but instead of dining he took a moderate dose of medicine and went to bed, and to sleep. At ten P. M. he awoke, called for a bowl of tea, and without other refreshment went immediately to work. To use his own phrase, 'the tapes had not been off the papers for more than a year.' He worked all night, and, as he has told me more than once, he thought he never on any occasion had so completely the free use of all his faculties. He hardly felt that he had bodily organs, so entirely had his fasting and the medicine done their work. At nine A. M., after eleven hours of continuous intellectual effort, his brief was completed. He sent for the barber and was shaved; he took a very slight breakfast of tea and crackers; he looked over his papers to see that they were all in order, and tied them up—he read the morning journals, to amuse and change his thoughts, and then he went into court, and made that grand argument which, as Judge Wayne said above twenty years afterward, 'released every creek and river, every lake and harbor in our country from the interference of monopolies.' Whatever he may have thought of his powers on the preceding night, the court and the bar acknowledged their whole force that day. And yet, at the end of five hours, when he ceased speaking, he could hardly be said to have taken what would amount to half the refreshment of a common meal, for above two and thirty hours, and, out of the thirty-six hours immediately preceding, he had for thirty-one been in a state of very high intellectual excitement and activity."

Probably, if we possessed as full a report of this argument as that which remains of the Dartmouth College case, we should be inclined to estimate it quite as highly. Certainly the difficulties to be overcome were as great, and the nature of the question demanded as much power of analysis and discrimination, and force of reasoning, as were required in the former case. The weight of judicial authority that was arrayed against the side which Mr. Webster had to espouse was far more imposing than in the college case. The question derived its chief difficulty from the apparent conflict of jurisdictions as between the State and the national governments, in respect to waters which are confessedly within the territorial limits of a State. But notwithstanding the locality in which these laws of monopoly were to operate, the question was, whether they were consistent with the grant to Congress of the power to regulate commerce with foreign nations and between the several States. The argument of Mr. Webster established the great positions that the commerce of the Union is a unit; that its regulation being vested in Congress, there is of necessity some legislative regulation, which is exclusively in Congress, and not concurrently in Congress and the States; and that a law granting a monopoly of navigation over waters where commerce is carried on, is a law regulating commerce, and is one of those regulations that can be made, if by any authority, only by the authority in which the regulation of that commerce is vested.

We have seen that Mr. Webster did not take a very strong personal interest in the topic that absorbed so much of the attention of members of Congress at this session—the approaching presidential election. On his arrival at Washington in December, 1823, he found the state of things to be this: The candidates were Mr. John Quincy Adams, General Jackson, Mr. Calhoun, Mr. Clay, Mr. Crawford, and Mr. Clinton. Each of these gentlemen seemed likely to command so many of the electoral votes as to prevent a choice of any one of them. Mr. Webster was satisfied, therefore, from the first, that the election would devolve upon the House of Representatives. He would have preferred Mr. Calhoun at this time, for the presidency, of all the candidates, if there had been a reasonable prospect that he could be elected. As the winter wore on, he saw that Mr. Adams and General Jackson would be the real competitors at last; and under these circumstances, so far as he gave any advice to his friends at home, it was to cast the electoral votes of New England so as to secure the election of Mr. Calhoun as Vice-President. In March he wrote to his brother, who had much influence in New Hampshire: "I hope all New England will support Mr. Calhoun for the vice-presidency. If so, he will probably be chosen, and that will be a great thing. He is a true man, and will do good to the country in that situation."

Mr. Webster's labors of this session, in the House, in its committees, and in two legal tribunals, had their effect even upon him, accustomed as he was to such exertions, and strong as was his physical constitution at the age of forty-two. Probably he never passed a winter at Washington of more constant and severe exertion than this, although he had no such cause for intense anxiety concerning the country as he afterward had, in 1830, in 1842, and in 1850. It was a winter of hard work; and, when the spring arrived, he admitted its effects. "We have had a busy time of it," he wrote to Judge Story, "since you left us. For myself, I am exhausted. When I look in the glass, I think of our old New-England saying, 'as thin as a shad.' I have not vigor enough left, either mental or physical, to try an action for assault and battery. However, the fine weather has come on, I have resumed the saddle, and hope to 'pick up my crumbs' again soon." To his brother, a little later, he writes: "I hope to get away by the 12th of May, and to be at home in season to see you at Dorchester the week before the General Court meets at Concord. The ensuing summer I shall do nothing but move about and play. I shall certainly spend a fortnight with you at Boscawen, and the rest you may spend with us. August we will pass together on Cape Cod. My wife wants some one to ride about with her, while I am shooting," etc.

But it was past the middle of June before he could get away. He was detained for some days after the termination of the session, to serve on a committee of investigation into certain charges made by a Mr. Ninian Edwards against the Secretary of the Treasury, Mr. Crawford. As this tedious business dragged its slow length along, he began to think of the birds that he ought to be following at Cohasset or Chelsea Beach, in company with his friend Mr. George Blake. He was not yet so reduced, he wrote, but that he "could walk with a bit of iron" on his shoulder, and he desired to know whether Mr. Blake was ever found driving with an "umbrella" in his chaise, as that quaint and most agreeable person was accustomed to call his fowling-piece when in its case.[1]

In the autumn of this year (1824), he was again elected a Representative in Congress from the Boston district, by a vote which is recorded in the newspapers of the time as "nearly unanimous." There was in fact no opposition of any importance.

Mr. Webster had hitherto possessed no permanent country residence, excepting his father's farm in New Hampshire, which, in the days when railways were as yet unknown, was at a rather inconvenient distance from Boston. In fact, he did not become the sole owner of this property until some years after this period, although he frequently went there. It was a place always full of tender recollections for him. But the farm was a small one, the rural resources were few; and, above all, it was remote from the sea, which always had for him very great attractions. "At Franklin," he used to say, "I can see all in two days."

It was in the autumn of this year (1824) that he first saw the spot on the southeastern shore of Massachusetts which afterward became his favorite home, and with which his name will be long associated; where, as he often said, he "could go out every day in the year and see something new." This house, situated about a mile from the ocean (which is in full view from it), and surrounded by a farm then embracing one hundred and sixty acres, was the property of Captain John Thomas. The month of August was passed by Mr. and Mrs. Webster and their children at Sandwich. On their way to Boston — Mr. Webster driving his

[1] The Hon. George Blake, a leading member of the Boston bar, for many years United States District Attorney for Massachusetts, was one of Mr. Webster's most intimate friends, and a frequent companion of his field-sports. He was a gentleman of many oddities, of excellent company, not specially diligent in his profession, and not always "prepared" for the trial of his causes. In the year 182–, the office which he occupied in Boston was burned, and he lost his library and papers. Mr. Webster used to say, that ever afterward, whenever Mr. Blake had a cause to try, which he did not wish to try, whatever was the date of its inception, he invariably began a dilatory motion with the words—"May it please your honors, the disastrous and ever-lamented fire in Court Street, which consumed every one of my papers in this cause, makes it necessary for me to throw myself upon the indulgence of the court," etc.

wife in a New-England "chaise"—they chanced to take the road which passed by the Thomas farm. As they descended the valley, Mrs. Webster was so much delighted by the quiet repose of this old house under its magnificent elm, and by the general beauty of the scene, that she begged her husband to turn in at the gate and pay a visit to the family. The call ended in their being invited to extend their visit to a few days; and, before they left, an arrangement was made, by which they became, in succeeding summers, regular inmates in the family of Captain Thomas. This continued to be their course of life for several years.

GREEN HARBOR—THE THOMAS ESTATE AT MARSHFIELD.

CHAPTER XI.

1824–1825.

VISIT TO MR. JEFFERSON AND MR. MADISON—DEATH OF HIS SON CHARLES—ELECTION OF MR. JOHN QUINCY ADAMS AS PRESIDENT—INTERNAL IMPROVEMENTS—CRIMES ACT OF 1825—CORRESPONDENCE WITH J. EVELYN DENISON, ESQ.—FIRST BUNKER HILL ORATION—JOURNEY TO NIAGARA.

AFTER passing the summer of 1824 in the relaxation which he had promised himself, it was arranged in the autumn that Mr. Webster should make a visit to Mr. Jefferson at Monticello, in company with Mr. Ticknor, who had been invited by Mr. Jefferson to assist him in regulating the course of studies at the University of Virginia. Mr. Ticknor has furnished me with the following account of their journey, and the incidents of their visit to Mr. Jefferson and Mr. Madison:

"Early in the autumn of 1824, I was one day dining with Mr. Webster at his own house, and talked about passing some time in Washington the next winter, as I had often done before. I told him that Mr. Jefferson had invited me to meet General Lafayette at Monticello, but that I did not think I should be able to do it. I thought, however, that, in the event of my going to Washington, I should endeavor, as Mrs. Ticknor would be with me, to take her to Mr. Jefferson's. He said he should like to be of the party. I replied that if he were in earnest, and could afford the time for it, I could easily arrange matters so that it would be agreeable for him to go. He held out his hand and said, 'It is a bargain, if you say so.'

"In consequence of this conversation, I wrote to Mr. Jefferson, intimating to him that Mr. Webster might visit Virginia with us. He answered immediately, under date of November 8th: 'Whether Mr. Webster comes with you, or alone as suits himself, he will be a welcome guest. His character, his talents and principles, entitle him to the favor and respect of all his fellow-citizens, and have long ago possessed him of mine.'

"We left Washington on the 9th day of December, and went by steamboat to Fredericksburg Landing. At Fredericksburg, a friend had made all the arrangements necessary for the journey, and we set off the next morning in a carriage and four horses and a gig, all very slovenly, after the Virginia fashion. The roads were very bad. The landlord of the house where we dined dropped his knife and fork with astonishment, as he was carving a very nice turkey, when he understood that he was talking with Mr. Webster of Massachusetts; but he was nothing daunted, and they had a great argument upon the question of internal improvement, the Virginian confessing that if the power were not in the Constitution, he wished it was. We were to pass the night at a tavern kept by a Dr. Tyrrel, but the days were short and the roads detestable, and it was long after dark before we reached our destination. Mr. Webster was very amusing, telling stories to keep our spirits up, singing scraps of old songs, and making merry like a boy. Our accommodations for the night were bad enough, but before we went to bed we prepared a note for Mr. Madison, which was to be dispatched the next morning at daylight, and informed him of our intended visit, for which President Monroe had prepared him. At Orange Court-House, five miles from Dr. Tyrrel's, we met our messenger, who brought us a kind welcome from Mr. Madison, and who was accompanied by Mr. Madison's coachman, whom he had sent to show us the way—a needful providence, where proper roads were none and landmarks very few.

"We were very hospitably received. Mr. Madison and Mr. Webster were old acquaintances, and evidently well pleased to see each other again. Mr. Madison talked well, and laid himself out to be agreeable to Mr. Webster. After a long and pleasant dinner, as we were going back to the saloon, Mr. Webster said to me, in an undertone, '*Stare hic;*' for he was afraid I might say something of going away the next day; but I had no such intention. We did not talk that evening very late, for we were tired, and late hours were evidently not the habit of the family. The next morning (Sunday), after breakfast, Mr. Webster and I, accompanied by Mr. Todd,[1] took a ride on horseback of eight or ten miles. When we had passed beyond the limits of Mr. Madison's domain, the country looked pretty cheerless. We rode through woods and across fields, Mr. Webster making himself merry as he had the day before with wondering where 'Phil Barbour's constituents could be,' for this was Mr. Philip Barbour's district. Before we returned, however, we made a visit to Mrs. Barbour, to whom Mr. Webster gave an account of her husband, whom he had left in Washington, which visibly interested her. The dinner that day was as agreeable as the one the day before. Mr. Madison told many stories with

[1] Son of Mrs. Madison, by a former husband.

much grace and effect. Mr. Webster was much interested in them, especially in those that had a political cast; for, though every thing of a party nature was avoided between persons whose opinions were so opposite, yet both were too much interested in the country and its history not to talk about its affairs. After we returned to Washington, Mr. Webster told me that he had been very much impressed by Mr. Madison's conversation, and that it had fully confirmed him in an opinion he had for some time entertained, that Mr. Madison was 'the wisest of our Presidents, except Washington.'

"We spent two days at Mr. Madison's, and then went to Mr. Jefferson's, which, though only thirty-two miles off, proved a journey of more than one day. At Charlottesville, before we went up to Monticello, Mr. Webster received a letter which changed his appearance and manner the moment he had read it. It was from Mrs. Webster, and gave him bad news of his youngest child, little Charles, who was thought ill, but not dangerously so. The change was the more apparent from his having previously been so gay. Only the evening before, at Mrs. Clarke's tavern, he had said, 'that without intending any compliment to his companions, he would say that he had not felt so free from care and anxious thought, as he did then, for five years.' (I find this in a memorandum made at the time.)

"We remained at Monticello four or five days, detained one day beyond our purpose by rains and the consequent swelling of the streams, which made travelling difficult in a country where bridges are rare. Mr. Jefferson had regular habits and fixed hours for every thing; but he was very attentive to Mr. Webster, and plainly liked to talk with him. Mr. Webster, on his part, was very respectful to Mr. Jefferson, and led him constantly to converse upon the doings of the old Congress and the period of the Revolution, on both which topics Mr. Jefferson was interesting and instructive. Mr. Webster enjoyed these conversations very much, and spoke of them afterward with great satisfaction.

"One day, after dinner, Mr. Webster told a story of himself, which was characteristic of him, and amused Mr. Jefferson very much. Mr. Jefferson remarked that 'men not unfrequently obtained more credit for readiness in command of their knowledge, and indeed for its amount, than they deserved.' He said it had happened to himself. Mr. Webster replied that he supposed it had happened to most men, and especially to lawyers. He said that, soon after going to Portsmouth as a young lawyer, a blacksmith brought him a case under a will; he was unable to give him a decided answer, and desired him to call again. Having little to do, he went to work upon the case, and found it a difficult one. He went through all the books in his own little collection, that could give him any light, and then borrowed what he could find relating to the point in question, in the libraries of Mr. Jeremiah Mason, and of Mr. Peyton R. Freeman, a curious black-letter lawyer in Portsmouth. His client called for an opinion, but he was unable to give him one—he had only got far enough into the matter to ascertain that the blacksmith's bequest was either a *contingent remainder* or an *executory devise.* He sent to Boston and bought Fearne's Essay on these two subjects, and other books, all together costing him fifty dollars. At last, after a month's hard work, and making out a very elaborate brief, he gave an opinion favorable to his client's claim, argued the case, won it, and received a fee of fifteen dollars; all that the amount in controversy would warrant him to charge.

"Years passed by, and the blacksmith and his case had almost passed away also from his memory. At length, being in New York on his way to Washington, Mr. Aaron Burr sent him a note, saying that he wished to consult him on a legal question of some consequence. Mr. Webster gave him an appointment, and, when Mr. Burr began to explain his case to him, he said that he knew in a moment that it was his blacksmith's case over again. He, however, heard Mr. Burr quietly through, and then, with the blacksmith's brief full in his mind, began to reply. He cited a series of cases bearing on the point, and going back, if I remember rightly, to a leading one in the time of Charles II. Mr. Burr listened to him for some time, and then interrupted him somewhat suddenly, by asking him whether he had been consulted in that case before. 'He evidently suspected,' said Mr. Webster, 'that I must have been of counsel to the other side. I assured him that I did not know there was such a case or such parties in the world till he explained it to me.' Mr. Webster said that he subsequently gave Mr. Burr a written opinion on his case, and made him pay enough for it to cover all his work for the blacksmith and something moreover for Mr. Burr's suspicion that he had been of counsel for the opposite party. He added, 'Mr. Burr, no doubt, thought me a much more learned lawyer than I was, and, under the circumstances of the case, I did not think it worth while to disabuse him of his good opinion of me.'

"Mr. Jefferson, though then eighty-one years old, rode constantly on horseback in fine weather. One day we rode with him to Charlottesville, about four miles, to visit the buildings for his university, which had not yet gone into operation, but was soon to be opened. It was the last great interest of his life, and Mr. Webster took much pleasure in witnessing the beginning of the enterprise. He did not, however, fail to discover some of the defects of the system; he especially suggested to Mr. Jefferson that a project he had introduced into his laws for the university, to train the scholars in military exercises with guns made wholly of wood, because he did not think it safe to trust them with the usual fire-arms, would fail from the ridicule of the young men. It proved so.

"Mr. Webster was impatient of our detention by the weather. He was very anxious to get news of his sick child, and could not hope for any letters till he should reach Washington. He wanted also to know what was going on in Congress; but Mr. Jefferson took no newspaper but the *Richmond Enquirer.* With the first fine weather, therefore, we descended the mountain. Several of the young gentlemen of the family accompanied us. On the banks of the Rivanna we found many wagons waiting to be ferried over; the stream was much swollen, and the passage difficult. Many had their turn before us, and, among the rest, a drove of pigs from Kentucky. The ferryman had but one person to assist him—an inefficient slave—they were both much exhausted, having been at work since day-break. While we were crossing, Mr. Webster, in his usual cheerful manner, began to talk to the ferryman, who found it very difficult to stem the sudden turbulence of the stream. 'You find it hard work enough this morning, I think,' said Mr. Webster. 'Yes, sir,' said the boatman, 'it puts a man up to all he knows, I assure you.' An apt phrase, which amused Mr. Webster very much at the time, which he was constantly using on all occasions through the rest of the journey, and which he often introduced in speaking and writing in after-years. In this way it has become a common phrase in our part of the country, where few persons know its origin.

"Of the rest of our journey back to Washington I remember nothing but that it was uncomfortable from the season of the year, and that Mr. Webster was depressed and anxious from the news he had received from home, and from what he feared he should receive."

To this account, which was written by Mr. Ticknor since Mr. Webster's death, I have to add a memorandum of Mr. Jefferson's conversation, that was prepared by both these gentlemen at the time of their visit, and which remained private until it was included in the first volume of Mr. Webster's correspondence, published by Mr. Fletcher Webster in 1857. It was dictated partly by Mr. Webster and partly by Mr. Ticknor at the inn where they passed the first night after leaving Mr. Jefferson's, Mrs. Ticknor acting as amanuensis, and adding her recollections of Mr. Jefferson's conversation to those of the gentlemen.[1] This paper will be found in the appendix to the present volume.[2]

[1] I mention these facts, because the biographer of Mr. Jefferson has doubted the accuracy of Mr. Webster's account of some of Mr. Jefferson's remarks, especially those relating to Mr. Wirt's Life of Patrick Henry. The facts are, that what was published in 1857, in Mr. Webster's correspondence as a "Memorandum of Mr. Jefferson's Conversation," was a very carefully-prepared paper, the result of the recollections of three persons, who assisted and corrected each other, and who composed the account immediately after leaving Mr. Jefferson's house. It was originally prepared for the purpose of preserving a private record of this most interesting visit; although it was doubtless supposed that the time might arrive when this account of their illustrious host, as he appeared in the last year of his life, could with propriety be given to the world. Thirty-two years after the death of Mr. Jefferson, and five years after the death of Mr. Webster, this paper was first published. I may be permitted to add, what will be confirmed by all who have known them, that, in strength and accuracy of memory there have been few men who excelled the two gentlemen who prepared this memorandum.

[2] *Post*, p. *et seq.*

After the return of the party from Mr. Jefferson's, Mr. and Mrs. Ticknor left Mr. Webster in Washington, and went to Baltimore to pass a short time. The following letter was the first they received from him:

[MR. WEBSTER TO MR. TICKNOR.]

"WASHINGTON, Sunday Evening.

"MY DEAR SIR: I send you three letters, which have been put into my hands for that purpose to-day.

"I find that you are really *gone;* and if I could tell you how sorry I am, I would. I passed the house yesterday, and gave a look to the windows, but saw no *inviting* faces. To-day I have been at home, except an hour passed with Mr. Tazewell. The general[1] has been to see me, and we have had a good long talk. I believe he hopes to catch a sight of your party at Baltimore.

"If my constituents accuse me of negligence and inattention this session, I shall lay it all off on Mrs. Ticknor. She had no right, I shall say, to be so agreeable as to draw my attention from the weighty affairs of state while she was here, and to create depression, or a kind of I-am-not-quite-ready-to-go-to-work feeling by her departure. What will State Street say to it, think you, if its affairs should be neglected, although Shakespeare be ever so well read, or all the versions of Sir John Moore's burial revised and corrected?

"Please to assure her that I shall put it to her account, if there should happen any dissatisfactions or disaffections hereafter—any mutterings of the 'vital commoners,' or 'petty inland spirits.' To-morrow, we shall have Niagara—Chesapeake Canal—Cumberland Road—and, in the Senate, a discussion on piracy.

"I have no news from Boston. Our mail is 'due and unpaid.' Send back Wallenstein.[2] I shall be happy to see him on two accounts: first, on account of himself; second, that I may see whether any of your visages are reflected from his face.

"I am shocked with the news of Mr. Harper's death. It is a public loss. He was a man of excellent feelings and much cultivation. His mind was rather comprehensive than profound, and his general power persuasion rather than logic. He wrote with much more of purity and of elegance than most of his contemporaries. His heart was true and kind in all cases, and I believe no man more loved or cherished his friends.

"I hope to hear from you by to-morrow's mail. Give my remembrances, regrets, good wishes, and whatever else is proper, to Mrs. Ticknor and Miss

[1] General Lafayette.

[2] Julius von Wallenstein, for several years an *attaché* to the Russian legation in Washington; a man of talent, and various but irregular culture. He was a German by birth, but had long been in the service of the Russian government. Mr. Ticknor first knew him in Madrid in 1818, where he held a position corresponding to that which he held in this country. He was a good deal in Mr. Webster's society.

Gardiner—and to Mr. Wallenstein if he be yet with you—but again I say, send him back as soon as you can spare him.

"I am, my dear sir, most truly yours,

"D. WEBSTER."

[MR. TICKNOR TO MR. WEBSTER.]

"BALTIMORE, Tuesday Evening.

"MY DEAR SIR: Your kind note of Sunday evening, by the unkindness of the Baltimore post-office, was put among the F's, and therefore did not reach its destination until this morning, though it was due, and arrived yesterday. Wallenstein, however, who went back in the coach, carried you a little note, which I trust you received early in the forenoon; and which will, at least, serve to assure you that we are not insensible to the kindness you have expressed for us during the last week. . . . General Harper's death has cast a gloom over this city, as such a great loss ought to. Wallenstein will have given you all the details. Old Mr. Carroll fainted when he heard of it; but is gradually recovering. We have seen Count Menou[1] several times, who is staying at old Mr. Carroll's to comfort him; and his feelings, on the loss of General Harper, who was once a great benefactor to him, do him great credit as a good man. . . . Savage says there is no excitement in Boston about the presidential election. Do let us hear from you as often as possible, if it be but a line, written in your place while some Ohio member is prosing; it will console us, for we have indeed a heavy miss of you. GEO. TICKNOR."

The child, whose illness cast the coming shadows of grief over Mr. Webster's enjoyment of his tour in Virginia, was born in Boston, on the 31st December, 1822. He died on the 18th of December, 1824. He was the youngest of Mr. Webster's children; loved with all the strength of the great heart of his father, and all the affection of the devoted mother.[2] The following letter, from Mrs. Webster to her husband, succeeded the first announcement of their loss:

[MRS. WEBSTER TO MR. WEBSTER.

"BOSTON, *December* 28, 1824.

"I have a great desire to write to you, my beloved husband, but I doubt if I can write legibly, as I can hold my pen but in my fingers.[3] I

[1] Count Menou was long a refugee French resident in Baltimore, and subsequently French minister in Washington.

[2] This child is said to have borne a stronger likeness to Mr. Webster than either of his other sons. Mrs. Lee says of him: "This lovely child indicated singular attractiveness of mind and character. His illness was short, and had hardly impaired the fresh beauty of his countenance; but shortly after his death, when the round contour of his cheeks had a little fallen away, his face and head were like a perfect miniature cast of his father. No marble bust can ever present a more perfect likeness of his noble father."—(*Correspondence*, i.)

[3] In consequence of an injury to the thumb of her right hand.

have just received your letter, in answer to William's,[1] which told you that little Charley was no more. I have dreaded the hour which should destroy your hopes, but trust you will not let this event afflict you too much, and that we both shall be able to resign him without a murmur, happy in the reflection that he has returned to his Heavenly Father pure as I received him. It was an inexpressible consolation to me, when I contemplated him in his sickness, that he had not one regret for the past, nor one dread for the future; he was patient as a lamb during all his sufferings; and, they were at last so great, I was happy when they were ended.

"I shall always reflect on his brief life with mournful pleasure, and, I hope, remember with gratitude all the joy he gave me; and it has been great. And, oh, how fondly did I flatter myself it would be lasting!

'It was but yesterday, my child, thy little heart beat high;
And I had scorned the warning voice that told me thou must die.'

"Dear little Charles! He sleeps alone under St. Paul's. I cannot express how much I regret that it did not occur to any one of us to have the dear remains of Grace removed. I thought much of it when the tomb of Mr. Sullivan was opened for Mrs. Sullivan's little boy. I regretted you were not here to consult upon the subject. Oh! do not, my dear husband, talk of your own 'final abode;' that is a subject I never can dwell on for a moment. With you here, my dear, I can never be desolate. Oh, may Heaven, in its mercy, long preserve you! And that we may ever wisely improve every event, and yet rejoice together in this life, prays your ever affectionate G. W.

"I ought to mention William's unwearied attention and kindness to dear little Charles. His grief is great at the loss. Poor Nancy came last Friday; she is much afflicted that she did not come in time to see the dear little boy once more. She begs you to accept her sympathy and love."

So far as I know, this was the last occasion on which Mr. Webster's emotions found relief in his own verse. It is needless for me to repeat that, even in private, he made no pretensions to be a writer of poetry. Yet, among all the productions in which the idea of the earlier immortality of a child has been mingled with parental grief, I have seen few that are more touching than some of the stanzas which he sent to his wife after he had learned the death of his son:[2]

[1] Mr. Paige.

[2] In a note to Mrs. Ticknor at Baltimore, enclosing a copy of these lines, he said: "I occupied a lonely hour on Saturday evening in composing these little stanzas, which I have sent to Mrs. Webster. I have made this copy for your eyes and your husband's—*and for no other human being's*."—(MSS. in the author's possession.)

"The staff on which my years should lean
Is broken ere those years come o'er me;
My funeral rites thou shouldst have seen,
But thou art in the tomb before me.

"Thou rear'st to me no filial stone,
No parent's grave with tears beholdest;
Thou art my ancestor—my son!
And stand'st in Heaven's account the oldest.

"On earth my lot was soonest cast,
Thy generation after mine;
Thou hast thy predecessor past,
Earlier eternity is thine.

"I should have set before thine eyes
The road to Heaven, and showed it clear;
But thou, untaught, spring'st to the skies,
And leav'st thy teacher lingering here.

"Sweet seraph, I would learn of thee,
And hasten to partake thy bliss!
And, oh! to thy world welcome me,
As first I welcomed thee to this."

The business of legislation, the demands of society, the responsibilities of the presidential election, then pending before the House, are reflected in his correspondence of this winter, together with the memory of this affliction. He carried a heavy heart into most of the scenes in which he participated during this session.

[MR. WEBSTER TO MRS. TICKNOR, AT BALTIMORE.]

"HOUSE OF REPRESENTATIVES, *January* 17, 1825.

"Mr. Wallenstein has given me, my dear Mrs. Ticknor, your very kind note, and I cannot well tell you how much it has gratified my feelings. You have inferred nothing, my dear lady, and can infer nothing, of my regard and affection for yourself and your husband, more than the truth, nor equal to the truth. And I beg you to believe that there are none in the world whose regard and kind feelings I wish more to cultivate and secure.

"Our six weeks' acquaintance has been to me a mixture of high enjoyment and severe suffering. The former I owe, mainly, to you and Mr. Ticknor; the last I take, and would wish to bear, as a common visitation of a kind Providence. Yet I have felt it more than might have been expected, and my spirits recover slowly. I am sure that Mrs. Webster and yourself are congenial and assimilated spirits, and that she will cultivate your acquaintance with delight. Let us hope that circumstances may favor an habitual intercourse. At any rate, be assured that the *principle* of regard and affection will live in my heart.

"I write this in the House, while Mr. Clay is speaking on the Cumberland Road. The ladies are all present, inside the House. I have not reviewed them; for I am sure there is none of them that I have lately seen or know, unless it may be Mrs. (A. H.) Everett. I see Wallenstein among them, as becomes a diplomatist. Mr. Clay speaks well. I wish you were here to hear him. The highest enjoyment, almost, which I have in life, is in hearing an able argument or speech. The development of *mind*, in those modes, is delightful. In books, we see the result of thought and of fancy. In the living speaker, we see the thought itself, as it rises in the speaker's own mind. And his countenance often indicates a *perception* before it gets upon his tongue. I have been charmed by observing this operation of minds which are truly great and vigorous; so that I sometimes am as much moved, as in reading a part of Milton and Shakespeare, by a striking and able argument, although on the dryest subject.

"Mr. Wallenstein says you are to leave Baltimore on Thursday. There is, as yet, no Northern mail to-day. Should there be one, and in it letters for you, they shall be forwarded in due season. I shall flatter myself with the hope of hearing from you, not once only, but often, before you reach the little peninsula of Boston. Pray ask your husband if he has written to Dr. Warren.

"Yours most truly,

"DANL. WEBSTER."

[FROM MR. TICKNOR, AT BALTIMORE.]

"BALTIMORE, *January* 19, 1825.

"MY DEAR SIR: We think it was rather hard in you to wait till we were just out of the district, and then make a great speech. We have heard all about it, and all Mr. Clay said, and all Mr. Livingston said, and all everybody said in its praise. We had no right to complain of the speaker's[1] taking such instant advantage of our absence; but we thought our own member might have given his constituents a chance to tell of him when they get home. But we will have our revenge of you by reading it twice over in a bad report of it.

"I spent the last evening at old Mr. Carroll's. He was well and cheerful—much more remarkably preserved for eighty-eight, than Mr. Jefferson for eighty-two. When he first heard of General Harper's death, the shock reached his mind, and his memory was affected for a few hours; but his perfect equanimity, which is a chief source of his unvarying health, soon restored him, and he is now able to talk on all subjects as usual and on his

[1] Mr. Clay.

recent loss with perfect composure. Indeed, as he well said and deeply felt, a loss of this sort at eighty-eight is very sure to be soon made up. I was much gratified with my visit, and intend to go again this evening, to meet General Lafayette. It is hard, however to go without Anna, for I was more desirous she should see Mr. Carroll than anybody in Baltimore. But she shall see him yet.

"I entirely forgot to tell you yesterday, that I had written to Dr. Warren. I did it the day after you told me you would be faithful to the 17th of June, for I remembered the old rule of striking while the iron is hot. I have written too to Mr. Quincy, telling him he may probably have the general[1] for July 4th by asking for him.

"Anna desires her love, and we all desire to hear from you as often as may be. We have few amusements here, for I do not care to go abroad alone, and your letters are as apples of gold set in pictures of silver.

"Yours always,

"GEO. TICKNOR."

[TO MR. TICKNOR, AT BALTIMORE.]

HOUSE OF REPRESENTATIVES, *January* 20, 1825.

"MY DEAR SIR: I owe you for two very kind letters, and the only painful circumstance they mention is Mrs. Ticknor's health. I am truly sorry that any thing should interrupt her enjoyment of the society of Baltimore. You must certainly stay long enough for her to see Mr. Carroll. The opportunity may not again occur.

"We are to-day engaged on the canal. Several speeches have been *filed in*. Mr. Breck is now speaking. It must have been the good Wallenstein who wrote you about my little speech—for it was a very little one. We think our Eastern candidate grows a little stronger in the prospect of the presidency. As the time draws near, we hear more conversation on the subject; but every thing is yet uncertain.

"I go to-night to pass the evening with Wallenstein. My friend Dr. Sewall has proposed him as a member of the 'Columbian Institute;' so the doctor and I are going to pick a pheasant's wing on the occasion.

"I have to-day no letters from Boston—and hear little news from that quarter, since the great explosion. Mr. Gannet has gone to-day to Mount Vernon. He left me a card without *notation* of place, and I know not where to seek for him.

"Give my best and most true regards to Mrs. Ticknor. I should be glad to read Shakespeare—or Mr. Tucker—or Mrs. Hutchinson—or any thing else to her, that would make her forget the oppression of her cold. I hope to hear from her soon, and hear that she is better.

"Yours always truly,

"D. WEBSTER.

"I sent you one letter, enclosed, yesterday—have none to-day."

[1] Lafayette.

[TO MR. TICKNOR, AT BALTIMORE.]

Tuesday evening, 8 o'clock.

"My dear Sir: This is all I have for you. I expect, indeed, something further, as Wallenstein said he should inquire at the P. O. about this time. If it comes, I shall enclose it to you.

"I have been to dine with Mr. Calhoun. He talked to me, among other things, of your good fortune in picking up a *companion* on the road of life. I did not think that a subject on which I was bound to quarrel with a Secretary of War, whatever I might think of the matter. Mr. Calhoun is a true man.

"Shall I learn, to-morrow, when you leave Baltimore?

"God bless you and yours!

"D. W."

[FROM MRS. WEBSTER, AT BOSTON.]

Saturday morning, *January* 22, 1825.

"My dear Husband: I was sitting alone in my chamber reflecting on the brief life of our sainted little boy, when your letter came enclosing those lines of yours, which to a 'mother's eye' are precious. Oh, my husband, have not some of our brightest hopes perished! 'Our fairest flowers are, indeed, blossoms gathered for the tomb.' But do not, my dear husband, do not let these afflictions weigh too heavily upon you; those dear children who had such strong holds on us while here, now allure us to heaven:

On us with looks of love they bend,
For us the Lord of life implore;
And oft from sainted bliss descend,
Our wounded spirits to restore.

"Farewell, my beloved husband! I have not time to write more, only to say I regret you have lost the pleasure of Mr. and Mrs. Ticknor's society, which you so much need. I fear Mrs. Dwight is not much benefited by her voyage, so the last accounts appear; though at first they thought her better.

"The children are tolerably well, though not free from colds.

"Your ever affectionate

"G. W."

[TO MRS. TICKNOR, AT PHILADELPHIA.]

House of Representatives, *February* 4, 1825.

"My dear Lady: I am right glad to find a little place left for me in Mr. Wallenstein's letter, and to find it so flatteringly filled. I use the present moment to acknowledge this favor, while Mr. McDuffie is making a very warm speech, I hardly know why or wherefore; but it relates to the rules of proceeding in electing a President next week, and he, being a pretty ardent Jackson man, seems inclined to make a kind of Jackson speech. I told Mr. Wallenstein to tell you that I should write you during the first long speech—and, depend upon it, the act of *writing* is, in such cases or most of them, less onerous than the act of *listening*. The Hall of Congress is an admirable situation to cultivate the powers of an organ which has been generally too much neglected in its *education*; I mean the *ear*. Now I have so disciplined this little member that, on being informed that I am not particularly concerned to know what is said, and requested to 'bring me no more reports,' it very faithfully performs its duty, and leaves me quite at ease to pursue any vocation I may choose. The 'enclosed petty spirits' are left entirely undisturbed by what prevails without. This is an admirable improvement on the old maxim, 'Hear with both ears.' I hear with *neither*.

"Times have a good deal changed with me, my dear lady, since your departure. The business of Congress has become more urgent—the event draws near—the session is wearing off—I begin to see *home* at the end of no long prospect, and all these things create a little activity and bustle, which serve, in some poor measure, to fill up such portions of time as I usually passed in your house, while you remained here.

"I am glad to learn that you are entered so favorably into the society of Philadelphia. I think you will find it very intelligent and agreeable; but am not afraid, nevertheless, that it will lead you to be dissatisfied with a little peninsula running into Massachusetts Bay.

"Give my love to your husband. There seem to have been proceedings about the college, which must interest him. I hope he is satisfied with the result. Remember me also to Miss Gardiner.

"Yours most truly,

"D. WEBSTER.

"Mr. Sturgis says he had the pleasure of passing a very gratifying hour at your room in Philadelphia. Let me have a letter from you before you leave Philadelphia."

[TO MR. TICKNOR, AT PHILADELPHIA.]

February 4, 1825.

"I have only time to send love. W. has been a little unwell—I have not seen him for two days, but expect him this evening. I thought of you all day yesterday, during the storm. I hope you were and are well and safe. I should have felt less concern but for Mrs. Ticknor's cold.

"It is confidently believed that New England will give a President, *Kentucky concurrente.* D. W."

[TO MR. TICKNOR, AT BOSTON.]

SENATE, Wednesday, 3 o'clock (*February* 11).

"MY DEAR SIR: I have been looking in vain for your promised letter. Be assured, I am anxious to hear from you, and to know how yours and

Mrs. Ticknor's health is. Pray find or make opportunity to give me a line.

"We have just returned from counting the votes and announcing the election. General Jackson arrived here at nine this morning. I have not seen him nor anybody that has seen him.

"With great love to Mrs. Ticknor, and in the hope of hearing from you,

"I am yours,

"D. Webster.

"Mr. Quincy has not yet arrived."

The presidential election of 1825, which is referred to in the last note, should not be passed over without giving at least a brief account of Mr. Webster's relation to it. Of the four principal candidates, General Jackson had 99 electoral votes, Mr. Adams 84, Mr. Crawford 41, and Mr. Clay 37. Mr. Calhoun had been chosen Vice-President by the electoral colleges, by a very large majority. The election in the House being determined by the votes of States, and the choice being confined by the Constitution to the three highest candidates on the list of the electoral votes, Mr. Clay was not before the House; but it soon became apparent that, if he and his friends were to give their votes to Mr. Adams on the first ballot, the choice must lie between Mr. Adams and General Jackson; but, if they gave their votes to Mr. Crawford, the final choice would be between that gentleman and General Jackson. Mr. Webster had no strong personal preferences for Mr. Adams; and, so far as there were any remains of old party distinctions or connections, he was not likely to favor Mr. Adams's election. As one who respected the old Federal party and who had himself acted with it, Mr. Webster might have remembered Mr. Adams's efforts to bring it into disrepute; nor was he, although a Representative from Massachusetts, personally intimate with Mr. Adams. But Mr. Adams had received the electoral votes of all the New-England States, and Mr. Webster felt bound to give effect to this expression of the popular voice in that region, so far as he could consistently with his convictions of what the welfare of the country required. Between Mr. Adams and General Jackson, moreover, he would have preferred the former, for the principal claims of the latter on the office were those of a popular military chieftain, a class of men from whom Mr. Webster was always unwilling to select a President. But, of all the prominent men then before the country, Mr. Webster would have preferred Mr. Calhoun for the presidency, if he could have had a free and unrestricted choice. He had a very high estimate of Mr. Calhoun's abilities and patriotism, and there was then no fundamental difference in their opinions on great constitutional questions. But, in the present condition of things, Mr. Calhoun could not become President, unless the office should be devolved on him by the failure of the House to elect a President before the 4th day of March. The election was fixed for the 9th of February.

Under these perplexing circumstances, Mr. Webster consulted his friends at home, and especially his brother, on whose calm and solid judgment, in all things public or private, he placed great reliance, as to what was proper to be done in two or three contingencies. To his brother he stated the contingencies thus:

1. "If on the first or any subsequent ballot Mr. Adams falls behind Mr. Crawford, and remains so a day or two, shall we hold out to the end of the chapter, or shall we vote for one of the highest?

2. If for one of the highest, say Jackson and Crawford, for which?

3. Is it advisable, under any circumstances, to hold out and leave the chair to Mr. Calhoun?

4. Would or would not New England prefer conferring the power on Calhoun, to a choice of General Jackson?"[1]

The advice which Mr. Webster received, and which entirely concurred with his own judgment, was, that the votes of New England ought to be given to Mr. Adams on the first ballot, and thenceforward steadily, so long as there should be a reasonable chance of his election. Mr. Adams was elected on the first ballot. This result was fortunate for the country; for, although his election was followed by a charge of corrupt coalition between Mr. Clay and himself, the evils and mischiefs and heart-burnings of that unfounded accusation were not to be compared to the dangers that would have ensued from a prolongation of the contest. Mr. Webster, who had no particular connection with the interests of Mr. Adams or Mr. Clay, was, of course, never involved in that charge. He never believed

[1] Correspondence, i.

that it had any foundation, although he considered that some of the steps taken by Mr. Clay in repelling it were not well judged.

There was one interview, and I believe but one, between Mr. Adams and Mr. Webster, on the subject of this election, which places in a very striking light the objects which Mr. Webster sought from Mr. Adams, in case of his election, and the extent of the whole understanding between them respecting Mr. Adams's course. Mr. Webster desired to see an administration of the Government that would not seek to revive or perpetuate the old party distinctions by a distribution of offices of trust among men called by one party denomination. He thought that the welfare of the country required this abnegation of party, and that it could be sufficiently signified by one clear and distinct case of an appointment of a Federalist to office, which would show that the having been of that party was not to operate as a cause of exclusion. The result would be, that the Administration would be left free to call to the public service the best ability and the purest character. Entertaining these opinions, Mr. Webster, on the 3d of February, received a letter from Mr. Warfield, one of the Representatives from Maryland, who had been a Federalist, and whose political friends at home feared that Mr. Adams would build up again the old landmarks of party distinction. Oppressed with the responsibility of his position in his own delegation—since his vote might decide the vote of his State—this gentleman desired Mr. Webster's opinion as to the mode in which he ought to act. Two days afterward, Mr. Webster returned him the following answer:

[MR. WEBSTER TO MR. WARFIELD.]

"House of Representatives, *February* 5, 1825.

"My dear Sir: I have received your note of yesterday, and reflected on its contents, and am very willing to answer it, as far as I can, without incurring the danger of misleading you in the discharge of the delicate and important trust belonging to your present situation.

"I must remark, in the first place, that my acquaintance with Mr. Adams, although friendly and respectful, I hope, on both sides—certainly so on mine—is not particular. I can say nothing, therefore, on the present occasion by any authority derived from him.

"Being in a situation, however, not altogether unlike your own, I have naturally been anxious, like yourself, to form an opinion as to what would be the course of his Administration in regard to the subject alluded to by you. For myself, I am satisfied, and shall give him my vote cheerfully and steadily. And I am ready to say that I should not do so if I did not believe that he would administer the Government on liberal principles, not excluding Federalists, as such, from his regard and confidence.

"I entertain this feeling, not because I wish to see any number of offices, or any particular office, given to those who have been called Federalists; nor because there is a number of such, or any one, that I particularly desire to see employed in the public service; but because the time is come, in my opinion, when we have a right to know whether a particular political name, in reference to former parties, is, of itself, to be regarded as cause of exclusion.

"I wish to see nothing like a portioning, parcelling out, or distributing offices of trust among men called by different denominations. Such a proceeding would be to acknowledge and to regard the existence of distinctions; whereas my wish is, that distinctions should be disregarded. What I think just and reasonable to be expected is, that, by some one clear and distinct case, it may be shown that the distinction above alluded to does not operate as cause of exclusion. Some such case will doubtless present itself, and may be embraced probably in proper time and manner, if thought expedient to embrace it, without prejudice to the pretensions or claims of individuals. The Government will then be left at liberty to call to the public service the best ability and the purest character. It will then be understood that the field is open, and that men are to stand according to their individual merits. So far as this, I think it just to expect the next Administration to go. At any rate, it is natural to wish to know what may probably be expected in this regard.

"While with these sentiments, which, my dear sir, are as strong in my breast as they can be in yours, I am willing to support Mr. Adams, and to give him my vote and influence, I must again remind you that my judgment is made up, not from any understanding or communication with him, but from general considerations; from what I think I know of his liberal feelings, from his good sense and judgment, and from the force of circumstances. I assure you, very sincerely, that I have a full confidence that Mr. Adams's Administration will be just and liberal toward Federalists as toward others; and I need not say that there is no individual who would feel more pain than myself, if you and the rest of our friends should ever find reason to doubt the solidity of the foundation on which this confidence rests.

"Note.—I read this, precisely as it now stands here, to Mr. Adams, on the evening of February 4th. He said, when I had got through, that the letter expressed his general sentiments, and such as he was willing to have understood as his sentiments. There was one particular, however, on which he wished to make a remark. The letter seemed to require him, or expect him, to place one Federalist in the administration. Here I interrupted him, and told him he had misinterpreted the writer's meaning. That the letter did not speak of those appointments called Cabinet appointments particularly, but of appointments generally. With that understanding he said the letter contained his opinions, and he should feel it his duty, by some such appointment, to mark his desire of disregarding party distinctions. He thought either of them, if elected, must necessarily act liberally in this respect. In consequence of this conversation, I interlined, in this letter, the words 'in proper time and manner.' I made no other alteration in it."

What Mr. Webster's opinions were on the subject of internal improvements, and under what circumstances they were formed in 1816, the reader has seen. At this session a very interesting debate took place in the House upon a bill to provide for the continuation of the Cumberland road to Zanesville, in Ohio; a national road, commencing at Baltimore, and then completed as far as Wheeling. The bill was opposed by Mr. McDuffie, of South Carolina, as partial and sectional. He considered that the true course for Congress was to wait until a general system could be devised and put into operation as a whole, with reference to an expenditure graduated somewhat according to the amount of national revenues paid in the particular region to be benefited. Mr. Webster took part in this discussion, and said that, on this subject, as on all others, he wished to bring to the discussion a right feeling, that is, a truly national feeling. It mattered nothing to him who was to be immediately benefited. *Tros Tyriusve*, whether an inhabitant of the banks of the Merrimac of New Hampshire, or the Merrimac of Missouri, he cared not; provided he be a subject of our legislation, he has claims, said Mr. Webster, on my impartial consideration. If he had been led, since the discussion of 1816, to alter his opinion on any part of the general subject then debated, it was that which respects an equal distribution of the public expenditures through the different parts of the Union according to their population. He doubted extremely the propriety and even the power of Congress to carry on legislation on the principle of balancing the local interests of different sections of the country. If the business of legislation had been committed to Congress at all, the whole subject is in its power and under its discretion. . . . When Congress legislates at all, it must legislate for a whole, not for twenty-four parts. The idea had been brought forward as being calculated to prevent a merely local legislation; but it was, in truth, itself a local idea. Such a system would rest on a foundation essentially vicious. When going into a system of improvement, the House has simply to inquire, Where is improvement most needed? He cared not whether it was beyond the Alleghanies or beyond the Missouri; wherever it was most needed, there it must first be made.

Mr. Webster further defended the present object, by contending that the opening of these Western roads had a tendency to settle the public lands, which he regarded as a national object. This again called up Mr. McDuffie, who declared himself opposed to the policy of selling the public lands at the minimum price of one dollar and twenty-five cents per acre, when they were fairly worth fifteen dollars per acre, and would sell at that price if the market were not glutted. This policy had the tendency, he said, to drain off the population of the old States, and it was accompanied by an artificial system of grinding tariffs to counteract the effect of reducing the population of those States. He drew a somewhat melancholy picture of the impoverishment of the Southern States; but, so far as that apprehended decay depended upon a tariff policy, he did not allude to the South Carolina origin of that policy. Mr. Webster replied that he was not in favor of selling the public lands at a price that would throw them into the hands of speculators, but he desired to have them offered at rates that would encourage their settlement. He did not regard it as desirable to prevent the laboring classes of the Eastern States from going to any part of our territory where they could better their condition. The emigration was the natural condition of a country densely populated in one part and possessing in another a vast tract of unsettled lands. The plan of the gentleman, he said, went to reverse the order of Nature, vainly expecting to retain men within a small and comparatively unproductive territory, who have "all the world before them where to choose." For his own part, he was in favor of letting population take its own course; he should experience no feeling of mortification if any of his constituents liked better to settle on the Kansas or the Arkansas, or the Lord knows where, within our territory; let them go and be happier if they could. "The gentleman says our aggregate of wealth would have been greater if our population had been restrained within the limits of the old States; but does he not consider population to be wealth? And has not this been increased by the settlement of a new and fertile country? Such a country presents the most alluring of all prospects to a young and laboring man; it gives him a freehold—it offers to him weight and respectability in society; and, above all, it presents to him a prospect of a permanent provision for his children. Sir, these are inducements which never were resisted, and never will be; and, were the whole extent of country filled with population up to the Rocky Mountains, these inducements would carry that population forward to the shores of the Pacific Ocean. Sir, it is vain to talk; individuals will seek their own good, and not any artificial aggregate of the national wealth; a young, enterprising, and hardy agriculturist can conceive of nothing better to him than plenty of good cheap land."

How Mr. Webster's course in this Congress was regarded in the West, will appear from the following letter, addressed to him by one of the Representatives of Ohio:

[FROM THE HON. JOSEPH VANCE.]

"URBANA, *March* 29, 1825.

"DEAR SIR: From the interest you took during the last Congress in favor of some of the important measures of the West, you have not only a claim on the gratitude of this people, but are entitled to know the political feelings of this section of the Union, both as it respects yourself personally, as well as those growing out of the late presidential election.

"On my way home I passed through our State diagonally, and was everywhere met by our citizens with that cordiality and good feeling which spoke in a language not to be misunderstood that our stand in favor of Mr. Adams was not only approved but received with a degree of enthusiasm unequalled in our State since its admission into the Union. This enthusiasm and good feeling was no doubt as much the result of a well-grounded confidence in our political institutions owing to the manner in which the question was settled in the House of Representatives, as it was to that of the elevation of the present incumbent to the chief-magistracy of the nation.

"As it respects yourself, permit me to say, that with our people no man in this nation stands on more elevated ground, and so far from a wish to proscribe any of the old Federal party, their paramount wish is, that talent, integrity, and worth should be the only passport to office, regardless of party names or sectional distinctions.

"In conclusion, permit me to say, that, among the many valued friends I have made in Congress, none stands higher than yourself, and that nothing would afford me more pleasure than a conscious ability to serve you in attaining under this government a standing equal to your merit.

"Give my respects to friend Baylies, and accept for yourself the sincere regard of your friend,

"JOSEPH VANCE.

"Mr. Webster."

At this session, Mr. Webster introduced and carried through the House the Act for amending the criminal code of the United States, which has sometimes been called by his name, and which is now generally referred to as the "Crimes Act of 1825." The undertaking was a difficult one; for it related to a subject on which jealousy of Federal jurisdiction was quite certain to be aroused. The criminal law of the United States had remained substantially where it was left by the first Congress that sat under the Constitution. It had very serious defects and omissions; yet these could not be supplied without exciting much opposition. Mr. Webster, by his address and by the fulness of his learning and experience, succeeded in overcoming that opposition, and the result was the establishment of a criminal code for the United States, which forty years of practical working have stamped as one of the great monuments of criminal legislation.

The new Administration commenced on the 4th of March, 1825. Mr. Clay became Secretary of State; Richard Rush, of Pennsylvania, Secretary of the Treasury; and James Barbour, of Virginia, Secretary of War. The following members of Mr. Monroe's Cabinet remained in office: Mr. Southard, of New Jersey, as Secretary of the Navy; Mr. McLean, of Ohio, as Postmaster-General, and Mr. Wirt as Attorney-General. Mr. Webster, who, as we have seen, sought nothing for himself or any one else at the hands of the new President, anticipated that this would be a liberal Administration, and considered that it was his true course to support it.

During the years 1824 and 1825, four young English statesmen—the Earl of Derby, then Mr. Stanley, Mr. John Evelyn Denison, the present Speaker of the House of Commons, the late Lord Wharncliffe, then Mr. Stuart Wortley, and the late Lord Taunton, then Mr. Labouchere—travelled extensively in this country, and were much in the society of Mr. Webster and Judge Story. From that period is to be dated a strong friendship between Mr. Webster and Mr. Denison, which continued through Mr. Webster's life. I avail myself of Mr. Denison's permission, to print some portions of their correspondence:

[FROM MR. DENISON.]

"NEW YORK, *April* 27, 1825.

"MY DEAR SIR: We got here last night from our tour in Virginia, which the long distances and bad roads made more of an undertaking than we had anticipated. I write to you, as I promised, without a moment's loss of time, but it is to tell you that all our hopes of another week with you at Boston are over. We have only eight days more on these shores, and intend to sail by the British packet on the 5th. It is not without great regret that I give up this last chance of seeing you in this country, and I certainly would have contrived it in some way if it were not for the good assurances I have that we shall meet at no very distant period in England, where I may pass much more time, and many hours of much more leisure in your company, than a hurried visit at Boston now would allow me. Mr. Rufus King's appointment appears to have given very general satisfaction, in which I heartily join, and, out of many reasons, for none more than because I imagine it will fall in well with your views, and further the prospects you once mentioned in a conversation to me. I should be very glad to have this confirmed by you. I have written to our most excellent Judge,[1] as he desired me when we parted at Philadelphia, to tell him the day we sail, and how impossible it is for us to visit Salem again, but I have insisted that this is not to be a solemn leave-taking, and that the vision which now floats before my eyes, of our active and vigorous friend surveying his robed, and ermined, and gouty brothers of Westminster Hall, is to be realized. He is to see Lord Eldon on his woolsack, and we are to wander together through the aisles of Westminster Abbey.

"I don't know what to expect about the continuance of the session of Parliament after our arrival in England. They have done a great deal of most important business; but I do not regret my absence from England, or think I could have spent one moment of my time better than in this country. You see we are verifying your predictions to Congress in April, '24,

[1] Mr. Justice Story.

as fast as we can reasonably be expected, by our policy at home and abroad. By the time you pay us a visit, Mr. Robinson will let us make you tipsy on good French wine almost for nothing. The first branch of Huskisson's new proposals for the regulation of colonial trade appears to me the most important measure produced for many years, as well as the most convincing proof of the real disposition of our Government. The way in which the people of England appear to be conducting themselves about the Catholics is still more important. I really believe that an effective cry of 'No Popery' could hardly now be raised in the country. If it is so, the mighty change can be attributed only to the diffusion of light and knowledge among the people, and to the long and open discussion of the question. The triumph of discussion will be greater in this case, than even in the case of the emancipation of slaves. After this, Right and Truth need never despair.

"I will not fail to write to you. You will direct me by your letters to the subjects about which you feel the greatest interest. Wortley and Labouchere desire their best remembrances to Mrs. Webster and you.

"Believe me,
"With great truth and friendship,
"Most sincerely yours,
"J. EVELYN DENISON.

"I find an English road-book brought by accident among some others with us. As it is the best we have, and a late and correct edition, I thought you might like to have it. You may now travel from Liverpool to London with the same ease as you used to do from Hyde Park corner to the Bank, and learn the names of all the country-seats by the way."

[TO MR. DENISON.]

"BOSTON, *May* 2, 1825.

"MY DEAR SIR: I have received yours of the 27th of April, and most sincerely regret that we shall not see you again among us before you leave our continent. The good Judge will be inconsolable. He is now in Maine, in the discharge of official duties, and will not, I fear, be home in season to write you before your departure. You must try to keep our little Boston alive in your recollections. It will not be disagreeable to you, I hope, when you return to your own country, and to the midst of your own associations there, to know that there are those on this side the globe, wholly unknown to you a year ago, who entertain much regard for your welfare. For me, I shall take care to keep myself in remembrance, I shall contrive pretences to write you often, and I hope to hear from you sometimes.

"Mr. King's appointment gives very general satisfaction; I like it very much. He is a gentleman of great worth and respectability, a little too much advanced in life, perhaps, to be expected to remain long in the situation. I think the President's selection fortunate on all accounts.

"I assure you, my dear sir, it is my fixed intention to see England, within two or three years. No disappointment, not connected with my own health, or that of my family, can be allowed to prevent the accomplishment of this purpose. Your acquaintance and friendship form not only an additional inducement, but an important reliance and resource, in relation to such a visit.

"You will doubtless find Parliament still sitting, although many great questions will be disposed of before you will be able to show yourselves at Westminster. I have read the proceedings of the session thus far with great interest, especially Mr. Robinson's speech, on bringing forward the Budget, and Mr. Huskisson's two speeches, on the subject of the proposed changes in the laws of trade. There appears to me to be, in each of these gentlemen, so much clearsightedness, so much enlightened liberality, united to so much general ability, as to fit them well to be leading ministers in your government at this most interesting period of the world. I regard not only England, but all the civilized states, as greatly their debtors, for having set an example of a policy so wise, and so beneficial, in the intercourse of commercial states. Their success thus far has been greater, I think, than even they themselves anticipated; and I most sincerely partake in the gratification it produces.

"I hope you will remember to send me any distinguished Parliamentary speeches that may happen to be separately published. I believe I have not omitted this particular in the memorandum you were good enough to take. I believe I shall not receive, except through your agency, the volumes of Parliamentary Debates, of which you took a note. On this subject, however, I will shortly write you, to your address in London.

"I shall be very glad of the road-book you mentioned. If the present rage continues, one will need no *road-books;* when I arrive at Liverpool, I expect to embark on a *railway* for London.

"I beg you to make my best remembrances to Mr. Wortley and Mr. Labouchere. Mention me also to Colonel Dawson, if he be now with you. I saw less of him here than I wished. When you meet Mr. Stanley in England, be kind enough to remember my regards to him. I expect to see a speech from him, yet, before the close of the session. Adieu, my dear sir, and I pray you to be assured of my

"Faithful friendship and entire esteem.

"DANL. WEBSTER.

"Mrs. Webster desires me to give her farewell to you and your friends, Wortley and Labouchere. She wishes you fair winds, a prosperous voyage, and a happy meeting with your friends.

"If Mr. Stratford Canning should return to England, I beg you to make acceptable to him my best regards."

[FROM MR. DENISON.]

"NEW YORK, Evening of the 4th (*May*), 1825.

"MY DEAR SIR: I have just got your letter, and cannot refrain from thanking you, and sending you a few more last words from this side the water. I am much gratified by the assurances you give me that I shall not be forgotten by some of your countrymen, in whose remembrances I shall be very anxious and proud to have a place. This year of my life will be deeply engraven on my memory; and the strongest and deepest lines will be those that record the hours spent in your company, and in that of our good Judge and some of your townsmen—I will take care of the Parliamentary Debates, among your other orders.

"Wortley and I drove over this morning to Mr. Rufus King's, who had desired to see us before we sailed. We found him in good health and spirits. He told us that he did not look forward to a long stay; that he had hesitated much, before he accepted the appointment, and that nothing but the strong and pressing language of Mr. Adams, and his own wish to second the President's endeavors to adjust all points of difference between the two countries, and to unite them, as far as in him lay, in one common interest and in mutual good-will, would have induced him to undertake the mission. No man is better fitted to bring about so desirable an event; and I am much mistaken if he will not find our Government readily and cordially meet him in all his advances.

"Pray thank Mrs. Webster for her kind wishes, and give her mine for the health and prosperity of all around her.

"Colonel Dawson joins us in best remembrances. Mr. Canning and Stanley shall have your messages, and I know both will be proud of them.

"We sail to-morrow in the middle of the day.

"Yours with sincere friendship,

"J. EVELYN DENISON"

[TO MR. DENISON.]

BOSTON, *June* 6, 1825.

"MY DEAR SIR: You perceive that I do not intend to allow you time to forget your Cisatlantic friends before you hear from some of us. I use this opportunity the more cheerfully, as my friend Mr. Dutton, of this city, goes by the same conveyance, and although I believe he has a letter to you from your very good friend the Judge, and although I believe also you saw him here, I must beg to solicit your attention and regard to him, if he should happen to come where you are in England. He is a very respectable and worthy man.

"We all regretted here very much that you and your friends did not come here to give us a parting look. Nevertheless, we have prayed for prosperous gales, and an agreeable voyage for you all. For myself, I have been very quietly at home, since I returned from Washington, but the

Judge and myself are thinking of making an excursion, to commence in the course of this month, to Niagara. Since the adjournment of Congress we have little political news. Mr. Clay is gone to Kentucky, and expects, I believe, to be well received by his friends, notwithstanding some complaints, probably not general, for the support which he gave to the President. We look for Mr. Rush next month. Mr. King has already sailed to take his place. We have hopes of seeing Mr. Addington so far North as this place during the summer. Wallenstein is already at New York. I believe Mr. Hopkinson and Mr. Walsh intend us a visit this month.

"When you shall have composed yourself, my dear sir, and settled your brain, disturbed as it must be by such a whirl as you have made round so great a part of our continent, I shall hope to hear from you. We have accounts from London to April 21st. Mr. Canning's last speech on the Catholic question is, I think, a most admirable performance. Some men, and he seems to be one of them, show great powers under the pressure of great responsibility. Certain it is, that his late parliamentary efforts far exceed any thing which is to be found of his at an earlier date. I go far enough back, of course, to include among his great efforts his speech at Liverpool.

"I am for the Catholic emancipation; but I should think, nevertheless, that its friends overrate its utility and importance by about as much as its enemies overrate its mischief and danger. You must excuse this expression of opinion on a matter, of the merits of which I know so little. If the leading speeches on this (and other) subjects should be published in pamphlet form, I should be very glad to have them. I have made an arrangement with Mr. Burdett, bookseller of this place, by which his correspondents in London will receive, pay for, and transmit hither any books which you may procure or order for me. The names and address of these correspondents are, Messrs. Peter, William, and George Wynne, stationers, Paternoster Row. When you took my memoranda, it was left a little doubtful whether I should rely on you to be able to complete my set of Parliamentary Debates. My other hope has *failed*, and I now wish you to take the trouble to order what will complete my set, according to the minutes taken at Washington. I think of nothing in particular to be added to the list, with which I troubled you, but will thank you to exercise a pretty liberal discretion, in regard to such occasional publications, especially in the department of politics, as you think may interest me. I would like well enough to see Sir Egerton Brydges's book. The books, however, which I mean to trouble you to obtain, are only such as I should hardly be able to get otherwise, and therefore I shall not at present swell the list.

"I pray you to remember me to your fellow-travellers in America. We cherish the hope that you sometimes think of us. Mrs. Webster joins me in remembrance and regard to you. I shall be likely to trouble you often, and trust you will let us know of your safe arrival. I shall expect, of course, that if any friend of yours shall be induced to visit America, you will allow me to be known to him.

"I am, dear sir, yours very truly and sincerely,

"DANIEL WEBSTER."

An association for the erection of a monument to commemorate the battle of Bunker Hill had been for some time in existence in Boston and its neighborhood, of which Mr. Webster was now president. As the fiftieth anniversary of the battle approached—the 17th of June, 1825—it was determined that the corner-stone of the monument should be laid on that day, with appropriate ceremonies; and Mr. Webster was unanimously requested by his fellow-trustees to deliver the address. General Lafayette was then making that tour through the United States which became, in its progress, the most remarkable ovation ever given in this country to any man, and the arrangements of his journey were so made as to admit of his being present on this occasion. Among the reminiscences furnished to me by Mr. Ticknor, I find the following description of the scene, the orator, and the address:

"*June* 17, 1825.—Mr. Webster delivered the oration on laying the corner-stone of the Bunker Hill Monument. He was president of the association, and, as such, presided at the meeting of the trustees when he was appointed. On the evening when he was chosen, being present as one of the trustees, he took me aside, and asked me if I supposed all the trustees would prefer to have him deliver the address. I told him I thought there was no difference of opinion on the point. He then asked if I thought it would be well for him to accept, doubting whether he were well fitted for it, or whether the president of the society should be its orator. I told him that I thought he would fulfil public expectation better than any one else; and that I thought his place rather called on him to perform the duty than otherwise.

"He often talked with me of the work afterward, and seemed quite anxious about it, especially after it was decided that General Lafayette could be present. A few days before he delivered it, he read it over to me. The magnificent opening gave him much concern; so did the address to Lafayette; but about that to the Revolutionary soldiers, and the survivors of the battle, he said that he felt as if he knew how to talk to such men, for that his father, and many of his father's friends, whom he had known, had been among them. He said he had known General Stark, and that the last time he saw him was in a tavern, in Concord, not long before he died, when he said to him: 'Daniel, your face is pretty black, but it isn't so black as your father's was with gunpowder at the Bennington fight.' He added, that it seemed to him as if he was peculiarly familiar with those men and those times.

"The day of the 17th was very propitious for laying the corner-stone. The occasion and the presence of General Lafayette had brought together immense crowds of people from all parts of the country. The procession was formed at the State-House, in Boston, and, just as it moved, an easterly breeze came up, that tempered the air delightfully through the rest of the day. We arrived in good season on the hill, where more than twenty thousand people were collected. The platform from which Mr. Webster spoke was at the bottom, and temporary seats for several thousand persons were arranged on the rising hill-side, while, near the brow above, stood a dense black mass, most of whom could hear what was said. His voice was very clear and full, and his manner very commanding. Once, owing to the great press, some of the seats and barriers gave way, and there was a moment of considerable confusion, notwithstanding the efforts of those whose duty it was to preserve order. One of these gentlemen said to Mr. Webster: 'It is impossible, sir, to restore order.' Mr. Webster replied with a good deal of severity: 'Nothing is impossible, sir; let it be done.' Another effort was made, and silence was obtained.[1]

"The passage about the rising of the monument and the address to the survivors of the battle were the most effective parts of the oration. The shouts at the first were prolonged until it seemed as if they would not stop; the address brought tears into the eyes of many, and bowed down the heads of the veterans themselves to conceal their emotion.

"When it was all over, Governor Barbour, of Virginia, said to me: 'If that address had been delivered in Virginia, I should say that the person who made it was sure of the first prize in the national lottery.'

"The dinner, under the great awning on the neighboring hill, was a scene of much confusion, and, although Mr. Webster, General Lafayette, and some other persons gave toasts, very little was heard of what they said.

[1] I was present (then a boy), in the outskirts of that vast audience, and well remember that, when order was restored, after the confusion described by Mr. Ticknor, Mr. Webster's clarion voice was distinctly heard at the spot where I stood. His voice, in public speaking, was a very peculiar one. Whether speaking in the open air, or under a roof, he could make himself heard to a great distance, apparently without much effort, and without being unpleasantly loud to those who were near him. This was partly due to the *quality* of his voice, which was naturally pitched at a high key, but which was tempered by such a richness of tone that it was never in the smallest degree shrill. It was due also to what might be called the *quantity* of his voice. He had an unusual capacity of chest and vocal organs, and hence his voice was one of extraordinary volume. It was, moreover, so entirely under his control, when his vocal organs were in full play, that it never broke, however high it might rise in the scale of its natural compass, or whatever might be the state of his emotions. At the same time, there was a peculiarity about his organs of speech that I have heard him describe as a momentary paralysis. It sometimes happened to him, on rising to speak suddenly, that they utterly refused to perform their office until moistened by a slight draught of water. As soon as this was done, the inability vanished, and did not return upon him.

In the evening there was a grand reception at Mr. Webster's, in Summer Street, Colonel Thorndike, who occupied the adjoining house, kindly cutting a door to connect Mr. Webster's house and his own, so that the crowd might find room. It was not like the reception immediately after his address at Plymouth, when the spontaneousness with which people gathered round him, and his freedom from all care and responsibility, filled him with such a natural and beautiful excitement. He was on this occasion the host, dignified and agreeable, but nothing more.

"The address was immediately published. He placed it at the disposition of the Bunker-Hill Monument Association, and I sold the copyright to Hilliard & Gray for three hundred dollars. He desired me, as he was going directly to Niagara with Mrs. Webster, Judge and Mrs. Story, and others, to superintend the publication. The day before he went away, he came to see me at my house, about a passage he wanted to alter; he took the proof-sheet, and went to work, but did not satisfy himself with what he wrote. He grew very impatient; he thought he could do better by dictating; and walked about the room uneasily, reading the proof-sheet and his changes over and over again, dictating new matter, which satisfied him no better. At last I suggested something as a substitute, and he desired me to put it in writing, throwing himself upon the sofa in a sort of despair. I did as he desired. It took perhaps five minutes, and, when I turned round to read what I had written, I found him fast asleep; a change not surprising in him, for he could, almost at any time, dismiss any subject, however exciting, and compose himself to sleep. When I waked him, he seemed much relieved to find the matter arranged; and I did not see him again till he returned from Niagara, long before which time the country was ringing with the power of the oration. From Worcester, however, he wrote me a note, still troubled about words and phrases."[1]

Mr. Fletcher Webster has related an amusing anecdote of the place where the first Bunker-Hill Oration was chiefly composed before it was committed to paper. By an extract from Mr. Webster's Autobiography, contained in a previous chapter of this volume, the reader has learned that he was much in the habit of preparing formal speeches in the solitudes of Nature. It seems that the celebrated passage, in which he addressed the surviving veterans of Bunker Hill, was first heard by the trout in Marshpee Brook. Mr. Fletcher Webster says:

"The Marshpee River flows from a large lake, called Wakeby Pond, in Barnstable County, into the ocean on the southeast coast of Massa-

[1] The passage which troubled him was that relating to the position of Colonel Prescott in the battle. As he originally spoke it, he did not give credit enough to Prescott, and, even as it was altered and printed, it did not wholly satisfy some persons, who were supposed to know much about the battle.

chusetts. It is a short and rapid stream, running in a deep valley, or rather ravine, with high, precipitous sides, covered with a thick growth of small pines, and various kinds of brushwood and shrubs.

"The only method of fishing it, is by wading along the middle, and throwing under the banks on either side, it being unapproachable otherwise, owing to the trees and underbrush.

"It was, as he states in his Autobiography, while middle-deep in this stream, that Mr. Webster composed a great portion of his first Bunker-Hill Address. He had taken along with him that well-known angler, John Denison, usually called John Trout, and myself. I followed him along the stream, fishing the holes and bends which he left for me; but, after a while, I began to notice that he was not so attentive to his sport, or so earnest as usual.

"He would let his line run carelessly down the stream, or hold his rod still while his hook was not even touching the water; omitted trying the best places under the projecting roots of the pines; and seemed, indeed, quite abstracted and uninterested in his amusement.

"This, of course, caused me a good deal of wonder, and, after calling his attention once or twice to his hook hanging on a twig, or caught in the long grass of the river, and finding that, after a moment's attention, he relapsed again into his indifference, I quietly walked up near him, and watched. He seemed to be gazing at the overhanging trees, and presently advancing one foot, and extending his right hand, he commenced to speak: 'Venerable men,' etc., etc. He afterward frequently referred to this circumstance, as he does in the above letter." [1]

From a brief note now before me, addressed by Mr. Webster to Mr. Ticknor, on the day on which he completed the writing of this address, it appears that he was not well satisfied with it, and quite misjudged the effect that it was likely to produce:

"I did the deed this morning, i. e., I finished my speech; and I am pretty well persuaded it is a speech that will *finish* me, as far as reputation is concerned. There is no more tone in it than in the weather in which it has been written; it is 'perpetual dissolution and thaw.'"

It would be a work of supererogation if I were to enter upon extended criticisms of Mr. Webster's productions, as they successively arise in the course of his history; and certainly it is unnecessary for me to endeavor to guide the judgment or instruct the taste of the reader in respect to this one. He himself, as perhaps I have already said, was always inclined to

[1] Correspondence, ii., 257, note.

regard the Plymouth Discourse as the best of his efforts of this class. In point of breadth, and of the reach to which he carried the subject, and in the massiveness of its colossal proportions, the Plymouth Discourse may stand at the head of his orations. But the thrilling eloquence of the address to the old soldiers of Bunker Hill, and of the apostrophe to Warren, and the superb reservation of eulogy with which he spoke of and to General Lafayette—" reluctant to grant our highest and last honors to the living, honors we would gladly hold yet back from the little remnant of the immortal band"—were perhaps unequalled, surely never surpassed by him on any other occasion. The consummate skill of composition and delivery, which afterward gave to a supposititious speech of John Adams all the effect of a real utterance of that patriot, in the eulogy at Faneuil Hall, was an exhibition of power of quite another kind.

The illustrations given by Mr. Ticknor of Mr. Webster's literary care in respect to this class of his public efforts call for some further remark concerning his habits in this respect. He would sometimes make an important speech in Congress or in court, and pay no attention to the dress in which it might be laid before the world; insomuch that his friends, as we have seen, often considered him careless about his reputation as a speaker. But, with these formal orations, which he regarded as coming within the domain of scholarship, and on which he was conscious that his fame as an orator was, in part, to rest with present and future generations, he was extremely careful, as they were passing through the press. He would correct them with a severity of taste that was far more rigorous than any standard that the public was likely to apply to them; and, when he failed to satisfy himself, he would resort to the aid of others. The late Mr. Thomas Kemper Davis, a son of one of his intimate friends, and a good scholar himself, was a student-at-law, in Mr. Webster's office, at the time when he delivered his eulogy on Adams and Jefferson. He has told me that, on the morning after its delivery, Mr. Webster entered the office, and threw down the manuscript before him, with the request: "There, Tom, please to take that discourse, and weed out the Latin words." Such was his love of the Anglo-Saxon element in our language, that he preferred to avoid a word of Latin origin, if he could do so without impoverishing his style. At the same time, he was a Latin scholar, and a constant reader of the Latin classics.

There are those who may be inclined to regard this trouble about words and phrases as something a little beneath a great statesman; and, perhaps, as evincing less of the practical, and of what is sometimes affectedly called the "business" character of mind, than has been displayed by other eminent men, who have taken, or have been supposed to take, no thought of such refinements. But there are several obvious answers to this kind of cavil, at least when it is applied to Mr. Webster. In the first place, if a thing is to be done, whoever is to do it, it is better to have it done well than ill, in point of manner as well as of substance. In the next place, a man who occupies a very conspicuous public position, is bound to look farther than a merely selfish regard for his own reputation might lead him. The effect of his example on the culture of his time and country is to be considered, in matters of style, as well as in the sentiments that he speaks or writes. Public speaking, in this country, has never been so pure and correct as to make it unimportant whether the best models are or are not found in the performances of those who are regarded as the ablest thinkers and most eloquent speakers of their time. In the third place, demonstrative oratory, in a cultivated age, is one of the departments of letters in which a correct and carefully-polished style, or the want of it, is especially conspicuous. Finally, in the case of Mr. Webster, no one, who is conversant with what he could do and did, as a statesman, a legislator, and a lawyer, will be inclined to rate his business capacities the lower, because he was nice and long in the correction of discourses that were to live after him, and to be read with delight by the lettered and the unlettered in periods very remote from his own. Instead of contracting, it should enlarge our estimate of his powers, to know that, while he was capable of moving, or convincing, or instructing men to a degree in which he was not excelled, certainly, by any of his contemporaries, he was not indifferent to the language in which he clothed his thoughts. One great secret of the directness with which he reached the minds of men lay in the simplicity and purity of his style; a simplicity that was the result of the clearness and vigor of his thought, and a purity that was the result of a highly-cultivated and disciplined taste.

Mr. Ticknor observes that, long before Mr. Webster's return from Niagara, the country was ringing with the power of the Bunker-Hill Oration. It was no less rapidly circulated on the Continent of Europe. General Lafayette wrote to Mr. Webster from La Grange: "Your Bunker Hill has been translated in French and other languages, to the very great profit of European readers. My gallant and eloquent friend, Foy, has lived long enough to enjoy it."[1]

The journey to Niagara, mentioned by Mr. Ticknor, occupied the remaining portion of June and nearly the whole of July. The party consisted of Mr. and Mrs. Webster, Judge and Mrs. Story, and Miss Buckminster, afterward Mrs. Lee. Forty-five years ago, when this tour was undertaken, there was, of course, not a single mile of railway between Boston and Niagara. Mr. Webster and his friends travelled in the coaches of that period, and in the passenger-boats of the Erie Canal, which, saving their slowness, were not a disagreeable mode of locomotion. At Albany, Mr. Webster and Judge Story were invited to meet General Lafayette at a public dinner, given to him in the capitol; and, in the evening, the whole party attended the theatre, where the General was present, and remained until he had taken his leave to go on board a steamer, and descend the river.[2]

The letters of Mr. Webster, written from Niagara to his friends at home, are nearly all embraced in the first volume of his printed correspondence. They were chiefly addressed to Mrs. George Blake, to whom he endeavored to impart as vivid a description of that sublime spectacle as words can convey. It was the first time he ever looked upon it. The following passage, in one of his letters to Mrs. Blake, may be quoted here, as one of the best specimens of his manner of describing a scene which has awakened similar emotions in all thoughtful minds that have beheld it, while it has per-

[1] Correspondence, i., 400.

[2] Life of Judge Story, i., 455.

haps rarely touched such a power of expressing the feelings that it excites:[1]

"We went this afternoon a little lower down the river than the upper staircase, almost, indeed, down to the ferry, and, getting out on a rock, in the edge of the river, we thought the view of the whole falls the best we had obtained. If, at the bottom of the staircase, instead of descending farther, we choose to turn to the right, and go up the stream, we soon get to the foot of the fall, and approach the edge of the falling mass. It is easy to go in behind for a little distance between the falling water and the rock over which it is precipitated; this cannot be done, however, without being entirely wet. From within this cavern there issues a wind, occasionally very strong, and bringing with it such showers and torrents of spray, that we are soon as wet as if we had come over the Falls with the water. As near to the fall, in this place, as you can well come, is perhaps the spot on which the mind is most deeply impressed with the whole scene. Over our heads hangs a fearful rock, projecting out like an unsupported piazza. Before us is a hurly-burly of waters, too deep to be fathomed, too irregular to be described, shrouded in too much mist to be clearly seen. Water, vapor, foam, and the atmosphere, are all mixed up together in sublime confusion. By our side, down comes this world of green and white waters, and pours into the invisible abyss. A steady, unvarying, low-toned roar thunders incessantly upon our ears; as we look up, we think some sudden disaster has opened the seas, and that all their floods are coming down upon us at once; but we soon recollect that what we see is not a sudden or violent exhibition, but the permanent and uniform character of the object which we contemplate. There the grand spectacle has stood for centuries, from the creation even, as far as we know, without change. From the beginning it has shaken, as it now does, the earth and the air; and its unvarying thunder existed before there were human ears to hear it. Reflections like these, on the duration and permanency of this grand object, naturally arise, and contribute much to the deep feeling which the whole scene produces. We cannot help being struck with a sense of the insignificance of man and all his works compared with what is before us:

'Lo! where it comes like an eternity,
As if to sweep down all things in its track!'"[2]

After his return from Niagara, Mr. Webster passed the remainder of the summer and a portion of the autumn (1825) at Sandwich, on Cape Cod.

[1] In the Life of Judge Story is a series of very interesting letters, written by him on this journey, which describe its incidents more minutely than those of Mr. Webster.

[2] Correspondence, i., 389.

CHAPTER XII.

1825-1826.

CORRESPONDENCE—AMENDMENT OF THE JUDICIAL SYSTEM—SPEECH ON THE CONGRESS OF PANAMA—EULOGY ON ADAMS AND JEFFERSON—REËLECTED TO CONGRESS.

MR. WEBSTER arrived in Washington, to attend the first session of the Nineteenth Congress, before the 1st of December, 1825, with a great stock of health and strength, which he had gained at Niagara and at Sandwich. Mrs. Webster and the children, Daniel, Julia, and Edward, were all with him. Before entering upon the business of the session, I quote some portions of his correspondence, extending through this winter, and I add to it a letter written by Mrs. Webster, because it will give my readers a pleasing impression of that cultivated and gentle lady, and because it is the only production of her pen among the papers before me.[1]

[MRS. WEBSTER TO MRS. TICKNOR.]

"WASHINGTON, *December* 24, 1825.

"I am unwilling a single day should pass, my dear Mrs. Ticknor, without telling you how much I feel indebted by the kind interest you take in our welfare. It is indeed pleasant to feel assured that, though absent, we are still remembered, and I have the great happiness of telling you we are all well. We had a very good journey; having neither heroes nor heroines, no incident worth relating occurred. Julia took a severe cold in the renowned city of New York, which, added to the fatigue of the journey,

[1] The letters of Mrs. Webster, quoted in a previous chapter, were printed in the first volume of Mr. Webster's correspondence.

made her look quite ill. I was very unhappy for a time; but she soon began to mend, and is now very well. Mr. Webster is in very good health. He got a headache yesterday in consequence of his exertions to put out the fire which was discovered in the library of the capitol the night before. As the newspapers, I see, made 'honorable' mention of him, together with the fire, I need say little about it.

"Washington is the same as when you were here. I see very little or indeed no change. There are, however, some changes in the inhabitants, and some have changed places—all else appears precisely the same.

"Mrs. Adams looks well in her new station, and the President now and then sheds a tear, which looks *benign.*[1] Things are under much better regulation in the palace than formerly. There is a little of Northern comfort. Instead of shivering and shaking in that immense cold saloon, we were shown into a good, warm parlor, with a nice little white damsel to take care of our coats, etc. I said there were no changes in the appearance of things here; there have been several new houses, which ought not to be passed over, but the distances are so immense they are hardly perceptible. The furniture at the palace below-stairs is precisely as it was. I believe all the appropriations have been confined to the second story. There are many things below that want renewing. I wish I could send you an inventory of the furniture as it was when Mrs. Adams came into possession —it's a curiosity.

"Mr. Wallenstein I do not see so often as I should like to. His visits unfortunately happen, most of them, when I am out. I saw him, however, yesterday and the evening before; he was in fine spirits, and very amusing with his remarks upon the ladies. I shall have great pleasure in presenting him your kind remembrances. My husband, I am sure, will be very happy in giving you his opinion of the President's message, or any thing else which may serve as an apology for writing you. I have much duty to perform in the way of visits this morning, which I must beg you will accept as an apology for this hasty letter. Pray remember me very affectionately to your husband, and give much love and a kiss to little Anna. And believe me very truly and affectionately yours,

"G. WEBSTER."

[MR. WEBSTER TO MR. TICKNOR.]

"WASHINGTON, *January* 8, 1826.

"MY DEAR SIR: It is a poor return for your kindness to remain so long dumb. Your letter has stood up here before me these three weeks, like another conscience, giving me a rebuke ever and anon. I had thought that for the first month of the session I should have much leisure, and had meditated divers great things. But I have found some small matter or

[1] Mr. Adams was subject to an affection of the lachrymal duct, and hence he occasionally had the appearance of weeping.

other forever in the way. I stay at home to-day while my wife is gone to hear '† John, Bishop of Charleston,' preach in the capitol, that I may have time to write to Mr. Denison (England), and yourself, and some other friends in the United States.

"Pretty near the whole of Washington is reflected in 'Gales and Seaton;' so that there is not much to talk about out of the newspapers. Mr. Adams's mission to Panama is opposed in the Senate, and will be in the House, when the money is asked for. It is not unlikely it may be the first measure which shall assemble the scattered materials of opposition. But I entertain no doubt about the result. From what I learn of the causes which led to Mr. Adams's agreement to the proposal, I am convinced he acted right; and, in addition to that, the popular topics lie on that side.

"Mr. Clay appears to get on very well in the discharge of his duties. I believe the whole diplomatic corps entertain much respect for him, and what I have seen of his diplomatic correspondence shows great cleverness.

"I am greatly pleased with your friend Mr. Vaughan.[1] He has been very civil to me, for which I have to thank you. He speaks of you much, and is very desirous to see you. What has continued to puzzle him, he says, is how you could contrive, in so short a time, to master so much Spanish literature. I find he is brother of Mr. Sergeant Vaughan, one of the leading lawyers in England, whose bar speeches Judge Story and I have been reading (like the rest of our brethren) any time these twenty years. The Judge will be pleased with Mr. Vaughan the more, as he is thus collaterally connected with the law. We have a Dutch minister in the person of Mr. Huygens, apparently a respectable man; and in other respects the corps remains much as it was.

"In the way of private affairs, I believe you must rely on my wife for a knowledge of what little there is stirring. The drawing-room is agreed by all to have received great improvement. When I was there it was absolutely warm, within a very few degrees, to the point of comfort. I even saw gentlemen walking in the great hall of entrance, with apparent impunity, without their great-coats on! (This is for Mrs. Ticknor.) We have even dined at the White House—a very good dinner and a very good time. But not liking large dinner-parties at all, I think they are hardly better for having ladies. It is a solemn time, when we are at a dinner-table, where numbers prevent us from being social, and politeness forbids us to be noisy. On the whole, however, the domestic presidential arrangements are approved. (For Mrs. Ticknor.)

"We had a discourse yesterday from Dr. Watkyns, of the Columbian Institute. It was, I thought, a very creditable performance, and will doubtless be printed.

[1] The English minister at Washington. Mr Ticknor knew Mr. Vaughan in Madrid in 1818, where that gentleman was secretary of embassy to Sir Charles Wellesley, afterward Lord Cowley, at whose house they constantly met during that summer. He had recently arrived in Washington.

"When you see the Judge, tell him I am in a peck of troubles for want of his promised letter.

"Adieu! Have you had any more fires? With my love to Mrs. T.,

"Yours truly, D. W."

[MR. WEBSTER TO MR. TICKNOR.]

"WASHINGTON, *March* 1, 1826.

"MY DEAR SIR: I owe you for two very kind letters; and, although I do not pay the debt, it is but fair to acknowledge it. To begin with affairs: I immediately called at the War Department, and suggested an idea about West Point.[1] It was received not only kindly but with much apparent satisfaction and pleasure. As great men are apt to have short memories, I have written a note on the subject, addressed to the Secretary, which will go on file, of course, and will recall the matter to his mind at the proper time. I already envy you and your wife the pleasure of Catskill.

"Our Philadelphia matter remains as when I wrote you last; all being, I believe, quiet and gratified.

"Judge Story was sick on his way—and is again a little unwell here. But his present illness is only a little sick headache; one of the ways, perhaps, in which the great enemy influenza makes his attacks. Wallenstein is mourning according to law, and as well and happy as a man can be who belongs to an empire that has so suddenly lost a *pretty good* head and got another rather doubtful one.[2] I speak, however, of those only in this empire whose honors, or whose bread, depend on this same head of the empire; for, as to the masses, I suppose they care not whose head is lost, so it be not their own. When quite a boy I remember reading some verses of a song, which had some sense though not much poetry. I have looked for them often since in vain. Their moral is as applicable to emperors as others, more striking of course in the case of the great than of the small. I can recall only these few doggerel lines:

"'When you and I are dead and gone,
This busy world will still jog on,
And laugh and sing, and be as hearty,
As if we still were of the party.'

[1] Mr. Ticknor had written to Mr. Webster as follows: "And *apropos* of this, I want to see the establishment at West Point. Thayer, the superintendent, was my classmate, and this makes it more interesting to me. In 1822, I was asked to go as a visitor; but it was impossible for me, and I declined. Last winter Mr. Calhoun asked me again; but I foresaw what would be the situation of my family, and again declined. Next summer, however, as far as I can now see, we shall be on the North River within a week of the examination. I do not doubt I shall be present at it; and if the Secretary of War chooses to ask me to go as a visitor, I should be glad of it, because I can in this way get more of the practical details and information that will be useful at Cambridge, and besides get it in a more agreeable way. At any rate, I think I shall be there, whether the secretary sends me his compliments or not, and Thayer will, perhaps, be quite as glad to see me as if I were an official visitor."

[2] This alludes to the death of the Emperor Alexander of Russia, who was succeeded by his brother the late Emperor Nicholas, in December, 1825.

This is melancholy, but it is true; and, if a dead man finds any thing, the autocrat of all the Russias will find it is true.

"As to politics, we have little *stirring*. All goes on smoothly except the Panama mission; that sticks in the Senate. The incongruous materials of opposition assimilate better on that subject than they are likely to on most others. I believe the measure will prevail, however, by a slight majority in the Senate. In our House we shall have a debate on it, and I shall make a short speech, for certain reasons, provided I can get out of court, and provided better reflection should not change my purpose. At present, the H. R. is *riding at anchor* on the Constitutional Amendment question. I seize the occasion *to go ashore* and dispatch my concerns in Supreme Court.

"As to parties, dinners, etc., we have enough and to spare. My wife is a good deal dissipated. So is Mrs. Blake. The ball of the 22d was a grand affair. But I learn that Mrs. Webster intends to write a dispatch soon to Mrs. Ticknor, which will, of course, discuss all these questions at large.

"And now of Governor Cass.[1] Lewis Cass is a native of Exeter, New Hampshire. His father was an officer in our army, long ago. Lewis was educated at Exeter 'in my time,' and went with his father to Ohio about 1798 or 1800. He there read and practised law—took a military command at the commencement of the late war, and, on the peace, was appointed Governor of Michigan. He is what we call in New England *a clever fellow*, good-natured, kind-hearted, amiable, and obliging. His education was imperfect; but he seems to have done something for himself in the Western wilds. He has been here this winter, and I have brightened old chains with him. He is of the age of Saltonstall,[2] who was with him at Exeter, equally good-humored, more talkative, and twice as fat. In Ohio he was always found, I am told, on the side of sound principles. He is probably not overlearned in Indian languages—perhaps is superficial—but I confess I was astonished to find he knew so much. But I ought to say that I am a total unbeliever in the new doctrines about the Indian languages. I believe them to be the rudest forms of speech; and I believe there is as little in the languages of the tribes as in their laws, manners, and customs, worth studying or worth knowing. All this is heresy, I know, but so I think.

"Adieu, my dear sir. Pray remember me most sincerely to Mrs. Ticknor. I go seldom to Williamson's. It is dreary and solitary. Mrs. Webster joins me in her remembrances, and will shortly have the pleasure of writing to Mrs. Ticknor.

"Adieu.—Yours always most truly,

"D. W."

Among the topics that required Mr. Webster's immediate

[1] Mr. Ticknor had inquired about him.

[2] The late Hon. Leverett Saltonstall, of Salem.

attention at this session, the judiciary system was the first. In the last preceding Congress, he had been able to do nothing more on this subject than to prevent the adoption of measures which he regarded as inexpedient and injurious. It now became necessary for him to introduce a bill that should amend the judicial system, as it then existed, in several very important respects. The number of the judges of the Supreme Court was then seven. They were allotted to seven circuits, six of which embraced the Atlantic States. The seventh circuit consisted of the States of Kentucky, Ohio, and Tennessee. All the other Western and Southwestern States had only District Courts, exercising the powers of Circuit Courts. Great complaints came from these States, while upon the Atlantic seaboard there was no pressing necessity for any change. Mr. Webster desired to frame his measure so as to meet the exigencies arising from the great expansion of the country, with as little disturbance as possible to the general principles on which the judicial system had been long conducted. In doing this he proceeded in a mode that was one of his most remarkable characteristics. He was not at all accustomed, in important public affairs requiring the adjustment of very wide relations, to set forth with previously-fixed opinions, unless some constitutional principle was involved; nor did he, even in such cases, adopt his opinions hastily. One of his most marked intellectual traits was his deliberate habit of mind and action. He omitted no source or opportunity of information; he conversed with every well-informed person who had any idea upon the subject to impart; he weighed every thing; he digested the whole with the results of his own observation, experience, and reflection. When he spoke, therefore, as he could speak, with a clearness and precision that were generally felt to be unequalled, it was found that his opinions were wise because they were formed with so much care, and with such comprehensive attention to the opinions of others. Mr. Calhoun once said that he had never seen any man who gave the views of an opponent so fairly as Mr. Webster was in the habit of stating an argument to which he intended to reply, and that he often stated the position of an adversary better than the adversary himself could have given it. This predominance of intellect over the mere *fevers* of jealous anxiety for display—this superiority to the weak trickery of misrepresentation—gave Mr. Webster, in debate, a very uncommon power. Men felt that, if what he said admitted of an answer, that answer must be made with great care; that one who had manifestly looked with equal attention on all sides of a subject was not likely to be self-deceived, or to aim at deceiving others; and they yielded their convictions to his arguments, because conviction is an intellectual process, that is largely influenced by the feeling that he who seeks to produce it is above the use of sophistry and incapable of unfairness.

He had never more need of these peculiar powers than he had in conducting this judiciary bill through the House of Representatives in the winter of 1825–'26. It was not a measure of a party character; and, if it had been, he had no special party to rely on. It was a measure affecting the working of the judicial department of the Government, which, as originally organized, the country had outgrown. There were serious dissatisfactions to be encountered, and there was a great conflict of opinions respecting the proper mode of meeting them. On the one hand, the members of the Supreme Court itself, consisting of Marshall, Washington, Todd, Johnson, Story, Duval, and Thompson, judges long accustomed to act together, and thus far generally harmonizing in their views of the constitutional questions arising in the exercise of their appellate functions, were naturally solicitous about the effect of any considerable increase of their numbers. Such an increase, however, was unavoidable, unless the judges were to be separated from the performance of circuit duties. The new measure, therefore was to be carried in a manner to conciliate the court, or, at all events, so as to prevent a feeling that the expansion of the system (in order to meet the wants of the great West) was not destined to injuriously affect the function of the Supreme Court as the conservative balance-wheel of the Constitution. The measure was to be carried, too, through a House of Representatives, where there were leading and important men, who entertained a good deal of jealousy concerning the power of the court to declare State laws unconstitutional, and who desired to restrict the exercise of that power by a statute provision that would require the concurrence of a majority of all the members of the court. There were others who objected to an increase of the number of the judges of the Supreme Court, and still others who wished to make it merely a court *in banc*, while many were opposed to removing them from all connection with the circuit business. To reconcile these discordant views, and to present a bill that would afford a uniform system to the whole Union, Mr. Webster yielded to the preference of his committee for an addition of three judges instead of two, the number which he preferred; provided that six of the ten judges should be a quorum for the transaction of business in the Supreme Court; distributed the judges to ten circuits, comprehending all the States in the Union, and established a Circuit Court for each of them. In this shape the bill was brought before the House on the 22d of December, 1825. The discussion on it continued at intervals for a month. The principal speeches made by Mr. Webster, in opening and closing the discussion, are to be found in the third volume of his Works. They contain opinions upon this subject which I believe he always continued to hold, especially those which relate to the expediency of having the judges of the Supreme Court perform circuit duties. The bill, as he advocated it, finally passed the House, on the 25th of January, 1826, and was sent to the Senate.

But in that body there was no one who favored it and who had the requisite skill and influence to conduct it to a successful vote, in an unimpaired condition. The Western members differed about the distribution of the circuits; and, from this and a real unwillingness to give the Administration the appointment of three new judges, the bill came back to the House so encumbered with amendments, that it was finally lost by the disagreement of the two bodies. Writing to Judge Story in May, while the bill still hung in uncertainty in the Senate, Mr. Webster said: "If the bill passes, well; if not, we have made a fair offer, and the court will remain at seven some years longer." [1]

That this measure should have been lost for want of Western support, is truly surprising. What was thought of it by

[1] Correspondence, i., 405.

one of the wisest men in New England, may be seen from the following letter:

[FROM MR. JEREMIAH MASON.]

"PORTSMOUTH, *February* 4, 1826.

"MY DEAR SIR: I congratulate you on the success of your judiciary bill. You have certainly carried it through your House handsomely, and had in the end a triumphant majority. The plan for circuit judges might possibly have better suited certain personal views, but, if such a plan had succeeded, there are ten chances to one all such views would, in the end, have been disappointed. On a measure of this importance, such considerations ought to have no manner of influence. I was amused with Mr. B———'s motion, intended, I suppose, for the special benefit of ———. The increased number of judges must, I think, bring additional strength and security to the Supreme Court, where more is wanted, in the determination of constitutional questions. By dividing it among a greater number of individuals, it will lessen the responsibility, which is certainly heavy. The *States* will be more apt to be satisfied with the decision of a tribunal consisting of an unusual number. When united, the influence of their opinion with the *public* will be increased by the increased number of judges. The chief danger to be feared is their division in opinions. I trust this will be guarded against in the only way it can be, by the selection of suitable men. This is of vast importance, and ought to be effectually attended to. Good judges will do well, under almost any organization, and bad ones will make poor work, however perfect the system may be. In the determination of mere legal questions in the Supreme Court, the increased number of judges can, as I think, do no good, and, should they all be fit for their places, it will do little, if any harm. But, should they, by reason of indolence or incapacity, fall into a habit of determining causes by major vote, or, for the sake of saving labor, of devolving the duty, by rotation, on a single member, the court will be ruined.

"The most important consequence of this measure is its tendency to satisfy and conciliate the Western States. It will lessen, if not destroy, their antipathy to the Supreme Court. The apparent union of sentiment between the East and West augurs well. The close union which has heretofore subsisted between the Southern Atlantic and the Western States has done us of the East much mischief. The present auspicious good liking ought to be carefully cultivated.

"I suppose the Supreme Court, or something else, will prevent your attempting the bankrupt system this winter. Were I in your situation, I would not attempt it, without pretty good prospect of success. The attempting it and failing would do the public no good, and might do you hurt. Of this, however, you are the best judge. You have often succeeded in what I deemed impossible.

"I began this with no intention of writing you a political lecture, but of requesting you to have the enclosed letter delivered to Colonel Williams, if he remains still at Washington, and, if not, to have it sent to him, wherever he may be. I am glad he has the appointment to his present situation, and wish it was better both in grade and emoluments.

"We have no news except the low state of the thermometer, which makes us rather more stupid than ordinary. Please to give my and Mrs. Mason's best regards to Mrs. Webster, and believe me as ever,

"Truly yours,

"J. MASON.

"Mr. Webster."

In the spring of 1825, soon after the inauguration of Mr. Adams as President, the Republics of Colombia, Mexico, and Central America invited the United States to be represented at a congress of the American nations to be assembled at Panama. At the time of this proposal, the independence of none of the Spanish-American States had been acknowledged by Spain, and the war between Spain and her former colonies was still going on; no part of these colonies, however, being in the actual occupation of Spanish forces. In reference to that war, the United States, although recognizing the new governments as governments *de facto*, as in other cases of civil war, had yet maintained from the first a position of neutrality. Still, it appeared to Mr. Adams and his Cabinet that, as there were objects of peculiar concern to the whole of this hemisphere, which could be usefully considered in such a meeting, the United States might take part in its discussions without entering into any questions concerning the war, or the belligerent operations or relations; and, subject to that understanding with the three republics which had extended the invitation, and with a general reference to the questions in the consideration of which the United States would consent to participate, Mr. Adams accepted the proposal to send commissioners to Panama. On the assembling of Congress in December, 1825, the President nominated Richard C. Anderson, of Kentucky, and John Sergeant, of Pennsylvania, as the envoys to be sent to the Congress of Panama, which had already met; and he asked the House of Representatives for an appropriation to enable him to carry out this diplomatic purpose.

Such was the simple origin of a proposal which encountered

a strong resistance, and led to protracted discussion in both Houses, and around which the scattered elements of a political opposition to the Administration were first arranged. Intrinsically, the project was not one of great importance; but it appeared to Mr. Webster that Mr. Adams had done rightly in accepting the invitation; and it was quite plain that the President had acted within the scope of his constitutional authority, in undertaking to enter into diplomatic relations with a body known to the usages of nations. Still, it is not probable that Mr. Webster would have taken any considerable part in the discussions on this measure, if it had not been for the turn given to it in the House of Representatives, where an effort was made which he regarded as an encroachment on the constitutional prerogative of the President, and which, with his characteristic watchfulness over the Constitution, he desired to prevent from becoming a precedent.

Upon a resolution which merely proposed to declare, as the sense of the House, that it was expedient to appropriate the funds necessary to enable the President to send ministers to the Congress at Panama, Mr. McLane, of Delaware, and Mr. Rives, of Virginia, moved amendments, which undertook to instruct the ministers what they should discuss, consider, or consult upon, with the representatives of other powers whom they were to meet. This led to the speech delivered by Mr. Webster, on the subject of this mission, upon the 14th of April, 1826.[1] It embraces an elaborate explanation of what the Congress of Panama was, as a diplomatic body, in the eye of the public law. Mr. Webster showed it to be an assembly of the representatives of certain nations met to deliberate upon their common concerns, in which it was competent to any nation to be represented to whom an invitation was extended; and he held that the appointment, and the instruction as well as the appointment, of ministers to such a body, was a matter in which the House of Representatives could have no voice. In its discussion of the constitutional relations of the different departments of our Government to diplomatic action, the speech has a general and permanent importance. It also embraces a full exposition of the real meaning and bearing of

[1] Works, iii. 178–217.

that declaration of Mr. Monroe, respecting the interference of European powers in the affairs of this continent, which has been popularly called the "Monroe Doctrine."

[FROM MR. DENISON.]

"LONDON, *February* 23, 1826.

"MY DEAR SIR: In writing to you at this moment, I might with justice say, as one of our friends of Rome said of old: '*Cum tot sustineas, et tanta negotia*—I should err against the public weal, if I should occupy your time with too long a discourse.' But, in truth, I am too much engaged just now myself to commit this fault. What prompts me to write at this moment is, that I was fortunate enough to hear yesterday from Mr. Rufus King that Captain Morris was now in London. With Mr. King's assistance I found him out this morning; and as he tells me he is about to return to Washington, where he expects to meet you, I cannot let him pass between us without a few lines of friendly remembrance.

"I received ten days ago the *National Intelligencer* containing your speech on the introduction of your proposition for the alteration of the judiciary, and about that time the first volume of the 'Debates of Congress.' I am much obliged to you for these two proofs of your kind remembrance. It does not fall within the compass of a hurried letter to enter upon the vast subject of your Supreme Court, the corner-stone of your whole edifice. I congratulate America that so solemn and weighty a subject has fallen into such hands as yours. Your speech commands my admiration, as your view of the question carries with it my concurrence. I am afraid you have fixed the last rivet in the chains of our friend the Judge. I shall be extremely sorry, indeed, to find that the hope of seeing him amongst his brethren here is utterly gone. Westminster Hall is swept and garnished for his reception, and there are many persons here who would be very happy to make the Judge's acquaintance, and in whose society mutual pleasure would be given and received.

"I hope you received safely your package of books, and one or two letters that I wrote to you last summer, and that the Judge received a book I sent to him and a letter written early in September, which I believe is the latest communication I can profess to have made.

"You will have been contemplating, not without astonishment, the extraordinary depression under which our affairs have been, and are laboring. Much of what has occurred was clearly foreseen, and plainly predicted by Mr. Huskisson and some others; the extent to which it has gone (and it has not yet reached its ultimate point) was hardly within the power of human calculation. It happens, very unfortunately for the interests of truth and sound policy, that these embarrassments, concurring in point of time with the alteration in our commercial laws, are by a large and powerful body in this country attributed mainly (though very falsely) to their enactment.

"*February* 28.—I wrote so far on the morning of the 23d—that afternoon I took Captain Morris with me to the House of Commons, where, though no very particular business was expected, fortunately a debate of great interest occurred. I shall leave Captain Morris to describe it to you. The first debate arose on a petition from the city, that a select committee might be appointed to inquire into the causes of the present commercial distress, and to devise, if possible, some remedy for it. This was the ostensible object; the real one was to induce the government to issue exchequer bills as a temporary relief. On this subject, Captain Morris heard Mr. Canning and Mr. Robinson speak shortly; he heard one disagreeable, foolish man coughed down; he heard a Scotchman, and some country gentlemen, and an alderman or two deliver themselves, each in his particular line.

"Then followed the question of retracing our steps on the silk laws. The subject itself was one of sufficient importance, and one of great immediate interest, from the pressing distress to which all branches of that trade are exposed through their own miscalculations. But much more was meant than met the eye, and through the sides of silk a deadly blow was aimed at the whole system of our new commercial regulations, and at Mr. Huskisson's character and fame. He rose under many disadvantages, at the close of a long debate, with a large party in the House hostile to his views, and with many of his friends faltering in their allegiance. He entered into a general review of the commercial policy of this country, past and present, and made the most masterly statement on the subject of trade that ever was exhibited before Parliament. By this he has accumulated a new load of reputation to his former great character. He has proved himself true, under the best of all proofs, a pressure of difficulties, and has raised himself to the second place, second only to Mr. Canning, in the House, and in the country. Captain Morris will tell you how his speech was received. If he thinks we were very tumultuous, we were so beyond our ordinary expression. I never recollect a speech received with such loud and unanimous cheering since I have been in Parliament. Certainly upon none have greater consequences depended. If he had failed in his defence—for upon his trial he stood before a House of Commons which had already sanctioned his measures—I verily believe we might have been driven back step by step to the old fastnesses of selfish prohibition. His speech turned the tide, raised his character higher than it has ever yet stood, and has confirmed his policy even beyond the power of prejudice to overthrow it. I hope this speech will be published. I will take care you have it immediately.

"I have been greatly delighted by receiving a very long and kind letter from Judge Story this afternoon. He gives me an account of your trip to Niagara, through the State of New York. I think the Trenton falls exceed any scenery of the same dimensions that I am acquainted with, in exquisite finished beauty, and the Falls of Niagara in their way surpass every thing in splendor and awful grandeur. He tells me, too, something of your political existence, of which I had partially informed myself through your papers, and from some private hands. I may well congratulate you on its general features. It is not right to meddle with the affairs of individuals, but I think some politicians have played safer games than a certain young —South Carolinian, is he not?—late of the War Department, is now playing at Washington. I must trust to you and the Judge to keep me in a certain degree on a pace with the changes and the progress of your striding country. If I remain stationary for a few years, you will be out of my sight, and it will be then too late to resume the chase. It seems not improbable that affairs may keep you at home for the present, and that you cannot be spared for your visit here. If so, I shall only look upon it as a pleasure delayed, and not taken away. For I feel sure that you will some day come and afford me the very sincere pleasure of conducting you around this little sea-girt land.

"Pray, say for me every thing most kind to the Judge, and give him my best thanks for his long and interesting letter. I wish we had him here to let us into the true secret of safe banking; we have all been racking our brains, and writing pamphlets, and making speeches on this subject, which practically we have certainly not administered well. We hope to go on sounder principles, and pursue them with a steadier course. I shall not answer the Judge's letter immediately, because you will give him my present thanks, and a short interval perhaps may produce something of greater interest. The commission which has been examining into the practice of our Court of Chancery has closed its inquiry, and framed its report. This will be published shortly, and shall immediately be sent for your and the Judge's examination. We shall do nothing this year about the Catholic question, or the Corn Laws. Both will be submitted to the new Parliament next year; the Corn Laws will probably be taken up by the government, the other has, I fear, made little progress in public opinion. I dare make uo prophecy as to when it may pass, and receive the triple sanction of Parliament. The condition of Ireland in the mean time is decidedly improving, and has already made most essential advances, but it is still such as no Englishman can contemplate without regret and shame, and no Irishman without still more bitter feelings.

"I am sorry to hear from the Judge's letter that a package of books I sent you, with one included to him, has never reached you. I shall send into the city immediately to make inquiries on the subject. I shall look out for a few pamphlets and books to send you by Captain Morris, who has been good enough to undertake to deliver them to you.

"I beg you will make my respects to the President, and assure all those, who may be good enough to have kept me in mind, of the grateful remembrance I entertain of their individual civilities, and of my general reception in the United States. You will know several to whom I would be specially remembered.

"I have seen Lord Stowell once or twice lately; he was much flattered by the assurances I felt authorized to give him of the great reputation he enjoys amongst you; he desired his best compliments to the Judge. The chancellor has lately rallied, which, if it was not treason to say so, I am almost sorry for.—Believe me,

"My dear sir,

"Your sincere friend,

"J. E. DENISON.

"Stanley is yet in the country with his wife, Wortley with his wife in town. He moved the address in a good and sensible speech this year. Labouchere is in town, and very well. I met Mr. Addington, too, the other day here, very well.

"I hear from the office through which the package to you was sent, that it was shipped, and the ship arrived safe at New York, probably in August last. It was sent to the care of Le Roy, Bayard & Co., and is now most likely lying in the custom-house, or some warehouse."

[TO MR. DENISON.]

"WASHINGTON, *May* 3, 1826.

"MY DEAR SIR: I received yesterday your letter of the 23d February, and am greatly obliged to you as well for the letter itself as for the valuable pamphlets with which you accompanied it. We are now within fifteen or twenty days of the end of our session, and, according to our custom (and I suppose according to yours also), these last days are exceedingly crowded with business. Upon the whole, it has not been a session in which we have dispatched many concerns of great moment. It has been a *talking* winter. The President's proposition to send ministers to the Congress at Panama has led to endless debates, especially in the Senate. The measure has met with much opposition, by which more was intended than the defeat of the measure itself. Various parties, not likely to act together often, united on this occasion in a close phalanx of *opposition*. The measure, however, has succeeded by a small majority in the Senate, and a large one in our House.

"Another long topic has been, a plan for amending the Constitution in the manner of electing President. This grew out of the event of the late election. After much tedious discussion, we leave the matter as we found it. Our other subjects have not been of particular interest.

"Mr. Randolph was elected last fall a Senator from Virginia. It was unexpected; but his great devotion to certain political opinions cherished in that State gave him the election. He is a violent opposer of the present Government, and has conducted his part of the discussions in the Senate in a way hitherto altogether unknown. The Vice-President has found out that he has no authority to call him to order, or restrain his wanderings; so he talks on for two, four, and sometimes six hours at a time, saying whatever occurs to him on all subjects. This course, and its indulgence by the presiding officer of the Senate, has produced a very strong sensation throughout the country. It is now said he will sail for England in a few days, to pass the summer.

"We hear that Mr. King is coming immediately home, on account of ill-health. I regret very much his sudden return. It is quite *unseasonable.* I hardly know what will be done, not having seen the President since the information arrived. I *hope*, however, somebody will be sent out to bring pending negotiations to a close, and should not be surprised if, with that view, *Mr. Gallatin* should be selected.

"I have read your debates thus far with great and peculiar interest. The questions in your House have been such as are connected with general principles of great importance. In my poor judgment, your friends are clearly right on the currency question, the silk-trade question, etc. On the silk question, Mr. Huskisson's speech is most admirable. I read it in the *Courier*, but am happy to have it, through your kindness, in a more correct form. I have read it a second time here in my study with real delight, and enjoyed his triumph, when he resumed his seat, almost as much as he himself could have done. Pray, tell him, what I hope he would not be displeased to know, that there are men on this side of the globe who admire his liberal principles, and the singular ability and excellent sense with which he recommends those principles to the adoption of his countrymen. His speech on the silk-trade question appears to me, on the whole, his greatest effort; and next to this I place that which he made several years ago, on what I thought a very wild proposition in your House, for the equitable adjustment of contracts.

"I entertain no doubt that the prohibition of the circulation of small notes is a good measure, and will produce all the benefit intended by it, although it may have some effect to continue the immediate pressure; or, rather, it may retard, in some degree, the natural progress of relief and restoration. As it is prospective, however, in its operation, and for the present deferred, perhaps this effect may hardly be perceptible. It is quite true that gold and paper will not circulate together. It is quite true also that two kinds of paper, of different values, cannot circulate together, however small the difference. We have much experience of this last truth. For example, we have in Massachusetts many country banks, all being incorporated institutions, well regulated, and in good credit. *Their notes are payable only where issued.* These notes get to Boston; they pass in the common exchanges, and for all ordinary purposes; yet, as they are payable fifty or a hundred miles from town, they are not quite so good as notes of the Boston banks. Now, the consequence is, that these country notes fill up the whole circulation. Hardly is there a Boston note to be seen; and, in order to correct this, it has been found necessary that these country banks should make provision for the redemption of their notes in Boston, as well as on their own counters at home. You will experience, as I should think, the same thing in England, if you establish country banks, making their notes payable only where issued. These notes will be so good that they will be taken, and yet not so good, quite, as Bank of England notes, or the notes of London bankers,[1] because the bank and London bankers will not receive them, in deposit, as cash. They will still pass, in all small payments, at all the shops in London, and the consequence will be that bankers will take them up, at small but different rates of discount, for gold or Bank of England notes. York notes will be at one rate, Welsh notes a little higher, Worcestershire a little lower, etc., according to distance from London.[2] Let me tell you a short story. A year or two ago, a client of mine, a trader, came to my rooms to pay me for a legal opinion. The sum was fifty dollars. He handed me ten five-dollar notes on a country bank, in good credit, but a hundred miles from Boston. He was a good-natured man, and I addressed him thus: 'You give me this fee in country notes; now, I wish to tell you what I suspect. I suspect that, when you left your counting-house, you filled up a check on a Boston bank, for fifty dollars; you put it in your pocket, and, on your way hither, you have called at a broker's, sold your check for these country notes, and have received a premium of one or one and a half per cent.—say fifty or seventy-five cents, with which it is your intention to buy a leg of mutton for dinner. Now, sir, that mutton is mine; you shall not dine at my expense in your own house. The legal opinion which I gave you was not *below* par; I will not be paid in any thing which is—sit down and draw me a check for fifty dollars.' He at once admitted that the process had been as I stated, very nearly.

"I have, indeed, understood, that heretofore the notes of country bankers would not pass in London. Possibly that may continue to be the case, but I should expect that they would make their way, and, if so, I have no doubt the same evil will be felt, in time, which we have experienced here. But, my dear sir, I am talking upon what you must understand much better than I do, and I will tax you no further.

"We have a countryman of yours here, a Captain Wylde, of the artillery, who, I had the pleasure to find, is a Nottingham man, and an acquaintance of yours.

"I have forgotten to tell you that my books all arrived safe, soon after I wrote you last. I hardly yet know what accident detained them, but they arrived in good time, nevertheless.

"You have a busy summer before you. I suppose you will be *dissolved* next month and have a warm July of it. I should admire to be in England during a general election. It must be an occasion, I should think, in which one could see a good deal of the true Mr. Bull. I trust your Catholic vote will not endanger your seat, as you thought it might if the elections had come on earlier. It would be unkind in your constituents to let their resentment, on account of that vote, be *felt*. I shall continue to rely on your friendship to send me occasionally such speeches,

[1] "I believe your London bankers do not issue notes."

[2] "This is, of course, conjectural, but such has been our experience."

pamphlets, etc., as you may happen to notice, and as you may think interesting.

"Mrs. Webster is with me here. She commands me to make her remembrances to you. I had occasion lately to write Mr. Stanley, but must beg you to renew as well to him, as Mr. Wortley and Mr. Labouchere, my assurances of regard and attachment.

"Pray what has become of Colonel Dawson?

"I am, my dear sir,

"Most truly yours,

"DANIEL WEBSTER.

"I shall see the good Judge by 25th instant, in his court in Boston. He will be most glad to hear from you."

[FROM MR. MASON.]

"PORTSMOUTH, *May* 7, 1826.

"DEAR SIR: I have just received your letter. I regret exceedingly that Mr. King is to return so speedily, for many reasons. It is unfortunately timed for him. His bad state of health, of which I was before aware, is doubtless the chief cause. If, however, he knew it was determined at Washington to send Mr. Gallatin out to aid him in his negotiations, it is possible that might influence him in requesting leave to return sooner than he otherwise would have done. Unless his feelings toward Mr. Gallatin are now different from what they were ten years ago, it would not be entirely pleasant to be associated with him.

"It seems to me that you cannot, under existing circumstances, assert your claim at the present time. Should the Government offer you the appointment, I think you ought not to refuse it. But, if I mistake not, it will be thought you cannot at this time be spared from the House of Representatives. And, as far as I understand the state of that body, I am inclined to think your presence there at the ensuing session very important.

"In my opinion, you have a right to insist that such arrangements be made, if they can be without injury to the public interests, that you shall not be defeated of that appointment eventually, and *at a period not more than two years distant.* How this arrangement is to be made I do not know. If Mr. Gallatin should be appointed for a special mission, and go out before Mr. King's return, I suppose all the duties of a minister resident would, of course, be devolved on him. I see no inconvenience in such a mission continuing for two or three years, unless there should be something in court etiquette forbidding it. A continuance of two years probably would not be unpleasant to Mr. Gallatin. Should he be appointed as regular minister resident, it may be doubtful whether he would be desirous of returning as soon as may be wished. He remained in France several years after he first began to talk of returning.

"Our Circuit Court sits to-morrow, when I expect from Judge Story a stock of Washington news. With Mrs. Mason's and my best regards to Mrs. Webster, and wishing you a safe return home,

"I am truly yours,

"J. MASON.

"I have read your Panama speech, which has reached here. It is all that it should be. It is read with eagerness, and abundantly praised. The opposition can gain nothing on this subject. They misjudged in attempting to attach such vast importance to it. What I chiefly regret in that matter is the course adopted by Mr. McLane. I fear it is an indication of his inclination favorable to the opposition."

From the commencement of this session of Congress in December, 1825, to its termination in May, 1826, Mr. Webster's occupations were incessant. On the 8th of May he wrote to Judge Story that since the first day of December he had not been an "inch" from his place, till the previous Saturday, when he rode a few miles on horseback. He went home about the middle of May. His health, however, was good, and it well needed to be so, for there was awaiting him, in the near but as yet undeveloped future, another of those occasions on which no voice but his could speak to the country as its emotions demanded.

On the 4th of July, 1826, John Adams, at Quincy, and Thomas Jefferson, at Monticello, died within a few hours of each other, each conscious of the day that was his last on earth. This extraordinary coincidence, which, it has been well said, is unparalleled in history, produced a most profound impression throughout the country. Commemorative services were everywhere held. In Boston the municipal authorities requested Mr. Webster to pronounce a public discourse on the lives and services of these great leaders of the Revolution; and, in compliance with this request, the eulogy which is so well known was delivered on the 2d of August, 1826. Again I must resort to the same pen from which I have borrowed the description of the Plymouth Oration and the Address at Bunker Hill:

"In 1826," observes Mr. Ticknor, "when Mr. Webster was preparing his discourse in commemoration of Adams and Jefferson, he talked with me much about it. It seemed to embarrass him in several parts, and to satisfy him less in the composition than he had been satisfied in preparing the address on Bunker Hill the year before. He showed me no part of it while he was writing it, but, when he considered it as finished, he read me the whole. Of course, I had nothing but gratification to express. The very day, however, before he was to deliver it, he sent for me early in the forenoon to come to his house (next to Colonel Thorndike's, in Summer Street). He was walking up and down his room when I went in, a good deal excited, and at once proceeded somewhat abruptly to repeat the two speeches attributed to an opponent of the Declaration of Independence and to Mr. Adams in reply to him. He said that he had just written them, and that he was quite uncertain whether they were the best or the worst part of the discourse. I had no doubt about the matter. I told him that I did not know whether they were better than the description of eloquence which preceded them or not, but that there was certainly nothing else equal to them in the whole of it.

"The next day, the 2d of August, the weather was fine, and the concourse to hear him immense. It was the first time that Faneuil Hall had been draped in mourning. The scene was very solemn, though the light of day was not excluded. Settees had been placed over the whole area of the hall; the large platform was occupied by many of the most distinguished men in New England, and, as it was intended that every thing should be conducted with as much quietness as possible, the doors were closed when the procession had entered, and every part of the hall and galleries was filled. This was a mistake in the arrangements; the crowd on the outside, thinking that some space must still be left within, became very uneasy, and finally grew so tumultuous and noisy that the solemnities were interrupted. The police in vain attempted to restore order. It seemed as if confusion would prevail. Mr. Webster perceived that there was but one thing to be done—he advanced to the front of the stage, and said, in a voice easily heard above the noise of tumult without and of alarm within, '*Let those doors be opened.*' The power and authority of his manner were irresistible—the doors were opened, though with difficulty, from the pressure of the crowd on the outside; but, after the first rush, every thing was quiet, and the order during the rest of the performance was perfect.

"Mr. Webster spoke in an orator's gown, and wore small-clothes. He was in the perfection of his manly beauty and strength; his form filled out to its finest proportions, and his bearing, as he stood before the vast multitude, that of absolute dignity and power. His manuscript lay on a small table near him, but I think he did not once refer to it. His manner of speaking was deliberate and commanding. When he came to the passage on eloquence, and to the words, 'It is action, noble, sublime, godlike action,' he stamped his foot repeatedly on the stage, his form seemed to dilate, and he stood, as that whole audience saw and felt, the personification of what he so perfectly described. I never heard him when his manner was so grand and appropriate.

"The two speeches attributed to Mr. Adams and his opponent attracted great attention from the first. Soon they were put into school-books, as specimens of English and of eloquence. In time men began to believe they were genuine speeches, made by genuine men who were in the Congress of '76; and at last Mr. Webster received letters asking whether such was the fact or not. In January, 1846, he sent me from Washington a letter he had just received, dated at Auburn, begging him to solve the doubt. With it he sent me his answer, which is published in his works, saying, 'The accompanying letter and copy of answer respect a question which has been often asked me. I place them in your hands to serve if similar inquiries should be made of you.'[1] Two months after, in March of the same year, he sent me a letter from Bangor, in Maine, asking the same question, beginning the note which accompanied it with these words: 'Here comes another; I cannot possibly answer all of them one after another.' Indeed, he continued to receive such letters until the edition of his works was published in 1851, though the matter was repeatedly discussed and explained in the newspapers. The fact is, that the speech he wrote for John Adams has such an air of truth and reality about it, that only a genius like Mr. Webster's, perfectly familiar with whatever relates to the Revolution, and imbued with its spirit, could have written it."[2]

President Fillmore informs me that he once asked Mr. Webster, in familiar conversation, what authority he had for putting this speech into the mouth of John Adams, the Congress at that period having always sat with closed doors. Mr. Webster replied that he had no authority for the sentiments of the speech excepting Mr. Adams's general character, and a letter he had written to his wife, that had frequently been published. After a short pause, Mr. Webster added, "I will tell you what is not generally known. I wrote that speech one morning before breakfast, in my library, and when it was finished my paper was wet with my tears."

[FROM MR. J. E. DENISON.]

"LONDON, *July* 11, 1826.

"MY DEAR SIR: I received the other day your agreeable and instructive letter, through the hands of Mr. J. King. I was very sorry to miss Mr. Dutton; he came to London while I was engaged in election matters in Staffordshire, and before my return he had left it. Colonel Dawson was fortunate enough to fall in with him, and I believe explained to Mr. Dutton the cause of my absence, and Wortley's, and Stanley's. You follow the course of our public business so closely, and remark upon it so justly, that it is really superfluous in me to attempt to give you any information.

[1] The answer may be found in his Works, i., 149.

[2] MS. Recollections of Mr. Webster, by Mr. Ticknor.

"I predicted truly the effect my Catholic vote would produce at Newcastle. I could not have carried my seat without a severe contest and a great expenditure. I declined it under such circumstances; secured the return of my friend and colleague, Mr. Wilmot Horton, and myself shall be elected for Hastings at the opening of the session, when the gentleman now returned means to retire. I am happy to say the result of the elections is upon the whole not unfavorable to the Catholic concessions. They have gained in Ireland and lost something in England, and, as far as prospective calculations can be relied upon, there will be a majority of about twenty or twenty-five for sending the bill to the Lords. How will they conduct themselves? If the Parliament sits four sessions, and the House of Commons sends the bill up every session, I am inclined to think the Lords must make a great gulp and swallow it. I was very much obliged to you for the information contained in your letter about the system of banking with you. I am collecting all the information I can on the very important question of the currency. Should I be asking you a very troublesome favor, if I was to beg that you would send me over a detailed account of the banking system in Massachusetts? I do not mean to put so heavy a tax on your time, as to ask for a description of it under your own hand. But you could perhaps send me the general laws that regulate the banks, and the principles on which they are conducted. How is the paper kept at par? We find here convertibility not to be a sufficient check. How are over-issues controlled or rectified? Is there any general understanding among the banks, and a mutual interchange and exchange of each other's notes, as is the case in Scotland?

"I much regret that I did not look more closely into all this while I was at Boston. Pray furnish me with such facts as may enable me to comprehend the merits of your system, which I know to be so very good. I dined with Mr. Huskisson the other day, and took the liberty of showing him your letter; he desired me, when I wrote to you, to make you his best compliments, to thank you for your obliging message, and to say how greatly struck he had been with your speech on the tariff, which he had read with the greatest pleasure. I went yesterday to Sadbrook, near Richmond, a villa of Mr. W. Horton's, where Mr. Huskisson dined, and Mr. Randolph, your notorious Virginian. I had not the pleasure of his acquaintance in America, but we had a good deal of conversation in the course of the evening, and I brought him back to London in my carriage. He is certainly an extraordinary man; with a very accurate memory, stored with minute facts. As you and I agree in politics, naturally he and I did not. He astonished me by some of his doctrines about slavery, and by recommending the policy and maintaining the practicability of cutting the throat of every inhabitant of the Island of Hayti. After what I saw in the papers, I expected to see him put on his hunting-shirt, but was disappointed.

"I leave England the day after to-morrow, cross to Calais or Ostend, and shall pass up the Rhine into Switzerland, where I shall spend two months in the neighborhood of Lausanne with my friend Lord Sandon, who has taken a country-house for the summer. October and November I shall pass at Paris, and return to look about me in England for two months before the meeting of Parliament. I fear it will be a winter of great distress. Indeed, it must be one of extreme pressure and difficulty. The unprecedented drought has heightened and aggravated every cause of preëxisting distress. The hay-harvest, which generally affords employment to so many laborers, has passed over in a few days; cattle are perishing for want of water and pasture; the spring crops, oats, barley, and beans, have failed almost universally. Wheat still looks well, but, after so long a drought, we fear a rainy harvest. Prices are continually falling, and the manufacturing interest does not yet begin to revive; and add to all this, the potato crop must fail in Ireland. I have drawn you a gloomy but faithful picture of the present state of this country. We cannot quite agree among ourselves as to the cause of all this. Some maintain that it arises purely from overtrading, some purely from the fluctuations in the currency; one proposes a metallic circulation; one a paper circulation, and the more depreciated the better. I much question myself whether great attempts will not be made in Parliament to reconsider the amount of depreciation during the war, and to try to accommodate the present standard of money to that rate. It will be a most important session. The Corn Laws, the Catholic bill, the currency, the new commercial system, will be violently attacked, and almost every weighty matter will come under discussion; West Indies again, and what is to be done with the colonial Legislatures. I most earnestly hope the negotiations pending between our countries will be speedily and satisfactorily concluded. Your Government has a character in Europe for an encroaching and aggrandizing spirit, which makes it difficult to treat with it on even terms. I wish all men in your country, or at least the prevailing party, held the language that you do. As an American, I think I should be quite satisfied with the tone of dignified importance that you properly think becoming the situation of the United States. As a neutral, I should think stronger language hardly consistent with friendly intercourse. I write freely to you, as I should do to an intimate friend in England. Certainly, my earnest wish is for the establishment of a perfect understanding between the two countries, that would be for the honor and interest of both, as a bad understanding would be injurious to both, and to many of the greatest and most important interests of the world.

"I was much obliged to you for the speeches you were good enough to send me. Mr. Huskisson's speech on the shipping interests of the United Kingdom is not yet published in a separate pamphlet, nor is there any thing very new or worth your attention.

"I shall be really obliged to you for the information about the Massachusetts banks, particularly since some conversation that I have had with Mr. Huskisson about them. If you read the report of the Chancery Commission, I should very much value your opinion. I must insist on having the Judge's opinion at length. You may vote upon it in the House of

Commons, if you please. If you agree in a common judgment, I will confirm it by my vote, for I am sure I shall not have time to read it myself, or knowledge of the subject, or patience of investigation, to form an opinion.

"Thank Mrs. Webster for her kind remembrances, and give all assurances of my esteem. I am writing in a great hurry; it is now midnight, and at four in the morning I am to be on board the steamboat that is to convey me to Calais. You say nothing of your visit to England. If you will come, I don't know but I will enter into a compact to visit you at Boston again, some summer agreed upon between us.

"Best remembrances to the good Judge,

"And believe me

"Your sincere friend,

"J. E. Denison."

[FROM MR. HOPKINSON.]

"Philadelphia, *August* 30, 1826.

"My dear Sir: I am much obliged by your sending your 'Commemoration Discourse,' which requires not the partiality of friendship to obtain for it unqualified applause. Mr. Walsh begs me to offer you his suffrage in its behalf. He has briefly noticed it in the *Gazette* of last evening, and wishes me to explain the reason of his not speaking more largely of its merits at this time. He has been for several weeks in deep anxiety and affliction. His excellent wife has been and continues to be struggling with a most distressing, painful, and dangerous malady. I think there is but little hope of her recovery.

"Mr. Walsh and myself, without any previous communication, were both struck with the circumstance that the *argument* given against the Declaration of Independence is much stronger than that in support of it. This confirms an opinion I have long held, that, *as things then stood*, and putting the result out of the case, the strength of all human reasoning was with those who opposed the measure, although every elevated and noble feeling was in favor of it. It was one of those bold and lofty steps which outstripped the process of calculation, and set at naught the conclusions of logic. Great spirits were made for such occasions; and when they embark in them they must firmly resolve to 'sink or swim, live or die, survive or perish.'

"Remember me affectionately to all your household, but to the lady particularly.

"Yours truly,

"Jos. Hopkinson."

[FROM THE HON. RICHARD RUSH.]

"Washington, *August* 30, 1826.

Dear Sir: Yesterday's mail brought me your discourse in commemoration of the lives and services of Adams and Jefferson, pronounced at

Boston on the 2d of this month, and I have just finished reading it. If I were to say that it is able and eloquent, I should give it only the common praise of common productions. It takes much higher rank. It is full of commanding thoughts, full of elevated patriotism, full of profound criticism applied to the great subjects, individual and moral, that you had in hand. It is disencumbered of all that is little, in its facts, of all that is of every day's hearing, in its reflections. The former are well chosen, and we have not too many of them; the latter are rich, condensed, elementary. There were parts that thrilled me. I read them to my family, and they thrilled them too. The speech beginning at page 38 made my hair rise. It wears the character of a startling historical discovery, that bursts upon us at this extraordinary moment, after sleeping half a century. Curiosity, admiration, the very blood, all are set on fire by it. Nothing of Livy's ever moved me so much. Certainly, your attempt to pass the doors of that most august sanctuary, the Congress of '76, and become a listener and reporter of its immortal debates, was extremely bold, extremely hazardous. Nothing but success could have justified it; and you have succeeded.

I pray you, sir, not to regard this letter as idle compliment. I intend it not in that spirit, but only as a momentary record of the true feelings with which I have risen from the perusal of so admirable a specimen of discriminating and philosophical eulogy; of a composition which I have found all over as animating as it is intellectual. With my thanks for the copy you have had the goodness to send me, I ask permission to tender you the assurances of my high respect and esteem.

"RICHARD RUSH.

"Hon. Daniel Webster."

[FROM MR. MASON.]

"PORTSMOUTH, *September* 3, 1826.

"MY DEAR SIR: I am truly sorry that I was unable to comply with your advice to be at Cambridge to hear Judge Story's oration. For a fortnight past I have been much indisposed, occasioned by our most extraordinary weather. I was fearful it would end in downright sickness. That, I trust, is warded off. I infer from the newspaper reports that the Judge acquitted himself very ably, and to the entire satisfaction of his auditors.

"Of your oration there seems to be but one opinion. Without saying any thing of its merits, in point of eloquence, I really think you have managed the subject with most admirable address, of which no small share was necessary, considering your own situation. I do not see that you have exposed yourself to serious abuse from any quarter. . . .

"Faithfully yours,

"J. MASON."

Mr. Webster was elected to Congress in the autumn of this year, for the third time, as the Representative of the Boston district in the Twentieth Congress, by a majority of votes as large as in the preceding elections. He was now nominated and voted for by the "Republican" party; comprehending that portion of the old Democratic party which supported in general the Administration of Mr. Adams, and which was not merged in the organization then forming for the elevation of General Jackson to the presidency.

CHAPTER XIII

1826–1827.

BANKRUPT LAW—CASE OF OGDEN *VS.* SAUNDERS—DIFFICULTIES IN GEORGIA—COLONIAL TRADE—SPANISH CLAIMS.

AT the second session of the Nineteenth Congress, which commenced in December, 1826, Mr. Webster, as chairman of the Judiciary Committee of the House, reported a bill for the establishment of a uniform system of bankruptcy, which he had founded on a bill received from the Senate at the last session, and into which he had also very carefully incorporated such provisions of the recent English bankrupt law as were applicable in this country. At this precise time, the condition of the question, as to State laws of insolvency discharging debtors from their contracts, was, that the Supreme Court of the United States had already decided that such laws are constitutionally invalid to discharge contracts made before their passage; but the question in relation to their effect on contracts made after their enactment was now pending in that court, and was expected to be argued at its approaching session. Mr. Webster said, however, that, whatever might be the decision of this question, it would not deter him from laboring to obtain the adoption of a national system of bankruptcy. The Constitution having given to Congress power to regulate this subject, he was always of opinion that there should be a standing bankrupt law, to operate uniformly throughout the country. His bill was read a second time, and referred to a Committee of the Whole, but it was not acted upon.

It may be stated in this connection that in the case of *Sturges* vs. *Crowninshield*, decided by the Supreme Court of the United States in 1819, it had been held that a State law, which undertakes to discharge debtors from contracts made before its enactment, is a law that impairs the obligation of a contract, and is, therefore, prohibited by the Constitution of the United States. The question presented in the case of *Ogden* vs. *Saunders*, which was argued in the Supreme Court at the January term, 1827, and in the discussion of which Mr. Webster took part, was whether a contract, made after the passage of a State law which undertakes to discharge debtors on a surrender of their property for distribution among their creditors, is not equally within the prohibition of the Federal Constitution. Mr. Webster argued against all this distinction between past and future contracts, maintaining that it was the purpose of the Constitution to prohibit State Legislatures from passing any law impairing the obligation of any contract, and that a law which discharges a debt, whenever contracted, in the constitutional sense impairs its obligation. He contended that Congress alone is vested with authority to discharge from the payment of debts, as Congress alone can provide the medium in which a debt is to be paid.[1] But a majority of the judges held that an insolvent law of a State does not impair the obligation of *future* contracts between its own citizens.[2]

At this session it became necessary for Mr. Webster to take a very firm and decided stand in relation to a dangerous controversy that had sprung up between the United States and the State of Georgia. In 1825 a treaty had been made between the United States and the Creek Indians, at a place called Indian Springs, by which that tribe had ceded to the United States their title to certain lands lying within the limits of the State of Georgia. If this treaty had taken effect, the lands, pursuant to an agreement between Georgia and the United States, would have become the property of Georgia. But, previous to the period assigned for the operation of this treaty of

[1] See the argument in the case of *Ogden* vs. *Saunders*. Works, vi., 24, *et seq.*

[2] Chief-Justice Marshall and Mr. Justice Story dissented from the opinion of the majority, and were of the same opinion with Mr. Webster in respect to the meaning of the Constitution. See 12 Wheaton's Reports, 213.

Indian Springs, the Creek nation complained to the Government of the United States that it had been negotiated by persons not duly authorized, and that they were dissatisfied with its provisions. A new treaty was thereupon negotiated and ratified, the first article of which declared that the treaty of Indian Springs was annulled. In the mean time, however, the State of Georgia, claiming that the first treaty had operated to vest in her the lands embraced in it, and now contending that the later treaty had not divested that title, and also claiming that, if the former treaty had been annulled, the repeal did not operate upon the whole tract, sent surveyors upon a certain portion of the territory to lay out the lands as part of the property of the State. By the last treaty, the United States had guaranteed to the Indians protection in all their lands lying beyond a certain line, which was the line over which the officers of the State had now encroached; and there was an existing law of the United States which punished the acts of citizens of the United States, whether as trespassers or as surveyors, who should interfere to run lines on lands guaranteed by treaty to the Indian tribes. The State had threatened to support its officers by military force, and the Government of the United States had no alternative, if this course were persisted in, but to repel the aggression by the same means.

In this posture of the affair, President Adams sent a message to Congress, communicating the facts, intimating with great distinctness what it might become his duty to do, and submitting to Congress to determine whether further legislation was necessary to meet the emergency.

The reading of this message in the House was followed by an excited discussion, in which Mr. Forsyth, of Georgia, and other members, resisted all reference of it to any committee, but, if it should be determined to refer it at all, they insisted that it should go to a Committee of the Whole, or to a Select Committee, and not to the Committee on the Judiciary. The course of the Administration was denounced as "infamous;" and it was boldly asserted by a member from Mississippi that his State would extend its legislative power over the Indians within its limits, and at its own pleasure. Mr. Webster having said that the States would so act at their peril, he was assailed as the organ of the Administration fulminating threats against sovereign States. He then felt it to be his duty to come forward and carry the reference of this message through the House with a firm hand. Repeating the rebuke he had already administered, he explained the peril which a State would incur by resisting the execution of a treaty of the United States, stated both sides of the question between Georgia and the United States with equal fairness, and confessed his willingness to appropriate money to extinguish the Indian title to the lands in controversy. But he demanded a reference of the message to a Select Committee, and carried it without a division of the House. The following extracts from his remarks will exhibit the manner and the spirit with which he met the attack:

"Mr. Webster said, on rising, that he was not much concerned what course this communication should take, or whether it should be referred to one committee or another; but he was not contented that it should be supposed, either here or elsewhere, that there existed an entire unanimity of opinion with the gentleman from Georgia on this subject. The gentleman from Georgia must know that there were two sides to this question between Georgia and the United States; and he would tell the gentleman from Georgia that there existed two opinions also, not only on that question, but on the conduct which that gentleman had designated as 'base and infamous.'

"This, Mr. Webster said, was strong language, but not argument. The gentleman had told the House that nothing prevented every thing from going right in Georgia but the interference of the General Government. The gentleman denounced such interference, saying in effect, 'Hands off for the present; leave the Indians to the remedy of the courts.' But, Mr. Webster said, he would tell that gentleman, that if there were rights of the Indians, which the United States were bound to protect, that there were those in the House and in the country who would take their part. If we have bound ourselves by any treaty to do certain things, we must fulfil such obligation. High words will not terrify us—loud declamation will not deter us from the discharge of that duty. For myself, the right of the parties in this question shall be fully and fairly examined, and none of them with more calmness than the rights of Georgia. In my own course in this matter, I shall not be dictated to by any State, or the Representative of any State on this floor. I shall not be frightened from my purpose, nor will I suffer harsh language to produce any reaction on my mind. I will examine with great and equal care all the rights of both parties. Occasion had been taken on the mere question of reference of this communication, he would not say for argument, but for the assumption of a position, as a matter perfectly plain and indisputable, that the Government had been all in the wrong in this question, and Georgia all in the right. For his own part, Mr. Webster said, he did not care whether the communication did or did not go to a Committee of the Whole on the state of the Union, nor how soon it went there, and was there taken up for discussion. When he went into that committee, he should go there not in a spirit of controversy, nor yet in a spirit of submission, but in a spirit of inquiry, calmly and deliberately to examine the circumstances of the case, and to investigate the rights of all parties concerned. But he had made these few remarks to give the gentleman from Georgia to understand that it was not by bold denunciation, or by bold assumption, that the members of this House are to be influenced in the decision of high public concerns.

"The gentleman from Mississippi had reason to know that he (Mr. Webster) was disposed to use all proper authority of the United States to extinguish Indian titles to lands within the States. But he must tell the gentleman from Mississippi that the States would act on their own responsibility, and at their own peril, if they undertake to extend their legislation to lands where the Indian title has not been extinguished. If any such measure was contemplated in the State which the gentleman represented, Mr. Webster hoped that gentleman would lose no time in warning his friends against making any such attempt. The relation which the United States held to these tribes, of parental guardianship over the remnant of mighty nations now no more, was a very delicate relation. Its general character was that of protection, and, while every facility was given to the extinguishment of the Indian title, let not that circumstance be so far presumed on that the States should attempt to exercise authority within the Indian limits. Any such course would be attempted at their own responsibility. Mr. Webster concluded by saying that he was ready to do all that could be done to extinguish the Indian title in the States, and particularly in the States east of the Mississippi. But this disposition, common to all parts of the country, should not be so far presumed upon as that any State should undertake of its own mere motion to exercise an authority over the lands to which the Indian title is guaranteed by treaties."

In the course of this discussion on the Georgia controversy, Mr. Forsyth, speaking of Mr. Webster, referred to "the great and commanding influence which he too often exercises here." That influence had to be again exerted on the introduction of a bill from the Senate regulating the very difficult and complicated subject of trade with the British colonies. The bill had been framed, as Mr. Webster thought, with an insufficient comprehension of a system of laws that extended back to the year 1818. It provided that, if, before the 31st of December,

1827, the English Government should open the colonial trade to us without discriminating duties on their part, the President might issue a proclamation opening the trade on equal terms on our part. But it overlooked the effect of our former legislation, which, in the event of an adherence by Great Britain to her present system of exclusion, would, after the 31st of December, open our ports to vessels coming from her colonies without any discriminating duties. In the House an amendment was offered, providing that, if no arrangement should take place by treaty before the 31st of December, nor any Act of Parliament, or Order in Council, should meet our offers of reciprocity embraced in this bill, our former laws excluding British vessels from the colonies should be revived, and put in force. Mr. Webster deemed it his duty to have this amendment adopted, and adhered to by the House, preferring the defeat of the bill to its passage without the amendment. But, in order to effect this, it was necessary for him to enter upon an elaborate explanation of a matter that was very imperfectly understood. He succeeded in causing the adoption of the amendment, and in subsequently leading the House to adhere to it; in consequence of which the bill was lost, and a great blunder was prevented.

At this time, of so much activity in public business, while giving his attention to many subjects not within the ordinary range of a lawyer's studies, and supplying, by the fulness of his knowledge, the deficiencies of others, Mr. Webster, it must be remembered, was engaged in a very large practice in the Supreme Court of the United States, and, when not in Washington, was constantly employed in his profession elsewhere. He had also been for several years the leading counsel for the prosecution of claims under the Florida Treaty of 1819, for indemnification on account of the spoliations committed by Spanish cruisers on American commerce in 1788–'89. The commissioners appointed to adjudicate these claims sat at Washington at various times from 1821 to 1826. Not only was the investigation long protracted, but the business was extremely intricate, and the labor required for it was proportionably great. Mr. Webster had a very large number of the claims committed to his hands, and, when the awards were finally made and paid, his fees amounted to about seventy thousand dollars.

In the winter of 1826 his engagements in the Supreme Court of the United States were unusually heavy. It appears that, among the regularly reported cases of this term, he argued fifteen; in which number are not included the arguments made on motions.

As this was the period when the transfer of Mr. Webster from the House of Representatives to the Senate began to be considered, some idea should be formed by the reader of the personal sacrifices he was called upon to make by that change of his position. Indeed, by being in public life at all, and, for that reason alone, he failed to do what he might easily have done, that is, to earn the largest professional income of his time in the United States. So long as he continued in the House of Representatives, he could still discharge his public duties, sustain by far the heaviest burden that rested upon the shoulders of any one member of that House during Mr. Adams's administration, and yet maintain a remunerating practice in the Supreme Court, and in the special tribunals that from time to time sat in Washington. But events were approaching which were to render his position in the Senate one that would make still greater inroads upon his professional income.

CHAPTER XIV.

1827–1828.

ELECTED TO THE SENATE OF THE UNITED STATES—ILLNESS AND DEATH OF MRS. WEBSTER AT NEW YORK—HER FUNERAL IN BOSTON—RETURN OF MR. WEBSTER TO WASHINGTON—VISITED BY MR. TICKNOR AND MR. PRESCOTT—SPEECH FOR THE REVOLUTIONARY OFFICERS—SPEECH ON THE TARIFF—PUBLIC DINNER IN BOSTON—THE PRESIDENTIAL ELECTION—PROSECUTES FOR A LIBEL—ADDRESS BEFORE THE BOSTON MECHANICS' ASSOCIATION.

THE relation of Mr. Webster to the administration of Mr. John Quincy Adams did not, as we have seen, commence as the relation of a partisan. At the time of Mr. Adams's election, by the House of Representatives, parties had not yet formed themselves into a distinct division; but the "era of good feeling," which had prevailed under Mr. Monroe, was certain to be followed by divisions among the public men of the country, that would lead to the formation of defined parties, animated by a spirit of hostility the more rancorous, because the opposition was to be made up from previously discordant elements, and fragments of former parties, for the purpose of elevating to the presidency a distinguished military chieftain, who had been one of the defeated candidates at the late election. Mr. Webster desired to postpone the evil day of such parties as long as possible. His general views respecting the principles on which the administration of the Federal Government should be conducted had never been those of the extreme

Federalists, although he had formerly acted with the Federal party; and, satisfied with the impartial spirit of Mr. Adams, and believing that his administration would be conducted without personal objects, he desired to prolong, if possible, the state of things that had existed under his predecessor. But, as the "scattered elements" began to arrange themselves into a decided opposition, Mr. Webster was drawn more and more into a kind of representative relation to the Administration, in the House, because he stood beyond all comparison the foremost man in that body, and because he was the most important and efficient friend that the administration possessed in Congress. His great talents, learning, and experience made the administration the strongest side of the House in point of ability, as it was numerically the largest. In the Senate, the weight of ability, and perhaps of numbers, was already on the side of the opposition. Certainly, there was no one friendly to the Administration, who could be regarded as filling a position in the Senate corresponding to that of Mr. Webster in the House, at the termination of the first session of the Nineteenth Congress, in the spring of 1826.

There soon occurred, however, in the failing health of Mr. Mills, one of the Senators from Massachusetts, a necessity for considering the question whether Mr. Webster should not be transferred to the Senate. The period, therefore, which we are now approaching, is undoubtedly to be regarded as a turning-point in his life; for, whatever may have hitherto been his inclination or his power to withdraw from all public station, his entrance into the Senate must be considered as having fixed for the remainder of his days, and fortunately or unfortunately for his personal happiness and welfare, his position as a statesman who belonged to the country, and for whom, henceforth, private life was to be a matter of intervals and episodes. We may speculate, with varying conjectures and conflicting feelings, on what might have been the course of his existence if he had never entered upon the new career that was awaiting him in the Senate. But the real clew to his life was correctly expressed by one of his friends, the Hon. William Tudor, at this time United States consul at Lima: "I have, in fact, long apprehended," writes Mr. Tudor, "that the business of law and politics, and a leading station in both, will abstract you entirely from the more amiable interests of private life, and make you a huge Colossus, the wonder of contemporaries, and admiration of posterity. But however I may lament such a result, *it is in vain to resist destiny.* 'Some achieve greatness;' and Mrs. Webster and I and I. P. D., and others, who would have liked to have possessed you ourselves, must be content to be chilled in the increasing shadows you cast. Be it so."[1]

This complaint, a little querulous, perhaps, on account of long silence toward an old friend, shows how well that friend understood the case of one whose great powers were the real arbiters of his fate.

Still we shall find that, in proportion as the public life became more and more exacting, the private life became more and more full; that its enjoyments were the more keenly coveted and relished; that its pursuits and interests became extremely various, and that those who stood in "the shadows" really basked in the sunshine, whenever the world and the world's cares could be shut out. We must, in fact, look to the requirements of a great nature which no public ambition could satisfy, and no fame could fill, for the key to a life of a totally different character, which led him to the large and pecuniarily unprofitable interests of agriculture, to the exercise of a free hospitality, to the delights of the fowler's gun and the angler's rod, to the society of those who were neither of the great, the distinguished, nor the ambitious, and to the converse and the solace of humble friends, who served him with their homely virtues, amused him by their native originality, and loved him with a love unselfish and unalloyed. When we follow him to the places where his private life was passed, we shall see how much it took to occupy and to gratify such a nature, and we shall find the explanation, if not the excuse, for the fact that, with almost unparalleled opportunities for amassing a great fortune by his profession, he died poor.

When Mr. Webster left Boston to attend the session of Congress, which commenced in December, 1826, it was feared that Mr. Mills was in a very precarious condition of health, and

[1] Letter from William Tudor, dated at Lima, November 15, 1827, complaining that Mr. Webster had not written to him in four years.

some of the members of the Legislature of Massachusetts, about to assemble, were anxiously considering whom to make his successor. Mr. Webster, in the following January, having been written to on the subject by one of these members, made the following reply:

[MR. WEBSTER TO MR. JOSEPH E. SPRAGUE.]

"WASHINGTON, *January* 10, 1827.

"MY DEAR SIR: I am quite obliged to you for your letter, although I confess it has caused me some uneasiness. I cannot persuade myself that the Legislature, under present circumstances, will omit to reëlect Mr. Mills. Here, I assure you, we are all of one mind on the subject. We think there is nothing in his health to make it improper, and that every thing else is in favor of it. If the Legislature will not agree to that, I hope the election will be postponed. For mercy's sake, do not weaken our power in the Senate! When all the Philistines are against us, do let us have all the strength we can have. If Mr. Mills lives, he is second to no man in the Senate among our friends. Why, then, should he be now superseded? We shall know more of his health in June; and June is early enough for the election. But, as I will answer for it that he will not hold the office any longer than he is able to discharge its duties, I should hope he would be now reëlected.

"Having so settled an opinion as to what is fit to be done, namely, to reëlect Mr. Mills, or postpone the choice, I really have not thought of what would be best in case neither of these two things can take place. Of that, my dear sir, you can better judge than I. I only say that if you are governed by a disposition to sustain Mr. Adams, and help on the public business, you will, in all events, elect a man of the very best talents which are at your disposal. I pray you let no local, nor temporary, nor any small consideration induce you to refrain from electing the fittest man that can be found, and that can possibly be prevailed on to take the place. The present moment, be assured, is a crisis in the affairs of Massachusetts and all the North.

"I am, dear sir, very truly yours,

"DANIEL WEBSTER."[1]

On the 13th of February (1827), the State Senate made choice of the Hon. Levi Lincoln, then Governor of the State, for the senatorial term that was to commence in March, and communicated their action to the House. Governor Lincoln, in a communication addressed to the Speaker of the House, declined to be considered a candidate, and the subject, in that branch of the Legislature, was postponed.

[1] Correspondence, i., 424.

At that period, the Legislature held two sessions in the year; and when the June session was approaching, and the action of the State Senate remained without change, it became necessary for Mr. Webster to meet the desire expressed to him by many members of the Legislature, and by many persons at Washington, that he would allow himself to be transferred to the Senate of the United States. His own preference was for Governor Lincoln, as will be seen from the following correspondence:

[MR. WEBSTER TO GOVERNOR LINCOLN.]

"BOSTON, *May* 22, 1827.

"MY DEAR SIR: It was my misfortune not to see you on your late visit to this place, owing partly to engagements in and out of town, and partly to a misapprehension as to the time of your leaving the city. Disappointed, then, in the expectation and hope of a personal interview, I now adopt this mode of making a few suggestions to you on a subject of some interest; I mean the approaching election of a Senator in Congress. The present posture of things, in relation to that matter, is so fully known to both of us, that I need not trouble you with much preliminary observation. I take it for granted that Mr. E. H. Mills will be no longer a candidate. The question then will be, who shall succeed him? I need not say to you that you yourself will doubtless be a prominent object of consideration in relation to the vacant place, and the purpose of this communication requires me to acknowledge that I deem it possible also that my name should be mentioned, more or less generally, as one who may be thought of, among others, for the same situation. In anticipation of this state of things, and more especially since I have been awakened by its probably near approach, I have not only given it a proper share of my own reflection, but have also consulted with others in relation to it, in whose judgment and friendship I have confidence. The result is, that there are many strong personal reasons, and, as friends think (and as I think, too), some *public* reasons, why I should decline the offer of a seat in the Senate, if it should be made to me. Without entering, at present, into a detail of these reasons, I will say that the latter class of them grow out of the public station which I at present fill, and out of the *necessity* of increasing rather than of diminishing, in both branches of the national Legislature, the strength that may be reckoned on as friendly to the present Administration. I hope you will understand what I would now wish to communicate, without imputing to me the vanity of supposing that my *services* to the Administration or to the country, in the House of Representatives, are of any particular importance, or, on the other hand, that it is matter of option with me to change that place for another. I think quite differently in both respects. Nevertheless, however inconsiderable the first of these things may be, and however contingent or improbable the last, they are such as to make it convenient at the present crisis to act upon the one as though it were of some consideration, and to regard the other as if it might probably or possibly happen. To come, therefore, to the main point, I beg to say that I see no way in which the public good can be so well promoted as by *your* consenting to go into the Senate. This is my own clear and decided opinion; it is the opinion, equally clear and decided, of intelligent and patriotic friends here, and I am able to add that *it is also the decided opinion of all those friends elsewhere, whose judgment in such matters we should naturally regard. I believe I may say, without violating confidence, that it is the wish, entertained with some earnestness, of our friends at Washington, that you should consent to be Mr. Mills's successor.* You will probably, as soon as you arrive here next week, learn the same thing through another channel. I need hardly add, after what I have said, that such also is my own wish. We are in a *crisis*, and it requires all the aid that can be mustered. If I have not misunderstood you, on some former occasion, you do not desire a long continuance in your present situation. If so, this occasion is an apt and convenient one to resign it. If you should find your employment at Washington not agreeable, that also may be relinquished, without particular inconvenience, in a short time. The 'crisis' will terminate, one way or the other, about the end of the next session, or by the beginning of the next ensuing. You will then be able to regard your private wishes, probably, as to prolonging your official service there.

"A professional engagement will take me to New York at the end of this week. I hope to return by the 5th or 6th of June, but possibly may be detained longer. If you wish to address me soon, please enclose your letter to Nathan Appleton, Esq., of this city, and he will forward it to me wherever I may be. Mr. Appleton is one of our few *Representatives*. He is intelligent and perfectly well disposed, and I shall leave him possessed with my confidence, and with power to communicate my views on this subject to other friends, as convenience may require. He is well known to you, I suppose; if he is not, you may safely regard him as a man of high honor, and fit to be treated with confidence.

"I am, dear sir, very truly yours,

"DANL. WEBSTER.

"His Excellency Governor Lincoln."

[GOVERNOR LINCOLN TO MR. WEBSTER.]

"WORCESTER, *May* 24, 1827.

"To the Hon. DANIEL WEBSTER,

"MY DEAR SIR: I hasten, on the moment of the receipt of your letter, to a reply, in the hope that it may reach you before you leave the city on your proposed journey. Believe me, my dear sir, I am strongly impressed with a sense of the confidence and kindness of my friends. Your opinions, too, came to me with the added weight of suggestions of friendship. But I have to regret that, under existing circumstances, I cannot feel at liberty to yield a conformity to them. My course, in reference to the subjects to which you allude, was originally directed by considerations, over some of which I had no power of control, and others had relation to the situation of friends, and to what I believed was due to public sentiment. The expressions of *personal disinclination* to the office of United States Senator were sincere, and, from the delicacy of my position last year, were called for, and openly and repeatedly made. Indeed, it became necessary for me to say that I should absolutely decline the place, if offered to me. I have since believed and am now confirmed in the opinion (Mr. Mills being out of the question) that the *transfer* to which *you object* should be made. In the expression of this sentiment I have no disguise. If the strength and support of the Administration are regarded, it should most certainly be done. To your private interests, it seems to me, it could produce no additional prejudice. The sacrifice of business and of domestic duties and enjoyments is no greater in the one place than the other. To the Administration, this arrangement must be all-important. I consider the deficiency of power in the Senate as the weak point in the citadel, the breach already made in the walls. The force should there be immediately strengthened. No individual should be placed there who was not *now* in armor for the conflict; who understood the proper mode of resistance, who personally knew, and had measured strength with the opposition, who was familiar with the political interests and foreign relations of the country, with the course of policy of the Administration, and who would be prepared, at once, to meet and decide upon the character of measures which should be proposed. This, I undertake to say, no *novice* in the national council could do. At least, I would not promise to attempt it. I feel deeply that I could not do it successfully. I should disappoint the expectations of my friends, and do injustice to the little reputation I might otherwise hope to enjoy. There is no affectation of humility in this, and, under such impressions, I *cannot suffer myself* to be thought of in a manner which may make me responsible for great mischief in defeating the chance of a better selection.

"As to the objection which I have heard urged from your present situation in the House, it has force, but is yet susceptible of a satisfactory answer. Even from the Senate that influence would continue to be *felt indirectly where* it has heretofore been *effectually exercised.* It could not but be selfish, I had almost said *cowardly*, in the host which will remain to the side of the Administration in the popular branch, to avoid that responsibility which their numbers, and I am well persuaded their *talents*, will enable them triumphantly to meet.

"But I have already written more and with greater haste than I should. I have to repeat that I beg not to be considered a candidate for the station, to which, I feel, that the best and kindest motives of friends would assign me, but which I venture to assure them, upon such explanation as I might more fully offer, they would excuse me this time for declining. In this act it will be among the first of my wishes to retain that good opinion with which you have so highly honored me.

"I shall have pleasure in seeing Mr. Appleton, and hope that he may favor me with an opportunity on my arrival in the city.

"With sentiments of the most respectful and friendly consideration,

"Your obedient servant,

"LEVI LINCOLN."

[MR. WEBSTER TO GOVERNOR LINCOLN.]

"NEW YORK, *May* 30, 1827.

"DEAR SIR: I have received here your letter communicated through Mr. Appleton. I could have very much wished that you might have arrived at a different conclusion on the question of going into the Senate. Nevertheless, I see that there is weight in some of the reasons which you mention, and I am aware also that there are other considerations, not stated by you, which, however little they affect your own mind, very naturally would create in others regret at your leaving your present situation. Under existing circumstances, I feel it my duty to leave it to others to decide how the place shall be filled. If a satisfactory appointment can be made without removing me from the place I am in, it will be highly agreeable to me; *if it cannot*, the matter must be disposed of as others may deem best.

"I am, my dear sir,

"With most true regard,

"Your obedient servant,

"DANIEL WEBSTER.

"His Excellency Governor Lincoln."

When the Legislature was reassembled in June, Mr. Webster, without any regular nomination from any quarter, was elected to the Senate of the United States, for the term of six years, from the 4th of March, 1827, by large majorities.[1]

The following letters will explain the reasons which led many of his friends to desire his remaining in the Lower House of Congress—reasons which the Legislature of Massachusetts felt it to be their duty to overrule:

[FROM MR. CLAY.]

"WASHINGTON, *14th May*, 1827.

"MY DEAR SIR: I duly received your favor of the 7th instant, and on the interesting subject of it I have conversed with the President.

[1] In the House, Mr. Webster received 202 votes out of 328, and, in the Senate, 26 out of 39. The Legislature at this time was composed, by a very large majority, of members of the old Republican party of the country, to which the Governor and most of the members of the Executive Council also belonged.

"I had previously written to Mr. Silsbee that the *pros* and *cons* on the question of your translation from the House to the Senate were so nearly balanced that I thought you might safely pursue the bent of your own inclination. The public interests require you in the House, and you are wanted in the Senate. So far as your personal interests are to be advanced, I incline to think you had better remain where you are. If your place could be supplied in the House, then I should say go to the Senate. Oakley or Sergeant might enable the Administration to get along in the popular branch, but the course of one and the election of the other are uncertain. If neither of them come to our aid, we *possibly* may do without them, should you be compelled to accept a place in the Senate. The Administration loses much, directly as well as morally, for want of such abilities as you would carry into that body; directly, by the array of talents on one side (which it must be owned the opposition there exhibits) without an adequate counterpoise on the other, which has the effect of disheartening friendly Senators; morally, by the extraneous effect on the country of this unequal contest.

"What the President would be glad to see is, that Mr. Lincoln should come in place of Mr. Mills, as the state of this latter gentleman's health dees not admit of his longer serving; and if, as it is said to be probable, Mr. Silsbee should resign, in consequence of his being elected Governor, or from any other cause, that you, after the ensuing session, should take his place. But if Governor Lincoln cannot be prevailed upon to accept a seat in the Senate, then the President decidedly prefers your coming in at the next session as Mr. Mills's successor.

"From McLane I have heard directly nothing. I have hoped that if Delaware should send to the House of Representatives next fall a friend to the Administration, and no very adverse events should occur elsewhere, Mr. McLane might see that it was his interest to adhere to his principles, and disentangle himself from his new associates; and I had thought that the probability of his adopting a correct course might be influenced by the consideration of his being the leader of one party, instead of being eclipsed in the ranks of the other. But all this is speculation, and, should you go into the Senate, he may still find that his future advancement lies rather on the side of working with you than against you. Unless I am much deceived, Delaware will send to the House of Representatives a friend to the Administration.

"The recent changes in the British ministry are very great, and they must have been the result of a radical difference of opinion on some important subject. We have no explanation of them from Mr. Gallatin, from whom I have received no letter subsequent to the resignations. The most obvious cause is that of the Irish Catholics. On the last day of March, Mr. Huskisson remained too unwell to resume the negotiation with Mr. Gallatin. He was trying to settle a preliminary point, respecting our Northeastern boundary, with Mr. Addington, but was able to make very little progress. I should think that the new ministerial arrangements would occasion some further delay. I see, therefore, but little prospect of Mr. Gallatin's speedily coming home.

"I have very little late political news. The meeting in Baltimore was all that we could have desired it to be. The progress of correct thinking in Pennsylvania continues to be encouraging, and in New York our friends are as confident of success as they need be. They are about to establish a newspaper, edited by Mr. Leake, formerly senior editor of the *Argus*, and I hope they will not fail in that object. It is much wanted.

"From Kentucky, my friends write me in good spirits. We shall, however, have warm work there, growing out of our 'Free bridge' question, *alias* the relief system.

"I have written a short letter to Silsbee, communicating the preceding views in regard to the Senate.

"I am making efforts to get off to Kentucky in about a fortnight. Unless there should be some unexpected occurrence, I think I shall go about that time.

"Yours cordially,

"H. Clay.

"D. Webster, Esq.

"P. S.—Your late speech at Faneuil Hall is all that it should have been. It presents the true condition of the existing state of things, and points out clearly the only correct line of policy. In spite of all the carpers, it will have good effect. H. C."

[MR. SILSBEE TO MR. CLAY.]

"Salem, *May* 23, 1827.

"Dear Sir: Absence from home has prevented an earlier acknowledgment of your letter of the 15th instant.

"It has long been proverbial here that 'Boston folks are full of notions,' and the Republicans of the other sections of the Commonwealth have too often found this to be the case with their political friends of the metropolis; but, independent of this natural propensity to pursue a course counter to that of their friends, the divisions which have been evinced in the recent elections may be attributed to other causes, and principally to the recent decisions of the State government upon the bridge and lottery questions, which have caused some excitement throughout the Commonwealth, and much in the vicinity of Boston; and the opponents of the Administration are unwearied in their efforts to make these divisions subservient to their purposes, the effect of which will not be such as may be apprehended at a distance.

"It is yet quite uncertain who will be elected to the United States Senate in place of Mr. Mills. It seems to be the wish of a large majority of our friends in this town that Governor Lincoln should be the man, but it is apprehended that he will not consent to be a candidate, and it is the opinion of some that he ought not to, while others yet entertain a hope that he may be prevailed on to consent to a nomination when he sees (as he will) that Mr. Mills declines. I have a letter now before me from Mr. Lincoln (in reply to one written to him on the subject), in which he says, 'I know full well that the policy of a transfer from my present office, at this time, is much doubted by a large proportion of our Republican friends; and the circumstances which existed, and the manner in which I was sustained by the people of the Commonwealth, in the late election, impose on me the highest obligation to respect this expression of their sentiments. I, therefore, beg leave to be permitted explicitly to repeat *my entire disinclination* to be considered a candidate for the place to which you refer. *It is an arrangement to which I cannot consent.* There are reasons, both of a public and private character, which I am sure might satisfy you of the propriety of this determination.

"Notwithstanding this communication, I have promised some friends here that I will see the Governor the moment he arrives in Boston, and endeavor to remove his objections to a nomination, but really I see but little hope of success. If he persists in declining, Mr. Webster will, I think, be selected, though at this moment doubts are expressed of the expediency of removing him from the House to the Senate. So far as my own feelings are concerned, I should prefer seeing Mr. Webster in the Senate, at this time, to any individual that could be sent from the State; but fears are entertained by many that his removal may be productive of more injury than benefit, especially if Mr. Oakley, from New York, should be found in the opposition. The 'divisions and commotions' which now exist in Boston will, I am afraid, operate unfavorably to the removal of Mr. Webster, as many of his constituents are apprehensive that they may not be able, at this time, to elect a Representative with whom they should be satisfied, and some of them think a new election quite too hazardous to be attempted. As soon as the Legislature meets, efforts will be made toward a suitable nomination. No one *avowedly* unfriendly can succeed. The exertions of the opposition will, therefore, be directed toward one whom they may think most susceptible of conversion.

"Anxious as I am to resign, and great as will be the sacrifice to me, both of interest and of inclination, by omitting to do it, yet I shall not resign unless the result of the election about to take place is such as to show, satisfactorily, that it can be done without hazard.

"With the highest respect, your obedient servant,

"NATHL. SILSBEE.

"Hon. Henry Clay."

[FROM MR. CLAY.]

"WASHINGTON, 28*th May*, 1827.

"MY DEAR SIR: I received your favor under date the 18th instant, from Boston. I regret the state of things there which defeated the election, but it will have no bad effect on the general scale.

"Governor Lincoln, I fear, will not be prevailed upon to run as Senator, I transmit you a letter this day received from Mr. Silsbee on that subject. The Governor, I believe, is well apprised of the President's anxious desire that he should be in the Senate. I know not of any further exertions that can be made to induce him to alter his determination. Should he adhere to it, I have ventured to express the opinion that it would be expedient that you should be sent. Should Oakley be friendly, that will abate the objections to your transfer, although, as it regards yourself personally, I do not think they will be entirely removed.

"The condition of affairs in New Hampshire is to be regretted. But, if you are right in supposing four-fifths of the Republican party in that State to be favorable, Mr. Hill cannot effect much. And sooner or later he must meet with the fate which he merits. I have always supposed that New England, in all its parts, was so friendly as not to leave any doubt of its final decision. I have not a single regular correspondent in New Hampshire. I think Governor Bell (with whom I have occasionally exchanged a letter) may be entirely confided in.

"From the West, and from Pennsylvania and Maryland, the current of news continues to run in a good channel. They are getting very warm in Kentucky, but, unless I am entirely deceived, there is no uncertainty in the final issue.

"I *wish* to leave here about the middle or last of next week. I shall go by Pittsburg, where I anticipate a cordial reception.

"I shall be glad to hear from you while you are in New York.

"The affair of Rio is much less serious in fact than it is represented to be in the papers. I think Mr. Raguet acted rather precipitately. And I hope we shall be able to arrange it satisfactorily.

"I am always

"Cordially your friend,

"H. CLAY.

"D. Webster, Esq."

[FROM THE HON. J. C. WRIGHT, ONE OF THE REPRESENTATIVES FROM OHIO.]

"STEUBENVILLE, *24th May*, 1827.

"D. WEBSTER, Esq.:

"MY DEAR SIR: Your favor of the 30th ultimo reached me some days since, during my absence of a week attending court, and to the giving certain men the proper political impetus in a neighboring county. This absence has occasioned the delay in acknowledging your letter.

"I had understood from another quarter that our friends in the 'Bay State' had it in contemplation to send you and some other 'strong man' to the United States Senate. . . . This information had occasioned me to reflect on the probable effect of removing you to the Senate, and had really given me much trouble. It is useless to disguise the fact, your presence in the House has been thought essential in sustaining our cause in that body, and although Providence, or exertion, might bring forth men, if you were absent, equal to any emergency, yet no one can say where they are to come from, or point out the men now in the House to supply your place. Your absence will be sensibly felt by our side, and will inspire our adversaries with new hope and courage. Should Oakley be against us, and Phil. Barbour be active and zealous on the same side, they, with McDuffie, Ingham, and Buchanan, aided by the sarcasms of the crazy Randolph, even if Forsyth should be elected Governor and Wickliffe fail, will give us a hard tug. I fear Oakley more than any of them, and am exceedingly anxious to have him with us, though I am yet unable to learn how he is. It is equally useless to attempt to deceive ourselves as to the fact that our opponents array more energetic operating talent on their side in the Senate than we do on ours. I do not intend to disparage our friends there, but the world says, and we have all *felt* the inferiority of our force in that body. We ought to have there some of our most powerful minds. I have been astonished that New England has not placed in that station some men of more force. But we must look at the body as it is. We must recruit our force there, and where have we the men at command? *You, we want in both places.* It is difficult to see how we can get along in either House without you. In the Senate, there is little hope of renovating the present members, and imparting to them increased moral energy and exertions. In the House, we have, I think, better ground to rest our hopes on—our men are younger, have more elasticity of mind, and, perhaps, pressing necessity may bring out talents and exertions equal to any emergency we shall be called to encounter. If *Oakley and Phil. Barbour* be warmly against us, they, with McDuffie, Buchanan, and Randolph (with his dreaded sarcasm), even if Forsyth should be Governor, and Wickliffe have liberty to stay at home, will present a force we cannot despise—a force requiring strong power and efficient discipline to conquer. Yet, I incline to the opinion the chance for us in the House is better than in the Senate. And, though not without great distrust of the correctness of my opinion, I think you should go to the Senate. If it be true that Mr. Silsbee will retire, who will succeed him? Give us a strong man, and when you are about 'improving the condition' of the Senate, suppose some of you put W—— out of the humor of continuing any longer, that his place may be supplied by M——. Who will succeed you? Boston ought to be able to supply one of the first order of intellect.

"The New-Hampshire plan of sustaining the Administration party, without the aid of Federalists, is certainly injudicious; the cry of old party names, at this day, is of no use except to demagogues; honest men ought to discountenance it. I regret your views in Boston were opposed by any local and selfish views—those seem to have prevented an election of part of your Representatives. Although your city is denominated 'headquarters of correct principles,' you can't boast much of union in this last election. I hope for the success of the remainder of your ticket on the next trial. I see Baylies has *agreed* to try his luck again. Cannot one of the Administration opponents be induced to retire, and the other be elected? . . .

"Truly yours,

"J. C. WRIGHT."

[FROM THE HON. CHARLES MINER, MEMBER OF CONGRESS FROM PENNSYLVANIA.]

"WEST CHESTER, *June* 13, 1827.

"MY DEAR SIR: The mail last night brought the account of your election to the United States Senate. How can we possibly spare you from our House? Who, when the storm is up and the billows roll, can we see at the helm, and each one feel that the vessel is safe? Well, they need a pilot in the Senate. I have felt that our friends there needed aid of a kind no one is so able to afford them; for the opposition happen to be strong in talent there. Believing the public good will also be promoted, I congratulate you sincerely on this accession to your well-deserved honors—on this gratifying testimonial of confidence from your noble State. The feeling of my heart is, *onward*, and may the highest honors be awarded to the greatest merit.

"With sentiments of perfect respect,

"CHARLES MINER.

"Hon. Daniel Webster."

[TO MR. DENISON.]

"BOSTON, *July* 28, 1827.

"MY DEAR SIR: It is a great while since you have heard from me; but this you must impute, not at all to forgetfulness, nor altogether to procrastination. I wrote you a long letter at Washington, and when I supposed you had already received it, it was brought back to me, having been dropped in the street by my servant on his way to the Department of State, and taken up by another servant, who kept it for a month or two, on the supposition, I imagine (he being an ignorant black), that it might contain money.

"The last letter which I had the pleasure to receive from you was dated in April, and forwarded by your brother and Captain Hall.[1] I have not yet had the good fortune to meet either of those gentlemen, but on the strength of your letter I have written to Captain Hall, now in Canada, solicited the honor of his acquaintance, and expressed the hope that we should see him here; and communicated through him my respects and salutations to your brother. Captain Hall writes me that he will pay us a visit, and I hope he may bring your brother along with him.

"I thank you for the pamphlets, etc., which you were kind enough to send me. All such things I read with much interest, and shall be more and more obliged by every such instance of your recollection.

[1] Captain Basil Hall.

"The recent political events in England have produced a good deal of sensation and speculation on our side the Atlantic. It is quite astonishing how extensively the debates and proceedings in your Parliament are read in the United States. Our interior papers, back to the shores of the Mississippi, contain more or less of them, and they everywhere excite some degree of attention. We are very generally on Mr. Canning's side of the question, although we have a suspicion that he does not love us Americans with quite all his heart. The general tenor of his political sentiments, especially so far as they regard the state of the world, and the cause of liberal opinions, and free governments, is, of course, highly acceptable and gratifying to us republicans. For one, however, I regret the secession of *some* of the ministers who have retired, and I suppose you must also. Among them is Mr. Peel, who seems to have established a high character, as a man of useful and solid talents. I feel pain also that Lord Eldon should not otherwise have terminated his long career. Perhaps something of the professional feeling mingles in my regrets, on his case, for I confess I have the most profound admiration for his judicial character. Nothing in your prints has disgusted me more than the fierceness of some, and the wantonness of others, of the innumerable attacks on the character of the ex-chancellor. Of Lord Bathurst I know nothing, and of Lord Westmoreland I suppose there is not much to be known, except that he is a peer, a respectable person, and with powerful influence of property and connection. These noble lords, I suppose, could be spared, if such were their pleasure; but I should think it would have been desirable that the Duke of Wellington should have remained. Of course, I am a very incompetent judge, but I must say I have seen no proofs of that *incapacity* which some of your journals charge upon the duke, in regard to the discharge of official duties. He does not appear to me to be a weak man, and I think his speech in the House of Lords made out a better case than was presented by any of his seceding colleagues. At any rate, considering his unequalled military achievements, in hours of peril and darkness, your countrymen, many of them, will regret an arrangement which *appears* to place him out of the favor of the crown.

"I congratulate you most heartily, my dear sir, on your own accession to office, and the career that seems so auspiciously opening before you. I have looked after you in the debates, but have seen little of you this session. Our dates are now only to the 13th June. We do not know yet what the *Lords* have done with the Corn Law, and perhaps the Lord only knows what they may do.

"Since you last heard from me, we have become involved in a very warm canvass for the next presidency. General Jackson's friends have made, and are still making, very great efforts to place him in the chair. He is a good soldier, and I believe a very honest man, but some of us think him wholly unfit for the place to which he aspires. Military achievement, however, is a very visible and palpable merit, and on this account the general is exceedingly popular in some of the States. The election will be close, though my present belief is that Mr. Adams will be again elected.

"The good people here have seen fit to transfer me from the House of Representatives to the Senate. This was not according to my wishes, but a state of things has arisen which, in the judgment of friends, rendered the measure expedient, and I yielded to their will. I do not expect to find my situation so agreeable as that which I left. Mr. Gorham, a highly respectable man, who was also my predecessor, succeeds to my place as Representative from this city. Our next session, we fear, will be stormy. There is nothing new of an exciting character, either in our foreign relations, or our domestic condition; but the pendency of the President's election is likely enough to produce heats, as it has already created parties in both Houses of Congress.

"Your excellent friend, the Judge, is very well: I believe he has recently written you. He always speaks of you with great regard and kindness.

"We have heard, my dear sir, that you are soon to cease writing yourself bachelor. If this be true, it is another topic on which we all send you our congratulations. Mrs. Webster accepts the tender of your remembrance with pleasure, and bids me reciprocate respect and good wishes from her.

"Let us not be forgotten by your fellow-travellers in America, but give them our regards, as you may see them. I shall send you a little package of such things as may be most likely to interest you; and, in the hope of hearing from you ere long,

"I am, dear sir,

"Most truly yours,

"DANIEL WEBSTER.

"J. E. Denison, Esq.,
"2 Portman Square, London.

"Your new chancellor, Lord Lyndhurst, was born in this town, and christened in Trinity Church July or August, 1772. His mother was a direct descendant from one of the first *comers*, viz., one of the company of the May Flower, landed on Plymouth Rock, *December* 22, 1620. So you see there is a little of the blood of the Puritans in him. Being at Plymouth the other day, their village antiquarian gave me this last part of the information."

But the honor which had come to Mr. Webster by the general voice of the people of Massachusetts, and with the approbation of the whole country, was not to be shared by her who had been the proud and happy partner of all his advances in public consideration, and who had adorned every circle, private or official, into which he had conducted her, since the day when their lives were united in a little New-Hampshire village. In the summer of 1827, Mrs. Webster's health had not been good, but she had apparently been restored by the air of Sandwich, where they had passed several weeks. When they left Boston in the latter part of November, to proceed to Washington, she was again far from well. Still, it was not then imagined that she was suffering from a fatal malady. The journey to New York increased her debility, and on their arrival in this city, a consultation by Dr. Post and Dr. Perkins resulted in a very unfavorable opinion of the case. Its progress to the sad termination, the alternations of hope and discouragement, the patient resignation of the sufferer, and the bearing of him who was to be thus bereaved, are brought vividly before us in the correspondence of those two trying months of December and January:

[TO MR. PAIGE.]

"NEW YORK, *December* 5, 7 P. M., 1827.

"DEAR WILLIAM: I must now write you more fully upon the afflicting state of Mrs. Webster's health. Dr. Post, a very eminent physician and surgeon, has to-day been called into consultation with Dr. Perkins. Their opinion, I am distressed to say, is far from favorable. I believe they will recommend her return to Boston as soon as convenient. They seem to think that it is very uncertain how fast or how slow may be the progress of the complaint; but they hold out faint hopes of any cure. I hope I may be able to meet the greatest of all earthly afflictions with firmness, but I need not say that I am at present quite overcome. I have not communicated to Mrs. Webster what the physicians think. That dreadful task remains. She will receive the information, I am sure, as a Christian ought. Under present circumstances, I should be very glad if you could come here, although I would not wish you to put yourself to too much inconvenience. I should be very glad myself to go to Washington, though it were but for a single day, but I should not do that unless, in the mean time, Mrs. Webster should be on her return. I shall now make no move until I hear from you in answer to this letter. If you come on, I think the best way will be to take the mail stage-coach, with the chance of finding an evening boat at New Haven. You must let Fletcher[1] know, without alarming him too much, that his mother's health is precarious, and that she will probably return home. I am not yet able to write, as you see, though I think I am getting better.

"Yours truly,

"DANIEL WEBSTER.

"P. S. Eight o'clock.—I would fain hope that the foregoing is of too alarming a character. I have since seen Mrs. Webster, and told her the

[1] Daniel Fletcher Webster had now dropped the name of Daniel, although he continued to be so called occasionally by some of his father's friends.

doctors' opinions. She says she still has courage. If you can come on so as to accompany Mrs. Webster home, it will not be necessary that you should set out the very day you receive this. But I shall not myself go to Washington until I hear from you that you can come to take Mrs. Webster home, if need be."

[TO MR. TICKNOR.]

"NEW YORK, *December* 9, 1827.—Sunday Evening.

"MY DEAR SIR: We have received your very kind letter of the 7th (intended to be brought by Mr. Paige) through the mail. Mr. Paige, we suppose, took the boat, and may probably be kept back by this thick weather. We look for him to-morrow.

"I am most happy to say that the physicians to-day think Mrs. Webster's case is apparently *better* than when they made a joint examination three days ago. She is certainly far more free from pain, and, in all respects, more comfortable. Yesterday, I wrote an urgent letter to Dr. Warren to come here, and see her, if possible. To-day, she consents that that request may be withdrawn for the present, and I have written the doctor accordingly. Will you have the goodness to see him, or send him a note, on receipt of this, by way of caution, lest *his* letter should have happened to miscarry.

"Our hope now is, that Mrs. Webster, by staying here until Mr. and Mrs. Story come along, may then be able to go with them to Washington. At any rate, we think she must stay until some further change, as rest, quiet, and repose, seem now essential to her. Will you have the goodness to signify this state of things to Judge Story? I hope to write him myself in a day or two; but writing is, at present, not easy to me. I am, however, getting along, and so far well that my own case deserves no regard.

"Mrs. Webster desires her fervent love to Mrs. Ticknor, and her very best regards to yourself. She thanks you both abundantly for your kindness and friendly concern. Pray, make my best remembrances to Mrs. Ticknor, and believe me, as I am always,

"Yours most truly,

"D. WEBSTER.

"Mr. Ticknor."

[FROM MR. TICKNOR.]

"BOSTON, *December* 10, 1827.

"MY DEAR SIR: Your packet, covering three letters, came safely yesterday (Sunday). The one addressed to Mr. Paige, and marked *private*, was carried home by Daniel, who locked it up unopened; the one to Dr. Warren was sent to him at once; and the one from Dr. Perkins to Mr. Paige was opened by Daniel, who afterward brought it to us. The last two have given us very unwelcome news about Mrs. Webster; but I am happy to find that Dr. Warren looks very cheerfully on the case, though that is not the professional habit of his mind; and, when she arrives here, we will do all we can to make the winter comfortable for her. It would relieve her of some of her pain at this moment if she could see how bright Daniel looks at the thought of her coming home, and of his being able, as he expresses it, 'to go and see her every day.' He is gone this morning to let Hannah[1] know it, and I advised him also to tell Mrs. Lekain, that she might not let her rooms, which are now empty, until your intentions are known. Mr. Paige's visit could not have been better timed, and, indeed, kindness like his is as sure as instinct.

"We are very glad to hear, from Dr. Perkins's letter, that you would probably be well in three or four days from its date. Pray send us notice, somehow or other, how you get on, when Mrs. Webster is likely to come, and all other matters about which you know we are anxious to learn. Daniel is quite well, and has interested us very much by the delightful feeling he has shown under his late anxiety, and his present happiness at the thought of seeing his mother again.

"Remember us particularly to Mr. Paige, who promised to write to us, and remember us most affectionately to Mrs. Webster. Can we do any thing to prepare for her coming? Let us know, and it shall go hard but your wishes shall be fulfilled.

"Yours very faithfully,

"G. T."

[TO MRS. TICKNOR.]

"NEW YORK, *December* 11, 1827.

"MY DEAR MRS. TICKNOR: Mr. Paige arrived this afternoon, bringing your very kind letter to Mrs. Webster, for which she desires to return you a thousand thanks. It would fatigue her too much to undertake the answering of it herself, and, therefore, she employs me in the grateful service. It is very good in you and your husband to remember us in our unfortunate detention here, and to give us so much sympathy for the causes which have produced it. I wrote Mr. Ticknor the evening before last. Yesterday, Mrs. Webster continued better, in a degree answering to the increased hopes of the physicians. She thinks, however, that she must have taken some little cold, as her limb has been uneasy and felt stiff to-day, and she has at times had very severe pain. She hopes that she shall sleep to-night, and be better again to-morrow. She is indeed very sick, and suffers much. Her spirits are, however, pretty good, and she bears all with great fortitude and patience. She is much gratified to see her brother.[2]

"As for me, I am yet in-doors, but am tolerably well. If I felt like leaving Mrs. Webster, I could be moving along slowly toward Washington, but I shall wait a little longer, in the hope of leaving her more comfortable. At any rate, I should return immediately, unless a decidedly favorable change should take place in her condition.

[1] A favorite servant.

[2] Mr. Paige.

"Mrs. Webster has also letters from Mrs. Hale and Eliza. Will you send them word that I will write them to-morrow and next day, instead of this evening; so that you may hear from us daily. This is a poor apology I have for not answering the letters of such friends immediately, but I am not yet so free from my complaint as to make writing entirely easy. The children are well, and pray papa to send their love to Mr. and Mrs. Ticknor and little Anna.

"I am, my dear lady, with most true regard, yours,

"D. WEBSTER.

"Mrs. Ticknor."

On the 13th of December, the symptoms were so far favorable, that Mr. Webster felt justified in proceeding to Washington, leaving Mrs. Webster in the care of Dr. and Mrs. Perkins, in their own house, and surrounded by other affectionate and devoted friends.

[TO MR. EZEKIEL WEBSTER.]

"WASHINGTON, *December* 17, 1827.

"DEAR EZEKIEL: I arrived here but last night, and have to say that I left my wife sick at New York. Her complaint, which is partly local, has been of some time standing, but we did not think much of it till lately. I fear now it is dangerous. She was much more comfortable when I left New York than she had been for a fortnight; but whether permanently better, I know not. Mr. Paige is now there with her, at Dr. Perkins's. If she should get so well as to be able to travel, I shall go back for her. On the other hand, if she grow worse, I must go and stay with her. I know not how Providence will dispose of this threatening case; but at present it fills me with the keenest anxiety.

"I find here two letters from you, and have received another to-day. As soon as I have been here long enough to learn what is the state of things, I will write you on political matters.

"I find our friends here not despairing.

"Yours as ever,

"D. WEBSTER."

[TO JUDGE STORY.]

"WASHINGTON, *December* 18, 1827.

"MY DEAR SIR: Yours of the 13th, addressed to New York, has followed me hither. My own health was so far restored, that, on Thursday, the 13th, I ventured to set forth, and arrived here Sunday evening, the 16th, without inconvenience, and with far better health than I had when I left New York. I do not now write myself an invalid.

"I left Mrs. Webster at New York. Her health was bad, though better than it had been. I know not whether you are acquainted with the nature of her complaint; though Dr. Warren or Mr. Ticknor will readily explain it to you.[1] My last letter, December 16th, says she is, on the whole, 'better than at any time before since she came to New York.' I am still in great hopes of her being able to join me here. Mr. Paige is now with her, and will stay till Christmas. If she should be able to travel, I expect to go for her, and bring her along. I desired Mr. Paige to keep you informed.

"Our rooms I found all ready, and in order; and, notwithstanding Mrs. Webster's illness, they will be kept for her, and for you and Mrs. Story. Our good landlady has done all in her power to prepare for us; and, if my poor wife had health, I should look forward to a happy session. And, as it is, I hope for the best. You say you shall set out by the 29th. I have given that information this morning to Mr. Silsbee's and Mr. Crowninshield's families, and they hope only that it may be earlier. I am sure Mrs. Story will find herself pleasantly situated here. As to political affairs, I have not been here long enough to learn much. I find our friends not discouraged. Virginia appears to be showing great strength for the Administration, and many hopes are entertained of her final vote that way. The weather has been so bad, I have as yet seen very few persons since I came here.

"I am glad Mason succeeded in the Argonaut. It is a good cause, whatever Judge P—— may think of it, and must finally prevail. It would not give rise to a serious doubt in any other part of the Union. At least, I think so.

"I shall write you again shortly; and, in the mean time, am, with all my heart,

"Yours,

"D. Webster.

"P. S.—Remember my regards to Mrs. Story."

[TO MR. PAIGE.]

"Washington, *December* 25, Christmas, Noon, 1827.

"Dear William: Your letter of Sunday has this moment reached me, in which you say Mrs. Webster would be glad if it should be quite convenient for me that I would come to New York to meet Judge Story; and I certainly shall do so. I cannot go for a day or two, because my cold is too severe; but there is nothing to prevent my setting off so soon as I am quite well. Judge Story wrote me that he should probably set out about the 29th, which is next Saturday.

"Possibly I may not leave here before Monday, the 31st; but, even then, I shall be in New York as soon as the Judge. On receipt of this I will thank you to write me, saying whether Mrs. Webster wishes me to bring any of hers or the children's things along with me. Your letter, if written on Friday morning, will be here on Sunday, so that, if I happen to stay till Monday, I shall get it. Probably I shall go off before Mon-

[1] Mrs. Webster's disease was a tumor.

day; this depends a little as well on the weather and the state of the public conveyances as on my getting rid of my cold.

"I hope, if it be not too inconvenient, you will stay till I come, and then we can talk about Grace's going to Boston or Washington. The tone of your letters, for three or four days, has been so much more favorable than before, that I feel encouraged. It will be dull for her, I fear, to be left by me again, after you are gone; but, then, I must come here, dispatch some few things, and return to her again. I shall let no business, public or private, prevent my attention to her, as the first duty.

"My cold is better to-day; but still I am not quite well. Indeed, so much of rheumatism, and then so severe a cold, have rather reduced this corporeal system of mine to some little degree of weakness. Two or three days of good weather, which I know not when we shall see again, would do me a great deal of good.

"You will, of course, send this to Grace, as I shall not write another to-day.

"Yours always truly,

"D. WEBSTER.

"P. S.—Again to-morrow.

"My Christmas dinner is a handful of magnesia and a bowl of gruel."

[TO MR. MASON.]

"WASHINGTON, *December* 26, 1827.

"MY DEAR FRIEND: I cannot write you now a political letter, but must tell you something about me and mine. I came here the 17th, pretty free from rheumatism, but have since had a violent and obstinate cold, which finally has brought me to keep house. It is now, I think, better; but, it will be two or three days before I shall be well again, at best. Mrs. Webster, as you know, I left in New York, quite sick. She has been perhaps, on the whole, from the time of my departure to the date of my last letter, a good deal more comfortable and free from pain than for the fortnight I was in New York. I cannot say that her substantial cause of illness is better, but Mr. Paige writes on the 23d that he thinks more favorably of the future progress and final result of the complaint than I did, when I left New York. It is a tumor of rather anomalous character, and the best surgeons look upon it with much fear of consequences. It seems to have a tendency to break out; this they dread, and try to disperse it, although its real character, perhaps, can only be fully known when that shall take place. I would not alarm myself or my friends unnecessarily; but, to say the truth, my dear sir, I fear the worst. I shall leave here, if I am well enough, on Saturday, for New York. There I expect to meet the Judge and Mrs. Story. Whether I shall return hither with her, or stay at New York, or endeavor to get Mrs. Webster home, must be decided by the state of things which I shall find existing when I get there. If it should be probable, which the surgeons somewhat incline to suppose, that my wife may remain for considerable time without essential change, I do not see that the superior duty of being with her must not lead to the vacation of the situation which I fill here. I should be very glad to hear from you, directed to New York, care of Dr. Perkins, Fulton Street.

"I am, dear sir,

"Most truly yours,

"DANIEL WEBSTER."

[TO MR. SILSBEE, HIS COLLEAGUE IN THE SENATE.]

"NEW YORK, *January* 4, 1828.

"MY DEAR SIR: I arrived here yesterday at eleven o'clock, after a very tolerable journey, and without having added any thing to my cold. Indeed, I think it is better than when I left Washington.

"I find Mrs. Webster more comfortable, on the whole, than I expected. She has now enjoyed more rest and repose, and more freedom from pain, for three days together, than in any equal time since we came here six weeks ago. She has lost flesh since I left her, however, and is now feeble.

"As to the original cause of her illness, I do not know exactly what to think of it. Some symptoms are certainly a little more favorable. I cannot help getting a little new hope, on the whole, though I fear I build on a slight foundation.

"I find here Judge Story and his wife. They are in very good health. He has not looked so well for a long time. It is a great thing to get him out of his study. They set off this afternoon, being anxious to get over the Chesapeake before the boat stops. They will take possession of the rooms at Mrs. McIntyre's, where I hope to join them soon. Mr. Paige went to Boston yesterday. As soon as he shall be able to return, which I think will be in a few days, I shall return to Washington, if Mrs. Webster remains as comfortable as at present.

"I am, my dear sir, with most true regard yours,

"DANIEL WEBSTER.

"P. S.—Mr. Clay's address seems to meet with universal approbation."

[TO MR. EZEKIEL WEBSTER.]

"NEW YORK, *January* 8, 1828.

"DEAR EZEKIEL: I came here from Washington on Friday, the 4th. There are so many friends to write to on the subject of Mrs. Webster's health, that I fear I may neglect some; and hardly know how long it is since I wrote you. William, however, has written occasionally to his friends in your vicinity.

"I cannot say any thing new in regard to Mrs. Webster. Her case is most serious. It is one of rare occurrence, no physician here, but Dr. Perkins, thinking he ever saw one like it. The tumor has not yet broken out, but threatens it, and will, doubtless, soon. Its character will be then better known and I fear the worst. Dr. Nathan Smith, Dr. Physick, etc., have been written to for opinions and advice; and I have written an urgent letter to Dr. Warren to come here. After all, the case is very much out of the reach of medical application or surgical aid. . . . Internal remedies do not reach it, and external applications have little effect. The result must be left with Providence; but you must be prepared to learn the worst. For three or four days she has been more free from pain than for some time before; but yesterday she was a good deal distressed again. William Paige went home the day I came. He thinks he can return in a week or ten days, and stay till I make a visit to the court at Washington, if Mrs. Webster should be so as to allow of my leaving her. You will, of course, not alarm your wife and Mrs. Kelly, and Nancy, too much in regard to Grace. There is yet a hope; but I have thought it best to tell you my real opinion.

"My own health has suffered from continual colds and catarrhs. Though not quite well even yet, I have no dangerous or bad symptoms. I feel no inflammation of the lungs, or soreness of the chest, nor any febrile symptoms. An epidemic cold is all about here, and I partake in it; but it appears to be getting better, and I have no doubt that two or three clear days would finish it. Julia and Edward are pretty well; they go to school. Grace and the children desire their best love to Mrs. Webster and the little girls, as well as to you.

"Yours always truly,

"DANIEL WEBSTER."

[TO MR. MASON.]

"NEW YORK, *January* 15, 1823.

"MY DEAR SIR: I thank you for your kind and friendly letter, and wish I could feel justified in confirming those favorable hopes which your friendship leads you to form in regard to my sick wife. Would to God I were able to encourage my own hopes, and yours also! But I fear, greatly fear, that Providence has not so ordered it. Although she is better one day than another, that is, more comfortable, more free from severe pain, yet I do not see any material change in that which has occasioned her illness. . . .

"After all, my dear sir, we have a ray of hope. I try to keep up my courage, and to strengthen hers; but it is due to our friendship that I tell you the whole truth. I have endeavored to prepare myself for that event, of all others the most calamitous to me and to my children.

"I thank you for your advice as to myself, and shall certainly follow it. In all probability I shall stay here for some time yet. I fear circumstances will not be such as that I can leave, even after Mr. Paige comes, nor am I very anxious to do so. There seems nothing important in Congress, and I must try to make some arrangement of my business in court.

"My health, though not entirely confirmed, is daily improving. I have the remnant of an epidemical cold, a little loose cough and catarrh; no soreness of breast, nor inflammation of lungs, nor any feverish tendency. Be assured, my dear sir, I shall take all possible care of my own health.

" *Ten o'clock*, P. M.—Mrs. Webster is now asleep, and is free from severe pain, but breathes not easily. She is a good deal inclined to sleep. I leave space to tell you how she may be in the morning.

" *Wednesday morning, eight o'clock.*—Mrs. Webster passed rather a comfortable night. She had less cough than I apprehended, and seems calm and quiet this morning. She thinks she breathes a little easier than yesterday. Her voice is faint, but natural in its tones.

"Yours truly,

"DANIEL WEBSTER."

[TO MR. EZEKIEL WEBSTER.]

"NEW YORK, *January* 17, 1828.

"MY DEAR BROTHER: I cannot give you any favorable news respecting my wife. She is no better, and I fear is daily growing weaker. She is now exceedingly feeble. Dr. Perkins thinks she has altered very much the last three or four days.

"The prospect nearly confounds me; but I hope to meet the event with submission to the will of God.

"I expect Mr. Paige to-morrow morning. He or I will write you again soon.

"Yours affectionately,

"DANIEL WEBSTER."

[TO MR. E. WEBSTER.]

"Monday Morning, *January* 21.

"DEAR BROTHER: Mrs. Webster still lives, but is evidently near her end. We did not expect her continuance yesterday, from hour to hour.

"Yours affectionately,

"D. W."

[TO MR. MASON.]

"Monday Morning, nine o'clock.

"MY DEAR SIR: Mrs. Webster still lives, but cannot possibly remain long with us. We expected her decease yesterday from hour to hour.

"I received Mrs. Mason's letter, but could not communicate it.

"Yours,

"D. WEBSTER."

[TO MR. EZEKIEL WEBSTER.]

"Monday, quarter-past two o'clock.

"DEAR BROTHER: Poor Grace has gone to heaven. She has now just breathed her last breath.

"I shall go with her forthwith to Boston, and, on receipt of this, I hope you will come there if you can.

"I shall stay there some days. May God bless you and yours!

"D. WEBSTER."

[TO MR. TICKNOR.]

"Quarter-past two o'clock, P. M., Monday, *January* 21, 1828.

"MY DEAR SIR: All is over. My blessed wife has just expired. With the leave of Providence, I shall soon see you, and receive your condolence.

"May God bless you.

"D. WEBSTER.

"Mr. Ticknor."

Mr. Ticknor observes in his Reminiscences:

"Mr. Webster came to Mr. George Blake's in Summer Street, where we saw him both before and after the funeral. He seemed completely broken-hearted. At the funeral, when, with Mr. Paige, I was making some arrangements for the ceremonies, we noticed that Mr. Webster was wearing shoes that were not fit for the wet walking of the day, and I went to him and asked him if he would not go in one of the carriages. 'No,' he said, 'my children and I must follow their mother to the grave on foot. I could swim to Charlestown.' A few minutes afterward, he took Julia and Daniel in either hand, and walked close to the hearse through the streets to the church in whose crypt the interment took place. It was a touching and solemn sight. He was excessively pale."

Mrs. Webster's remains were placed in a tomb belonging to her husband, beneath St. Paul's Church, in Boston, with those of her children, Grace and Charles. I continue the correspondence which followed this event:

[FROM JUDGE STORY.]

"WASHINGTON, *January* 27, 1828.

"MY DEAR SIR: I received in the course of the mail your letter announcing the melancholy news of the death of Mrs. Webster. It has sunk Mrs. Story and myself in deep affliction. And, prepared as we were for the heavy intelligence, it came at last with a most distressing power over our minds. We do, indeed, most sincerely and entirely, from our whole hearts, sympathize with you, and partake largely of your sorrows. We have long considered Mrs. Webster one of our best and truest friends, and, indeed, as standing to us almost in the relation of a sister. We have known her excellent qualities, her kindness of heart, her generous feelings, her mild and conciliatory temper, her warm and elevated affections, her constancy, purity, and piety, and her noble disinterestedness, and her excellent sense. Such a woman, and such a friend, must be at all times a most severe loss, and to us, at our age, is irreparable; we can scarcely hope to form many new friendships, and our hope, our dearest hope, was to retain what we had. We have so hoped in vain. I can say with Young, in deep humiliation of soul:

"'Our dying friends come o'er us like a cloud,
To damp our brainless ardor, and abate
That glare of life, which sometimes blinds the wise.'

"Of the loss to you, I can and ought to say nothing. I know that, if we suffer, your sorrows must be unspeakable. And I can only pray God to aid you by His consolations, and to suggest to you that, after your first agony is over, her virtues and your own admirable devotion to her cannot but be sources of the most soothing recollection to you. I know well that we may do mischief by intermeddling with a heart wounded by grief; and it must be left to itself to recover its powers, and to soften its anguish. What some of us think of the dead, you may read in the *National Intelligencer* of Saturday.[1]

"In going to Boston, and attending the funeral obsequies, I entirely agree with your own judgment. I should have done the same, under like circumstances, as most appropriate to my own feelings and to public propriety. We have in spirit followed your wife to the grave with you.

"I do not urge your immediate return here. But yet, having been a like sufferer, I can say that the great secret of comfort must be sought, so far as human aid can go, in employment. It requires effort and sacrifices, but it is the only specific remedy against unavailing and wasting sorrow; that canker which eats into the heart, and destroys its vitality. If you

[1] Obituary (written by Mr. Justice Story).—"On Monday last, at New York, where her journey to Washington was arrested by the disease that terminated her life, Mrs. Grace Webster, wife of the Hon. Daniel Webster, of the Senate of the United States. The death of this excellent woman has spread a general gloom among her numerous friends. Few persons have been more deservedly or more universally beloved; few have possessed qualities more attractive, more valuable, or more elevating. Her manners carried with them a winning grace and ease, expressive at once of benevolence and respect. Her heart was open to every call of human affliction, and her charity was of that Christian power which blesses them that give and them that take. Her talents, naturally fine, had been cultivated by study and a large intercourse with society; and her conversation diffused a charm which belongs only to the purity and refinement of the best female minds. Her life was filled up in the conscientious discharge of duty: in devoted attachment to her family and friends; in deep, sincere, and unobtrusive piety; in holiness of purpose and conduct; and, in affections which, beginning in this world, belong also to eternity. Such a life, too brief indeed for our happiness, ought to leave nothing by its close but regrets for our own loss, while it should afford the highest consolations from the connections which it adorned, and the virtues which it illustrated. To her husband and children, we too painfully know that the loss must be irreparable."—(*National Intelligencer* of January 26, 1828.)

will, therefore, allow me to advise, it would be that you should return here as soon as you can gather up your strength, and try professional and public labors. Endeavor to wear off that spirit of despondency which you cannot but feel, and which you will scarcely feel any inclination to resist. Saying this, I have said all that I ought, and I know that you can understand what is best, better than I can prescribe.

"Mrs. Story desires her most affectionate regards to you and the children, and I join in them, being always affectionately

"Your friend,

"JOSEPH STORY."

[TO DR. PERKINS.]

"BOSTON, Monday, *January* 28, 1828.

"MY DEAR SIR: You have learned, by Mr. Paige's letter, that we reached Boston on Friday evening; and, on Saturday, committed Mrs. Webster's remains to the tomb. We used the occasion to bring into our own tomb the coffin containing the remains of our daughter Grace, who died January 23, 1817. My dear wife now lies with her oldest and her youngest; and I hope it may please God, when my appointed hour comes, that I may rest by her side.

"Mrs. Bryant came immediately to see me and the children, and manifests her kindest sympathy in the calamity which has befallen us. She is an excellent woman, and one whom Mrs. Webster very much regarded and loved. All our friends have received us with a sincerity of condolence and sympathy which we can never forget. The children are well. Daniel will resume his usual residence and occupation in a day or two. Mrs. Lee (Eliza Buckminster), Mrs. Ticknor, Mrs. Hale, Mrs. Appleton, and others, have offered, in the most friendly manner, to take care of Julia and Edward for the winter. We have not yet decided how we shall dispose of them.

"I pray you to give my most affectionate regards to Mrs. Perkins. I never can express how much I feel indebted to her kindness and friendship. If Mrs. Webster had been her sister, she could have done no more.

"In a few days, I intend to set out for Washington. If there should come a flight of snow, so as to make sleighing, I shall immediately improve the occasion to get over the hills to New Haven.

"I am, dear sir, most truly,

"Yours always,

"DANIEL WEBSTER."

[TO MR. MASON.]

"BOSTON, *January* 29, 1828.

"MY DEAR SIR: I thank you for your kind letter of yesterday. It would give me great pleasure to see you; but I do not expect you to make a journey hither at this season. I know also that your engagements must be pressing. I am, at present, at Mr. Blake's, with the children. My brother came down yesterday. It is my purpose to stay till toward the end of this week, or to the first of next, according to the weather, and then proceed South. My own health is pretty good, although I feel, in some measure, fatigued and exhausted. I shall travel slowly, and must necessarily stay two or three days in New York.

"As to my children, I think I shall dispose of them in this town for the present, without inconvenience. Daniel is perfectly well disposed of where he is. Mrs. Lee (Eliza Buckminster) lays claim to Julia, of right, and would be glad of Edward; also, Mrs. Ticknor, Mrs. Hale, Mrs. Appleton, and others, have kindly offered to take them. I feel a reluctance to separate these two little ones, but still incline to think the best thing will be to let Julia go to Mrs. Lee's, and turn Edward, for the winter, into Mrs. Hale's little flock.

"As far as I have thought at all of my future arrangements, my inclination is to make no more change in my course and mode of life than the event necessarily produces.

"I think I shall leave orders to have the furniture put up in the house, with the view of taking home the children when I return, and, with the aid of Mr. Paige, keeping the family together. Except, perhaps, that it may be best that Julia should stay principally with Eliza, or in some other family where there is a lady. Very probably both the little children may pass the summer at their uncle's.

"I pray you give my most affectionate remembrance to Mrs. Mason. Mrs. Webster spoke of her often, and always with the strongest sentiments of esteem and affection. Her last letter was received, I think, before Mrs. Webster's death; but when she was not in a condition to read it or hear it.

"In regard to this calamity, my dear sir, I feel that every thing has conspired to alleviate, as far as possible, the effects of the calamity itself. All was done that could be done; the kindness of friends had no bounds; and it is now continued, also, toward me and the children. The manner of the death, too, was, in all respects, such as her dearest friends would have wished.

"Adieu, my dear sir,

"Yours, always truly,

"DANIEL WEBSTER."

[TO MR. FLETCHER WEBSTER.]

"SENATE-CHAMBER, Tuesday, *February* 17, 1828.

"MY DEAR SON; I have received a letter from you to-day, before I have found time to answer your last. That gave me singular pleasure, as it contained a very gratifying report from Mr. Leverett.[1] I have nothing more at heart, my dear son, than your success and welfare, and the culti-

[1] Master of the Latin School, Boston.

vation of your talents and virtues. You will be, in the common course of things, coming into active life, when, if I live so long, I shall be already an old man, and shall have but little left in life but my children and their hopes and happiness. In contemplation of these things, I look with the most affectionate anxiety upon your progress, considering the present as a most critical and important period in your life.

"Such reports, as that last received, give me good spirits; and, I doubt not, my dear son, that the consciousness that your good conduct and respectable progress in your class, and among your fellows, gives me pleasure, will stimulate your affectionate heart, with other motives, to earnest and assiduous endeavors to excel. I pray Heaven to bless you and prosper you.

"At present my time is exceedingly occupied between the Senate and the court, and I suppose it will continue so to be till the 3d of March. It is very cold here; much the severest winter I ever experienced at Washington.

"Yours most affectionately,

"D. WEBSTER."

[TO MR. PAIGE.]

"WASHINGTON, Sunday Evening, —— —, 1828.

"DEAR WILLIAM: I found divers letters of yours here yesterday, and have another to-day; for all which I thank you. A line from you, as often as you can write one, will always give me pleasure and satisfaction. I sometimes feel as if I were troubling you too much with so much care of the children, and so much attention to my concerns. But I trust you will not suffer me to wear out your patience and kindness. Notwithstanding the blessed spirit, that has so long been the common bond of union between us, is now on earth no more, you will ever be to me one of the nearest and dearest objects in life; nearer and dearer, indeed, from this very calamity. Enough!

"I find Judge Story and his wife very well. Mrs. Story has had the company of Mrs. Lawrence, and has not been therefore lonely. But, alas! it is not such a winter as she promised herself. I have not been out of the house to-day. A great many people have been to see me. To-morrow I shall probably go into court.

"Yours, dear William,

"Most faithfully,

"D. WEBSTER."

[TO MR. PAIGE.]

"WASHINGTON, Wednesday Evening, —— —, 1828.

"DEAR WILLIAM: I have received to-day your letter of Saturday, which makes me feel a good deal better. I have seldom been five days before without hearing from home; and, although I have lost what mainly made home dear to me, there is yet that in it which I love more than all things else in the world. I could not get along without cherishing the feeling that I have a home, notwithstanding the shock I have received. You must try to make the children write when you cannot, so that I may hear from some of you; once every two or three days at least.

"This morning was devoted to General Brown's funeral; and I went into court at one o'clock. For some days to come, indeed, as long as the court continues, I expect no leisure. Time has been when I should not have cared much about it; and, as it is, I shall get through somehow or other.

"The arrangement you suggested some time ago, as to the children's all dining with you on Sunday, and occasionally with our other friends, pleases me well. I hope they are happy. Edward, I am sure, is as well off as he can be; and, since you cannot spare him, I am content he should remain where he is.

"Riley's trunk is here. I shall send it the very first opportunity. He will receive it, I trust, in a week or two. I am sorry to hear Mary is sick, and hope her illness will not be of long duration.

"Remember me kindly to Mr. Blake. I would write him, if I had time, to-night, but must put it off for a day or two.

"Give my love to all the children. I wish I had one of them here.

"Good-night.

"D. WEBSTER."

[TO MR. TICKNOR.]

"WASHINGTON, *February* 22, 1828, in Supreme Court.

"MY DEAR SIR: I find myself again in the court, where I have been so many winters, and surrounded by such men and things as I have usually found here. But I feel very little zeal or spirit in regard to the passing affairs. My most strong propensity is to sit down, and sit still; and, if I could have my wish, I think the writing of a letter would be the greatest effort I should put forth for the residue of the winter. I suppose, however, that a sort of necessity will compel me to be here for ten days or a fortnight, and to appear to take an interest in the business of the court. My own health, I think, is a good deal better than when I left home. Indeed, it is very good, and I have nothing to complain of in that respect.

"The Judge and Mrs. Story are getting along very well. She has complained a little of *dyspepsia*, but now seems to be well, and enjoys Washington society with reasonable relish. They dine to-day (birthday) at the President's.

"I hear that my children are frequent visitors at your house, much to their gratification. I know, my dear sir, with how much kindness you and Mrs. Ticknor treat us all; and feel how greatly we must lean on our friends under our present circumstances. I feel a much greater inclination, or, to speak more properly, a much greater necessity, of being at home than ever before; not at all on account of the children at present, as I know they are well disposed of, but for my own comfort and solace. There is little here to administer that, which I find I most need. But I did not intend, my dear sir, to write you a gloomy letter. My object was mainly to notify my safe arrival, to keep myself in remembrance, and to thank you for all your kind deeds. Both you and Mrs. Ticknor are persons to whom the art of writing is known, and the exercise of it not afflicting. I flatter myself, therefore, that one or the other of you will sometimes favor me with a few lines. I pray you make her my most grateful and kind remembrance. Mention me also to Mr. and Mrs. Hale.

"Yours ever faithfully,

"DANL. WEBSTER.

"G. Ticknor."

[TO MRS. LEE.]

"WASHINGTON, *March* 15, 1828.

"DEAR ELIZA: I return you Mr. Parker's[1] letter, which I have read, as you may well suppose, with great pleasure. Nothing is more soothing and balmy to my feelings than to dwell on the recollection of my dear wife, and to hear others speak of her who knew her and loved her. My heart holds on by this thread, as if it were by means of it to retain her yet here. Mr. and Mrs. Parker were always kind to us, and are among those Portsmouth friends whom time and distance never separated from our acquaintance and affection. Mrs. Webster had very high esteem for them both.

"I hear from Mr. Paige and from Julia and from Edward that you are well. Julia has told me all about your party, and how long she sat up. I hear from others, as well as herself, that she is happy as possible under the protection of your care and kindness. You will love her, I know, for her mother's sake, and, I hope, for her own also; and I trust she will make herself agreeable to your husband. You are kind enough to say that concern for Julia need not lead me to forbear any purpose which I might otherwise have of crossing the water. It would be unpleasant, certainly, to leave the children, and especially a little girl of Julia's age; but I should not feel uneasy about her at all while under your guardianship. There are other considerations, however, which are well to be weighed before I am water-borne. Even if what you allude to were supposed to be at my own option, and, however desirable it might be in itself, times and circumstances may, nevertheless, be such as 'give me pause.' This is all I can say about it at present, except that I am now too old to do any thing in a hurry. I believe this is almost the only time I have alluded to the subject to any one; and would not wish to be quoted as having said one word respecting it.

[1] Rev. Dr. Parker, a clergyman of Portsmouth, an excellent man, with a brilliant wife, who is again mentioned, *post*, in the year 1848.

"Mrs. Story left us the day before yesterday. The Judge goes in a day or two. I shall be sorry to lose him, though quite willing to have the court break up.

"I have a very kind letter, indeed, from Mrs. Everett, respecting the name of her youngest daughter; I wish uncle would carry Julia out to see her.

"Is your husband a document-reader? I should be glad to send him some of our papers, speeches, etc., but have been afraid he would vote it a bore. Pray give my love to him; and believe me, as

"Ever, yours,

"DANL. WEBSTER."

[TO MR. HADDOCK.]

"WASHINGTON, *March* 21, 1828.

"MY DEAR NEPHEW: I thank you for your kind and affectionate letter, and assure you its suggestions are all in accordance with my own feelings. It does not appear to me unreasonable to believe that the friendships of this life are perpetuated in heaven. Flesh and blood, indeed, cannot inherit the kingdom of God; but I know not why that which constitutes a pure source of happiness on earth, individual affection and love, may not survive the tomb. Indeed, is not the principle of happiness to the sentient being essentially the same in heaven and on earth? The love of God, and the good beings whom He has created, and the admiration of the material universe which He has formed, can there be other sources of happiness than these to the human mind, unless it is to alter its whole structure and character? And, again, it may be asked, how can this world be rightly called a scene of probation and discipline, if these affections, which we are commanded to cherish and cultivate here, are to leave us on the threshold of the other world? These views, and many others, would seem to lead to the belief that earthly affections, purified and exalted, are fit to carry with us to the abode of the blessed. Yet, it must be confessed, that there are some things in the New Testament which may possibly countenance a different conclusion. The words of our Saviour, especially in regard to the woman who had seven husbands, deserve deep reflection. I am free to confess that some descriptions of heavenly happiness are so ethereal and sublimated as to fill me with a strange sort of terror. Even that which you quote, that our departed friends 'are as the angels of God,' penetrates my soul with a dreadful emotion. Like an angel of God, indeed, I hope she is, in purity, in happiness, and in immortality; but, I would fain hope that, in kind remembrance of those she has left, in a lingering human sympathy and human love, she may yet be, as God originally created her, 'a little lower than the angels.'

"My dear nephew, I cannot pursue these thoughts, nor turn back to see what I have written. Adieu.

"D. W."

[TO MRS. TICKNOR.]

"WASHINGTON, *March* 23, 1828.

"I received your husband's letter, my dear Mrs. Ticknor, some time ago, and your postscript, and thank you both for taking the pains to think of me. My children write me often, and do not fail to let me know how constant is your kindness toward them. You feel an interest in them, I know, for their mother's sake, and I hope they may be able in due time to awaken a feeling of regard and kindness on their own account. I do not feel over-anxious about them, knowing that they are in safe hands, and well disposed of; yet they necessarily occupy my mind a great deal, and bring reflections and thoughts which I cannot shut out, and which come also through many other channels. I did not intend, however, my dear friend, to write you a melancholy letter, or in depressed spirits; but so it is, that whenever my mind falls into communion with those whom I know to take a concern in its recent sorrows, it hastens back to the past, and claims to be indulged in the enjoyment of a friend's condolence and sympathy. But of this, no more.

"My health has become very tolerably good, and, now that the court has closed its session, I do not expect to find myself involved in a great pressure of affairs, and certainly shall do nothing that I am not absolutely obliged to do.

"It is probable Congress will rise the middle of May.

"Mr. Ticknor gave me a very good account of Boston matters, up to the date of his letter. There have been some more recent occurrences, about which I know nothing more than the newspapers tell. I allude especially to a great meeting of Federalists, which is said to have taken place to aid General Jackson's election, against Mr. Adams. I did not hear that your husband was there. If he was, he does not appear to have made a speech.

"I can tell you very little about Washington, as I do not go out, and see nobody except in the halls of Congress. Mr. Vaughan has been two or three times to see me. He looks rather thin and pale, though he counts himself well. Wallenstein is here, a perfect hermit. He does not go even to Congress or the court. His health seems not good, and they say he is in love, which, you know, may either mend or mar it, according to circumstances.

"I must pray you to give my love to Mr. Hale's family, with the assurance that it shall be one of my first efforts to write to them. I see that Mr. Hale is the president or vice-president of all the internal improvements in the Commonwealth.[1]

"Give my love to your husband, and believe me, my dear Mrs. Ticknor, most truly and sincerely yours,

"DANIEL WEBSTER.

"Mrs. Ticknor."

[1] The late Mr. Nathan Hale, one of the founders of the railroad system of New England, and editor of the Boston *Daily Advertiser*.

In the next month Mr. Webster was cheered by a visit from Mr. Ticknor and Mr. Prescott,[1] which he seems to have anticipated with great pleasure.

[TO MR. TICKNOR.]

"WASHINGTON, *April* 18, 1828.

"MY DEAR SIR: I received yours of the 13th this morning, and never executed commission with more alacrity and pleasure than this of looking up rooms for you and Mr. Prescott. It delights me to hear that you are coming, and I shall certainly keep you a fortnight.

"The rooms are engaged. They are not strictly in the house I live in, but in the same block, and quite proximate. My landlady has engaged them, and I am to have the pleasure of your company at my table. When you arrive in this far-famed metropolis, please direct the coachman to set down at Mrs. McIntyre's, Pennsylvania Avenue, nearly opposite Gadsby's National Hotel, a little this side, precisely by the side of a pump, at a large wooden platform which supplies the place of a stepping-stone. Inquire for Mr. Webster. If he is out, ask for Charles ——, and the rest will follow in regular sequence. I shall see that there is dinner for you at two o'clock on Sunday; and, if that day should not bring you, at four o'clock on Monday.

"Yours always truly,

"D. WEBSTER."

This visit I find alluded to in the following passage of Mr. Ticknor's Reminiscences:

"In the spring of 1828 I made a short visit in Washington, for the purpose of breaking up a cough which had teased me for some time. Prescott went with me. Mr. Webster provided rooms for us in the house adjacent to the one where he lived, but we shared his parlor and his table. He was much out of spirits, from the death of Mrs. Webster a few months before, but he was very busy and very interesting. There was much talk of his going minister to England, and I think he might have had the place about that time if he had chosen. Talking of it with him one day, he said he could not afford the expense, and besides he thought he was more useful in his place in the Senate. I think he believed he could render the country more service there than anywhere else. Indeed, he intimated as much, more than once, particularly in a conversation with Mr. Storrs, of New York, who, till Mr. Webster undeceived him, believed he had been nominated to the place that very morning. Mr. Webster was undoubtedly right. If he had gone to England then, he could not have made the speech in answer to Mr. Hayne in January, 1830."

[1] The historian.

[TO MRS. TICKNOR.]

"WASHINGTON, Friday, five o'clock, *May* —, 1828.

"MY DEAR MRS. TICKNOR: I thank you for your letter, enclosing your husband's. He is dressing to go to the President's, and I shall go with him rather than stay to my lonely dinner. He and Mr. Prescott leave me to-morrow. I shall feel their loss very seriously, I assure you, but I cannot persuade them to stay longer. Nothing resists the attraction of wives and children.

"You are very kind to tell me about my three little ones. I have the greatest happiness in knowing that they are well, and in feeling how much my friends care for them, and think of them.

"In next month I hope to see you all.

"Adieu. Ever very truly yours,

"D. W."

Washington was not the scene from which he could derive the consolations that he needed. He longed for the society of his children and the friends of his home. The following letter to Mrs. Lee expresses the state of his feelings, as the session drew to its close, and his escape became nearer:

[TO MRS. LEE.]

"WASHINGTON, *May* 18, 1828.—Sunday Evening.

"MY DEAR FRIEND: Your very kind letter of the 12th was received to-day. I cannot thank you sufficiently for your goodness and affection toward Julia. Certainly you come nearer supplying her loss than any one else. I believe she loves you best of any; and it is my wish, my dear friend, that you should make her as much your own as your feelings prompt you to do. She cannot be better than with you, and I incline to leave it very much to your choice how much she shall be with you, and when it is best for her to be elsewhere. You have a right to her, if you choose to have her, which nobody else will ever divide. You have been among our dearest friends from the day of our marriage, and, as Julia is left motherless, I know not what to do for her so well as to leave her with you, whenever it is agreeable to you to have her with you. If you think her education would not suffer, I should be quite willing she should be with you most of the summer; though I hope to have her with me some of the time.

"I thank you, my dear friend, for all your kind remembrance and good wishes. Your regard and friendship are among the objects which make me willing to live longer, and which I shall never cease to value while I do live. You say Mr. Sullivan thought me depressed. It is true. I fear I grow more and more so. I feel a vacuum, an indifference, a want of motive, which I cannot describe.

"I hope my children, and the society of my best friends, may rouse me; but I can never see such days as I have seen. Yet I should not repine; I have enjoyed much, very much; and, if I were to die to-night, I should bless God most fervently that I have lived.

"Adieu, my dear friend; I hope to be in better spirits when I see you.

"DANIEL WEBSTER."

This correspondence has been spread before the reader, because nothing else can so well disclose the trial to which this portion of Mr. Webster's life was subjected, as nothing else can so well exhibit his religious nature, his tenderness, and his self-control. Nor could there be a better tribute to the character of a wife and a mother than the evidence which is here afforded of the blank in his existence which this loss created. The "applause of listening senates" became as nothing to him, when he remembered that it could not be shared by her who had witnessed all his triumphs, and whose quick and intelligent sympathies had crowned them all. The thought of remaining in public life, with his children cast upon the care of others, rich as he was in friends, oppressed him. His sons might be placed where the work of education could be well performed; but there was a daughter, inheriting some of the father's intellect and all of the mother's gentleness, whose bereaved condition filled him with anxiety. Yet for them, as for himself, he could see no way but to trust in the vigilant affection of those who loved him for his own sake, until he could determine whether there remained aught for him in the paths of fame that could compensate, in the good he could do his country, for the loss that was to fall on himself and his, by continuing in the public service.

As the narrative of Mr. Webster's life goes on, it will be seen that while his career was marked by great success, while his reputation as a statesman rose constantly higher and higher before the eyes of men, while the exercise of his public talents afforded him pleasure, and the applause that followed him was a source of happiness, and while new exigencies in public affairs constantly multiplied his distinctions, he was yet a man who suffered perhaps more than the ordinary share of human sorrows. If we would know what it was that carried him on, to the last, in public life, and prevented him from seeking in a private station for that repose which is at once rest and obscurity, we must look for something deeper than mere ambition. Undoubtedly he was ambitious. It would not be a true view of his character or nature to claim for him an exemption from that attribute, whether it be a virtue or a vice. But it will be found, and it will be allowed, by all who shall understand and embrace the whole circle of motives which actuated him at the several most critical periods of his life, when retirement from public station came prominently before his thoughts, that we must admit him to have been chiefly controlled by patriotic reasons, or we cannot fully estimate his character.

There is a low type of supposed wisdom, which always assigns the actions of public men to a selfish origin, and which complacently assumes that it has sounded all the depths of human nature, when it has made this common suggestion. But such vulgar shrewdness does not penetrate beneath the surface.

Among the measures of this session was one in which Mr. Webster took a deep interest, notwithstanding his present affliction. This was a bill for the relief of the surviving officers of the Revolution. In the Senate, the discussion on this measure had been watched by him with great solicitude, until it appeared that there was likely to be an equal division upon it. He had not intended to speak upon the subject until it was probable that the bill would be lost. He then came forward and delivered the speech now contained in the third volume of his works.[1] The bill became a law. Among the letters addressed to Mr. Webster by the surviving patriots whose cause he had espoused, the dignity and elevation of the following from General North, of Connecticut, render it too striking to be omitted. All my readers may not be aware that the case of these officers involved an unfulfilled contract on the part of the country, which had remained neglected for more than fifty years. It was this feature of their claim that Mr. Webster especially enforced, in one of the most beautiful and impressive speeches that he ever made.

[1] A speech delivered in the Senate, April 25, 1828, on the Bill for the Relief of the Surviving Officers of the Revolution.—(*Works*, iii., 218.)

[FROM GENERAL NORTH.]

"NEAR NEW LONDON, *May* 13, 1828.

"Permit me to offer my thanks and grateful acknowledgments to you, sir, and to the other gentlemen of the Senate, who, with you, under adverse circumstances and great discouragements, have steadily and with force advocated the claims of the remaining Revolutionary officers; and for the delicacy with which the unfortunate situation of many of them has been alluded to. During the short period allotted to us, I trust we shall forget whatever has been unpleasant, whatever we may have thought unjust, remembering only the benefits received from those who, had it been possible, would have bestowed a gift without alloy.

"What may be the ultimate fate of the bill, time will show. Our hope has been long deferred, it may be soon extinguished; but the soldier of the Revolution possesses that which none can take away—the thought of having labored in erecting a temple, under the ample roof of which our posterity may repose in safety, and the oppressed of other climes find shelter.

"With great respect,

"I am, sir, your obedient servant,

"W. NORTH."

At this session, a debate took place in the Senate on the subject of the tariff, which was the forerunner of the discussions that not long afterward introduced into the Senate the doctrines of "Nullification." The pending bill of 1828 was one making extensive alterations in the existing rates of duties, and, of course, it was filled with multifarious details. The general policy and principle of protection, and the sectional interests affected by it, as well as the propriety of the several changes proposed, entered as usual into the discussion. It was, however, on this occasion, that the assertion was first made, by General Hayne, of South Carolina, that the interests of the Southern States had been sacrificed, "shamefully sacrificed," to the selfish policy of other sections, and especially of New England. Mr. Webster, on the 9th of May, took part in this discussion, principally for the purpose of showing that the original tariff policy, entered upon in 1816, was not a New-England measure; that the present bill was not one originating with her; and that some of its provisions were likely to benefit no interests anywhere excepting the interests of the Treasury. This is the second principal speech made by Mr. Webster in

Congress on the subject of the tariff, and it is contained in the third volume of his works.[1]

Several of the provisions of this bill were extremely injurious to some of Mr. Webster's constituents, and there were great differences of opinion and feeling concerning it among his immediate fellow-citizens in Boston. But he voted for it, because, finding himself under the constraint of an unprecedented mode of legislation, obliged to deal as a whole with a measure containing good and bad provisions relating to different subjects, he believed that the good preponderated over the evil, having in view the general welfare of the country. His colleague in the Senate, Mr. Silsbee, voted the other way, as did the Representative of the Boston district, Mr. Gorham.[2]

Mr. Webster returned from the first session of the Twentieth Congress in May, 1828. He was greatly depressed. If it is true, as perhaps it is, that in seasons of such affliction as that from which he now suffered, occupation is one of the best medicines to the mind, the remedy is one that requires accompaniments which he could not have in Washington. He was necessarily separated there from his children, and from the friends who could best minister the solace that he needed. On reaching Boston, he gathered his children once more under his own roof; leaving his daughter, however, for the greater part of the time, with Mrs. Lee, in Brookline. He was obliged at once to enter on some professional engagements, and also to accept from his fellow-citizens the compliment of a public dinner, which took place in Faneuil Hall on the 5th of June.

In this expression of the confidence and respect of his friends and neighbors, all the principal persons in the city participated, and among them were those who disapproved of his vote on the tariff bill of the last session. They respected him for the uprightness of his character, and the exercise of his independent judgment; and it was long, very long, before Boston ever had many prominent citizens who were not ready to give a candid interpretation to any act of his. On this occasion, notwithstanding his general depression, he spoke, in reply to the com-

[1] The first was the speech of April 1 and 2, 1824.—(*Works*, iii., 94.) *Ante*, chap. 9.

[2] The principal reason that led Mr. Webster to vote for the bill of 1828 was, that it gave woollens the protection which Congress had pledged itself to give by the law of 1824.

plimentary toast, with his usual spirit, dignity, and force, accounting for his vote on the tariff, alluding to the measure for the relief of the Revolutionary officers, and to the subject of internal improvements.[1]

The following letter from Mr. Clay was received after the dinner:

[FROM MR. CLAY.]

"WASHINGTON, 13*th June*, 1828.

"MY DEAR SIR: Notwithstanding your kind permission given me in your letter of the 8th instant, to abstain from addressing you, I cannot deny myself the gratification of expressing the satisfaction which we all felt here with the proceedings and speeches of the Boston dinner. I was particularly delighted with two or three circumstances: 1. The harmony which prevailed in respect to the tariff, or, rather, the acquiescence in the measure. 2. Your felicitous defence of your vote. 3. The notice, truly national and patriotic, which you took of the great interest of internal improvements. And 4. The New-England feeling to which you so urgently appealed, and which the whole proceedings were well calculated to excite. Good will come of your work.

"I have a letter from General Porter, who will be here in two or three days. He postpones his decision until he comes here; but I think it will be to accept.

"My health continues as it was when you left here. I commence my journey next week, from which I anticipate the best effects. I have been rendered very happy by the company of my only surviving daughter, who joined us a few days ago, and who is one of the best of girls. She brought with her her two children, whom I had never seen.

"Our news from Kentucky continues good.

"You will have seen a report on the secret service fund. It was a necessary explanation for the West. I must be held exclusively responsible for its publication, which the President approved at my instance. I hope it will meet your approbation.

"My best regards to Everett, Gorham, and Mr. J. Mason.

"Cordially your friend,

"H. CLAY.

"D. Webster, Esq."

Into the excitements of the presidential election, then approaching, Mr. Webster did not enter. That contest, of a bitterness then unexampled, in which General Jackson obtained a majority of ninety-five electoral votes over Mr. Adams, and

[1] See the speech in Works, i., 163, *et seq.*

sixty-seven electoral votes above the number necessary to a choice, was not one in which Mr. Webster could take an active part. His chief regret at the state of things arose from the fact that persons holding opposite opinions on the constitutional powers of the Government, and on the leading measures of Mr. Adams's Administration, had united to overthrow it. An opposition founded, not on the measures of Government, but on other and chiefly personal causes, he regarded as dangerous and alarming. He foresaw in it that rage for office, and that dedication of the offices of the country as a fund for the reward of personal partisanship, which speedily followed, and which have entered more or less into every succeeding renewal of the contest for the executive power, bringing us nearer and nearer to that catastrophe in which he feared that this experiment of confederated government would sooner or later end. "It is my opinion, Mr. President," he said, at the dinner in Faneuil Hall, "that the present Government of the United States cannot be maintained but by administering it on principles as wide and broad as the country over which it extends. I mean, of course, no extension of the powers which it confers; but I speak of the spirit with which those powers should be exercised. If there be any doubts whether so many republics, covering so vast a territory, can be long held together under this Constitution, there is no doubt, in my judgment, of the impossibility of so holding them together by any narrow, local, or selfish system of legislation. To render the Constitution perpetual (which God grant it may be), it is necessary that its benefits should be practically felt by all parts of the country. The East and the West, the North and the South, must all see their welfare protected and advanced by it. While the Eastern frontier is defended by fortifications, its harbors improved, and commerce protected by a naval force, it is right and just that the region beyond the Alleghanies should receive fair consideration and equal attention, in any object of public improvement, interesting to itself, and within the proper power of the Government. These, sir, are in brief the general views by which I have been governed on questions of this kind; and I trust they are such as this meeting does not disapprove."

Nevertheless, Mr. Webster was an object of virulent attack

from many members of the old Republican party, who had entered into the new organization for the support of General Jackson's claim to the presidency. In this warfare, the persons who assailed him did not evince their "Republican" consistency. As a mere Federalist of a former day, they would have passed him by unmolested, or have courted his favor. Upon all grounds of party consistency, aside from his personal eminence, he was entitled to their respect and confidence. His election to the House of Representatives in 1822 had not been opposed by the Republicans; in 1824, he was unanimously selected as the Republican candidate; and, in 1826, that party again united in supporting him as their Representative in Congress. When elected to the Senate in June, 1827, he was chosen by a Legislature in which a great majority of the members were of the same Republican party. His whole course, therefore, in the support which he had given to the measures of Mr. Adams's Administration, had received the sanction of a party which had been the ancient opponents of the Federalists; for Mr. Webster, in truth, was regarded as a statesman whose political principles, in respect to the constitutional powers of the Government and the proper mode of administering them, were such as in that day were considered to be "Republican." His transcendent abilities and patriotism, added to this political sympathy with his opinions on public questions, disarmed, with many of the old "Republicans," the prejudice that might otherwise have arisen from his former connection with the now extinct Federal party.

Still, there were individuals among his constituents who could not overlook the fact that he had supported Mr. Adams's Administration, and now desired his reëlection. It is needless to revive or recall these personal attacks. But, as there was one of them which Mr. Webster thought fit to bring before a court of law, it is proper that an exact account should here be given of the causes which led him to this departure from a rule which he followed upon all other similar occasions throughout his life.

In the autumn of 1828, Mr. Webster prosecuted a gentleman of high social standing in Boston by indictment for a libel. The facts were these: During the canvass for the presidential election of that year, there appeared in the party newspapers of the day what purported to be a letter written by Mr. Jefferson to the Hon. William B. Giles, in 1825, in which Mr. Jefferson referred to disclosures made to him by Mr. John Quincy Adams in 1807 or 1808, concerning the action of the leaders of the Federal party in New England at the time of the Embargo. Mr. Adams was stated in that letter to have accused those leaders of the design, in their opposition to the Embargo, of effecting a dissolution of the Union, with a view of uniting the New-England States to the British provinces.

Mr. Adams immediately caused an article to be published in the *National Intelligencer* at Washington, denying that he had made such disclosures in any interview with Mr. Jefferson, but admitting that, in a correspondence with Mr. Giles in 1807–'8, he had said that he thought the opposition to the Embargo would become so open and violent as to require forcible suppression; in which case he had "unequivocal evidence" that the Federalist leaders would attempt to form a separate confederacy of New England, and call in Great Britain to their aid; for he knew it had long been their design to bring about such a dissolution of the Union.

Mr. Jefferson's letter and Mr. Adams's admissions elicited a great deal of acrimonious discussion and comment both from the political opponents of Mr. Adams and from those who had hitherto been his political friends. In a newspaper published in Boston, under the name of *The Jackson Republican*, there appeared an article, on the 29th of October, 1828, referring to Mr. Webster by name as one of the Federalist leaders who had been charged by Mr. Adams in 1807–'8 with this treasonable design. Mr. Webster was naturally indignant at such a use of his name, which pointed at *him* a charge that Mr. Adams never could have thought of levelling at him; for, in the time of the Embargo and of the New-England resistance to it, Mr. Webster was a young lawyer in New Hampshire, and had no personal connection with the gentlemen who were named by the article as the obnoxious plotters against the Union, all of whom were citizens of Massachusetts. Mr. Webster's own course, moreover, respecting the Embargo, was well known, or could be easily ascertained; and, if there was any thing treasonable in the proceedings or design of the subsequent Hartford Convention, it was quite notorious in Boston, in 1828, that he had never had any thing to do with it, and had disapproved of it. He had other reasons for feeling deeply hurt by the publication. He knew well, as every one else knew, that the New-England resistance to the Embargo was a constitutional resistance; that the law was subjected to a constitutional test of its validity, in a court of the United States, and was upheld, and that the people who suffered by it submitted. The eminent men who were charged with fomenting treasonable projects had since become his personal friends, and his name was now coupled with theirs in an infamous charge, founded on statements said to have been formerly made by a man filling the exalted position of President of the United States, and whose reëlection Mr. Webster now favored. In all the tactics of party warfare, there has scarcely been a greater accumulation of personal injustice; and this injustice was surrounded by circumstances which, in Mr. Webster's opinion, and that of friends who were no way involved in the charge, made it his duty to call for the author of the article, and to prosecute him for libel.

The name of the author was given up by the publishers of the paper, and the grand jury found a bill of indictment against him, which was tried in the Supreme Judicial Court of Massachusetts, Chief-Justice Parker presiding, on the 16th and 17th of December, 1828. Before the trial came on, the defence intimated that the course which they should take would lead to important developments concerning the political period of the Embargo; but they abandoned this design, and contented themselves with an effort to show that the article was no libel upon Mr. Webster, as no malice was intended toward him, the whole being a fair comment on the statements and conduct of Mr. Adams. The jury did not agree. Ten were for convicting and two were for acquitting. The case was never pursued further.[1]

Probably it happens to all conspicuous public men to be much importuned by colleges and literary societies to appear as their

[1] A clearer case of libel could not well exist. The name of Mr. Webster had not been introduced, nor had he been alluded to, in Mr. Adams's correspondence with Mr. Giles, or in the letter attributed to Mr. Jefferson. The writer of the newspaper article, therefore, *originated* a charge of treason against Mr. Webster, and did not comment on one made by somebody else. But the whole affair was mixed up with the party feelings of the day, and it is not surprising that there should have been two recusant jurymen on the panel.

"orator" at their anniversaries. Many such applications, addressed to Mr. Webster at this time, are now before me, some of them couched in the language of young men, who, ingenuously occupied with the concerns of associations filling a large space in their thoughts, apparently supposed that an "honorary membership" should be a sufficient inducement to draw from a great statesman a very large donation of his time and thoughts; and sometimes it was added that the invitation was sanctioned by the college "faculty."

The truth is, the curiosity to see and hear Mr. Webster, intense among all classes of our countrymen at all times in his life after his distinction was attained—a curiosity that arose not only from his great intellectual reputation and his power as a speaker, but from his singularly impressive aspect and the majesty of his person—was not likely to be less strong among those who were engaged in intellectual pursuits, than it was among the general multitude. But, of course, it was necessary to return a civil refusal to nearly all such requests. There did occur, however, occasions when the public importance of his influence, in promoting the objects of particular associations designed to advance popular intellectual culture, made it necessary for him to discharge duties that were somewhat foreign from his habitual studies and pursuits. Such was the occasion when he consented to deliver the introductory lecture before "The Boston Mechanics' Association," on the 12th of November, 1828. The subject of this discourse was the relations of science with the practical arts.[1]

For similar reasons, he presided in the month of November at a preliminary meeting of the gentlemen who founded the "Boston Society for the Diffusion of Useful Knowledge," of which in the following year he became president.

[FROM MR. CLAY.]

"WASHINGTON, *24th October*, 1828.

"MY DEAR SIR: Although some of the Congressional results in Ohio are to be regretted, my belief is unshaken that we shall get the State by a large majority. The returns in Whittlesey's, Bartlett's, Vinton's, and McClure's districts are not yet fully received. In them, our majorities will

[1] *Vide* Works, i., 176, *et seq.*

be very great. Trimble will be reëlected by many thousands, and he, you know, was the Administration candidate for Governor.

"My intelligence from Kentucky continues good, very good. I have heard of the safe reception there of what you sent. All has been done, and will continue to be done, that honorable men can or ought to do.

"I yet think that Mr. Adams will be reëlected; but it is mortifying and sickening to the hearts of the real lovers of free government that the contest should be so close; and that if Heaven grants us success it will be perhaps by less than a majority of six votes.

"I thank you for the hint about Mr. B., who has not yet called.

"Always cordially your friend,

"H. CLAY.

"D. Webster, Esq."

The presidential election terminated, as Mr. Webster had foreseen it would, in the choice of General Jackson. He had not participated in the sanguine belief entertained by Mr. Clay, that Mr. Adams was to be reëlected. Still, he had done what he could by diffusing correct information respecting the real merits of Mr. Adams's course; and it was in a great degree a consequence of his exertions in this way that Mr. Adams received all the electoral votes of New England. But they were given from what Mr. Ezekiel Webster afterward well described as "a cold sense of duty, and not from any liking of the man." "The measures of his Administration," he added, "were just and wise, and every honest man should have supported them, but many honest men did not, for the reason I have mentioned."

[FROM MR. CLAY.]

"WASHINGTON, 30*th November*, 1828.

"MY DEAR SIR: As I understand that you are not to be here for a month, I wish to say some things which I had intended for a personal interview.

"We are beaten. It is useless to dwell on the causes. It is useless to repine at the result. What is our actual position? We are of the majority in regard to measures; we are of the minority in respect to the person designated as Chief Magistrate. Our effort should be to retain the majority we have. We may lose it by imprudence. I think, in regard to the new Administration, we should alike avoid professions of support or declarations of opposition, in advance. We can only yield the former, if our principles are adopted and pursued, and, if they should be, our honor and our probity afford a sufficient pledge that we shall not abandon them. To say beforehand that we will support the President-elect, if he adheres to our systems, is to say that we will be honest; and that I hope is a superfluous proclamation. On the other hand, if we were now to issue a manifesto of hostility, we should keep united, by a sense of common danger, the discordant confederates who have taken the field against us. They cannot remain in corps but from external pressure. The dissensions among them this winter, the formation of the new Cabinet, and the inaugural speech will enable us to discover the whole ground of future operations. Above all, I think *we* ought not to prematurely agitate the question of the succession. The nation wants repose. The agitations of the last six years entitle it to rest. If it is again to be immediately disturbed, let others, not us, assume the responsibility.

"We shall here all calmly proceed in our various spheres to discharge our duties until the 4th of March. The message is good. It makes no allusion to the late event. Its strongest features are the support of the tariff, and disapprobation of sentiments of disunion.

"I shall retire to Ashland after the 4th of March, and there consider and decide my future course. I do not mean to look at it until there.

"You have all my wishes for success in the prosecution against ——. I regretted the publication here which led to the libel; but most certainly I never supposed you to be alluded to in that publication. In the midst of all the heats of former times, I believed you, as I have since found you, faithful to the Union, to the Constitution, and to liberty.

"Under every vicissitude, believe me

"Sincerely your friend,

"H. CLAY.

"D. Webster."

CHAPTER XV.

1828–1829.

INAUGURATION OF PRESIDENT JACKSON—DEATH OF MR. EZEKIEL WEBSTER—SECOND MARRIAGE.

THE second session of the Twentieth Congress found Mr. Webster, in December, 1828, again in the Senate and in the Supreme Court. Great uncertainty prevailed at Washington concerning the course likely to be taken by the President-elect. General Jackson remained in Tennessee, answering very few of the multitude of letters that were sent to him, urging him to make a general removal of the incumbents of the public offices. It was not known who were to form his Cabinet. Of this state of "syncope," arising from ignorance of the views of the new President, Mr. Webster writes, in January, 1828:

"My opinion is, that, when he comes, he will bring a breeze with him. Which way it will blow, I cannot tell.

"He will either go with the party, as they say in New York, or go 'the whole hog,' as it is phrased elsewhere, making all the places he can for his friends and supporters, and shaking a rod of terror at his opposers.

"Or else he will continue to keep his own counsels, make friends and advisers of whom he pleases, and be President upon his own strength.

"The first would show boldness where there is no danger, and decision where the opposite virtue of moderation would be more useful. The latter would show real nerve, and, if he have talents to maintain himself in that course, true greatness.

"My fear is stronger than my hope.

"Mr. Adams is in good health, and complains not at all of the measure meted out to him.

"Mr. Clay's health is much improved, and his spirits excellent. He goes to Kentucky in March, and, I conjecture, will be pressed into the next House of Representatives. His chance of being at the head of affairs is now better, in my judgment, than ever before.

"Keep New England firm and steady, and she may make him President if she chooses.

"Sundry important nominations are postponed, probably to know General Jackson's pleasure.

"The above contains all that is known here at this time."

General Jackson arrived in due time, and the "breeze" which he brought and the direction in which it blew are well known. Mr. Webster was disposed to look on calmly; and he was certainly much amused with whatever was going on, as well as greatly anxious about what was to ensue.

[TO MRS. EZEKIEL WEBSTER.]

"SENATE-CHAMBER, *February* 19, 1829.

"MY DEAR SISTER: I must begin with apology; or, let me rather say, with confession; for, though I am willing to confess great and censurable omissions, I have little to urge by way of apology, and nothing which amounts to justification. Let me pray you, therefore, in the exercise of your clemency, to adopt the rule which Hamlet prescribes for passing judgment on the players. Do not treat me according to my deserts, for, if so, 'who would escape whipping;' but, according to your bounty and dignity, the less I deserve forgiveness, the more will forgiveness exalt your forbearance and mercy.

"The children, under your good superintendence, have written me continually, day by day, very good letters. Mr. Paige, also, has been kind, as he always is.

"Your own letters have completed my circle of domestic correspondence, and I must say that it has been very punctual, and highly gratifying. And now what can I tell you worth hearing?

"General Jackson has been here about ten days. Of course, the city is full of speculation and speculators. 'A great multitude,' too many to be fed without a miracle, are already in the city, hungry for office. Especially, I learn, that the typographical corps is assembled in great force. From New Hampshire, our friend Hill; from Boston, Mr. Greene; from Connecticut, Mr. Norton; from New York, Mr. Noah; fron Kentucky, Mr. Kendall; and, from everywhere else, somebody else. So many friends ready to advise, and whose advice is so disinterested, make somewhat of a numerous council about the President-elect; and, if report be true, it is a council which only 'makes that darker which was dark enough before.' For these reasons, or these with others, nothing is settled yet about the new Cabinet. I suppose Mr. Van Buren will be Secretary of State; but, beyond that, I do not think any thing is yet determined.

"For ten or twelve days our Senate has been acting, with closed doors, on certain nominations to office by Mr. Adams. What we have done is not yet known, though one day it will be, probably.

"The general spirit prevailing here, with the friends of the new President, is that of a pretty decided party character. It is not quite so fierce as our New-England Jackson men are actuated by; still, I think it likely to grow more and more bitter, unless, which is highly probable, the party itself should divide.

"We have all read the dispute between Mr. Adams and the Boston gentlemen. Thus far, I believe, the universal feeling is, that Mr. Adams has the worst side of it. I hear, however, that he is about to reply in another pamphlet!

The fashionable world is, and has been, full and gay. Crowds have come, and are coming, to see the inauguration, etc. I have been to three parties—to wit, Mrs. Adams's last, Mrs. Clay's last, and Mrs. Porter's last. Mrs. Porter, wife of the Secretary of War, is a fine woman, whom we visited at Niagara, when there four years ago. With these manifestations of regard for the setting sun and stars, I have satisfied my desire of seeing the social circles. If there should be a ball on the 22d, I shall attend as usual, to commemorate the great and good man born on that day.

"Judge Story is well, and in his usual spirits. The court is deeply engaged, and, as soon as I get rid of these secret sessions of the Senate, I have enough to do in it.

"We are looking to New Hampshire; I shall not engage lodgings for you and your husband next winter, till I see the returns.[1]

[*Conclusion cut off.*]

[TO MRS. EZEKIEL WEBSTER.]

"WASHINGTON, *March* 4, 1829.
"First year of the Administration of Andrew Jackson, and the first day.

"MY DEAR SISTER: I thank you for yours, received to-day; and thank you both for the letter itself and for your pardon which it contains, and of which I stood in so much need. Your benignity is memorable and praiseworthy. To be serious, however, my dear sister, let me say, once for all, that I have a very affectionate regard for you, that I am very glad you are my sister, and the wife of the best of all brothers; and if, like him, I am not the most punctual of all correspondents, I am like him in sincerity and constancy of esteem. If you find in your connection with my own

[1] Mr. E. Webster had reluctantly consented to be a candidate in New Hampshire for a seat in Congress; but he was not elected.

little broken circle but one-half as much pleasure as you bestow, you will have no reason to regret it. Your presence with my children through the winter has relieved me from a pressing weight of anxiety.

"To-day we have had the inauguration. A monstrous crowd of people is in the city. I never saw any thing like it before. Persons have come five hundred miles to see General Jackson; and they really seem to think that the country is rescued from some dreadful danger.

"The inauguration speech you will see. I cannot make much of it, except that it is anti-tariff, at least in some degree. What it says about reform in office may be either a prelude to a general change in office, or a mere sop to soothe the hunger, without satisfying it, of the thousand expectants for office who throng the city, and clamor all over the country. I expect some changes, but not a great many at present. The show lasted only about half an hour. The Senate assembled at eleven; the judges and foreign ministers came in; the President-elect was introduced, and all seated by half-past eleven. The Senate was full of ladies; a pause ensued till twelve. Then the President, followed by the Senate, etc., went through the great rotunda, and all became confusion. On the portico, in the open air, the day very warm and pleasant, he read his inaugural, and took the oath. A great shout followed from the multitude, and, in fifteen minutes, 'silence settled deep and still.' Everybody was dispersed. As I walked home, I called in at a bookstore, and saw a volume which I now send you; it may serve to regulate matters of etiquette at Boscawen.

"I hope to write Edward to-night. If not, I shall not fail to do so to-morrow.

Yours very sincerely and truly,

"D. WEBSTER."

[TO MR. EZEKIEL WEBSTER.]

"WASHINGTON, Sunday Evening, *March* 15, 1829.

"DEAR EZEKIEL: The Senate will probably adjourn to-morrow, and I hope the court will rise, or, at least, will dismiss me by Wednesday or Thursday. I shall be immediately off. My books are in trunks. I shall hear from New Hampshire to-morrow, and dispose of them according to circumstances. If no change takes place in my own condition, of which I have not the slightest expectation, and if you are not elected, I shall not return. This, *inter nos*, but my mind is settled. Under present circumstances, public and domestic, it is disagreeable being here, and to me there is no novelty to make compensation. It will be better for me and my children that I should be with them. If I do not come in a public, I shall not in a professional character. I can leave the court now as well as ever, and can earn my bread as well at home as here.

"Your company, and that of your wife, would make a great difference. I have not much expectation that you will be returned. Our fortune is, as connected with recent and current events, that, if there be opposite chances, the unfavorable one turns up. You had a snow of five feet, which of itself might turn the election against the well-disposed and indifferent, and in favor of the mischievous and the active. I shall not be disappointed if I hear bad news.

"I make my point to be home the first day of April, when I trust I shall meet you. We will then settle what is best to do with the children. I shall want Julia and Edward to stay a little while with me. Edward, I think, should then go to Boscawen. I hardly know what I shall think best to do with Julia.

"Yours, as ever,

"D. Webster.

"P. S.—We have had one important cause here. It is from New York, respecting what is called the Sailors' Snug Harbor. I have made a greater exertion in it than in any other since *Dartmouth College* vs. *Woodward*, or than it is probable I shall ever make in another."

But this was the last of the hopes that turned on the future society of his brother and the excellent lady who had had the care of his children through the preceding winter. Mr. Webster arrived at his own house, in Boston, in the second week in April, 1829. Mrs. Ezekiel Webster was there, with her eldest daughter. At three o'clock in the morning of the eleventh a messenger brought the sad intelligence that Mr. Ezekiel Webster had died suddenly on the previous day. His death, which was instantaneous, occurred in the court-house at Concord, New Hampshire, while he was addressing a jury.[1] I borrow the words of his son-in-law, Professor Sanborn, of Dartmouth College:

"Mr. Webster was speaking, standing erect, on a plain floor, the house full, and the court and jurors and auditors intently listening to his words, with all their eyes fastened upon him. Speaking with full force, and perfect utterance, he arrived at the end of one branch of his argument. He closed that branch, uttered the last sentence, and the last word of that sentence, with perfect tone and emphasis, and then, in an instant, erect, and with arms depending by his side, he fell backward, without bending a joint, and, so far as appeared, was dead before his head reached the floor."[2]

He was at the age of only forty-nine at the time of his death. He was a man of high talent, much professional learning, and

[1] He died of a disease of the heart, of which Mr. Daniel Webster had long known the existence, although I am not aware that they ever spoke of it to each other.

[2] Correspondence, i., 42.

great solidity of character. From their earliest youth, the younger and more brilliant of these two brothers was more dependent on the sound judgment of the elder, while he lived, than he was on that of any other man with whom he was ever connected. "He has been my reliance through life," is the weighty testimony borne by the survivor to him who had been thus snatched away. The qualities of Ezekiel Webster were of a kind eminently adapted to produce this feeling in one who, however great and wise, was embarked on the stormy sea of public life, and in whom the powers of genius were united with its dangers. The elder brother was a man whose days were passed in the less exciting scenes of a country life; and if, from a sense of duty, he was sometimes drawn into politics, it was without personal ambition. While he pursued his profession as a lawyer with diligence and success, he enjoyed the tranquillizing influences of agricultural tastes and knowledge, a department in which his public spirit, his intelligence, and his foresight, were of great service to his native State.[1] At the same time, his intellectual culture was always maintained at the high point at which he left the college, where he received the education that he obtained with so much painful exertion. Indeed, it is said, by those who should know, that his classical attainments and general reading were far more extensive than is common with men engaged earnestly and early in active life. Before his brother left New Hampshire, he was not willing to put himself forward in the public exhibition of his professional talents; but, after such a comparison was no longer likely to be suggested, he became eminent as an advocate. He was a man

[1] It is worthy of commemoration, that when Mr. Daniel Webster delivered his Phi Beta Kappa Oration at Dartmouth, in 1809, New Hampshire did not possess a single agricultural society. On that occasion, after speaking of the like destitution in the matter of historical societies, he said: "Is it not still more incredible that, in a community where agriculture is the great leading interest of all classes, no two minds should combine their powers to facilitate its improvement? That there should be no union of effort, no concert, no comparison of experiments? That all should be left to individual enterprise, and the few improvements which are made should owe their existence to chance or accident? The tillers of the soil have certainly a right to expect that men of science will lend them the aids of their knowledge. An agricultural society, formed on principles broad enough to embrace such objects of natural history as are connected with husbandry, is an establishment which long, long ere this, should have been effected."

This strong recommendation did not remain unheeded. Ezekiel Webster became the most active founder and afterward the president of the Merrimac Agricultural Society.

of strong religious faith and sincere piety. His loss was long and deeply felt by the community in which he had always lived.[1]

In person he was tall, standing nearly six feet; of a full muscular development, and commanding presence. If the testimony was partial, it was sincere: "He appeared to me," Mr. Webster said, in 1846, "the finest human form that I ever laid eyes on. I saw him in his coffin; a tinged cheek, a complexion clear as the heavenly light;"[2] and another, less near to him, but who knew him well, speaks of a "magnificent form, crowned with a princely head, that in his last years was thickly covered with snowy hair."[3]

Such was the man who, in an instant, was snatched away from a community that had known and trusted and honored him from his earliest manhood. By Mr. Webster his loss was felt to be irreparable; nor was it ever repaired. Valued friends, dear and trusted friends, he still had, and others came afterward to be acquired. But that tie—that fraternal tie—stretching backward to the old days of their self-sacrificing parents, to their youthful struggles for education, to their early successes, and forward into the unbounded mutual confidence of their maturer years, could not be replaced. Mr. Webster never sought the advice of any man as he sought that of his brother. At the time of his brother's death he was peculiarly dependent on him, as we have seen. Was it not true, as I have already said, that he was severely tried?

[TO MR. MASON.]

"BOSTON, *April* 19, 1829.

"MY DEAR SIR: I thank you for your kind letter. You do not and cannot overrate the strength of the shock which my brother's death has caused me. I have felt but one such in life; and this follows so soon that it requires more fortitude than I possess to bear it with firmness, and, perhaps, as I ought. I am aware that the case admits no remedy, nor any present relief; and endeavor to console myself with reflecting that I have

[1] I have already referred to the beautiful memoir of Mr. Ezekiel Webster, by Professor Sanborn, embraced in the first volume of Mr. Daniel Webster's Correspondence.

[2] Letter to Mr. Blatchford, Correspondence, ii., 228.

[3] Quoted by Professor Sanborn, in his Memoir.

had much happiness with lost connections, and that they must expect to lose beloved objects in this world who have beloved objects to lose. My life, I know, has been fortunate and happy beyond the common lot, and it would be now ungrateful, as well as unavailing, to repine at calamities of which, as they are human, I must expect to partake. But, I confess, the world, at present, has for me an aspect any thing but cheerful. With a multitude of acquaintance, I have few friends; my nearest intimacies are broken, and a sad void is made in the objects of affection. Of what remains dear and valuable, I need not say that a most precious part is the affectionate friendship of yourself and family. I want to see you very much, indeed, but know not whether I shall be able soon to visit Portsmouth. You will be glad to know that my own health is good. I have never, for ten years, got through a winter without being more reduced in health and strength. My children, also, are well. Edward is at Boscawen, where he will probably stay through the summer, or as long as the family may be kept together there. Daniel hopes to go to college in August. Julia proposes to pass the summer, or a part of it, with Mrs. Lee, and must afterward be disposed of as best she may.

"This occurrence is calculated to have effect on the future course of my own life, and to add to the inducements, already felt, to retire from a situation in which I am making daily sacrifices, and doing little good to myself or others. Pray give my love to your family.

"Yours, affectionately and entirely,

"DAN'L WEBSTER."

A considerable part of the ensuing summer was passed by Mr. Webster in the new cares and duties which the death of his brother devolved upon him. He was now the sole survivor of a large family. The farm at Franklin, thenceforward to have a melancholy attraction for him, because there were the tombs of his parents and of his brothers and sisters, became his own property, by an arrangement with the guardian of his brother's children. His inclination at this time to retire from public life was almost insurmountable. But the depressing feeling, that he was doing little good to compensate for the sacrifices that he was making, was not destined to last long. There was awaiting him one of those opportunities and duties which occur but once in the life of any statesman; when he was to perform that public service which constitutes, perhaps, the greatest of his senatorial achievements, and which has forever connected his name with the security and perpetuation of the Constitution of the United States

There was also awaiting him a very important and happy

change in his domestic condition. In the autumn of 1829 he passed a considerable time in the city of New York, for professional purposes, and, of course, he was a much-honored guest in its best circles. Although such a connection was not long anticipated,[1] he was married in December, to Miss Caroline Le Roy, the second daughter of Jacob Le Roy, Esq., a wealthy merchant, descended from one of the early settlers of New York. This event was thus announced to his eldest son, who was then a Freshman in Harvard College:

[TO MR. FLETCHER WEBSTER.]

"NEW YORK, *December* 14, 1829.

"MY DEAR SON: You have been informed that an important change in my domestic condition was expected to take place. It happened on Saturday. The lady who is now to bear the relation of mother to you, and Julia, and Edward, I am sure will be found worthy of all your affection and regard; and I am equally certain that she will experience from all of you the utmost kindness and attachment. She insists on taking Julia with us to Washington, thinking it will be better for her, and that she will also be good company.

"We shall leave New York in about a week. I read your first letter, which gave me pleasure, and hope to have another from you before I leave New York. You will not fail to write me once a week, according to arrangement. The enclosed note you will of course answer. If you dispatch your answer at once, without waiting for the keepsake, it will arrive here before our departure. Let it come enclosed to me. The 'keepsake' is an elegant gold watch. You must send for it to Mr. Paige, by a careful hand. Mr. Paige will not be home under ten days from this time.

"I hope, my dear son, that I shall continue to hear good accounts of you.

"I am always, with much affection, your father,

"D. WEBSTER."

[1] [To Mrs. E. WEBSTER.] "I parted with you, I think, the first day of October, not at all foreseeing what was to happen to myself in so short a time. I am now here settled down for the session, with Mrs. Webster and Julia. When I left home I did not expect to bring Julia farther than New York. She was to have returned with Mr. Paige; but Mrs. Webster chose to have it otherwise, and I believe it is much better as it is. Julia seems exceedingly happy. Her health is better than I ever saw it, and she is much attached to her new mother. With this last personage I am sure you will be pleased. You will find her amiable, affectionate, prudent, and agreeable; as these are good, sober words, you must take them as used for what they ought to mean, and not as the rhapsody of a new husband. It will not be many months, however, I hope, before I shall bring her and yourself face to face, and then you can judge for yourself."—(*Correspondence*, i., 484.)

In the month of June of this year occurred the visit of Mr. Wirt to Boston, on a professional engagement, in which he was employed as the leading counsel against Mr. Webster, in a cause of some importance in the Supreme Court of Massachusetts. Mr. Wirt's gratification at his reception by Mr. Webster is expressed in the warmest terms in his letters, given in his Life by Mr. Kennedy.[1]

[1] Kennedy's Life of Wirt, ii., 268–272.

CHAPTER XVI.

1829–1830.

POWER OF REMOVAL FROM OFFICE—NULLIFICATION—THE TWO SPEECHES ON FOOT'S RESOLUTION—REPLY TO HAYNE.

AT the first session of the Twenty-first Congress, one of the subjects that earliest demanded Mr. Webster's anxious consideration was the President's supposed power to remove the incumbents in public office without consulting the Senate. The inauguration of General Jackson had been followed by a sweeping change in the executive offices, not only in all the departments at Washington, but throughout the country. The state of things thus produced at the capitol was entirely without precedent; for, while it had always been understood, since the origin of the Government, that, with every change of the person of the President, the new Executive was at liberty to select new heads of the principal departments, because those officers form what is by usage called the "Cabinet," it had never been customary to regard the subordinate places as a fund for the reward of personal partisans, or to remove faithful and competent public servants merely because their political opinions did not coincide with those of the successful party. The wise forbearance that had been exercised by most of our former Presidents had left in the several subordinate stations a body of trained and experienced men, who possessed the knowledge of official business essential to the successful working of any government, and who were, in general, men of unexceptionable characters. This degree of permanency of official life in Washington formerly had an important influence on the prosperity and growth of the city; for men who felt that they were secure in their places so long as they properly discharged their duties to the Government, could afford to seek permanent homes for their families where their salaries were earned. All this was suddenly changed; and it was changed with a disregard of the claims of meritorious public servants, and with the employment of excuses to effect their removal from office, on which all candid men, of whatever political connection, must now look back with regret and disapprobation, as a course alike unworthy of those who then assumed the administration of the Government, and injurious to the future welfare of the country. In multitudes of cases it was not pretended that there was any other cause for the removals than the demands of party. It was a very common occurrence for a secretary, at the head of one of the departments, to inform a subordinate that no complaint could be made of the manner in which he had discharged his duties, but that the place was wanted for a political or personal friend; and, where this kind of frankness was not used, the private and trivial and casual conversation of some inferior clerk, involving an alleged disrespect toward the new President, and often reported anonymously, was duly laid before the Cabinet, and gravely acted upon.[1] In the course of the first two years of General Jackson's first presidency he made two thousand removals from office.

The influence of this new method of administration on the material prosperity of the city of Washington was the least of the evils that attended it. The opponents of President Jackson's government saw in it a long train of public mischiefs; and scarcely any wise man will now question that they were right. But whether this credit will be generally conceded to them or

[1] I state these miserable facts, withholding names and particulars, on the authority of a letter, written to Mr. Webster by a private citizen of Washington, in no way connected with the Government. It bears date in May, 1829; so soon had the "reform" done its work. The writer describes a total suspension in the business of erecting private houses, and observes: "Confidence in the stability of office is so much shaken, that the clerks and other officers of the Government will hereafter consider themselves as only visitors among us, and not make any investment in real estate. We already realize the influence of this feeling. . . . . I could not have believed that your predictions were so correct, and that your foresight was so extensive as I now find it to have been." But it is scarcely necessary for me to quote private testimony to that which has long been historical and notorious.

not, they considered it their duty to subject to close public scrutiny the question whether the President possesses, under the Constitution, power to remove a subordinate civil officer without assigning a cause to the Senate, and without taking its assent.

It must be regarded as a strong proof of Mr. Webster's fairness of mind, and of his unwillingness to assert an extreme principle for party objects, that, in the midst of such a state of things as had been produced by the course of General Jackson's Administration, he approached this question with very great deliberation, and, finally, formed opinions concerning it contrary to his original views. If the question, in 1830, had been entirely new, he would have held that the power of removal, as a distinct power, and as residing in the President alone, does not exist. This was his own opinion, as it was also that of Chancellor Kent, apart from the construction that had been put upon the Constitution by some precedents, by a declaratory resolution of Congress, in 1789, and by an acquiescence of half a century. It is true that Mr. Webster might have argued down the precedents, which were not numerous, and not of great force; while the cases before him were enormous in number, and flagrantly unjust; some of them comprehending men of entire fitness and capacity, who, to official merit, added the strongest of claims upon the country for Revolutionary services. He might have contended that the congressional construction of the Constitution, by the First Congress, besides being wrong in the abstract, had been given when no such sweeping and irresponsible power, as was now exercised, had ever been claimed for the President; and he might have urged that the public acquiescence had never related to any but extreme cases of public exigency, arising from incapacity or misconduct. But it was not his habit to be ingenious in considering how the Constitution ought to be construed. He felt bound to remember that the Constitution expressly provides for the action of the Senate only when an appointment is to be made; and although it may fairly be argued that this power of appointment determines the pleasure of the appointment when all else is silent, and, consequently, that the President alone cannot terminate an appointment, and call upon the Senate to confirm a new nominee without making the cause of the removal of the old incumbent a part of the question of such new appointment; yet, that this course of reasoning, although strictly logical, was too abstract to countervail what had occurred since the Constitution went into operation. He therefore, in what he said in the Senate in 1830, and ever afterward, refrained from denying the President's power to remove from office without the consent of the Senate; and maintained that the abuses of this power were mischiefs to be corrected by public sentiment; or, in a case of extreme corruption, by the power of impeachment. This was the view of Mr. Madison, who held that the President's power exists in cases of clear and absolute necessity, but that its exercise in any other case is an abuse.[1]

[1] The most plausible ground on which to vindicate the political application of the too famous maxim, that "to the victors belong the spoils," is this—Parties are organized in free and elective governments, in order to give effect in administration to certain political opinions, which those who lead in political action sincerely hold to be essential to the public interest, which is a much larger object than the individual interest of any office-holder. The public patronage is a powerful means of influencing men to labor for the success of certain political opinions; and, if the power to use it for this purpose exists in the constitutional arrangements of official power, such use is legitimate, because the patronage, in the hands of those who use it, is an instrument for the promotion of the public good according to the judgment of those who have the official right to shape the measures of Government. Without considering how far this reasoning borrows aid from the maxim that the end justifies the means—a rule that is wholly unprincipled, and generally productive of mischief when it is resorted to—it is clear that it overlooks some very important things which are true, and assumes some things which are not true. In the first place, it makes no account of the direct tendency of such a principle of action to render the political principles of parties matters of subordinate, and the enjoyment of public patronage a matter of primary, concern with the electors. We know, as a matter of fact, that candidates have been elected who would not have succeeded, and that parties have triumphed whose principles would not have received the sanction of the people, if this kind of corruption had been kept out of our elections. We know this, because we know that there have been successful candidates who were without superior merit, and successful parties whose principles and measures were unworthy of popular support, and have proved to be mischievous. In the next place, this reasoning disregards the fact that the offices of a great government will be less well filled when they are made a reward for the party services of the most active and energetic politicians; for the simple reason that this class of men will rarely embrace the most competent of those who may desire public office as a means of livelihood. In the third place, frequent and periodical changes in all the administrative offices of a great government deprive it of the strength that is derived from accumulated official experience and knowledge, and render any proper system of promotion impracticable. Finally, a general degradation of the tone of political discussion and action is sure to take place under a government in which the public patronage is thus used. All these evils our experience has proved; and when they are connected, as they are, both as cause and effect, with the system of nominating candidates for the chief executive office by party conventions, on the prin-

But a far deeper question—one that concerned the particular interests of no party, and that involved, in truth, the continued existence of the Government—soon but not unexpectedly claimed of Mr. Webster services of a very peculiar character. It may be justly said of General Jackson, that if he was not the only man in the country who, in the executive office, could have met the crisis of 1830–'33 as it required to be met, yet that it was fortunate for the country that a person of his inflexible firmness and perfect courage was then in the office of President; and it should for similar reasons be said of Mr. Webster, that he was better fitted than any other man in the Union to encounter in debate the new doctrines that now threatened the overthrow of the Constitution, and that it was, therefore, as fortunate that he was still a member of the Senate as it was that General Jackson was President. If he had not been there, it can scarcely be imagined that the hands of the Executive could have been strengthened by the public refutation of a heresy which threatened a direct obstruction to the laws of the United States; a refutation that was the necessary forerunner to executive action, in a Government largely dependent upon popular opinion and inevitably influenced by it.

It is difficult to account for the origin and growth of what were called the doctrines of nullification, which originated in South Carolina, without touching upon the peculiar mental characteristics of one of her statesmen, who was their reputed author, and who, by his great abilities, the purity of his personal character, and the persuasiveness of his address, exercised a vast influence over many of the public men of his time.

ciple of availability, it is impossible to deny, and not easy to exaggerate, the injury that has been done to our political institutions. That injury is a direct refutation of the claim that the success of the principles of a party is an object that justifies the use of such means of attaining it. Nor is it true, as the justification assumes, that such means are within the legitimate control of those who hold the executive power for the time being. If a party in power were to make a great and unnecessary increase of public offices, by regular enactment of law, for the purpose of securing the predominance of its political principles, no one would be hardy enough to justify this use of the public money. How, then, is the practice any more to be justified which makes use of the *whole* body of existing and necessary offices as a fund for the reward of partisan services on a change of parties? As a general rule, it may be quite right for an administration, in case of a vacancy, to prefer a political supporter to a political opponent. But this is a very different proceeding from the creation of thousands of vacancies, in order to bring the influence of public station and of the public money to bear on future elections.

In May, 1828, a meeting of the South Carolina delegation in Congress was held in Washington, at the rooms of General Hayne, one of the Senators of that State, to concert measures against the tariff and the protective policy which it embodied. From the history of the times, and the disclosures subsequently made, it is apparent that some violent things were said at this meeting, but it broke up without any definite plan. In the course of the following summer, there were many popular meetings in South Carolina, largely attended, at which the tariff of 1824 was treated as an act of despotism and usurpation, which ought to be openly resisted. The tone of these meetings was not unlike that which has since been heard elsewhere, when laws of the United States have been distasteful to local feelings or in conflict with local interests. They occasioned anxiety and regret among the friends of the Union throughout the country, though nothing more. But, in the autumn, the Legislature of South Carolina adopted an "Exposition and Protest,"[1] which

[1] In a memorandum now before me, in Mr. Webster's handwriting, I find the following analysis of this document:

"But the most bold and imposing form in which the doctrine of nullification has been presented, is doubtless to be found in the Exposition and Protest of the Legislature of South Carolina in December, 1828. It seems to have been judged expedient at that time to put forth the nullifying power of the State in bold relief. This exposition is a labored argument for the power of nullification; and, whatever may be thought of its train of reasoning, its conclusions and results are at least clearly stated. Its purpose is not disguised. The general understanding assigns its authorship, not to the committee, but to a distinguished citizen of South Carolina, holding at present a very high place in the Government of the United States.

"The doctrines clearly announced in it are: 1. That it is a most erroneous and dangerous proposition to maintain that the Supreme Court of the United States has constitutional authority to decide on the extent of the powers of a State government; its decisions being final only when applied to the authorities of the departments of the General Government. 2. That 'universal experience' (lest we should seem to do the distinguished author injustice, we cite the very words)—that 'universal experience, in all ages and countries, teaches that power can *only* be met by power, and *not* by reason and justice, and that all restrictions on authority, unsustained by any equal antagonist power, must forever prove *wholly* insufficient in practice. Such,' he adds, 'also has been the decisive proof of our own short experience.' 3. That the right of judging and finally deciding on the extent of their own powers is an essential attribute of sovereignty, of which the States are not and cannot be divested. 4. That power being divided between the General Government and the State governments, it is impossible to deny to the States the right to decide on the infraction of their own rights, and the proper remedy to be applied for their correction. 5. 'But the existence,' here we quote the very words again, lest it should seem incredible that such a position had been taken—'but the existence of the right of judging of their powers, clearly established from the sovereignty of the States, as clearly implies A VETO OR CONTROL ON THE ACTION OF THE GENERAL GOVERNMENT, on contested points of authority; and *this very control is the remedy which the Constitution has provided to prevent the encroachment of the General Government on the reserved rights*

gave form and substance to the doctrines which thenceforward became known as "Nullification." In order to understand them, however, as a theory of the Federal Constitution, it is necessary to state the theory to which they are opposed, and to overthrow which they were brought forward.

The Government of the United States, under the Constitution, had hitherto been administered upon the principle that the extent of its powers is to be finally determined by its supreme judicial tribunal, not only when there is any conflict of authority between its several departments, but also when the authority of the whole Government is denied by one or more of the States. According to the view of the framers of the Constitution, the General Government was endowed with a judicial department, and the Constitution and the laws passed in pursuance of it were made the supreme law of the land, for the very purpose of withdrawing from the States all final cognizance of questions relating to the extent of the powers of Congress. If there had been any opinions supposed to have been entertained by important persons, that were in conflict with this theory, prior to 1830, that supposition perhaps had its origin in erroneous constructions of the public documents in which such opinions were alleged to be found. For example, the famous Virginia and Kentucky resolutions of 1798, which had asserted the right and duty of the States to interpose, in a case of "deliberate, palpable, and dangerous" exercise of powers not granted to the General Government by the Constitution, had not distinctly asserted, as the opinion of their authors, that there could be a constitutional interposition by a State, in the shape of resistance to the execution of a law enacted by Congress, whenever the State believed such a law to be an exercise of power not warranted by the Constitution. If, on the other hand, there was language in those resolutions which seemed to

of the States.' 6. The practical result of the foregoing doctrines is then stated in the following words: 'That there *exists* a case (the tariff) which would *justify* the interposition of this State, and thereby *compel* the General Government to abandon an unconstitutional power, or to make an appeal to the amending power to confer it by express grant, the committee do not in the least doubt, and they are equally clear in the *existence* of a *necessity* to justify its exercise, if the General Government should continue to persist in its improper assumption of powers belonging to the State; which brings them to the last point which they propose to consider—When would it be proper to exercise this high power?'"

imply a right to resort to forcible resistance, their principal authors had not sanctioned an interpretation which would look to any other right of resistance than that which is commonly described as the right of revolution, and which is allowed to be held in reserve by all communities against acts of intolerable oppression.

But aside from the authority of these resolutions—an authority that was doubtful, because their interpretation was not clear—there had been no important assertion of the principle that a State can determine for its citizens whether they are to obey an act of Congress, by asserting its unconstitutional character, and that the right to do this is implied as a right inherent in a State, under the Constitution, and results from the nature of the Government. This, however, was what the advocates of nullification now undertook to establish. The remedy which they sought, against acts which they regarded as usurpations, was not revolution, and not the breaking up the Union, as they claimed; but it was a remedy which they held to exist within the Union, and to have been contemplated by the people of the States when they established the Constitution. How far they considered such a theory compatible with the continued existence of the Union, I am not aware that they undertook to explain. Having obtained the means of resisting one exercise of authority by the General Government, it was clear that the same rule would serve to defeat any other.

Such was the foundation and such was the doctrine of the asserted right of nullification. It assumed that the Constitution, by reserving to the States, or the people, all the powers not vested in the General Government, contemplated some means of checking and controlling the action of that Government on contested points of authority. It assumed that the Constitution, being only a compact between sovereign States, all questions respecting the extent of the powers conferred by it necessarily touched the extent and nature of the powers reserved to the States. It assumed that the right of judging and finally deciding on their own reserved powers was an essential attribute of sovereignty of which the States had not been and could not be deprived; and hence it declared that the control by State interposition was the remedy which the Constitution had contemplated to prevent the encroachments of the General Government on the reserved rights of the States.

Although the Legislature of South Carolina had thus propounded a theory of resistance, and held that there was then a case in the tariff which would justify a resort to it, no steps were yet taken toward the immediate exercise of the asserted power. Whether these doctrines were introduced afterward into the Senate of the United States, as in the nature of a warning, or were brought there without premeditation, it is a fact that, on the 29th of December (1829), Mr. Foote, a Senator from Connecticut, introduced a resolution to inquire respecting the sales and surveys of the Western lands. Mr. Webster was then absent from Washington, but he took his seat in the Senate two days afterward. An important discussion of this resolution took place, which continued at intervals, but without eliciting any thing of special interest, until the 19th of January. On that day, General Hayne, of South Carolina, delivered an elaborate speech, calling in question the conduct of the New-England States toward the interests of the West; accusing them of a selfish design to retard the growth of the Western States—a design originating, he said, in the policy of the tariff, which required the New-England States to keep their population from emigrating to the new States; and endeavoring to show that there existed a natural sympathy between the Southern and Western States, upon the distribution and sale of the public lands, which ought to make those sections natural allies against the tendencies and consequences of the tariff policy.

Such a tone had seldom been heard in the Senate. Whatever may have been the political sins and failings of New England, a narrow and illiberal policy toward the West had not been one of them; and it was quite new in the Senate of the United States, at that day, to hear appeals made to a supposed identity of sectional interests between the South and the West, on account of any injustice toward either of them on the part of the Eastern States. Mr. Webster entered the Senate from the Supreme Court just as Mr. Hayne rose to speak. His engagements in the court were at that time pressing and important, and he had no thought of taking part in this debate on the public lands.[1] But Mr. Hayne's speech he considered worthy of a reply, and, as soon as that gentleman had finished, he rose to answer it. Mr. Benton, however, after complimenting Mr. Hayne on his speech, moved an adjournment, to which Mr. Webster consented. The latter, of course, was entitled to the floor on the next day.

On that day, the 20th of January, Mr. Webster delivered his first speech on Foote's resolution, which is now contained in the third volume of his works. The notes for this speech—all that were ever made—were prepared in the night of the 19th, or more probably on the morning of the 20th.[2] They are now before me. They occupy, loosely written, three sheets of ordinary letter-paper. The speech, as it was delivered and reported, fills more than twenty pages of the octavo volume. It did not follow closely the written notes. On the contrary, the notes contain minute and accurate references to the history of the public lands and the legislation concerning them, which no one, not as familiar with the subject as Mr. Webster was, could have gathered at a single sitting. It seems to have been his purpose, in making these notes, to place before his own mind the historical facts from which he was to argue, rather than to place those facts in their details before the Senate. But one of his principal purposes, in making the speech, was to repel the charge made by Mr. Hayne, that the Government, especially so far as it might have been under the lead of New England, had acted with a narrow and illiberal policy toward the West. He had no thought of provoking a discussion on the power of the General Government to establish tariffs for the protection of manufactures, or on the authority of the Government to enforce

[1] The important controversy between John Jacob Astor and the State of New York was to come on in the Supreme Court on the 20th, and the argument was, in fact, begun on that day. This controversy is known as the case of *Carver's Lessee* vs. *Astor*, and is reported in the fourth volume of Peters's Reports.

[2] Mr. Webster was always an early riser. It was his habit, when he had any important work to do, to rise about four o'clock in the morning, light his own fire, and continue his occupation until the hour of breakfast, or until he chose to go out, as he was very fond of doing, before most people were abroad. In Washington, he could be frequently seen in the market-house, before any other inhabitant of the city, conversing with the tradesmen there, and securing the best choice from their stalls. Every butcher, and fisherman, and country produce-dealer, white or black, man or woman, free or slave, knew him well. Perhaps they did not know to what themes his early morning chats with them were parentheses. It was at such times, however, that his important labor was chiefly performed before people in general had begun the day.

its laws against the opposition of States; although he did incidentally allude to the prevalence of opinions and feelings, in some quarters, adverse to the Union, which, he said, had caused him regret, and which he hoped the gentleman from South Carolina did not share.

On the following day, January 21st, Mr. Chambers, of Maryland, moved an adjournment of the debate, as it was well known that Mr. Webster had urgent business which required him to be in the Supreme Court. Mr. Hayne objected, saying:

"He saw the gentleman from Massachusetts in his seat, and presumed he could make an arrangement that would enable him to be present here during the discussion to-day. He was unwilling that this subject should be postponed, until he had an opportunity of replying to some of the observations which had fallen from the gentleman yesterday. He would not deny that some things had fallen from the gentleman which rankled here (touching his breast), from which he would desire at once to relieve himself. The gentleman had discharged his fire in the face of the Senate. He hoped he would now afford him the opportunity of returning the shot.

"Mr. Webster: I am ready to receive it. Let the discussion proceed."

Mr. Benton then rose and finished a speech, in reply to Mr. Webster, which he had commenced on the previous day. An adjournment of the Senate was then moved and negatived.

Mr. Hayne then commenced his reply to Mr. Webster, which, in consequence of an adjournment of the debate, he did not finish until Monday, the 25th. His speech ranged through a great variety of topics. He assailed New England; called in question Mr. Webster's consistency, and depreciated the patriotism of Massachusetts. He then concluded with a highly-ingenious and acute exposition and assertion of the doctrines of nullification. One part of the speech was caustic and extremely personal; the residue was argumentative and able—so able, that without immediate refutation it would have done mischief.

Mr. Webster took notes while Mr. Hayne was speaking, and manifestly intended a rejoinder. As soon as Mr. Hayne had concluded, he rose, but an adjournment of the Senate was moved, which gave him the floor for the next day. This discussion had now been going on for so long a time, that strangers had come to the capital on purpose to witness it. When the Senate-chamber was opened on the morning of Tuesday, the 26th of January, the galleries, and even the floor, therefore, were crowded. Ladies were admitted to the seats of the members, and such was the extraordinary eagerness to hear Mr. Webster, that all rules had to give way to the interest and importance of the occasion. The House of Representatives was so deserted, that no business could be transacted, although the Speaker remained in his chair. Every inch of available space within the Senate-chamber, for sitting or standing, was occupied, and the crowd extended out into the lobbies and down the staircases, far beyond the sound of Mr. Webster's voice. He has himself said that he "never spoke in the presence of an audience so eager and so sympathetic."[1] In truth, that great assembly, composed of many of the most intelligent and cultivated men and women of the land, felt that, on that day, the Constitution of the United States was on trial.

On this occasion Mr. Webster again had but a single night in which to make preparation to answer the really important parts of the preceding speech of his opponent; for that speech was not concluded until a late hour of the session of the 25th, and it was on that day that General Hayne made his argument on the constitutional right of State nullification of the laws of the United States. Such written preparation as Mr. Webster, in fact, made for the speech that is called his "Second Speech on Foote's Resolution," and which embraces the celebrated answer to the doctrines of nullification, was made after the adjournment of the Senate on the 25th, and before the hour of its assembling on the next day. These notes are also now before me. Like those which he prepared for the "First Speech on Foote's Resolution," they are written with great brevity on common letter-paper, and extend through five sheets. The printed speech, as reported by a stenographer, fills seventy pages of the octavo edition of Mr. Webster's Works.[2] The notes

[1] Correspondence, i., 494.

[2] It was reported by Joseph Gales, Esq., the senior editor of the *National Intelligencer*, who, aware of the importance of the occasion, and being himself an accomplished stenographer, was unwilling to intrust this duty to any other hand. In the memorandum above referred to, Mr. Webster says: "Notes of this speech, in short-hand, were taken by Mr. Gales, the senior editor of the *National Intelligencer*. They were written out by another hand, and the report was most remarkably accurate. It was in the possession of Mr. Webster a part of one day for revision, and then the speech was sent to the press." I believe the report is still in the possession of Mrs. Gales.

contain no hint of the impressive exordium with which the speech was opened. They commence with the words:

> "No man hurt. If his 'rankling' is relieved, glad of it."
> "I have no 'rankling,' fear, anger, consciousness of refutation."
> "No 'rankling,' original or received—bow not strong enough."

It has been said that Mr. Webster needed no preparation to answer the heresy of nullification. In one sense this is true. From his first entrance into public life, he had been familiar with the historical facts on which any true theory, respecting the nature of the Constitution of the United States, must be based. His opinions on the subject had been formed long before the crisis of 1830–'33 had arisen; and if it is to be suggested that those opinions were such as were usually held by the best minds in New England, it is to be remembered that they constitute the sole ground on which the supremacy, claimed by the Constitution as the supreme law of the land, can be maintained. His long experience, too, in the argument of constitutional questions at the bar of the Supreme Court of the United States, commencing in 1819, had given him a training in the handling of such subjects which few men have possessed who have ever taken part in them; and he had, what few great lawyers have ever had, the power of adapting himself as effectively to parliamentary as to forensic discussion. So far, therefore, as the exigencies of this occasion required any study of the fundamental principles of our Constitution, Mr. Webster's preparation was made long before this occasion arose. But the marshalling of his subject in the order in which it was necessary to treat it, the special answers required by the special arguments of his adversary—the conception and the framework of the speech—all this did require labor, and that labor was performed after the adjournment of the Senate, late on the 25th, and before it reassembled on the 26th.

At the conclusion of Mr. Webster's argument, on the 26th of January, General Hayne, who had taken notes, rose to reply; and although one of his friends proposed an adjournment, he declined to avail himself of it, and addressed the Senate for a short time upon the constitutional question. Mr. Webster then rose again, and, after alluding to the "vain attempt" of his opponent to "reconstruct his shattered argument," restated both sides of the controversy with great force, giving General Hayne the benefit of that clear setting forth of the position of an adversary which none could do better than Mr. Webster, and which none could doubt was the strongest method of stating it; and then following it step by step with the appropriate answer. This was the reduction of the whole controversy into the severest forms of logic.

Mr. Webster's "Second Speech on Foote's Resolution," comprehending the memorable reply to General Hayne, has been compared to the oration of Demosthenes on the Crown. That it is the masterpiece of American as that is of Grecian debate, is, perhaps, not questioned. There is, too, some further parallel between them. The speech of the great Athenian was the public defence of a policy with which his own reputation had been identified for a period of twenty years; and this personal element, mingled with a grand patriotism that is exceeded in no recorded language, gives to it, as we read, even now, scarcely less than the interest with which it must originally have been heard. The American statesman was not, indeed, called upon to vindicate his claim to a civic crown; but he had to defend his own character and fame as a man, in repelling an attack made at once upon himself and upon the region of the country which he immediately represented, and to show that the course of the Government, whose existence was threatened by the doctrines advanced by his opponent, and his own participation in that course, had been national, just, and patriotic.

The first portion, therefore, of this speech, may well be compared to the oration of Demosthenes, and it will not suffer by the comparison. But here the parallel ends: for the American speech was no funeral *éloge* over the dead body of public freedom, as the Athenian's was over the lost liberties of Athens and of Greece. Demosthenes spoke to his countrymen when he could only speak of what once was, when he could recount what he had wished to strive against Philip, who was dead, and when the living and terrible son of Philip, then conquering the world, could crush Athens, and all that Athens sheltered, as he had crushed Thebes. The American statesman, on the contrary, had to deal not only with the past, but with the present and the future; for he was to show that, if the principles asserted by his opponent were a true explanation of the political Constitution of the country, we had no Constitution, we had made no advance from the inter-state league of the Revolutionary period, and the Government of the United States, notwithstanding its nominally direct legislative authority, existed at the pleasure and was subject to the control of each State. In this respect—in the fact that the accepted character of a great government turned on an argument to be made by a single statesman in a public body—this speech is unlike any other in the history of parliamentary or popular eloquence.

That such was the crisis is apparent from all that had gone before, from all that was then transpiring, and from all that has since followed. If the doctrines asserted by the statesman of South Carolina had not been triumphantly answered in that very debate, it would have been in vain to point to the general fact that the Constitution of the United States had hitherto been administered upon the principle that its powers are held directly of the people, and that they are not subject to the control of the State governments. Such had been, doubtless, the generally-received judicial and administrative interpretation; but the opposite theory had been now brought forward in a very imposing form; in fact, in an attitude of direct resistance taken by a State, supported with great dialectic ability by men of high and pure personal characters. It is true that no action could have been taken by the Senate, as a sequel to this debate, to affirm or to reject the South Carolina doctrine; for the discussion was really foreign to the question actually pending. But the introduction of the doctrine into the Senate had fixed upon it the attention of the whole country, and when Mr. Webster spoke, he spoke to the popular tribunal and the public judgment, as well as to the administrators of every branch of the Government. According to his success or his failure in convincing the understandings of men that the principles of State interference and nullification were wrong, the Government would thenceforward be able or unable to enforce its laws through its own judicial interpretation of their constitutional validity, and to maintain or not to maintain the Union in case of future forcible attempts to break it up; since these issues in truth depended, for all future time, upon the popular acceptance of the one or the other theory of the Constitution, as well as upon the convictions of the public men of the country respecting the real merits of this controversy. The results that, as we now know, followed this discussion, make it apparent that the responsibility of Mr. Webster's position embraced all that is here ascribed to it.

He comprehended and felt this in its full force. But he was always equal to the occasion, whatever it might be, and responsibility always stimulated his powers in proportion to the pressure that came upon him. As he approaches this part of the subject, he is evidently conscious that he is about to speak to the sense of the whole nation, and he frames his argument so that it may be comprehended by all intelligent men, as well as by publicists and statesmen; using in this consciousness a "studied plainness of speech." Throughout the argumentative portions of this grand division of the speech, he employs no reasoning that is not level to the understanding of a popular tribunal, although he is speaking in the presence of a singularly intelligent audience, and is addressing himself immediately to a body of Senators; and it is one of the most remarkable peculiarities of this speech that, upon a constitutional question of fundamental law, it satisfies alike the technical and the untechnical intellect. Nothing short of this could have accomplished the work he had to do; for we can now see that, if the argument had failed to convince the popular mind, the Constitution of the United States would ere this have been numbered among the things that were.

The celebrated peroration of this speech has been criticised as too elaborately rhetorical; and Mr. Webster once made this criticism himself. But it is, in the first place, quite certain that it was unpremeditated, and was drawn from him in the excitement of feeling caused by the evident sympathies of the great and eager audience, of both sexes, that drank in every word that fell from him, with an interest so intense that the pleasure and the pain of listening struggled strangely in their breasts. The very meagre notes from which he spoke contain nothing to show that he had previously wrought out the magnificent passage at the close of the speech which was soon ringing from all the college platforms of more than half the Union.[1] In the next place, it is to be observed of this and other passages of similar eloquence interspersed through the argument of this speech—of which his "brief" affords no sign—that if they had been the work of the most artistic closet preparation, he could have done nothing better adapted to fix popular attention upon the speech, and especially to give it that hold upon the popular heart, and that interest for the educated youth of the country, which caused it to do its work in after-years, and led the national intellect into the appreciation and acceptance of its political doctrine. These results would scarcely have followed if there had gone forth nothing more than an argumentative discussion of principles, however logical and convincing the statement, without those bursts of feeling, highly ornamented and rhetorical as they are, which sustain the interest and carry along the attention of the common reader. Yet, from the notes which he used, one would have expected to hear nothing but a very

[1] The writer of a life of Mr. Webster, published in the "American Biographical Library," has made the following assertions:

"A very foolish endeavor has been made, by some of Mr. Webster's friends, to create the impression that the great orations and speeches which have carried his celebrity all over the world were made with little effort and trifling preparation. Even so judicious a writer as Mr. Everett seeks to confirm the statement of Mr. March, that the reply to Hayne was the result of at most a few hours' reflection, and that all the notes he made for it were contained upon one side of a sheet of paper. This latter statement is true, so far as the notes from which he *spoke* are concerned; but the general impression conveyed in these representations is unjust to Mr. Webster, and calculated to induce very injurious theories and habits in the minds of the young. Mr. Webster had prepared himself for that debate with all his usual care. He knew a fortnight beforehand the points that would be made, the positions that would be assumed, and the parties that would be assailed. And we have no doubt that all those magnificent passages, which live in the memory and glow in the heart of all who read them, were prepared beforehand with the utmost care, and the nicest discrimination in the choice of words. And the same thing is certainly true of many other of his celebrated speeches."

I have no theories to maintain concerning Mr. Webster's capacity to make the speech in question with comparatively little written preparation. His general habits, in this respect, varied a good deal, but he invariably *wrote* much less than most public speakers commonly do, unless he was to pronounce one of those formal discourses, which are always written; and, when these came to be printed, he corrected and polished them with great care. With regard to the Reply to Hayne, as well as the First Speech on Foote's Resolution, I have given the facts, not only from my own examination of the public records, but also from a detailed memorandum which I possess, in Mr. Webster's own handwriting, stating the whole history of that debate. In this paper he says: "It is *evident* that the occasion was unexpected;" and when he adds that he "made such preparation as is usually made for such subjects," he refers to each of the briefs which he prepared at the times I have mentioned in the text. These were the notes which he used in speaking, so far as he used any; and he afterward presented them to Mr. Ticknor. What, then, are the proofs that these were the only notes which he made in preparing

dry discussion of a constitutional question, with perhaps a little play of fancy concerning the allusion to Banquo's ghost and the march of the South Carolina militia upon the custom-house. Perhaps one of the most efficient means which he employed to bring the position of his opponent to the appreciation of common minds was the introduction, among the severer forms of logic, of a lighter tone of illustration, by running out the practical application of the South Carolina doctrine into the results and the inconvenient vulgar consequences of mere treason. If ridicule be not always the test of truth, it certainly is, when logically correct in its argument, and used without personal discourtesy, a very powerful auxiliary.

The effect of this speech upon the country, that immediately followed its delivery, it is not easy for us at the present day to measure. We are to remember that this was the first time that the two opposite views of the nature of the Constitution had come into public discussion in Congress, and that the political

those speeches? The proofs are: 1. That he had no time to make any other written preparation for either speech. 2. When he gave these notes to Mr. Ticknor, he gave them as *all* that he had put on paper before speaking. 3. They are precisely the kind of notes which a speaker of great practice usually prepares when he has to make an important speech on the following day; and the internal evidence shows that they are the notes from which he spoke.

To say of Mr. Webster's reply to Hayne that he "knew a fortnight beforehand the points that would be made, the positions that would be assumed, and the parties that would be assailed," contradicts the recorded history of the debate, and Mr. Webster's own testimony. That he knew previously the general grounds on which the nullifiers claimed to rest their theory of the Constitution, is certainly true. But Mr. Hayne's argument was very far from being a common-place repetition of what had been uttered or printed by others; his points could not have been anticipated, nor could the persons or parties whom he was to assail have been previously known.

With regard to the opinion of this writer, that "all those magnificent passages which live in the memory," etc., "were prepared beforehand with the utmost care," etc., I have reason to believe that none of them were prepared beforehand, but that they were elaborately corrected on Mr. Gales's report, after they were spoken. There is no note or sign of the magnificent imagery of the peroration to the second speech on the written brief. When Mr. Webster, in uttering that peroration, depicted "the gorgeous ensign of the Republic—still full high advanced, its arms and trophies streaming in their original lustre," there was floating in his mind Milton's sublime description of the unfurling in the lower regions of

"Th' imperial ensign, which, full high advanced,
Shone like a meteor streaming to the wind,
With gems and golden lustre rich emblazed,
Seraphic arms and trophies."

There is no doubt whatever that he used this image in speaking, with more or less adoption of Milton's language; and I have reason to know that, after the speech was delivered, a friend asked him to look at Milton's lines, and that he did so, and corrected the passage as it now stands. (For a very graphic description of the scene, and Mr. Webster's manner on this occasion, see an extract from Mr. March, in the Biographical Memoir by Mr. Everett, in Works, i., 92–97. Compare March's Reminiscences of Congress, 132–148.)

relations of several eminent men were such as to make this and the three following years an era of great peril. Mr. Calhoun, the real author of the doctrine of State nullification—a man whom Mr. Webster always regarded as the ablest of the public men whom he had ever been called to oppose, and whose personal character always commanded his entire respect—had been chosen Vice-President of the United States at the time when General Jackson became President; and, as Vice-President, he, of course, occupied the chair of the Senate during this debate. He was naturally regarded by his friends as the probable successor of General Jackson; and, in the event of the death of the President, he would be the constitutional incumbent for the residue of the official term. But the relations of General Jackson and Mr. Calhoun were not friendly, notwithstanding their official positions, and the fact that they had been elected to them by the same general political combination. Mr. Van Buren had become the head of General Jackson's Cabinet, as Secretary of State, and it was well known that he was the person whose aspirations to the presidency General Jackson was most disposed to favor. Mr. Calhoun, however, was strong in friends, and, in his own State, his sway over the minds of a large majority of her people was supreme. His opinions, on the expediency of protective tariffs, and on the constitutional power of Congress to impose and enforce them, had undergone a complete revolution; and he had, in the full conviction that Congress was not likely to abandon them, constructed for himself, and for those who followed him, the theory of State nullification as the last and only remedy against their oppressive operation. General Hayne, in the debate of 1830, although a man of undoubted ability and accomplishments, was the mouthpiece of Mr. Calhoun.

When, therefore, this memorable discussion took place, there was, in these personal relations, and in the immediate subject on which the doctrine of nullification was first asserted, cause for great anxiety on the part of friends of the Union everywhere, and this anxiety was heightened by the character of the constitutional question. For it is not to be denied that there is much plausibility in the argument that makes the Constitution a compact between sovereign States, of whose infraction they are to judge; and although it is an argument which omits to give due weight to that part of the Constitution providing for a judicial arbiter of its own, with the express intention of withdrawing such questions from the final cognizance of the States themselves, and which also deals imperfectly with some of the other very important facts respecting the origin of the Constitution, it was by no means clear, beforehand, how far the popular mind of this country could be relied upon to embrace and give effect to its appropriate refutation.

It is not surprising, therefore, that this speech of Mr. Webster should have been more extensively read, within the six months following its delivery, than any other speech that had been made in Congress since the establishment of the Constitution. Men, everywhere, were aware that a new and startling doctrine, respecting the Constitution, had assailed its very foundations, and they were eager to possess and to understand the answer to it; knowing well that, if that answer were not complete, their own minds, and the minds of others, would be left in a painful and perilous uncertainty. Vast numbers of Mr. Webster's speech were therefore published and circulated in pamphlet editions, after all the principal newspapers of the country had given it entire to their readers. The popular verdict, throughout the Northern and Western and many of the Southern States was decisive. A great majority of the people of the United States, of all parties, understood, appreciated, and accepted the view maintained by Mr. Webster of the nature of the Constitution, and the character of the government which it establishes.

A singular occurrence, which took place during this debate, presents a striking proof of the practical operation of certain opinions held by the statesmen of South Carolina on the powers of the Federal Constitution. Perhaps it may, in part, account for the introduction of some of the topics on which Mr. Webster deemed it necessary to reply to General Hayne, in his first speech on Foote's Resolution. It has generally been overlooked in the various accounts which have been given of this great discussion.

Among the earliest of the railroad enterprises projected in this country, was one in South Carolina, to extend from

Charleston to the western boundary of the State, at a point opposite to the city of Augusta, in Georgia. It was a scheme in which were embarked some citizens of South Carolina, who did not share the constitutional opinions of their congressional representatives concerning the power of Congress to promote what were called "internal improvements," and who believed that this enterprise embraced relations which made it a proper object for the exercise of that power. The petition of the corporation of the "South Carolina Canal and Railroad," asking a Government subscription to its capital stock, was sent to Mr. Webster, to be presented in the Senate, accompanied by the following letter from the president of the company, which sufficiently suggests the reasons for asking his aid, and fully explains the grounds on which the directors of the corporation believed they were entitled to the assistance of Congress. It will be observed that the letter is dated early in January. The petition was presented in the Senate, by Mr. Webster, on the 18th, the day before that on which General Hayne made his first speech to which Mr. Webster felt called upon to reply:

[FROM THE HON. WILLIAM AIKEN.]

"OFFICE OF THE SOUTH CAROLINA CANAL AND RAILROAD COMPANY,
"CHARLESTON, *9th January*, 1830.

"The Hon. DANIEL WEBSTER,
"United States Senate.

"SIR: The directors of the South Carolina Canal and Railroad Company have instructed me respectfully to request from you the favor to present their petition to the Senate of the United States, praying the General Government in furtherance of the objects of their institution.

"The subject is fully developed in the petition and documents accompanying it, which will be presented to you by General Hayne, of this State, and we trust every point of difficulty touching the completion of this work, and our ability to effect that object should the General Government aid the enterprise to the extent prayed for, will be removed by Colonel Blanding, of this State, at present on a visit to the city of Washington.

"In soliciting your aid in behalf of our institution, it is due to the gentlemen who are Senators from our State, to inform you that objections predicated on constitutional grounds will induce them to oppose the object of our petition, and some reluctance to present it, therefore, must be experienced, on which we are not inclined to trespass.

"The quality of the enterprise as it relates to the General Government is obviously calculated to acquire for it the most indulgent consideration. The purpose is not less to give a particular direction to the produce of this and a sister State, than to procure for commercial operations certainty and confidence. The deepening of our bar, or improving the facilities of our port, would not more certainly advance the interests of the merchant than in communicating assurance of a prompt execution of their orders. The present season, with almost all the past, evidence the uncertainty and losses incident to an exclusive reliance on our rivers for the transportation of produce. For, until within a very few days, this harbor has been crowded with ships, and our country warehouses with cotton—the planter and the merchant incurring heavy charges, and deprecating the disappointments and delays to which they are subjected. In a military point of view, the contemplated road will subserve highly-essential objects. The United States arsenal at Augusta would be rendered more generally and promptly useful, and confer protection, when under present circumstances the emergency would pass, before the relief required from it could be obtained. Still more important would be the facility of transporting troops from the dense population of the interior to the Atlantic border of our State. These advantages are not unworthy of the patronage of the General Government, whether they refer to foreign invasion or domestic insurrection. As a post-road, its benefits will be most extensively conferred, nor will it admit of doubt that, in a much shorter period than works of such magnitude have hitherto been accomplished, it will, under the fostering care of the General Government, be made to constitute a link of union with the rising States of the West, attaching them more strongly, through the powerful influences of interest, to their Atlantic brethren. These, however, are subjects on which we will not dilate.

"Should you, sir, approve our purposes, believing that the General Government does legitimately possess the power to aid works (of great public utility) in the way intimated, you will confer an obligation which we shall most sensibly feel, by bestowing on it the acknowledged influences of your attention and talents. We would gratefully add yours to the name of the patrons of our infant institution, and the record of the service will be found in the general advantage resulting to our city and State.

"With sentiments of high consideration,

"I remain, sir,

"Your most obedient servant,

"WM. AIKEN,

"President South Carolina Canal and Railroad Company."

The following report of Mr. Webster's remarks, on presenting this petition, is taken from the "Register of Debates:"

"Mr. Webster said he rose to present the petition of 'the South Carolina Canal and Railroad Company,' praying Congress to authorize a subscription, on the part of the Government of the United States, of two thousand five hundred shares of the capital stock of that company. The railroad, contemplated by the petitioners, was to extend from Charleston to Hamburg, in the vicinity of Augusta; and the petition sets forth the practicability of the intended work. The enterprise was certainly one of a very laudable nature, such as had, in other instances, met encouragement and assistance from the Government of the United States, and it was with pleasure that he presented it to the consideration of the Senate. It had been confided to his hands from no disrespect, certainly, toward the honorable gentlemen who were Senators from South Carolina, but solely because the petitioners were unwilling to trespass on the reluctance which the honorable Senators from South Carolina naturally felt, or might be supposed to feel, to presenting petitions for aid from the Government of the United States in cases in which their known opinions, as to the constitutional powers of Congress, would oblige them to oppose the prayer of the petitioners. For his own part (Mr. Webster said), it was well known that, during the whole time in which he had had any connection with Congress, he had been uniformly in favor of what was called internal improvement, when applied to objects of sufficient magnitude and importance to be properly called national. And, while he admitted the necessity of great caution and wisdom in the exercise of the power, he must still say that every day convinced him more and more of the necessity of such exercise in suitable cases. He would take occasion to add, that he was a thorough convert to the practicability and efficacy of railroads. He believed that the great results which the power of steam had accomplished, in regard to transportation by water, were not superior to those which it would yet accomplish in regard to transportation by land. The only doubt was as to the amount of cost; and that was a point which experience would shortly solve, he hoped satisfactorily. He would only add, that while he felt pleasure in presenting this petition, he looked forward with equal pleasure to the time, he hoped not distant, when it would be his duty, in conjunction with his colleagues, to ask a subscription by Congress to the Massachusetts railroad, a contemplated work, which, if executed, would facilitate intercourse between several States, and be felt, in its beneficial effects, all the way from the Bay of Massachusetts to the mouth of the Ohio. When the proper time should come, he doubted not the Senate, and the other branch of the Legislature also, would give to the enterprise such aid and assistance as it should be entitled to by the consideration of its magnitude, and its obvious public utility and importance."

Mr. Webster then presented the petition, and it was referred to the Committee on Roads and Canals.

I now add some further selections from Mr. Webster's correspondence during a part of this session—a correspondence that lies before me in such masses, that it is difficult to adjust my space to what may be the demands of my readers.

[FROM MR. CLAY.]

"ASHLAND, *6th January*, 1830.

"MY DEAR SIR: I offer you hearty congratulations on a late event, which I hope, and have no doubt, will conduce to your happiness. The most favorable accounts of Mrs. Webster reach me from all quarters. You have avoided an error too frequent, in second marriages, of a great disproportion in the ages of the parties. Rumor says that the late event is the prelude to another, that of your removal to New York.[1]

"I am about proceeding to New Orleans, where I purpose passing a portion of the winter with my daughter and son-in-law. The effect of a southern climate will be agreeable, and I trust may prove beneficial to my health, which, though improved, still requires care. I shall be thus placed farther than ever from the scenes now passing at Washington. My correspondents there keep me pretty well informed of the actual state of things; but as yet no important movements appear to have been made in either branch of Congress. I am curious to know the issue of the nominations, which, if not already, must be shortly sent in. One of the strangest among them, from this quarter, is that of ——. I had hoped that the appointment of minister to Mexico would have been conferred on ——, a most excellent fellow, and one of good capacity. But these are not the times in which such men are employed.

"Cordially your friend,

"H. CLAY.

"The Honorable D. Webster."

[FROM THE HON. J. H. PLEASANTS, OF VIRGINIA.]

"RICHMOND, *4th March*, 1830.

"DEAR SIR: Permit me to congratulate you on your speech, on the great sensation it has produced in this quarter, so flattering to your feelings, and its effects so honorable to the consistency of your public conduct, and your ability to defend it. The knowledge that you have completely vindicated yourself, floored your antagonist, and gained a complete victory so far as argument goes, is nearly universal. . . .

"I am, sir, with great respect,

"JNO. H. PLEASANTS."

[FROM GOVERNOR LINCOLN.]

"WORCESTER, *March* 17, 1830.

"MY DEAR SIR: I cannot consent to forward the accompanying official papers without improving the same opportunity to express to you my grateful sense of your kind recollection and attention, in transmitting vari-

[1] For this rumor I believe there was no sufficient foundation.

ous documents during the present session of Congress, and especially copies of your speeches on Mr. Foote's resolution. As a New-England man, I thank you for the able defence of this much-abused part of the country; as a citizen of Massachusetts, I thank you for the vindication of her character for patriotism, for attachment to the Federal Union, for services, sacrifices, and undeviating and devoted regard for the interest of a common cause and country—and as a Republican—ay, and as an *old-fashioned Jefferson* Republican, too! I feel the weight of obligation to you for asserting the consistency of principle and the integrity of purpose with which we oppose despotism in every shape, and however exercised—whether from a foreign source or under the abuse of domestic authority. If any thing can rouse the people of the United States to a sense of their danger, and a timely protection of themselves and their free institutions, it must be the appeals to their intelligence and virtue which have been addressed to them from the Senate-chamber. I pray God they may be effectual. They have awakened attention, and there must be safety in the result. . . .

"With great respect and esteem, most truly,

"Your obedient and obliged servant,

"LEVI LINCOLN.

"To the Hon. Daniel Webster."

[FROM MR. TICKNOR.]

"*April* 4, 1830.

"MY DEAR SIR: The enclosed letter will sufficiently explain itself. It is only necessary to add that Mr. Allston wrote it without any request or suggestion from any one; that the opinion he expresses in it of Greenough's talent is one entertained by all the artists in this quarter; and that neither Allston nor myself has any interest in Greenough except on account of his genius. Verplanck, I understand, has been written to on the same subject, and probably Everett, Gorham, and some other of our friends, would be influenced by Allston's opinion in such a matter—that is, if it ever comes to the question whether anybody shall be employed to make a statue of Washington. But enough of this. Allston's letter contains the whole.

"Judge Story is at home and well, with two words to say to his friends, and no more. From him, more distinctly than we knew it before, we have heard of your great labors this winter, and the burdensome occupation of your time. But I trust Congress will rise early in May, that you may be relieved and come home to us before you are worn down by the hot weather.

"I had a letter from you some time since, and a copy of your truly great speech, for both of which I desire to thank you. If your health should freely permit, I hope you may, on some suitable occasion, make another speech this session. I hope it for two reasons: in the first place, it seems to me that the nation is in a condition to listen to the discussion of such questions as it is your peculiar province to discuss, there being now no great party questions or interests to excite the passions of men and absorb their attention; and, secondly, because I am sure they are disposed to listen respectfully and carefully to whatever you may say. It seems to me, therefore, that it is an occasion to speak for the public good.

"But I hear you have more letters every day than you can read, and so I will not add to the oppression of the number.

"Yours very faithfully,

"GEO. T—

"R. Gilmore, of Baltimore, knows Greenough, and would, I think, interest himself in his behalf. Greenough's plan was the one adopted for the Bunker Hill monument."[1]

[TO MR. TICKNOR.]

"WASHINGTON, *April* 8, 1830.

"MY DEAR SIR: If Congress should proceed so far, in my time, as to vote a statue to Washington, I will make an effort for Greenough. But at present the business has proceeded no further than a report. I have no belief any thing will be done. After this faint ebullition of national gratitude and national pride, the whole subject will probably sleep another ten years. "See nations slowly wise," etc.

"I have read Tom Moore's first volume of Byron's life. Whatever human imagination shall hereafter picture of a human being, I shall believe it all within the bounds of credibility. Byron's case shows that *fact* sometimes runs by all fancy, as a steamboat passes a scow at anchor. I have tried hard to find something in him to like besides his genius and his wit, but there was no other *likeable* quality about him. He was an incarnation of *demonism.* He is the only man, in English history, for a hundred years, who has *boasted* of infidelity, and of every practical vice, not included in what may be termed (what his biographer does term) meanness. Lord Bolingbroke, in his most extravagant youthful sallies, and the wicked Lord Littleton, were saints to him. All Moore can say is, each of his vices had some virtue or some prudence near it, which, in some sort, checked it. Well, if that were not so in all, who would escape hanging? The biographer, indeed, says his worst conduct must not be judged of by the ordinary standard! And that is true, if a favorable decision is looked for. Many excellent reasons are given for his being a bad husband, the sum of which is that he was a very bad man. I confess, I was rejoiced then, I am rejoiced now, that he was driven out of England by public scorn; for his vices were not in his passions, but in his principles. He denied all religion

[1] This letter, and Mr. Webster's reply to it, which follows, relate to the statue of Washington, afterward executed by the late Horatio Greenough, and placed in front of the Capitol.

and all virtue from the house-top. Dr. Johnson says there is merit in maintaining good principles, though the preacher is seduced into violation of them. This is true. Good theory is something. But a theory of living, and of dying, too, made up of the elements of hatred to religion, contempt of morals, and defiance of the opinion of all the decent part of the public, when, before, has a man of letters avowed it? If Milton were alive, to recast certain prominent characters in his great epic, he could embellish them with new traits, without violating probability.

"Walter Scott's letter, toward the end of the book, is much too charitable.

"I find in one of Lord Byron's letters a suggestion that a part or the whole of 'Robinson Crusoe' was written, while in prison, by the first Lord Oxford (Robert Harley), and by him given to Defoe. Is there any such suggestion anywhere else? I do not believe it. Defoe's (his true name was Foe) other works show he could write 'Robinson Crusoe.' Harley has left no proof of his capacity for such a work. While on the subject of books, whither I have strayed, I know not how, allow me to say there is one I want to see. It is Johnson's 'Shakespeare.' I covet a sight of that book, just as S. J. left it. His first edition was about 1765 or '66. Did he publish a second? You are not only a man for books in general, but for Shakespeare in particular, and can tell me. If you have the book, I shall get a reading of it; if you have it not, I wish you would order it on my account, the next time you write Mr. Rich. I suppose the first edition was folio, but know not.

"We have the April number of the *North American* here, and I have run over its articles. I think them good, generally speaking, but am not satisfied with that on Mr. Jefferson's correspondence. Early diplomatic history is interesting.

"I shall make no more speeches. What I have done, even, was not with malice prepense. Make our best regards to Mrs. Ticknor, and believe me always truly yours,

"D. WEBSTER."

[FROM MR. STORER, OF OHIO.]

"CINCINNATI, OHIO, *April* 11, 1830.

"MY DEAR SIR: Our friend Judge Burnet will hand you the retainer for our city, and I will, at an early day, transmit you a full statement of the case.

"I have just been relieved from a few weeks' session of our court, and feel too much fatigued to prepare so full a history of the matters involved in our suit as I wish.

"It has yielded me the most unmingled pleasure to read, in your late address in the Senate, the defence of our fathers, and the principles of our fathers. There cannot be a New-Englander whose soul has not kindled up within him, whose energies have not been awakened, if he has perused your triumphant vindication of his country and his countrymen. If there is a recreant spirit, let him go down to infamy with the 'scavenger' whom you have 'damned to everlasting fame.' Thank Heaven, we hold but few of these degenerate men in our political communion, and we should be an exception to all governments if we did not; yet it gives us in the West great cause for exultation that no son of New England, who has left the land of his nativity and cast his lot with the people of any other State, has ever publicly vilified his country. There has been something so sacred connected with early associations that it has protected his birthplace from moral and political profanation. If the blow has been struck, the parricide is not an emigrant.

"The intimation in your letter, that you had strong hopes of visiting us during the summer or autumn, has been communicated to many of your friends. I say friends, for *we all claim you*, and we anticipate the pleasure of welcoming you to a 'free and independent State,' whose prosperity and happiness have been mainly secured by the intelligence and wisdom of Nathan Dane, of Beverly.

"Shall I ask the favor of you to transmit me Mr. Clayton's speech, if it is published in pamphlet. The '*rari nantes in gurgite vasto*' of the opposition I can read in the newspapers.

"I am, very respectfully and truly, yours,

"Bellamy Storer."

[from mr. clay.]

"Ashland, *29th April*, 1830.

"My dear Sir: I received to-day your very acceptable favor of the 18th instant. The copies of the speech to which it refers have not been received, but probably will come safe to hand. If they do not, it is to be hoped that the seed may not fall on barren ground. I congratulate you on the very great addition which you have made during the present session to your previous high reputation. Your speeches, and particularly that in reply to Mr. Hayne, are the theme of praise from every tongue; and I have shared in the delight which all have felt. I trust that they will do much good. It is a great consolation to the honest patriot that, whatever may be his own fate, his principles will stand, and his country, sooner or later, derive the benefit of their illustration and establishment. To that consolation you will be eminently entitled.

"I have attentively observed the course of measures and events in and out of Congress. If all shall not have been, much will be, done to bring the public mind back to soberness and truth; and I yet see no cause of despair. It is greatly to be regretted that the Senate has not better fulfilled its high duties incident to the power of appointment. It ought to have rejected all nominations made to supply persons dismissed for political cause; all to replace those whom they approved at the last session;

most of the printers, and most of the members of Congress. If it has left undone some things which it ought to have done, we ought to be thankful for some of its rejections. Those of Lee and Hill are especially entitled to the public gratitude; and I hope it will place us under a similar obligation for the rejection of Kendall and Noah.

The importance of rejecting certain nominations does not consist in the exclusion merely of unworthy men from office, although that is far from being a minor object; but it shows that Jackson is not infallible nor invulnerable. The character of an eminent public man resembles a fortification. If every attack is repelled, if no breach on any point be made, he becomes impregnable. But if you once make a breach, no matter how small, the work may be carried. Considering how many of his recommendations in his opening message have failed, or are likely to fail, if to their defeat could be added that of some of his more obnoxious nominations, it seems to me that the effect on the public would be very great. Indeed, whatever may be the result of his nominations not disposed of at the date of your letter, the effect of his miscarriages has been considerable. He still shows game, appears stout and strong; but I think his strength is that of the buck, mortally wounded, who springs boldly forward while he is internally bleeding to death.

"In this view of the matter, I must respectfully doubt that policy which would surrender to his party their undisturbed course on any subject respecting which they were believed to be wrong. Success too often sanctions; and their success, in reference to the defeat of the power of internal improvement, for example, would, I fear, tend to produce acquiescence in the surrender of the power. If, indeed, they can defeat, at present, the power, after all proper exertions by our friends, good might result from that. We should have done our duty; and the great body of the nation would then see that it was not our fault that they did not get the benefit of the exercise of the power; and that, if they wished for that, they must support us.

"My observation induces me to believe that there is a great reaction in respect to the present administration; and that the exercise of the power of patronage is condemned by a vast number of the Jackson party as well as by our own friends. It is true, as you justly remark, that there is less public disapprobation expressed of the dismissions than could have been expected. But, I believe, nevertheless, that it exists very extensively. I speak confidently on this subject as it regards the valley of the Mississippi.

"I have noticed the movements at Harrisburg and Albany. The former, if we are rightly informed, was an abortion; and the latter may, I suppose, be considered as essentially Mr. V. B——'s. That Jackson will be again a candidate is highly probable. If he can unite in his support Virginia, Pennsylvania, and New York, opposition to his election will be vain. If either of those States can be detached from him, he may be beaten. What is the probability of their union? You are better judges at

Washington than I can be. My information from the western part of Pennsylvania is very flattering; and something may come out of the late celebration of Mr. Jefferson's birthday.

"In considering the expediency of using my name in opposition to General Jackson, I desire that every interest and feeling which I may be supposed to cherish in respect to myself should be entirely discarded. The question ought to be examined and decided exclusively in reference to our cause, and, which is the same thing, the great interests of our country. No personal or private considerations ought to have the smallest influence in its determination. If I could make an honorable retreat from public life, forever, it would cost me much less effort to do so than will be believed.

"After saying so much, it is scarcely necessary to add that I shall acquiesce—most cheerfully acquiesce—in whatever line of policy my friends may mark out at Washington.

"There are three courses: 1. Assuming that Jackson will be a candidate, to abandon all opposition to his reëlection; 2. To hoist our banner, and proclaim, prior to the close of the present session, our candidate; 3. To wait until the next session of Congress.

"I shall not discuss the advantages and disadvantages of each. My friends at Washington are more competent, from their superior information, and more impartial than I am, to compare and weigh them.

"Even if the second of the suggested courses should be deemed expedient, the question would not be free from difficulty as to the time when and the place where our candidate should be announced. . . .

"I shall be glad to hear from you again before the session closes.

"I am, ever truly your friend,

"H. CLAY.

"D. Webster, Esq."

[TO MR. DENISON.]

"WASHINGTON, *May* 10, 1830.

"I begin, my dear sir, by confessing my faults. It is long since I wrote you, and I have no apology but the evil habit of omitting to-day that which may be done to-morrow. Let me assure you I never forget you, nor lose sight of you; from the moment when you last wrote me, when you were just going, but did not go, on a little 'family party' to India, to the present, whether in office or out, I have kept a watchful eye upon you. My friend Mr. Rush spoke of having seen you in his late visit to England; and I am indebted to you for a copy of your brother's very sensible and manly dissertation on confederacies, received last autumn.

"For the four years (or five, I believe, it may be) since I saw you, my own fortunes have been no otherwise remarkable than as I have experienced domestic changes. I am now the husband of another wife.

Some three years ago our good people thought I had become old and grave enough for a Senator; wherefore they transferred me to that

House of Congress. Mr. Gorham became my successor as representative from Boston.

"Our political affairs just now are destitute of any particular interest. We have our party quarrels—our ins and our outs, our likes and dislikes—and we change men and dynasties; but the Government still keeps on, and holds us thus far safely together. Our foreign relations, like those of our neighbors, are very quiet. We should be glad you would let us into your colonial trade; but, if you do not, we shall not quarrel with you on that account. Expensive living, heretofore, the great reduction of prices now, and the vast overstock of supply of every kind beyond the demand, produce, what we call here, *hard times;* and the country is at present divided in relation both to the cause and the remedy. A portion of the South lays all the evil to the *tariff;* the Middle States deny this. The former insist on the repeal of all protecting duties; the latter warmly resist it; and the New-England States, though not originally in favor of the protecting policy, having now become deeply interested in manufacturing establishments, are not inclined to change back again. All New England, or all with few exceptions, voted against the tariff of 1824. It is now nearly unanimous against repeal or reduction. But I must send you a speech of mine to explain this; and I will relieve you from further detail here, leaving you to be edified by the speech aforesaid. You will see strong symptoms of *oppugnation* in the South, especially in South Carolina. There is, however, I trust, no great danger of violent irregularities. The tariff will not at present, certainly, be either repealed or reduced.

"Your friend Judge Story has been made a professor of law, and has gone to live at Cambridge. He and his brothers of the bench left us a month ago. The Chief Justice, now almost as old as Lord Mansfield at his retirement, enjoys excellent health, and seems to experience no decay of mind or faculties. We shall break up here in all this month, and, for one, I shall be very glad to be off. Summer and sea-shore are a coincidence of time and place very favorable to my health and enjoyment.

"I shall pack up our blue-book, a speech or two of the session—such as I think will best bear reading across the Atlantic—add one of my own, and ask the favor of Mr. Vaughan to put them together with this letter in the way of reaching your hand. When you see Mr. Stanley, Mr. Wortley, Mr. Labouchere, and Colonel Dawson, pray assure them that we hold them in fresh remembrance on this side of the globe. Let not my past omissions forfeit me your future kindness. Pray make my most respectful compliments to Lady Charlotte; and believe me ever, my dear sir, with

"Sincere and true regard,

"Cordially yours,

"Danl. Webster.

"J. E. Denison, Esq.,
"2, Portman Place, London."

In the summer and autumn of 1830, Mr. Webster was engaged, with the Attorney-General of Massachusetts, in one of the most remarkable criminal prosecutions on record. The following is a summary of the facts:

"On the morning of the 7th of April of that year, the town of Salem was thrown into a state of intense excitement by the intelligence that Mr. Joseph White, one of the wealthiest and most respectable citizens of that town, a retired merchant, eighty-two years of age, had been found murdered in his own bed. This gentleman was not known to have an enemy; a large amount of money and other valuable property in the house was left undisturbed, and popular conjecture was baffled in its attempt to assign a motive for this atrocious crime. Meetings of the citizens of Salem were called; a committee of vigilance was organized, consisting of twenty-seven of the most reputable citizens of the town, and every effort was made to ferret out the perpetrators of this enormity. For a long time the most persistent investigations of the ministers of justice were unavailing; but at length a rumor came to the ears of the vigilance committee of Salem that a prisoner, by the name of Hatch, in the jail at New Bedford, seventy miles away, had thrown out some intimations that he could let light into this strange mystery. The Attorney-General immediately had the man brought up before the grand jury, and on his testimony an indictment was found against Richard Crowninshield, of Danvers, for the murder; and several associates of his, including his brother George, were indicted on the testimony of other witnesses. Richard Crowninshield was a dark and desperate character, a man who shunned the public ways, but was well known as a cool and subtle villain.

"About two weeks after the arrest of this desperado and his companions, Captain Joseph J. Knapp, a shipmaster and merchant of good character, received a strange note from a man in Belfast, Maine, signing himself Charles Grant, Jr., which threw out vague intimations and threats of exposure if a demand for money which the note conveyed was not complied with. The writer of this mysterious letter said: 'I merely tell you that I am acquainted with your brother Franklin, and also the business he was transacting for you on the 2d of April last; and that I think that you was very extravagant in giving one thousand dollars to the person that would execute the business for you.' This letter was a complete riddle to Captain Knapp, and he showed it to his son, N. Phippen Knapp, a young lawyer of Salem, who was equally at a loss to understand its meaning. Captain Knapp, with this son, then set out to consult his other sons, John Francis Knapp and Joseph Jenkins Knapp, Jr., who resided in Wenham. The wife of Joseph J. Knapp, Jr., was the daughter of a niece of the late Mr. White, who had acted as his housekeeper prior to the murder. When the letter from the mysterious Grant was shown to this son Joseph, he said it 'contained a devilish lot of trash,' and told his father to hand it over to the committee of vigilance. This blundering disposition of the letter on the part of young Joseph Knapp was the first step in a train of evidence which brought himself and his brother Frank to the gallows. No sooner had the committee of vigilance received Grant's letter, than they sent a trusty messenger to Maine to find out the writer. This proved to be one Palmer, who had served a term in the State prison, and had associated with the Crowninshields during some part of the preceding winter, having been concealed in their father's house at Danvers. On the 2d of April, he said, he saw Frank Knapp and a young man by the name of Allen ride up to the house, and afterward go away in company with the Crowninshields; and when they returned, he heard George Crowninshield tell Richard that Frank Knapp wished them to undertake to kill Mr. White, and that J. J. Knapp, Jr., would pay them one thousand dollars for the job. Palmer said he had been asked to be concerned in the matter, but had declined.

"There had already been a strange occurrence connected with these Knapps since the murder, but the excitement then prevailing in the community had not allowed public attention to rest on it. A report had been circulated that, on the night of the 27th of April, Francis and Joseph Knapp had been attacked by highway robbers, on their way from Salem to Wenham, and had escaped with their lives only after a desperate struggle. The account of this bold attempt at highway robbery, in a hitherto undisturbed community, was published in the newspapers of Salem, as reported by the Knapps, with the comment that 'these gentlemen are well known in this town, and their respectability and veracity are not questioned by any of our citizens.' It afterward appeared, however, that this story was a pure fabrication, intended to divert attention from the real perpetrators of the murder at Salem; but, with the usual imprudence of guilt, the criminals only furnished additional ground for suspicion by this improbable and gratuitous narrative.

"On the testimony of Palmer, a warrant was issued for the arrest of John Francis Knapp and Joseph J. Knapp, Jr., and they were held in custody to await a thorough investigation of the evidence in their case. On the third day of his imprisonment, Joseph Knapp made a full confession. He had found that Captain White, by his will, intended to leave to his (Knapp's) wife but fifteen thousand dollars, while he supposed that if Captain White died intestate she would inherit one-half of his property as the sole representative of his sister, although a brother of Mr. White had left four sons, all of whom were living. Under this impression, he determined to destroy the will, and to compass the death of the old man. Frank agreed to hire an assassin, and Joseph was to pay one thousand dollars for the bloody service. The agent employed was Richard Crowninshield, who entered the house on the night of the 6th of April by a window which had been prepared by the care of Joseph Knapp for the purpose, and made his way to the chamber of Mr. White, where he dealt him a deadly blow on the temple with a bludgeon, and then gave him no less than thirteen stabs with a dagger. So coolly did he accomplish his devilish purpose, that, as he afterward declared, he paused to feel the old man's pulse to see if life was extinct. While this horrid business was going on in the house, Frank Knapp was waiting the issue; but Joseph had that day got possession of the will, and gone home to Wenham, leaving the perpetration of the crime in the hands of his hirelings.[1]

"When Richard Crowninshield learned that the Knapps were in custody, and that Joseph had made a confession, he committed suicide by hanging himself to the bars of his cell with a handkerchief. A special term of the Supreme Court was held at Salem on the 20th of July, and continued in session till the 20th of August, with a brief intermission.[2] Indictments for murder were found against John Francis Knapp as principal, and Joseph J. Knapp, Jr., and George Crowninshield, as accessories. The Attorney-General obtained the assistance of Mr. Webster in conducting the prosecution, and, at the trial of Francis Knapp, in August, leave of the court was asked and obtained that he might assist in the management of the case, and close the argument on the part of the government. The prisoners were defended by Mr. Franklin Dexter and Mr. W. H. Gardiner, advocates of great learning and ability, who omitted no exertions which could help the case of their clients. Francis Knapp was convicted of the murder, as principal, and sentenced to death. Joseph Jenkins Knapp, charged with being an accessory before the fact, was tried at the November term of the court, and was convicted and sentenced to share the fate of his brother. On this trial also Mr. Webster assisted the law officers of the State. George Crowninshield proved an *alibi*, and was acquitted."

Mr. Webster's appearance for the prosecution, on these trials, gave rise to some complaints on the part of the prisoner's counsel, as it was supposed that he was retained for the purpose by Mr. Stephen White, who was a nephew and residuary legatee of the gentleman murdered. The facts are these: The Attorney-General and the Solicitor-General were both persons quite advanced in years, and they desired Mr. Webster's services on the trials. On the trial of John Francis Knapp as principal, leave was obtained from the court that Mr. Webster should aid the law officers of the State, and no objec-

[1] A peculiar circumstance about this strange murder was the series of blunders of which Joseph Knapp was the victim. In the first place, his mother-in-law would not be heir to more than one-fifth of Captain White's property at best; the *ruse* of the highway robbery was a stupid piece of business; the giving up of Grant's letter to the committee of vigilance, when he might easily have destroyed it and hushed up the Maine convict, was a remarkable instance of the want of sagacity of criminals; and, finally, the will which he had seen, and which he carried away on the day of the murder, was not the *last* will of Captain White.

[2] Capital trials in Massachusetts always take place before, at least, three judges of the "Supreme Judicial Court," the highest court of the State; so that points of law are ruled upon the trial by more than one judge.

tion was interposed by the prisoner's counsel. But, in addressing the jury, Mr. Dexter complained that Mr. Webster had been brought there to "hurry the jury against the law and beyond the evidence." It does not appear, however, that on this trial any suggestion was publicly made that Mr. Webster had received, or was to receive, a fee from any private quarter. In opening his argument to the jury, Mr. Webster said that "although he could well have wished to shun this occasion, he had not felt at liberty to withhold his professional assistance, when it was supposed that he might be in some degree useful in investigating and discovering the truth respecting this most extraordinary murder," and that "in that court nothing could be carried against the law, and an intelligent and just jury could not by any power be hurried beyond the evidence."[1]

On the trial of Joseph Knapp, as accessory, the prisoner's counsel (the same gentlemen who had defended Francis Knapp) objected to Mr. Webster's appearance for the government. They referred to a statute, which placed public prosecutions under the direction and control of the law officers of the State, and which prohibited them from receiving any fee or reward from or in behalf of any prosecutor. They stated that they "had understood that Mr. Webster was to receive a compensation for his services from a private prosecutor, and they questioned the right of a private individual to retain counsel to aid the law officers of the government in effecting a conviction for a crime punishable with death." Mr. Webster rose and said that "he appeared solely at the request of the Attorney-General, and without any pecuniary inducement." These are the statements of what occurred, as they are found in the official report.[2] On the following day, the court delivered its opinion on the application, through Mr. Justice Putnam, as follows:

"In the present case, Mr. Webster avows that he is induced to aid the Attorney-General merely at his request, and without any other consideration, so that this case presents the question whether a counsellor may, at the request of the Attorney-General, be admitted to aid him in the prosecution, without any pecuniary consideration being paid to him, or any

[1] Works, vi., 51, 52.

[2] 10 Pickering's Reports, 477.

other consideration which may be supposed to influence him, excepting a disinterested regard for the public good. And we all think that, under these circumstances, the application should be granted.

"It is to be recollected that, at the trial of John Francis Knapp, Mr. Webster was, at the request of the law officers, appointed to aid them, and that there was no objection then made by the prisoner's counsel. And although that appointment strictly was for the then pending trial, yet, if the other trials had followed immediately, the counsel for the government would have had reason to suppose that they were to receive his assistance in those trials, unless good objections should have been made. It is said by the law officers that the preparations for this trial have been made under similar circumstances, and no objection was made to this measure until the jury were empanelled."

On the same day on which this decision was pronounced, Mr. Webster wrote to Mr. Justice Story in these words:

"SALEM, Wednesday, one o'clock.[1]

"MY DEAR SIR: J. J. Knapp's trial commenced yesterday. The A. M. yesterday was occupied in empanelling a jury; the P. M. mainly in debating whether the Attorney-General had a right to bring in other counsel; on this question their honors deliberated, and this morning agreed to let me in, I having stated to them that I appeared at the request of the Attorney-General, and had not received, and should not receive, any fee in this case, which, of course, was and is true. This A. M. has been employed in discussing the admissibility of the confessions, and the court holds the point under advisement. I expect they will be ruled out."[2] . . .

It is quite evident that the court understood Mr. Webster as denying that he had received or expected any fee *in the case then on trial.* The application before the court involved no inquiry into the relations in which Mr. Webster had stood in the case of Francis Knapp, who had been tried, convicted, and sentenced three months previously; and Mr. Webster's own report of his language on the trial of Joseph Knapp is, that he had not received, and should not receive, any fee *in that case.* Judge Story was connected by marriage with Mr. Stephen White, the supposed private prosecutor, and doubtless knew under what circumstances Mr. Webster originally came

[1] In the first volume of Mr. Webster's Correspondence, published in 1857, by Mr. Fletcher Webster, the date of this letter is given as of August 11, 1830. This is clearly an error. The context shows that the letter was written on the second day of *Joseph* Knapp's trial, and this was November 10th.

[2] Correspondence, i., 506.

into the case of Francis Knapp, the principal, and that in the case of Joseph Knapp, the accessory, Mr. Webster's statement was strictly true. Moreover, in the case of Francis Knapp, Mr. Webster assisted the Attorney-General at his request, and without any previous fee, or promise of a fee, from any quarter; although I believe it to be true that, after the trial and conviction of Francis Knapp, Mr. Stephen White offered Mr. Webster, and the latter received, pecuniary compensation for his services on the trial of Francis.

The circumstances which led to the request for Mr. Webster's services on these trials were entirely unprecedented. Joseph Knapp was the person who instigated the murder. He had two objects to accomplish: one to destroy a will which it was known Captain White had executed, and which gave the greater part of his property to his nephew Stephen; the other, to kill Captain White before the destruction of his will could be known to him. In the event of Captain White's dying intestate, Joseph Knapp supposed, erroneously, that his mother-in-law would inherit a moiety of the estate. Through the agency of his brother Frank, he hired Richard Crowninshield to kill the testator, and himself abstracted *a* will (but not the last will) from a strong-box in the chamber of the deceased, and prepared the house for the entrance of the assassin. The three were, therefore, concerned in a joint conspiracy to compass the death of Captain White, and, after the confession of Joseph, the details of this conspiracy, and the part played in it by each of them, became known to the Attorney-General, who obtained the confession by promising immunity to Joseph, on condition that, when brought into court as a witness for the State, he should testify fully and truly. But, after the suicide of Crowninshield, it became necessary to convict Frank Knapp as a principal in the murder; for, as the law of Massachusetts then stood, no one could be convicted as an accessory until there had been a conviction of some one as principal. But, when it was found that Frank was to be put on trial as a principal, Joseph retracted his engagement with the Attorney-General, and refused to testify. This was done upon the calculation that, as Crowninshield alone had entered the house, the prosecution would not be able to prove that Frank's participation amounted to that of a principal in the murder. He was no nearer to the house, at any time, than a distance of three or four hundred feet; and, although he was in the street at the rear of the house, at some time during the night, and at a position from which he could see when all the lights were extinguished, it was very doubtful if the prosecution could show, by independent testimony, whether he was there before Crowninshield entered, or while the latter was within the house, or when he came out. In order to convict Frank as a principal, it was necessary for the prosecution to convince the jury that he was present in the street at the time of the murder, aiding and abetting the person who dealt the fatal blow. To produce this conviction, Mr. Webster put forth all his strength, and it was all needed. No one of less ability in the handling of evidence could have succeeded in satisfying the jury that Frank Knapp was *present* at the murder for the purpose of rendering aid, if necessary. Mr. Webster's argument rested mainly on two positions: first, that there was a conspiracy to murder the deceased, and that Frank Knapp was one of the conspirators; second, that, as a conspirator, he was present in the street, by agreement, to countenance and aid the perpetrator. This would make him a principal. The force of Mr. Webster's argument convinced the jury that Frank was, in this sense, present at the murder.[1] But the fact was otherwise; and if Joseph Knapp had not refused to testify, and had told the whole truth, neither of them would have suffered for the murder. It would then have appeared that, at the time Crowninshield started to commit the murder, he told Frank to go home and go to bed; that Frank did so; but that he afterward rose, from anxiety to know what had been done, went toward Captain White's house, and met Crowninshield, after the murder had been committed. If Frank had not been convicted as principal, Joseph could not have been convicted as accessory.

On the trial of Joseph Knapp, as accessory before the fact, Mr. Webster's task was of an entirely different nature. Having refused to testify on the trial of his brother, Joseph had forfeited his right to the immunity promised to him by the Attorney-General, and was, therefore, rightfully put upon trial him-

[1] Mr. Webster's address to the jury is contained in his Works, vi., 41–105.

self. But he could not be convicted without the use of the confession which he had made under the promise of favor. Mr. Webster had to satisfy the court that the confession was admissible, although made under these circumstances. He argued that, as against himself, the prisoner's confession was admissible, because made freely and voluntarily; for, having obtained the Attorney-General's promise of immunity before he made the confession, he had no motive falsely to accuse himself, although he might have a motive falsely to accuse his accomplices. The court permitted the confession to go to the jury. Mr. Webster then had to convince the jury that the confession was credible. The prisoner was convicted.

Nothing was more remarkable in Mr. Webster than the manner in which he kept distinct, in his own person, the characters of the statesman and the lawyer. A stranger, hearing him in the forum, would not have imagined him to be any thing but a lawyer; one who should have heard him in the Senate would rarely have suspected that he was one of the very first lawyers of his time and country. It was always observed of him, by his contemporaries of the bar, that he brought into the forum neither the habits of mind, the modes of reasoning, nor the kinds of eloquence, which belong to the discussions of statesmen; nor did he carry into the Senate the peculiarities of reasoning and analysis and proof which are alone effective in judicial tribunals. In the latter, his great renown as a public man no doubt helped to fasten the attention of judges and jurymen, and sometimes aided the ascendancy which his intellect enabled him to obtain over the intellects of those he addressed. But Mr. Webster was generally encountered at the bar by men who were able to overcome any influence of this kind, by rendering it necessary for him to exert all his powers in the mode which the forensic habit demands, and which is peculiar to the discussions in courts of justice. His ability to do so was never affected by the habits acquired in legislative bodies. On the trials of which I have here given an account, he produced convictions of the prisoners because of this power to discharge the functions of a lawyer, as if he were never any thing but a lawyer.

CHAPTER XVII.

1830-1831.

MR. WEBSTER'S POPULARITY—CHARACTER OF GENERAL JACKSON—MR. CLAY'S CLAIMS TO THE PRESIDENCY—ANTI-MASONRY—DINNER TO MR. WEBSTER IN NEW YORK—GIVES UP A JOURNEY TO THE WEST—NOMINATION OF MR. CLAY AS THE CANDIDATE OF THE NATIONAL REPUBLICANS—RELIEF OF INSOLVENT DEBTORS OF THE UNITED STATES—MISCELLANEOUS CORRESPONDENCE.

WE are now arrived at the period in Mr. Webster's life when he began to be considered, by a part of the people of the North and the West, and by many in the South who were politically opposed to the reëlection of General Jackson, the most suitable person to be brought forward as a candidate for the presidency. Aside from the public questions which were about to separate the people of the United States into two parties, many of the best minds in the country had come to place their hopes for the success and perpetuity of its institutions upon the power and the willingness of the nation to call to the chief magistracy a statesman whose extraordinary civil services, whose intellect, whose broad national politics, and whose moderation and elevation of character, pointed him out as the most fit person in the Union to be intrusted with the executive office. It is quite unnecessary for me to insist that this was not an undue partiality. We have to deal with facts; and it is one of the facts which constitute Mr. Webster's justification for allowing himself to be drawn into that long candidacy, in respect to which he was destined to be always unsuccessful, that some of the best and wisest men of his time—men who had the least that was selfish and the least that was local in their political wishes and conduct—originally awakened this desire in his breast. It will not be questioned, by even the most philosophic or the most severe judgment, that the ambition was a worthy one. To preside over the government of a great country, by the suffrages of a free people, and to attain that position without mean compliances, and through the public confidence and respect, might well be admitted by any man to be among the objects for which he lived. Nor were there wanting to Mr. Webster, from the first, large elements and striking proofs of that popularity for which mere politicians will look, in the selection of a leader under whose political banner they may seek to array themselves. Wherever he went, the popular interest in him was sure to manifest itself; not only because of his intellectual celebrity, but because he was everywhere regarded as a man who was serving the country from profound convictions respecting its true policy, and with a wise and far-seeing devotion to the Union and the Constitution. His opinions, sentiments, and character, were as well known in the remotest West, or in the farthest South, as they were in New England. Every man in the country, who read any thing of public interest in the current political affairs of the nation, had read his most important Congressional speeches. Every such man knew how he had voted on questions that concerned the general interest, and could tell almost with certainty where he could be found on any question that was likely to arise. From quarters very remote from the region which he represented, and from a great variety of associations, whose members could scarcely hope that he would ever visit their locality, or evince a personal interest in their affairs, and who could have had no special political motive, there came to him expressions of a desire for the honor of enrolling him among their nominal patrons or members. If such evidences of popularity mean any thing —and, undoubtedly, they mean a great deal, both in the calculations of mere political managers and in the judgments of those who look for solid proofs of the estimation in which a statesman is held by his contemporaries—Mr. Webster undoubtedly possessed them in an abundance that would make them important to any body. They now lie before me in forms so numerous and so various—the spontaneous and untainted expressions of popular respect—that the details would inconveniently encumber my pages if they were to be set forth.[1]

General Jackson's administration of the Government commenced and was continued under circumstances that produced in him two opposite tendencies. He was elected to the presidency through the agency of that class of public men who were most disposed to a strict construction of the powers of the Federal Constitution; and it so happened that many public questions arose in the first term of his official service, which involved the assertion or the denial of specific powers of the utmost importance. At the same time, he was called to encounter a doctrine which threatened the entire overthrow of the Constitution; and the arguments by which this doctrine was supported were, to a considerable extent, the same with those which lead to a denial of the particular powers that came into prominent consideration during this period. General Jackson finally saw that it was his duty to defend the Constitution from the heresy of State "nullification;" and, when the crisis came, he executed that duty with all the firmness that belonged to his character. But he did not see

[1] Among these indications of popular strength—to use the cant of politics—I know of none that can be more significant, because there can be none more genuine and unalloyed, than the numerous requests which came to Mr. Webster from associations that were not political in their character, to permit the enrollment of his name among their honorary members, or to address them upon the subjects which formed the objects of their organization. Of these, I should select those coming from the colleges scattered through our country, as affording a very striking evidence that a public man, who elicited such proofs of regard from the young who were coming forward into the ranks of educated life, or from the older guides of public opinion, had laid a very broad foundation for what is commonly called "popularity." I have counted a very great number of such communications, at this period, coming from the most eminent as well as the least known of such institutions, and from many different States, both in and out of New England. Such applications, too, came from numerous popular societies in no way connected with the collegiate institutions, and in whose objects Mr. Webster could scarcely be expected to take an active part. Whether it was the great Bible association, whose headquarters were in the city of New York, or a society of the angling-rod, who wet their lines in the streams of the Ohio, and from all kinds of associations that might be classed in dignity and importance between these two extremes, the solicitations and invitations were constantly accumulating. If it is true that, in many such cases, the chief object was to draw public attention by a great name, let it be remembered that the recognized power of that name to move public attention is a very weighty proof of what might have been done by it in political action, if the right steps had not been thwarted by untoward causes or by the notorious doctrine of "availability."

with equal clearness that the rules of constitutional interpretation are closely connected with the political doctrine that maintains the supremacy of the Constitution as a fundamental law; or that the Constitution itself provides for an authorized judicial interpreter, whose decisions respecting the extent of its powers ought to be his guide; or that a uniformity of interpretation and action, from the time of the origin of the Constitution to any given period, ought to be regarded, under a Government like ours, as the best evidence alike of the national will and of the just construction of such an instrument. In all these respects, he and his supporters belonged to one political school, and his opponents to another. Moreover, there grew up in his time, partly as the effect of his own imperious temper, to which the food of adulation was abundantly administered, and partly from the loose ideas of the Presidential office that then prevailed among his followers, very enlarged views of executive discretion. A man of his temperament, whose purposes were patriotic, and whose intentions always were to promote the glory and welfare of his country, but who had not been much accustomed to consider the boundaries of departmental power, was very likely to embrace the idea of a sovereignty of the people, acting through the President in the control of all the operations of Government. General Jackson did embrace it. He had been elected by an immense popular majority, and he came to regard himself as the direct and immediate constitutional representative of the people, forgetting that, under a fixed constitution, which distributes political functions among distinct departments, and grants specific powers to each, the present popular will on any particular subject has no just relation to the authority of any one of those departments, as it can have no just influence in determining what are the constitutional powers of the whole Government.

These well-known facts and truths are alluded to here, for the purpose of showing why Mr. Webster could not become a general political supporter of President Jackson, or of any one of those who might be made the succeeding candidate of the same party. But why was it, posterity will ask, that this very eminent statesman was never presented to the suffrages of his countrymen, for the highest office in their Government, by the political party who shared his opinions, and with whom he acted? The civil history of this country, for the two and twenty years commencing in 1830 and ending in 1852, must furnish the answer to this question. In that period Mr. Webster acted a great and a very conspicuous part. Whether it in truth detracts any thing from his just fame that he never became the candidate of his party for the office of President of the United States, will depend on the judgment that may be formed respecting his own relation to the causes which prevented his selection. If it is true that he was right in the public conduct which lost him the support of those on whom he had claims of the highest nature; if his well-earned popularity waned through the influence of that which was in him a merit and not a fault; if he served his whole country with soundness of judgment and singleness of purpose, at cost to himself; if events have shown that in matters of moment he made no mistakes, sacrificed no principles, was true to his own character, and would have averted great evils from his country if his advice had been followed—no one can regret, for him, that an ambition which he unquestionably possessed was never gratified.

It is important to a correct view of Mr. Webster's whole conduct on the subject of the presidency, that he was from the first always willing to admit the claims of Mr. Clay while there was any prospect that the selection of Mr. Clay as a candidate would be wise. In the winter of 1829, after the first election of General Jackson, as the reader has seen, he wrote to his brother that, if New England could be kept firm and steady, she could make Mr. Clay President, if she should choose to do so.[1] In the spring of 1830, after General Jackson had been in office a year, he wrote from Washington to Mr. Pleasants, of Virginia, in reference to the course of the opposition, in these words:

"As to future operations, the general idea here seems to be this: to bring forward no candidate this year, though, doubtless, the general impression is, that Mr. Clay stands first and foremost in the ranks of those who would desire a change. I do not think there is the least abatement of the respect and confidence entertained for him. As to the other Western gentleman whom you mention, he must not be thought of, for he is not

[1] *Ante*, chap. xvi.

with us. Depend upon it there is a negotiation in train to bring him out as Vice-President, to run on the ticket with Mr. Calhoun. In my opinion, he has very little weight or influence in the country, and that is fast declining. Our friends in the West will quit him, of course, in that event, as he must give up their interests. I write now to say that two things must not be omitted when we speculate on the future; first, that General Jackson will certainly be a candidate again, if he live and be well; I say certainly—I mean only that I have no doubt of it. Second, that we cannot now foresee what events will follow from what is passing in Pennsylvania and New York, on the subject of antimasonry. This matter, be assured, is not to be disregarded."[1]

This was written to a gentleman of much political activity in the ranks of the opposition, after Mr. Webster had electrified the whole country by his defence of the Constitution, at the very time when he was an object of the strongest popular interest, and when he might well have been justified if he had availed himself of the demonstrations made toward him, so as selfishly to advance his own claims as the leader of a party which was to seek the overthrow of the party of the Administration. But he placed himself in no such attitude; on the contrary, he carefully observed the evidences of Mr. Clay's position in the public regard, willing, if necessary, to follow that gentleman as the person who might displace from the Government a party whose principles he could not espouse, and restore it to what he believed to be its true policy. But his attention was very early arrested by the formidable disturbance of all political calculations that was about to be made by the antimasonic movement—a phenomenon that requires a brief explanation.

This popular agitation had its origin in the excitement produced by the abduction and supposed murder of one Mor-

[1] Correspondence, i., 492.

He had previously written to Mr. Mason, in February, 1830, as follows:

"Calhoun is forming a party against Van Buren, and as the President is supposed to be Van Buren's man, the Vice-President has great difficulty to separate his opposition to Van Buren from opposition to the President. Our idea is to let them pretty much alone; by no means to act a secondary part to either. We never can, and never must support either.

"While they are thus arraying themselves for battle, that is Calhoun and Van Buren, there are two considerations which are likely to be overlooked, or disregarded by them, and which are material to be considered. 1. The probability that General Jackson will run again; that that is his present purpose, I am quite sure. 2. The extraordinary power of this antimasonic party, especially in Pennsylvania." — (*Correspondence*, i., 488.)

gan in 1826.[1] The masonic lodge that he had left was supposed to be responsible for this act. This agitation spread through the country, drawing largely from the ranks of those who were opposed to the reëlection of General Jackson. The party that led, and should have comprehended, all the effective opposition to Jackson, had taken the name of National Republicans. Being of recent origin, and having never yet acted in a general election, it was not very thoroughly organized. It was to hold a national convention, however, in December of this year (1831), at Baltimore, for the purpose of nominating its candidates for the presidency and vice-presidency. No doubt would have been felt anywhere respecting the selection of Mr. Clay as its candidate for the first office, if it had not been for this antimasonic excitement. But Mr. Clay was what was called, in the cant of the time, an "adhering Mason," that is to say, having been a member of a Masonic lodge, he had not chosen to withdraw from it, and to renounce Masonry. The new party that had undertaken a crusade against the Freemasons was violently intolerant and proscriptive. It had grown to be powerful, as a third party, in the States of New York and Pennsylvania, and to be capable of doing much injury elsewhere to the cause of those who desired a change in the administration of the General Government. Some honest and high-minded men had been drawn into it, led away by imaginary evils that were believed to be the fruits of Freemasonry; speculating and intriguing politicians had joined in, and were using it; and the whole mass of those who constituted its rank and file were acting under a delusion about an institution which had no possible relation to the questions of national policy that should alone have absorbed their attention in a national election.

Mr. Webster regarded this movement from the first with

[1] William Morgan was abducted from the village of Batavia, in the western part of the State of New York, and was supposed to have been sunk in the waters of Lake Ontario. On the one side it was charged that he was about to print a book, revealing the secrets of Masonry, and that for this treachery the Masons had murdered him. On the other side, the Masons asserted that the whole story was a fraud, and that the man was still living. That he was abducted and drowned, because of his supposed treachery to the obligations of Masonry, was, I suppose, not doubted by impartial people who attended to the material facts at the time they transpired.

serious concern. He knew that it was formidable, but he was always unwilling to make it an issue in national politics. He had never been a Mason; and he did not believe that in modern society there is any real necessity, in order to subserve any useful purpose, for secret societies with pass-words and cabalistic ceremonies. He was, in fact, disposed to consider the Masonic institutions as objectionable, so far as they imposed on their members duties to each other that might conflict with their general duties as citizens. But, as a national statesman, it was impossible for him to consent to the introduction, among the important questions of national politics, of an issue so irrelevant to the great concerns of the country as that presented by antimasonry. He was willing to go as far as in honor he could go, to reconcile this schism in the body of those who sought to take the Government out of its present hands; but he was not willing to forego the hope of electing a President upon the principles professed by the National Republican party, and thus founding a political organization that would be permanently useful to great national ends.

He was solicited to discourage the nomination of Mr. Clay at Baltimore. Great efforts were made to convince him that Mr. Clay could not be elected, in consequence of the determination of the antimasons not to vote for him. Their leaders made known to Mr. Webster this determination in the winter of 1830–'31, and their purpose to nominate a candidate of their own. Gentlemen in different parts of the country, who earnestly desired the election of Mr. Clay, also informed Mr. Webster of the dangers attending the rise, the progress, and the proscriptive spirit of this new organization. His own opinion concurred with theirs, that, if this movement went on, it would very seriously endanger the election of Mr. Clay. He knew that his own claims were equal at least to those of Mr. Clay, and he received constant assurances from many important persons that there was nothing they so much desired as to make him President of the United States, if he could in any way produce a union between the National Republicans and the antimasons.

Under these circumstances, Mr. Webster, had he chosen to do so, might have said to the friends of Mr. Clay, that the latter could not be elected; and that, if defeated in 1832, he could not again be brought forward as a candidate in 1836. To the antimasons he could have said, that no one but himself had the smallest prospect of being elected in opposition to General Jackson, and that their project of nominating Mr. Wirt as their candidate was futile. He might thus have caused himself to be presented as a candidate on whom both branches of the opposition could unite; and, from the mass of correspondence that is before me, I am authorized to say that this view was presented to him again and again.

What, then, were the reasons that prevented Mr. Webster from seeking the Baltimore nomination, to the exclusion of Mr. Clay?

It has already been said that Mr. Webster had hopes for the country, which looked to the success of a party founded on definite principles that concerned the interests of the country. He considered Mr. Clay as a suitable leader of that party; and, although he had seen reason, during the past year, to regard Mr. Clay as less strong politically than he had formerly been, he was aware that Mr. Clay had a large body of attached friends throughout the Union, whose defection, if caused by a rejection of his claims to the Baltimore nomination, would render it impracticable to preserve the National Republican party and to make it useful to the country. Moreover, he had long known that Mr. Clay expected this nomination, and that he cherished the sanguine belief that he could be elected. They had been in a free and friendly correspondence on the subject.

But Mr. Webster could not forego all the public demonstrations of respect and admiration that were tendered to him at this period, merely because of this pending nomination for the presidency. At the close of the session of Congress, a public dinner was given to him in the city of New York, which was intended as a special recognition of the services he had rendered to the country and to its constitutional law, in the debate of 1830 on the doctrines of nullification. Circumstances had made it inconvenient for him to accept this compliment until after the adjournment of Congress, in March.[1] With great fitness to the nature of the occasion, Chancellor Kent was selected to preside. In the following introductory speech, proposing

[1] The dinner was given March 10, 1831, at the City Hotel.

the health of Mr. Webster, he avoided all topics of a party character:

"New England has been long fruitful in great men, the necessary consequence of the admirable discipline of her institutions; and we are this day honored with the presence of one of those cherished objects of her attachment and pride, who has an undoubted and peculiar title to our regard. It is a plain truth, that he, who defends the Constitution of his country by his wisdom in council, is entitled to share her gratitude with those who protect it by valor in the field. Peace has its victories as well as war. We all recollect a late memorable occasion, when the exalted talents and enlightened patriotism of the gentleman to whom I have alluded were exerted in the support of our national Union, and the sound interpretation of its charter.

"If there be any one political precept preëminent above all others, and acknowledged by all, it is that which dictates the absolute necessity of a union of the States under one government, and that government clothed with those attributes and powers with which the existing Constitution has invested it. We are indebted, under Providence, to the operation and influence of the powers of that Constitution for our national honor abroad, and for unexampled prosperity at home. Its future stability depends upon the firm support and due exercise of its legitimate powers in all their branches. A tendency to disunion, to anarchy among the members, rather than to tyranny in the head, has been heretofore the melancholy fall of all the federal governments of ancient and modern Europe. Our Union and national Constitution were formed, as we have hitherto been led to believe, under better auspices, and with improved wisdom. But there was a deadly principle of disease inherent in the system. The assumption by any member of the Union of the right to question and resist, or annul, as its own judgment should dictate, either the laws of Congress, or the treaties, or the decisions of the Federal Courts, or the mandates of the Executive power, duly made and promulgated, as the Constitution prescribes, was a most dangerous assumption of power, leading to collision and the destruction of the system. And if, contrary to all our expectations, we should hereafter fail in the grand experiment of a confederate government, extending over some of the fairest portions of this continent, and destined to act, at the same time, with efficiency and harmony, we should most grievously disappoint the hopes of mankind, and blast forever the fruits of the Revolution.

"But, happily for us, the refutation of such dangerous pretensions on the occasion referred to was signal and complete. The false images and delusive theories, which had perplexed the thoughts and disturbed the judgments of men, were then dissipated, in like manner as spectres disappear at the rising of the sun. The inestimable value of the Union and the true principles of the Constitution were explained by clear and accurate reasonings, and enforced by pathetic and eloquent illustrations. The result was the more auspicious, as the heretical doctrines, which were then fairly reasoned down, had been advanced by a very respectable portion of the Union, and urged on the floor of the Senate by the polished mind, manly zeal, and honored name of a distinguished member from the South.

"The consequences of that discussion have been extremely beneficial. It turned the attention of the public to the great doctrines of national rights and national union. Constitutional law ceased to remain wrapped up in the breasts, and taught only by the responses, of the living oracles of the law. Socrates was said to have drawn down philosophy from the skies, and scattered it among the schools. It may, with equal truth, be said that constitutional law, by means of these senatorial discussions and the master genius that guided them, was rescued from the archives of our tribunals and the libraries of lawyers, and placed under the eye and submitted to the judgment of the American people. *Their verdict is with us, and from it there lies no appeal.*"

Mr. Webster spoke for an hour and a half on this occasion, entirely with reference to the dangers to which the Constitution was exposed, and to some of the interesting and important incidents connected with its history.[1] He did not deem it fit to use this opportunity to "break ground" against the Administration, as some of his friends elsewhere had desired; for the crisis had not fully passed by, and it was essential that he, who was now universally regarded as the "Champion of the Constitution" in the halls of Congress, should be in a position to render to the Administration of General Jackson all the aid it could need or would receive from him in the future possible collision with the party of nullification. He spoke with reference to this matter as follows:

"Seeing the true grounds of the Constitution thus attacked, I raised my voice in its favor, I must confess, without preparation or previous intention. I can hardly say that I embarked in the contest from a sense of duty. It was an instantaneous impulse of inclination, not acting against duty, I trust, but hardly waiting for its suggestions. I felt it to be a contest for the integrity of the Constitution, and I was ready to enter into it, not thinking or caring, personally, how I might come out.

"Gentlemen, I have true pleasure in saying that I trust the crisis has, in some measure, passed by. The doctrines of nullification have received a severe and stern rebuke from public opinion. The general reprobation of the country has been cast upon them. Recent expressions of the most

[1] The speech is contained in the first volume of his Works, 195–215.

numerous branch of the national Legislature are decisive and imposing. Everywhere, the general tone of public feeling is for the Constitution. While much will be yielded—everything, almost, but the integrity of the Constitution and the essential interests of the country—to the cause of mutual harmony and mutual conciliation, no ground can be granted, not an inch, to menace and bluster. Indeed, menace and bluster, and the putting forth of daring, unconstitutional doctrines, are, at this very moment, the chief obstacles to mutual harmony and satisfactory accommodation. Men cannot well reason and confer and take counsel together about the discreet exercise of a power with those who deny that any such power rightfully exists, and who threaten to blow up the whole Constitution if they cannot otherwise get rid of its operation. It is matter of sincere gratification, gentlemen, that the voice of this great State has been so clear and strong, and her vote all but unanimous on the most interesting of these occasions in the House of Representatives. Certainly, such respect to the Union becomes New York. It is consistent with her interests and her character. That singularly prosperous State, which now is, and is likely to continue to be, the greatest link in the chain of the Union, will ever be, I am sure, the strongest link also. The great States which lie in her neighborhood agree with her fully in this matter. Pennsylvania, I believe, was loyal to the Union, to a man; and Ohio raises her voice, like that of a lion, against whatsoever threatens disunion and dismemberment. This harmony of sentiment is truly gratifying. It is not to be gainsaid that the union of opinion in this great central mass of our population, on this momentous point of the Constitution, augurs well for our future prosperity and security."

Immediately after this dinner, however, it became necessary for Mr. Webster to decide what he should do in regard to a long contemplated journey to the West, where he had never been, and where the desire to see him was exceedingly strong among the people at large.[1] Such a tour, at this time, however, was very likely to be regarded with jealousy by the friends of Mr. Clay; for the question, in relation to the expediency of Mr. Clay's nomination by the National Republicans, was an exceedingly delicate one; and Mr. Webster's purposes, in making this journey, would certainly have been liable to misconstruction. He decided not to undertake it, although it was urged upon him with much earnestness, and although its present renunciation was a postponement of his own long-cherished desire to see the Western States, and to converse with their people. He sub-

[1] The letters on his files, at this time, begging him to visit the West, are extremely numerous and pressing. He gave up the journey with great reluctance.

stituted for this tour a journey through the State of New York and to the Canadas.

As the time approached for the decision of the question whether Mr. Clay should be presented as the candidate of the National Republicans, or whether such a concession should be made to the antimasons as would enable them to dictate the candidate to the whole opposition, and thus to reduce the character of that opposition to the level of their own unimportant issues, Mr. Webster made up his mind concerning his personal duty. He advised against that concession, and did all he could to dissuade influential persons who were delegates to the Baltimore Convention, and who would there have insisted on the nomination of Mr. Wirt instead of Mr. Clay, from attending that body. To the suggestions that were made to him, that, if Mr. Wirt were chosen President, he could have any place in the Cabinet that he might desire, with the advantage of being the agreed candidate to succeed Mr. Wirt, or that he could now place himself in a position to command the support of the whole body of those who were opposed to General Jackson and his party, he gave no countenance. The following selections from his correspondence during the period that immediately preceded Mr. Clay's nomination fully explain his course in this respect:

[FROM MR. JOSEPH GALES.[1]]

"*March* 27, 1831.

"DEAR SIR: I have regretted, since writing you a few days ago, that I did so at all; and especially as, under the excitement of surprise, I may have considered Judge Spencer more committed to the scheme of his son than he is. I regret it the more since I see, by the account of the dinner, how you prize his political and personal character. I desire to state more precisely how far I suppose the matter to have proceeded. . . .

"Of all men (I can say in writing what I would not to your face) I should prefer you to any other for the presidency. I hope in God the time will come which will give to that station 'one Roman more.' At present Mr. Clay is so prominently before the public, and so identified with Western feeling (as you will find him), and, through you and other friends, so acceptable to the East, and so qualified by experience, and so allied,

[1] The senior editor of the *National Intelligencer*, and a person of great political consequence then and for a long period afterward.

and, as it were, endeared by late associations, that we must go for him if we go alone. I, for one, cannot bear the idea of any other being thought of by those who approve his politics; and, I believe, I cannot mistake in supposing your views to be the same, though only this day I have been told that the contrary is reported.

"Can nothing be done to save New York? Are there no high-minded men, who, like you, are not Masons, and who can say, we, too, are anti-masons, but we cannot sacrifice our country to our prejudice against a sect, not more *persecuting*, in the main, than any *religious* sect in the country? Being no Mason myself, and always considering its mummeries absurd, I may be believed when I give it this character. Let me beg of you to do what you can to heal this division among our friends. Could it be done, the day would be ours!

"Most respectfully, I am,

"Yours faithfully,

"JO. GALES, JR.

"P. S.—I would not copy the report of your speech by 'a stenographer,' which has come on in the *Daily Advertiser* and the *Commercial* of to-day. A speech of an hour and thirty-five minutes reported in the compass of a column! I admire your gallantry (and good conduct, too) in vindicating and eulogizing the fame and character of Hamilton. Few men at this day are magnanimous enough to dare it.[1]

[FROM JUDGE SPENCER.]

"NEAR ALBANY, *April* 19, 1831.

"MY DEAR SIR: You will recollect that I promised to write you, when I had the high gratification of seeing you in New York, and partaking of the dinner given to you for your patriotic and unrivalled efforts in defence of the Constitution; and I cannot omit saying that, on no former occasion during my life, have I been more honored or gratified. You will believe me when I say that my motives for attending that dinner were my high and sincere regard for you, and also to give my support to the doctrines you advanced, and which gave rise to the dinner. Little, indeed, did I expect, because I feel that I did not merit, the delicate but high compliment paid to me conjointly with Chancellor Kent; and I beg you to accept the unfeigned assurances of a most grateful heart that the impression is indelible.

"I did myself the pleasure of calling on Mrs. Webster the last week, and gave her some assurance that I should visit Boston during the season; and was pleased to learn that you and she contemplated a visit to this part of the State during the summer, and have her promise to see us.

"The result of the New-York charter election is auspicious, and will

[1] The allusion here is to the magnificent passage in the speech at the New-York dinner, in which Mr. Webster described the power of Hamilton over the national resources.—(See Works, i., 198, *et seq.*)

have great influence on our fall elections. Indeed, I perceive everywhere indications of returning sobriety and good sense on the part of the people, and am encouraged in the hope and belief that the public will appreciate justly the abominations of the present administration of the General Government.

"But, my dear sir, I am pained to tell you that, after several interviews with leading antimasons, if they are correctly informed, and I fear they are, the antimasons in this State will never support Mr. Clay. We know he cannot renounce his Masonic principles without ruin and dishonor, and they say that unless he does he cannot be nominated. Antimasonry is gaining rapidly in this State, and they feel conscious of their strength and importance. I think they will make nominations, in September, of candidates for President and Vice-President. Some of them, I have reason to believe, are favorable to me for the latter office; but I shall remain perfectly passive, being a Mason of the third degree, but not having attended a lodge in more than thirty years, but determined to remain, as I have been, perfectly neutral between the Masons and antimasons.

"If the tickets of electors are nominated in this State (the election being by general ticket, and determined by a plurality), I fear that Jackson electors would be chosen. Should that event appear probable, the only course to be pursued to prevent that result would be for the opponents of Jackson to vote for the antimasonic ticket. This would probably, and I think certainly, defeat the choice of Jackson electors, and bring the choice into the House. How it would be decided there, or whether any choice would take place, depends on the result of elections to be held this spring and summer. I merely give you some loose speculations founded on the present state of things.

"Having mentioned my own name to you, who were among the first to suggest the idea, I need scarcely say to you that I am incapable of playing any deceptive game, or acting at all with a view to my own election. I am as indifferent to the subject as any man can be; if I can be serviceable to the country, I am nothing loth to be so, but any office must come unsought by me.

"I heartily concur in the election of Mr. Clay, not that I think him the only fit, or even the fittest, man for the station of President (for he has erred in judgment on some very important points), but because he seems to be called for by the great mass of those opposed to Jackson; and union is essential to success. Lest I should be misunderstood in imputing to him *errors*, I do not mean his general principles of government, but those that are of a personal character, such as his acceptance of the office of Secretary of State under Mr. Adams, and his duel with Randolph, etc., etc.

"You will, I am sure, excuse me for thus trespassing on your time. In the hope and expectation of seeing you somewhere or somehow during the summer, believe me,

"Most sincerely yours,

"A. SPENCER."

[FROM COMMODORE STOCKTON.]

"PRINCETON, *August* 19, 1831.

"MY DEAR SIR: We have had recently but little communication on the subject of politics, and this letter may not perhaps be acceptable.

"The present posture of public affairs, however, tempts me to communicate to you some views which I, in common with many friends here and at the South, entertain. Mr. Calhoun's friends, I presume, no longer hope for his success; his last address to the public has, in my opinion, settled that matter. Mr. Clay cannot, in my poor opinion, succeed. The popularity of General Jackson is on the wane. If you can get back to your free-trade notions of 1824, and to the old Federal doctrine in relation to the judiciary, and to some point on the subject of internal improvement where the funds of the nation may be used safely for that purpose, without encouraging the system of 'log-rolling,' so dangerous to all honest legislation, your chance is good.

"Most truly,

"R. F. STOCKTON."

On the back of this letter is the following indorsement, in Mr. Webster's hand-writing:

"Answered August 25. Glad to receive his letter. As to getting back, difficulty is not in *my* position, but in that of the country. Country cannot go back—cannot bear violent change. Said at the time (1824) I would not vote to change back again.[1] As to judiciary, never altered my opinions, that it is in danger."

[FROM MR. GALES.]

"WASHINGTON, *October* 19, 1831.

"DEAR SIR: I do not know that I am able, in reply to your late favor, to afford you any encouraging information. The nomination of Mr. Wirt, as far as I can perceive, will produce no defection from the ranks of Mr. Clay's friends, but rather seems to have rallied them to his support. If the antimasons do not eventually also support him, they will have the honor of reëlecting General Jackson; for, as to yielding to the fanatical spirit of that party which excludes all non-conformists from public employ, from the jury-box, the witness-stand, and the communion-table, the thing is too revolting, if it were possible. But the fact is, that, if our convention were to yield every thing, it would accomplish nothing for the country. The strength of Mr. Clay is not transferable. You will find, in the end, that he has a strength in some States greater than the cause.

[1] This refers, of course, to the tariff. I have not been able to obtain from the representatives of Commodore Stockton Mr. Webster's full answer. But what it was in substance the reader can easily see, and can see how it must have expressed the *character* of this statesman, whose opinions were never varied to suit the exigencies of nominations, at any time in his whole career.

"If we have been *forbearing*, it is because we would not incur the reproach of sacrificing the cause to our own personal feelings. We have been deeply mortified at the course of Mr. R——, Mr. A——, Mr. Wirt (if, in fact, he be with them), and such persons as Mr. B—— and Mr. S——, who have sacrificed to their pride and supposed personal interest their principles and their friends. We are most unfortunate in finding in the front rank against us those who ought to have led our own forlorn hope. You may have heard before now that your own name was used as authority for the impossibility of electing Mr. Clay. Mr. B—— denied to me having used it; but it was used by somebody. —— is the father of the intrigue which procured the nomination of Mr. Wirt, which was literally made *de talis circumstantibus*, as Mr. Walsh says, with the hope of forcing the December Convention to take a candidate of their selection. If there be any mischief brewing in which he could have a hand, this promising young gentleman is always at the bottom of it. He is the serpent that tempted Mr. Wirt, whether he succeeded in seducing him or not, of which I am not yet certain. Poor Mr. R——!

"The worst that can befall us is that the antimasons will force the reëlection of General Jackson. This is bad enough, to be sure; but is it not better than to subject the nation to the rule of a frantic fanaticism, or of still more frantic Jacobinism, by the name of Nullification, even under the cloak of Free Trade? The General has a *decent* Cabinet at last (though I have no sympathy whatever even with them), and it may be hoped would not be allowed *further* to disgrace the country. We do not feel so confident of what would happen under an antimasonic or nullification dynasty, and would rather 'bear the ills we have than fly to others that we know not of.

"We hope yet for the best. The antimasonic party, I think, except in Vermont, is not on the increase; in some parts it is on the wane. If it can feel this, and especially if Mr. Wirt can feel it, there is yet a faint hope for our cause. But, if there be not, let us die with harness on our backs, having the consolation at least of the company of a noble army of martyrs.

"Upon these views, or any other, I shall be happy to have the advantage of your information and counsel. They are my own purely, made up in my daily rides between my cottage and my office.

"With true respect and the highest consideration, I am

"Yours faithfully,

"JO. GALES, JR.

"Hon. D. Webster."

[FROM JUDGE SPENCER.]

"ALBANY, *November* 24, 1831.

"MY DEAR SIR: I am very much obliged by your friendly letter of the 16th, and finding that we concur in opinion that, from my opinions, my attendance on the Baltimore Convention would not be advisable, I shall not attend.

"I hope I may be mistaken in believing that Mr. Clay's nomination ensures the reëlection of General Jackson. I cannot, even in deference to you, renounce the belief that, were Mr. Clay to decline, and should Mr. Wirt be nominated at Baltimore, he would probably be elected. I can easily conceive that some of our friends may now declare their preference of Jackson over Mr. Wirt, yet I do not believe, unless they are insane, they would execute their threats.

"I feel anxious not to be misunderstood in recommending the course I have, and I believe you do me justice. It appeared to me that the first and greatest object was to defeat the reëlection of General Jackson, and that our proceedings were to be subservient to that end. I believed, and yet believe, that every well-informed man must be sensible that Mr. Clay cannot be elected, because, in his support, the votes of the great body of General Jackson's opposers cannot be united, for various causes, but principally from the prevalence of antimasonry in this and several other States. I may labor under false impressions as to some of the States, but I think I know something of this State, and here I know he cannot get the electoral vote.

"I did not think Mr. Clay's friends so irrational as to persevere in nominating him, when his defeat and consequent depression were so apparent.

"I could not perceive any reasonable objection to Mr. Wirt or his principles. Indeed, I thought that his nomination was a providential act to save the nation from further dishonor and injury, and that all men who detested Jackson and his administration would cheerfully unite in his support.

"I do not understand it to be the antimasonic creed, 'that antimasonry alone is a principle broad enough to save the country and maintain the Government.' Their creed is that the practical evils of Masonry, as illustrated in New York, are of such an alarming nature, and so vitally concern all good government, that it must be put down by public opinion. They think, and certainly with a show of reason, that this can be done in no other way than through the ballot-boxes. Mr. Wirt expressly disclaims every thing like persecution, or making Masonry or antimasonry a test for office. In short, as I understand the matter, he has done all that they ever expect of him; he has borne his testimony to the supremacy of the laws and the free course of justice.

"It is undoubtedly true, as you suggest, that, even in New York, the high Masons will not support Mr. Wirt, and would not under any circumstances; this we disregard, because their defection would be more than compensated by antimasons from the Jackson ranks.

"I hope a part at least of New England will be found, a year hence, sound in Mr. Clay's support, but I confess your recent election, especially after Governor Lincoln's satisfactory letter, gives demonstration somewhat alarming as regards your own State.

"It is our duty to offer up earnest supplications 'for long life to all good men in office.' Bad men, however, have a remarkable tenacity of life, and I fear they will live long enough, not, indeed, absolutely to ruin the country, but to bring on disorders and confusion, to put us back, God only knows how long. We may live to see the Bank of the United States put down and the judiciary destroyed. We now see, and feel, too, the many evils already pressing on us by the misrule of this corrupt, mean, and wicked Administration.

"I have one consolation: I have done all I could to avert these evils.

"I may avail myself of your kind invitation to write you, and I certainly will if I can say aught useful or interesting.

"With high respect and regard,

"Your obedient servant,

"A. SPENCER.

"Hon. Daniel Webster."

The National Republican Convention, which assembled at Baltimore, nominated Mr. Clay for the Presidency, with great unanimity and enthusiasm, and placed the name of John Sargeant, of Pennsylvania, on the same ticket for the Vice-Presidency. I am indebted to one of the members of that body, the Hon. Hiram Ketchum, of New York, an intimate and much-loved friend of Mr. Webster, for the following statements:

"I have no letters from Mr. Webster in respect to Mr. Clay's nomination for the Presidency in 1831, but, previous to that nomination, I had very full and free conversations with him in respect to it. He did not favor the nomination of Mr. Clay, and I know that he desired the nomination for himself. I then, as in all subsequent time, was in favor of Mr. Webster's nomination; but National Republican friends here, with whom I acted, overruled my preference, and I was compelled to say so to Mr. Webster himself. He acquiesced, and the Convention, of which I was a member, unanimously, by open nomination, every man rising in his place and naming his candidate, put Mr. Clay in nomination for President, and John Sargeant for Vice-President. During the session of the Convention Mr. Webster passed through Baltimore, on his way to Washington, and visited one of its sessions. After the convention had finished its work, quite a large number of its members, I among them, went to Washington. Mr. Webster and Mr. Nathan Appleton, then a member of the House of Representatives from Massachusetts, invited us to meet Mr. Clay at dinner. Several distinguished persons were present; among them, the late Alexander H. Everett, Governor Bradish, Senator Johnson, of Louisiana, etc. I think there was very little confidence in the success of our ticket, yet I went into the canvass with all the ardor of youth. Mr. A. H. Everett, on that visit, dined with Mr. John Quincy Adams, who made no allusion to the work of the Convention."

The session of Congress which followed this nomination of Mr. Clay for the Presidency was not an eventful one. The only subject in reference to which Mr. Webster made any considerable exertion was that of a bill for the relief of insolvent debtors of the United States, introduced and carried through the House by Mr. Buchanan; to whose zealous devotion to this object, and his successful lead in its accomplishment, Mr. Webster paid a high compliment in the Senate. After the termination of the session, the following correspondence took place between them in reference to the bill, which had become a law:

[FROM MR. BUCHANAN.]

"LANCASTER, *September* 13, 1831.

"DEAR SIR: I enclose you the copy of a letter which I have addressed to the Secretary of the Treasury, because I have taken the liberty of using your name in it. If you consider the reference incorrect, it will afford me pleasure to correct it immediately. In looking over your remarks on the bill for the relief of insolvent debtors, I was forcibly struck with the liberal and kind expressions which you used in relation to my exertions in the House. Rest assured that they are duly appreciated by me, and that I consider it 'praise, indeed, to be praised by you.'

"Should your recollection correspond with mine in relation to this bill, if you thought proper to interpose, a word from you would have a powerful effect in correcting the error into which the Attorney-General and Secretary of the Treasury have fallen.

"Please to present my respectful compliments to Mrs. Webster, and believe me to be truly yours,

"JAMES BUCHANAN.

"Hon. Daniel Webster."

[TO MR. BUCHANAN.]

"BOSTON, *September* 24, 1831.

"MY DEAR SIR: I have the honor to acknowledge the receipt of your letter of the 18th instant, enclosing the copy of one from yourself to the Secretary of the Treasury, relative to the construction of the act of the last session for the relief of certain insolvents. Your communication furnished me with the first information of the construction, proposed to be put on that act, at the departments. I confess I am quite surprised by it. No such construction ever occurred to me as being possible, nor was ever suggested, to my knowledge, by any one. The language of the act appears to me to be, as it was intended it should be, general, and unambiguous. I must acknowledge I can see no ground, upon which its application can be restricted in the manner proposed, which I am quite sure would be, as you say, quite at war with the intentions of every one of those who concurred in the law.

"With the most unfeigned respect for the opinions of the Attorney-General, I cannot persuade myself to think that he has taken the right view of the provisions of the act. If he has done so, we were very clumsy law-makers.

"I am, dear sir, with regard,
"Your obedient servant,
"DANIEL WEBSTER."

[TO MR. BUCHANAN.]

"BOSTON, *September* 24, 1831.

"DEAR SIR: The decision at the Treasury, on our (or more properly on *your*) act of the last session, astonished me. I had never dreamed of any such thing. If you think the enclosed expression of opinon will do any good, you are at liberty to communicate it.

"I thank you for your kind and friendly expressions; and, as I did you no more than justice, in regard to your agency in the passing of the Insolvents' Relief Bill, I trust I shall on no occasion do you less. I would express the hope of seeing you at Washington, in the winter, if it were not that such an expression might imply an expectation that you are not to be elsewhere at that time. Not knowing at all how that may be, I must confine myself to the tender of general good wishes, and to the assurances of esteem and regard.

"D. W."

The following letters relate to the purchase of his father's farm; to the fragment of his autobiography which he wrote this year; to the strong interest which he took in the removal of Mr. Jeremiah Mason to Boston, and to the marriage of his brother-in-law, Mr. Paige.

[TO HIS NEPHEW, MR. C. B. HADDOCK.]

"WASHINGTON, *February* 6, 1831.

"MY DEAR NEPHEW: I heard from you at the early part of the session, and have omitted to answer longer than I intended. I was at Salisbury after I saw you, and gave directions about the farm. I think it best to put an end to separate interests there as soon as convenient. I suppose you have by this time obtained your license to sell. My hope and expectation now are to be in Boston the first day of April; perhaps a little earlier. If you could arrange the sale for about the middle or 20th of April, I could conveniently attend it, as I propose to visit Salisbury in that month. In

May and June I doubt whether it will be in my power. If events come about according to my wishes, I hope to run away to Ohio about the 1st of May.

"Partly on my own motion, and partly at the request of friends, I have been putting into writing something of my early history, dates, incidents, etc., touching early years. I have not made much progress, nor is there, indeed, much to be said, but I have run over a few sheets of paper. It has occurred to me, in connection with this subject, to suggest to you the expediency, as of your own motion, of writing to Rev. Dr. Wood, of Boscawen, who, I hope, is yet living. He may have few or no incidents to relate, but his general recollection may possibly be worth preserving. I need not enlarge; you will understand me. It may be well to tell him that the object is to preserve materials, not to be used in his lifetime or mine. I wish he would say something of my brother, whom he knew so well and so long.

"The book,[1] I have seen. It is well enough, except the awful face, which seems to be placed in the front of the volume, like a scarecrow in a cornfield, to frighten off all intruders.

"Pray, let me hear from you, and tell me all you have to say, *de omnibus rebus*. We have a most severe winter here; this is as frosty a morning as might become the neighborhood of Kearsarge. Mrs. Webster desires her regards, and I am

"Dear Charles, always truly yours,

"DANIEL WEBSTER."

[TO MR. MASON.]

"NEW YORK, *April* 26, 1831.

"MY DEAR SIR: I came here Saturday, to bring my wife back to Boston, after spending a few days here with her friends. Having leisure this P. M., I incline to give it to the purpose of writing to you; but I am not about to speak on the subject of the resignation of our wise ministry at Washington, or any other public subject. It is to talk of yourself. Before I left home last fall, I had resolved to make one more effort to bring you up to Boston. For particular reasons then existing, I was induced to postpone the mentioning of the subject. I write now simply to execute that intention; and to entreat you, earnestly, to consider the expediency of such a measure. I will not presume to enter into the considerations which recommend it, at least in my opinion; but I will say that my opinion is strong and decisive on the point. I am persuaded a removal will add to your happiness, and that of your family. You will find as much professional employment as you may wish to engage in; and you will find yourself surrounded by warm friends, who estimate you as you deserve to be estimated. Your boys are now provided for. Your daughters are better

[1] A volume of Mr. Webster's speeches.

at Boston than Portsmouth; at Boston, you will find associations, topics, congenial minds, and objects of greater interest than now surround you. New York, perhaps, might be still better. But Boston is something.

"I am persuaded you dislike the idea of removal, and that that is the main obstacle. But that is a thing of a week. Once settled, and all that thing is over.

"My dear sir, although it would add greatly to my happiness that you should come to Boston, I would not advise it, certainly, if I did not think it would promote yours, and promote it greatly. Indeed, I reproach myself for not having urged this point with you oftener. I wish to do it now with earnestness; I am sure I do it with sincerity.

"Ever truly and affectionately your friend,

"DANIEL WEBSTER."

[TO MRS. A. P. WEBSTER.[1]]

"BOSTON, *June* 14, 1831.

"MY DEAR SISTER: Your letter has come to hand quite apropos. It is our intention to set off on Thursday morning for Boscawen, by way of Nashua village. Weather being favorable, we may be expected Thursday afternoon at Nashua, and shall be happy to have you go north with us. I am under the necessity of being at Concord at noon on Friday, so that I shall be obliged to put you to the distress of an early rising on that day. In addition to Mrs. Webster, Julia will come along. Edward begins to beg hard to go, and, as his mother is on his side, he also may prevail. We shall have room for you. This is a great day with us, as Mr. Paige is to be married this evening.

"The dawn is overcast, etc."

"The happy pair set out to-morrow or next day for the Springs, the Falls, and other points of the grand tour.

"Give my best regards to Mrs. Abbott.

"Yours always affectionately,

"D. WEBSTER.

"P. S.—Julia wrote you yesterday, so that, probably, your household will learn our intentions, that is to say, provided you have left a secretary to attend to your correspondence."

In the course of this year, Mr. Walsh, the editor of the *Philadelphia Quarterly Review*, desired to have an article reviewing Mr. Webster's recently published speeches. It was written for him, at the request of Judge Story, by Mr. Ticknor, and appeared in his eighteenth number. It was subsequently

[1] Then at Nashua.

reprinted, and largely circulated in pamphlet. The following correspondence relates to the article and the reprint:

[TO MR. TICKNOR.]

"Saturday Morning.

"DEAR SIR: I received a copy of the *Quarterly*, but, before I had read the article, lent it to Mr. Dutton. He has returned it with this note. Yesterday, I went carefully through the article. It is all that I could possibly desire. There is nothing that need be changed. If it should be printed separately, *room* would be more at command, and there are possibly one or two points which might be a little more expanded. I have made some attempt to see you; which I shall renew so soon as the 'all-conquering sun shall intermit his wrath.' I hope you are alive to-day.

"Yours,

"D. W."

[TO MR. TICKNOR.]

"Thursday Morning.

"DEAR SIR: I believe things will be put in train for a reprint, and, as you have leisure, will beg of you to think of the expediency of expanding two topics a little more.

"1. The nullification topic, about which we have conversed.

"2. The finance topic, with a pretty cogent page or two, in favor of maintaining the national bank.

"In mustering over some old papers the other day, I found a *speech*, on the subject of the present bank. I did not stop to read it, and, like everybody else, had quite forgotten it. It may contain something. I will send it to you on my return.

"We are off at nine o'clock for Boscawen.

"Yours truly,

"D. WEBSTER.

"Mr. Ticknor."

[TO MR. TICKNOR.]

1831.

"MY DEAR SIR: I have had time to add but very little to the sheets you have already had, and no time to read over any thing. But I will endeavor between this and nine o'clock this P. M. to bring the important narrative down to 1816.[1]

"Yours,

"D. WEBSTER.

[1] The autobiography, which was, from its first inception, in the possession of Mr. Ticknor, to whom it was entrusted sheet by sheet, as it was written.

"N. B.—I have seen no such Congress for talents as the fourteenth. It commenced its first session December, '15, and terminated its second March, '17. If you run over the Journal, you will see that the House of Representatives was particularly strong.

"I do not know whether there is any thing of mine, Congressional, earlier than my return to Congress in 1823, of interest, beyond what you have.

"I had a hand, with Mr. Eppes and others, in overthrowing Mr. Monroe's *conscription*, 1814, and [there is] a long speech on that subject, in manuscript.[1] But I do not think it worth while to notice it.

"So of my resolutions in 1813. They were right—our Government was completely cajoled by France, but whether it is worth while to allude to that now, I know not, but I doubt whether it is. I will be at home this evening, if you want to *talk*, and will send me word.

"D. W."

[1] The speech is now lost.

CHAPTER XVIII.

1831-1832.

MODIFICATION OF THE TARIFF—BILL TO RENEW THE CHARTER OF THE BANK—PRESIDENT JACKSON'S "VETO"—SPEECH ON THE PRESIDENT'S OBJECTIONS—REJECTION OF MR. VAN BUREN AS MINISTER TO ENGLAND—REPORT ON THE APPORTIONMENT OF REPRESENTATIVES—FIRST PURCHASE AT MARSHFIELD.

THE session of Congress which commenced in December, 1831, and extended to July, 1832, was fruitful in events and in discussions that were to affect the country for a long period of time. It was at this session that an effort was made to overthrow the tariff system; that the bill to renew the charter of the Bank of the United States was passed by Congress and "vetoed" by the President; and that the Senate refused to confirm the nomination of Mr. Van Buren as Minister to Great Britain.

The tariff system under which the manufactures of the country had been carried on since 1824 had established the general principle of protection as a settled policy. On this ground, and because the legislation of Congress had strongly tended to force capital into manufactures, Mr. Webster supported the system. He was unwilling to go back, because he was satisfied that the industrial pursuits of the country could not bear the change. In the winter of 1831-'32, the subject was first introduced into the Senate by Mr. Clay, who offered a resolution, declaring that the duties on imported articles, which did not come into competition with similar articles made or produced in the United

States, ought to be forthwith abolished, except the duties on wines and silks, and that these ought to be reduced. He proposed that the Committee of Finance be instructed to report a bill accordingly.

Mr. Clay was led to this step toward the abolition and reduction of certain classes of duties by the fact that the public debt was nearly extinguished, and that the Government would no longer need such a revenue as it was now receiving. But he meant to take the step without abandoning the principle of protection. Accordingly, in the elaborate speech which he delivered in support of his resolution, he declared, repeatedly and emphatically, that this principle was not to be surrendered, either by a sudden or a gradual abolition of the duties on the protected articles. A long and occasionally angry discussion ensued—a gathering of the clouds that portended the coming storm. The political party which, in general, supported the Administration of General Jackson, and which intended to reëlect him to the Presidency, was then divided into two sections, in the Senate, on the subject of a protective tariff. One of these sections adhered to the protective system; the other was bitterly hostile to it. The latter was led by Mr. Hayne, of South Carolina, who, in answering Mr. Clay, reopened the whole subject, attacking both the policy and the constitutional right of protection, and throwing out many intimations of the dangers that threatened the Union if the protective system should be retained. He did not, however, again directly introduce the doctrines of nullification.

As the discussion proceeded, the subject became complicated with that of the proceeds of the sales of the public lands, and with the question, to what committee Mr. Clay's resolution should be sent. At length, with many other propositions, the whole subject was referred to the Committee on Manufactures. Mr. Dickerson, of New Jersey, chairman of that committee, reported a bill to reduce the duties on certain articles which were not in competition with articles manufactured in this country, and reserving the other subjects for a further report. This was assailed by the antiprotection party as a virtual indorsement of Mr. Clay's plan, and a confirmation of the protective system. Another long and exciting discussion followed, and, on the suggestion of constitutional doubts whether a bill for reducing duties could originate in the Senate, the bill, on the 30th of March, 1832, was laid upon the table, to await the action of the House of Representatives.

A bill from the House afterward came into the Senate, which made considerable changes in the existing duties. In the Senate it was amended, and on these amendments the two houses disagreed; but the result of a conference was that the bill was finally passed, the Senate receding from its amendments. It reduced the duties to what might be called a revenue standard, on many articles, leaving woollen and cotton goods and iron as they previously stood. It was, therefore, denounced by Mr. Hayne as an adherence to the protective system, which, he said, it recognized as the settled policy of the country. It was, he asserted, "neither more nor less than the resolution of the Senator from Kentucky reduced to the form of a law." He concluded with the declaration that "the hopes of the South are at an end, and, as far as their prosperity is dependent on Federal legislation, their ruin is sealed."

In all this discussion Mr. Webster took no other part than to intervene occasionally for the proper adjustment of particular duties, and to express his disapprobation of the manner in which the conference committee of the Senate had receded from an amendment raising the existing duties on woollens. He was, in truth, watching this discussion with great but almost silent anxiety, as he well knew it to be the forerunner of events in the South that he had long anticipated as possible, and because the relations to this subject of many of the supporters of the Administration were to have a serious effect on the future peace of the country. Mr. Calhoun occupied the chair of the Senate as Vice-President. Upon some remark by Mr. Clay concerning his opinions, in the course of this debate, he broke the silence of the Chair so far as to say that he held the protective system to be unconstitutional. He had already put forth a pamphlet, which contained a labored defence of nullification, which Mr. Webster regarded as "far the ablest and most plausible, and therefore the most dangerous, vindication of that particular form of revolution which has yet appeared."[1] Mr. Calhoun had

[1] Correspondence, i., 526.

been elected Vice-President by the same conglomerate party that had elected General Jackson to the presidency; and what the effect of an attempt at nullification of the tariff might be upon that party, and upon the course of the Administration, was at this moment entirely problematical. To enter, therefore, at this time, upon a labored defence of the principle of protection, and the constitutional right of Congress to enforce it, appeared to Mr. Webster both superfluous and inexpedient. He was himself in no degree responsible for its original introduction into the policy of the country; and now that there were a considerable number of the leading friends of the Administration in Congress determined to continue it—a number sufficiently large, when added to the votes of the opposition, to uphold it as the decisive determination of Congress—he considered it to be rather his duty to forecast the measures by which the authority of Congress was to be upheld against the threatened nullification, and by which the President and his supporters should be induced and enabled to encounter that resistance.

But there were other discussions and measures of this session in respect to which Mr. Webster felt obliged to take a part that necessarily prevented any close political sympathy, at this time, between him and the President, or the President's party, which might otherwise have sprung out of Mr. Webster's refutation, in 1830, of the doctrines of nullification. He was not only acting with the opposition, which had nominated Mr. Clay for the presidency, but, at the very beginning of that long warfare respecting the Bank of the United States, which was now about to enter so largely into the politics and the legislation of the country, his convictions respecting the utility and necessity of such an institution led him to support the application of the existing bank for a renewal of its charter, and, consequently, to encounter the hostility which General Jackson directed against it.

It is quite unnecessary, to any elucidation of Mr. Webster's course on this subject, to inquire who was responsible for the original antagonism between President Jackson and the bank. On the one side, it was charged that the Administration had been foiled in an attempt improperly to control the election of a local board of directors of one of the branches of the bank for electioneering purposes. On the other side, it was said that the managers of the bank had entered the field of politics for the purpose of using it as an instrument to defeat the reëlection of General Jackson, and that its application for a renewal of its charter at the present session of Congress, more than three years before its charter would expire, was designed to embarrass the Administration with a question on which its friends would be divided, and to throw that question into the excitements of the presidential election in such a manner as to make it operate in favor of the prospects of Mr. Clay. Into these personal controversies Mr. Webster did not choose to enter. I have discovered no evidence, either in public or private sources, that he advised an application for the renewal of the bank charter at the present session; but he was undoubtedly of opinion that, if the bank was not to be continued, the period was not a day too long to enable it to wind up concerns of such vast magnitude, affecting the interests and business of the whole country. He told the Senate that he desired to have the question treated as a great public subject; to have it considered as statesmen should consider it, and with as little mixture as possible of all minor motives. He reminded them of the fact that, two years and a half previously, the President of the United States had called the attention of Congress to the subject of the continuance of the bank; that this invitation had been more than once repeated; that the subject had been everywhere discussed, and that the public interest now demanded a decision upon it.

The truth in respect to the course of President Jackson on this subject is that, when the bill for continuing the charter of the bank was brought into Congress at this session, it was not known that he entertained opinions hostile to the constitutional power of Congress to create such an institution. If he had such opinions, they were not known to his own political friends in Congress any more than they were to his opponents; and there was, therefore, no reason, on this or other grounds, to anticipate that the bill would not meet his official approval. Accordingly, Mr. Webster, in the first speech which he made on this subject, on the 25th of May (1832), entered into no direct argument on the point of constitutional power, but confined himself almost wholly to the expediency of renewing the charter. He did, however, express an opinion on the power of the States to create banks of issue, which had an important bearing on the duty of Congress to regulate and control the paper currency of the country, by maintaining a bank capable of having this effect. As an original question, unaffected by the practice of forty years, he considered it very doubtful whether the States had any constitutional authority to authorize the circulation of bank paper. The Constitution having conferred upon Congress exclusive power to provide and regulate the metallic currency, it was, in Mr. Webster's view, necessary to regard this power as including that of deciding how far any other currency should take its place, or act as its substitute, and what the substitute was to be. Congress can only do this through the agency of a bank established by its authority. Beyond the statement of this position, and its appropriate illustrations, he did not enlarge upon any of the constitutional aspects of the subject, but confined his argument to the necessity and usefulness of the bank, treating the question as purely one of public, national, and universal interest, and making no allusion whatever to any of the party topics connected, or supposed to be connected, with it. The speech is contained at length in the third volume of his works, and is very important.

Able and instructive as it was, on all the financial and prudential questions embraced in the question of continuing the bank, it was followed, in a few days, by another speech, which contained some very profound and searching views respecting the power of Congress to confer on the States authority to tax a franchise created by Congress in the exercise of its constitutional powers. This topic came into consideration in consequence of an amendment of the charter of the bank, offered by Mr. Moore, of Alabama, to authorize the States to tax the offices and branches of the bank, according to the amount of their loans and issues, as other banks or other property are liable to taxation. It will be remembered that the Supreme Court of the United States had decided, in reference to the existing charter, that the States could not tax the bank or its branches; and it was now proposed that this power should be expressly given to the States. Mr. Webster resisted this proposition, not only because it would enable the States to drive the bank out of their limits, but because he did not admit that Congress has the power to confer upon a State authority to tax a franchise created by Congress for national purposes. His argument on this subject, condensed into a single sentence, rested upon the position that the restraint against taxing a national franchise is imposed upon the States by the *Constitution*, and not by any *law* which Congress may enact; that, as the restraint does not originate with Congress, but with a higher authority, viz., the Constitution, Congress cannot dispense with or remove it. On this point he expressed himself with great earnestness, and he succeeded in preventing the adoption of the amendment.[1]

The bill to continue the charter of the bank passed both Houses of Congress by decisive majorities,[2] and was sent to the President. He returned it without his signature, and with a message assigning his reasons for not approving it. This "veto" message for the first time made known to the country that General Jackson held the bank to be unconstitutional; and that he held himself at liberty to act upon this opinion, against the whole current of congressional legislation on the subject, and against an express decision of the Supreme Court of the United States. It opened a chasm between the Presi-

[1] This very striking argument appears to have arrested the attention of Chief-Justice Marshall, who, in acknowledgment of the receipt of Mr. Webster's speeches on the bank, wrote as follows:

[FROM CHIEF-JUSTICE MARSHALL.]

"RICHMOND, *June* 6, 1832.

"MY DEAR SIR: I thank you very sincerely for the copy, with which you favored me, of your speeches on the bill for renewing the charter of the Bank of the United States. I need not say that I consider an accommodation of the tariff question itself as scarcely more interesting to the country than the passage of that bill. Your argument presents the subject in its strongest point of view, and to me seems unanswerable. Mr. Ritchie, in his *Inquirer*, informs the people of Virginia that Mr. Tazewell has refuted you completely. This he may have done, in the opinion of Mr. Ritchie. I have not seen Mr. Tazewell's speech, and do not understand from the *Inquirer* whether his refutation applies to your speech in favor of the bill, or to that against the amendment offered by Mr. Moore. By the way, your argument against that amendment is founded in an idea which to me is quite novel. I had often heard it advanced that the States have no constitutional power to establish banks of circulation, but never that Congress might not introduce into the charter a restraining principle, which might prohibit branches altogether, or require the assent of a State to their introduction, or a principle which might subject them to State taxation. This may be considered not as granting power of taxation to a State, for a State possesses that power, but as withdrawing a bar which the Constitution opposes to the exercise of this power over a franchise created by Congress for national purposes, unless the constitution of the franchise in its creation has this quality engrafted on it. I, however, am far from undertaking to dissent from your proposition; I only say it is new, and I ponder on it.

"With great and respectful esteem, I am your obedient servant,

"J. MARSHALL.

"P. S.—I only meant to express my obligation for your attention, and I have betrayed myself into the politics of the day."

[2] The vote in the Senate stood 28 to 20. "We are all aware of what we owe to the admirable pilotage which carried us through the Senate."—(General T. Cadwallader to Mr. Webster, July 7, 1832. MS.)

dent and Mr. Webster which could never be filled or passed; for the doctrines of the message were diametrically opposite to all the views respecting the powers of Congress, and respecting the office of the Supreme Court as the interpreter of the Constitution, which Mr. Webster had held from his first entrance into public life, and which were as inseparable from his public character as they were thoroughly incorporated into all his intellectual habits. As he had taken the leading part in conducting the bill through the Senate, it appeared to devolve on him to examine the grounds of the veto message. There was little probability that the bill could obtain the requisite constitutional vote of two-thirds of the members of each House, in order to make it a law notwithstanding the objections of the President. But the doctrines of the message could not be passed by in silence.

The speech which Mr. Webster delivered on these doctrines, upon the 11th of July (1832), was grave, and as courteous toward the President as could be demanded, but it was exceedingly plain and emphatic. It was not answered then, nor has it ever been answered since. The position taken by the President, that every official, who takes an oath to support the Constitution, swears to support it "as he understands it," and that, if he understands it differently from the construction that has been given to it by the Supreme Court of the United States, he is at liberty, in his official action, to follow out his own convictions,[1] was, it is right to say, refuted by Mr. Webster. It has never commended itself to the sound judgment of the most enlightened portion of the nation, of any party; and, although it has been occasionally reasserted by public men, in justification of particular acts, it has never been successfully defended. In the excitement of the time, the party that followed General Jack-

[1] The following is the position of President Jackson's celebrated "veto" message: "Each public officer, who takes an oath to support the Constitution, swears to support it as he understands it, and not as it is understood by others. It is as much the duty of the House of Representatives, of the Senate, and of the President, to decide upon the constitutionality of any bill or resolution which may be presented to them for passage or approval, as it is of the supreme judges, when it may be brought before them for judicial decision. The opinion of the judges has no more authority over Congress than the opinion of Congress has over the judges; and on that point the President is independent of both. The authority of the Supreme Court must not, therefore, be permitted to control the Congress, or the Executive, when acting in their legislative capacities, but to have only such influence as the force of their reasoning may deserve."

son yielded their assent to this doctrine, because it was advanced *by him;* but it did not become a permanent dogma in their political creed, and it will never attain that rank in the opinions of any party that means to give a just effect and operation to the provisions of the Constitution.

In order to a correct understanding of the grounds of Mr. Webster's denial of the President's position, it is proper to explain the precise situation to which the President applied the claim of the Executive to judge of the constitutional validity of laws presented for his approval. The existing charter of the bank had been pronounced by the Supreme Court to be a valid law, duly enacted under the Constitution. It was, therefore, a statute, in force as the law of the land, when a bill was sent to the President to continue it for a further term of years beyond its existing limitation. The President refused to sign this bill, upon the ground that the original charter was unconstitutional. A large part of the message was taken up with an argument to refute the decision of the Supreme Court affirming the constitutional validity of a law now in operation. The claim of the President thus came to be, that the Executive, when called upon in his legislative capacity to sign a bill continuing a law that has been pronounced constitutional by the Supreme Court, is at liberty to deny that it is, or was, a valid law, and *therefore* ought not to be continued. Taken in connection with the language of the message, and its broad position respecting the meaning of the oath to support the Constitution, this doctrine was regarded by Mr. Webster as disorganizing and revolutionary; for it could be extended to the execution of laws, just as readily as to their reënactment or continuance, and would leave every public officer to judge what laws he would carry into effect.

Mr. Webster never denied that the President, when called upon to decide whether a law is *to be* enacted, may apply his own judgment to the question whether it is within the scope of the Constitution, although all other branches of the Government have repeatedly decided that similar laws are constitutional. He did, indeed, always hold that decisions of the Supreme Court have a greater force, in concluding questions of constitutional power, than is accorded to them by simply weighing their reasoning. In his view, the Supreme Court was created for the express purpose of acting as the official interpreter of the Constitution; yet he did not deny that, when a law is proposed to be enacted, all who are to perform a part in that enactment must judge of its constitutional validity, for the purpose of governing their legislative action. But this was not the limit to which the President confined himself. He claimed the right to say that an existing law, pronounced constitutionally valid by the Supreme Court, was constitutionally invalid, and for this reason to refuse to sign a bill continuing it in force. He, or the writer of the message, failed to see that there is a clear distinction between such a case and a case where the President is called upon, in his legislative capacity, not to continue a law that has been expressly pronounced constitutional by the Supreme Court, but to act upon a law on the same subject that has not itself been submitted to the adjudication of that tribunal. Overlooking this distinction, the message took an extreme and untenable ground, which makes the official oath to support the Constitution nothing but a declaration that it is to be supported as the person taking the oath understands it, in respect both to laws that have been enacted and have been directly adjudicated as constitutional by the Supreme Court, and in respect to laws that are to be enacted and have not been subjected to that judicial revision.

Such, in substance, was the commencement of the famous controversy between President Jackson and the Bank of the United States—a controversy that was destined to agitate the country for many years. Mr. Webster's early relation to it was limited to what I have now described. From convictions of public duty, he carried the bill, to recharter the bank, through the Senate. From convictions of what he owed to the Constitution and its just interpretation, he resisted the doctrines of the "veto" message. Time has made all that was personal or merely political in these controversies of very little importance. But it has not seen the powers of Congress to create banking institutions, as those powers were maintained by Mr. Webster, finally abandoned or renounced by the nation; nor has it seen a national sanction given to the doctrine that the constitutional decisions of the Supreme Court of the United States are not binding upon the other departments of the Government, in respect to the matters which they decide.

On the 20th of July, 1829, Mr. Van Buren, Secretary of State in General Jackson's first Cabinet, gave instructions to Mr. McLane, then going to the court of England as minister of the United States, on the subject of colonial trade. By the convention of 1815, reciprocity of intercourse was established between the United States and Great Britain, but this arrangement was not extended to the British West Indies. The result was the passage of various discriminating and retaliatory acts on both sides. At length, in 1825, the English Parliament passed an act, offering reciprocity in the West India trade, so far as the mere carrying-trade was concerned, to all nations that might accept the offer within one year. The Administration of Mr. John Quincy Adams did not avail itself of this offer, preferring to accomplish by treaty the free admission of our *products* into the British islands for consumption, and not regarding the admission of our *vessels* as an object that ought to be severed from that of our productions. This purpose had not been accomplished when Mr. Adams went out of office, and the direct trade between the United States and the British West Indies remained closed in consequence of the mutually retaliatory legislation. Mr. McLane was instructed by Mr. Van Buren to reopen this subject, and in these instructions the Secretary said:

"The opportunities which you have derived from a participation in our public counsels, as well as other sources of information, will enable you to speak with confidence (as far as you may deem it proper and useful so to do) of the respective parts taken by those to whom the administration of this Government is *now* committed, in relation to the course heretofore pursued upon the subject of the colonial trade. Their views upon that point have been submitted to the people of the United States, and the counsels by which your conduct is now directed are the result of the judgment expressed by the only earthly tribunal to which the late Administration was amenable for its acts. It should be sufficient that the claims set up by them, and which caused the interruption of the trade in question, have been explicitly abandoned by those who first asserted them, and are not revived by their successors. If Great Britain deems it adverse to her interests to allow us to participate in the trade with her colonies, and finds nothing in the extension of it to others to induce her to apply the same rule to us, she will, we hope, be sensible of the propriety of placing her refusal on those grounds. To set up the acts of the late Administrations as the cause of forfeiture of privileges which would otherwise be extended to the people of the United States, would, under existing circumstances, be unjust in itself, and could not fail to excite their deepest sensibility. The tone of feeling which a course so unwise and so untenable is calculated to produce would, doubtless, be greatly aggravated by the consciousness that Great Britain has, by order in council, opened her colonial ports to Russia and France, notwithstanding a similar omission on their part to accept the terms offered by the act of July, 1825. You cannot press this view of the subject too earnestly upon the consideration of the British ministry. It has bearings and relations which reach beyond the immediate question under discussion.

"I will add nothing as to the impropriety of suffering any feelings, that find their origin in the past pretensions of this Government, to have an adverse influence upon the present conduct of Great Britain."

On the dissolution of General Jackson's first Cabinet, Mr. Van Buren was appointed by the President as minister to Great Britain. He had gone abroad, and been accredited by the government to which he was sent, before his nomination could be acted upon by the Senate. The instructions which he had given to Mr. McLane were regarded by the whole opposition as an appeal to the favor of the British Government, grounded upon reflections on the past conduct of the preceding Administration in a matter of foreign intercourse, and conveying intimations that those *now* in power in this country did not intend to assert pretensions which had by their assertion deprived us of privileges accorded to other nations. For these reasons, Mr. Van Buren's nomination was rejected by the Senate. The part taken by Mr. Webster in this rejection may be fully understood by examining his remarks explanatory of the vote he intended to give.[1] He placed that vote entirely upon the party tone and character which he found in the instructions given by Mr. Van Buren, as Secretary of State, to Mr. McLane, in reference to a claim advanced by our Government in diplomatic intercourse. Speaking of Mr. Van Buren's letter, he said:

[1] Works, iii., 357, *et seq.*

"Sir, I submit to you, and to the candor of all just men, if I am not right in saying that the pervading topic through the whole is, not American rights, not American interests, not American defence, but denunciation of past pretensions of our Government, reflections on the past Administration, and exultation and a loud claim of merit for the Administration now in power. Sir, I would forgive mistakes; I would pardon the want of information; I would pardon almost any thing where I saw true patriotism and sound American feeling; but I cannot forgive the sacrifice of this feeling to mere party. I cannot concur in sending abroad a public agent who has not conceptions so large and liberal as to feel that, in the presence of foreign courts, amidst the monarchies of Europe, he is to stand up for his country, and his whole country; that no jot nor tittle of her honor is to suffer in his hands; that he is not to allow others to reproach either his Government or his country, and far less is he himself to reproach either; that he is to have no objects in his eye but American objects, and no heart in his bosom but an American heart; and that he is to forget self, and forget party, to forget every sinister and narrow feeling, in his proud and lofty attachment to the republic whose commission he bears.

"Mr. President, I have discharged an exceedingly unpleasant duty, the most unpleasant of my public life. But I have looked upon it *as a duty*, and it was not to be shunned. And, sir, however unimportant may be the opinion of so humble an individual as myself, I now only wish that I might be heard by every independent freeman in the United States, by the British ministry and the British king, and by every minister and every crowned head in Europe, while, standing here in my place, I pronounce my rebuke, as solemnly and as decisively as I can, upon this first instance in which an American minister has been sent abroad as the representative of his party, and not as the representative of his country."

It has often been said that this rejection of Mr. Van Buren was a political mistake on the part of the opposition; and doubtless it was made afterward to contribute to his subsequent elevation to the presidency. But Mr. Webster's participation in it is to be judged, not by the lower standard of political expediency, in reference to which the rejection may have been a political error, but by the higher standard of public propriety, in reference to which Mr. Van Buren's letter to Mr. McLane was clearly open to the complaints that were made of it. Mr. Webster was, of course, aware that, by voting against the nomination of Mr. Van Buren, he might give to a political opponent the benefit of a grievance. But he considered the preservation of an elevated and national tone in our diplomacy to be a thing of too much consequence to allow him to avoid a disagreeable duty. Whatever may be the opinion with which the criticisms upon Mr. Van Buren's course are now viewed, there can be no doubt that this occurrence has had an important influence in restraining the introduction of party differences into the diplomatic relations of our Government with foreign powers, and that it has taught other Secretaries to remember that they represent the nation and not the parties or factions into which it may be at any time divided.[1]

[1] Among the forgotten topics of this affair was the origin of what Mr. Van Buren in his letter to Mr. McLane called "the past pretensions of this Government." This related to the claim for a free reciprocity in the colonial trade; a claim which had been, in fact, advanced by Mr. Monroe's Administration. One of the objects of the law passed by Congress, in 1823, was to prevent Great Britain from availing herself of our productions sent circuitously through her colonial ports. For this purpose, the third section of that law enacted that, on proof being given to the President that goods imported in the British colonial ports in American vessels were subjected to no other duties than the like goods imported into the same ports "from elsewhere," the President might, by proclamation, establish the same privilege for British colonial importations into our ports. In the discussion on Mr. Van Buren's nomination, it was said that the effect of this provision was not understood, at the time of its passage, as demanding a free reciprocity. Mr. Van Buren was a member of the Senate when the act of 1823 was passed. To clear up this point, Mr. Webster wrote to Mr. Barbour the following letter, and received the subjoined answer:

"WASHINGTON, *February* 8, 1832.

"MY DEAR SIR: I send you a newspaper, containing the remarks of General Smith, in the Senate, on Mr. Van Buren's nomination, for the purpose of drawing your attention to that part of them in which he speaks of the act of March 1, 1823.

"He seems to think, as you will perceive, that the important provision, respecting equality of duties, contained in that act, passed unnoticed by any one. Such a thing is, of course, exceedingly improbable, since it is the main provision in a principal section of the act. I am told, too, by those who were here at the time, that not only was this provision perfectly well understood in Congress, but that it attracted the notice of persons not in Congress; and that, as soon as the bill was printed and published, and while yet on its passage, the British minister suggested to the Department of State his views of it.

"I have looked for the debate in the Senate on this bill. All I have been able to find is in the *National Intelligencer* of the 26th or 27th of February, if I rightly remember the day. It is there stated that the bill was introduced by you, as Chairman of the Committee of Foreign Relations, and its principles and provisions explained; and that Messrs. Smith, Lloyd, etc., took part in the discussion of its details. My object now is, to inquire whether you are able to recollect what occurred in the Senate respecting this provision of the third section of the bill; and whether that third section, with the word 'elsewhere,' and all its other words, was explained by you, and its object stated, in your general speech on introducing the bill?

"You will see that one of the gentlemen's remarks would seem to imply that *I* was present at the passage of the bill, and was silent. In this, as well as in other particulars, it would have been better, perhaps, if the worthy member had been a little more distrustful of his own memory. I was not a member of either House of Congress when the bill passed.

"I pray you to accept, my dear sir, assurances of my cordial regards.

"DANIEL WEBSTER.

"Hon. James Barbour,
"Barboursville,
"Orange Co., Va."

[TO MR. WEBSTER.]

BALTIMORE, *February* 17, 1832.

"DEAR SIR: Your letter of the 8th instant was received by me just as I was setting out for this place to visit my family. I avail myself of the first moment which circumstances afford to furnish my reply.

"Although I am aware that one should speak with diffidence of events long past, of which there is no memorial but a frail memory, still, from my peculiar relation to the subject-matter of your inquiry, I think I can speak with some degree of confidence as to the facts regarding which you ask for information. You are aware that, immediately after the war, the United States determined

A great deal of attention was given by Mr. Webster at this session to the subject of the apportionment of representatives to the several States. By the rule hitherto followed, and now proposed to be repeated under the census of 1830, by a bill which came from the House, a ratio was adopted, giving one representative for a *fixed* number of persons. This representative ratio was proposed by the present bill to be forty-seven thousand seven hundred. The application of the ratio to the several States left much larger unrepresented fractions, or residuary numbers, to some of the smaller States than it left

to adopt perfect reciprocity as a fundamental principle of its commercial intercourse with all nations—that while Great Britain had reluctantly yielded to this principle in our intercourse with her European possessions, she pertinaciously refused it in our trade with the West India colonies, and her efforts were incessant to mould the intercourse to her peculiar advantage. It is also known to you that our minister at London at that time continually impressed on the American Government that, so long as we permitted, without resistance, a course of things to be pursued so injurious to us and so beneficial to Great Britain, remonstrance would be in vain. Our remedy was to be found only in a vigorous countervailing policy. I happen to know that this was the opinion of both Mr. Madison and Mr. Monroe. Hence the commencement of the war of regulations between the two powers—a policy which was then, I may say, universally approved of, judging by the votes in both Houses on the bill which was first enacted on the subject; and it was also believed in the sequel that to this course was to be ascribed the relaxation, on the part of Great Britain, of her exclusive pretensions. Eventually, in the session, '22-3, the progress of affairs called for a new enactment. At that time it was my lot to be the Chairman of the Committee of the Senate on Foreign Relations. The bill as it passed, I believe, was furnished by the Administration. When it was presented to the committee, our attention was drawn to these same notorious words 'from elsewhere;' we understood them in the sense which has ever been ascribed to them. I was directed, however, by the committee to have an interview with the Secretary of State, for the purpose of ascertaining if our interpretation of these words was the one designed, and also to obtain all the information in the possession of the Administration, and its views on the whole matter. I obeyed their instructions by calling on Mr. Adams, and communicating the wishes of the committee. He went fully into the matter. First, by stating that the policy on which the bill was formed was the result of the deliberate consideration of the whole Cabinet, and had its unanimous approbation. He proceeded to develop the reasons which had brought them to that result. These, it is unnecessary to state. It may be proper, however, to refer to one of them as connected with the more particular object of your inquiry. Were the words, said he, 'from elsewhere,' stricken out, it would leave to Great Britain the power of fixing such high discriminating duties in favor of the products of her continental colonies that similar products of the United States, it was to be feared, would be sent to the ports of these colonies, to profit by a fictitious naturalization so as to be relieved from the burden of the alien duty, and from thence to be transported in *British bottoms* to the places of consumption, and thereby Great Britain would monopolize the whole of the navigation between the continent and her islands to our entire exclusion. Mr. Adams closed his remarks by saying he would ask the President to bring the subject again under the consideration of the Cabinet, and that, if in two or three days I would call again, he would inform me of the result of their deliberations. I did so, and he informed me that they were unanimous in advising the adoption of the measure, and in particular the words 'from elsewhere.' The committee was convened again, and I communicated all the information I had obtained. As well as I recollect, they unanimously recommended reporting the bill. I think I cannot be mistaken in saying that Mr. Rufus King was a member of the committee. When we reflect on his very extensive capacity, and his intimate and profound knowledge of our commercial affairs, to say nothing of other most respectable members of the committee, it furnishes a very satisfactory assurance that so important a measure could not have passed without a due consideration and a perfect understanding of the subject. It devolved on me, from my relation to the committee, to present to the Senate the whole subject, and all the information which the committee had obtained—that duty I discharged. I am, therefore, at a loss to conjecture on what ground the assertion, that it was little understood, is to rest; and I heard with surprise that a deliberate enactment of the United States of America in Congress assembled was stigmatized as a silly pretension. Although I cannot speak from my own knowledge of the course of the British minister in regard to the measure during its pendency in Congress, yet, I believe, from my recollections, that he did express his opinions on it.

"I hope to be in Washington on next Monday, when I promise myself the pleasure of seeing my friends, among whom I take great pleasure in permitting myself to believe I may rank you.

"I offer you my respects.

"James Barbour."

to the larger ones; and, as the process produced a House of two hundred and forty members, the assignment of members made by the bill to the several States gave to New York, for example, forty members, while she was entitled, out of the whole mass presented by the number two hundred and forty, according to her population, to but thirty-eight. Forty members for the State of New York gave her eight times as many members as the process assigned to Vermont, although her population was not eight times that of Vermont by more than three hundred thousand. These and many other glaring inequalities, operating throughout the Union, led Mr. Webster to make a very careful examination of the whole subject, in order to discover a rule that would better effect the purpose of the Constitution. The mandate of the Constitution required representatives and direct taxes to be apportioned among the several States according to their respective numbers, but limited the number of representatives to not more than one for every thirty thousand, and allowing, however, at least one member to every State, although its representative population might fall short of thirty thousand. But the Constitution prescribed no process by which its mandate was to be carried out. Mr. Webster considered that the true course was, to regard the Constitution as directing an equality of representation between the States, *as near as may be*, since absolute equality is impracticable. He embodied his views in an elaborate report, which he made to the Senate on the 5th of April. It is contained in the third volume of his works.[1] Its principles were not adopted by Congress at that time, but they were carried out under the census of 1850.

His principal object in this report, and in the amendment which he proposed to the bill as it came from the House, was to get rid of the idea that the Constitution requires or authorizes Congress, in apportioning the representation of the States, to adopt a fixed integer or any common number of constituents for every member of the House. Such a process necessarily results in fractions or residuary numbers, and renders it exceedingly difficult, and sometimes impracticable, to attain that approximate equality which the Constitution con-

[1] Works, iii., 369.

templates. On this subject he received the concurrence of Chancellor Kent, expressed in the following letter:

[FROM CHANCELLOR KENT.]

"NEW YORK, *April* 21, 1832.

"DEAR SIR: I have perused the report you made to the Senate, and sent me, on the apportionment of representatives. Its clear and severe logical reasoning has struck me forcibly. I am not a mathematician, and not well versed in the application of divisors. I have looked at the Constitution and your argument again and again, and I see nothing unconstitutional, but great justice and reason in your amendment, and the principle on which it is founded, that Congress are bound to apportion among the States according to numbers *as near as may be*. Perfect equality is impracticable, and the allowance of a representative to fractions exceeding a moiety of the ratio would seem to me to make the best approximation; and that the results and irregularities in the bill, as it came from the other House, were unjust and intolerable. So it strikes me; and I see no infraction of any rule in the Constitution, but a conformity to its spirit and equity (which is *equality*), in the amendment.

"JAS. KENT.

"Hon. D. Webster.

"Be so good as to send me one copy out of the *five thousand* copies of Mr. Clay's land papers."

In the course of this year Mr. Webster became the owner of the estate at Marshfield, which I have already said was the place of his summer residence after 1824. As Captain Thomas approached the age of seventy, the care of his farm became irksome to him. His means were not large, and it was thought best for his children that he should sell this property. Mr. Webster purchased it in the autumn of 1831, but the deed was not taken until April, 1832. Nor would Mr. Webster then consent that Captain Thomas should leave the house. The old gentleman continued, in fact, to live there until his death, which occurred on the 27th of July, 1837, at the age of seventy-three. While he lived, Mr. Webster continually spoke of the affairs of the farm as if it were still the property of its former owner; saying, "Captain Thomas has this," or "Captain Thomas is going to do that," while it was Mr. Webster who ordered, and Mr. Webster who paid; for the fees of the great lawyer went lavishly into extensive plantations, noble barns, and many other improvements. But the family of Captain Thomas did not continue to reside there as the result of any bargain. It was simply Mr. Webster's wish that they should remain. "Captain Thomas and Mrs. Thomas," he used to say, "are a part of Marshfield, and it can never be the same without them." Hereafter we shall see this feeling extending itself to their children.

CHAPTER XIX.

1832–1833.

NULLIFICATION—CONDUCT OF SOUTH CAROLINA—SPEECH AT WORCESTER IN OCTOBER, 1832—REËLECTION OF GENERAL JACKSON—MR. CALHOUN'S POSITION—THE PRESIDENT'S PROCLAMATION—MR. CLAY'S COMPROMISE BILL—THE FORCE BILL—MR. WEBSTER'S VIEWS OF THE PROPER COURSE TO BE PURSUED—DEBATE WITH MR. CALHOUN ON THE NATURE OF THE GOVERNMENT—PRESIDENT JACKSON'S VISIT TO NEW ENGLAND—MR. WEBSTER'S VISIT TO THE WEST — GENERAL JACKSON'S SENSE OF MR. WEBSTER'S SERVICES—CORRESPONDPNCE.

MR. WEBSTER was well advised, when, at the dinner given to him in New York, in March, 1831, he intimated that the crisis of nullification was not wholly passed by. Congress met in December, 1831, and adjourned in March, 1832, without surrendering the policy of protection, and without renouncing the constitutional power to lay duties of discrimination for the purpose of fostering American manufactures. Notwithstanding the general acceptance of the views maintained by Mr. Webster in the debate of 1830, concerning the nature of the Constitution, many of the statesmen, and a majority of the people of South Carolina, adhered with unshaken pertinacity to the conviction that a State can constitutionally and rightfully arrest the operation of an act of Congress within her own limits, when she believes that it transcends the powers of Congress. Events were now to bring this doctrine to the test of an actual collision; and, according as that collision should be met by the

General Government, the Constitution would be freed in all future time from further hazards to its authority, or the necessary assertion of that authority might have to be undertaken at some future period amid the perils and sufferings of civil war. What part Mr. Webster acted in this emergency, what were his opinions respecting the steps that ought to be taken, and the attitude in which the Government ought to be left in reference to this whole subject, must now be explained.

In November, 1832, a State convention assembled at Columbia, in South Carolina, and adopted an ordinance declaring the revenue laws of the United States to be null and void within the limits of that State; and making it the duty of the Legislature to pass such State laws as would be necessary to carry the ordinance in question into effect from and after the 1st of February, 1833. The Legislature assembled on the 27th of November, and the Governor laid before them the ordinance of the convention, now become "a part of the fundamental law of South Carolina." In his message, he said that "the die has been at last cast, and South Carolina has at length appealed to her ulterior sovereignty as a member of this confederacy, and has planted herself on her reserved rights. The rightful exercise of this power is not a question which we shall any longer argue. It is sufficient that she has willed it, and that the act is done; nor is its strict compatibility with our constitutional obligation to all laws passed by the General Government, within the authorized grants of power, to be drawn in question, when this interposition is exerted in a case in which the compact has been palpably, deliberately, and dangerously violated. That it brings up a conjuncture of deep and momentous interest is neither to be concealed nor denied. This crisis presents a class of duties which is referable to yourselves. You have been commanded by the people, in their highest sovereignty, to take care that, within the limits of this State, their will shall be obeyed. . . . The measure of legislation which you have to employ at this crisis is the precise amount of such enactments as may be necessary to render it utterly impossible to collect, within our limits, the duties imposed by the protective tariffs thus nullified." He proceeds: "That you shall arm every citizen with a civil process, by which he may claim, if he pleases, a restitution of his goods, seized under the existing imposts, on his giving security to abide the issue of a suit at law; and, at the same time, define what shall constitute treason against the State, and, by a bill of pains and penalties, compel obedience, and punish disobedience to your own laws, are points too obvious to require any discussion. In one word, you must survey the whole ground. You must look to and provide for all possible contingencies. In your own limits, your own courts of judicature must not only be supreme, but you must look to the ultimate issue of any conflict of jurisdiction and power between them and the courts of the United States."

In prompt compliance with this and other recommendations in the Governor's message, the Legislature passed acts providing for the replevin of goods that might be seized under the revenue laws of the United States; inflicting heavy punishments upon any persons who might undertake to execute those laws; and raising military forces to resist the collection of the revenue of the United States, and to repel any efforts of the General Government to coerce the State into a submission to their execution. On the 20th of December the Governor issued his proclamation, giving notice that he was ready to accept the services of volunteers for this purpose. Thus the whole revenue system of the United States was obstructed, and apparently overthrown, in South Carolina; so that, if these measures were left without being defeated and suppressed, foreign merchandise, of any description, could be introduced into the ports of that State without the payment of any duties whatever. No period was assigned for the operation of this state of things. Nothing was left for the United States by this State legislation but unconditional submission. In an address, however, issued by the Convention of South Carolina to the people of the United States, they said: "Having now presented, for the consideration of the Federal Government, and our confederate States, the fixed and final determination of this State in relation to the protecting system, it remains for us to submit a plan of taxation in which we would be willing to acquiesce, in a spirit of liberal concession, provided we are met in due time and in a becoming spirit, by the States interested in the protection of manufactures."

Mr. Webster had to perform a very delicate duty, before the

meeting of Congress, which, while it would present to the country the grounds on which he called in question the general policy of the Administration, would signify what was to be expected of that Administration in regard to the impending collision with South Carolina. It was highly important, on the one hand, that, in criticising the conduct of the Administration, he should not place himself in such a position toward it that his aid could not be sought when the time should arrive for asserting the just authority of the Constitution; and, at the same time, it was, on the other hand, equally important that the country should understand that he did not consider the Constitution free from dangers arising from the course of the Administration itself. It was his habit, when requested to address bodies of men assembled for the purpose of promoting the objects of party organization, to speak with great circumspection, to seek to influence public opinion, and, through public opinion, to act upon men in official stations. Such an opportunity presented itself by the assembling of a political convention of the National Republican party of Massachusetts, at Worcester, on the 12th of October (1832), preparatory to the annual elections in that State, and to the presidential election, in which, it will be remembered, Mr. Clay was the candidate of this party.

In his speech on this occasion, Mr. Webster called the attention of the country, and of General Jackson himself, to the attitude in which the latter stood in reference to some of the powers of the Constitution. After adverting to the fact that, in South Carolina, the execution of the revenue laws of the Union was openly threatened with resistance, and that in Georgia a decree of the Supreme Court of the United States, directing the deliverance of individuals held in prison by the State authorities, was set at naught, he proceeded to show that the manner in which the President had treated the powers of the Constitution was signally unfavorable to their present execution and their future stability. He contrasted the President's annual message of 1830, which asserted the constitutional power to protect and foster domestic manufactures, with the recent "veto" message, which treated laws of protection as "a prostitution of our government to the advancement of the few at the expense of the many;" and he adverted to the fact that the tariff act of 1824, now the object of attack in all the warfare waged against the protective policy, was voted for by the President, who was then a Senator in Congress. Taking the present opinions of the President, however, as more important than any question of his personal consistency, Mr. Webster believed that they were hostile to the constitutional power of Congress to establish and maintain the system of protection, in whole or in part. The presidential election, which occurred soon afterward, resulted in the defeat of Mr. Clay, and in the reëlection of General Jackson by a very great majority of the electoral votes.[1]

Whatever might have been General Jackson's personal opinions respecting the tariff, a duty was cast upon him which he certainly exhibited no desire to avoid. He regarded the ordinance of South Carolina and the acts of her Legislature as sufficient notice to him that the collection of the revenue was to be forcibly resisted in that State; and, on the 10th of December, he issued his celebrated proclamation, which, adopting entirely the views that had been maintained by Mr. Webster (in the debate of 1830) concerning the nature of the Constitution and the powers of Congress, directed the officers of the revenue to discharge their several duties, warned the people and authorities of South Carolina of the consequences of their resistance, and frankly making known that, in his opinion, the time had arrived when the alleged inequality of laws, "which," he said, "may have been unwisely, not unconstitutionally passed," could be removed, he expressed the hope that they would retrace their steps. At the same time, he distinctly and firmly informed them that the acts which they meditated were treason, that the laws of the United States must be executed, and that all opposition to them must be put down.

It had become apparent, before the assembling of Congress in December, that the public men of South Carolina, who controlled the action of the State, were resolved to maintain the asserted right of nullification. Mr. Calhoun had been elected to the Senate of the United States, and had determined to resign the vice-presidency, and to take his seat in that body.

[1] Mr. Clay obtained the States of Massachusetts, Rhode Island, Connecticut, Delaware, Maryland, and Kentucky—forty-nine electoral votes. The vote of South Carolina was given to Mr. Floyd, of Virginia. General Jackson had all the other States—two hundred and nineteen votes.

His pamphlet on the right of nullification, in the form of a letter to the Governor of South Carolina, was regarded by Mr. Webster as a paper that required an answer. It was his purpose to make that answer in a similar form, by addressing a public letter on the subject to Chancellor Kent;[1] but the announcement of Mr. Calhoun's intention to be upon the floor of the Senate at the approaching session led Mr. Webster to prefer encountering his doctrines there.

Mr. Webster was on his way to Washington, in the month of December, after the proclamation had been issued for several days. At an inn in New Jersey he met a traveller, to whom he was not known, and of whom he inquired the news. The stranger, who was fresh from Washington, answered that General Jackson had made a proclamation, taken altogether from Mr. Webster's speech of 1830, in reply to General Hayne. The proclamation was written by Mr. Edward Livingston, then Secretary of State.[2] On his arrival at Philadelphia, Mr. Webster met there Mr. Clay, who informed him that he had prepared a plan for settling the tariff difficulty, which he would make known to Mr. Webster when they reached Washington. He did not learn it, however, directly from Mr. Clay, but a copy of Mr. Clay's intended bill, in the handwriting of Mr. Clay, was placed in Mr. Webster's hands by a third person, in the early part of the session. It contained a preamble, reciting that differences of opinion on the policy of protecting manufacturing industry, by duties on similar articles when imported, were agitating the public mind, and threatening serious disturbances, which it was desirable to prevent. The first section then proposed to enact that the existing tariff laws should remain in force until March 3, 1840, and that then all should be and "hereby are" repealed. The second section provided that, until March 3, 1840, no higher or other duties than those now existing shall be laid; "and from and after the aforesaid day, all duties collected upon any article whatever of foreign importation shall be equal, according to the value thereof, and solely for the purpose and with the intent of providing such

[1] Correspondence, i., 526.

[2] MS. memorandum by Mr. Webster, in the possession of Hon. Hiram Ketchum, of New York. This and some other papers derived from Mr. Webster will be cited hereafter as "Ketchum MS."

revenue as may be necessary to an economical expenditure of the Government, *without regard to the protection or encouragement of any branch of domestic industry whatever.*" When Mr. Clay offered his bill, however, in the Senate, the words here printed in italics were not embraced in it, and other modifications were made, as will be seen hereafter. But, either with or without these words, the measure was not one that could receive Mr. Webster's support. For the original introduction of the policy of protection he was in no degree responsible. But it had been made the policy of the country; and, since the tariff act of 1824, the great stimulus it had given to manufactures had caused very large masses of capital, and also a great aggregate of smaller amounts, to be invested in establishments which represented not merely the interests of the rich, but the interests of those who could by no means be classed in that category. It was no longer a question, in Mr. Webster's view, as it was in 1817, whether an original policy of free trade is best for such a nation as ours. That question had been settled; a long course of legislation had established the opposite policy; and it was, therefore, with Mr. Webster simply a question whether, for the mere purpose of conforming his present public conduct to theoretical opinions which he had expressed seventeen years before, in a very different state of things, he should lend his aid to overturn a system, in the continuance of which he believed the interests of the country to be now deeply involved.

Moreover, with respect to the constitutional power of Congress to so collect its revenues as to discriminate in favor of our domestic industry—a power which Mr. Webster never at any time questioned, and which was all that he ever contended for—much important information, respecting the purposes of those who founded and the people who ratified the Constitution, had been added to what was known when the policy of protection was first resorted to. In 1830–'33, there was no prominent statesman in the party with which Mr. Webster acted who doubted the existence of this power; and least of all men did he doubt it. There were, in truth, many important men in the opposite party, who held it as firmly as he did, and upon the same grounds.

There was still another reason why Mr. Webster could not

be a party to any abandonment of this policy, or to any renunciation of the constitutional power. The laws of the Union were resisted. The whole revenue system was, in South Carolina, threatened with direct nullification. The President of the United States had a duty to perform, which he could not perform unless his hands were strengthened by appropriate legislation. At such a time to undertake a modification of the existing laws, which would carry in itself an immediate or prospective renunciation of the constitutional power on which those laws had been passed—passed with the concurrence of men who differed about almost every thing else—appeared to Mr. Webster to be highly inexpedient and dangerous. In all the discussions on Mr. Clay's "compromise" measure, as, when introduced, it came to be regarded, and in all the changes that it underwent from Mr. Clay's original plan, it will be seen that Mr. Webster's chief objection was aimed at what he regarded as an unwise and unworthy surrender of a constitutional power, as an unjustifiable attempt to control its future exercise, and as an impracticable effort to settle the degree of protection which it would be necessary to afford to the manufacturing industry of the country at the end of eight or nine years.

The situation of affairs at Washington in the early part of the session was thus described by Mr. Webster to two of his friends:

[TO MR. WM. SULLIVAN.]

"WASHINGTON, *January* 3, 1833.

"MY DEAR SIR: I am glad to receive your letter. We are surrounded with difficulties here, of various sorts; and it is not a little uncertain how we shall get out of them. At the present moment, it would seem that public opinion, and the stern rebuke by the Executive government, had, in a great measure, suppressed the immediate danger of nullification. As far as we see the results of the legislation of South Carolina, her laws limp far behind her ordinance. For aught that appears, nothing will interrupt the ordinary collection of duties, after February 1st, unless some individual chooses to try the nullifying remedy. If any importer should suffer a seizure to be made, and should endeavor to replevy, under the State process, the collector would probably not deliver up the goods to the sheriff, nor suffer his own goods to be taken *in withernam*. This, probably, would bring on a trial of strength.

"But our more imminent danger, in my opinion, is that, seizing on the occasion, the anti-tariff party will prostrate the whole tariff system. You will have seen the bill reported by Mr. Verplanck. Great and extraordinary efforts are put forth to push that bill rapidly through Congress. It is likely to be finally acted upon, at least in the House of Representatives, before the country can be made to look on it in its true character. On the other hand, our friends will resist it, of course, and hold on to the last. A vigorous opposition will, at least, it may be hoped, be made, and, as I believe, produce the necessity, on the part of the supporters of the measure, to make some beneficial amendments in it, before even it can get through the House of Representatives.

"Under these circumstances, it seems to me it would be extremely useful that the Legislature of Massachusetts should express its temperate but firm opinion, first against the doctrine of nullification; secondly, on the violation of the public faith, which would be perpetrated by this thorough and sudden prostration of the protective system.

"On this ground of vested interest we can make, if well sustained at home, the most efficient stand against the threatened ruin. We mean to occupy this ground, and to make the most of it.

"If the bill were now in the Senate, it would not pass; but, how far individuals may be brought over by party discipline in the drill of a month, it is impossible to say.

"I do not believe the President himself wishes the bill to pass. *E contra*, I fancy he would prefer the undivided honor of suppressing nullification now, and to take his own time hereafter to remodel the tariff. But the party push on, fearing the effect of the doctrines of the proclamation, and endeavoring to interpose, and to save Carolina, not by the proclamation, but by taking away the ground of complaint.

"But against this, again, there is some degree of undercurrent, because there are some who think that surrendering the tariff to the menaces of nullification would be voting a triumph to Mr. Calhoun, at the expense of Mr. Van Buren's expectations, etc.

"I shall be glad to hear from you and other friends, especially if you can give me any good advice.

"Yours ever truly,

"DANIEL WEBSTER."

[TO CHIEF-JUSTICE LIVERMORE, OF NEW HAMPSHIRE.]

"WASHINGTON, *January* 5, 1833.

"MY DEAR SIR: Your letter of December 29th is received, and has given me pleasure. I regard you, my dear sir, not only as an acquaintance of many years' standing, but also as one whose countenance and kindness were important to me in youth. I shall be sure to send you any thing which I may think you would like to receive, and I beg of you not to take the trouble to acknowledge receipts. It will be quite enough that I understand generally that such communications are welcome.

"The impression here to-day seems to be that nullification has assumed a less threatening aspect; at least, the danger of immediate collision appears less. The act passed by the Legislature of South Carolina to carry the ordinance into effect does not come up to the ordinance. It may happen that, notwithstanding the ordinance and the act, things may go on much as they have done.

"Nothing is more uncertain than the fate of the new Tariff Bill. It will pass the House if the President desires it; but that is doubtful. If it were now in the Senate, it would be postponed from indisposition to act again on that subject so soon; but I do not know what will be done with it should it come to us a month hence.

"It is sometimes said that, in so changing a world, if people will but stand still, others, sooner or later, will come to them. Were you not struck with this truth in seeing the proclamation?

"I am, dear sir,

"With constant regard, yours,

"DANIEL WEBSTER."

In his annual message, at the opening of the session, President Jackson had suggested that it might become necessary for him to recommend certain measures to enable him to meet the threatened resistance to the laws of the Union. On the 16th of January he sent a special message to Congress, communicating, officially and in detail, what had occurred in South Carolina, and recommending the measures which he deemed necessary to meet the emergency.[1] He asked that provision might be made, that whenever, by unlawful combination or obstruction, in any State or port, the collection of duties had become impracticable, the President should be authorized to change the collection districts and ports of entry, and to establish the custom-house at some secure place, where vessels and cargoes could be detained in the custody of the collector until the duties were properly paid or secured, and to protect that custody by the employment of the land and naval forces. To shield the officers so acting from suits in the State courts, he asked that provision be made for the removal of such cases to the Federal tribunals, where they should be tried and determined as if they had been originally instituted there. Mr. Calhoun had now taken his seat in the Senate. On the motion to refer the message to the Committee on the Judiciary, he made some remarks that exhibited a great deal of feeling, and indicated his purpose to con-

[1] Mr. Webster was apprised of this message before it was sent.

test strenuously the propriety of the President's course. The message, however, was quietly referred to the Judiciary Committee, and in less than a week their chairman, Mr. Wilkins, reported a bill, "further to provide for the collection of duties on imports," which became known and has since been called the celebrated "Force Bill." Its consideration was fixed for Monday, the 28th of January, as the special order of the day. Mr. Calhoun, appreciating what was impending, immediately made a movement to interpose what he denominated a "plea in bar," against this use of force. He offered certain resolutions, for the purpose of testing the principles on which the bill rested, expressing his views of the nature and extent of the powers of the Federal Government.[1] They were ordered to be printed. Mr. Calhoun pressed them on the consideration of the Senate. Mr. Webster professed his readiness to meet the discussion at any proper time, but did not think they should be allowed to interfere with the progress of the bill. They were laid on the table, and the revenue collection bill was proceeded with; Mr. Calhoun saying that he had a deep conviction of the truth of his propositions, and Mr. Webster replying in his seat, "I do not doubt it."

The "Force Bill," when originally introduced into the Senate,

[1] The following are the resolutions:

"*Resolved*, That the people of the several States composing these United States are united as parties to a constitutional compact, to which the people of each State acceded as a separate sovereign community, each binding itself by its own particular ratification; and that the Union, of which the said compact is the bond, is a union between the States ratifying the same.

"*Resolved*, That the people of the several States, thus united by the constitutional compact, in forming that instrument, and in creating a General Government to carry into effect the objects for which they were formed, delegated to that Government, for that purpose, certain definite powers, to be exercised jointly, reserving, at the same time, each State to itself, the residuary mass of powers, to be exercised by its own separate Government; and that, whenever the General Government assumes the exercise of powers not delegated by the compact, its acts are unauthorized, and are of no effect; and that the same Government is not made the final judge of the powers delegated to it, since that would make its discretion, and not its constitution, the measure of its powers; but that, as in all other cases of compact among sovereign parties, without any common judge, each has an equal right to judge for itself, as well of the infraction as of the mode and measure of redress.

"*Resolved*, That the assertions that the people of these United States, taken collectively as individuals, are now, or ever have been, united on the principle of the social compact, and as such are now formed into one nation or people, or that they have ever been so united in any one stage of their political existence; that the people of the several States composing the Union have not, as members thereof, retained their sovereignty; that the allegiance of their citizens has been transferred to the General Government; that they have parted with the right of punishing treason through their respective State governments; and that they have not the right of judging in the last resort as to the extent of the powers reserved, and, of consequence, of those delegated; are not only without foundation in truth, but are contrary to the most certain and plain historical facts, and the clearest deductions of reason; and that all exercise of power on the part of the General Government, or any of its departments, claiming authority from so erroneous assumptions, must of necessity be unconstitutional, must tend directly and inevitably to subvert the sovereignty of the States, to destroy the federal character of the Union, and to rear on its ruins a consolidated Government, without constitutional check or limitation, and which must necessarily terminate in the loss of liberty itself."

was wholly an Administration measure. Its conduct through the Senate was left principally to the charge of Mr. Grundy, of Tennessee; but many of General Jackson's friends recoiled from its support. In this condition of things, other aid became essential; and, among the President's friends in the House of Representatives, there was much inquiry as to "where Mr. Webster was." Several of these gentlemen sought and obtained personal interviews with him. At length, as the discussion proceeded in the Senate, Mr. Webster being absent, from engagements or ill health, a member of the President's Cabinet visited him at his lodgings, and earnestly requested him to take an active part in the defence of this measure, and in preparing and making all necessary amendments to it.[1]

In a few days Mr. Webster appeared in his place in the Senate, and found this bill an object of attack from some of the Administration members. Having interposed for the purpose of saying a few words against a motion to postpone the bill, and urging that the Senate continue its discussion until all who desired had been heard upon it, Mr. King, of Alabama, said that, if the Senator from Massachusetts wished to deliver his sentiments upon the bill, he should be happy to listen to him at any length. Mr. Webster simply replied that he appreciated this kindness, but that, under existing circumstances, he had no disposition to address the Senate on this bill, then or at any future time.[2] As the bill was now the special order for each day at 12 o'clock, it was called on the following day (February 8th), when Mr. Webster rose and said:

"He wished to interrupt the course of the debate for a single moment, in order to set one matter right, if he could. Since a warm controversy was rising, he thought it but proper that we should understand between what parties the controversy existed.

"Soon after the declaration of war by the United States against England, an American vessel fell in at sea with one of England, and gave information of the declaration. The English master inquired, with no little warmth of manner and expression, why the United States had gone to war with England. The American answered him, that difficulties had existed for a good while between the two Governments, and that it was at length thought in America to be high time for the parties to come to a better understanding.

[1] Ketchum MS.

[2] July 7th.

"I incline to think, Mr. President, that a war has broken out here, which is very likely, before it closes, to bring the parties to a better understanding. But who are the parties? Will you please to remember, sir, that this is a measure founded in Executive recommendation? The President, charged by the Constitution with the duty of executing the laws, has sent us a message, alleging that powerful combinations are forming to resist their execution; that the existing laws are not sufficient to meet the crisis; and recommending sundry enactments as necessary for the occasion. The message being referred to the Judiciary Committee, that committee has reported a bill in compliance with the President's recommendation. It has not gone beyond the message. Every thing in the bill, every single provision, which is now complained of, is in the message. Yet the whole war is raised against the bill, and against the committee, as if the committee had originated the whole matter. Gentlemen get up and address us, as if they were arguing against some measure of a factious opposition. They look the same way, sir, and speak with the same vehemence, as they used to do when they raised their patriotic voices against what they called a 'coalition.'

"Now, sir, let it be known, once for all, that this is an Administration measure; that it is the President's own measure; and I pray gentlemen to have the goodness, if they call it hard names, and talk loudly against its friends, not to overlook its source. Let them attack it, if they choose to attack it, in its origin.

"Let it be known, also, that a majority of the committee reporting the bill are friends and supporters of the Administration; and that it is maintained in this House by those who are among its steadfast friends of long standing.

"It is, as I have already said, the President's own measure. Let those who oppose it, oppose it as such. Let them fairly acknowledge its origin, and meet it accordingly.

"The honorable member from Kentucky (Mr. Bibb), who spoke first against the bill, said he found in it another Jersey prison-ship; let him state, then, that the President has sent a message to Congress, recommending a renewal of the sufferings and horrors of the Jersey prison-ship. He says, too, that the bill snuffs of the alien and sedition law. But the bill is fragrant of no flower except the same which perfumes the message. Let him, then, say, if he thinks so, that General Jackson advises a revival of the principles of the alien and sedition laws.

"The honorable member from Virginia (Mr. Tyler) finds out a resemblance between this bill and the Boston port bill. Sir, if one of these be imitated from the other, the imitation is the President's. The bill makes the President, he says, sole judge of the Constitution. Does he mean to say that the President has recommended a measure which is to make him sole judge of the Constitution? The bill, he declares, sacrifices every thing to arbitrary power; he will lend no aid to its passage; he would rather 'be a dog and bay the moon, than such a Roman.' He did not say 'the old Roman.' Yet the gentleman well knows that, if any thing is sacrificed to arbitrary power, the sacrifice has been demanded by the 'old Roman,' as he and others have called him; by the President whom he has supported, so often and so ably, for the chief magistracy of the country. He says, too, that one of the sections is an English Botany Bay law, except that it is worse. This section, sir, whatever it may be, is just what the President's message recommended. Similar observations are applicable to the remarks of both the honorable gentlemen from North Carolina. It is not necessary to particularize those remarks. They were in the same strain.

"Therefore, sir, let it be understood, let it be known, that the war which these gentlemen choose to wage, is waged against the measures of the Administration, against the President of their own choice. The controversy has arisen between him and them, and, in its progress, they will probably come to a distinct understanding.

"Mr. President, I am not to be understood as admitting that these charges against the bill are just, or that they would be just if made against the message. On the contrary, I think them wholly unjust. No one of them, in my opinion, can be made good. I think the bill, or some similar measure, had become indispensable, and that the President could not do otherwise than bring it to the consideration of Congress. He was not at liberty to look on and be silent, while dangers threatened the Union, which existing laws were not competent, in his judgment, to avert.

"Mr. President, I take this occasion to say that I support this measure, as an independent member of the Senate, in the discharge of the dictates of my own conscience. I am no man's leader; and, on the other hand, I follow no lead but that of public duty and the star of the Constitution. I believe the country is in considerable danger; I believe an unlawful combination threatens the integrity of the Union. I believe the crisis calls for a mild, temperate, forbearing, but inflexibly firm execution of the laws; and, under this conviction, I give a hearty support to the Administration in all measures which I deem to be fair, just, and necessary. And, in supporting these measures, I mean to take my fair share of responsibility; to support them frankly and fairly, without reflections on the past, and without mixing other topics in their discussion.

"Mr. President, I think I understand the sentiment of the country on this subject. I think public opinion sets, with an irresistible force, in favor of the Union, in favor of the measures recommended by the President, and against the new doctrines which threaten the dissolution of the Union. I think the people of the United States demand of us, who are intrusted with the Government, to maintain that Government, to be just, and fear not; to make all necessary and suitable provisions for the execution of the laws, and to sustain the Union and the Constitution against whatsoever may endanger them. For one, I obey this public voice; I comply with this demand of the people. I support the Administration in measures which I believe to be necessary; and, while pursuing this course, I look unhesitatingly, and with the utmost confidence, for the approbation of the country."

The Senators, who were thus put upon their good behavior toward the President of their own choice, made disclaimers of their belief that the President had asked for such powers; and one of them, Mr. Bibb, commenting on the first and fifth sections of the bill, expressed his doubt whether any President would have had the "daring effrontery" to ask for such powers, and desired to know what was the "secret connection" between the message and the bill. Mr. Webster replied that there was nothing in the bill which was not recommended in the message; and then, looking at Mr. Bibb, he added, "I will tell the gentleman that the President *has* had the 'daring effrontery' to ask for these powers, no matter how high may be the offence."

This evidence that Mr. Webster was to act with the Administration, in upholding the execution of the laws and the authority of the Constitution, caused dismay in several quarters. To the Administration Senators who were inclined to resist the passage of the bill, the revelation of Mr. Webster's purpose, and of his complete accord with the President, showed that their opposition would be fruitless, and that their attempt to throw the *onus* of the bill upon Mr. Webster would not succeed. The well-known determination of General Jackson's character, acting in the same direction with Mr. Webster's forensic power, and his weight in the country, gave Mr. Calhoun much uneasiness. He saw that great forces were closing around him, and that his position was one of much peril. But he was a very able tactician, and having, as Mr. Webster thoroughly believed he had, undoubting confidence in the truth of the positions he had taken in his resolutions, he was very anxious to bring on their discussion in the Senate before the "Force Bill" could pass. But, before this could be done, he had reason to be alarmed. It became known that General Jackson had used, in private, very strong language in regard to the leaders in the South Carolina movement. In periods and scenes of excitement, he had not always been willing to wait for the due course of law, and his temperament was well understood to be one that might suddenly visit the leaders of nullification with extreme personal danger. He had received great provocation; for, on the 11th of January, a series of resolutions, adopted by the Legislature of South Carolina in answer to his proclamation, had been laid before the Senate of the United States, bitterly denouncing him, and breathing a spirit of open defiance. His resentments were never slow to kindle, and, on this occasion, he took no pains to conceal them. In this attitude of affairs, Mr. Calhoun sought the interposition of Mr. Clay. An interview took place between these gentlemen, at which Mr. Calhoun obtained the promise of Mr. Clay's interference.[1] On the 11th of February, the "Force Bill" being still pending, Mr. Clay announced in the Senate that on the following day he should introduce a bill to modify the tariff.

This sudden and unexpected movement changed the entire aspect of affairs. Up to this moment, it was not imagined that there could be in the Senate more than two parties in reference to the question of executing the revenue laws as they stood: the one consisting of all who held to the duty of upholding the authority of the Government, and the other comprehending those who meant to resist it. It now appeared to be Mr. Clay's purpose to take an intermediate position, by removing what was put forward by South Carolina as the grievance which justified her resort to nullification. The dangers attending this step were manifest. On the one side, it might cause the Administration to be placed in the apparent attitude of asking for unnecessary powers, and might throw upon them the odium of seeking the personal humiliation and political ruin of Mr. Calhoun and his friends. On the other side, considering the attitude taken by South Carolina, her threats of resistance, and her military preparations, a sudden reversal of the long-established policy of Congress, by a repeal or modification of the laws which she proposed to resist, was not unlikely to be claimed as a triumph of the principles which Mr. Calhoun had advanced as the true theory of the Constitution. To Mr. Webster, this movement of Mr. Clay left nothing but the consideration of what was most fit to be done when a State had announced her purpose to obstruct the execution of the laws of the Union. He could not join in Mr. Clay's proposed "compromise," for he had, in the most

[1] My authority for this statement is the late Mr. Crittenden, who once related to me the particulars of the interview.

public manner, expressed his opinions that the hands of the Executive ought at once to be so strengthened by legislative action, that the threatened nullification could be met by peaceful means and judicial remedy, but that, if force were ever resorted to, South Carolina must be the aggressor. He considered the future stability of the Government involved in this crisis, and he had reason to know that the Executive Department, while desirous, as he was, to avoid the dire result of civil war by every means that did not sacrifice the just authority of the Constitution, had determined firmly to maintain that authority.

It is now necessary to go back to an earlier period in the session, in order to see what had taken place in the House of Representatives on the subject of the tariff. On the 27th of December, Mr. Verplanck, of New York, from the Committee of Ways and Means, to which was referred a part of the President's annual message relating to the finances and to a further reduction of the revenue, reported a bill to reduce and otherwise alter the duties on imports. This bill was called up on the 8th of February, and was under discussion in the House when Mr. Clay offered his own bill in the Senate.

Mr. Clay began his speech, on the introduction of his bill, by declaring it to be his purpose to save the tariff, which he believed to be in imminent danger, and which, even if it should be preserved during the present session, must, he thought, fall at the next. He therefore sought, he said, to find some principle of mutual accommodation, in order to satisfy, as far as practicable, both the friends and the opponents of the tariff, to increase the stability of legislation, and, at some distant day, to bring down the rate of duties to that revenue standard for which the adversaries of the tariff had long contended. This, he maintained, was not an abandonment of the constitutional power of protection, but a suspension of it. If the power and the principle of protection were to be preserved, it was necessary, he said, to carry *now* some measure of modification, with the assent of all parties; and if that assent were *now* yielded, the circumstances of the transaction would afford a guaranty that future legislation would give all the protection that could be reasonably required. To secure such a guaranty, concessions must be made on both sides; and he claimed that his measure was founded on the great principle of compromise which had given birth to the Constitution itself, and which had always regulated the affairs of the Union.

Alluding next to the attitude of South Carolina, Mr. Clay said that at the commencement of the session he felt a very strong repugnance to any legislation on this subject, believing that South Carolina had arrogantly demanded of Congress at once to abandon a system which had long been the settled policy of this country. But he had since found that South Carolina was making only an experiment; to prevent by a course of legislation, not by force, the execution of the laws of the Union within her limits, in order to have the question of constitutional power determined by the courts. After expressing his belief that the course of the State was both wrong and impracticable, he concluded by deprecating strongly any action by Congress at the present session that might plunge the country into a civil war; and, making an eloquent appeal to a spirit of mutual forbearance and conciliation, he asked leave to introduce his bill.

When read, the bill was found to contain the following provisions: It proposed to enact that, on all existing duties which exceeded twenty per cent. on the value of the articles on which they were laid, the excess should undergo a certain reduction at every period of two years until September 30, 1842, at which time, by the process of reduction, the excess over twenty per cent. would be extinguished; that until September 30, 1842, the existing duties, as proposed to be modified, should be collected; that after that date all duties upon imports should be paid in cash, and be laid for the purpose of raising such revenue as may be necessary to an economical administration of the Government, and that for that purpose they should be equal upon all articles according to their value; that until otherwise directed by law, from and after September 30, 1842, the rate of duties shall be twenty per cent. *ad valorem*, reserving, however, power to raise the rate in the event of war with any foreign power. The bill also enlarged and modified the free list, especially in relation to raw materials and articles used in manufactures.

Before the bill had been formally read, however, but after Mr. Clay had explained its provisions, Mr. Webster rose and said:

"That as, by its title, the bill appeared to be a bill merely to modify the existing revenue laws, it could hardly be rejected as a bill for raising revenue, which ought to originate in the other House, since there are many particulars in which all the existing revenue laws might be modified, without raising more or less revenue. As the bill has not been read (said Mr. Webster), we seem to know no more of it, regularly, than its title purports. That *title* describes a bill which may constitutionally originate in the Senate; I shall, therefore, vote for the leave.

"But I feel it my duty, Mr. President, to say a word or two upon the measure itself. It is impossible that this proposition of the honorable member from Kentucky should not excite in the country a very strong sensation; and, in the relation in which I stand to the subject, I am anxious, at an early moment, to say that, as far as I understand the bill, from the gentleman's statement of it, there are principles in it in which I do not at present see how I can ever concur. If I understand the plan, the result of it will be a well-understood surrender of the power of discrimination, or a stipulation not to use that power, in the laying of duties on imports, after the eight or nine years have expired. This appears to me to be a matter of great moment. I hesitate to be a party to any such stipulation. The honorable member admits that, though there will be no positive surrender of the power, there will be a stipulation not to exercise it; a treaty of peace and amity, as he says, which no American statesman can hereafter stand up to violate. I propose, so far as depends on me, to leave all our successors in Congress as free to act as we are ourselves.

"The honorable member from Kentucky says the tariff is in imminent danger; that, if not destroyed this session, it cannot hope to survive the next. This may be so, sir. This may be so. But, if it is so, it is because the American people will not sanction the tariff; and if they will not, why, then, sir, it cannot be sustained at all. I am not quite so despairing as the honorable member seems to be. I know nothing which has happened within the last six or eight months changing so materially the prospects of the tariff. I do not despair of the success of an appeal to the American people, to take a just care of their own interests, and not to sacrifice those vast interests which have grown up under the laws of Congress.

"But, sir, out of respect to the economy of the time of the Senate, I will pursue these remarks no further at present; but I will take an opportunity to-morrow to lay on the table resolutions expressing my general opinions on this interesting subject."

On the next day (February 13th), Mr. Webster offered the following resolutions, which were ordered to be printed:

"*Resolved*, That the annual revenues of the country ought not to be allowed to exceed a just estimate of the wants of the Government; and that, as soon as it shall be ascertained, with reasonable certainty, that the rates of duties on imports, as established by the act of July, 1832, will yield an excess over those wants, provision ought to be made for their reduction; and that, in making this reduction, just regard should be had to the various interests and opinions of different parts of the country, so as most effectually to preserve the integrity and harmony of the Union, and to provide for the common defence, and promote the general welfare of the whole.

"But, whereas it is certain that the diminution of the rates of duties on some articles would increase instead of reducing the aggregate amount of revenue on such articles; and whereas, in regard to such articles as it has been the policy of the country to protect, a slight reduction on one might produce essential injury, and even distress, to large classes of the community, while another might bear a larger reduction without any such consequences; and whereas, also, there are many articles the duties on which might be reduced, or altogether abolished, without producing any other effect than the reduction of revenue: therefore,

"*Resolved*, That, in reducing the rates of duties imposed on imports by the act of the 14th of July aforesaid, it is not wise or judicious to proceed by way of an equal reduction per centum on all articles; but that as well the amount as the time of reduction ought to be fixed, in respect to the several articles, distinctly, having due regard, in each case, to the questions whether the proposed reduction will affect revenue alone, or how far it will operate injuriously on those domestic manufactures hitherto protected—especially such as are essential in time of war, and such, also, as have been established on the faith of existing laws—and, above all, how far such proposed reduction will affect the rates of wages and the earnings of American manual labor.

"*Resolved*, That it is unwise and injudicious, in regulating imposts, to adopt a plan, hitherto equally unknown in the history of this Government, and in the practice of all enlightened nations, which shall, either immediately or prospectively, reject all discrimination on articles to be taxed, whether they be articles of necessity or of luxury, of general consumption or of limited consumption; and whether they be, or be not, such as are manufactured and produced at home; and which shall confine all duties to one equal rate per centum on all articles.

"*Resolved*, That, since the people of the United States have deprived the State governments of all power of fostering manufactures, however indispensable in peace or in war, or however important to national independence, by commercial regulations, or by laying duties on imports, and have transferred the whole authority to make such regulations, and to lay such duties, to the Congress of the United States, Congress cannot surrender or abandon such power compatibly with its constitutional duty; and, therefore,

"*Resolved*, That no law ought to be passed on the subject of imposts, containing any stipulation, express or implied, or giving any pledge or assurance, direct or indirect, which shall tend to restrain Congress from the full exercise, at all times hereafter, of all its constitutional powers, in giving reasonable protection to American industry, countervailing the policy of foreign nations, and maintaining the substantial independence of the United States."

On the two following days, Mr. Webster was prevented, by the discussion on the "Force Bill," from addressing the Senate on his tariff resolutions. On the 15th, the "Force Bill" being under consideration, Mr. Calhoun commenced the great speech in which he resisted the passage of that bill, developed his views on the nature of the Constitution, and the right of State nullification, as embodied in his resolutions, and explained the attitude taken by South Carolina. The doctrine of this very able speech maintained the Union to be a confederacy of sovereign States, in contradistinction to a consolidated Government; that the States, being sovereign—having reserved all powers not granted to the General Government—reserved to themselves, among other powers, that of judging of any infractions of the Federal compact, which power, from the necessity of the case, could exist nowhere else; and that, when a State, in its sovereign capacity, has solemnly pronounced an act of the General Government to be unwarranted by the Federal Constitution, the paramount allegiance of the citizens of the State is due to her authority, and she stands between the citizen and the Federal Government to protect him from the consequences of resistance. As an exposition of the doctrines of nullification, this speech was of a far higher order than that of General Hayne, to which Mr. Webster replied in 1830. It was the embodied result of all Mr. Calhoun's political studies and teachings of many years; and it is not to be doubted that it sowed the seeds which in another generation produced the opinions that made the right of secession from the Union a firm political faith, which multitudes of men have sealed with their blood on the battle-fields of a civil war. The occasion on which the speech was made was the last time when these doctrines came prominently into discussion on the floor of Congress; the last in which they were to be subjected to that forensic ordeal, which was to fix the convictions of a majority of the nation on the one side or the other, before they were to be, at some unknown day, submitted to the final and dread arbitrament of arms.

Mr. Webster felt the full importance of the occasion, but he felt also the great vantage-ground he had gained by the debate of 1830. His reply to General Hayne had been accepted as conclusive, not merely by the quarter of the country which he represented, and the political party with which he was connected, but by a large part of the people in the Central and Western States, and by many of the ablest public men in the party to which he did not belong. Moreover, the doctrines which he then maintained respecting the Constitution had been adopted by the President of the United States in the most important state paper that had proceeded from his Administration, and had thus received the full sanction of an Executive who was the head of the largest and most powerful party in the Union. As might have been expected, therefore, the speech in reply to Mr. Calhoun was far less rhetorical than that in reply to Mr. Hayne. The thesis was substantially the same; but the subject was not so new as on the former occasion, and there was not the same feverish anxiety in the public mind respecting the result of the debate.

As soon as Mr. Calhoun had concluded, Mr. Webster rose and delivered the speech which now stands in the third volume of his works, under the title, "The Constitution not a compact between sovereign States." It comprehended and maintained the following propositions:

"1. That the Constitution of the United States is not a league, confederacy, or compact between the people of the several States in their sovereign capacities; but a government proper, founded on the adoption of the people, and creating direct relations between itself and individuals.

"2. That no State has authority to dissolve these relations; that nothing can dissolve them but revolution; and that, consequently, there can be no such thing as secession without revolution.

"3. That there is a supreme law, consisting of the Constitution of the United States, and acts of Congress passed in pursuance of it, and treaties; and that, in cases not assuming the character of a suit in law or equity, Congress must judge of and finally interpret this supreme law so often as it has occasion to pass acts of legislation; and, in cases capable of assuming, and actually assuming, the character of a suit, the Supreme Court of the United States is the final interpreter.

"4. That an attempt by a State to abrogate, annul, or nullify any act of Congress, or to arrest its operation within her limits, on the ground that, in her opinion, such law is unconstitutional, is a direct usurpation on the just powers of the General Government, and on the equal rights of the States, a plain violation of the Constitution, and a proceeding essentially revolutionary in its character and tendency."

Perhaps there is no speech ever made by Mr. Webster that is so close in its reasoning, so compact, and so powerful. Whoever would understand that theory of the Constitution of the United States which regards it as the enactment of a fundamental law, must go to this speech to find its best and clearest exposition. Whoever would know the doctrine that enabled the Government of the United States, thirty years later, to call forth the physical energies of a population strong enough to encounter and to prevent the dismemberment of this Union by the secession attempted in 1861, and finally suppressed in 1865, must find it in the position maintained by Mr. Webster in 1830 and 1833.

But what was then taking place in the Senate of the United States rendered it morally certain that at some future time this great issue would be transferred from the arena of forensic discussion to the theatre of war. The idea of putting into the hands of the Executive the means of compelling obedience to the laws of the Union, and at the same time of modifying those laws so as to retract the principle on which the authority of the Union had been asserted and was now resisted, was regarded by Mr. Webster in a very different light from that in which it presented itself to Mr. Clay. Gifted with powers of persuasion that have rarely been excelled by any statesman in our annals, that distinguished person embraced with eagerness the part of a pacificator, and was led on by the captivating thought that he could put an end to all *future dangers* by removing the causes of *present discontents*. This is a mode of action, in free governments, which has succeeded, and has failed, according to the degree in which essential principles have been preserved, or relaxed, in dealing with factious resistance. It is a mode of action in respect to which statesmen of equal purity and patriotism will differ, according to their estimate of what is involved in present concessions, and of what will remain for the assertion and vindication of authority in future. Between Mr. Webster and Mr. Clay, on this occasion, there was precisely such a difference. Posterity must judge, will judge, the motives of each of them, with equal liberality. The one aimed at a great settlement of an immediate difficulty, by calling on the contending parties to make mutual sacrifices. The other believed that the proposed settlement surrendered fatally a principle of the Constitution. It was not the reduction of duties to which Mr. Webster objected; it was to the effort to bind the Government not to exercise the power of discrimination in raising its revenues on imports, and to the enactment of such a stipulation in the face of a threatened resistance to an important constitutional power, which Mr. Clay held to be as clear as Mr. Webster or any one else. How far Mr. Webster had grounds for his opinion, will be seen from the further history of this memorable discussion and its consequences.

The discussion between Mr. Calhoun and Mr. Webster would seem to have convinced Mr. Clay that a vote from him against the passage of the "Force Bill" would be unbecoming. He would not speak in its favor, and he so declared in the Senate. While he admitted that such a law might with propriety be upon the statute-book, he declined to vote for it. It was finally passed on the 20th of February.[1]

The previous action of the Senate on Mr. Clay's bill to modify the tariff act of 1832 had resulted, on the 13th of February, in referring it to a select committee, of which Mr. Clay was chairman. On the 19th, it was reported with amendments. On the 21st, the amendments were adopted by the Senate. On the 22d, on motion of Mr. Clay, the principle of home valuation was added, and on the 24th the bill was engrossed. Before this occurred, Mr. Webster had suggested that it was not a bill that could originate in the Senate, as it was a money bill, whether it increased or diminished the revenue. Mr. Clay combated

[1] Mr. Tyler, of Virginia, alone recorded his vote against the passage of this bill. The votes in its favor were thirty-two. The vote was taken at a late hour of the evening session on the 20th. Mr. Calhoun and Mr. Clay withdrew from the Senate before the final vote was taken on the bill.

this position, and regretted that there should be any disposition to oppose a measure of conciliation and compromise. On the 25th, the question being on the final passage of the bill, Mr. Webster addressed the Senate in opposition to it.

Of this speech, there is but a meagre account remaining. The reason that led Mr. Webster to refrain from putting it afterward into a full report will be seen hereafter. But enough remains to inform us that he resisted its passage upon the following grounds: First, that it undertook to bind future Congresses, in respect to the measure of protection to be given to domestic manufactures. Second, because it reduced the duties on the protected articles below twenty per cent. *ad valorem*, while it prohibited their being raised above that rate. Third, because it surrendered, and would be claimed to have surrendered, the constitutional power of protection. Fourth, because it gave up specific duties, and adopted a system of valuations, which he regarded as objectionable. Practically, he contended that this measure surrendered the interests of all the smaller capitalists, and made concessions in favor of the overgrown monopolists. As a measure of finance, he considered it inefficient, and did not anticipate that it would be acquiesced in as a permanent settlement. With respect to the attitude of South Carolina, he said that, if her object was merely to enter into a law-suit with the United States, there was no necessity for this sacrifice of great interests. In conclusion, he said that, when the point of necessary revenue should become known, any Congress would be able to make a tariff that would suit the country, if the constitutional power to discriminate were not given up.

Mr. Clay closed the discussion, in reply to Mr. Webster, and enforced the passage of the bill in an impassioned and eloquent speech. On the 26th, the Senate bill being still pending, Mr. Clay suggested that the House of Representatives had just then passed a similar bill, and, as this would obviate the constitutional objection to his own bill, the Senate, on his motion, adjourned.

What had occurred in the House of Representatives was the introduction, by Mr. Letcher, of the same bill then pending in the Senate. It was passed rapidly through the forms of the

House, without the allowance of amendments, and, on the 26th, was sent to the Senate for its concurrence.

On that day Mr. Calhoun called up his resolutions on the nature and power of the Government, and commenced an elaborate reply to Mr. Webster, reasserting the doctrines of State nullification. Mr. Webster immediately rejoined, terminating the discussion as follows:

"Mr. President, turn this question over, and present it as we will—argue it as we may—exhaust upon it all the fountains of metaphysics—stretch over it all the meshes of logical or political subtlety—it still comes to this: Shall we have a General Government? Shall we continue the union of the States under a *Government*, instead of a *league?* This is the upshot of the whole matter; because, if we are to have a Government, that Government must act like other governments, by majorities; it must have this power, like other governments, of enforcing its own laws and its own decisions; clothed with authority by the people, and always responsible to the people; it must be able to hold its course, unchecked by external interposition. According to the gentleman's views of the matter, the Constitution is a league; according to mine, it is a regular popular Government. This vital and all-important question the people will decide, and, in deciding it, they will determine whether, by ratifying the present CONSTITUTION AND FRAME OF GOVERNMENT, they meant to do nothing more than to amend the articles of the old Confederation."

The Compromise Tariff Bill finally passed the Senate on the 1st day of March, Mr. Webster, with fifteen other Senators, voting against it.[1]

In 1838, Mr. Webster wrote the following private letters to a friend, for the purpose of explaining his own course on this subject, and in order that there might remain a permanent record of his sentiments in regard to it—sentiments which I happen to know he never changed:

[TO MR. KETCHUM.]

"WASHINGTON, Monday Morning, *January* 18, 1838.

"DEAR SIR: In December, 1832, on my way to Washington, I fell in with Mr. Clay at Philadelphia. He then told me he had conceived a plan for quieting the tariff question, which he would communicate to me when we should reach Washington. In the early part of the session I learned what the plan was. It was first explained to me by Mr. Letcher, to whom I expressed my astonishment at hearing of any intention, by Mr.

[1] The votes in its favor were twenty-nine.

Clay, to bring forward such a proposition. It was a good deal talked over, privately, among friends. Mr. Clay put the proposed bill into the hands of Mr. Davis, my present colleague, then in the House of Representatives. Mr. Davis handed it to me, *in Mr. Clay's handwriting*, and I copied it; and that copy you have. When the bill was afterward introduced, those words which you speak of were left out. The bill was discussed in the Senate, referred to a committee (of which I was one), and again reported to the Senate; and it became understood that it would pass the Senate. I had, however, suggested that it was not a bill which could constitutionally originate in the Senate; and, this opinion appearing to gain ground, the proceeding in the Senate stopped all at once, and Mr. Letcher introduced the measure into the House, had it referred to the Committee of the Whole, as the rules require, *but with instructions to report the same bill, without amendment, back to the House.* This was done accordingly; the bill immediately passed; came to the Senate, and passed there also. In a day or two I will send you a copy of the bill, as Mr. Clay first introduced it into the Senate, and such other facts, from the journals, as may place you in possession of the exact history of the bill. But if you will look at the law, as it now stands, you will find that it completely negatives all idea of protection:

1. Because it expressly confines revenue to the wants of Government.

2. Because it expressly rejects *discrimination*, which is the *only* true and practical mode of protection.

Yours truly,

"DANIEL WEBSTER.

"Mr. Ketchum."

[TO MR. KETCHUM.]

"WASHINGTON, *January* 20, 1838.

MY DEAR SIR: I enclose you a copy of Mr. Clay's bill, in 1833, as originally prepared by him. The copy was made by me, from the original, in Mr. Clay's own handwriting. Some alterations took place before the measure was formally brought forward, as others, during its progress in Congress. Nevertheless, if you examine the law, it is now, in truth, an attempt by Congress to surrender the protecting power, and strike it out of the Constitution. I opposed this bill in every stage, and so did three-fourths of the tariff interest in both Houses. All the South went for it; Mr. Clay's personal friends went for it, and a few good men from the North and the Centre, from various motives, went for it also; for example, Mr. Bell, of New Hampshire, and Mr. Frelinghuysen.

"The bill passed at the end of the session. I took my notes, etc., along with me, and, staying a day or two at Philadelphia, sat down to write out my speech at length. A friend happened to come in, and, finding out what I was about, dissuaded me from it. He said the act was done, the thing was settled; and the publication of my speech would only prove a wide difference to exist among friends. I acquiesced, which I have ever since regretted. When I reached New York, I had conversation on the subject with Mr. C. King. *I left with him my notes.* I wish they could now be had. I think he once told me he could lay his hands on them. This copy of Mr. Clay's original proposition I wish you to preserve. I can send you, if you wish it, a list of ayes and noes on the passage of the bill in both Houses. All Massachusetts went against it.

"Yours truly,

"DANIEL WEBSTER."

The Ordinance of South Carolina, which undertook to nullify the revenue laws of the United States, was never repealed. That State rested satisfied, as Mr. Webster said she would, with what she had gained; satisfied that she had extorted from Congress at least a suspension of the power to discriminate in favor of domestic manufactures when levying duties on foreign merchandise. When it is remembered that this concession was contemporaneous with the assertion on the floor of Congress of the doctrine of State nullification, we can see that the public men who ruled the action of South Carolina had no reason for regarding the passage of the "Force Bill" as a defeat, and no special cause for putting that measure to the test of execution. As years flowed on, the teachings of Mr. Calhoun became the political creed of her rising youth. They led directly to the belief in the right of State secession from the Union—a belief that, in the succeeding generation of public men in the South, spread far beyond her own limits. Had she been told by the unanimous voice of the country, as represented in Congress, that no concessions could be made to her menaces, we cannot now say that the theory of nullification and its cognate doctrines would not have continued to have advocates and followers. But it is not probable that such a theory could have attained the proportions which it afterward reached, or that it would ever have culminated, as it did at the end of another quarter of a century, in an attempted disruption of the ties that bound the Southern States to the Union. In seeking for the explanation of revolutionary movements, we are too apt to regard them as inevitable, and to consider that they have flowed from events and causes independent of the conduct of men and parties. But all who would understand Mr. Webster's opinions on this momentous subject, or who would do him justice—all who may be inclined to think that he leaned on this occasion too strongly to the side of authority, and too little to the side of conciliation—must endeavor to stand where he stood, and to look, as he looked, into the future. They must recognize what presented itself to his con victions; which was no less than the certainty that the Southern quarter of the Union would not alone be the theatre of factious resistance to law; that the day would come when *that section* would have cause to invoke and depend upon the same principle of supremacy in the Constitution which he had now so signally displayed and vindicated; and that, if this principle were weakened *now*, the character of the Government, at some distant day, would have to be asserted by more than the power of argument. All, too, who would rightly estimate his subsequent career, must learn how this occurrence threw upon him, afterward, the necessity, in following out his constitutional principles, of encountering the popular feeling of his own community, when it arrayed itself in opposition to the just authority of the fundamental law. He now saw, or believed that he saw, that authority remitted to an uncertain future, in which the prevalence of error would be wider, the motives for discontent would be multiplied, and the love of the Union would be enfeebled. For the exigencies of that hour, which he always feared was in store for us, he made all the preparation that any human intellect could make, by the maintenance and elucidation of the principles on which he believed that the political institutions of this country rest. He was never called to look upon that scene of fraternal strife in which those principles had to be enforced in the shock of armies. He prayed that such a scene might never open on his vision; and his prayer was heard. But he always feared that it would come, and it did come.

[TO MR. PERRY, OF SOUTH CAROLINA.]

"BOSTON, *April* 10, 1833.

"MY DEAR SIR: I was gratified by the receipt of your letter of the 1st of this month, and thank you for the favorable and friendly sentiments which you express in regard to an effort of mine, at the late session of Congress, in a cause which I deemed all-important to the country, and to which I had already learned you were as much devoted as myself. I am not at all surprised, my dear sir, at the opinions you express, as to the ultimate object of those who have raised the flag of nullification. Circumstances, full of meaning, attracted my attention to it early; and, in December, 1828, I became thoroughly convinced that the plan of a Southern Confederacy had been received with favor by a great many of the political men of the South, especially of your State.

"I agree with you also entirely in the opinion that the danger is not over. A systematic and bold attack, now but just begun, will be carried on, I apprehend, against the just and constitutional powers of the Government, and against whatsoever strengthens the Union of the States.

"For my own part, I look forward to an animated controversy on these points for years to come; and if we can sustain our side of the controversy, my dear sir, with success, as I hope and believe we may, we shall transmit to posterity an inheritance above all price.

"I do not apprehend any further difficulty with Georgia. There was not the slightest reference to the Georgia case in my mind, or ever, as far as I know, in that of any other gentleman, in preparing and passing the bill for the better collection of the revenue. It is true that some of the provisions of the bill ought, in my judgment, to be permanent. If they had previously existed, the idea of putting the doctrines of nullification in practice, in the mode recently adopted at least, would probably not have been entertained. I have expected what I see now publicly announced, that the effort will be to repeal this law so soon as Congress shall assemble.

"It is probably expected that, since the occasion has passed by, many will be willing to repeal the law, although they were in favor of its passage at the time; and it is hoped that, by the repeal of this act, it may be considered as decided that Congress is hereafter to take no step to execute any laws which are resisted by State authority.

"The high regard which I feel for the patriotic gentlemen with whom you act in your State, and the respect which I have been led to entertain for yourself, induce me, my dear sir, to express a wish to hear from you, on the interesting subjects which at present occupy the public attention, whenever your convenience may allow.

"With friendly salutations, I remain,

"Your obedient servant,

"DANL. WEBSTER."

The reader may now turn from these public events, in which Mr. Webster performed so conspicuous and important a part, to the following letter from his daughter, at this time of the age of sixteen, written with much of the father's admirable simplicity and correctness of style—a style which he may be said to have imparted to all his children, for Fletcher, Julia, and Edward, all wrote through life the same unaffected and easy English that belonged to him. The mention of her brother Fletcher's "part" at "exhibition" relates to a college performance. He was graduated from Harvard College in the autumn of this year:

[FROM MISS JULIA WEBSTER.]

"BOSTON, *March* 3, 1833.

"MY DEAR FATHER: I received your beautiful present a few days since, and was very much pleased with it. I think it contains some very fine faces, and I like the stories much better than those usually found in "souvenirs" or "annuals." Your letter preceded it a few days, and I beg you, my dearest father, to accept your little daughter's best thanks for them both.

"I am staying with Cousin Eliza, and am passing my time most pleasantly. I find it very convenient as regards my school, as I am never late now, which used sometimes to be the case. I have not commenced any new study since I last wrote you. I think I should like to study Italian very much, as I have not much to do.

"I hope we shall soon see you in Boston, as Congress has risen; and we are very anxious to see you at home once more. Although spring has in reality begun, you would not imagine it to be so by the weather, which is intensely cold; the ground is covered with snow, and the thermometer last night was eleven degrees below zero.

"Fletcher dined with us yesterday, it being Saturday. I suppose you have heard he is to have a part at the next exhibition. Dr. and Mrs. Kirkland dined here to-day; the latter had, as usual, a good deal to say. I saw Edward yesterday; he was very well.

"I went, on Wednesday, with Cousin Eliza to hear a lecture on hieroglyphics, delivered by Mr. J. Pickering. It was very interesting; but he did not tell us as much upon the principal subject as I should have liked to have heard. A considerable part of it was upon the necessity of attention, which he addressed principally to his younger hearers.

"I heard two very good sermons to day from Mr. Greenwood, one of which I shall make an abstract of for my composition. It was upon the resignation of the Shunamitish woman when she lost her only son. Cousin Eliza says she wishes you would come home, for she thinks if you were here we should not think any more of the snow or the cold, for it would make sunshine in Boston. She also unites with me in a great deal of love to you; and, believe me ever, dear father,

"Your affectionate daughter,

"JULIA WEBSTER."

[TO MISS JULIA WEBSTER.]

"WASHINGTON, *Ma*[illegible] 1833.

"MY DEAR DAUGHTER: I have this moment received your letter of the 3d instant. It is so kind and good a letter that I will not omit for a moment to answer it, although I am expecting a summons to go directly into court. Notwithstanding your mother's absence, I have felt quite easy about you since I learned you were to spend your time at Cousin Eliza's. Everybody is happy where she is.

"I am glad to hear that Fletcher has a part at exhibition. You do not mention the time; I fear it will be before I get home.

"We have the same cold weather here, at least in some degree, of which you speak. The last ten days have been the severest part of the winter. Some signs of relenting begin now to appear.

"I heard yesterday from your mother in New York. I have written her, preferring that she should meet me in Philadelphia, as I shall be obliged to stay there on business for a day or two.

"The court will rise about the fifteenth, and, by the end of next week, say by the sixteenth, I hope to take leave of Washington.

"I must pray you to remember me most kindly to Mr. and Mrs. Lee. Give my love also to Edward and to Uncle Paige and Aunt Henriette, not forgetting the amiable Miss Paige.

"Adieu, my dear daughter.

"Ever your most affectionate father,

"DANIEL WEBSTER."

Mr. Webster returned to Boston at about the middle of April, to make preparation for his long-intended journey to the West. He soon heard, however, of General Jackson's proposed visit to the Eastern States, and was a good deal embarrassed by the probability of his own absence from Boston at the time of the President's arrival. He wrote to General Cass, the Secretary of War, to explain the cause of his intended absence, from whom he received the following answer, and to whom he wrote again in reply:

[FROM GENERAL CASS.]

"WASHINGTON, *April* 17, 1833.

"MY DEAR SIR: I have just received your kind letter, and sincerely thank you for your recollection of me. I think the President will visit New England this season; if he does, he will leave here about the first of May, and he is desirous that I should accompany him. I shall accordingly do so; and I presume we shall be in Boston not far from the 20th of June.

I cannot ask you to postpone your intended journey till after this time, as it might expose you to much inconvenience. Still, I will confess to you that the hope of meeting you, and of revisiting with you the scenes and friends of our youth, has dwelt upon my mind since we first conversed together on the subject. Nothing could give me greater pleasure than such an occasion; and, if more pressing engagements should require your absence at the time I have mentioned, I shall look forward at a future day to realize this hope.

"With sincere regard, I am, my dear sir,

"Truly your friend,

"LEWIS CASS."

[TO GENERAL CASS.]

"MY DEAR SIR: I have received your letter of the 17th instant. A journey to the West has long been in contemplation by me, but I have not yet been able to accomplish it. Every other year the session of Congress has been so far protracted as to forbid the undertaking for that season, and professional duties have allowed me no leisure, hitherto, in the intervening years. In addition to these causes, the political state of things has, for some time, been such that the motive and objects of such a tour would have been very likely to be misinterpreted and misunderstood.

"In this last respect, the present moment seems favorable; and, as I have found myself able to make the necessary arrangements with my professional engagements, I have thought it not well to defer longer the execution of that which has been already a good while postponed.

"Nevertheless, I am very unwilling to miss your visit to New England: and, although I might even make that sacrifice in the hope that you would, as you suggest, hereafter repeat your visit, I still feel great reluctance in being from home when the President comes to Massachusetts. In the first place, it would give me pleasure to see him, and to extend to him and his party the hospitalities of my house, as well as to unite with my friends and neighbors in such manifestations of respect as are due to him; and, in the next place, my absence on such an occasion, when it was known that a visit from him to this part of the country was intended, may be liable to much misconstruction.

"I am inclined, therefore, at all events, to be at home by the time the President reaches Boston. My plan has been to return by the 1st of July, if I shall not be able to accomplish all I intend, and return earlier than that day. But, under present circumstances, I shall abridge the extent of my travels, so as to be able to return to Boston by the 20th of June.

"D. W."

Mr. Webster arrived at Albany, accompanied by his wife and daughter, and by his friend Mr. Stephen White, in the latter part of May. Agriculture was, as I have said, one of his passions; and at Albany he was a delighted visitor of the celebrated farm of Mr. Buel. From Albany the ladies returned to Boston, and Mr. Webster went on his way to the West. On the 4th of June he was at Utica, where all political distinctions were forgotten by the citizens in their manifestations of respect to this great man, whom few could have ever before seen, and whom all were anxious to honor. He tarried long enough in the rich valley of the Genesee to examine and enjoy its magnificent agriculture, strongly contrasting with that of less fertile New England. On his arrival at Buffalo he was invited to a public dinner, but declined it, preferring an unrestrained and unceremonious intercourse with the citizens of the place. He was present at the launching of a steamboat that was to be called by his name, and the local courts that were in session at the time were adjourned in honor of the event. Here, too, he received an address from the mechanics and manufacturers, to which he replied in some remarks expressing his views of the tariff policy. At Columbus he declined another public dinner, but at Cincinnati he was obliged to accept one that was tendered to him by a general meeting of the citizens, held at the Exchange on the 15th of June. The dinner took place a few days afterward. The toast expressed the feelings of a great company of intelligent persons toward "the profound expounder of the Constitution, the eloquent supporter of the Federal Union, and the uniform friend and advocate of the Western country." Mr. Webster spoke in reply for more than an hour, but the speech is not preserved.

At Cincinnati, invitations of the most earnest kind poured in upon him from the surrounding States. But it was impossible for him to go farther. The cholera was then prevailing in many of the Western towns, and the season was so far advanced that he deemed it prudent to return through Pennsylvania. Before he left Cincinnati, he received the subjoined cordial letter from Mr. Clay:

[FROM MR. CLAY.]

"ASHLAND, 17*th June*, 1833.

"MY DEAR SIR: The mail brought me to-day your letter of the 10th, from Columbus, and also the intelligence of your safe arrival in

Cincinnati. I had been tracing in the papers your progress with much interest.

"I regret extremely that you should find us, in so many places, suffering with cholera. Its visit to Lexington has been frightful. Its mortality there has been exceeded in degree at no other point in the United States, New Orleans, perhaps, excepted. The shops and stores and principal hotel have been all closed. The pestilence, within the two or three last days, has considerably declined, and in a few more will, I think, have disappeared. Happily, in a family of about sixty, we have as yet sustained no loss, and are not sure that we have had one case of genuine cholera.

"I shall be mortified and disappointed if you do not visit Kentucky and Lexington; but I hardly know how to advise you. You will certainly go to Louisville, where there is no danger. At that place daily intelligence is received from Lexington, and you can hear whether there has been such an abatement of the cholera as to enable you to visit us without hazard. I hope the state of things will admit of your coming, and I request that you and Mr. White will come directly to Ashland, and any other gentlemen, if there be any other in your party, where, judging from the past, you will be secure, if the disease should even continue to prevail at Lexington. It is not at Frankfort, the principal intermediate point, and where, as everywhere else, your visit has been anticipated with great pleasure.

"As for myself, I shall not leave home for the North until between the 10th and 15th July, if I go at all.

"Poor Johnston's untimely fate has filled me with grief. I fear Mr. White has not survived.

"Favor me with a line from Louisville as to your movements; and believe me always faithfully,

"Your friend,

"H. CLAY.

"The Honorable D. Webster.

"P. S.—I write in duplicate to Louisville and Cincinnati."

He left Cincinnati on the 20th of June. In Pennsylvania, at Washington, and at Pittsburg, public dinners awaited him, both of which he accepted. At the latter place, the demonstration was of a very imposing character. Of the whole tour, the *National Intelligencer*, of the 13th of July, said: "Mr. Webster has wrought little less than a miracle upon the party feuds and divisions of the Western country. He has fairly extinguished the one and obliterated the other;" and it spoke of the complete political amalgamation perceptible in the list of the committee which invited him to Nashville, the home of President Jackson, in Tennessee. It was a time of very bitter political divisions, and these divisions in the West were of the most extreme character. But men forgot their divisions, forgot their personal and party rancors, wherever Mr. Webster came, and, where he could not come, they united frankly and earnestly in expressing their regrets that any circumstances whatever should have prevented them from manifesting their respect and regard for him. These multiplied public proofs of the consideration in which he was held by large numbers of his political opponents were looked upon with much jealousy by a certain class of their associates in the East. When connected with what soon became known respecting the sentiments of the President himself, and of some of the principal statesmen about him, toward Mr. Webster, these occurrences stimulated a purpose to prevent the latter, if possible, from acquiring further influence with General Jackson. This purpose found the means by which it could be accomplished. The following memorandum, dictated by Mr. Webster in 1838, discloses, in the concluding sentence, the peculiar topic that was made the means of opening a new subject of difference between him and the President, which would render it necessary for him to oppose with renewed vigor the measures into which the Administration was led.

"General Jackson took an early opportunity to thank Mr. Webster *personally* for his support of the Administration on this occasion [the "Force Bill"]; and Mr. Livingston expressed his own sense, and that of General Jackson's friends, repeatedly, and in warm terms. Before the end of the session, a member of the Senate, of General Jackson's party, asked Mr. Webster to look at a list of applicants for an office from the Eastern States. This Mr. Webster declined, as he did not wish to place himself under any obligation. In May, 1833, Mr. Webster set out on a journey to the West, and returned in June [July]. On his return, he met Mr. Livingston in New York, who was then preparing to depart on his mission to France. It was understood at that time, in private and confidential circles, that, before leaving Washington, Mr. Livingston had frequent conversations with General Jackson respecting Mr. Webster, and expressing the hope that he would be able to continue his support of General Jackson's Administration. These conversations were stated to Mr. W. On many points of what was then the proposed future policy of the Government, there was no great difference of opinion; but there was an irreconcilable difference on the great question of the currency." [1]

[1] Ketchum MS.—It has been stated by Mr. Everett that, on the day when Mr. Webster replied to Mr. Calhoun on the "Force Bill," the President's carriage was sent to Mr. Webster's lodgings, with a message borne by the President's private

Mr. Webster knew in the summer of 1833, before he went on his journey to the West, that the President had determined to remove the public deposits from the Bank of the United States as soon as he could effect it. But he could not speak publicly of this information; and, therefore, when he had occasion, at Pittsburg, to refer to the President, he confined himself to that part of his conduct which related to his action against the "Nullifiers," on which Mr. Webster said:

"Gentlemen, the President of the United States was, as it seemed to me, at this eventful crisis, true to his duty. He comprehended and understood the case, and met it as it was proper to meet it. While I am as willing as others to admit that the President has, on other occasions, rendered important services to the country, and especially on that occasion which has given him so much military renown, I yet think the ability and decision with which he rejected the disorganizing doctrines of nullification create a claim, than which he has none higher, to the gratitude of the country and the respect of posterity. The appearance of the proclamation of the 10th of December inspired me, I confess, with new hopes for the duration of the Republic. I regarded it as just, patriotic, able, and imperiously demanded by the condition of the country. I would not be understood to speak of particular clauses and phrases in the proclamation; but I regard its great and leading doctrines as the true and only true doctrines of the Constitution. They constitute the sole ground on which dismemberment can be resisted. Nothing else, in my opinion, can hold us together. While these opinions are maintained, the Union will last; when they shall be generally rejected and abandoned, that Union will be at the mercy of a temporary majority in any one of the States.

"I speak, gentlemen, on this subject without reserve. I have not intended, heretofore and elsewhere, and do not now intend here, to stint my commendation of the conduct of the President in regard to the proclamation and the subsequent measures. I have differed with the President, as all know, who know any thing of so humble an individual as myself, on many questions of great general interest and importance. . . . But all these differences afforded, in my judgment, not the slightest reason for opposing him in a measure of paramount importance, and at a moment of great public exigency. I sought to take counsel of nothing but patriotism, to feel no impulse but that of duty, and to yield not a lame and hesitating, but a vigorous and cordial support to measures, which, in my

secretary. The carriage being at the door at the time when Mr. Webster was about to go to the Capitol, it conveyed him to the Senate-chamber.—(Biographical Memoir, prefixed to Mr. Webster's Works, i., 109.)

conscience, I believed to be essential to the preservation of the Constitution."

The present chapter may be closed with some selections from Mr. Webster's private correspondence during the winter and spring of this year:

[FROM MR. J. E. DENISON.]

"OSSINGTON, NEWARK, *January* 21, 1833.

"MY DEAR SIR: It is a long time since I have written to you, and I say it with the more shame, as in the interval I have received a very friendly letter from you. I trust our friendship is sufficiently deep-rooted not to suffer materially from an occasional drought. We have had two or three years of difficulties and troubles, and of great labor and anxiety to all connected in any way with public affairs. You have been moving on for the same time in a course of even prosperity which I have rejoiced to contemplate, and sometimes, perhaps, allowed myself to envy. The late movements in your affairs have excited, of course, great interest in this country. The latest document I have seen is General Jackson's proclamation. I cannot bring myself to believe that your differences will be allowed to run to very extreme lengths. My sense of the justness of public opinion throughout the United States, and of its uncontrollable power, convinces me that you will settle the question in dispute without violence, and certainly without a dissolution of your Federal Government. In both countries just now separation is the cry. I prove my confidence in American good sense in confessing that I think Governor Hamilton and nullification will be more easily settled than O'Connell and repeal.

"The subject and the occasion will be worthy of your powers, and I look forward with delight to their display, instructing your countrymen and mankind.

"We are breathing in this country more freely and calmly than we have done for some years; a sort of repose after the excitement of the great fight for reform, and the celebration of the victory in the elections. I have been tossed about among two or three constituencies, and am at last quietly settled among my neighbors as the representative of the south division of the county of Nottingham. My colleague is Lord Lincoln, the eldest son of the Duke of Newcastle; he has had a public education at Eton and Oxford, and, with a very good disposition, is much more a man of the world than his father, and likely to keep out of scrapes, and to lead an easier life. Our friend Wortley, who took a decided Tory line, is thrown out of Parliament and public life for the present. Stanley is, as you know, a Cabinet minister and Secretary for Ireland. Labouchere is a Lord of the Admiralty, and I occupy the place of an independent country gentleman, and M. P. for my own county. I declined taking office under Lord Grey when I had the offer of Secretary for Indian Affairs. I acquiesced in the Reform Bill, and supported it through all its leading provisions, but declined further identifying myself at that time with its authors. We now stand at the commencement of a new era; and the first question will be, whether the impulse given to the movement party (to use a French phrase) can be resisted by those who gave the first impulse to the movement. Can Lord Grey and his colleagues put a drag-chain on their own car? I shall lend them all my aid to enable them to do so. Great changes in church and in almost every department must and ought to follow. But the check wanted is no further change in the constitution of the House of Commons. The movement party cries out for the ballot, for triennial Parliaments, for household suffrage. At present I am quite sure the mass of the country, nine-tenths of the property and education and respectability, do not want further change, but, on the contrary, entirely deprecate it. A very great deal turns on the discretion of the Government, and I am not sure that of that quality there is in some of its members a very large stock.

"I wish you would enlighten me on the ballot. I did not, while in America, pay very much attention to its real working and effect. I heard various opinions about it, but did not examine them minutely. Some said the ballot did not effect secrecy, that people's votes were still known. What should you say about it?

"I am very curious, too, about the success of some of your experiments in prison discipline. How does the plan adopted at Auburn answer? Perhaps you could get our friend the Judge to write me a letter on this subject.

"I hope you have not given up all idea of paying us a visit here. It would give me the greatest pleasure to see you, and I would devote myself to you to make your time pass as agreeably as I could.

"With my best remembrances to the Judge, and to any of my friends who may keep me in their memory,

"Believe me,

"Yours very sincerely,

"J. E. Denison."

[TO MR. PAIGE.]

"Washington, Friday, P. M., *March* 5, 1833.

"Dear William: I give you great joy at the birth of a daughter! There is no event on which I could more sincerely congratulate you. A daughter is one of Heaven's best and sweetest gifts to man. It delights me to hear of her dark hair, dark eyes, and high forehead, although it costs me an involuntary tear, by the recollection of poor little Grace. My dear sir, I share your feelings, and partake your joy. May a thousand blessings hover over the little stranger! I beg to be most particularly remembered to Harriette. What a new world this has become to her by the events of a year! Pray give her my love.

"I shall write a note forthwith to the Judge,[1] and send Charles off with it. I met Mr. Appleton between the House and my seat in the Senate, he bringing me the news, I carrying it to him. So you see the young lady makes a stir in Washington already. I thank you for your continued attention to my land matters, etc.

"I would be glad to help poor Edward along with his hard lessons, if I were at home. Tell him to keep good courage. Making Latin is hard work, but it will grow easier.

"Yours most truly always,

"D. WEBSTER."

[TO MR. PAIGE.]

"WASHINGTON, *March* 10, 1833.

"DEAR WILLIAM: I have been exceedingly glad to hear from you from day to day, with accounts of Harriette and Miss Paige. I rejoice to think that, by the time you receive this, Harriette will be at the head of her own table again; for

'What is a table, richly spread,
Without a lady at its head?'

"Although not a passionate lover of children, that I know nothing about, yet I really long to see this little specimen of humanity.

"Mr. Appleton and Mr. Dutton seem much pleased with the result of the sales. They think it was better than was to be expected. They both perused the catalogue, etc., many an hour, while I read the newspapers. Mr. and Mrs. Dutton leave us on Monday next.

"I hear that Mrs. Webster was at Baltimore last night; and, while I write this, I am expecting every moment to see her. Charles keeps watch at the door.

"Pray dispatch Mr. White by the 15th. I want to see him, but do not let the girls suppose I am desirous of seeing them.

"P. S. Six o'clock.—Mrs. Webster came into this great city at three, with Mrs. Edgar, Herman Newbold, and Mr. Hamilton Fish. All well.

"I write to Mr. White by this post; if he shall have left you, you may either send it after him to New York, or put it into the fire, no matter which.

"Yours,

"D. W."

[TO MR. PAIGE.]

"WASHINGTON, Tuesday Morning, *April* 24, 1833.

"DEAR WILLIAM: I have received yours respecting the lining of the chaise. I do not like a dark lining; such linings look hot in summer, and

[1] Judge Story, uncle to Mrs. Paige.

in winter I go in a sleigh. I reject blue; therefore, the body and carriage being dark, I suppose a light drab would not answer, and dark drab looks dull. On the whole, I am for a brown, or a claret, though, if I know what a claret is, it is rather darker than I should like, yet I think it will do very well. Please ask Harriette whether it shall be a claret or a brown, and decide according to her response, as I hope she will sometimes do my new chaise the honor to take a drive in it.

"I hear that Mr. White and daughters left Baltimore yesterday morning. Of course, Mr. A. and Mrs. White did not reach them there. They will, doubtless, overtake them this night at Philadelphia. I am happy to say that my letters this morning, dated Sunday morning, represented Mrs. Jones as a great deal better.

"Yours truly,

"D. WEBSTER."

CHAPTER XX.

1833-1834.

MR. WEBSTER'S FINANCIAL VIEWS—REMOVAL OF THE GOVERNMENT DEPOSITS FROM THE BANK OF THE UNITED STATES—MR. CLAY'S RESOLUTIONS OF CENSURE—MR. WEBSTER'S REPORT ON THE REMOVAL OF THE DEPOSITS—INTRODUCES A BILL TO MEET THE CRISIS—THE PRESIDENT'S PROTEST AGAINST THE RESOLUTIONS OF THE SENATE—SPEECH IN ANSWER TO THE PROTEST—PERSONAL RELATIONS TO THE BANK—RISE OF THE WHIG PARTY.

THE "irreconcilable difference on the great question of the currency," between Mr. Webster and the Administration of General Jackson, is a topic that requires to be carefully understood by the reader. To this understanding, a statement of Mr. Webster's opinions on the subject of the currency is here essential.

He was in Congress when the last bank of the United States was created, in 1816, and, after an interval of five or six years, he had been in public life ever since. The opinions which he held in 1816, respecting the duty of the General Government toward the currency of the country, and concerning the means of discharging that duty, had been confirmed by the whole experience of the period that had since elapsed. His financial system rested, for its corner-stone, on the principle that the Government should not permit its revenues to be paid in any bank-paper that was not in fact as well as in theory convertible at once into specie. This he regarded as the only efficient means of repressing a circulation of depreciated paper money. He caused this principle to be acted on by the Government, and it had been successful through the whole period of seventeen years. To a national bank, with a suitable capital, carefully guarded against the suspension of specie payments, either at the dictation of the Government or by its own action, he was not opposed in 1816. He believed then that the paper of such a bank could be made eminently useful in the exchanges of the country, and that it could be an important fiscal agent of the Government, relieving it of the necessity of moving great masses of specie from one part of the country to another whenever payments were to be made or balances were to be settled. But, so far as such a system rested upon the use of credit, or involved the use of credit, it was with Mr. Webster a cardinal principle that the paper instruments of that credit should be based on immediate convertibility into specie at the pleasure of the holder. This point being secured, he held that there was no reason why the Government should use gold and silver, exclusively, in its own transactions. On the contrary, from the magnitude of the public transactions, and their relation to the commercial exchanges of the country, he held it to be essential that there should be a mixed currency, alike capable of use by the Government and by individuals, consisting of specie and of bank paper securely representing specie. The existence of the State banks, with the power of issuing paper for a circulating medium, he regarded as an evil; but as an evil which it was better to regulate than to endeavor to suppress. Such regulation, of an indirect nature, could be exercised by a national bank, the effect of whose operations would be to limit the area over which the paper of such local banks would circulate, and thus their tendency to make excessive issues would be checked.

Mr. Webster was not, therefore, what is called a "hard-money man," in the sense which banishes all paper circulation; but in the sense that admits of the use of bank-paper, and yet which requires it, by suitable provisions of law, to be kept always and practically at the par of its nominal specie value, he was, as he always claimed to be, a "bullionist." Although the Bank of the United States, chartered in 1816, had some features which, as we have seen, caused him to vote against it, its operation and effect, coupled with the influence of his specie resolutions of the same year, had been entirely successful in producing a sound state of the currency. We have his recorded opinion, expressed in 1831, that "the United States have had a currency perfectly sound and safe, and more convenient, and producing local exchanges at less expense, than any other nation is, or ever was, blessed with."[1]

It is not probable that this condition of the currency would have been disturbed, if political events had not intruded an element of a personal nature into the question of renewing the charter of the Bank of the United States. General Jackson had refused his assent to a bill for renewing the charter of the bank, in 1832, previous to the election in which he was again a candidate for the presidency. He believed that the bank had entered the political field for the purpose of preventing his re-election; and he came to the discharge of the duties of his second presidency with a determination to prevent the bank from obtaining any prolongation of its existence. The belief which he and some of his friends entertained, naturally led to the conviction that a moneyed institution, possessed of so large a capital, and having certain practical powers over the whole paper circulation of the country, was a dangerous instrument, capable of political uses, and therefore capable of abuse. The effect of this conviction was, when it came to be acted on, to place a great moneyed capital in a struggle with the Executive Government for the retention of the privileges which it had enjoyed, and for which it claimed to have paid, and to be still paying, an ample equivalent in the benefits which its incorporation and its use, as regulated by law, conferred on the Government and the country. Whatever might be the result, the controversy was one that must necessarily cause great mischiefs to the public; for it was a controversy that could scarcely be tried upon its true merits, and it was very likely to lead to measures that were merely experimental and tentative, because there could be no transition from the existing financial system of the Government to another equally sound, convenient, and safe, while there was so much difference of opinion as to what the substitute ought to be, and while the immediate changes were so liable to be dictated by personal and party considerations.

[1] *Ante*, chap. vii., p. 150.

From this unfortunate attitude, and from the exposure to be led into immediate steps disastrous to the country, Mr. Webster would have saved the Administration of General Jackson, if he could have done so. There could have been no doubt entertained by any one that Mr. Webster's general system on the financial questions involved was the correct one. But an impartial consideration of principles was out of the question in the state of feeling which then existed. The President and many of his friends had come to entertain the belief that the bank must be compelled to wind up its affairs, and surrender its existence; and, consequently, that other modes of treating the relations between the Government and the currency, and of transacting the fiscal business of the United States, must be resorted to.

When, therefore, Mr. Livingston, in the summer of 1833, held the important conversation with Mr. Webster, in the city of New York, which developed the only irreconcilable difference between the latter gentleman and the Administration, as its future policy was stated to him, it is quite easy to see what that difference was. In the first place, Mr. Webster did not approve of the refusal to continue in existence the Bank of the United States; nor did he believe that, if the Executive hostility were not directed against it, it would be misused for political purposes. In the next place, he knew that the condition of the currency, dependent on the practical benefits secured by the operation of the bank, was perfectly sound and healthy; he held that this condition ought not to be disturbed by experimental efforts to find some other mode of managing the public finances; and that it could not be disturbed without producing universal commercial derangement and distress. He saw that the Administration, if the determinations of the President were persisted in, would be committed to a course of measures that were far more likely to be dictated by accidental circumstances, than they were to be the steps of a comprehensive policy that perceived distinctly the objects at which it meant to aim, and that grasped the principles on which a new system was to be based, so as to bring them into operation without serious injury to the business interests of the community. In the result Mr. Webster proved to be right. What the President was determined to prevent was, the renewal of the bank charter. What he did not foresee, and had not settled, was, the system that was to take its place.

It is probable that Mr. Livingston, in his conversation with Mr. Webster, must have alluded to the plan, which the President had already entertained, of removing the Government deposits from the Bank of the United States. At all events, Mr. Webster was aware of it, although it was not publicly known at the time of the interview between those gentlemen. The fact was, however, that, in the previous May, the President had consulted his Cabinet in regard to this measure, at a time when Mr. Louis McLane was Secretary of the Treasury. Two of the Secretaries had given written opinions in favor of the removal, and two had given their written opinions against it. Mr. McLane, by whom alone the removal could be ordered, was opposed to it. He was induced to accept a diplomatic appointment, and Mr. William J. Duane, of Pennsylvania, was made Secretary of the Treasury on the 29th of May. Although his known opinions were against the bank, he did not accept the office with a pledge that he would order the removal of the deposits, if required to do so.

This was the attitude of the Executive Department when the President went on his tour to the Eastern States, at a time when Mr. Webster was absent from home. The President left Washington early in June, remained in Boston and its neighborhood through that month, and reached Washington on his return on the 4th of July. Before his return, his purpose to have the deposits removed from the bank had become irrevocably fixed. If Mr. Webster had been in Boston during the President's visit, the latter would have had an opportunity, if he had chosen to use it, to sound Mr. Webster on the subject; or, if that is to be regarded as an improbable occurrence, it could scarcely have happened that the President, with the general confidence which he felt in Mr. Webster, and his acknowledged obligations to him, would not have held conversations with him that might have cleared the Executive mind of many delusive ideas, and rendered it less open to the influence of persons who had an object in misleading it. For, that General Jackson was misled when he was induced to take this step—that it was a step fraught with incalculable mischiefs to the country, and that it impelled the President into measures that ultimately cost his party the control of the Government—can now be seen with entire distinctness. All these consequences could have been pointed out by Mr. Webster, if General Jackson had been wise enough to have consulted a statesman who was personally disposed to aid him in what concerned the welfare of the country, and whose advice would have been given on purely public grounds. Undoubtedly, General Jackson's victory, as it has been accounted, over the Bank of the United States, has been regarded by many as his most famous civil achievement, and as entitling him to the gratitude of his contemporaries and of posterity. But this is a subject which has more than one side. We are here concerned with the view taken of it by Mr. Webster, and with his action in regard to it.[1]

By the charter of the bank, which was still in force as a law of the land, the moneys of the United States were required to be deposited in the bank or its branches, subject to a power of removal in the Secretary of the Treasury, who was required immediately to lay his reasons for such removal before Congress, if in session at the time, and, if Congress was not in session, as soon as it had assembled. In consideration of being made the depositary of the public funds, the bank had paid to the Government a million and a half of dollars, and had bound itself to make the necessary transfers of the public money,

[1] It is a remarkable fact, now generally overlooked, that President Jackson, who came into office in March, 1829, and who announced in his inaugural address that the great object of his Administration would be the reform of abuses, which he specified, did not mention the Bank of the United States as unconstitutional, unnecessary, or dangerous. In his annual message of December, 1829, he advanced the opinion that the *true bank for the use of the Government of the United States would be one founded on the revenues and credit of the Government itself.* When, therefore, it is claimed for General Jackson, as the great merit of his official career, that he severed the Government from all connection with a bank, and taught us the dangers of such a connection, two things should be remembered: First, that he was the first President who ever propounded the idea of an executive bank founded on the revenues and credit of the Government; second, that the plan to which he resorted after he had removed the public deposits from the Bank of the United States, namely, to unite certain State banks in a fiscal agency for the Government for the collection and disbursement of its revenues, was in substance the same kind of executive bank which he recommended in December, 1829. Moreover, it was a system which, without any sanction of law, brought the whole money power of the Government under the direct management and control of the Executive. It certainly effected no divorce of the Government from banking institutions; although it did divorce the connection between the Government and one particular bank.

throughout the country, for the payment of the public creditors, without any charge or allowance on account of differences of exchange. Although, at the last session of Congress, the bank had failed, in consequence of the President's opposition, to obtain a prolongation of its charter, the present charter would not expire until the year 1836, and the legal and fiscal relations between the bank and the Government remained unchanged.

Soon after the return of the President to Washington, it began to be publicly rumored that an irresponsible cabal was trying to induce him to order the removal of the public deposits from the Bank of the United States, and to place them in certain selected State banks. Before the end of July, it was announced in the official newspaper that an agent had been appointed by the Secretary of the Treasury, under the direction of the President, to ascertain from the State banks in the principal cities on what terms and in what manner they would be willing to perform the services hitherto rendered by the Bank of the United States, if the Government should think proper to remove the deposits. This inquiry was actively conducted in August and September. On the 18th of September, the President read a paper to his Cabinet, announcing the final conclusions of his own mind, and the reasons on which they were founded. In this paper, he made known to them that the measure was his own, and that he assumed the responsibility of it. He did not require their concurrence, but he made it very plain that he would not brook opposition. He named the first day of October as the period when the removal was to take place, or sooner, provided the necessary arrangements could be made with the State banks.

The Secretary of the Treasury, Mr. Duane, believing that the law referred to his judgment, and not to the judgment of the President, the question whether the custody of the public moneys should at any time be changed, and not concurring in the President's reasons for this act, declined to order the removal.[1] The President dismissed him from office on the 23d

[1] That there was no reasonable ground for the apprehension that had been excited in the breast of the President, is apparent from the fact that, at the recent session of Congress in the winter of 1832–'33, the House of Representatives, after in-

of September, and on the same day, Mr. Taney, afterward Chief Justice of the United States, was appointed Secretary of the Treasury. Before this occurrence, namely, on the 20th, the official newspaper was authorized to state that the deposits would be removed from the Bank of the United States and placed in the State banks as soon as the necessary arrangements could be made. This intelligence was received in the city of New York, the commercial centre of the United States, on the 21st, with extraordinary sensations of alarm and reprehension. On the 26th, Mr. Taney signed an official order removing the deposits.

There was no existing law authorizing the selection of the State banks as custodians of the public money, and no authority in the Secretary of the Treasury to make contracts with the State banks for the performance of the duties of fiscal agents of the Government, excepting as such a power could be inferred by remote implication from the Secretary's authority to change the custody of the public funds when Congress was not in session.

When these occurrences afterward became known to the country, it appeared very plainly that while a Secretary of the Treasury was in office who held it to be his duty not to remove the deposits until Congress could consider the propriety and expediency of the step, the President had determined that the removal should be made, and that he changed the officer in order to secure obedience to his will. It also appeared that the President had considered no other plan for the custody of the public funds and for the performance of the fiscal agency for the Government, hitherto performed by the Bank of the United States, and regulated by the law contained in the charter of that bank, except that the custody and the fiscal agency should be intrusted to certain State banks, to be selected by the Executive. When this measure was resolved on and executed, the project which was afterward developed, for dispensing with all bank agency, and conducting the fiscal operations of the Government by the direct action of the Treasury, as well as the further plan of making gold and silver the sole medium of circulation, had not become parts of the Administration scheme.

vestigation, had pronounced the bank to be a well-conducted institution, and had expressed the opinion that the public moneys were entirely safe in its keeping. When Mr. Taney assigned his reasons for removing the deposits, he did not rest his justification upon the charge that they were not in safe custody.

When, therefore, Congress assembled in December, the country was undergoing the effects of this sudden change in the relations of the Government to the Bank of the United States, and had entered upon the experiment of substituting State banks for the performance of the various duties imposed by law upon the national institution. The removal of the public deposits from the Bank of the United States was immediately followed by a contraction of its loans, and a general panic; and so great was the commercial distress, that, as soon as Congress was assembled, memorials from all quarters of the country were poured upon its tables urging a restoration of the public moneys to the institution to which the law had confided them. The experiment, too, of making use of the State banks as fiscal agents of the Government had already failed to command the public confidence, while it had pushed the selected banks into a position in which they were certain to become the instruments of wild speculation in the hands of their managers, which was to ruin many of them in the end, entailing a long course of disasters upon the several communities within the spheres of their operation.

Yet the condition of the public mind was at the very time of these events in some respects favorable to the change. Perhaps no man has ever held the office of President of the United States with more personal power than General Jackson. Among great masses of the people there was such a conviction of his patriotism and honesty, that, while they disapproved of his acts, and saw their arbitrary or illegal character, they gave him credit for wisdom and integrity in his ends, and were willing to overlook the objectionable character of his means. Over the public men who belonged to his political party, and over the party itself, he exercised an almost absolute sway. Few dared to withstand a will that was at once so inflexible and so imperious. He was, too, a great and most adroit politician in the personal management of those whom he had occasion to influence; knowing well when to restrain and when to unbridle his own temper, and holding its manifestations under the guidance of an instinct that enabled him to perceive when they would be useful, or when they would be misapplied. It must ever be regarded as a striking proof of the mere power which he exercised over the people of this country, that two such statesmen as Mr. Webster and Mr. Clay put forth the exertion of every faculty that they possessed, each in his own characteristic way, to convince the people that the measures of General Jackson were often wrong, both in point of constitutional authority and in point of present expediency; and yet he always carried them, and the great men who opposed them had to wait for the recognitions of the future, and for that popular conviction which comes only after public suffering has enforced the truth.

On the assembling of Congress, Mr. Webster was chosen chairman of the Senate Committee on Finance. He had made up his mind that there was but one course that ought to be pursued. Congress, he thought, would have to act for the relief of the country from the prevailing and increasing distress. It would have to regulate, in some form, the custody of the public money, and not leave it to the discretionary control of the Executive. He did not believe in the capacity of the State banks to fulfil the functions which had been performed by the Bank of the United States; and he foretold with the utmost distinctness how that incapacity would, as it did, reveal itself. Although he held that the only suitable remedy for the existing state of things was, to continue the national bank in existence for a short period beyond its present charter, until Congress could more deliberately determine on the financial system best adapted to the wants of the country and of the Government, he considered it to be the first duty of Congress to act upon the reasons assigned by the Secretary of the Treasury, in his official report, for the removal of the deposits, and to vindicate its own authority over the subject against the assumption by the Executive of powers not vested in it by the Constitution and the laws. This action, he maintained, should not be allowed to be mixed with or influenced by the question whether there was or was not to be in the future a national bank. At the same time, he did not hesitate to declare his own opinion to be, that a national bank, in some form, was a national necessity, and that the period could not then be foreseen when it would cease to be so. But the first thing to be done was to decide whether the deposits should be restored to the Bank of the United States, or whether they were to be left in the custody of the Secretary of the Treasury without the sanction and regulation of law. These were the opinions with which Mr. Webster entered the Senate at this momentous session.

On the 26th of December, Mr. Clay introduced two resolutions, the first of which declared that the President, by dismissing the late Secretary of the Treasury because he would not, contrary to his own sense of duty, remove the public deposits from the bank, and by appointing his successor to effect such removal, which had been done, had assumed the exercise of a power over the Treasury not granted to him by the Constitution and the laws, and dangerous to the liberties of the people. His second resolution pronounced the reasons assigned by the Secretary of the Treasury for the removal unsatisfactory and insufficient.[1] During a long and excited discussion which en-

[1] The Secretary of the Treasury, Mr. Taney, assumed the ground, first, that the power to remove the deposits was vested in him, and that Congress, under the stipulations in the charter of the bank, could not direct it to be done; second, that the exercise of his power did not depend merely on the safety of the public money in the hands of the bank, nor on the fidelity with which it had conducted itself, but that he had the right, and that it was his duty, to remove the deposits whenever the public interest or convenience would be promoted by the change. He assumed, as the basis of his action, that the refusal of the President, at the former session, to assent to the bill renewing the charter, and his reelection since, had settled the question that the charter was to expire on the 3d of March, 1836. On these premises, his reasons were, that the public interest required that the deposits should not be continued in the bank to the close of its existence; and that the bank had been guilty of actual misconduct, which chiefly consisted in its attempt to influence the late elections. He claimed that the power to remove the deposits from the Bank of the United States carried with it the power to select other depositaries, and to make contracts with them. The State banks which he had selected for this purpose were, he said, by agreements among themselves, "providing a general currency at least as sound as that of the Bank of the United States, and [one that] will afford facilities to commerce, and in the business of domestic exchange, quite equal to any which the community heretofore enjoyed..... Every object," he continued, "which the charter to the present bank was designed to attain, may be as effectually accomplished by the State banks." Nothing could more strongly mark the entirely empirical character of this measure than this hazardous assertion; and that it was made and acted on, exhibits the power of party over the judgments of public men in a very striking light. The whole experience of the country for forty years had demonstrated that the State banks were incapable of doing for the community and the Government what the Secretary here claimed for them; and a very short period was now again to demonstrate the same thing. The truth is, that of disinterested advisers who understood this subject, General Jackson had not one in his Cabinet. If there was ground for the opinion that a national bank, constituted as the existing bank was, and with such powers over the currency, was an instrument that could be used for political purposes, the true corrective for statesmen to apply did not require the commission of such a blunder as suddenly throwing the public deposits into the hands of the State banks, upon the delusive idea that they could make a reliable national currency by the operation of their contracts with each other. I am aware that General Jackson's justifica-

sued upon these resolutions, memorials on the subject were frequently presented, coming from every part of the country, representing the general commercial distress; assigning the removal of the deposits as the cause, and praying Congress to direct their restoration to the Bank of the United States. The friends of the Administration in the Senate denied the existence, in any extraordinary degree, of monetary pressure, and asserted that these memorials were dictated by party spirit, or were got up at the instance of the bank. Day after day the Senate resounded with charges and counter-charges, intermingled with debates of great ability and scope on some of the financial questions involved. In this attitude of affairs, Mr. Webster had occasion, on the 20th of January, to present a series of resolutions passed by a public meeting in Boston, which was attended by members of both the political parties, and con-

tion depends upon the suggestion that this bank was so powerful and so determined to perpetuate its power, that it was necessary to destroy it by an extreme measure, *coûte que coûte*, and that nothing less than a direct blow such as he aimed at it, would have answered the necessary purpose. But leaving out of consideration entirely the personal feelings in which his hostility to the bank was said to have originated, the true answer to this suggestion is, that whatever may have been the aims of the Bank of the United States, and the conduct of its chief manager, before the removal of the deposits, its charter could have been extended, or another bank could have been created, under provisions which would have obviated all the supposed political dangers. The bank that was presided over by Nicholas Biddle never did, and never could have, exercised so much power as to prevent a statesman like Mr. Webster from incorporating into its renewed charter, or into the charter of another bank, all the necessary safeguards which the purity of elections and the independence of public men may have required. Mr. Webster was always ready to do this, and no one can doubt his ability, with his long experience and his thorough acquaintance with the subject of public finance, to have formed a national bank that would have continued the advantages of a sound national currency, without being capable of being made the political instrument of a party. But such were the prejudices and the state of crimination and recrimination excited at once by the step taken by the Administration, that Mr. Webster, in whose impartiality and uprightness the nation would in any other condition of the public mind have been entirely disposed to confide, could effect nothing beyond leaving upon record, for future guidance, the evidence that his own principles on these financial questions were the true ones. The result was that experiment after experiment, to which this and the succeeding Administration were led, failed to accomplish any thing of importance in reference to the currency; that a state of prejudice on the question of a national bank was perpetuated until it became impossible to create one; that a great national emergency afterward found us without a national currency other than gold and silver, and drove the Government into the issue of a currency consisting of its own paper divorced from all relation to the precious metals excepting that which was to be measured by its speculative value as a promise to pay; and that we have never yet reached the means by which the paper issues of private corporations can be maintained as a national currency at a par with gold and silver, or even be made a general medium of exchange, without being enforced by the direct credit of the Government itself.

sisted of men engaged in all the active pursuits of life, recommending, as the appropriate remedy for the present commercial distress, a restoration of the relation in which the bank had heretofore stood to the Government. His remarks, in presenting these resolutions, were exceedingly grave and pointed, but without any asperity. He dealt with the present condition of things as a crisis fraught with the most important issues for the Government and the community. The great evil, he said, arose from the new attitude in which the Government had placed itself toward the bank. Every thing was in a false position. The Government, the Bank of the United States, and the State banks, were all out of place, deranged, separated, and jostling against each other, each acting on the defensive, and the public interest crushed between the upper and nether millstones. All this should have been foreseen. It was idle to say that these evils might have been prevented by the bank, if it had exerted itself to prevent them. The quarrel was an unnecessary one; and it was one that had given a great shock to the whole currency system of the country, deranging the internal exchanges, which had hitherto been accomplished by the Bank of the United States with great facility, and at a rate unprecedentedly cheap.

The public moneys, he continued, were now out of the Bank of the United States, and in the custody of the Secretary of the Treasury, without regulation of law, to be kept where he pleased and as he pleased. This state of things Congress could not suffer to remain. His own opinion was, that the deposits should be restored to the Bank of the United States. This question was entirely unconnected with the controversy whether that bank should be rechartered or any new one created. But looking beyond the question of the immediate custody of the public funds, he asked, What is to take the place of the bank as a means of exercising that salutary control over the currency of the country which it was the unquestionable purpose of the Constitution to devolve on Congress? There were but four opinions or suggestions as to what might thereafter be expected or attempted. One was, to leave things as they stood, with the whole subject under the control of the Executive; another, to do away with paper entirely, leaving only a metallic currency.

Both of these he dismissed as impracticable. There remained only the rechartering of the present bank, or the creation of a new one. The last could not be effected before March, 1836. Entertaining the opinion that a well-conducted national institution was essential to guard against the excessive issues of nearly four hundred State banks, and to furnish a sound and uniform currency to every part of the United States, he was ready to recharter the present bank, with such modifications as would meet and reconcile the different states of opinion on the subject, so as to remove all reasonable grounds of jealousy in all quarters. These suggestions, he declared, were made without the knowledge of the bank, and with no understanding or concert with any of its friends, or with any one heretofore opposed to it. In conclusion, he demanded of those who proposed to continue the discussion concerning the removal of the deposits, to let the country see their plan for the final settlement of the present difficulties.

Such in substance were the views that were repeated by Mr. Webster more than once, as he had occasion to speak upon the several memorials or resolutions of public bodies that were presented by others or by himself. He tendered to the opponents of the bank, to the Administration, and to the country, all his aid in reconstructing the bank so that the general sense of the people would be satisfied that the Government would have a safe depositary for the public treasure, an important auxiliary in its financial operations, and a sound national currency, without the possibility of political abuses of the powers conferred.

But it soon became apparent that his aid for this purpose was not wanted by those who had the power to obstruct any such healing measure. On the 30th of January, it became evident, from some remarks made by Mr. Wright, one of the Senators of New York, that the Administration had determined that the public moneys should remain in the State banks, and that the public revenues should be collected through their agency; that no law on the subject should be passed, and that the point was to be established that Congress has no power to create a national bank. This aroused all Mr. Webster's energies. From this date he entered into the discussion of the whole subject with the utmost earnestness. It is impossible to give here a detailed account of the speeches which he made in the course of this discussion, which lasted until the adjournment of Congress in June, 1834, occupying a part of nearly every day. Between the 20th of January and the close of the session, he addressed the Senate on this subject sixty-four times, besides making the report of the Committee on Finance in relation to the Secretary's reasons for the removal of the deposits, and delivering his great speech in answer to the Protest which the President sent to the Senate. In these various speeches there is embraced a most extensive range of subjects; comprehending practical questions of finance and currency, an exposition of the constitutional relations between the different departments of our Government, and a searching and profound analysis of the office of those checks and balances which the principles of civil liberty have established as barriers against the encroachments of arbitrary power. How all this should have grown out of the mere executive act of removing the public moneys from the custody of one bank into that of several other banks, can be understood only by observing the character of the pretensions asserted by the Executive Department, and the necessity that existed for resisting them. The merely financial and prudential features of this controversy would not alone have called out such a discussion of the principles on which Mr. Webster put forth his peculiar powers. But the President's act rendered it necessary, in Mr. Webster's opinion, for the Senate to express its firm and decided condemnation. This drew from the President claims of executive authority so high and transcendent, that an answer to them became necessary for the future preservation of the principles of constitutional government. The whole attitude of affairs was not unlike some of the collisions between Charles I. and his Parliament, and it produced discussions that are not less important than were those memorable debates, in which the prerogatives of the crown came into conflict with the rights of the legislature.

On the 4th of February, Mr. Clay's second resolution, censuring as unsatisfactory and insufficient the Secretary's reasons for removing the deposits from the bank, was referred to the Committee on Finance. On the 5th of February, Mr. Webster brought in the report of the committee. It embraced a full and elaborate examination of the legal relations between the Government and the bank, the powers of the Secretary of the Treasury, and the reasons which he had assigned for the removal. It negatived the claim of the Secretary to an absolute and unqualified control over the question of removal, and maintained that the provision of the law which required him to give an account of his reasons to Congress, constituted Congress the final judge, by way of appeal, of all his reasons, both as they affected the interests of the bank and the interests of the public. After an elaborate examination of the Secretary's reasons, the report concluded with a recommendation that the resolution referred to the committee be adopted by the Senate. It was finally voted upon on the 28th of March, and was carried by twenty-eight yeas against eighteen nays. Immediately afterward, Mr. Clay modified his first resolution, which was then passed by twenty-six yeas against twenty nays, in the following terms: "That the President, in the late executive proceedings in relation to the public revenue, has assumed upon himself authority and power not conferred by the Constitution and laws, but in derogation of both."

It had become apparent to Mr. Webster, before the middle of March, that while he and those who acted with him could carry a measure through the Senate, nothing could be done for the relief of the country, unless the President and a majority of the House of Representatives would concur in what might be proposed. The Administration would do nothing. It was important, therefore, that no one should be able to say that what was to be proposed by an opponent of the Administration would insure the continuance of the Bank of the United States, and it is important now, to those who mean to understand Mr. Webster's course on this subject, to know that he meant to give that bank no claim to a renewal of its charter, by the bill which he introduced on the 18th of March. It was the purpose of this bill to give the Bank of the United States sufficient time to wind up its affairs, without distressing the public by a too rapid collection of its debts; to have the public deposits restored to it after the 1st of July, subject to removal at any time by order of Congress; and to reserve to Congress perfect liberty to create any new bank at any time after March, 1836. He also proposed, in order to increase the circulation of gold and silver, that, when the States would direct their own banks not to issue notes of a less denomination than five dollars, Congress should direct the Bank of the United States to issue no notes below twenty dollars. This he regarded then, and always, as a very important object. On asking leave to introduce this bill, he delivered an impressive speech, which is to be found in the fourth volume of his Works, and which he closed as follows:

"I have thus, sir, stated my opinions, and discharged my duty. I see the country laboring and struggling and panting under an enormous political evil. I propose a remedy which I am sure will produce relief, if it be adopted, and which seems to me most likely to obtain support. And now, sir, I put it to every member of Congress, how he can resist this measure, unless by proposing another and a better. Who, among the agents and servants of the people assembled in these Houses, is prepared, in the present distressed state of the country, to say that he will oppose every thing and propose nothing? For one, sir, I can only say that I have been driven to this proposition by an irresistible impulse of obligation to the country. If I had been suddenly called to my great reckoning in another world, I should have felt that one duty was neglected, if I had had no measure to recommend, no expedient to propose, no hope to hold out to this suffering community.

"As to the success of this bill, sir, or any other, I have only to repeat what I have so often said, that every thing rests with the people themselves. In the distracted state of the public counsels, any measure of relief can only be obtained by the decisive demand of the public will.

"By an exercise of executive power, which I believe to be illegal, and which all must see to have been injurious, by an unrelenting adherence to the measure which has thus been adopted, in spite of all consequences, and by the force of those motives which influence men to support the measure, though they entirely disapprove it, the country is brought to a condition such as it never before witnessed, and which it cannot long bear. But it is not a condition for despair. Nothing will ruin the country, if the people themselves will undertake its safety, and nothing can save it, if *they* leave that safety in any hands but their own.

"Would to God, sir, that I could draw around me all these twelve millions of people! Would to God that I could speak audibly to every independent elector in the whole land! I would not say to them, vainly and arrogantly, that their safety and happiness require the adoption of any measure recommended by me. But I would say to them, with the sincerest conviction that ever animated man's heart, that their safety and happiness do require their own prompt and patriotic attention to the public concerns—their own honest devotion to the welfare of the State. I would say to them that neither this measure, nor any measure, can be adopted except by the cogent and persisting action of popular opinion. I would say to them that the public revenues cannot be restored to their accustomed custody, that they cannot be again placed under the control of Congress, that the violation of law cannot be redressed, but by manifestations, not to be mistaken, of public sentiment. I would say to them that the Constitution and the laws, their own rights and their own happiness, all depend on themselves; and, if they esteem these of any value, if they were not too dearly bought by the blood of their fathers, if they be an inheritance fit to be transmitted to their posterity, I would beseech them, I would beseech them, to come now to their salvation."

But it was impossible even for Mr. Webster to remove the vast weight of executive will which obstructed every measure that sought to change the present state of things. The President had determined that nothing should be done. In this determination he was supported by a great party, in which some acted from conviction, some gave up their convictions, and all were fearful that any yielding would be accounted a political victory over their chief; yet it is as certain as the motives of any statesman can be made certain by what he aims to do, and by the spirit in which he acted, that Mr. Webster, throughout this controversy, sought no political victory over General Jackson. He regarded the President as a man who had precipitated the country, needlessly, into a condition from which it was necessary that it should be rescued. To rescue it, he would have given his aid to the President, cheerfully and frankly, as he gave it in the crisis of nullification. But, unfortunately, the state of things was such that he could reach the mind of the President only as he could reach the mind of the country, namely, from his place in the Senate; and, whatever was uttered there, came to the President's ear mingled with the utterances of those to whom he felt personal hostility, and was associated to him with the obnoxious bank. Demonstration, argument, eloquence, could effect nothing. Mr. Webster did not press his bill to a vote, because a vote of the Senate, sustaining it, would have led to no practical result.

Another event, too, of a character entirely unprecedented, soon obliged Mr. Webster to deal with this whole controversy in a manner in which he had not hitherto treated it. He had concurred in the vote of the Senate which had censured the control assumed by the President over the public funds as a violation of the Constitution; and, as the reader has seen, he had, in a formal report, recommended the expression of that opinion by the Senate. On the 17th of April the President sent to the Senate a protest against that proceeding. This was a document written with great ability, and with a sustained dignity. The character and station of the President, and his vast popularity and influence, gave to the doctrines embraced in it an importance which they could not have had if advanced from any other source.

Our country, in the different vicissitudes through which it has passed, has exhibited very striking proofs of the manner in which the popular power forces its way into the working of our Constitution, alternately raising and depressing the spheres of its several departments. When the executive office has been filled by a man of strong characteristics and great popularity, it has been exalted into an undue and unconstitutional predominance over the Legislature. When the President has not been a man of extraordinary force of character, and the popular sympathy has been with Congress, the tendency in the other direction has been equally marked, and Congress has absorbed the executive powers, besides exercising its own. It is justly to be claimed as one of the great merits of all that Mr. Webster has left to us, that his whole public career was mainly occupied in expounding the Constitution; that his doctrine was never partial or defective; that he gave no distorted interpretations; that he elevated no department at the expense of any other; that he comprehended and ever kept in view the just relations of all parts of the Constitution; and that he regarded its observance as paramount to all other considerations.

General Jackson's Protest embraced claims of executive power and views of the presidential office, which had never been asserted before since the Constitution was established. Nothing so closely resembling the prerogatives of English kings, as they were held in former ages, had ever been broached in this country. Construing the Constitution of the United States as if it had intended, by vesting the executive power in the President, and by placing in his hands the power of appointment to office, to give him discretionary control over all subordinate executive officers, the Protest claimed it to be the right and duty of the President, by virtue of his general executive power, to supervise and control the Secretary of the Treasury in relation to the custody of the public funds. It thus appeared that, in the judgment of the President, the law establishing the bank did not, and could not, change the relation between the President and the Secretary; and that, notwithstanding the law had vested in the Secretary the power to determine whether the public funds were to be removed from the bank, on reasons to be rendered to Congress, the President could interpose his own judgment, order the Secretary to remove the deposits, and dismiss him from office if he did not comply. It was upon this ground, chiefly, that the President denied the right of the Senate to censure his act; and that he protested against that censure as an unwarrantable interference with the executive power.

A true judgment cannot be formed respecting this controversy, without remembering that the law had prescribed a duty to be performed by the Secretary, and to be performed in a particular manner. The President did not deny this; but he claimed that his paramount *executive* authority enabled him to control the Secretary, if the latter did not act in the execution of the law as the President thought he should act. It would be difficult to imagine a case in which a law of Congress could more explicitly vest in a subordinate officer a function to be performed by him, independent of the President, than had been done in this case. The issue, therefore, between the President and the Senate was, whether the general executive power of the President is of such a character that legislation cannot direct a subordinate officer to perform duties which are executive in their nature, without subjecting that officer, in the performance of those duties, to the control of the President.

This issue, in the excitements of the time, was more or less obscured by the collateral topics and personal criminations that attended its discussion. A debate followed the reading of the President's Protest, which did not satisfy Mr. Webster's conceptions of the manner in which it should be met. He was reluctant to enter again into the subject, for the occurrences of the last session were fresh in his recollection, and he did not desire, from public reasons, to be obliged to make further opposition to General Jackson, whose hands he had recently sought to strengthen against a dangerous attack upon the Constitution. But the Constitution itself was ever the first object in his thoughts, the one constant motive of all his public acts, whenever its meaning and operation were called in question. He regarded the President's ideas of the nature and extent of his authority as entirely untenable. The personal popularity of the President, who had advanced this claim, made it the more necessary, in Mr. Webster's opinion, that it should be answered upon its own merits, and in a becoming spirit. After listening for some days to a very unprofitable and angry discussion in the Senate, he wrote to Mr. Jeremiah Mason: "I fear I shall be obliged to make a speech on the Protest. I have heard nothing, as yet, which puts the case on such grounds as you and I should approve." The result was the delivery of his speech on the President's Protest, which is printed in the fourth volume of his Works.[1]

How entirely it was in his power to lift himself above the heated atmosphere of party, in the discussion of topics that involved constructions of the Constitution, this speech is a signal proof. The most important of the doctrines asserted by the Protest related to the nature of the executive power, which the Constitution vests in the President, and to the relation of the power of appointment to the general executive function. According to the Protest, the supreme executive of the Constitution is a department in which is vested all the authority for executing the laws that can exist in any government. As the laws are to be executed by public agents, the Protest derived the power of their appointment from the general executive power; and from the same source it deduced the power of removing them from office. Hence it appeared to be the view of the Protest, that the appointing power, being originally and inherently in the Executive, and including the power of removal, remained absolutely in the hands of the President except so far as the Constitution has restrained it. From this

[1] Delivered May 7, 1834.

position, it followed that the Legislative Department cannot impose upon an inferior officer the performance of duties which are executive in their nature, so that he shall be beyond the control of the President, who may remove him from office at pleasure. Reasoning from these premises, and assuming, further, that the custody of the public money is an executive function—belonging to the Executive by force of the constitutional creation and nomination of that department—the Protest, which claimed authority in the President to control all public officers holding the public funds, necessarily asserted that Congress could not place the money of the Government where its custody was not at all times subject to the will of the President.

Mr. Webster's answer to this doctrine presents a view of the Constitution which must at all times be regarded as of the utmost importance. After adverting to the fact that, in all our American constitutions, as in other governments, the general distribution of powers into the legislative, the executive, and the judicial, does not of itself fix precise definitions, he proceeded to show that the Constitution of the United States, in conferring powers on all the departments, proceeds by specific enumeration, and not by general definition of what constitutes legislative, executive, or judicial power. The general principle of the distribution is, he said, of inestimable value, but the Constitution does not give a general definition of the executive any more than of the legislative or the judicial power. We are to seek for the extent and scope of each of these departments in the specific powers which the Constitution confers upon them. Following this rule, it will be found that the denomination of the Executive Department does not necessarily confer upon it the power of appointment; but that this power is the subject of a specific grant, to be exercised under certain restrictions, and in a prescribed mode; nor does it follow, from the President's power to appoint public officers, that they are, and must be, under the Constitution, removable at his pleasure, so that Congress cannot regulate the tenure of office.

The doctrine of the Protest, that the custody of the public money belongs, by the Constitution, to the Executive, was all founded on the asserted power of the President over those who might be appointed to hold that custody. It amounted, therefore, to the practical denial of all power in Congress to place the public treasure in the hands of officers whom the President could not control; and this claim was asserted in it in express terms. Having shown that the Constitution did not vest in the President absolute control over all public officers, so that Congress cannot prevent the removal of an incumbent by the President, Mr. Webster contended that, whether the individual officer is to be changed by the President, or is to be removed only as Congress may prescribe by law, it is entirely competent for Congress to direct that whoever is in the office shall perform its duties without the interference of the President. If the President may change the officer, the duties of the office remain, and they must be performed by the successor, as Congress has by law directed them to be performed. This had been the state of the case in regard to the public deposits, which the law had directed to be kept in the bank, subject to removal by the Secretary, for reasons which he was to render to Congress. But the President had not left this duty to be performed by the officer as the law required it. He had removed one officer who would *not*, to make room for another who *would*, change the custody of the public money; and he had publicly declared it to be his own act, and to have been done at his command. That command, rested upon the paramount control of the supreme Executive Magistrate over all public officers and upon the further claim that the custody of the public money is necessarily an executive function, was what Mr. Webster regarded as a violation of the Constitution, because of its encroachments on the powers of the Legislature.

That the Senate, as one of the branches of the legislative power, had an unquestionable right, and was bound by its duty, to defend the legislative power, and that it could do so by an expression of its opinion on any act of the Executive which it deemed an encroachment, Mr. Webster held to be clear.

The residue of this speech was devoted to a refutation of the doctrine put forth by the Protest, that the President is responsible for the conduct of all executive officers, and may discharge them when he is no longer willing to be responsible for their acts. Misled by foreign analogies, as Mr. Webster held the writer of the Protest to have been, it was necessary to point out that our American constitutions are not checks imposed upon a preëxisting authority, but that they are grants of specific powers, for the extent of which we are to look to the grants themselves. In this portion of the speech he has left the most important guide that we possess for the discussion of our American questions of constitutional power, by keeping in view the broad distinction between our systems and the precedents or analogies drawn from foreign states.

The excitements of the period in which this speech was delivered have passed away, and another generation has succeeded. More than thirty years have elapsed since General Jackson, by the mere force of his will, could cause a great party to accept, for the moment, the doctrines of his remarkable protest. But there is not one of those doctrines that has survived the temporary passions which gave them a brief political ascendency. They have received no subsequent sanction from the people of this country. As constructions of the Constitution, or as explanations of the nature of our institutions, and the distribution of political functions, they have been, in fact, rejected; and they stand in our political history in no other rank than that which belongs to assertions of power that have derived their force from the peculiarities of individual character, backed by the personal devotion of a party to whose general political creed they were as uncongenial as they were to the spirit of the age, and to the provisions of the fundamental law of the land.

But the personal and temporary triumph of General Jackson was complete; for, while the Senate recorded their rejection and official condemnation of the doctrines of his protest, there was no legislation effected, at this session of Congress, restoring the public deposits to the Bank of the United States, or controlling in any way the financial experiment which the Executive Government was determined should be tried.

Before leaving this subject of the Bank of the United States, it is proper to refer to a base attempt that was made to fasten upon Mr. Webster an imputation of interested motives.

It is rare that a slander of this kind does no mischief. Contemporary refutation or rejection seldom does the work of complete vindication to all whom the imputation has reached. There is, to this day, a vague popular belief that Mr. Webster was under an extraordinary personal bias toward the bank, which colored all his opinions, and influenced his acts on this occasion. It is so clearly my duty to him, and to the influence of his public principles, to notice this imputation, that my readers will expect no other reason to be assigned for laying before them the facts.

It had happened to Mr. Webster, in former years, to be employed by the bank, in his professional capacity, to argue important causes in the Supreme Court of the United States. He was one of the counsel for the bank in the celebrated case of *McCulloch* vs. *Maryland*, as early as 1819, which involved the question of the power of the States to tax the bank or its branches; and he had been engaged by the bank in other causes in subsequent years. He was not a professional adviser of the bank, in relation to its application, in 1831–'32, for a renewal of its charter. His correspondence with Mr. Biddle, its president, at that time and subsequently, is in my hands; and it was solely in his public capacity, as a Senator of the United States, who held that the public interest demanded the existence of such an institution, that he wrote to Mr. Biddle for information, or received any letters from him. In his former occasional relation of an advocate, in certain causes in which the bank had an interest, all men could see that the weight of obligation must have been on the side of the bank; and it must have required a high degree of credulity and prejudice for any man to have supposed that it was a matter of any personal importance to Mr. Webster whether this bank was to be continued in existence, or whether its capital was to take some other form of investment, unless he was one of its debtors. But there is always, among a part of mankind, a great amount of both credulity and prejudice. What it received and listened to on this occasion had an origin; and, as not unusually happens, the imputation became transformed in shape and substance, until what was originally intended as a charge of having received exorbitant fees as *counsel*, amounting to bribes for his public influence, was converted into the statement that he was an extraordinary *debtor* to the bank. For neither of these imputations was there any rational foundation. Mr. Webster was too wise and circumspect, and too great a man, to place himself under peculiar obligations to any corporation which might have interests liable to be acted upon by him in his public capacity; and it is my firm belief that he never was influenced, in any public act or opinion, by any private relation that may have subsisted even between himself and any portion of his immediate constituents or of his personal friends. I am not unconscious of what this remark implies; and hereafter I shall proceed to justify it, in relation to another topic, concerning which full information will be given to my readers. At present, I must ask their attention to the miserable origin of the particular charge that is here adverted to.

On the 17th of March, 1834, the Vice-President, Mr. Van Buren, communicated to the Senate a paper containing the proceedings and resolutions of a meeting, held in York County, Pennsylvania, by "friends of the Administration," in favor of the removal of the deposits from the Bank of the United States, and against the recharter of that institution. Mr. Webster had been furnished with evidence, from the same locality, that this paper misrepresented the sentiments not only of the bulk of the people in the county, but of the persons who attended the meeting; and he presented this evidence to the Senate. A discussion thereupon ensued, in the course of which Mr. Poindexter, of Mississippi, made known the fact that, when this paper reached the hands of the Vice-President, it contained, as part of its preamble, a gross libel on Mr. Webster, which had been stricken from it before it was presented by the Chair. Explanations were then made, from which it appeared that the Vice-President had pointed out the offensive paragraph to the Senators from Pennsylvania, and that it had been stricken out by them. It was read in the Senate, Mr. Webster himself calling for it, and was in these words:

"One word in conclusion. Daniel Webster, now a Senator, and a champion of the bank, was, at its creation, a member of the House of Representatives. Then the bank was not his client, and he was opposed to it. His unbiassed opinion, as a representative of the people, was in direct opposition to what he now holds; but now he is 'concerned for the bank' (in legal phraseology), and no doubt finds it a good fat client, as it has already disposed of more than fifty thousand dollars in the shape of fees. In 1816 he was alarmed at the dangerous powers such an institution could make its own, and he raised his voice for a sounder currency than mere 'promises to pay,' with nothing wherewith to fulfil such promises. He then said, 'Gold and silver currency was the law of the land at home, and the law of the world abroad; and that, in the present state of the world, there could be no other currency.'"

Mr. Webster, thereupon, rose and said:

"That he had been informed that a statement of the proceedings of this meeting would be presented, and that it would present an altogether false account of it; and he was requested to lay the evidence of this misrepresentation before the Senate. He had been told, at the same time, that there was one part of the paper, about to be presented, which contained matter scandalous in reference to himself. He had said then, what he had always felt, that he felt much reluctance in laying this evidence before the Senate, because he should have regarded it as more consistent with self-respect to have taken no notice of such idle and ridiculous scandal. He had consented, however, to lay the paper in his hand before the Senate, knowing that the sentiments of the respectable citizens of York would be misrepresented here by this truly miserable statement of the proceedings.

"He considered it due to the Vice-President to say, that he was this morning informed by that gentleman of the offensive character of the reference to himself. He had told the presiding officer he was aware of the existence of the offensive paragraph, and that he considered it unimportant whether it was read or not. The presiding officer had said that the paragraph was highly improper, and that he would not present the proceedings unless this part of them was stricken out. When the paper was read, he had not heard the offensive clause, and, of course, he concluded that it had been expunged. As to the resolutions, he had not read them, or seen them, until to-day. He considered them as obnoxious to the charges which the Senator from Mississippi had alleged against them. They did contain offensive imputations as to members of the Senate. But, as this was a subject which would take up some time, he would, if the gentleman from Mississippi had no objection, move to lay the proceedings on the table, to give the Senators from Pennsylvania time to look into the character of the statement. If they should afterward determine to renew the motion to refer and print, the further discussion of the matter might then take place."

A debate, however, followed upon the question of receiving

the paper at all, in the course of which the Vice-President and the Senators from Pennsylvania made further explanations of their respective agencies in having the paper modified before it was sent to the Senate. On all sides the greatest respect was manifested toward Mr. Webster; and those who caused the offensive paragraph to be stricken out were very explicit in their declarations that they had assumed a questionable responsibility in relation to a paper that fell within the category of petitions, because it contained grossly indecent imputations against a member of the Senate. It was finally rejected by a decisive vote.

Such were the contemptible source and shape of the charge that Mr. Webster was acting under a bias as the paid advocate of the bank, and such was the manner in which this charge first came into public notice. It was a charge made by low politicians of a distant borough, prompted or unprompted, and calling themselves "friends of the Administration." It was not much more than a twelvemonth since that Administration had been obliged to ask this great statesman's aid in a perilous crisis of its affairs; and well might public men of honor and character, who were in his presence, blush for the baseness of their partisans. But official rebuke of such a slander does not kill it. It possesses a vitality that can adapt itself to other shapes; and it soon came to be said, that although the charge that the bank was his "client" could not shake public confidence in Mr. Webster, the fact that the bank was his "creditor" was, at all events, good ground of attack. In this form the calumny has still perhaps living believers.[1] They may be gratified to know, under his own hand, precisely what his pecuniary relation to the Bank of the United States was then, and had been previously. Two letters are extant, in which he has taken notice of this form of the imputation. One of them was addressed to Mr. Everett, who was at the time serving on a committee of the House of Representatives to investigate the condition of the bank. It has been published heretofore. The

[1] I am inclined to think that, in respect to sums, the supposed disbursements of the bank, in the shape of *fees*, assumed by the politicians of "York," became, traditionally, *loans*. I have sometimes heard Mr. Webster's indebtment to the bank stated at the sum of fifty-six thousand dollars, by persons who were children when the events described in the text occurred.

other was a private letter, in answer to a gentleman in New Hampshire, an old college friend of Mr. Webster, but a political opponent, who had occasion, in the autumn of this year, to borrow money at the Branch Bank of the United States, in Boston. I believe it has not been made public before.

[TO MR. EVERETT.]

"WASHINGTON, *April* 26, 1834.

"DEAR SIR: I am obliged to you for your letter of the 23d. If, in the course of your investigations, the committee should incline to notice my name, I wish you to state, on my authority, that I never had any particular or unusual accommodation from the bank to the amount of a single dollar; that, since I went to Boston, in 1817, I have kept my account and done my necessary banking business at the Boston office; and notes, bills of exchange, etc., etc., with my name on them, have been collected and discounted, etc., as often as occasion required, precisely as would have been done in the case of any other person, and not otherwise. I hear reports of mortgages, standing loans, etc., etc., between the bank and myself, in all of which there is not a single word of truth. I never gave the bank any mortgage, and never had any standing loan or any other accommodation, except in the way of discount of bills and notes, as at other banks.

"As to Mr. Connell's notes, etc., they arose in a strictly professional transaction. He obtained the agency of the claims of our Boston merchants and insurance offices under the French treaty. They made it a condition of the bargain, that he should secure my professional services in all cases; and, having the agency for a vast amount of other claims, Mr. Connell engaged my professional aid in the whole as matter of contract, and the notes were given in pursuance of this contract.[1] That is the whole matter. You may make any use of these facts, public or private, which you deem proper. . . .

"Yours truly ever,

"D. WEBSTER."

[TO MR. HUBBARD.]

"BOSTON, *November* 18, 1834.

"MY DEAR SIR: I have received your two letters. The note accompanying the last I have indorsed, and sent to the bank, where it will be doubtless discounted, according to your wishes.

"Will you allow me to say, my dear sir, that I had one objection,

[1] This refers to professional services before the commissioners appointed to distribute the money to claimants under the treaty.

though a trifling one, to indorsing your note. You know what stories have been circulated (and nowhere more diligently than in New Hampshire) of my pecuniary obligations to the Bank of the United States, heavy mortgages, etc., etc. Now, the truth is, that the bank never discounted or advanced to me a cent in the world, except in the ordinary way as they have done for others; and, at this moment, the indorsement of your note, and one other signed by another gentleman, constitutes nearly, if not entirely, my whole liability to the bank; and, to put an end to such slanders, and to have been enabled myself to say that the bank did not hold my name for a dollar, I should, perhaps, if you had lived here, have suggested to you the obtaining of some other name instead of my own. But, as you lived in the country, it might have been inconvenient to you; and, after all, I suppose there would be just as much libellous matter published, let the facts be one way or the other. Mr. Frothingham will probably write you. I hope you will find the rogue that took such liberties with your name.

"Yours with regard,

"DANL. WEBSTER.

"Hon. Henry Hubbard,
"Charlestown, New Hampshire."

It was at this period that the term "Whigs" sprang into use, as a designation of that portion of the people who were opposed to the high prerogative ideas of the executive office which General Jackson and his friends maintained, and who sought to uphold the proper functions of the Legislature against executive encroachments. The party which had supported Mr. Clay for the presidency in the election of 1832, known as National Republicans, naturally remained in opposition to his successful rival. But the name of their party had never been significant of any well-defined political principles, and it was no longer suited to the circumstances of the times. In those circumstances, it was now felt instinctively that, in the existing struggle between the parties actually arrayed against each other, and in the principles and doctrines of those who were in power, there was a peculiar fitness in the revival of a term which, on both sides of the Atlantic, had been historically associated with the side of liberty against the side of power. This revival of the name of Whigs was sudden, and it was a spontaneous popular movement. In progress of time, it enabled the public men who were leading the opposition to the party of the Administration to consolidate an organization of distinct political principles, and to strengthen it by accessions from those who had found reason to be dissatisfied with the opinions prevailing among the friends of the President. From this period, in all his party relations, Mr. Webster was known as one of the great leaders of the Whigs.

CHAPTER XXI.

1834–1835.

NOMINATED FOR THE PRESIDENCY BY THE WHIGS OF MASSACHUSETTS—VARIOUS POPULAR DEMONSTRATIONS IN OTHER STATES—CORRESPONDENCE WITH THE ANTIMASONS OF PENNSYLVANIA—GENERAL HARRISON NOMINATED BY THE WHOLE OPPOSITION IN PENNSYLVANIA—DIFFICULTIES WITH FRANCE—WAR AVERTED—DEFEAT OF THE FORTIFICATION BILL—FRENCH SPOLIATIONS BEFORE 1800—SPEECH ON THE POWER OF REMOVAL FROM OFFICE—MR. BENTON'S "EXPUNGING" RESOLUTION—REGULATION RESPECTING TREASURY DRAFTS ON THE DEPOSIT BANKS.

SUCH a session of Congress as that described in the last chapter could have had no other effect than to develop parties, and to bring about a designation of candidates for the presidency. The separation of Mr. Calhoun from General Jackson, long since complete, and the avowed wishes of the latter to make Mr. Van Buren his successor, left scarcely any doubt that Mr. Van Buren would be the candidate of the party which supported the Administration. Among the opposition, Mr. Webster was the person most naturally to be regarded as the first choice. Mr. Clay was scarcely in a position to be selected a second time, immediately after his unsuccessful candidacy of 1832; and if he was to be regarded as out of the question, on this occasion, the opposition had no statesman who was for a moment to be compared to Mr. Webster, in respect to ability, to past services, to reputation, and to popularity. The tendencies of thoughtful men in different quarters of the Union toward Mr. Webster, in the summer and autumn of 1834, are abundantly proved by the mass of correspondence that lies before me, which shows that nothing was wanting to the opposition, in order to have made him their candidate, but a compact organization, and a definite unity of political objects. But the opposition was composed of heterogeneous materials. The National Republican party of 1832 had been embarrassed by antimasonry. The Whig party, which was substantially identical with the National Republican, was now embarrassed by the same cause; for men who earnestly desired to change the administration of the national Government, and who condemned the measures of General Jackson and his political supporters, still thought it necessary to worry themselves and to vex the politics of the country about "secret societies," to maintain a special party for this purpose, and to withhold their coöperation from all public men who did not regard this topic as of the first importance.

In Massachusetts, where the party of General Jackson, which now became known as the Democratic party, had never been very strong, there was an almost universal desire to take some step which would place Mr. Webster in a position to be regarded through the country as the candidate of the whole opposition. But the Whigs had not yet devised for themselves the machinery of a national nominating convention. No such meeting was contemplated; and, if it had been contemplated, the existence of the third party of Antimasonry would have been a serious obstacle to its harmonious action. The only step that could be taken by the Whigs of Massachusetts was, to nominate Mr. Webster for the presidency by a legislative caucus. In the Legislature they were the strongest of all the parties in numbers and in weight of character; and it was supposed at this time that such a nomination, proceeding from Massachusetts as the general voice of her people, would be followed by similar movements in other States.

The following letters, selected from Mr. Webster's most confidential correspondence with his personal friends, relate to this movement and its consequences:

[TO MR. MASON.]

"WASHINGTON, *January* 1, 1835.

"DEAR SIR: Whether it is or will be best for Massachusetts to act at all on the subject of a nomination, is a question which I leave entirely to the judgment of others. I cannot say that I have any personal wishes about it, either one way or the other. A nomination by Massachusetts would certainly be one of the highest proofs of regard which any citizen can receive. As such, I should most undoubtedly esteem it. But, in the present condition of things, and with the prospects which are before us, a nomination is a questionable thing to one who is more desirous of preserving what little reputation he has than anxious to grasp at further distinction. I have made up my mind, however, to be passive, and shall be satisfied with any result.

"But I have a clear opinion on one point; and, as I promised you to communicate my sentiments freely, I will state that opinion frankly. It is, that if Massachusetts is to act at all, *the time has come.* I think the proceeding, if one is to be had, should be one of the first objects of attention when the Legislature assembles. In Ohio, Mr. McLean is already nominated, I presume, according to late accounts. Many Whigs, who do not prefer him, fall into the measure (in Ohio) simply because they have no other choice. It is expected, or at least hoped, that New Jersey will second this nomination. Movements are in preparation in other places; but, as far as I know, nothing is yet proposed anywhere in which there could be a general union, or in which Massachusetts would be likely to agree.

"If a resolution to make a movement in Massachusetts should be adopted, not only should the thing itself be done as soon as practicable, but in the mean time notice of the intention should be given to friends in the neighboring States, and especially in New York, that they may prepare for it. Let us know *here* the moment any thing is determined on.

"It looks at present as if Mr. Clay would not do or say any thing. He declares himself in nobody's way; but still it is evident that his particular friends are not prepared to act heartily and efficiently for anybody else.

"Be sure to *burn* this letter, and assure yourself also that I write such letters to nobody else.

"Yours truly,

"D. WEBSTER.

"The committee of the House of Representatives will not report in conformity to the recommendation of the message on French affairs. Probably no report will be made, till further intelligence from France."

[FROM MR. ABBOTT LAWRENCE.]

"BOSTON, *January* 5, 1835.

"MY DEAR SIR: I wish I could see you for ten minutes, that I might say to you many things that cannot be written. Yet, I cannot omit the present time to say that I have been called upon within the last few days by many prominent individuals (your particular friends), who would be glad to know your wishes in relation to the future.

"There is a strong disposition to make a nomination early, by a Legislative caucus, of President of the United States. This will take place beyond a doubt, and it is to be hoped other States may follow in the course of the winter. Supposing such an event to take place, is it your intention to resign your seat in the Senate? If you have not made up your mind on this point, your friends here hope you will not do so without very mature deliberation, as your services in the Senate appear to be almost indispensable during this and the next session of Congress. I know full well that your sacrifices have been great, and I am the last individual to require of you a continuance of them if, in your judgment, your interests are to be promoted by retirement; at present I am not clear upon this point. There is hardly any thing, I believe, that your friends will not be ready to do in either case, whether you remain or whether you retire. I ask now, in candor and frankness, and in perfect confidence, as I have consulted with but one individual, in case your sacrifices *professionally* can be made more *reasonable*, whether you do not think it will be best, all things considered, to remain in your present situation till we see how matters stand a year hence, and then take such a course as circumstances may make expedient. I do not see that it is incumbent on you to resign in consequence of your nomination; perhaps, however, I may not see the whole ground. Others, I find, have the same opinion.

"You have doubtless marked out a course of action for yourself. I would not certainly undertake to divert you from it, as you have much more practical wisdom upon these matters than myself. I esteem the point at which you have arrived, however, one of vast moment to the country as well as to yourself, and feel an indescribable interest, that nothing should be done by which yourself or your friends shall hereafter feel that a mistake was made at this particular period of your political life.

"If you can do yourself politically more good by retirement, you can promote the good of the country by the same course. I leave the subject with a hope that, whatever your decision may be, it will be one which will lead to a life devoted to the public interest. This should be your *destiny*, and your friends ought in justice to do for you all that may be required.

"I remain, dear sir,

"Truly yours,

"A. L."

[TO MR. MASON.]

"Washington, *January* 10, 1835.

"Dear Sir: I have received your letter of the 4th. It seems generally understood here, that a nomination will be forthwith made in Boston. The proceedings in Ohio seem to make it necessary; and I believe friends here have found it expedient to signify to gentlemen in different parts of the country what may be expected to transpire in Massachusetts.

"On the subject of Senator, I have said little, and nothing publicly; as all the gentlemen who have been named are quite fit for the place, and would do credit to the State. Since you ask my private opinion, however, I am willing to say, in entire confidence, what I think about the question.

"There is no man who can come into the Senate, in my opinion, with so much prospect of being useful as Governor Davis. He is well known here, stands high in reputation for talents, and enjoys universal confidence as a man of honor and probity. And, if a candidate, such is his popularity at home, that I suppose he would be elected by general consent.

"Then, the objection arises, which you mention, from the difficulty of finding a successor to him in his present office.[1] This objection is serious, and they who are on the spot can best judge whether it be insurmountable. I have heard nobody much talked of for Governor, in case Mr. Davis should be Senator, but Mr. E. Everett. It has been thought his nomination would bring back a great portion of the Antimasons to a union with the Whigs. Certainly, that is a very important object. We need our whole strength in Massachusetts, and a cordial coöperation of the Antimasons in Massachusetts, *in other things*, would have greatly beneficial effects in New York and Pennsylvania.

"I have no question that Mr. Everett would make a perfectly safe Governor. He has been here ten years, and no man has acted with more faithfulness toward friends, or more devotion to the good cause. I should entirely confide in his integrity and ability in the government of the State. He has good principles, good feelings, good associations, and is no more likely to appoint a bad judge, for instance, or do any other thing leading to great public mischief, than Governor Davis himself.

"How extensively Mr. Everett may be thought of, I do not know. He is mentioned frequently here, in case Governor Davis should come to the Senate; and I have seen letters from home which suggest the same thing. If practicable, a pacification of the antimasonic question is, doubtless, highly desirable.

"I send you Mr. Clay's report. The committee of the House will not report at present; and nothing will be done here till we hear further from France.

"We are almost frozen up here. The weather is cold and the snow deep, quite beyond all my experience.

"Yours with great truth and sincerity,

"DANIEL WEBSTER.

"Hon. Mr. Mason."

[1] Governor of the State.

[TO MR. MASON.]

"WASHINGTON, *January* 22, 1835.

"DEAR SIR: I have received yours of the 14th. There has been some impatience here, in regard to proceedings in Boston, on account of the daily inquiries by friends in other quarters, as to what might be expected; but I presume things have gone on as fast as they well could.

"Mr. McLean's nomination appears to take but little. It is coldly received even in Ohio; so much so, indeed, that General Harrison's friends are holding meetings in that State, for the purpose of bringing *him* forward. Letters received to-day, from Columbus and Cincinnati, ask urgently what is doing or to be done in Massachusetts.

"The *schism* in the Jackson party proceeds. It appears to me that nothing is likely to stop its progress. If we *Whigs* had union and energy, we have now before us a prospect no way discouraging.

"You will have heard of a duel to-day between Mr. Wise, of Virginia, and his predecessor, Mr. Coke. I hear the former is badly wounded. I am busy in the court. Mr. Taney is yet before us. Probably will not be confirmed; but that is not certain.[1]

"Yours truly,
"D. WEBSTER.

"Mr. Mason."

[TO MR. MASON.]

"WASHINGTON, *February* 6, 1835.

"MY DEAR SIR: It is true that I have looked forward to the events which the approaching election might bring about as likely to furnish a fit occasion for my retirement from the Senate. I have fixed on no particular time, nor made, indeed, any such determination as may not be changed by the advice or wishes of friends. As I am now placed, I shall certainly not leave my place till the time arrives when I may think that its relinquishment will not be unsatisfactory to *Massachusetts*.

"I do not affect, my dear sir, to desire to retire from public life, and to resume my profession. My habits, I must confess, and the nature of my pursuits for some years, render it more agreeable to me to attend to political than to professional subjects. But I have not lost all relish for the bar, and can still make something by the practice; and, by remaining in the Senate, I am making sacrifices which my circumstances do not justify. My residence here so many months every year greatly increases my expenses, and greatly reduces my income. You know the charge of living here with a family; and I cannot leave my wife and daughter at home, and come here and go into a 'mess' at ten dollars a week.

"I find it inconvenient to push my practice in the Supreme Court while

[1] The nomination of Mr. Taney, as Chief Justice of the United States, to succeed Chief-Justice Marshall, was at this time before the Senate.

a member of the Senate; and am inclined, under any view of the future, to decline engagements hereafter in that court, unless under special circumstances. These are the reasons that have led me to *hope* for a fit occasion of leaving the Senate; when I can quit with the approbation of friends, I shall eagerly embrace the opportunity. In the mean time, I shall say nothing about it.

"I ought this spring to go to the West, as far at least as Kentucky and Indiana. I am fully persuaded it would be a highly useful thing. My friends urge it upon me incessantly, and I hold back from promising compliance with their wishes only from an unwillingness to lose six weeks more, after the session closes. On this point, however, as nothing is decided, I say nothing at present. There will be no cause in court, I think, to detain me after the 3d of March.

"We have nothing new here. A base attempt has been made to ascribe the *madness* of Lawrence[1] to the speeches, etc., of the Senate. An inquisition, if it may be so called, has been had upon Lawrence by two physicians, who have signed a report, and returned it to the marshal. It proves a clear case of insanity. The report will not be published so long as its publication can be withheld.

"We shall pass through the Senate a pretty good bill for reorganizing the post-office.

"I saw lately a strange letter from Washington in the *Boston Gazette*, about an express from the New York Whigs, and a coldness between Mr. W. and Mr. Clay. Both stories are equally and entirely groundless. There has been no express here from New York. On the contrary, *all* the Whig papers of the city (except Noah's) will soon be out (or we are misinformed) in the direction you would desire.

"Yours truly,

"D. Webster.

"Mr. Mason."

The nomination contemplated by the Whigs of Massachusetts was made in February. Mr. Webster had a strong body of friends in Pennsylvania, who desired him to come among them immediately after the adjournment of Congress. He was in Harrisburg on the 19th of March, where the Legislature was in session, and received from a committee of the members an invitation to a public dinner, which was tendered as a mark of respect for his public services and his character as an American statesman. This honor he felt obliged to decline. In August, being at Bangor, Maine, on a professional engagement, he accepted an invitation to a public entertainment, and afterward addressed an immense concourse of people who had

[1] A person who attempted to assassinate the President.

come from far and near to see and to hear him. In October occurred the imposing ceremony of the presentation to him, by his fellow-citizens of Boston, of a massive silver vase, in the presence of an audience of four thousand persons.[1] In November, he received an invitation to a public dinner from leading citizens of Philadelphia, and in December there came another from Baltimore; both of which he declined. From Vermont, from New York, from Ohio, from Louisiana, and from many other regions remote from New England, there came letters, often numerously signed, expressing the hopes of the writers that an opportunity might be secured for electing him to the presidency. This opportunity seemed most likely to be afforded by the action of the opposition in Pennsylvania. Public meetings were held in the counties of Chester and Alleghany, in November, to elect delegates to a State convention. In the former, the Whigs and Antimasons united, and appointed delegates in favor of the nomination of Mr. Webster. In the latter, the meeting was chiefly composed of Antimasons, but they instructed the delegates to vote for the nomination of Mr. Webster in the State Convention. But here the objectionable practice of interrogating public men, who were supposed to be candidates for public position, came into unfortunate activity. Men of entire honesty of purpose and of great respectability, ardently desiring to make Mr. Webster President of the United States, could not content themselves with the sufficiency of his character as a statesman, with his known sentiments on all really important public questions of the time, but they thought it necessary to press him on the point of Masonry. They wanted him to be their candidate, but they wanted him to be an *Antimasonic* candidate. Accordingly, the Pennsylvania State Committee of this party, as well as lesser organizations of the same kind, addressed to him specific and pointed inquiries as to his opinions about secret societies, and what he should deem the duty of a Chief Magistrate in respect to appointments to office.

This was undoubtedly one of the greatest trials of this peculiar kind to which Mr. Webster was ever subjected; and, in order to show why it was so, and to exhibit the manner in

[1] This vase is now deposited in the Public Library of the city of Boston.

which it was met, some explanation of the state of things in Pennsylvania, at this time, is here necessary. The Whigs of Pennsylvania were acting with great prudence, for the Antimasonic party was large, excited, and jealous. Without a co-operation of these two branches of the opposition, neither Mr. Webster nor any other man could obtain the popular vote of the State. Mr. Webster's Whig friends, therefore, although they regarded all this excitement on the subject of Masonry as eminently unnecessary, were very willing, and indeed earnest, to have him satisfy the sentiment to any reasonable extent.

On the other hand, he had many warm friends among the Antimasons, whose private communications to him revealed the intensity of their desire to have him made the candidate of their party, but who did not perceive that they exacted from him a pledge which it would have been unbecoming in him to give. To gratify such a body of men, on the eve of a very important election, without sacrificing his own character, was certainly a delicate task. It is not needful to ask the judgment of my readers as to the success with which Mr. Webster could play the part of a politician; but I can give the means of determining his rank as a statesman and a patriot. The conventions, the ballots, the parties of this and every other period of his life, are among the dead things of the past. His character remains—one of our great and imperishable treasures, to which we may point as a proof that our institutions sometimes produce men who can act with dignity and independence.

In the public answer which he made to the Antimasons of Pennsylvania, he did not hesitate to say that he regarded secret societies, the members of which take upon themselves extraordinary obligations, and are bound together by secret oaths, as objectionable; and he commended highly the sentiment which the Antimasons had adopted, of "the supremacy of the laws." [1] But to the inquiry of what he would deem the duty of a Chief Magistrate in making appointments to office, he made no answer. This topic he reserved for a private letter to one of the gentlemen who had addressed him. Let it be understood that Mr. Webster earnestly desired to be President of the United States; that he wished to receive the nomination and support

[1] For the public letter, see his published Correspondence, vol. ii.

of his Antimasonic friends in Pennsylvania; and that it would have been quite easy for him to have caused it to be believed, in that particular region, that as President he would appoint none but Antimasons to office; which was in fact what he was desired to say.

[TO MESSRS. WALLACE AND OTHERS.]

"BOSTON, *November* 30, 1835.

"GENTLEMEN: I have received your letter of the 16th instant. A desire to know my opinions concerning any public question, which proceeds from so highly respectable a source, would at all times command my respectful and prompt attention. Before the receipt of your letter, however, a correspondence had taken place between friends of yours in another part of Pennsylvania and myself, on the same general subject. That correspondence, I presume, is to be laid before the convention at Harrisburg, and may render a particular answer to your letter unnecessary. I will observe, however, that on the subject of all secret societies, bound by secret oaths, I concur entirely with what I suppose to be the sentiments of the Antimasons of Pennsylvania, as I have said on various occasions heretofore; and there can be no question of the constitutional right of those, who believe secret societies to be either moral or political evils, to seek to remove those evils by the exercise of the elective franchise, as well as by other lawful means. The expediency of such exercise of the elective franchise, in a given case, must be decided by the electors according to their own sense of the magnitude of the evils which they seek to remove, and a conscientious regard to those other great interests of the community which are more or less affected by every exercise of that franchise.

"I pray you, gentlemen, to accept the assurance of my personal regard and cordial good wishes.

"Your obliged friend and fellow-citizen,

"DANL. WEBSTER.

"To Messrs. J. Wallace and others."

[TO W. W. IRWIN.]

"BOSTON, *November* 30, 1835.

"MY DEAR SIR: I enclose you copies of a letter received by me from members of your State Committee, and my answer.

"If my letter to yourself and your associates had not appeared to supersede the necessity, I should have found no difficulty in answering the first two questions proposed to me in this letter. But I should doubt the prudence of directly replying to the third; because, in the situation in which I stand, that question might appear to others to be little else than asking me whether, on the happening of a certain event, I would confine myself to Antimasons in nominations to office. Although the question, in form, asks only what I think would be the duty of a Chief Magistrate, yet, in effect, it might be thought, or represented, as a mere request of a *promise* from me. I wish, my dear sir, you would take occasion to explain this point, in conversation, with the writers of the letter, and with other friends. What a Chief Magistrate must do, and ought to do, so far as he is elected on Antimasonic principles, and in regard to portions of the country where those principles prevail, can be no matter of doubt to you or to me, or to any man who reflects, and who means to act with candor and honesty toward those who support him. I hope no one hesitates to believe that I am altogether incapable of disappointing, in that respect, any natural and just expectations which friends may form. But it does not consist with my sense of duty to hold out promises, or any thing that might be regarded as equivalent to promises, particularly on the eve of a great election, the results of which are to affect the highest interests of the country for years to come. I authorize you, my dear sir, to make the substance of this letter known to your friends and mine; but it is still to be regarded, of course, as a private and confidential letter.

"Yours truly,

"DANIEL WEBSTER.

"Wm. W. Irwin, Esq., at Harrisburg, Pa."

On the 16th of December separate State conventions of the Whigs and the Antimasons assembled at Harrisburg. In the latter, nearly all men admitted that Mr. Webster was their first choice. But, alas for these nominating bodies, men could not act upon the conviction that a statesman of preëminent abilities and character was the fittest—nay, the only fit person to be designated for the presidency. To use the cant of these occasions, with which the private letters of the time are filled, they "could not carry him;" and it appears that the reason most generally assigned was that he had been a Federalist. The nomination was given to General William Henry Harrison, of Ohio, whose popularity, founded on the part he had taken in the late war with England, was supposed to be sufficient to encounter the pretensions of Mr. Van Buren. On the following day the Whig Convention adopted the nomination of General Harrison. A private letter, written on the spot, expressed the indubitable fact that this step only increased the chances of Mr. Van Buren's election.

But to return. Mr. Webster was in his place in the Senate

at an early period of the session which began in December, 1834. It was the commencement of the last year of General Jackson's Administration; and matters of great moment were pending in relation to our foreign as well as our domestic relations. There was no small danger of a war with France about an affair of money; and the whole subject of the custody and regulation of the public funds remained as it was left at the end of the last session.

Rarely have two great nations incurred a more unnecessary danger of coming to blows than did the United States and France in the year 1835. By a convention concluded in 1831, the French Government had bound itself to pay the Government of the United States twenty-five millions of francs, to liquidate certain claims of citizens of the United States;[1] and on the 2d of February, 1833, the first instalment of this sum became due. A bill of exchange was drawn by the Secretary of the Treasury on the French Minister of Finance for the amount of the instalment, and was sold to the Bank of the United States. On its presentation at the French Treasury, payment was refused, on the ground that the Legislative Chambers had made no appropriation to meet the instalment. The bill was taken up in Europe for the honor of the Bank of the United States, and was returned to this country protested. The bank claimed the usual damages of the Government, as in any other case of a protested bill which had been sold by the drawer. In his annual message at the commencement of the session of Congress in December, 1833, President Jackson made an official communication on the subject, and stated that he had dispatched an envoy to the French Government to attend to this matter, in regard to which he had received assurances that, at the next meeting of the Chambers, the subject would be presented and satisfactorily disposed of. The President added that, if he should be disappointed in the hope that he entertained, the subject would again be brought to the notice of Congress, "in such a manner as the occasion may require."

Perhaps it would have been well to have confined this affair, at first, to diplomatic action; since, in its attitude at that time,

[1] These claims were for spoliations committed on our commerce from 1800 to 1817. The French spoliations before 1800 were not embraced in this convention.

there was nothing for Congress to do in regard to it, and the course of the French Government might be susceptible of satisfactory explanation.

The Government of King Louis Philippe was at this time hampered by a truculent and turbulent opposition. That opposition contrived to make the treaty unpopular. When the President's message of December, 1833, was received in Paris, there was a general outcry against the execution of the treaty under what seemed a menace. Although the subject was several times brought before the Chambers, it was not until the month of April, 1834, that a vote upon it was obtained, and then the appropriation necessary to carry the treaty into effect was refused.[1] The ministry then dispatched a national vessel to this country, bearing the assurances of the King that, as soon after the election of new members as the charter would permit, the Chambers should be called together, and that the whole influence of the Executive Government should be exerted to procure the necessary appropriation, in season to be communicated to our Government before the assembling of the present Congress. The new Chambers met on the 31st of July, but the subject was not acted upon, and they were prorogued to the 29th of December. New assurances were given to the President by the King's Government that, at the ensuing session, the appropriation should be pressed.

This was the situation of the affair when President Jackson made his annual message of December, 1834. He laid before Congress the entire history of the negotiation, commented with a good deal of severity on the conduct of all branches of the French Government, and recommended that a law be passed authorizing reprisals upon French property, in case provision should not be made for the payment of this debt at the approaching session of the French Chambers. This message was received in Paris early in January (1835). It was there, of course, regarded as a threat. The French minister at Washington was recalled, and, on the 13th of January, Mr. Livingston, our minister at Paris, was informed that his passports were at his disposal. At the same time, the French ministry intro-

[1] The Duc de Broglie, who was then the Minister of Foreign Affairs, immediately resigned.

duced into the Chambers a bill for the necessary appropriation. What ensued can be best described by quoting the following private letter, addressed to Mr. Webster from Paris, by one of his personal friends and constituents, the Hon. Thomas H. Perkins, of Boston:

[FROM THE HON. THOS. H. PERKINS.]

"PARIS, *April* 21, 1835.

"Hon. DANIEL WEBSTER:

"DEAR SIR: I have been here some days, and shall leave to-morrow for Italy, to return to England in September, and hope to see you before you go South. Our question was brought before the Chambers on the 9th or 10th, and, until the last day of the discussion, it was doubtful how the question would go. It was passed on Saturday, with an amendment that I presume will defeat the payment of the stipulated sum, as it is not probable that the President will make an apology for the words used toward France. There is a great sensation among the people in general against America, as they believe every thing that has been asserted by the opposition, who have handled us 'without mittens.' The opposition consider the amendment as the success of their efforts. Has France a right to demand of the Executive the *amende honorable* for words addressed to the American people? I should think not. At any rate, they have paid us well in words, as there has been nothing left unsaid that could dishonor the country. They say we are not in a situation to go to war; that we are too avaricious to abstain from intercourse with them; and that we shall be glad to accept the amendment, which I hope will not be the case. My own opinion is, that many of the opposition would be glad of a war. There are, I am told, thirty general officers in the Chambers, and many naval men. The only thing that would bring them to accede to the payment, without conditions, would be a non-intercourse act, and making the manufactures or products of France liable to confiscation, if attempted to be introduced, after a given time, and that should be no longer than to enable goods already ordered to get home. A great part of this Chamber, and, indeed, of France out of the manufacturing towns, are ignorant of the fact that the United States take more than one-third of all they export to all countries. Non-intercourse would drive the manufactures of Lyons, Rouen, etc., into Switzerland and Germany, and create great distress in France generally. What the course of Mr. Livingston will be, I do not know. It is said he will go home in the Constitution, now in the Channel. I have not seen him since the action of the Chambers. Our latest dates are to the 16th from America. If there is no extra session, you will know all before you are called upon to act.

"Ministers have doubtless acted in good faith toward us in this matter, and I have no doubt the King would rather the bill had passed without any condition, but they were afraid to act upon the bill without accepting the amendment.

"Your friend and servant,

"T. H. PERKINS."

Before these occurrences could be known in this country—indeed, as soon as the President's message of December was communicated to Congress—the Senate's Committee on Foreign Affairs, of which Mr. Clay was chairman, determined that it would be inexpedient and improper to adopt the President's recommendation; and, on the 14th of January, the Senate, by a decisive vote, sanctioned the determination of their committee. The course of Mr. Webster, on this occasion, is sufficiently explained by the following letter, written by him in February:

[TO MR. WILLIAM SULLIVAN.[1]]

"WASHINGTON, *February* 23, 1835.

"DEAR SIR: . . . There are three parties in Congress on this question: the Jackson party proper, which, like its chief, feels very warlike; the

[1] This gentleman had written to Mr. Webster, on the 21st of February, as follows:

"You know by the papers that went last night (if in no other way) that a Senator is chosen. You know probably, to-day, that the ministers are recalled. I am reminded of a country milliner who was called to a duchess; to prepare herself for the interview, she inquired what she must say, and was answered, 'Your Grace.' Wherefore, on coming into the presence, she courtesied, and said: 'God bless us, and what is provided for us!' . . . There is here to-day much of that sort of feeling which one may suppose to exist among persons who dwell around the base of Vesuvius or Ætna, when the black smoke begins to ascend, and sparks to fly. Our Executive has no *metre*, to announce what is to come next, any more than a burning mountain has, to disclose when the lava will run, in what course, or in what quantity. Deplorable as a war with France would be in the present condition of the world, it is much more to be dreaded from its effects on our own institutions. In the feverish state of the slaveholding South, what will its duties and interests seem *to itself* to be? What is to be the character, and the will, of the military power to be embodied in this country, and by whom is its physical force to be directed, and to what objects? How entirely uncalled for is all this combination of probable evils! You stand acquitted of all responsibility, eminently. If your speech at Worcester, in October, 1832, could have found its way to the understanding of the country, things would not have been as they are. Is there not some reason to fear that restive, unquiet France, and perplexed England, and vindictive Spain, may think a good opportunity has arisen to dispose of that 'food for gunpowder' which a long peace necessarily prepares in Europe, and which must be sent abroad, to prevent mischief at home. Then, in what condition is this country for a violent or protracted struggle, even if another class of rulers had the power. This you know better than anybody, but every thinking man in Massachusetts knows that this State was never in a worse condition to meet such a crisis. The pulpit, peace societies—a sickly sort of philanthropy—a bad militia system, mischievously perverted, have combined to extinguish the noble spirit of independence, and to palsy the power of self-defence, which once gave Massachusetts a proud preëminence. Add to this (as I know from what I saw in the long session of the nominating committee at Worcester, October, 1833), there is not a man in the State on whom one-quarter of the qualified voters would combine, and to whom they would give the direction of its affairs. I remember to have heard you say, on one occasion, 'Providence may be better to us than our fears;' and, if not, I must again say, with the milliner, 'God bless us, and what is provided for us.' . . .

"I was interrupted here by an old gentleman named Goodhue, who is one of your admirers, and to whom (he says) you once gave four or five books. He has closed a somewhat long, profitless, and tedious discourse, with a phrase which I think I may well use to close a letter to which, perhaps, you may give a like character: 'I hope you will not impute any thing that I have said to any thing worse than weakness.'

"Your respectful friend,

"WM. SULLIVAN.

"Hon. Mr. Webster."

Southern anti-Jackson men, who seem to me to be in the other extreme—witness Mr. Calhoun and Mr. Poindexter, who speak of the whole matter only as a debt, and recommend an action of assumpsit, instead of war, etc.; and then there is the rest of us, who desire to say and do nothing to encourage France in her neglect of our rights, and who are not willing, nevertheless, to hazard the peace of the country without absolute necessity. We wish to show to France that there is but one sentiment in the United States as to the justice of our side of the question; one sentiment as to the propriety of insisting on the fulfilment of the treaty, but, at the same time, a great reluctance to come to an open rupture, and, in order to avoid that, a disposition to give France full time to consider well of her course."

Two days before this letter was written, he had occasion to interpose in a somewhat earnest discussion which sprang up on the presentation of one of the memorials on the subject, and which he thus quieted:

"Mr. Webster said he was surprised that such a debate should arise on a motion to print a memorial, considering the importance and delicacy of the question, and the state of the information before the Senate. He was not in his place, not having come from the committee-room, when his colleague presented the paper, but he found, from remarks of gentlemen since he had taken his seat, that the occasion had been taken to express strong opinions on the subject of our relations with France. He hoped, most sincerely, the discussion would not be pursued at present. If it were, he should be quite obliged to express his own sentiments, because he was bound to say that they differed from the sentiments which had already been uttered by those for whom he entertained much respect. He could not consider the question between us and France a mere question about a debt—a controversy only about so much money. He thought, certainly, that the question was of a much graver and higher character. He was anxious, most anxious, to preserve the peace of the country, without sacrificing, at the same time, its honor and dignity. He still hoped that these objects were not incompatible; he still trusted that peace might be maintained, without discredit or reproach, and without sacrificing any right, or any interest of this country, or any of its citizens. That, however, depended much on the course adopted by others. But, at present, the Senate was in no condition to discuss or consider this high subject. No official communication was before them. All they had was a paragraph from a French newspaper. It seemed to him, in all points of view, to be much wiser to wait till official communications shall be received, in the usual and regular way. He earnestly hoped the discussion would not proceed."

But this affair connected itself with another measure, in regard to which Mr. Webster felt it to be his duty to take a very decided stand. On the last night of the session (March 3d), the annual appropriation bills being under consideration in the Senate, a message was received from the House of Representatives, proposing to amend one of the Senate's amendments to the Fortification Bill by adding the following section:

"That the sum of three millions of dollars be, and the same is hereby, appropriated, out of any money in the Treasury not otherwise appropriated, to be expended, in whole or in part, under the direction of the President of the United States, for the military and naval service, including fortifications and ordnance and increase of the navy: provided such expenditures shall be rendered necessary for the defence of the country prior to the next meeting of Congress."

This proposition, which led to the loss of the whole Fortification Bill, was instantly opposed by Mr. Webster, upon the two plain grounds, that it had not been recommended or asked for by the Executive, and that the proposed grant specified no objects to which the money was to be applied. He rested both of the objections upon provisions of the Constitution. He spoke with great earnestness and animation. The result was, that the Senate rejected the amendment. The House then sent another message, insisting on its amendment, and the Senate, on Mr. Webster's motion, adhered to its refusal. The entire Fortification Bill failed to become a law, in consequence of the neglect of the House to act on the report of a committee of conference, through which Mr. Webster proposed to make specific appropriations for arming the fortifications, and repairing and equipping the ships-of-war.[1]

[1] Mr. Webster, from the committee of conference, reported that the two committees had agreed, in lieu of the amendment of the House, to recommend the adoption of the following appropriations:

"As an additional appropriation for arming the fortifications of the United States, three hundred thousand dollars.

"As an additional appropriation for the repairs and equipment of the ships-of-war of the United States, five hundred thousand dollars."

The House having possession of the bill and papers, the Senate could not act on the report until it heard from the other House.

After waiting some time, on motion of Mr. Webster, the Senate adopted the following resolution:

"*Resolved*, That a message be sent to the honorable the House of Representatives, respectfully to remind the House of the report of the committee of conference on the disagreeing votes of the two Houses on the amendment of the House to the amendment of the Senate to the bill respecting the fortifications of the United States."

The Senate then waited still a good while longer, and, not hearing, sent still another message, informing the House that they, the Senate, had no further business before them. No answer coming to this message, the Senate, after waiting a considerable time longer, and hearing nothing from the bill, adjourned *sine die.*

From these statements, the reader will understand the attitude of the French question, and the position which the Senate occupied in relation to military preparations, at the close of the session in March, 1835. Mr. Webster's personal relations to these subjects will be resumed in the next chapter.

At this session he brought before Congress the subject of French spoliations on American commerce, committed before the year 1800. This was a judicial question between citizens of the United States and their own Government; for these claims on the Government of France had been released on the part of the United States in the convention of 1800, by a mutual renunciation of all adverse claims between the two countries, which left the American sufferers in the position of parties whose right to demand indemnity from France had been, for public and national reasons, cut off by their own Government. The whole subject was fully examined by Mr. Webster in a speech which he delivered on the 12th of January (1835), and which is printed in the fourth volume of his Works. Before its delivery, he was charged, in a letter written from Washington to a newspaper in Albany, with having a direct personal interest in these claims, as counsel employed upon a contingent compensation. He caused a friend in Albany to demand of the editor the name of the writer; but no information could be obtained beyond the fact that the letter was written by a member of Congress. When he rose to speak upon the subject, he took occasion to say that he had never been retained, or even spoken to, as counsel, in the course of his life, in relation to these claims. He was placed by the Senate at the head of the committee on this subject, at the last session, without his own wish and without his own knowledge.

At this session, also, he made a very important speech on the President's power to appoint and remove public officers, upon a bill that was intended to reduce the influence exerted by the Executive through the public patronage. In this speech he took occasion to express fully his views of the construction given to the Constitution in 1789, by which Congress had then decided that the power of removal belongs to the President as the Executive. It has already been said that, as an original proposition, Mr. Webster did not concur in this construction.

He now placed upon record the grounds of his dissent from it. So far as the decision of 1789 implied a power of removal in the President separate from the action of the whole appointing power, which consists of the President and the Senate, he held that the decision was wrong; that Congress possesses the power to regulate the tenure of all offices the tenure of which is not fixed by the Constitution; and that it is competent for Congress to provide, as a regulation of that tenure, that the incumbent shall be removed only on reasons to be stated by the President to the Senate, and to be acted upon by both.[1] But, while he held that it is in the power of Congress to reverse the decision of 1789, which so construed the Constitution as to separate the power of removal from the power of appointment, he did not deny that under that construction the President possesses such a separate power, or propose to take it away. The bill which he now advocated, and which he considered sufficient to check the abuses of the power, required that when a nomination should be made by the President to the Senate, to fill a vacancy in an office caused by the President's having removed the former incumbent, the fact of the removal should be stated to the Senate at the same time when the new nomination is made, with a statement also of the reasons for making the removal.

On the 18th of February, Mr. Benton introduced a resolution to expunge from the Journals of the Senate its resolution of March 28, 1834, concerning the President's assumption of powers over the public revenue. On the last day of the session, the Senate, by a vote of thirty-nine to seven, struck out of Mr. Benton's resolution the words, "ordered to be expunged from the Journals." Mr. Webster immediately rose and said that this great vote had accomplished all that he had ever desired respecting this expunging resolution. Thereafter, propositions to pass resolutions inconsistent with that originally adopted on this subject must be met when they should arise. But the offensive and illegal act of tampering with the Journal of the Senate had now been most happily defeated by a nearly unanimous vote. He concluded with a motion, "which," he said,

[1] The speech is contained in the fourth volume of his Works, 179–199. Compare Madison's Works, iv., 342, 343, 368, 385.

"I forewarn friends and foes that I shall not withdraw"—that Mr. Benton's resolution be laid upon the table. This was carried by a vote of twenty-seven to twenty.

The occurrences of the last session had convinced Mr. Webster that the Bank of the United States could not be rechartered; that the experiment of making use of the State banks as fiscal agents of the Government must go on; and that, the day of argument being now passed, the new system must await the unerring result of experience. A bill to regulate the deposits of the public money being before the Senate, he took occasion to say that sooner or later the time must come when the country would feel the fullest conviction of the necessity for a national bank. But he did not purpose to propose another, until public opinion had demanded it. At present the ability of the State banks to furnish a circulating medium, or a safe system of exchanges capable of taking the place of those of the Bank of the United States, could not be tested, for the whole circulation of that bank was still employed in assisting the operations of the Treasury, facilitating exchanges, and enabling the deposit banks themselves to make use of a medium of universal credits. When the time should arrive for the substitution of the notes of the deposit banks in the place of the twenty millions of universally accredited paper of the national institution, the "experiment" of the Administration could be put upon its trial. What was likely to happen, however, was already foreshadowed. Treasury warrants drawn on the deposit banks had already begun, in a few cases, to be paid in *current bank notes*, which could not have the same value in all parts of the Union. To stop this on the threshold, he proposed and carried a provision making it illegal, and requiring the Treasury drafts on the deposit banks to be paid in gold and silver, if the holder should demand it.[1]

[1] February 26, 1835. Works, iv., 200.

CHAPTER XXII.

1835–1836.

THE INDEPENDENCE OF TEXAS ACHIEVED—MR. WEBSTER'S DESIRE TO HAVE HER REMAIN A NATION BY HERSELF—EARLY SPIRIT OF THE ANTISLAVERY MOVEMENT—OPINIONS OF MR. WEBSTER ON THE WHOLE SUBJECT OF SLAVERY—TREATMENT OF THE PETITIONS FOR ITS ABOLITION IN THE DISTRICT OF COLUMBIA—"INCENDIARY PUBLICATIONS"—ACKNOWLEDGMENT OF TEXAN INDEPENDENCE—LOSS OF THE FORTIFICATION BILL AT THE PREVIOUS SESSION—MR. WEBSTER'S DEFENCE OF HIS OWN COURSE—AN UNPUBLISHED SPEECH—CUSTODY OF THE PUBLIC FUNDS—REGULATION OF THE DEPOSIT BANKS—DISTRIBUTION OF SURPLUS REVENUES—SETTLEMENT OF THE DIFFICULTY WITH FRANCE—PRESIDENTIAL ELECTION OF 1836.

MR. WEBSTER is now to be observed in the position of a public man formally proposed as a candidate for the presidency of the United States by the State which he represented in the Senate. In what degree his public conduct was influenced or affected by this position the reader can judge. Topics were to come under discussion in Congress, in respect to which it was certainly in his power to conciliate popular sentiment in regions very far from New England; and there was no man in public life, at that day, whose words were carried farther, whose acts were more closely observed by the people of the United States, or whose sentiments were more likely to be known, when they were uttered, among both friends and opponents. In the remote Southwest, an excitement had already arisen, which was to test the strength of his character as a statesman, as it had not been tested or tried before.

The inhabitants of Texas were at this time engaged in the revolutionary war with Mexico, by which they had undertaken to establish their independence. The large emigration from the United States which had for some time been flowing into Texas, the sympathies which this emigration created between the people on our southwestern frontier and the people of that province, and the prospect of its separation from Mexico, attracted Mr. Webster's attention from the first, and gave him much anxiety. This whole subject appeared to him to be likely to bring into our politics new causes of embarrassment, and new tendencies to dismemberment.[1] The opinion, thus early formed, was based upon the consideration that the people of Texas, after driving out the Mexican power, must either be made a separate nation, or seek to become a part of the United States; that, however they might succeed for a time in maintaining the former character, the emigration that had entered Texas would make it a slaveholding country; that if it continued an independent nation, it would be one to which our Southern States would have strong tendencies whenever causes might spring up that would lead them to seek a separation from the Union; and that if Texas sought to become a part of the United States, its absorption into the Union would occasion new embarrassments, arising from the addition of an enormous territory to the slaveholding region of our confederacy, that could not take place and continue without bringing the Northern and Southern sections of our country, sooner or later, into collision, on the floor of Congress, in relation to the whole subject of slavery. There were, therefore, in his view, from the very first, serious difficulties to be encountered, springing from the success of the Texan Revolution. The course which he felt it to be his duty to take was one to be determined by a balance of all the evils arising out of the situation. He was very soon convinced that the paramount interests of the United States would be best secured by having Texas remain a distinct na-

[1] Letter to Mr. Everett.—(*Correspondence*, ii., 19. May 7, 1836.) The decisive battle of San Jacinto, which secured and practically established the independence of Texas, was fought on the 21st of April, 1836.

tion; that, if she could maintain herself in this character, we should avoid the internal dissensions that would be almost certain to follow her incorporation into the Union; and that, however it might be feared that her separate nationality would create some centrifugal tendencies in our Southern States toward her, such tendencies could be more easily encountered than the sectional collision which would be the sure consequence of her addition to the Union. It will be found, accordingly, that these views were the key-note of his whole policy on this subject, and that, so far as he could exercise any influence, publicly or privately, upon events, that influence was always exerted to promote the separate nationality of Texas, after she had succeeded, by the battle of San Jacinto, in expelling the Mexican power from her borders. Soon after that event, he received the following very graphic letter from Judge Catron, of Tennessee:

[FROM JUDGE CATRON.]

"NASHVILLE, *12th June*, 1836.

"MY DEAR SIR: An expression of yours in the Senate, when speaking of the propriety of recognizing the independence of Texas, has made a very strong impression in this country that England may endeavor to gain a footing in Texas by purchase from Mexico.[1] A large meeting was holden here yesterday, which resolved that Congress and the Executive should forthwith, and before the close of the session, recognize the independence of Texas; *and* use the means to end the war; and extend our boundary *west*, that is, acquire the country. This is proposed in effect, though not in terms.

"England will be drawn into the Texan war in this wise: The Mexican is driven from Texas with a terror upon him inconsistent with further fighting there. If the matter would end at this, it would be well. But the spirit is abroad through the whole valley of the Mississippi to march upon Mexico. All may emigrate to Texas who will. It is lawful. All who choose may buy Texas lands. This is lawful. The golden city presents temptations strong as in the days of Cortez. Men and money are to be had—the former in excess—to march upon it in the fall. The Mexican population consists of, say 7,000,000—3,000,000 native Indians an encum-

[1] Mr. Webster had said in the Senate, on the 23d of May, that he had received some information from a respectable source, which turned his attention to the very significant expression used by Mr. Monroe in his message of 1822, that no European power should ever be permitted to establish a colony on the American Continent. He had no doubt that attempts would be made by some European government to obtain a cession of Texas from the Government of Mexico.

brance, the like number of the mixed blood, worthless, or nearly so, as defenders, and one million of Spanish descent unmixed, who are poor soldiers, and divided at that between the parties of the priests and liberals. During the whole of the Mexican civil war, hardly a battle was fought respectable as a foraging skirmish of a well-appointed army of respectable size. Mr. Justin Chambers informs me (now here) that the companies of native Indians, and often of the mixed blood, are marched to the seat of war handcuffed by pairs, with a common chain extending through the middle, and when brought into battle put in front, with orders to shoot them in rear if they give way! That convicts always are managed in this wise, and were at the taking of the Alamo. There is not a boy, 'whose quiver and bow is scarcely terror to the crow,' in this great valley but believes this, be it strictly correct or not; and hardly one that does not ardently long to be of the army that is to conquer the priests, and divide the ill-gotten gold of the temple—to get his slice of the great lamp in the cathedral, or a foot's length of a silver pillar, and fame besides. It is not supposed there will be fighting enough for tolerable sport. My belief is, that this is but too true; but, whether true or fallacious, the effect must be the same. If the war continues, Texas will endeavor to conquer Mexico. England will aid the latter to resist; will aid her to invade Texas in turn; and depend on it, when she puts her hand into this work, Mexico shares the fate of India.

"Whether this be an evil-brooding fancy, you are the better judge; if not, now is the time for us to act as a preventive means. The object of this scrawl is to give the state of temperament in the West—uncontrollable as the Mississippi. It may be of use.

"The young fellows who fought in the battle of San Jacinto are dropping in daily, and are followed by crowds of young and old—for hardly any of us have escaped the felicity of having divers young kinsmen there of whom we are most anxious to hear—and the first question is, 'How did he fight?' with glistening eyes. '*Aye, aye!*' says the father, 'I thought so.' The boy may have run away, as many did; he is now the hero of the family, and all follow him who choose. No monk is needed to preach the crusade. The interference of yourself and Northern friends to check it would, I feel very sure, be a great service to the country. That the recognition of Texas, and the ending of the war, is the proper course, all must concur, and that another equal opportunity, *after* the close of the present session of Congress, to. fix our boundary west of the Colorado, will present, I think no well-informed man will believe.

"Most sincerely, I have
"The honor to be your
"Friend and obedient servant,
"J. CATRON.

"To the Hon. D. Webster,
Washington."

There were reasons less observed at this moment by the excellent man who wrote this letter than they were by Mr. Webster, which made it inexpedient for the United States to seek the acquisition of Texas. The agitation for the abolition of slavery was recently begun; and Mr. Webster had means of knowing in what spirit it had been begun, by many who had embarked in it, as well as the nature of the feeling which it was to touch in the breasts of the people of the North. An official letter from one of the antislavery societies addressed to him during the winter of 1836, transmitting to him some petitions for the abolition of slavery in the District of Columbia, which they wished him to present to the Senate, now lies before me; and, as the persons who subscribed and sent these petitions were among his constituents, they had a right to ask him to present them. It is quite apparent, however, from this letter, that the persons who caused it to be written intended to make no allowance for the feelings or apprehensions of the people of the slaveholding States; that the "Abolitionists" would, under no circumstances, refrain from pressing their points; that, if it should be found that Congress was unable, from any restrictions in the cessions by Maryland and Virginia, to abolish slavery in the District of Columbia, they intended to petition Congress to remove the seat of government; and that they designed to effect "the speedy and entire abolition of slavery," by the use of "moral means."[1] On all these points the letter was explicit, and it expressed the desire of the Antislavery Society that their determinations might be fully known. Mr. Webster knew, therefore, that an agitation had begun, which was to aim at a great organic change in the domestic relations of States which had never committed this subject to the control of the General Government, and that this agitation must inevitably make itself felt in the halls of Congress. Already the blunder had been committed of calling in question the *right* of citizens to petition Congress on this subject. Already there were manifestations of a purpose to exclude from the public mails, in the slaveholding States, printed matter in relation to slavery. Two opposite forces in the opposite sections of the Union were thus

[1] MS. letter from the corresponding secretary of the Massachusetts Anti-slavery Society to Mr. Webster, January 13, 1836.

arraying themselves for that long conflict that was finally to shake, if not to overthrow, the Constitution of the United States. Let it be remembered, therefore, that, at the very first moment of the success of the Texan Revolution, Mr. Webster had fixed his attention upon the dangers that would attend her absorption into this Union; and let it also be remembered what were the contemporaneous occurrences and tendencies that made him so unwilling to encounter that result.[1]

Having touched upon this topic, it is proper to indicate here the cardinal principles on which his course in regard to it was shaped from the first. In the first place, he held that all the guaranties which the Constitution had given to slavery, as a domestic institution of States in the Union, were to be strictly and faithfully observed; and, while he regarded it as a political, social, and moral evil, he did not allow that political action upon it, where it was not under the jurisdiction of the Federal Government, by citizens of non-slaveholding States, was legally or morally justifiable. In the second place, he maintained that any enlargement of its area, by the addition of new slaveholding States, was at all times and under all circumstances a question that concerned the whole Union; fit to be acted upon by Congress, and in his opinion never to be consented to. In the third place, he considered the existence of slavery in the District of Columbia as a matter wholly under the control of Congress, to be acted upon always with reference to the effect of such action upon the harmony and stability of the Union. But beneath all these opinions upon specific questions, lay his deep, abiding conviction that the Constitution of the United States was so founded in mutual concessions between the opposing interests and feelings of the two grand sections of the Union, that it could not be preserved but by acting under and administering it according to the letter of its provisions; and that when either section sought for additional advantages, not stipulated for in its formation, or when either refused to abide by any of its compacts, there could be no security for it in the future, and no means of preventing the dismemberment which the loss of its security must entail.

All men, who are accustomed to consider the boundary

[1] See the speech at Niblo's Saloon in New York.—(*Works*, i., 343, 354.)

which a statesman must regard as the line that forbids him to act upon purely moral considerations, will recognize in these opinions the just limitations of political conduct. An American statesman, living and acting in the period of Mr. Webster's public life, might well regard slavery as an evil, and a great moral wrong; he might even concur in the favorite phrase of those who assailed it as the "sum of all villanies," if he saw reason so to characterize it. But the question on which posterity are to judge Mr. Webster—on which many of his contemporaries were never willing to judge him fairly—is whether he could take part as a public man in administering the Constitution of the United States without acting up to his convictions of what it required at his hands. Few men, in all our history, have said more impressive things respecting the wrong of slavery and its inherent evils than he has. No man in our history has been more uniformly faithful as a statesman to the letter of the fundamental law, to the obligation of public compacts, and to the dictates of that public policy which results from the provisions of a fixed constitution. Let it be determined, by the fair judgment of mankind, whether such a character is marked by any inconsistency.

A debate on the reception of petitions for the abolition of slavery in the District of Columbia commenced in the Senate on the 7th of January, and was continued at intervals until the 11th of March. A great effort was made to prevent their being received at all; but the final decision of the Senate was to receive them, and then immediately to reject their prayer, without any reference to a committee. Mr. Webster voted against this method of action.[1] He had not participated in the long and excited discussion which preceded the vote, choosing to reserve the expression of his opinions upon the course proper to be pursued, until the Senate had made its decision. But he at once proceeded to give an opportunity for reversing it. On the 16th of March, he presented two petitions which had been sent to him from Massachusetts, and another from Michigan; and he then stated with great distinctness that, while the Government of the United States had no control whatever over slavery in the States, he held it to be entirely clear that Congress had

[1] The vote was thirty-four for the immediate rejection and six against it.

full control over it in the District of Columbia; that the prayer of these petitions was, therefore, not one that could be summarily rejected on the ground of want of power to deal with the subject; that the proper course to be taken with them was the usual course, namely, to refer them to a committee for consideration; and that in his opinion a report upon the subject, fairly discussing it in all its bearings, would produce a proper effect both in and out of the Senate. One of the Southern Senators who followed him referred to his having placed himself "at the head of the petitioners." He then rose and replied:

"The gentleman cannot be allowed, sir, to assign to me any place or any character which I do not choose to take to myself. I have only expressed an opinion as to the course which it is prudent and wise in us all to adopt in disposing of these petitions.

"It is true that, while the question on the reception of the petitions was pending, I observed that I should hold back these petitions till that question was decided. It is decided. The Senate has decided to receive the petitions; and, being received, the manner of treating them necessarily arises. The origin of the authority of Congress over this District, the views and objects of the States in ceding the territory, the little interest which this Government has in the general question of slavery, and the great magnitude which individual States have in it, the great danger to the Government itself of agitating the question here, while things remain in their present posture in States around us—these, sir, are considerations all intimately belonging to the question, as I think, and which a competent committee would naturally present to the Senate and to the public.

"Mr. President, I feel bound to make one further remark. Whatever gentlemen may think of it, I assure them that these petitions, at least in many cases, have no factious origin. Such may be the origin of some of them. I am quite sure it is not of all. Many of them arise from a sense of religious duty; and that is a feeling which should be reasoned with, but cannot be suppressed by a mere summary exercise of authority. I wish that all reasonable men may be satisfied with our proceedings; that we may so act in regard to the whole matter as shall promote harmony, strengthen the bonds of our Union, and increase the confidence both of the North and the South in this Government."

His advice was not followed. The capital error was committed of treating this subject of the abolition of slavery in the District of Columbia as a question that was not to be discussed in the legislative body which had plenary jurisdiction over it, and which was necessarily liable to be approached, in regard to it, by citizens of the United States, acting with various motives and purposes, but acting in the exercise of a right that could not be questioned. From this moment Mr. Webster saw that a great opportunity was lost. He would have had the subject so dealt with as to show to the whole country the clear line of its duty in regard to the institution of slavery as it existed in the States. He was well convinced that, if this occasion were suffered to pass without such a course of action as he recommended—if the Northern feeling, in regard to the presence of slavery at the seat of Government, was to be met by a refusal to consider the subject at all—a long agitation, constantly growing stronger, would produce a chronic irritation and alarm in the slaveholding States. He was fully aware that the introduction of Texas into the Union was already looked to as a means of increasing the political power of that section; and he knew that here would be a fresh provocative to the Northern sentiment, which was even now but too strongly stimulated by the efforts made to suppress it. But the wrong step was taken—taken against his earnest warning. His motion to refer the petitions was laid upon the table. Nothing remained for him, therefore, but to watch, as he had always watched, and to guard, as he had always guarded, against all attempts to give unwarrantable interpretations to the Constitution; and to prevent, so far as he could, the operation of causes that plainly tended to the increase of feelings which would assuredly weaken the bonds of the Union. It is certainly probable that, if the Senate had seen fit to refer these petitions to a committee, he would have been willing to undertake such a discussion as he desired should occur. Who can estimate the effect that would have followed, at that day, from a report proceeding from his pen, or a speech by him, on the topics which he desired to have treated? The result was that slavery, in the District of Columbia, was left until it could no longer be safely or successfully handled; it was left for thirty years as a perpetual cause of irritation, affording its own fuel to the flames that from other and similar sources kindled the fires of civil war.

Among the prominent occurrences of this session, which indicated the increasing irritation on the subject of slavery, and the causes which produced it, must be ranked Mr. Calhoun's bill concerning "Incendiary Publications." It proposed to prohibit the deputy-postmasters from delivering any printed matter touching the subject of slavery in States whose laws prohibited the circulation of such matter. Mr. Webster did not found his opposition to this measure on a denial of the evil complained of. He had not, he observed, a word to say against the objects of the bill; but, with constitutional lawyers, there was a great difference between the object and the means of carrying it into effect. His objection went to the means. Looking to the provision of the Constitution, which prohibits Congress from passing any law abridging the freedom of speech or of the press, he concluded that Congress had not the power to decide, from the character of a paper, whether it should be carried in the mail or not. Such a decision would be a direct abridgment of the freedom of the press. This was certainly a most important suggestion; and, perhaps, an equally important one was directed by Mr. Webster against the provision of the bill which looked to the destruction of papers, supposed to be prohibited by the laws of the States, if not withdrawn, on notice to the sender, within a certain time. This, it was proposed, should be done by the deputy-postmasters. Mr. Webster maintained the point that a paper sent in the mail is the property of the person to whom it is sent. If it is property, it cannot be destroyed without "due process of law," that is, without judicial trial. To make a deputy-postmaster the judge of whether it is such a property as the person to whom it is sent can lawfully possess, would be to constitute him a judicial officer to determine a question of property. He also considered the law unnecessary, because the States had full power to punish the deputy-postmasters for *circulating* incendiary publications in violation of their laws. Similar views were maintained by other Senators, especially by Mr. Clay, who made a strong opposition to the bill. It was rejected by a decisive vote.

On the 1st of July the Senate adopted a resolution, reported by Mr. Clay from the Committee on Foreign Affairs, declaring that the independence of Texas ought to be acknowledged by the United States, whenever satisfactory information should be received that it had in successful operation a civil government capable of performing the duties and fulfilling the obligations of an independent power. Mr. Webster advocated this course, and voted for the resolution, which was, in fact, unanimously adopted.

At this session the President, in his annual message, alluded to the loss of the Fortification Bill at the close of the last session, and said that "much injury and inconvenience have been experienced in consequence of" it. He added that "this failure was the more to be regretted, not only because it interrupted and delayed the progress of a system of national defence, projected immediately after the last war, and since steadily pursued, but also because it contained a contingent appropriation, inserted in accordance with the views of the Executive, in aid of this important object, and other branches of the national defence, some portions of which might have been most usefully applied during the past season."

This was the first intimation that had ever been given that the three million appropriation proposed by that bill was "in accordance with the views of the Executive;" and even this did not go so far as to suggest that the appropriation had been asked for or recommended by the Executive at the time it had passed the House of Representatives. The censure implied in the President's remarks fell, of course, upon the Senate; and for the Senate's rejection of the appropriation Mr. Webster was more responsible than any one else.

On the 14th of January, therefore, of the present session, he delivered a speech, embracing an elaborate account of all the facts attending the loss of the bill on the last night of the previous session, and restating the grounds of his opposition to it. He reminded the country that the proposed appropriation did not come before Congress with any Executive recommendation, and that its character was such that it would have vested in the President a naked discretion as to its expenditure, without specification of object or purpose, to the entire exclusion of the exercise of all judgment on the part of Congress. He then said: "The honorable member from Ohio,[1] near me, has said that, if the enemy had been on our shores, he would not have agreed to

[1] Mr. Ewing.

this vote. *And I say, if the proposition were now before us, and the guns of the enemy were pointed against the walls of the Capitol, I would not agree to it.*" [1]

On the 22d of January, a resolution was introduced into the House of Representatives for the appointment of a committee to inquire into the facts attending the loss of the Fortification Bill of the last session. In the course of the discussions on this resolution, Mr. Webster's remark, which is above printed in italics, was commented on with much severity. Although this was quite unparliamentary, Mr. Webster prepared himself to make a reply to it in his place in the Senate. He very deliberately wrote a speech, in defence of his observation, which he intended to read to the Senate at the first opportunity; but he was dissuaded from it by friends, who considered it both unnecessary and inexpedient. The paper, however, is preserved; and I make some extracts from it, of a very interesting character, which show his adherence, under all emergencies, real or pretended, to the requirements of the Constitution:

"Mr. President, I have no intention of entering again into this debate. The resolution itself, expressing the propriety of defending the country, I am quite ready to support by my vote, and, as to the various topics which have been discussed, I am willing to leave them without further remark from me.

"It might appear, however, affectation of dignity, rather than true dignity itself, were I to take no notice whatever of certain extraordinary occurrences which have taken place since I addressed the Senate on the 14th of January.

"In my speech, on that day, I gave my reasons for having opposed the vote of the three millions, on the last evening of the last session. I placed that opposition on constitutional grounds. I insisted that the proposed grant of money had no specified object; that it had no limit, within the broadest interpretation of whatever might be called military service; that it conferred on the President the power of deciding whether armies should be raised, or whether navies should be maintained, although these powers are expressly confided by the Constitution, not to the President, but to Congress; that, under this vote, the President might build ships, or buy ships, or levy troops, or do any thing which he might choose to think that the military service required.

"I endeavored to show that this mode of proceeding was, in no just sense, an *appropriation* of money; that it appeared rather to be a surrender of our own powers and our own duties to Executive discretion; that it

[1] A speech, Works, iv., 205.

was against fundamental principles, and the whole spirit of the Constitution; that it was a dangerous inroad on the Constitution, as it vested every power, great and small, respecting the military and naval service, in the President alone, without specification of object or limitation of purpose, and to the exclusion of the exercise of all judgment on the part of Congress.

"Holding this opinion of the proposed grant, fully believing it to be repugnant to plain constitutional injunctions, and a most alarming extension of the Executive authority, I declared that I could not agree in it; and added these remarks: '*The honorable member from Ohio, near me, has said that, if the enemy had been on our shores, he would not have agreed to this vote. And I say, if the proposition were now before us, and the guns of the enemy were battering against the walls of the Capitol, I would not agree to it.*

"'*The people of this country have an interest, a property, an inheritance, in this instrument, against the value of which forty capitols do not weigh the twentieth part of one poor scruple. There can never be any necessity for such proceedings but a feigned and false necessity, a mere idle and hollow pretence of necessity; least of all can it be said that any such necessity actually existed on the 3d of March. There was no enemy on our shores; there were no guns pointed against the Capitol; we were in no war, nor was there a reasonable probability that we should have war, unless we made it ourselves.*'

"Now, sir, whether I was right or wrong in my judgment of the true character of the proposed grant, no man, of common intelligence and common candor, can infer any thing from these remarks of mine but a conviction on my part of the great impropriety of the grant, a full belief that it was inconsistent with constitutional provisions, and a fixed resolution to prefer the safety and integrity of the Constitution to every political interest. I had only repeated, in other language, the sentiment of the gentleman from Ohio, to which nobody had thought of taking any exception.

"Gentlemen might say I was mistaken; that the proposed vote did not violate constitutional provisions; that it did not dangerously extend Executive power and discretion; all this gentlemen might say, and, undoubtedly, those gentlemen did so think who agreed to the vote themselves.

"But there is no member of the Senate who will say that, if he himself had honestly entertained the opinion which I expressed, he would have supported the grant, either to save the Capitol or to preserve any other public interest.

"No gentleman can say so, without admitting that he regards the integrity of the Constitution as a subordinate matter, a thing which may be surrendered in a political emergency like that of war and invasion. Every man must see that my expression was merely one of preference for the Constitution of the country over all other interests, and its preservation an object so vital, so paramount, in my judgment and feeling, as not to be hazarded in any emergency, real or pretended. This, sir, every man must see to have been my meaning, and my only meaning, and, if he is an honest man, he must acknowledge and admit it. . . .

"Sir, if I am guilty of idolatry toward any object on earth, it must be found in the homage I bear to the Constitution of the United States. I have been bred in the reverence and in the love of that Constitution. I think I have some knowledge of its history, its spirit, and its principles; but, however that may be, I am sure I have ample knowledge of its blessings in the prosperity which it has spread around us all at home, and in the national distinction which, under its fortunate star and beneficent guidance, we have attained abroad. These are the grounds of my attachment to it.

"It is not, sir, that this Constitution, or the Government established under it, has ever enriched or particularly benefited me or mine. I have never held an office, unless it be an office to represent the people in one or the other branch of this Legislature. I have received no favors, and asked no favors, at any time, or from any hand. Not one of those in whose veins there runs a drop of blood kindred to my own has enjoyed office, or profit, or patronage, or favor of any kind, under this Government.

"I have, sir, devoted no small labor, I have given the best years of my life, I have sacrificed professional emolument, and I have done all this cheerfully, for the honor of serving the people in Congress, with no other object than to secure their favor and confidence, and a desire, I hope not too ambitious, of being numbered among those who have done something, in their day and generation, to uphold the free institutions of the country, and to maintain the bond of our happy and glorious Union.

"With this unaffected attachment to the Constitution, with this sedulous care for it, with a habit, I confess, which leads me, on every great measure, and especially on every new and extraordinary proposition, to consider, first and mainly, its bearing on that great security for our liberties and our Union, I saw a grant of money to the Executive proposed at the last session, which I thought inconsistent with its fundamental provisions, and *dangerous* to its permanent safety. So thinking, I said in my place, the other day, that I could not have voted for it if the enemy were battering against the Capitol! And, so thinking, could I so vote, even in that state of things? Could any honest man, holding my sentiments, so vote, in that or any other emergency? . . ."

The financial measures of this session attracted a large share of Mr. Webster's attention, not merely from his position as chairman of the Finance Committee, but because he saw and foretold the approaching bankruptcies and distress which were to overspread the country, in consequence of the condition into which its currency had been brought. But it was not in his power, or in that of any other opponent of the Administration, wholly to prevent the mischiefs which he predicted. The condition of things was most extraordinary. By the President's refusal to continue the Bank of the United States, and by the removal of the deposits to the custody of certain State banks, the public funds were now under the control of the Executive. By the veto of the Land Bill of 1833, a bill which was designed to prevent an accumulation of money in the Treasury, there was now a large surplus, which was growing larger. These effects had led to a great increase in the number of the State banks, over whose excessive issues of paper money there was no existing check. These evils, Mr. Webster said, were begun, and could no longer be averted. They flowed from the disposition to submit every thing to the will of the Executive, and to permit the constitutional powers of Congress to lie dormant, because the Executive would not allow them to be exercised. In reference to this tendency, he said that the future historian of recent events in this country would find no topic more prominent and important than a review of the doctrines which had been advanced with regard to Executive power, and the means employed to increase it.[1]

In the latter part of April he brought this state of things to the attention of the Senate, in a striking manner, when speaking upon Mr. Benton's resolution to require payments for the public lands to be made in gold and silver. Two measures, he said, were then before the Senate, of the highest importance: one to diminish the public fund, the other to secure its safety. He desired to know what was to be done with these propositions. It was absolutely essential that the public money should be more equally distributed over the country than it then was.

The disposition which had prevailed among the supporters of the Administration, at the last session, to leave the public moneys on deposit in certain State banks, selected by the Executive, without regulation of law, now began to be relaxed. The effect of placing such large amounts of money in the hands of institutions not originally organized to receive and manage them had been, to stimulate a spirit of wild speculation, which was now, in fact, using the public money to buy up great quantities of Government lands in the West, paying for them with funds borrowed of the deposit banks, which, on being received at the land-offices, were again transferred by the Treasury, to

[1] Works, iv., 245.

be again deposited in the selected banks in the Eastern cities. It had become apparent that, at the end of the present year, the Government would have on hand a large surplus; but this surplus was in the hands of agents, who were under no regulation of law. Before the end of May, Mr. Webster had satisfied himself, by careful inquiry, that, at the close of the year, this surplus would amount to $40,000,000. Its existence in the hands of a few banking companies was of no real advantage to men engaged in regular business of any kind. Men in the ordinary avocations of life, whether commercial or agricultural, were subjected to embarrassment and difficulty in their pursuits, being unable to procure the facilities that were extended to speculators, whose employment of money which, in fact, belonged to the Government, resulted in the exchange of the public lands for unsound and unavailable bank credits.

Mr. Webster, as it has abundantly appeared, was in no degree responsible for this state of things. But he was not unwilling to give all his aid to counteract its mischiefs. He did not, indeed, believe that the State banks, as depositaries of the public money, could, by any thing that Congress might do with them, be made to furnish a sound general currency for the country, or a system of internal exchanges equal to the wants of the commercial community. He said that the deposit-bank system never could become the permanent system of the country, by any regulation that Congress could apply to it. Nevertheless, regulation was indispensable to prevent certain gross evils that were now apparent and pressing. Without assuming any lead in relation to a system which he disapproved, either in what might be done or omitted respecting it, he made known his opinions on two very important points when a bill to regulate the deposits of the public moneys was before the Senate. These opinions related to the increase of the deposit banks, so as to prevent the accumulation of large amounts of the public money in a few favored banks; to certain restraints to be imposed on the Secretary of the Treasury to prevent him from ordering funds from one bank to another, for any other reason than the exigencies of the public service; and to a requirement that each deposit bank should have at all times an amount of specie bearing a certain proportion to its debts and liabilities. These three regulations would, he said, bestow on these banks some power of useful action; although, having never been originally designed for any thing but local purposes, they could never be made into a perfect general system for the regulation of the currency of the country, and the facilitating of domestic exchanges. In relation to the disposition that ought to be made of the great surplus which it was quite certain the Government would have at the close of the year, while he held it to be on all accounts desirable to reduce the amount of money in the Treasury, he had an insuperable objection to the introduction of a settled practice of distributing the surplus revenues of the General Government among the States. "I cannot reconcile myself," he said, "to the spectacle of the States receiving their revenues, their means even of supporting their own governments, from the Treasury of the United States. If, indeed, the Land Bill could pass, and we could act on the policy, which I think the true policy, of regarding the public lands as a fund belonging to the people of all the States, I should cheerfully concur in that policy, and be willing to make an annual distribution of the proceeds of the lands, for some years at least. But, if we cannot separate the proceeds of the lands from other revenue, if all must go into the Treasury together, and there remain together, then I have no hesitation in declaring now that the income from customs must be reduced. It must be reduced, even at the hazard of injury to some branches of manufacturing industry; because this, in my opinion, would be a less evil than that extraordinary and dangerous state of things in which the United States would be found, laying and collecting taxes for the purpose of distributing them, when collected, among the States of the Union."

He limited himself, therefore, on this occasion, to a provision for depositing with the States the surplus that might be in the Treasury at the end of the present year; and for this purpose he introduced an amendment which in substance became a part of the law as it was finally passed.

Concerning the French question, it is only necessary to say that the President, on the 15th of January, recommended partial non-intercourse with France; but that soon afterward the Government of Great Britain offered its mediation, and that through this intervention the whole affair was finally adjusted.

Congress adjourned on the 4th of July, and Mr. Webster went immediately to Marshfield, where he remained through the summer and autumn. When the time for the general election drew near, it was understood in Massachusetts that a great majority of its citizens demanded the choice of presidential electors who would cast the vote of the State for Mr. Webster; although the want of coöperation elsewhere, arising from the imperfect organization of the Whig party, rendered it impossible that he should be chosen President. As soon as it was known that the body of electors, through whom this compliment was intended to be paid to him, had been appointed by the votes of the people of the State, the following correspondence took place between Mr. Webster and the gentleman who was placed at the head of the electoral body:

[TO MR. SILSBEE.]

"BOSTON, *November* 15, 1836.

"MY DEAR SIR: It appears highly probable that the election of yesterday has terminated in the choice of yourself and the other gentlemen on the same list as electors of President and Vice-President of the United States in behalf of the State of Massachusetts.

"This result, the relation in which I have stood to the people of the commonwealth during the contest, and events which have transpired or are anticipated in other States, have rendered it proper in my judgment that I should address you this letter to be laid before the electors when they shall assemble.

"My purpose is to say that, in the discharge of their high and most interesting trust, it is my earnest wish that they should act with entire freedom from all considerations merely personal to myself; and that they should give the vote of the State in the manner they think most likely to be useful in supporting the Constitution and laws of the country, the union of the States, the perpetuity of our republican institutions, and the important interests of the whole country; and in maintaining the character of Massachusetts for integrity, honor, national patriotism, and fidelity to the Constitution.

"I am, dear sir, with sentiments of the truest esteem, your friend and obedient servant,

"DAN'L WEBSTER."

[FROM MR. SILSBEE.]

"SENATE-CHAMBER, BOSTON, *December* 27, 1836.

"MY DEAR SIR: I have only time to say to you that, at the meeting of the electors yesterday afternoon (for organization, etc.), your letter was laid before them, and *well received* by all of them—it will appear, with the further proceedings of to-day, in the newspapers of to-morrow. The consultation which took place between the members of the college yesterday was such as to leave no doubt on my mind that the vote of the members will be unanimous for yourself as President, and Mr. Granger as Vice-President. In great haste,

"Yours truly,

"NATH. SILSBEE.

"Hon. D. Webster.

"One, P. M.—The votes have been taken, and declared as above."

CHAPTER XXIII.

1836–1837.

THE "SPECIE CIRCULAR"—A "CONSTITUTIONAL CURRENCY"—MR. BENTON'S EXPUNGING RESOLUTION—MR. WEBSTER'S PROTEST—SLAVERY IN THE DISTRICT OF COLUMBIA—RECEPTION OF PETITIONS—FARMING OPERATIONS—PROPOSES TO RESIGN HIS SEAT—RECEPTION IN NEW YORK—SPEECH AT NIBLO'S SALOON—JOURNEY TO THE WEST—SPECIAL SESSION OF CONGRESS IN THE AUTUMN OF 1837—MR. VAN BUREN'S FINANCIAL POLICY—CONTROVERSY WITH MR. CALHOUN—TEXAS SEEKS ADMISSION INTO THE UNION.

THE subjects of currency and finance, which had occupied so much of the attention of Congress and the country since the summer of 1833, still predominated over all others, when Congress assembled in December, 1836; and they were to be left by General Jackson to his successor, in an unfortunate legacy of temporary expedients, the effects of which were finally destined to bring their political opponents into power. Mr. Van Buren had been elected President, and it was understood that the policy, which had governed the administration of affairs since the experiment was instituted of dispensing with the agency of a national bank, was to be continued. In July of the year 1836, there was a large amount of the public money lying in the deposit banks, the accumulation of the customs receipts and the receipts at the land-offices. With the professed object of checking speculation in the public lands, of discouraging the excessive issues of bank paper, and of increasing the specie currency, the Secretary of the Treasury, on the 11th of July, issued the famous "Specie Circular," which directed that nothing but gold and silver should, after a certain period, be received at the land-offices, in payment for the public lands. The operation of this requirement, in the actual condition of the currency, was the reverse of its ostensible and intended purpose. The tendency was first to drain the specie of the country into the vaults of the deposit banks, by means of the land-offices, and then to keep it moving backward and forward through the country in masses. As this weakened the banks which were not depositaries of the public funds, and thus obliged them to curtail their loans, it produced a great scarcity of money in regions where money was most wanted. On the assembling of Congress in December, the internal exchanges of the country were much deranged, and a general suspension of specie payments by the banks seemed inevitable at no distant period. There was, therefore, an immediate necessity for ridding the country of this Treasury order; which had, in fact, no authority of law, since the Secretary of the Treasury had never been empowered to discriminate in respect to the *media* for payments at the land-offices and the custom-houses. In practical operation, too, it had no other effect than to increase the evils arising from the want of some competent regulator of the currency actually in use throughout the country.

Upon a resolution introduced into the Senate, at an early period of the session, to rescind the "Specie Circular," Mr. Webster delivered a speech on the 21st of December, which is now important chiefly for two reasons: First, because it contains a clear and succinct statement of his opinions respecting the constitutional relations of the General Government to whatever circulates as money; secondly, because it exhibits the mode in which an excessive circulation of bank notes results from a disturbance in the domestic exchanges, and is at the same time a cause of that disturbance. With regard to the relations of the Government to the circulating medium, he held that the legal standard of value, established in the regulated coin, can never be displaced;[1] but that an exclusive circulation of gold and

[1] The whole argument which denies the constitutional possibility of making any thing but gold and silver a legal tender, or of substituting any other stand-

silver is impracticable. He considered that a mixed currency, partly coin and partly bank notes, the notes not issued in excess, and always convertible into specie at the will of the holder, is, in the present state of society, the best practicable currency; but that it is always to be remembered that, in a great commercial country, bills of exchange necessarily perform a large part of the duty of currency, and hence arises the necessity of considering their function in the operations of business as a part of the currency. To prevent an excessive issue of bank notes, which even their convertibility into specie will not always check, and to prevent the effect of overtrading which will sometimes introduce great amounts of exchange not representing actual transactions of business, require the constant care, watchfulness, and superintendence of Government. The power of coinage, and the power and duty of regulating commerce, both external and internal, gave the Government of the United States, in his opinion, a rightful control over the whole mass

ard of values, is stated in a single paragraph of this speech, with a strength, simplicity, and cogency, that have never been surpassed: "But what is meant by the 'constitutional currency,' about which so much is said? What species or forms of currency does the Constitution allow, and what does it forbid? It is plain enough that this depends on what we understand by currency. Currency, in a large, and perhaps in a just sense, includes not only gold and silver and bank notes, but bills of exchange also. It may include all that adjusts exchanges and settles balances in the operations of trade and business. But if we understand by currency the legal *money* of the country, and that which constitutes a lawful tender for debts, and is the statute measure of value, then, undoubtedly, nothing is included but gold and silver. Most unquestionably there is no legal tender, and there can be no legal tender, in this country, under the authority of this Government, or any other, but gold and silver, either the coinage of our own mints or foreign coins, at rates regulated by Congress. This is a constitutional principle, perfectly plain, and of the very highest importance. The States are expressly prohibited from making any thing but gold and silver a tender in payment of debts; and although no such express prohibition is applied to Congress, yet, as Congress has no power granted to it, in this respect, but to coin money and regulate the value of foreign coins, it clearly has no power to substitute paper, or any thing else, for coin, as a tender in payment of debts and in discharge of contracts. Congress has exercised this power fully in both its branches. It has coined money, and still coins it; it has regulated the value of foreign coins, and still regulates their value. The legal tender, therefore, the constitutional standard of value, is established, and cannot be overthrown. To overthrow it would shake the whole system. But if the Constitution knows only gold and silver as a legal tender, does it follow that the Constitution cannot tolerate the voluntary circulation of bank notes, convertible into gold and silver at the will of the holder, as part of the actual money of the country. Is a man not only to be entitled to demand gold and silver for every debt, but is he, or should he be, obliged to demand it in all cases? Is it, or should Government make it, unlawful to receive pay in any thing else? Such a notion is too absurd to be seriously treated. The constitutional tender is the thing to be preserved, and it ought to be preserved sacredly, under all circumstances. The rest remains for judicious legislation by those who have competent authority."

of whatever circulates as money. From the peculiar condition of things in which he was then speaking—a condition which was yet to continue some time longer, and to end in great disaster—this control was entirely surrendered by the national Government to the eight-and-twenty States then composing the Union, and sixty or eighty millions of banking capital had been added to the whole mass since 1832; a thing that he had foreseen and foretold. Up to this point the great prosperity of the country, and the increase of its property, had prevented a depreciation of the currency, and the banks still maintained specie payments. But in the absence of any means of national control over the currency, and in the want of any national system of exchanges, the office of which must be supplied by sending masses of bank notes from place to place, he said that there must be an unnatural increase of paper circulation; an excess which had been foreseen, which the deposit-bank system had been entirely incapable of preventing, and which could not be prevented unless the national Government should exercise the powers conferred upon it. For the administration of the finances of the country, for the facility of internal exchanges, and for the due control and regulation of the actual currency, he still held a national institution, under proper guards and limits, to be the best means within the reach of Congress. With respect to the mode of removing the obnoxious Treasury circular, he was indifferent. A bill was passed for this purpose, but at so late a period in the session, that the President did not return it, and it failed to become a law. But two days before the bill was passed, Mr. Webster presented a petition, signed by fourteen or fifteen hundred mercantile firms in the city of New York, praying for the establishment of a national bank. On this occasion he reiterated his opinion that this would be found to be the true remedy for the existing disturbance in the monetary affairs of the country, and that the claim of power which the Administration had asserted, to use banking corporations in the fiscal concerns of the Government, necessarily conceded the power to create such corporations. But he repeated his determination not to make any movement toward the establishment of a national bank until public opinion should call for it. He acknowledged that the impression hostile to such an institution had become so general, that any action upon it in Congress would then be in vain. But he said that experience on these subjects would be likely to make the country wiser than it then was.

The resolution introduced by Mr. Benton during the last session, "for expunging" from the Journals of the Senate its resolution of December 26, 1833—which pronounced the control assumed by the President over the Treasury unwarranted by the Constitution and the laws—was now again brought forward under circumstances plainly indicating that it was to be passed. In any period of our history that has since elapsed, or in any that may occur hereafter while this form of government continues, it is not probable that intelligent and impartial men have been, or will be, able to deny that either House of Congress, holding the opinion that the Executive had usurped a legislative function, could rightfully express that opinion in the form in which the Senate in 1833 recorded in its Journal its opinion of the acts of President Jackson. Having recorded that opinion, the Constitution made the record sacred and indelible. Men might differ about the original propriety or justice of the record; but the Senate had decided on the question of right by passing the resolution. It stood among the recorded proceedings of the Senate; and the Constitution peremptorily required each branch of the Legislature to *keep* a Journal of its proceedings. But now, in deference to the President, who was soon to go out of office, his friends, who held a majority of votes in the Senate, resolved to have the Journal brought into the Senate by its secretary, and directed him to draw "black lines" *around* the obnoxious resolution, and to write across it, in "strong letters," the words "expunged by order of the Senate, this 16th day of January, in the year of our Lord 1837."

A proceeding so fantastic and theatrical could scarcely have been perpetrated in any other than a time of high party excitement, or from any other than party motives. To obliterate from history the fact that the Senate of 1833 had expressed a certain opinion of some of the President's acts, was of course impossible; and if the Senate of 1837 desired to soothe the feelings of the President by expressing their opinion that he had been unjustly censured, the two conflicting opinions might have gone down to posterity, and the last would have stood as a reversal of a legislative proceeding which is brought about by a change of men or of sentiments. But the friends of the President sought for what they considered an imposing form of stigmatizing the original record; and, in seeking for the means of doing this, they selected a mode which in express terms they dominated an "expunging" of the resolution from the "Journal," and thus plainly violated the Constitution. But for this, it is not at all probable that Mr. Webster would have said any thing on the subject. What his opinions were respecting the original resolution had been fully made known at the time; and now, in all the discussion which ensued upon Mr. Benton's resolution to expunge the record, he took no part, either to vindicate his former vote, or to go over the grounds which had led to the action of the Senate in 1833. But when the debate on Mr. Benton's proposition was closed, and it was about to be voted on, he rose in his place, and, in behalf of his colleague, Mr. Davis, and himself, read a solemn protest against the meditated violation of the Journal of the Senate. This paper will stand as long as the act against which it was directed shall be known—marking the character of a transaction by which a part of the original Journal of the Senate was sought to be stricken out of existence; presenting "to the common-sense and understanding of mankind" the plain meaning of the constitutional injunction which required the Senate "to keep" its Journal; and holding up to the view of future times the spectacle then exhibited, of respectable States instructing their representatives to vote for a mutilation of the records of one of the Houses of Congress.

"Mr. President: Upon the truth and justice of the original resolution of the Senate, and upon the authority of the Senate to pass that resolution, I had an opportunity to express my opinions at a subsequent period, when the President's Protest was before us.

"Those opinions remain altogether unchanged. And now, had the Constitution secured the privilege of entering a protest on the Journal, I should not say one word on this occasion; although, if what is now proposed shall be accomplished, I know not what would have been the value of such a protest, however formally or carefully it might have been inserted in the body of that instrument. But, as there is no such constitutional privilege,

I can only effect my purpose by thus addressing the Senate; and I rise, therefore, to make that protest in this manner, in the face of the Senate, and in the face of the country, which I cannot present in any other form.

"I speak in my own behalf, and in behalf of my colleague; we both speak as Senators from the State of Massachusetts, and, as such, we solemnly protest against this whole proceeding.

"We deny that Senators from any other States have power or authority to expunge any vote or votes which we have given here, and which we have recorded agreeably to the express provision of the Constitution. We have high personal interest, and the State whose representatives we are has also a high interest, in the preservation entire of every part and parcel of the record of our conduct as members of the Senate.

"This record the Constitution declares shall be *kept;* but the resolution before the Senate declares that this record shall be expunged. Whether subterfuge and evasion, and, as it appears to us, the degrading mockery of drawing black lines upon the Journal, shall or shall not leave our names and our votes legible, when this violation of the record shall have been complete, still the term 'to expunge,' and the term 'to keep,' when applied to a record, impart ideas exactly contradictory; as much so as the term 'to preserve,' and the term 'to destroy.' A record which is *expunged* is not a record which is *kept*, any more than a record which is *destroyed* can be a record which is *preserved*. The part expunged is no longer part of the record; it has no longer a legal existence. It cannot be certified as a part of the proceedings of the Senate for any purpose of proof or evidence. The object of the provision in the Constitution, as we think, most obviously is, that the proceedings of the Senate shall be preserved in writing not for the present only; not until published only, because a copy of the printed Journal is not regular legal evidence; but preserved indefinitely; preserved, as other records are preserved, till destroyed by time or accident.

"Every one must see that matters of the highest importance depend on the permanent preservation of the Journals of the two Houses. What but the Journals show that bills have been regularly passed into laws, through the several stages; what but the Journals show who are members, or who is President, or Speaker, or Secretary, or Clerk of the body? What but the Journals contain the proof necessary for the justification of those who act under our authority, and who, without the power of producing such proof, must stand as trespassers? What but the Journals show who is appointed, and who rejected, by us, on the President's nomination; or who is acquitted, or who convicted in trials on impeachment? In short, is there, at any time, any other regular and legal proof, of any act done by the Senate, than the Journal itself?

"The idea, therefore, that the Senate is bound to preserve its Journal only until it is published, and then may alter, mutilate, or destroy it at pleasure, appears to us one of the most extraordinary sentiments ever advanced. We feel grateful to those friends who have shown, with so much clearness, that all the precedents relied on to justify or to excuse this proceeding are either not to the purpose, or, from the times and circumstances at and under which they happened, are in no way entitled to respect in a free government, existing under a written Constitution. But for ourselves, we stand on the plain words of that Constitution itself. A thousand precedents elsewhere made, whether ancient or modern, can neither rescind, nor control, nor explain away these words. The words are, that 'each House shall *keep* a Journal of its proceedings.' No gloss, no ingenuity, no specious interpretation, and much less any fair or just reasoning, can reconcile the process of expunging with the plain meaning of these words, to the satisfaction of the common-sense and honest understanding of mankind. If the Senate may now expunge one part of the Journal of a former session, it may, with equal authority, expunge another part, or the whole. It may expunge the entire record of any one session, or of all sessions.

"It seems to us inconceivable how any men can regard such a power, and its exercise at pleasure, as consistent with the injunctions of the Constitution. It makes no difference what is the completeness or incompleteness of the act of expunging, or by what means done; whether by erasure, obliteration, or defacement; if by defacement, as here proposed, whether one word or many words are written on the face of the record; whether little ink or much ink is shed on the paper; or whether some part, or the whole, of the original written Journal may yet by possibility be traced. If the act done be an act to expunge, to blot out, to obliterate, to erase the record, then the record is expunged, blotted out, obliterated, and erased. And mutilation and alteration violate the record as much as obliteration or erasure. A record, subsequently altered, is not the original record. It no longer gives a just account of the proceedings of the Senate. It is no longer true. It is, in short, no Journal of the real and actual proceedings of the Senate, such as the Constitution says each House shall keep.

"The Constitution, therefore, is, in our deliberate judgment, violated by this proceeding, in the most plain and open manner.

"The Constitution, moreover, provides that the yeas and nays, on any question, shall, at the request of one-fifth of the members present, be entered on the Journal. This provision most manifestly gives a personal right, to those members who may demand it, to the entry and preservation of their votes on the record of the proceedings of the body not for one day or one year only, but for all time. There the yeas and nays are to stand forever, as permanent and lasting proof of the manner in which members have voted on great questions before them. But it is now insisted that the votes of members taken by yeas and nays, and thus entered on the Journal, as a matter of right, may still be expunged, so that that, which it required more than fourth-fifths of the Senators to prevent from being put on the Journal, may, nevertheless, be struck off, and erased the next moment, or at any period afterward, by the will of a mere majority; or, if this be denied, then the absurdity is adopted of maintaining that this provision of the Constitution is fulfilled by merely preserving the yeas and nays on the Journal, after having expunged and obliterated the very resolution, or the very question, on which they were given, and to which alone they refer; leaving the yeas and nays thus a mere list of names, connected with no subject, no question, no vote. We put it to the impartial judgment of mankind, if these proceedings be not in this respect also directly and palpably inconsistent with the Constitution.

"We protest in the most solemn manner that other Senators have no authority to deprive us of our personal rights, secured to us by the Constitution, either by expunging, or obliterating, or mutilating, or defacing the record of our votes, duly entered by yeas and neas; or by expunging and obliterating the resolutions or questions on which these votes were given and recorded.

"We have seen, with deep and sincere pain, the Legislatures of respectable States instructing the Senators of those States to vote for and support this violation of the Journal of the Senate; and this pain is infinitely increased by our full belief and entire conviction that most if not all these proceedings of States had their origin in promptings from Washington; that they have been urgently requested and insisted on, as being necessary to the accomplishment of the intended purpose; and that it is nothing else bnt the influence and power of the Executive branch of this Government which has brought the Legislatures of so many of the free States of this Union to quit the sphere of their ordinary duties, for the purpose of coöperating to accomplish a measure, in our judgment, so unconstitutional, so derogatory to the character of the Senate, and marked with so broad an impression of compliance with power.

"But this resolution is to pass. We expect it. That cause which has been powerful enough to influence so many State Legislatures will show itself powerful enough, especially with such aids, to secure the passage of the resolution here.

"We make up our minds to behold the spectacle which is to ensue. We collect ourselves to look on in silence, while a scene is exhibited which, if we did not regard it as a ruthless violation of a sacred instrument, would appear to us to be little elevated above the character of a contemptible farce. This scene we shall behold, and hundreds of American citizens, as many as may crowd into these lobbies and galleries, will behold it also; with what feelings I do not undertake to say.

"But we protest, we most solemnly protest, against the substance and against the manner of this proceeding; against its object, against its form, and against its effect. We tell you that you have no right to mar or mutilate the record of our votes given here, and recorded according to the Constitution; we tell you that you may as well erase the yeas and nays on any other question or resolution, or on all questions and resolutions, as on this; we tell you that you have just as much right to falsify the record, by so altering it as to make us appear to have voted on any question as we did not vote, as you have to erase a record, and make that page a blank in our votes, as they were actually given and recorded, now stand. The one proceeding, as it appears to us, is as much a falsification of the record as the other.

"Having made this Protest, our duty is performed. We rescue our own names, character, and honor from all participation in this matter; and whatever the wayward character of the times, the headlong and plunging spirit of party devotion, or the fear or the love of power, may have been able to bring about elsewhere, we desire to thank God that they have not, as yet, overcome the love of liberty, fidelity to true republican principles, and a sacred regard for the Constitution, in that State whose soil was drenched to a mire by the first and best blood of the Revolution. Massachusetts, as yet, has not been conquered; and, while we have the honor to hold seats here as her Senators, we shall never consent to the sacrifice either of her rights or our own; we shall never fail to oppose what we regard as a plain and open violation of the Constitution of the country; and we should have thought ourselves wholly unworthy of her if we had not, with all the solemnity and earnestness in our power, protested against the adoption of the resolution now before the Senate."

The reception of petitions for the abolition of slavery in the District of Columbia was again the subject of an excited discussion at this session. The former action of the Senate, in refusing to give such petitions a hearing, had greatly increased their number. They now came from many quarters of the country from which they had not come before; and it was apparent to most persons that the refusal to hear and to make a report on these petitions was the principal cause of the inundation that now came upon the Senate. On the 6th of February a great many of them were presented, and among them were some that had been sent to Mr. Webster. In presenting them, he repeated the opinions that he had expressed at the last session, especially in regard to the duty of the Senate to refer them, not only because this was a right which the petitioners could demand, but because it was wise to admit that right. At the same time, he declared that he meant to express no opinion on the expediency of legislating for the abolition of slavery in the District, a subject which he thought ought to be discussed by those who were most concerned in it.

But the representatives of the slaveholding States were now greatly excited, and thoroughly averse to any consideration of a petition which touched the institution of slavery in any of its aspects. Mr. Calhoun, who thought that the door ought to be peremptorily shut, obtained a ruling from the Chair,[1] that any objection made to the reception of a petition raised the question of reception, without a motion not to receive. As these petitions were successively presented, objections were made, and the question being stated on the reception, a motion to lay this question on the table carried the petition with it. In this way a large majority of the Senate thought fit to avoid a direct vote on the reception and reference of the petitions—a course which was as little adapted to allay the agitation then rising as the former rejection of the prayer of the petitions.[2] It was very apparent to Mr. Webster that the Senate would have to recede from this position, or to take another and further step in the wrong direction; and that, if it did the latter, an irretrievable error would be committed. What occurred in the next session will disclose the grounds of this opinion.

But, in the midst of this busy and important session, his thoughts were often away at "Green Harbor," with the "Thomases," with his fields, his cattle, his loads of "kelp," and his crops. Besides the original homestead of the Thomas family, he had, ere this, become the owner of several other properties, adjoining or near, and he had for several years been a systematic, although, it must be owned, a very expensive, farmer. The "temptations" to which he alludes in the following letter must not be ascribed to political aspirations. He was at this time meditating a dim project of a great farm in the West, and a retirement to it from professional and public life—a phantom of his brain that will reappear hereafter. But the truth undoubtedly is, that Marshfield owed its power to retain him, whenever he balanced its poorer soil against the richness of the prairies, to the attractions of the sea, and to the local associations with which that old "Pilgrim" region is filled. It is the neighborhood over which the company of the Mayflower and their immediate descendants first spread themselves, and their names, their lands, and their graves, are everywhere around. His own blood was not immediately of theirs, but he was of a kindred stock, and his feelings were always strongly moved by the traditions that clung to the soil where the sturdy Puritans

[1] Mr. King, of Alabama, President of the Senate *pro tempore*.

[2] Mr. Webster, of course, voted against this method of action.

"drove their teams afield," where they founded the early institutions of New England, and where, "each in his narrow cell forever laid," their simple monuments carried back public and private history to the infancy of the nation:

[TO CHAS. H. THOMAS, ESQ.]

"WASHINGTON, *February* 4, 1837.

"DEAR HENRY: Although I have no letter from you either yesterday or to-day, I must still commend your improved habits. You have certainly whipped up your spirit of letter-writing to new speed, so that I get two letters a week, at least. This is very pleasing. There have been times, since I saw you last, when I have doubted whether Marshfield and I could hold on together to the end of my life. I have felt in those moments as a *humility* looks when she spreads out her wings for flight. Even now some things are unsettled in my brain. I keep them, however, to myself, and, except you and one other, who has received a slight hint, nobody knows of the existence of any such notions. There are temptations, which, if Marshfield were not what it is, or if it were to cease to be what it has been, might induce me to look upon the last seven or eight years as a bright spot, in the journey of life, which I had passed *through*. All these things, however, are to be buried in the depth of your faithful bosom. And, in the mean time, I must say that even your slightest letters afford me pleasure. Amidst the toil of law and the stunning din of politics, any thing is welcome which calls my thoughts back to Marshfield, though it be only to be told which way the wind blows. I am suffering from a cold, and for two days have not been out of my room. Last night I was dreaming of you all night, which I hope you will consider as a very great compliment. My letters from Boston all speak of your mother. She seems to have made quite a sensation in Summer Street. Captain John Thomas will find it necessary to put his best foot forward when he goes to Boston, if he does not mean to have the *shine* taken off of himself by his spouse.

"In regard to farming matters, you appear to be doing well. Some of your kelp-drawing days have showed great results. If I have kept the account right, you have probably secured as much kelp as will be a decent dressing for all the corn-land you prepared to plant at Careswell. By-the-way, let us settle names. I am tired of the 'Soule Place,' and the 'Sprague Place,' and the 'Widow Winslow's Thirds,' and so many other names. Let us use some names *uniformly*, and we shall save time and breath. According to the proposed plans (which I hope are made), there are three places:

"1. The homestead—that is, 'Green Harbor;' and any man must be indicted for slander who gives it any other name.[1]

[1] This was the place bought of Captain Thomas.

"2. Those parcels which we have set apart for a mulberry farm. This may be called 'The Mulberry Farm,' or it may be called 'Winslow Place,' without the 'the,' or 'Pelham Place,' Pelham being a distinguished name in the pedigree of the Winslow family.[1]

"3. The Soule place—that is to say, the house and land bought of Mr. Soule, and what we have attached to it from the Sprague purchase—may be called 'Careswell,' which I do [not] much like, or 'The Summer Farm,' which I like better, or the 'Cottage Farm,' when we take down the big house.[2]

"Consult Captain John Thomas and Lucy, his wife, on these matters. Let me know what they and you and Edward[3] think, and we will give these places fixed names, and anybody who miscalls them is not to be answered when he speaks to us. Was Careswell the name of the Winslow property generally, or did it apply only to a part of it? Ask your mother to explain and expound. And now to return to the kelp.[4] I suppose the season may be pretty nearly over for it, but if it continue to come, you will be ready to seize it, and know what to do with it. When John Taylor comes down next August or September, I want him to lose himself in our cornfields.[5] I am thinking of using lime freely at Green Harbor, but this will depend on the cost. I understand it can often be had at less than a dollar a cask at Thomaston—sometimes lower than eighty cents. A cask is five bushels of unslacked lime. Of course, when slacked, there will be ten. Suppose the price a dollar a cask, the slacked lime would be ten cents per bushel, or equal to that, at the quarry. Now, what is the freight worth for a vessel to go direct, and to bring her cargo to the mouth of Green Harbor River? This, as well as the actual price at Thomaston, you can readily ascertain. Please make inquiries, and let me know. The Thomaston lime is a good deal stronger than the Pennsylvania lime, and yet, in the best counties of Pennsylvania, they will pay twelve or fifteen cents a bushel for lime, and haul it ten, fifteen, or twenty miles, for corn, clover, and wheat. Think of these things, and count the cost. If I had lime, in addition to using it with mud and other matter, I should use it by itself, thus: I should spread it, thirty or forty bushels to the acre, on old sward-land, like Stoughton Island, on the old orchard, or the sheep-pas-

[1] This farm, with a very old Puritan house, had become the property of Mr. Webster.

[2] This place Mr. Webster finally called "Careswell." He built a cottage-house upon it, which was occupied by his son Fletcher as a summer residence. It is about one mile distant from "Green Harbor."

[3] His second son, afterward Major Webster.

[4] Mr. Webster enjoyed the glory of being the first farmer on that coast to use "kelp," or sea-weed, as a manure. This was one of the local distinctions which were always conceded to him. Porter Wright, who was his "foreman" at Marshfield for many years, in giving his recollections of Mr. Webster, after his death, said, with delightful *naïveté*, "Nobody had ever used munhaden or kelp in this part of the country; he started both."

[5] John Taylor, one of the best specimens of the New-England yeomanry, was Mr. Webster's farmer and *factotum* at Franklin. It must have been tall corn for this man to lose himself in.

ture; plough it in, and plant the land with corn, potatoes, beans, or some other crop requiring the hoe, according to the natural strength of the land. The hoeing mixes the lime with the land, so that it affects the whole soil. On such land as the sheep-pasture, I should spread twenty-five bushels of unslacked lime to the acre; and on such light land I think I should plant beans. The next year apply manure from the barn-yard as plentifully as possible, get a crop of oats, and put in grass-seed. Field turnips would do well, instead of oats, or part might be put into each. On strong, clayey land, I should plant corn or potatoes. Ponder these matters.[1]

"We have made some mistakes, but must hope to grow wiser. *Never again sow small grains on long manure.* Put that down as one maxim. If I live, and am well, I must go home, either in March or the early part of April. Either time will be in season to settle some things. If I should be in Marshfield in March, I should expect to drive the team once off the beach with a load of kelp. The oxen which you destine for beef next fall you will, of course, ease off from their work so soon as you can, when the business of kelp is over. How many, and which is it best to turn out? 1. There are the old oxen, they must be fatted, of course. 2. The *off* oxen, bought of Captain Stevens (I wish we had the black ram to go with them), if not sold, these must be fatted. 3. Then there are the Princeton oxen, which are quite old enough to fat well. Now, I do not see how we are going *to sell* any thing, unless it be stock, and we must contrive to sell something, or we shall all be called on to make an assignment. These off oxen, I think, will make good beef, for Captain John Thomas and his wife Lucy, and for me and wife Caroline. Suppose, therefore, we devote them to the captain's 'powdering tub,' together with any other similar likely thing which John Taylor may happen to send down next fall? And then, suppose we fat the old oxen and the Princeton oxen for the market, loosing them from the yoke as early as we can, keeping them as well as we can through the summer, and keeping them on roots in the fall and winter, until they are fat enough to make people at Brighton 'open their eyes,' as Captain Thomas would say? All these things you must weigh. I don't mean you must weigh the *oxen;* they are too poor yet, but weigh these hints. But I must stop from these interesting topics, and pursue them no further. You owe the trouble of reading this long letter to my being unable, from my cold, to go either to the court or Senate, and to my having positively forbidden Charles to let any one in this day. I am tired, too, of reading, and so have run on with this incoherent scribbling. There is another matter on which I may write you in a few days; but, if I am well

[1] This reminds us of Burke, who, like Mr. Webster, was a practical farmer, and equally fond of the details of his work:

"BECONSFIELD, *October* 21, 1770.

. . . "Last year I sowed two acres with the same seed. . . . In the summer they were twice hand-hoed, I fear not sufficiently, but the crop is very large, and the carrots, though not so sightly as the sand carrots, full as rich in color, or, indeed, rather higher and finer; a most aromatic smell, firm and admirably tasted. I have sent two wagon-loads to London, for which I had six pounds, fifteen. The back-carriage of coal-ashes has paid my charges."—(*Correspondence of the Right Hon. Edmund Burke*, i., 246. London: 1844.)

enough to go out to-morrow, I shall have no more leisure to trouble you with a long letter for some time. Meanwhile, I hope you will not fail to write as often as you can. Give my best regards to your wife, and to Ann and the doctor, and to your father and mother, and my love to Edward. I suppose you all receive Charles's communications in sufficient abundance. Adieu! my good friend.

"DANL. WEBSTER."

Before this letter was written, however, he had determined to resign his seat in the Senate, and, at the end of January, he dispatched letters to Massachusetts, making known this purpose, in order that the Legislature might appoint his successor. His friends in Boston at once manifested their opposition to this step. In the city of New York the intelligence was received with no less concern. A meeting of his political friends was held on the 21st of February, at which Chancellor Kent presided, and which was attended by many of the principal persons in the city, for the purpose of inviting him to a public reception. If he was to resign, these gentlemen desired to mark their sense of his public services; and if his purposes might be modified by the wishes of a great body of citizens in the commercial metropolis of the country, they desired to present those wishes to him in the most imposing form in which they could be expressed. It was certainly a striking proof how entirely he belonged to the country, and how widely his importance was felt beyond the limits of the State which he represented, that the rumor of his intended resignation should have called forth such a demonstration as this. It was without precedent in the case of any man who had ever held a seat in the Senate of the United States; nor has it ever been since repeated in any other case. Even if we were now to regard it merely as the expression of a party to one of its great leaders, its significance is scarcely diminished. But it was not a mere party movement. It was his relation to the Constitution, his relation to the whole country, his extensive knowledge of public affairs, and his unwavering devotion to the Union, that led a body of men, who were not his constituents, to endeavor to influence, as far as they might with decorum undertake to influence, the course of his life. If such expressions induced further sacrifices of private convenience, if they postponed, as they did, again and again, the day for securing his personal fortunes until "a life devoted to the public service" became his unchangeable "destiny," we are to remember how earnestly and impressively he was appealed to, and how little he was left to regard his own personal interests, when they were to be weighed in the balance against the interests of the country.

When the invitation to a public reception in New York was about to be sent to him at Washington, he was in correspondence with his friends in Massachusetts on the subject of his resignation. The Legislature of the State was then in session, and it was his own opinion, and that of his friends in Washington, that the vacancy ought to be filled before its adjournment. He had important private interests in the West, connected with purchases of land which he had made in that region; and, without any political object, he desired to travel in his own country more extensively than he had hitherto done. Nor had he ever been in Europe. England, at least, he desired to see, and the desire to see him was not confined to the few Englishmen whom he had known here, although their letters to him constantly looked forward to the time when they might welcome him among them. All this, it seemed to him, could not be accomplished without some interval of uninterrupted attention to his private affairs. He expressed his willingness to return to the Senate at some future time, if that should be the wish of his constituents. But they were unwilling to receive his resignation, even on this understanding. A committee of the Whigs of the Legislature, with their Speaker, the Hon. Robert C. Winthrop, at the head of it, sent him a formal request to withdraw his resignation, or, at least, to postpone it for the présent. To this an overwhelming number of private wishes were added; so that when the New-York invitation was ready to be sent to him, and he was informally apprised of its tenor, nothing had been left for him to do but to signify his consent to hold the seat until the next meeting of the Legislature.

The public correspondence in relation to the proposed ceremony in New York is contained in the first volume of Mr. Webster's Works. The following private letter respecting the arrangements has been hitherto unpublished:

[TO PHILIP HONE, ESQ.]

"WASHINGTON, *March* 5, 1837.

"MY DEAR SIR: I had the pleasure to receive Mr. Ogden's communication, referred to in your letter of the 3d instant, and have made an answer to that communication, expressing, not half as fully as I feel, the honor conferred on me by this tender of respect and hospitality, made by political friends in New York.

"Such marks of approbation cannot but be gratefully received; and I have signified to Mr. Ogden the pleasure it will give me to meet these, and other friends, in the manner most acceptable to them.

"In answer to your inquiry as to the day of my arrival in New York, I have to say that I have not fixed on any day, and that such day may be named as may best suit the convenience of the committee, and of others. I shall be in Philadelphia on Thursday or Friday next, and shall be ready, I presume, to proceed to New York on Monday, the 13th. Tuesday, the 14th, or any day later than that, would, therefore, suit me. I can be at Jersey City Tuesday or Wednesday, or Thursday evening, as you may find most convenient, but rather preferring, myself, that it should not be later than Wednesday.

"I desire the committee to consult their own feelings and wishes, and not mine, in all things respecting the manner and forms of proceeding. It would be perfectly agreeable to me to dispense with all ceremony of reception, and to meet my friends after my arrival, in the ordinary way, in the city. But I leave all this in the discretion of others. You will have the kindness to write me, in Philadelphia, as soon as may be convenient, and to name day, and hour, and place, at which I may expect the honor of meeting with the committee.

"I must not close this short letter, my dear sir, without expressing the pleasure it gives me to receive expressions of your personal friendship and regard. Be assured, I reciprocate these sentiments, and cordially offer you renewed declarations of esteem and the most sincere good wishes.

"DANIEL WEBSTER.

"Philip Hone, Esq."

On the 15th of March the committee attended Mr. Webster at Amboy, and escorted him to the city; and in the evening he met a great assemblage of the people at Niblo's Saloon. The speech which he delivered on this occasion forms one of the chief landmarks in his political career, on account of the past, present, and future relations of the topics of which he treated, and the opinions which he expressed. He was at this time in his fifty-sixth year. It was very nearly a quarter of a century since he first entered Congress, and he had been fourteen years uninterruptedly engaged in public life. The Administration of General Jackson had just closed, through the whole of which, excepting in relation to the subject of "nullification," Mr. Webster had strenuously opposed the measures of the Executive. It was to be expected, therefore, that he would review the measures of that Administration; for the crisis which it was apparent that these measures had prepared for the country was upon it, and Mr. Webster owed it to himself to make it plain that his opposition had been founded in correct motives, and upon sound principles. The condition of affairs which I have described as existing during the past year remained substantially unchanged. The "Specie Circular" was still in operation, drawing the gold and silver of the country into the land-offices, and thence into the deposit banks, where it took the form of a debt to the Government, thus converting its revenues into bank credits. The seventy-five or eighty millions of specie in the country neither went abroad to pay the balance against us in foreign hands, nor was it so disposed of at home as to sustain the paper currency, the volume of which was increasing every day, without any regulator to control it. Besides that portion of the specie which was locked up from free circulation by the operation of the Treasury circular, large amounts had begun to be hoarded in private hands. Mr. Webster saw that an explosion must ensue, and that it could not be far off. He was, therefore, in this public address, to trace the causes that had brought about this state of things, and to point out to the public intelligence the little that could then be done toward arresting the catastrophe.

His review of General Jackson's measures relating to the currency, commencing from his first inauguration as President, was searching, but personally respectful. He spoke of the late President as a man who had done the country great service in the field; but whose usurpations of executive power, while administering the Government as President, had resulted in a total derangement of the currency and the business of the community. That this was a true description of the case, every one can now see who will look back to the year 1832, and will consider that, from that time down to the moment when Mr. Webster delivered this speech, in the spring of 1837, Congress had done nothing, and would do nothing, effectually to resist the control which the Executive had assumed over the currency. In 1832 the President vetoed the bill continuing the bank, and Congress would not pass it over the veto. In 1833 the President removed the public deposits from the bank, and, although Congress would not have voted for this measure, it would not direct their restoration. The Executive selected the State banks that were to take the place of the national institution; prescribed their duties, and committed to them the whole proceeds of the public revenues; acting all the while without any legislation or rightful authority on the subject. It was not until July, 1836, that Congress interfered at all to place the deposit banks under the regulation of law, and securing them against executive favoritism. But, in the mean time, great mischiefs had ensued. The public money, constantly accumulating beyond the wants of the Government, had become the means of speculation; banking capital and bank paper had vastly increased; there was no check on the paper circulation, and nothing to produce uniformity in its credit, and to sustain confidence in its security. As a means of effecting some diminution of these tendencies, Congress, in 1836, ordered the surplus in the Treasury to be distributed to the States. But now came in the Treasury circular, ordering nothing but gold and silver to be received at the land-offices—a thing which Congress had just previously refused to direct by law; and, although, in the winter of 1837, Congress passed a bill which was intended to rescind the circular, the President would neither approve nor disapprove of it, and, as it went to him within the last ten days of the session, it failed to become a law. Nearly every thing, therefore, in relation to the revenue and the currency, had been, from the beginning of the late Administration, entirely under the control of the President, and that control had resulted in bringing the country to the situation in which it now stood—on the verge of a suspension of specie payments by all its banks, including those which held every dollar of the public funds.

In the whole of that long contest, therefore, with the Administration of General Jackson, Mr. Webster was engaged in resisting a tendency of the Executive to absorb all political power, and especially all power over the currency; and it is because of the indisputable existence of this tendency, springing partly from the President's own temper, and partly from the new use of the public patronage then introduced, that Mr. Webster's opposition is to be judged. Certainly, he could have had no personal hostility to General Jackson. Their personal intercourse had always been mutually respectful, and Mr. Webster, notwithstanding his strong dissent from the President's measures, was a guest at the Executive mansion probably as often as any public man of the time who was so much occupied. But in that enormous enlargement of the Executive powers which grew up under President Jackson, in the control which he exercised over a great party, and in the manner in which Congress, when filled by a majority of his friends, surrendered its judgment to the executive will, Mr. Webster saw great dangers to the future stability of the Constitution; and it is quite apparent now that, if this had not been an exceptional case—if the succeeding Presidents had been men of sufficient force to have grasped and wielded the kind of sceptre that General Jackson left to them in the doctrines of executive power which he maintained—we should have had reason to know, practically, the significance of these warnings.

Moreover, this subject of currency and public finance was one that Mr. Webster well understood. He was not wrong when, in 1816, he insisted that the public revenues must be collected in the bills of specie-paying banks; and that a paper currency must be secured by being at all times convertible into specie. He was not wrong, twenty years later, when he said that the operation of the Bank of the United States, combined with the effect of his specie resolutions in 1816, had given us a better paper currency than any other country had ever possessed. He was not wrong when he maintained, as he always did, that there must be some paper circulation, and that no man of that generation would ever see an exclusive gold and silver currency. He was not wrong when he foretold that the State banks could not perform the functions of a national bank; when he said, after the removal of the public deposits from the Bank of the United States, that the exchanges of the country would become disordered; when he declared that the distribution of the public money to new agents, selected upon principles of favoritism, would end in over-trading and extravagant speculation; when he predicted that the disturbances in the internal exchanges would tend to the great increase of local paper money, which must be used to take the place of bills of exchange; and when, finally, as the last of the Executive projects came into operation, he pointed out the mischiefs that were to arise from placing the whole specie that was within the country where it could have no operation in strengthening and upholding its paper circulation, or be sent out of the country to restore the balance of trade by payment of its debts. Nor was he wrong when, on the 16th of March, 1837, he said, with caution, but plainly enough for wise men to understand, that "the worst is not yet." In less than three months from that time, all the banks in the country suspended the payment of their notes in specie,[1] and an almost universal bankruptcy overspread the country.

This speech is also memorable, because Mr. Webster availed himself of this, the earliest moment after the independence of Texas had been formally recognized by our Government, to express his opposition to its annexation to the United States—an opposition which he never changed nor relaxed. His reasons were these: In the first place, no necessity existed for extending the limits of the Union in that direction, and therefore the case was unlike that of Louisiana or Florida. In the next place, Texas was likely to be a slaveholding country, and he held that the people of the United States would not, and certainly should not, consent to add to the Union a territory large enough to make several new slaveholding States. On this subject he said:

"On the general question of slavery, a great portion of the community is already excited. The subject has not only attracted attention as a question of politics, but it has struck a far deeper-toned chord. It has arrested the religious feeling of the country; it has taken strong hold on the consciences of men. He is a rash man, indeed, and little conversant with human nature, and especially has he a very erroneous estimate of the character of the people of this country, who supposes that a feeling of this kind is to be trifled with or despised. It will assuredly cause itself to be respected. It may be reasoned with; it may be made willing, I believe it is entirely willing, to fulfil all existing engagements and all existing duties, to uphold and defend the Constitution as it is established, with whatever

[1] The suspension began in the city of New York on the 10th of June.

regrets about some provisions which it does actually contain. But to coerce it into silence, to endeavor to restrain its free expression, to seek to compress and confine it, warm as it is, and more heated as such endeavors would inevitably render it—should this be attempted, I know nothing, even in the Constitution or in the Union itself, which would not be endangered by the explosion which might follow."

At the same time he declared, in the strongest terms, that all the stipulations found in the Constitution in favor of the slaveholding States already in the Union ought to be fulfilled, and, so far as depended on him, should be fulfilled, "in the fulness of their spirit and to the exactness of their letter." Such was the attitude taken by him at the very commencement of an excitement which he forewarned the country was to be attended by the most serious consequences—an attitude that is most important to be remembered by the reader, because he will have occasion to see it again and again repeated, as often as Mr. Webster was called to act upon this subject. In this respect, it must now be conceded that, of all the statesmen of that period, he looked farther into the future, and comprehended more in the range of his vision, than any of the public men of his time. The Southern statesmen saw danger to that institution of their States which had received a qualified recognition, and some degree of direct guaranty in the Constitution of the United States; and they sought, by the enlargement of the number of slaveholding States, to strengthen their political power in the Government, as a means of defence against the growing spirit of aggression which had sprung up in the North. But they did *not* see that no amount of increase of their sectional power would be of any avail against a sentiment which was taking its hold upon private conscience. They miscalculated the effect of suppression and coercion, as they miscalculated the power of political combination or governmental action over the progress of opinion and feeling. The Northern statesmen, too, who thought that the Union could be strengthened by recasting the balance of power between the non-slaveholding and the slaveholding sections, equally failed to appreciate the fact that, after the latter had been increased, the movement itself—however it might, for a time, appear to be successful, by receiving the sanction of Northern constituencies—would, sooner or later, find those constituencies acting in the opposite direction, by the force which a moral sentiment always exerts over the restraints of political arrangements. All this Mr. Webster did see. The proof that he saw it is in the record of what he said, in the warnings that he gave, and in every one of his public acts relating to this subject, from this year 1837 to the close of his life. Let it be remembered that he entered upon this new era of the Union with a strong and clear conviction that causes were at work which were to expose it to great perils; and let every one of his particular efforts to avert those perils, when he could no longer control the causes, be judged by the existence of this conviction.

Mr. Webster's purpose to make an extended tour to the West, in the course of this spring and summer, having become known, Mr. Clay addressed to him the following cordial letter, in anticipation of his visit:

[FROM MR. CLAY.]

"ASHLAND, 28*th March*, 1837.

"MY DEAR SIR: I should like to know at what time we may expect the pleasure of seeing you in Kentucky, as I do not wish to be absent on that interesting occasion. I have no intention of leaving home during the spring, or before August, except to make an excursion to Missouri, to visit a young son whom I have established there. Without being bound to any specific time for this trip, I wish to make it toward the last of May; but, of course, shall be regulated by your movements, if I can know them.

"I am, truly and faithfully,

"Your friend and obedient servant,

"H. CLAY.

"The Hon. D. Webster."

The journey was begun in the early part of May, and on the 11th of that month he was at Pittsburg. Descending the Ohio, he was met by a hundred citizens of Wheeling, who had chartered a steamboat to ascend the river and escort him to that place. At the landing he was greeted by an immense throng of people, and, on the 17th, he accepted a public dinner. The news of the suspension of the Eastern banks reached Wheeling on the day of this entertainment. He had left a scene of commercial distress in the Atlantic cities, which, as he described it in his speech at this dinner, presented a mass of evil such as he had never expected to see, "except as the result of war, a pestilence, or some other calamity." He could not have avoided speaking of that which was in all men's thoughts, melancholy as the topic was. Nor was there any reason for avoiding an allusion to what all men spoke of—his own early and constant predictions of what had now occurred. From the year 1832 down to the last session of Congress, in every important debate, he had foretold and proclaimed the approach of this result, as a necessary consequence of the measures adopted in regard to the currency.

On the 17th and 18th of May he was at Maysville, in Kentucky, where he had a similar reception, great numbers of people coming in from the surrounding country to see and to greet him. On the 19th he was escorted into Lexington by a committee, chosen for the purpose at a general meeting of the citizens; and here another public dinner was given to him. At Louisville he was received at one of those peculiar entertainments which are known in that country as "barbecues," at which he addressed a vast crowd of people in a speech of two hours. Ascending the Ohio toward Cincinnati, he landed at North Bend, and paid a visit to General Harrison. On the 2d of June he arrived at Cincinnati, amid a great popular demonstration, and, on the 3d, he addressed the people of that city, being introduced by General Harrison. On the 9th, at St. Louis, he was received in a similar manner, and as no other man, according to the newspapers of the time, ever was received on the west bank of the Mississippi. On the 14th, he left St. Louis for Alton, in Illinois, where his arrival was greeted with a display of flags, ringing of church-bells, discharge of cannon, and a great turnout of the population. The next of these demonstrations was at Madison, Indiana; and here he was obliged, in consequence of the state of the country and the early meeting of Congress, to turn his course again toward the East. It would have occupied him for at least three months longer to have accepted the other invitations which poured in upon him from the great region that is covered by the States of Illinois, Indiana, and Ohio. But to the far greater part of all this outpouring of popular respect and interest he could only return his grateful regrets. From Madison he passed through Indiana to Chicago, where he was met by a cavalcade ten miles from the city, and was followed by a long train of carriages. Here he addressed a vast crowd assembled in front of the Lake House, and, on the following day, a festival was given in his honor. On the 1st of July he crossed the lower part of Lake Michigan to Michigan City, and passed thence to Toledo. On the 8th he reached Detroit, from which place he arrived on the 16th at Buffalo, where, on the 17th, there was a grand steamboat regatta on Lake Erie, in honor of his visit. On landing from this excursion, he was escorted to the park, and there addressed the public in one of his characteristic speeches. On the 26th he reached the city of New York, on his way to Massachusetts.

Such is a very imperfect outline of the last extended and public tour that Mr. Webster made to the West. It might have resembled the progress of a supreme ruler, if he had not been simply a member of the legislative branch of the Government; for the addresses which were presented to him, and which are now before me in great numbers, many of them coming from quarters which it was impossible for him to visit, almost always proceeded from formal meetings of the citizens, convened for the purpose of inviting him, and they mark the general sense of his public importance, while, with perfect freedom, they express the gratification and delight to be anticipated from his presence. It is quite apparent, from the tone of these addresses, that, on this tour, he exhibited his great social powers in their most attractive form, and that their fame spread far and wide through that vast region. It was a new experience in that country to see so much refinement and intellectual power, combined with a fascination and cordiality that put everybody at their ease, and yet lost nothing of personal dignity. Western society had heard of Mr. Webster's coldness, and coldness is not to its taste. It found him, to its surprise and delight, one of the most genial of men, capable of hearty enjoyment in the simplest pleasures of life, and feeling quickly and keenly all manifestations of sympathy and kindness. On him, too, the country and its people produced a very strong impression.

Mr. Van Buren, who received the administration of the Government in March, 1837, just as the great crisis in the monetary condition of the country, recently referred to, was rapidly developing itself, found himself obliged to summon Congress in a special session, to be holden on the 4th of September. The proclamation issued for this purpose met Mr. Webster while he was on his tour in the West. It rendered it necessary for him to shorten his journey; and, by the time he reached Boston, he had only the month of August remaining for rest and recreation at Marshfield.

The position of the new President was peculiar. Committed, by the circumstances of his election, to the policy of his predecessor, he had to accept the dogma that a national bank was a measure not to be resorted to under any circumstances. At the same time, nothing had been devised to answer the purposes of a substitute for such an institution. The deposit-bank system had broken down entirely; and, in the general crash which came by the suspension of specie payments, these banks, with the public funds in their custody, were alike involved. What had been called, under the former Administration, the "experiment," which had been founded in the expectation that the State banks could transact the financial business of the Government, and furnish a generally-accredited paper circulation for the uses of commerce, had completely failed. The new Administration, therefore, had to strike out for itself, and for the country, a policy that was destined to be somewhat of a paradox; for it was to coincide with that of the preceding Administration, and was yet to be unlike it. In refusing to go back to the policy of a national bank, Mr. Van Buren could adhere to the doctrines and example of General Jackson. But the latter had never renounced the duty of regulating the currency. He had, in fact, admitted this duty, by attempting to make the deposit banks a substitute for the Bank of the United States. But the alternatives from which Mr. Van Buren had now to choose were, either to return to the policy of a national bank, which had been the policy of the country for forty years out of the forty-eight which had elapsed since the Government was established, or to renounce all care of the national Government over the currency, excepting the coinage, and to disclaim all concern of the Government in the relations of commerce, of exchange, and of the money which the people must use in their ordinary dealings. This was a difficult path to tread; for if, on the one hand, it were to be considered that the peculiar agency of a national bank, as a regulator and source of a commercial currency, was out of the question, still it could not be easily seen how the Government was to extricate itself from its present embarrassments, and accomplish that divorce from the general concerns of the people, which alone remained for it to attempt, if no substitute could be found to discharge the functions that had so long been performed by a Bank of the United States.

Difficult, however, as the enterprise was, it was undertaken. The new Administration decided to disclaim the duty of providing a currency for commercial uses, or of exercising any control over the paper circulating medium; and it is in reference to this new policy, which was to confine the action of the Government to the care of its own interests alone, and to the mere collection and disbursement of its revenues, that Mr. Webster's opposition to Mr. Van Buren's measures is to be examined. Before it could be known what those measures were to be, Mr. Webster had said publicly, while on his tour in the West, that the country had now reached a point at which a great principle would have to be decided: whether the Government of the United States has any constitutional duty to perform in regard to the currency of the country, beyond the mere regulation of the gold and silver coins.

On the assembling of Congress, the message of the President and the report of the Secretary of the Treasury exhibited the deranged condition of the public finances, and disclosed the plan of the Administration. For the immèdiate relief of the Government, it was proposed to postpone the payment to the States of the fourth instalment of the surplus revenue, and to issue some millions of Treasury notes, to be used in paying the public creditors. Mr. Webster opposed the first of these measures as inexpedient, after the States had been led to expect that the money would be distributed to them; and he pointed out that the kind of Treasury notes proposed to be issued, to circulate on the credit of the Government, without interest, and with no fixed period of redemption, would be mere paper money. For the permanent plan of managing the public finances, the message proposed that the Government should no longer make any use whatever of banks, but that its revenues, after being collected, should be held by officers of the Treasury, and be paid out by them to the public creditors on Treasury orders. This scheme, which afterward became expanded into what was known as the "Sub-Treasury," was justified upon the ground that it was no part of the duty of the Government of the United States either to provide a paper circulating medium for the uses of the country, or to supervise and regulate that which is issued by corporations or individual bankers. A bill was soon introduced into the Senate, in accordance with the President's recommendation, for the purpose of carrying out the new plan of keeping and disbursing the public moneys; and to this bill Mr. Calhoun moved an amendment, providing for the gradual repeal of the resolution of April 30, 1816, so far as it authorized the receipt of the notes of specie-paying banks in payment of public dues. Mr. Calhoun, who, in 1816, advocated the creation of the last Bank of the United States, and, during the Administration of General Jackson, had been opposed to his measures, now became a convert to the doctrine that the Government has no right to have *any* connection with banks. He regarded himself as having formerly acted under the compulsion of necessity, in supporting a national bank; and, now that the connection between the Government and all banks was broken, he said that he was set at liberty to act upon his original opinions. It was in consequence of this change that Mr. Webster and Mr. Calhoun came into collision in the debate of this session upon the currency.

Mr. Webster's great speech on this subject was delivered on the 28th of September, in opposition to the bill embracing the first Sub-Treasury scheme, and to Mr. Calhoun's amendment. It was the most elaborate of all the arguments that he ever made in support of the constitutional duty of the General Government to see that a paper currency, of general credit, suitable to the wants of trade and business, as well as to the payment of debts due to the Government, be maintained and preserved. The capital sources of this constitutional argument were drawn from the coinage power of the Constitution, the prohibition on the States to issue their own paper for circulation, and the power to regulate commerce. Commencing with the great object of the coinage power, to provide a money for circulation that should be, at the same time, the standard of value, Mr. Webster contended that this power embraces authority to regulate and control any and all paper which either States or individuals may put into circulation in the place of coin. Passing thence to the prohibition on the States against issuing their own paper for circulation, he said that it had not been, and now cannot be held to prevent them from authorizing private corporations or individuals to issue notes for circulation on their own credit. Such notes were and would continue to be issued, and they filled all the channels of commerce, while they failed to be of universal credit. The power to regulate commerce here comes in, and is to be applied to the regulation and control of whatever, by circulating as money, is in fact an agent or instrument in the performance of commercial transactions; and from this power Mr. Webster deduced the duty of the General Government to provide a currency of general credit, equivalent in value to specie. Mr. Calhoun, who now denied this whole doctrine, appears to have anticipated a kind of Government paper circulation which we have seen since most extensively employed. While he contended that the entire banking system of modern times, so far as it involved the use of Government credit, was wrong and vicious, he was not able to suggest that the Government can wholly avoid the use of its credit in some form, or rely exclusively on the coinage. Credit, as the associate and assistant of the metals, he held to be both unobjectionable and necessary. But, in seeking the form in which the Government is to use its credit, he selected as "the most stable, the least liable to abuse, the cheapest, and that which combines all the requisite qualities of a credit circulation in the highest degree," a Government paper receivable in payment of the revenues, and to be issued as the wants of the Government should require. In the event of war, such a paper, he said, would open almost unbounded resources to carry it on, without the necessity of resorting to loans, which he was almost disposed to regard as a fraud. The increase of such bills would keep pace with the increase of taxes, and they would furnish the means of paying the taxes. Excepting that he did not suggest the making of this Government paper a lawful tender in the payment of private debts, the form in which Mr. Calhoun would have used Government credit, instead of using it in connection with banking institutions, was essentially the same scheme which we have since seen resorted to on a gigantic scale; and we have thus had some means of judging how far it can be made "the associate and assistant of the metals," and how far it combines "all the requisite qualities of a credit circulation."

The difference between Mr. Webster's financial system and that maintained by Mr. Calhoun as the best, can now be appreciated. Mr. Webster contended that it always had been and always will be impossible to maintain any paper circulation at par with specie that is not convertible into specie at the will of the holder; that if Government is to use its credit at all, in aid of the circulation, it must do it in such a form as to make the paper issues convertible at pleasure into coin; that its own paper, issued without any promise of redemption other than that of its being received for taxes, has no advantage over that issued by individuals; that the modern banking system leads to the circulation of paper as money which is founded on assigned capital and recognized credit, under an administration of citizens responsible, individually and corporately, to the laws. He held this system and form of credit to have been the great instrument which has elevated the condition of society in modern times, breaking down the influence which dead capital confers upon the few who possess it, lifting up those who have industry without having capital, and extending the property and business of the great mass of mankind. These principles, which he held to lie at the basis of the relation in which government stands to society, in regard to the circulating medium, were, in his opinion, those on which the Government of the United States must act; and he maintained, now and always, that the power to carry out these principles is in the Constitution, and that to deny it to be there is to reconstruct and rewrite the Constitution, to take it away and give us a substitute.

The bill to authorize the issue of Treasury notes was passed at this session. The bill to establish the Sub-Treasury was passed in the Senate, but did not pass the House.

It was at this period that the first formal overture of annexation to the United States was made by Texas, which now had an independent government that had been acknowledged by us. The offer was declined by President Van Buren, partly upon the ground that it involved constitutional questions which it would be inexpedient now to agitate, and partly because we had a treaty of amity and commerce with Mexico, the friendly purposes of which would appear to be disregarded by entertaining this proposal. Mr. Webster had received a great number of petitions against the annexation before the actual condition of this negotiation was publicly known. As soon, however, as it was known, he considered that the time had arrived when it was proper for our citizens to declare their sentiments on the subject, and he accordingly presented the petitions at this session.[1]

[1] October 12, 1837.

CHAPTER XXIV.

1837–1838.

PROJECT FOR A GREAT WESTERN FARM—SEPARATE NATIONALITY OF TEXAS — SLAVERY IN THE DISTRICT OF COLUMBIA — THE SUB-TREASURY—PREËMPTION RIGHTS FOR SETTLERS ON THE PUBLIC LANDS—THE COMMONWEALTH BANK, IN BOSTON—CORRESPONDENCE.

ONE of the effects of Mr. Webster's visit to the West, in the summer of 1837, was to confirm his desire for a great Western farm, and to lead him into other land speculations and projects of investment in that region. His fondness for agriculture, and his knowledge of it, found in that country the scope which they craved; for his preferences in this respect were for broad fields and large operations. He had become the owner of an extensive tract, to which he had given the name of Salisbury, from that of his native town in New Hampshire. This place is in Sangamon County, Illinois, not far from Springfield; on it he had placed, as his agent, Mr. Nathaniel Ray Thomas, a younger son of the family from whom he purchased the Green Harbor estate at Marshfield. After his return to Washington, in the winter and spring of 1838, he was occupied with a project for enlarging this tract, so as to carry out a plan which he had long entertained of making a Western farm of one thousand acres. There he sometimes believed that he should retire finally from professional and public life; sometimes, that he should make it a place of only occasional residence, in order to indulge his love of farming on a scale that suited the grandeur of his tastes, and on a soil such as he could not have in New England; and sometimes he imagined that a great fortune was to be made from the increased value of the property that was to arise out of the further settlement of that country. But, at this period, he had done nothing more than to make contracts for the enlargement of Salisbury, and for stocking it, as it would require to be stocked, according to the scheme that he had planned. He was to look for the means of carrying out this grand project hereafter.

At this session, another capital error was committed on the subject of slavery, and it is extraordinary that it should have been committed, and that the Southern statesmen should not have been content to accept the conservative and consistent views of Mr. Webster as the true ground on which to rest the rights and interests of their States, instead of obliging him to dissent from doctrines which it was out of the question for him to accept. His opinions were well known. He held that Congress could do nothing in regard to the institution of slavery in any State; but that, in the District of Columbia, inasmuch as the jurisdiction of Congress is plenary, it could deal with this subject as it might see fit, and that this legislative power necessarily involved the right of citizens of the United States to petition for the abolition of slavery in the District, and the duty of Congress to receive, refer, and consider the petitions. Nevertheless, Mr. Calhoun now undertook to have the Senate affirm, by resolution, that any act or measure of Congress, with a view to the abolition of slavery in the District of Columbia, would be a direct and dangerous attack on the institutions of all the slaveholding States; and Mr. Clay proposed to go further, and declare that such legislation would be a violation of the faith implied in the cessions of the District by Virginia and Maryland, a just cause of alarm to the people of the slaveholding States, and that it would have a direct and inevitable tendency to disturb and endanger the Union.[1] From this doctrine, of

[1] The following was the fifth of the resolutions moved by Mr. Calhoun, December 27, 1837:

"*Resolved*, That the intermeddling of any State or States, or their citizens, to abolish slavery in this District, or any of the Territories, on the ground, or under the pretext, that it is immoral or sinful, or the passage of any act or measure of Congress with that view, would be a direct and dangerous attack on the institutions of all the slaveholding States."

an implied faith involved in the cessions of the District as a restraint upon the legislative power of Congress, Mr. Webster expressed his dissent in the most decided, but temperate terms; at the same time saying, that whatever would stay the exercise of the power must be drawn from discretion, from reasons of justice and true policy, and from those high considerations which ought to influence Congress in questions of such extreme delicacy and importance.[1] How he regarded the effort of Mr. Calhoun and Mr. Clay is apparent from the following letter:

[TO MR. KETCHUM.]

"WASHINGTON, *January* 15, 1838.

"DEAR SIR: My speech on Mr. Clay's resolution will appear, I hope, in the *Intelligencer* to-morrow. I venture to say you will be satisfied with it. We are not slumbering here, but wish to act with circumspection as well as decision. I consider the proceedings of the Senate as having drawn a line which can never be obliterated.

"Mr. Clay and Mr. Calhoun, in my judgment, have attempted in 1838 what they attempted in 1833, *to make a new Constitution.*

"I am engaged to-day up to the chin, in committee on the new Sub-Treasury, and in court. To-morrow I will write you on the Hartford Convention, and on the Tariff Law of 1833.

"Yours,

"D. WEBSTER."

We have seen in the last chapter the grounds of Mr. Webster's dissent from the policy of Mr. Van Buren's Administration on financial subjects. It has been sometimes said, of late, that Mr. Webster's opposition to what was called the Sub-Treasury, if not the only error, was one of the chief errors of his political life. This opinion is founded in a superficial view of his doctrines respecting the power and duties of the General Government in regard to the currency, and in an assumed success of the Sub-Treasury in reference to things concerning which it had no success at all, and which remained, as he said

On the 10th of January, 1838, Mr. Clay moved the following as a substitute:

"*Resolved*, That the interference by the citizens of any of the States, with the view to the abolition of slavery in this District, is endangering the rights and security of the people of the District; and that any act or measure of Congress, designed to abolish slavery in this District, would be a violation of the faith implied in the cessions by the States of Virginia and Maryland, a just cause of alarm to the people of the slaveholding States, and have a direct and inevitable tendency to disturb and endanger the Union."

[1] See the speech, Works, iv., 371, *et seq.*

they would remain, unprovided for by the introduction of the plan of a separate custody and disbursement of the public funds, and uninfluenced by it. Undoubtedly, the plan of separate custody and disbursement has operated beneficially; but it is to be remembered that its introduction and establishment were accompanied by a denial of all power and duty of the General Government to exercise any control over the paper currency. This is the principal reason why Mr. Webster reiterated his opposition to the Sub-Treasury at the present session. The discussions on this subject led to another encounter with Mr. Calhoun.[1] The following note relates to it:

[TO MR. KETCHUM.]

"Monday Morning.

"DEAR SIR: I received yours last evening. The speeches will go to all the printers this mail, and you will get a copy also. The reply to Mr. Calhoun is nearly ready for the press. It will make a speech of twenty to thirty pages.

"The *speech* will not come quite up to expectation. It has been too much praised. If you can believe it, no reporter took down a single word of it. I had to gather it together from my own notes, my own recollection, other friends' recollections, and the letters of the letter-writers.

"I shall go to Boston the end of this week or early next; must see you for an hour as I go on, though I shall make no stay, or a very short one, in New York.

"Yours,

"D. WEBSTER."

Mr. Webster's visit to the West had made him acquainted with a condition of the frontier settlements for which he felt himself, on his return to his place in the Senate, bound to extend some relief. In parts of Indiana, Illinois, and Michigan, and especially in the region beyond the Mississippi, comprehended in what was then the Territory of Wisconsin, population had extended itself beyond the surveys of the public lands, and the actual settlers were consequently without any title to the land which they had cleared, and on which they had made improvements. Mr. Webster had satisfied himself that the cir-

[1] See the speeches on the Sub-Treasury, and the reply to Mr. Calhoun, Works, iv., 401–522.

cumstances under which these settlements had been made afforded some palliation for the intrusion on the public domain, and that the practical question of what was to be done with these settlers, their improvements, and the lands on which they were living, must be met by Congress in a spirit of liberality. He therefore supported, against Mr. Clay and his own colleague Mr. Davis, a bill to grant a preëmption right to every actual settler on the public lands, who was in possession on the 1st day of December, 1837, with certain restrictions and limitations. His speech on this subject is embraced in the fourth volume of his Works.

Among the mischievous abuses to which the system of depositing the public moneys in certain selected State banks had led, under the late Administration, a scandalous occurrence took place in Boston, in the payment, by the local disbursing officers of the United States, of pensions and fishing-bounties in the bills of a bank which was on the eve of failure, and the result was a total loss to a most meritorious class of public creditors. They were all entitled by law to be paid in specie or in the notes of specie-paying banks. This disgraceful affair was brought before the Senate by Mr. Webster, on the 17th of January; and he made it the occasion for pointing out that, while the general paper currency of the country was left depreciated and deranged for the want of some regulating and restraining power, the establishment of an exclusive system of gold and silver for Government use could not secure safety to the Government or its creditors; for, in spite of the provisions of law, the disbursing agents of the Government will always be tempted to offer, and the creditors be made to accept, paper which passes for money in the particular locality, and which is exposed at all times to the hazard of falling dead in the hands of its holders. He held the scheme of one kind of currency for the Government and another for the people to be both impracticable and dangerous.[1]

The following important letters may appropriately close the

[1] See his remarks on the affair of the Commonwealth Bank, Boston. Works, iv., 377, *et seq.* Some of the leading officers and managers of this bank were, at the same time, disbursing agents for the Government.

present volume, before we enter upon the period in which the stability of the Union was to be subjected to further perils, that were to demand of Mr. Webster, to the end of his career, a continued sacrifice of his private interests to the public good:

[TO MR. KETCHUM.]

"*May* 12, 1838.

"DEAR SIR: This Cherokee subject is difficult and delicate. The public sympathies are aroused *too late*. The Whig members of Congress, who have taken an interest in seeing justice done to the Indians, are worn out and exhausted. An Administration man, come from where he will, has no concern for Indian rights, so far as I can perceive. We shall endeavor to do something or to say something. We are all willing.

"You think that I ought to do some act to clear myself from the shame and sin of this treaty. My dear sir, I fought it a week in the Senate, on the question of ratification. We came near preventing it, and should have done so, if we had not been disappointed in Mr. Goldsborough's vote. We relied on him as a man of honor and religion; but he voted for the treaty, and turned the scale—mortified some of his friends severely—went home, and never returned.

"On all occasions, public and private, I pronounce the treaty a base fraud on the Cherokee Indians. What can I do more? Yet, I am willing to do more, if any good can be effected by it. . . .

"Yours,

"D. WEBSTER.

"P. S.—Please not to mention what I have said about the Cherokee Treaty in the Senate, because I do not know, now, whether the injunction of secrecy was taken off. I will look on Monday, and, if it was, will send you a list of *ayes* and *noes*. I think it was taken off, and that the *ayes* and *noes* have already been published.[1]"

[TO MR. PECK.]

"Senate-Chamber, *January* 11, 1838.

"MY DEAR SIR: I can have no possible objection to stating to you, in any manner you may desire, my opinions on the various branches of this great and agitating subject of slavery.

"In the first place, I concur entirely in the resolution of the House of

[1] This letter refers to the Treaty of New Echota, negotiated in December, 1835, which stipulated for the removal of the Cherokee nation to the West; the removal to be consummated by May 23, 1838. A large portion of the Cherokees were dissatisfied with the treaty, and claimed that it was negotiated in behalf of their nation by unauthorized persons, and was never ratified by a respectable number of the tribe. It was a most scandalous transaction.

Representatives, passed as early as March, 1790, at a calm and dispassionate period in our political history. That resolution is in the following words:

"'*Resolved*, That Congress have no authority to interfere in the emancipation of slaves, or in the treatment of them within any of the States; it remaining with the several States alone to provide any regulations therein which humanity and true policy may require.'

"In the next place, I entertain no doubt whatever that Congress possessing, by the express grant of the Constitution, a right to exercise exclusive legislation in all cases whatsoever over the District of Columbia, the same having been ceded by the States of Maryland and Virginia, and become the seat of the Government of the United States, have full authority to regulate slavery within said District, or to abolish it altogether, whenever, in their judgment, humanity and true policy may require it; and that they have full authority also to regulate or restrain the purchase and sale of slaves within said District in any manner which they may deem just and expedient.

"I am also clearly and entirely of opinion, that neither by acts of cession by the States, nor by the acceptance by Congress, nor in any other way, has the faith of Congress become pledged to refrain from exercising its constitutional authority over slavery and the slave-trade in said District. More than all, it is my opinion 'that the citizens of the United States have an unquestionable constitutional right to petition Congress for the restraint or abolition of slavery and the slave-trade within the said District; and that all such petitions, being respectfully written, ought to be received, read, referred, and considered in the same manner as petitions on other important subjects are received, read, referred, and considered; and without reproach or rebuke to the authors or signers of such petitions.'

"The right of petition, free, unqualified, and untrammelled, I hold to be of the very substance and essence of civil liberty. I can have no conception of a free government, where the people, respectfully approaching those who are elected to make laws for them, and offering for their consideration petitions respecting any subject, over which their constitutional power of legislation extends, may be repelled, and their petitions rejected, without consideration and even without hearing.

"Wherever there is a constitutional right of petition, it seems to me to be quite clear that it is the duty of those, to whom petitions are addressed, to read and consider them; otherwise the whole right of petition is but a vain illusion and mockery.

"I am, dear sir, with very true regard,

"DANIEL WEBSTER."

[TO MESSRS. KELLEY AND OTHERS, ERIE, PENNSYLVANIA.]

"WASHINGTON, *June* 4, 1838.

"GENTLEMEN: The cane made from the timber of the ship which bore the flag of the gallant Perry on the memorable 10th of September, and intended as a present to me from the citizens of Erie, has been delivered by your townsman, Mr. Freeman; and I have also since had the pleasure of receiving your letter intended to accompany the gift.

"To those who have united in this token of confidence and friendship, I beg leave to return my respectful and cordial thanks. Be kind enough to say this to them, as you may have occasion to see them, and assure them that I highly value their present, because of the associations connected with its material, and especially because it is their present, and because of the inscriptions which they have seen fit it shall bear.

"You have been kind enough to say, gentlemen, that you claim kindred with me as an American citizen.

"I admit and reciprocate this claim with great pleasure and sincerity. I recognize you and your neighbors as fellow-citizens, my own countrymen, embarked on the same political fortunes, enjoying the same liberty, and the same bounties and blessings of Providence as myself.

"Your homes are on the shores of one of our great inland seas, mine is on the ocean; but our substantial interests, the great elements of our prosperity, and, above all, our stake in that paramount treasure of a free people, a good and wise government, are the same. All these are under the protection and guardianship of that inestimable Constitution which our fathers framed and have delivered to us, as a bond of perpetual union.

"It affords me, gentlemen, much gratification to find that my political conduct, on trying occasions, now passed, and I hope passed forever, has met your approbation. The period to which you refer, you justly call the dark hour. I felt it to be my duty in that momentous crisis to disregard party and personal considerations, to act in the true spirit of the Constitution, and, without forgetting the propriety of moderation, or the laws of kindness and charity, to proceed, nevertheless, with a firm and inflexible resolution of upholding the authority of the laws and defending the Union. I am happy to know that in all this I appear to you to have discharged the duty of a good citizen.

"I am, gentlemen, your friend and obedient servant,

"DANIEL WEBSTER."

At this time the affairs of Texas assumed a new aspect, in consequence of a change in the purposes of the leading persons in that country, respecting its annexation to the United States. This change was especially welcome to Mr. Webster, who had always desired to see Texas establish and maintain a separate nationality; and when, in consequence of negotiations which the new minister of Texas opened with Mr. Nicholas Biddle, for a loan to his government of five millions of dollars, to be subscribed in the United States, that gentleman wrote to Mr. Webster, to ask his opinion on the whole subject of Texan independence, in its relations to the United States—Mr. Webster, without hesitation, sent him the following answer:

[TO MR. NICHOLAS BIDDLE.]

"BOSTON, *September* 10, 1838.

"MY DEAR SIR: I have received your favor of the 8th instant. The decision of the Government of Texas to withdraw its application for a union with the United States is, in my judgment, an event eminently favorable to both countries. She now stands as an independent state, looking to her own power and her own revenues to maintain her place among the nations of the earth; an attitude vastly more respectable than that which she held when solicitous to surrender her own political character, and become part of a neighboring country. Seeking thus no longer a union with us, and assuming the ground of entire independence, I think it highly important to the interest of the United States that Texas should be found able to maintain her position. Any connection with a European state, so close as to make her dependent on that state, or to identify her interests with the interests of such state, I should regard as greatly unfortunate for us. I could not but regret exceedingly to see any union between those parts of our continent which have broken the chain of European dependence, and the Governments of Europe, whether those from which they have been disunited or others. You remember the strong opinion expressed by Mr. Monroe, that the United States could not consent to the recolonization of those portions of this continent which had severed the ties binding them to a European connection, and formed free and independent governments for themselves; or to the establishment of other European colonies in America. The spirit and the reason of this sentiment would lead us to regard with just fear, and therefore with just jealousy, any connection between our near American neighbors and the powerful states of Europe, except those of friendly and useful commercial intercourse.

"It is easy to foresee evils, with which any other connection than that last mentioned, between Texas and one of the great sovereignties of Europe, might threaten us. Not to advert to those of a high and political nature, one likely to have a direct bearing on our commerce and prosperity is very obvious. I mean the effect of such a connection on the great staple of our Southern production. Texas is destined, doubtless, to be a great cotton-producing country; and, while we should cheerfully concede to her all the advantages which her soil and climate afford to her, in sustaining a competition with ourselves, we could not behold with indifference a surrender by her of her substantial independence for the purchase of exclusive favors and privileges from the hands of a European government.

"The competency of Texas to maintain her independence depends, I think, altogether on the character of her Government and its administration. I have no belief at all in the power of Mexico to resubjugate Texas, if the latter country shall be well governed. The same consideration decides also the question whether a loan to Texas would be safe. I have supposed that her new-found Government was gradually strengthening and improving in all the qualities requisite for the respectable exercise of national power. That, in institutions so recent, there should be for a time some irregularity of action, is to be expected. But, if those, to whose hands her destinies are now committed, shall look steadily to two great objects—first, real and absolute, as well as nominal national independence; and, second, the maintenance of a free and efficient Government, of which good faith shall be, from the beginning, a marked characteristic—I see nothing to render it less safe to negotiate money transactions with her than with the governments of other countries. On the other hand, if a spirit of speculation and project should appear to actuate her councils, if she should trifle with her public domain, involve herself in contradictory obligations, or seek to establish her prosperity on any other foundation than that of justice and good faith, there would then be little to be hoped, either in regard to her punctuality in pecuniary engagements, or to the probability of her maintaining an independent national character. My opinion on the whole is, that the prospects of Texas are now far better and brighter than they have ever been before; that the interest of our own country requires that she should keep herself free from all particular European connection; and that whatever aid can be furnished to her by individuals or corporations in the United States, in the present state of her affairs, to enable her to maintain a truly independent and national character, would tend to promote the welfare of the United States as well as of Texas herself.

"I am, dear sir, yours, with great regard,

"D. WEBSTER."

APPENDIX.

THE notes of Mr. Jefferson's conversation, referred to on page 226 of this volume, are given by the lady who wrote them, with the following explanation:

"These are notes about a visit of three or four days to Mr. Jefferson, in December, 1824. They were written down, on the very evening on which we left Monticello, at a little tavern kept by a Mrs. Clarke, where we stopped for the night, early in the afternoon, because it was the only tolerable inn within our reach. We had therefore a long winter evening before us, and we got rid of it by making these notes, which are here copied with care, and without a change of any sort, from the identical manuscript in which they were originally recorded, chiefly by Mrs. Ticknor, under the dictation of Mr. Webster and Mr. Ticknor. As far as what relates exclusively to Mr. Jefferson, his appearance and conversation, the work is Mr. Webster's. The rest was a sort of joint-stock contribution."

BOSTON, *May* 1, 1869.

NOTES.

MR. JEFFERSON is now between eighty-one and eighty-two, above six feet high, of an ample bony frame, rather thin and spare. His head, which is not peculiar in its shape, is set rather forward on his shoulders, and, his neck being long, there is, when he is conversing or walking, an habitual protrusion of it. His head is still well covered with hair, which, having been once red, and now turning white, is of an indistinct light sandy color. His eyes are small, very light, and now neither brilliant nor striking. His chin is rather long, not sharp; his nose small, regular in its outline, with the nostrils a little elevated. His mouth well formed, and still well filled with teeth, generally strongly compressed, bearing an expression of contentment and benevolence. His skin, formerly light and freckled, bears now the marks of age and cutaneous affections. His limbs are uncommonly long, and his hands and feet very large, and his wrists of a most extraordinary size. His walk is not precise and military, but easy and swinging; he stoops a little, not so much from age as from constitutional formation. When sitting, he appears low, partly from not holding himself erect, and partly from the disproportionate length of his limbs. He wears, in the house, a dark-gray surtout coat, kerseymere yellow waistcoat, with an under one, faced with a dingy red; his pantaloons are loose, very long, and of the same material as his coat. His stockings are gray, and his shoes of the kind that bear his name. His whole dress is not slovenly, but neglected. He wears a common round hat; when on horseback he wears a gray strait-bodied coat, and a long spencer of the same material, both fastened with large pearl buttons. When we first met him riding, he wore round his throat, in the place of a cravat, a knit white woollen tippet; and, to guard his feet, black velvet gaiters under his pantaloons. His general appearance indicates an extraordinary degree of health, vivacity, and spirit. His sight is still good, for he needs glasses only in the evening; his hearing is but slightly impaired, but a number of voices in animated conversation confounds it.

He rises in the morning as soon as he can see the hands of his clock, and examines his thermometer immediately, for he keeps a regular meteorological diary. Until breakfast he employs himself chiefly in writing; breakfasts at nine. From that time till dinner he is employed in his library, excepting that every fair morning he rides on horseback not less than seven miles, sometimes twelve or fourteen. He dines at four, retires to his drawing-room at six, passes the succeeding hours in conversation, and goes to bed at nine. His habit of retiring early is so strong, that it has become *essential* to his health. His breakfast is made of tea, coffee, and bread, in all the good Virginia varieties, of which he does not seem afraid, however new and warm. He enjoys his dinner well, taking with his animal food a large proportion of vegetables. In regard to wines, he may be said to excel, both in the knowledge and use. His preference is for the wines of the Continent, of which he has many sorts of excellent quality. Among others we found the following, which were new to us: L'Ednan, Muscat, Samian, and Limoux. His dinners are in the half Virginian half French style, in good taste, and abundant. No wine is served till the cloth is removed. Tea and coffee are served in the saloon between seven and eight.

His conversation is easy and natural, and, apparently, not ambitious; it is not loud, as challenging general attention, but usually addressed to the person next him. The topics, when not selected to suit the character and feelings of his auditor, are those subjects with which his mind seems particularly occupied, and these, at present, may be justly said to be—1st. Science and letters, especially the University of Virginia which is coming into existence, almost entirely from his exertions, and will rise, it is to be hoped, to usefulness and credit under his continued care. When we were with him, his favorite literary subjects were Greek and Anglo-Saxon; and 2d. Historical recollections of the times and events of the Revolution, and of his residence in France from 1783–'84 to 1789.

Mme. d'Houdetot's society was one of the most agreeable in Paris when I was there. She had inherited the materials of which it was composed from Mme. de Tencin and Mme. de Geoffrin. St. Lambert was always there, and it was generally believed that, every evening, on his return home, he wrote down the substance of the conversations he had held there with D'Alembert, Diderot, and the other distinguished persons who frequented her house. From these conversations he made his books.

I knew the Baron de Grimm very well; he was quite ugly, and one of his legs was considerably shorter than the other. But he was the most agreeable person in French society, and his opinion was always considered decisive in matters relating to the theatre and to painting. His persiflage was the keenest and most provoking I ever knew.

Mme. Necker was a very sincere and excellent woman, but she was not very pleasant in conversation, for she was subject to what we call in Virginia the "Budge;" that is, she was very nervous and fidgety. She could rarely remain long in the same place, or converse long on the same subject. I have known her get up from table five or six times in the course of one dinner, and walk up and down her saloon to compose herself.

PATRICK HENRY

WAS originally a bar-keeper; he was married very young, and, going into some business on his own account, was a bankrupt before the year was out. When I was about the age of fifteen, I left the school here to go to the college at Williamsburgh. I stopped some days at a friend's, in the county of Louisa. There I first saw, and became acquainted with Patrick Henry. Having spent the Christmas holidays there, I proceeded to Williamsburgh. Some question arose about my admission into the college, my preparatory studies not having been pursued in the school connected with that institution. This put off my admission about a fortnight, at which time Henry appeared in Williamsburgh, and applied for a license to practise law, having commenced the study at or subsequent to the time of my meeting him in Louisa. There were four examiners—Wythe, Pendleton, Peyton Randolph, and John Randolph. Wythe and Pendleton at once rejected his application; the two Randolphs were, by his importunity, prevailed upon to sign the license, and, having obtained their signatures, he applied again to Pendleton, and, after much entreaty, and many promises of future study, succeeded also in obtaining his. He then *turned out* for a practising lawyer. The first case which brought him into notice was a contested election, in which he appeared as counsel before a Committee of the House of Burgesses. His second was the "Parsons cause," already well known. These, and similar efforts, soon obtained him so much reputation that he was elected a member of the Legislature. He was as well suited to the times as any man ever was; and it is not now easy to say what we should have done without Patrick Henry. He was far before all in maintaining the spirit of the Revolution. His influence was most extensive with the members from the Upper Counties; and *his* boldness and *their* votes overawed and controlled the more cool, or the more timid aristocratic gentlemen of the lower part of the State. His eloquence was peculiar, if indeed it should be called eloquence, for it was impressive and sublime beyond what can be imagined. Although it was difficult, when he had spoken, to tell what he had said, yet, while speaking, it always seemed directly to the point. When he had spoken in opposition to my opinion, had produced a great effect, and I myself had been highly delighted and moved, I have asked myself, when he ceased, "What the devil has he said?" and could never answer the inquiry. His person was of full size, and his manner and voice free and manly. His utterance neither very fast nor very slow. His speeches generally short, from a quarter to a half hour. His pronunciation was vulgar and vicious, but it was forgotten while he was speaking. He was a man of very little knowledge of any sort. He read nothing, and had no books. Returning one November from Albemarle Court, he borrowed of me Hume's Essays in two volumes, saying he should have leisure in the winter for some reading. In the spring he returned them, and declared he had not been able to go farther than twenty or thirty pages in the first volume. He wrote almost nothing; he *could* not write. The resolutions of 1775, which have been ascribed to him, have been by many supposed to have been written by Mr. Johnson, who acted as his second on that occasion. But, if they were written by Henry himself, they are not such as to prove any power of composition. Neither in politics nor in his profession was he a man of business; he was a man for debate only. His biographer says: "He read Plutarch every year." I doubt if he ever read a volume of it in his life. His temper was excellent, and he generally observed decorum in debate. On one or two occasions I have seen him angry; his anger was terrible, and those who had witnessed it were not disposed to provoke it again. In his opinions he was yielding and practicable, and not disposed to differ from his friends. In private conversation he was agreeable and facetious, and, while in genteel society, seemed to understand all the decencies and proprieties of it; but in his heart he preferred low society, and sought it as often as possible.

He would hunt in the pine-woods of Fluvanna with overseers, and persons of that description, living in a camp for a fortnight at a time, without a change of raiment. I have been often astonished at his command of proper language; how he obtained the knowledge of it I never could find out, as he read little, and conversed little with educated men.

After all, it must be allowed that he was our leader in the measures of the Revolution in Virginia, and in that respect more is due to him than to any other person. If we had not had *him*, we should probably have got on pretty well, as *you* did, by a number of men of nearly equal talents; but he left all of us far behind. His biographer communicated the sheets of his work [to me], as they were printed, and, at the end, asked for my opinion. I told him it would be a question hereafter, whether his work belonged to the shelf of history, or of panegyric. It is a poor book, written in bad taste, and gives an imperfect idea of Patrick Henry. It seems written less to show Mr. Henry than Mr. Wirt.

BUFFON.

When I was in France, the Marquis de Chastellux carried me to Buffon's residence in the country, and introduced me to him. It was Buffon's practice to remain in his study until dinner-time, and receive no visitors under any pretence; but his house was open, and his grounds, and a servant showed them very civilly, and invited all, strangers and friends, to remain and dine. We saw Buffon in the garden, but carefully avoided him; but we dined with him, and he proved himself then, as he always did, a man of extraordinary powers in conversation. He did not declaim; he was singularly agreeable. I was introduced to him as Mr. Jefferson, who, in some notes on Virginia, had combated some of his opinions. Instead of entering into an argument, he took down his last work, presented it to me, and said, "When Mr. Jefferson shall have read this, he will be perfectly satisfied that I am right." Being about to embark from Philadelphia for France, I had observed an uncommonly large skin of a panther, at the door of a hatter's shop. I bought it for half a Jo [1] on the spot, determining to carry it to Europe, to convince M. Buffon of his mistake in relation to this animal, which he had confounded with the cougar. I sent him the skin, with a note. He acknowledged his mistake, and said he would correct it in his next volume. I attempted also to convince him of his error in relation to the common deer and the moose of America, he having confounded our deer with the red deer of Europe, and our moose with the reindeer. I told him our deer had horns two feet long; he replied, with warmth, that if I could produce a single specimen with horns *one* foot long, he would give up the question. Upon this I wrote to Virginia for the horns of one of our deer, and obtained a very good specimen, *four* feet long. I told him, also, that the reindeer could walk under the belly of our moose, but he entirely scouted the suggestion. Whereupon, I wrote to General Sullivan, of New Hampshire, and desired him to send me the bones, skin, and antlers of a moose, supposing they could easily be obtained by him. Six months afterward, my agent in England advised me that General Sullivan had drawn on him for forty guineas. I had forgotten my request, and wondered why such a draught had been made, but I paid it at once. A little later, came a letter from General Sullivan, setting forth the manner in which he had complied with my request; that he had been obliged to raise a company of nearly twenty men; had made an excursion toward the White Hills, camping out many nights; and had at last, after

[1] Jo is a Portuguese coin of eight dollars, common in this country at one period.

many difficulties, caught my moose, boiled his bones in the desert, stuffed his skin, and remitted him to me, horns and all. This accounted for my debt, and convinced M. Buffon. He promised, in his next volume, to set these things right also; but he died directly afterward.

THE VIRGINIA FAST.

About the time of the Boston Port Bill, the patriotic feeling in Virginia had become languid and worn out, from some cause or other. It was thought by some of us to be absolutely necessary to excite the people; but we hardly knew the best means. At length it occurred to us to make grave faces, and have a fast. Some of us, who were younger members of the Assembly, resolved upon the measure. We thought Oliver Cromwell would be a good guide in such a case. We accordingly looked into Rushworth, and drew up our resolutions, after the most pious and praiseworthy examples. It would hardly have been in character for us to present them ourselves. We applied, therefore, to Mr. Nicholas, a grave and religious man. He proposed them in a set and solemn speech. Some of us gravely seconded him, and the resolutions were passed unanimously. If any debate had occurred, or if they had been postponed for consideration, there is no chance that they would have passed. The next morning Lord Bottetourt, the Governor, summoned the Assembly to his presence, and said to them, "I have heard of your proceedings of yesterday, and augur ill of their effects. His Majesty's interests require that you be dissolved, and you are dissolved." Another election soon afterward taking place, such was the spirit of the times, that every member of the Assembly, without an individual exception, was reëlected.

Lord Bottetourt was an honorable man. His government had authorized him to make certain assurances to the people here, which he made accordingly. He wrote to the Minister that he had made those assurances, and that, unless he should be enabled to fulfil them, he must retire from his situation. This letter he sent unsealed to Peyton Randolph, for his inspection. Lord B.'s great respectability, his character for integrity, and his general popularity, would have enabled him exceedingly to embarrass the measures of the patriots. His death was therefore a fortunate event for the cause of the Revolution. He was the first Governor-in-Chief that had ever come over to Virginia. Before his time, we had received only Deputies, the Governor residing in England, with a salary of £5,000, and paying his Deputy £1,000.

Our fast produced very considerable effects. We all agreed to go home, and see that preachers were provided in our counties, and notice given to the people. I came to this county, and notified the people, who wondered what it meant, and came together in multitudes. I took care to provide a preacher for the occasion.

(In reply to a question of Mr. Webster.)

The Declaration of Independence was written in a house on the north side of Chestnut Street, between Third and Fourth—not a corner house. Heiskell's Tavern, in Fourth street, has been shown for it—(to Mr. Webster)—but this is not the house.

When Congress met, P. Henry and R. H. Lee opened the general subject with great ability and eloquence—so much so that Paca and Chase, delegates from Maryland, said to each other, as they returned from the House, "We shall not be wanted here; those gentlemen from Virginia will be able to do every thing without us." But neither Henry nor Lee was a man of business, and, having made strong and eloquent general speeches, they had done all they could. It was thought advisable that two papers should be drawn up, one, an address to the people of England, and the other an address, I think, to the King. Committees were raised for these purposes, and Henry was at the head of the first, and Lee of the second. When the Address to the people of England was reported, Congress heard it with utter amazement. It was miserably written, and good for nothing. At length, Governor Livingston, of New Jersey, ventured to break silence. After complimenting the author, he said he thought some other ideas might be usefully added to his draft of an address. Some such paper had been for a considerable time contemplated, and he believed a friend of his had tried his hand in the composition of one. He thought, if the subject were again committed, some improvement in the present draft might be made. It was accordingly recommitted, and the address, which had been alluded to by Governor Livingston, and which was written by John Jay, was reported by the committee, and adopted as it now appears. It is, in my opinion, one of the very best State papers which the Revolution produced.

For depth of purpose, zeal, and sagacity, no man in Congress exceeded, if any equalled, Sam Adams; and none did more than he to originate and sustain revolutionary measures in Congress. But he could not speak. He had a hesitating, grunting manner.

John Adams was our Colossus on the floor. He was not graceful nor elegant, nor remarkably fluent, but he came out occasionally with a power of thought and expression, that moved us from our seats.

THROUGHOUT the whole Revolution, Virginia and the four New-England States acted together. Indeed, *they made* the Revolution. They made five votes always to be counted on, and they had to pick up the remaining two for a majority, when and where they could.

RICHARD H. LEE moved the Declaration of Independence, in pursuance of the resolutions of the Assembly of Virginia, and only because he was the oldest member of the Virginia delegation.

I FEEL much alarmed at the prospect of seeing General Jackson President. He is one of the most unfit men I know of for such a place. He has had very little respect for laws or constitutions, and is, in fact, merely an able military chief. His passions are terrible. When I was President of the Senate, he was a Senator, and he could never speak, from the rashness of his feelings. I have seen him attempt it repeatedly, and choke with rage. His passions are, no doubt, cooler now; he has been much tried since I knew him, but he is a dangerous man.[1]

MARMONTEL was a very amusing man. He dined with me, for a long time, every Thursday, and I think told some of the most agreeable stories I ever heard in my life. After his death, I found almost all of them in his memoirs, and I dare say he told them so well because he had written them out before it, for this very book.

I WISH Mr. Pickering would make a radical Lexicon. It would do more than any thing else, in the present state of the matter, to promote the study of Greek among us. Jones's Greek Lexicon is very poor; I have been much disappointed in it. The best I have ever used is the Greek and French one by Planche.

[1] At the time of these conversations, the Presidential election was pending, and Mr. Jefferson favored the claims of Mr. Crawford.

END OF VOLUME I.

www.ingramcontent.com/pod-product-compliance
Lightning Source LLC
LaVergne TN
LVHW021103110826
845150LV00001B/159